Enhancing Missionary Vitality

In Memory of

Dr. Richard Weber Bailey
1926-2000

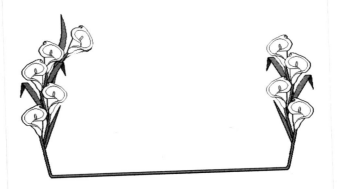

Enhancing Missionary Vitality

Mental Health Professions Serving Global Mission

Edited by

John R. Powell, Ph.D. and

Joyce M. Bowers, M.S.W.

MISSION TRAINING INTERNATIONAL

Cover design by Ann Rezny
Interior design by Joyce M. Bowers
Interior art used by permission from *Graphics for Worship 2.0*
   Minneapolis: Augsburg-Fortress Publishers, © 1999

Published by Mission Training International
P.O. Box 1220, Palmer Lake, Colorado 80133
Tel: 800/896-3710, 719/487-0111; Fax: 719/487-9350
E-mail: resources@mti.org Web site: www.MTI.org

ISBN Number: 0-942726-03-0

51442391

To presenters, participants, and hosts

Mental Health and Missions
Conferences

Potawatomi Inn, Pokagon State Park
Angola, Indiana

1980 - Present

Contents

PART IV: INTERFACES WITH SENDING AGENCIES

PART V: MODELS OF PREVENTIVE SERVICES

PART VI: CLINICAL INTERVENTIONS

PART VII: INNOVATIVE MODELS

PART VIII: ETHICS AND PROFESSIONAL STANDARDS

PART IX: APPLIED RESEARCH

PREFACE

Mental health and missions have not always coexisted comfortably in the same sentence. When the first small group of Great Commission mental heath professionals assembled at the Potawatomi Inn in northeastern Indiana more than a generation ago, the evangelical Christian community was just beginning to acknowledge the contribution the field of Psychology could make to hurting members of The Body. The notion that emotional instability was an indication of spiritual immaturity or faithless prayer was beginning to be questioned, mostly by people struggling alongside Christians who needed more help than "read your Bible and pray more."

It took godly psychologists like Dr. John Powell and others working faithfully and quietly on a variety of levels to build the trust and credibility necessary to enable the Christian community to extend an appreciation for biblically grounded mental health professionals to the missions community. Missionaries were assumed to be spiritually above the problems that confront ordinary Christians. The precarious pedestal of unrealistic expectations on which missionaries were placed was often the launching pad for devastating brokenness.

Far too many field missionaries and mission leaders reinforced those unrealistic expectations by isolating Philippians 4:13 from the rest of scripture and insisting that they, and those with whom they work, live up to that superhuman standard. The physical and mental destructiveness that often resulted from the "I can do all things..." approach to cross-cultural ministry became the special concern of Dr. Powell, Dr. David Wickstrom, and their colleagues who gathered each autumn at the Mental Health and Missions Conference.

Over the years this annual event became the forum in which some of the most perplexing challenges faced by the international missions community were addressed from the unique perspective of Christian mental health professionals. This book is a compilation of some of the seminal research, theological insights, models, and case studies gleaned from several years of Mental Health and Missions conferences. It is a wide-ranging resource for those who have an academic background in the field of psychology.

This is not intended to be a representative compendium of each Mental Health and Missions conference. Nor is it intended to be a comprehensive "how to" manual for everyone with missionary member care responsibilities. For example, it does not address the complexities of counseling across cultures. Its perspective is primarily North American and its examples and recommendations are predominately focused on the North American missions community.

A project of this scope requires the work and input of dozens of people. Each author has contributed far more than a manuscript. Their faithful and expert contributions to the annual conferences have made these events energizing and renewing experiences for the more than two hundred participants who attend.

Mission Training International has made it possible for this book to be published, but its commitment to the growth and continuity of Mental Health and Missions goes much deeper. The well being and effectiveness of the missions community is at the core of its mission as a training organization.

The patient and dedicated editorial work done on this book by Mrs. Joyce Bowers has been exceptional. Once again she has taken the thoughts, notes, and outlines of competent presenters and reworked them into readable text. Her organization, creativity, and detailed work on layout, so much appreciated in *Raising Resilient MKs*, are shown again here. Drawing on her mission service in Liberia as well as ten years of experience in member care, her incomparable catalytic work on this volume cannot be overstated.

The brilliance, expertise, and sweet spirit of Dr. John Powell are evident throughout this book. His insights and editorial suggestions have shaped the content as well as the direction of both Mental Health and Missions and this unique volume. It is with a deep sense of gratitude to God that we acknowledge the profound impact he has had on literally thousands of lives through his selfless service to his profession and to the Kingdom of God. The entire Great Commission community is in his debt.

Paul E. Nelson

Part I

The Mental Health and Missions Conference

1

The Annual Conference on Mental Health and Missions: A Brief History

John R. Powell and David L. Wickstrom

The Context of the Conference
The beginning of the Mental Health and Missions conference was predated by a growing interest in the use of mental health professionals to provide care for missionaries. In the 1960's, individual work was focused largely on pre-field clinical evaluations and counseling with missionaries both on and off the field with psychological and/or family issues. Missionary training seminars on topics such as family and marriage, interpersonal relationships, stress management and emotional well being were also led by mental health professionals.

Few Christian counseling organizations provided integrated help for missionaries, and little general knowledge existed pertaining to the psychological distinctives of mission service and culture. There was a paucity of empirical research in this area, and available research was largely anecdotal or based on master's theses and doctoral dissertations. However, the decade of the sixties saw emerging interest and growth in mental health and missions and set the direction for more rapid growth in subsequent decades.

By the seventies mental health professionals served missions in a variety of ways. Wycliffe Bible Translators Counseling Department was begun in the sixties and developed in the seventies and beyond. Instituted by Dr. Phil and Barbara Grossman, who had seen the desirability of counseling services for Wycliffe members, it was soon fully utilized and began developing additional activities relating to the understanding, care and development of missionaries (see Chapter 5 by Dr. Laura Mae Gardner).

The Mental Health and Missions conference began as a small, informal gathering of colleagues and friends in 1980. It has met annually for 23 years in Angola, Indiana. This chapter traces its history, including contributions participants have made to the development of mental health services in missions in the past two decades. Several innovative member care programs began as informal conversations at the conference.

3

Individual practitioners outside mission agencies were asked to share their expertise. Psychologists Dr. Henry Brant of Michigan and Dr. Clyde Narramore of California, each of whom established Christian counseling centers, sparked interest in missions and mental health by writings from field visits. These began to define needs, identify issues and outline opportunities which were soon built on by others. By the mid-seventies, both mental health professionals and mission leaders realized that a viable relationship was taking place. (See Chapter 3 by Dr. Frances White for a more extended history.)

Conference Beginnings

The conference known as Mental Health and Missions was birthed in November 1980. In the spring of that year, we (Dave and Johanne Wickstrom and John and Bev Powell) were sharing perspectives from our experiences in providing psychological services to missions. A strong desire was voiced to interact with others doing similar work, and the idea of an informal gathering emerged. We dreamed of what it would be like, considered some specific purposes and objectives, and brainstormed on a format. We wished it to be Biblically sound, spiritually deep, professionally inte-grated and have an atmosphere of openness and fellowship. We hoped that by being together we might collectively become better "handmaidens to missions" in our work.

Dave found that the Potawatomi Inn at Pokagon State Park near Angola, Indiana (within driving distance for both of us) would be an ideal meeting place. We decided to begin with the Friday evening meal and conclude with Sunday dinner, November 21-23, 1980. We contacted others doing similar work, shared our hopes and purposes, and strongly encouraged attendance with spouses. We invited participants to make presentations, to be followed by discussion. Time was available for informal interaction between the presentations. The gathering met the interests of virtually every participant and we were encouraged to arrange another.

Conference expenses followed a simple formula: the Potawatomi Inn computed total costs for meals, lodging, and the meeting room, and we divided it by the number of participants. Planners, presenters and participants all paid the same; total cost per person for the first conference was about $80! A few years later, growth necessitated adding a small factor to offset logistical expenses and copying of the *Proceedings*, which were distributed following the meetings.

Program planning was likewise simple. We talked with potential participants about their ideas, invited them to share, and trusted the Holy Spirit to accomplish God's purposes among us. Each year there was not only an excellent array of presentations but also the emergence of themes which directed further thought and exploration and informed practice. The warm fellowship, sharing, and effective networking between sessions and at meals added richness to the time together. Discussions around meal tables continued well beyond the satiation of appetites!

The twenty-one participants at the first conference represented several professions: nine psychologists, two psychiatrists, two missionary nurses (one having become a professor of missions), one social worker, one marriage and family therapist and one pastoral counselor. All were involved in providing services to missions and most had served in some capacity on the mission field. Seven presentations were made, including a time of worship on Sunday morning.

Presentations were compiled for a *Proceedings* booklet graciously paid for the first time by Health Integration Services (HIS) of Peabody, MA, represented by Dr. George and Kathi Ensworth, also of Gordon-Conwell Seminary. Conference papers were made available each year through 1998, after which the conference format was changed. The enthusiasm and success of this first conference, hardly imagined as the beginning of an annual international conference, cast the mold for the next 14 years.

The same format was followed annually. On Sunday mornings there were discussion groups around topics of interest and salient issues which emerged during the conference, followed by a worship service with a relevant sermon presentation. Participants involved in specific areas of work or who envisioned new possibilities or plans often scheduled meetings during free times. Time was set aside for announcements, news and updates on happenings in the broad area of mental health and missions, making the conference an informal clearing house of information.

To maintain the sense of openness and informal fellowship which was a hallmark of the conference, the number of participants was limited. By the early 1990's interest had grown, resulting in waiting lists even though only a single announcement letter was sent each year. To celebrate the 15th anniversary in 1994, an extra day was added and attendance limits were discarded. Attendance was over 100 and the extra day allowed for more presentations, discussion groups and free time. We felt the latter was especially valuable to model reasonable self-care during field visits. Though the format has changed since 1994, the time frame remains the same.

Some Personal Notes

Knowing something of a person's background helps to understand what they do and how earlier experiences fit with later career and life decisions. In that spirit, we share a bit about ourselves.

John: I grew up in small town in rural Missouri, attended a Christian liberal arts college, served in the U.S. military and worked two years in industry before experiencing a clear call into psychology in 1958. By 1980 I had been on the faculty at Michigan State University for 16 years and, as a psychologist, been providing consultation and services to missions since 1965. I often saw individual missionaries and their families in my off-campus private practice and made frequent trips overseas to provide a variety of psychological services.

Bev and I had meaningful exposure to missions during military years in Alaska during the 1950s. Alaska was then a U.S. territory and Fairbanks, where we lived, was a frontier town of some 10,000 population. We affiliated with a mission church made up largely of Eskimos and Indians, with a few military people like ourselves. We became friends with the missionary family serving that church and soon were exposed to a variety of issues and challenges of missionary life. We learned much from missionary families and indigenous friends both in Fairbanks and villages in the interior.

The seeds planted there grew into bigger hearts for missions and the hope of applying my psychological expertise. In 1965 I began providing pre-field clinical evaluations and counseling for missionaries. This soon expanded into broader activities both domestically and cross-culturally and has continued over the years as significant affirmations of our sense of call.

Dave and I met in the 1970s when he was completing doctoral work at Rosemead School of Psychology, where I consulted during its early development. Dave was researching the effects of boarding school on later personality development, and we had many common interests. Upon the Wickstroms' move to the midwest, we found occasions to be together as families. Working together in the conference and a variety of other venues provided spiritual and professional growth, deep friendship, and the joy of continuous learning.

Dave: I grew up as an MK in Nigeria, having virtually all my overseas schooling in boarding schools. Following undergraduate work at a small Christian college, my late wife Johanne and I were led to graduate school at Rosemead. Our hearts were directed toward serving missions by utilizing the psychological skills I was learning. We were involved in mission-related activities and found some peers from similar backgrounds and interests.

As John and I became acquainted we found many common interests, including MK development, my dissertation subject. While teaching at Grace College in Indiana and later serving at a community mental health clinic in northern Ohio, our families were within comfortable driving distance. The Mental Health and Missions confer-ence is a result of one of those visits. Having an independent practice in the Washing-ton, DC area for several years and later joining a Christian counseling group practice in Columbia, SC and teaching at Columbia International University have allowed increasing services to missionaries and led toward full-time service in this arena. Overseas trips, seeing many missionaries in my clinical psychology practice, and being involved in other areas of mental health and missions is deeply satisfying and affirming.

Several years after the conference began Johanne succumbed to cancer. Those were difficult days but the sense of community and the relationships developed at the conference, through church, and in other places was very encouraging as my children and I experienced the grief and transition of her loss. Later, in God's timing, Sharon and I met and were led into marriage. We both dreamed of being able to serve missions full time, and now do so. Sharon is able to use some of her skills on the field and we are able to travel together frequently.

The Evolving Conference

We had no idea that the informal gathering in 1980 would become an annual conference. We were simply seeking a time for mutual sharing, encouragement and edification in our work. The following year 40 participants came and in the third year (1982) there were 56. We began to realize that God had led us into something we needed to continue.

Missions and Mental Health Interfaces

At the first meeting we recognized that it would be valuable to invite mission leaders in order to learn from them and establish common objectives. This was verified by attendance of some missions leaders at the second meeting, and even more at the third. Even those of us with considerable experience realized that there was *much more* to learn through dialogue with mission agencies.

From the missions community, Rev. Peter and Mary Lou Stam of AIM-US, medical director Dr. John Bennett and his wife Shirley of TEAM, and psychologist/ pastor Dr. LeRoy Johnston and his wife Carol, at that time personnel director for C&MA, were particularly encouraging and helpful. Together, we sought ways to pursue our common objectives of enhancing missionaries by using our complementary skills and perspectives. Dr. Ken Williams, then director of Wycliffe's Counseling Department and Dr. Laura Mae and Dick Gardner, also of Wycliffe, were very encouraging in bringing their rich backgrounds and visions.

From outside missions, Dr. Frances White of Wheaton Graduate School's Department of Psychology, a veteran missionary in Zaire, brought keen insights both in applying psychological skills in serving missions and in showing us bridges between the world of missions and that of the mental health professions. Glenn Taylor, Director of Counseling at Missionary Health Institute (MHI) in Toronto brought many integrative theological insights intertwined with practical suggestions from field experiences (see Chapter 7).

Dr. Ken Gamble, MHI Medical Director, likewise brought rich insights from his practice in Toronto and his years of experience in Africa. These were especially helpful in understanding some of the intricacies in physical/mental health intersections and in broadening assessment skills to achieve better understanding of those with whom we worked (see Chapter 35).

Dr. Jarrett Richardson of the Mayo Clinic and Dr. Esther Schubert from New Castle, Indiana, each having grown up on the mission field, brought stimulating infor-mation and ideas from that background, their psychiatric practices and their contin-uing services to missions. Many, many others could be mentioned from these earlier years (and later!) and we are very grateful for each.

A Critical Decision

At our third meeting the idea of forming an organization was voiced. Perhaps a journal and/or newsletter could be published, other activities developed and more done to advance the relationship between mental health professionals and missions.

Yet, the spirit of the conference as a non-organization accomplished much in building relationships, establishing networks, stimulating thinking, and enhancing skills. Ideas and partnerships were developing without our steering them other than bringing people together. This approach economized effort and communication and allowed maximum freedom for participants to listen to God's leading.

At the conclusion of that conference we, along with Bev and Johanne and George and Kathi Ensworth, met to assess the conference and consider the "pros and cons" of an organizational structure. As the discussion progressed, so did the tension of uncer-tainty. What would be the best way of glorifying God in this situation? How should we proceed?

George Ensworth motioned for a pause, looked at us directly, and asked, "Are you willing to continue doing things just as you are?" That question made God's leading clear to each of us, and the non-organization which we had birthed continued in that manner for 18 years. We divided the workload and responsibilities between us, worked largely from our dining room tables, and enjoyed the responsibilities and results as truly a labor of love.

Further Developments

In many respects, the development of the conference and the content of formal and informal discussions reflected the development of mental health understanding and care in missions. There continued to be good representation of the disciplines involved, representation from mission organizations, an increasing number of students in mental health graduate programs, and excursions into new areas which informed both mental health professionals and mission representatives. Each year saw some meaningful international participation and there was never a dearth of participants willing to bring presentations or to interact energetically.

As the eighties unfolded, interest continued to grow as experience, knowledge and applications were made from psychology to missions. Drs. William Hunter and John Carter, co-editors of the *Journal of Psychology and Theology,* saw the trends of mental health professionals working with missions as worthy of more focus, and published a special issue on psychology and missions in Fall 1983. Five articles were based on presentations first made at the conference. According to Dr. Hunter, it was enthusiastically received with many orders for extra copies and reprints.

As the field grew, three subsequent special issues with this focus were published (Winter 1987, Spring 1993, and Summer 1999). Each contained articles based on presentations first given at the Mental Health and Missions conference. The *Journal of Psychology and Christianity, Evangelical Missions Quarterly, Mission Frontiers* and others have also given special focus to this area and published articles based on conference presentations.

It was becoming clear that mental health professionals had an important role to play with those serving in missions. In order to provide the best help, mental health professionals needed to understand the context of their work, distinctive features of mission culture, and the unique needs of missionaries. Increasingly, they were asked to provide preventive and educational programs as well as direct services. Broader consultation paradigms were developed regarding missionary care, assignments, satisfaction, growth, and restoration. At the administrative level more input was sought on personnel issues, responses to crises and emergencies and even organizational dynamics and policies.

The importance of interpersonal relationships, family life, sources of stress, leader/missionary interactions, and organizational practices was affirmed through individual work with missionaries. The value of preventive work and missionary enhancement through seminars on interpersonal skills, coping with stress, managing conflict, understanding emotions, marital and parent-child relationships, response to crises, etc. became significant for involvement by mental health professionals. Better continuity between mental and physical health care was also coming into focus. Conference presentations reflected these trends.

By the late eighties the accumulated experience of mental health professionals working with missions was made more widely available. Drs. Kelly and Michelle O'Donnell edited a seminal book, *Helping Missionaries Grow: Readings in Mental Health and Missions* (O'Donnell and O'Donnell, 1988). It covered a wide scope of areas pertaining to missionary growth and care, and contained some fifteen chapters based on presentations originally given at the conference, several of which had been published in journals. Presentations and discussions at the conference also broadened as more areas were developed and presented.

In the early nineties the term *member care* came into common use. It covers a spectrum of care and activities including that provided by mental health professionals. In its broadest sense, member care has always been a part of missions (Tucker and Andrews, 1992; Powell, 1992) but now was given greater attention and emphasis. Some mission organizations developed member care departments. More credentialed mental health professionals joined mission organizations. "Outside" mental health professionals served longer periods of time overseas, contributing to a better continuity of care.

New concepts and applications contributed to the growth, satisfaction and effectiveness of missionaries. These include and affirm much of the work of mental health professionals, but go well beyond their work in significant and cooperative ways. An excellent example of the combination of complementary skills, knowledge and experience and provision of relevant training is the West Africa Mobile Member Care Team. (See Chapters 39 and 47 by Dr. Karen Carr and Darlene Jerome).

A Critical Re-Affirmation

During the 1990's, presentations and discussions at the conference, including the *ad hoc* interest groups, reflected a broader array of content. The conference reflected the expansion of member care, but also honored its core purposes: to bring together mental health professionals serving missions and others both within and outside missions for cooperative growth and complementary understanding.

We developed themes with core elements for mental health professionals, but also of interest to member care workers and others within missions. It was important for mental health professionals to learn of broader areas of interest and care and to maintain mission/mental health professional dialogues. By simply following what we believed to be God's leading, we found the Holy Spirit bringing people together for Kingdom work.

A Design Shift

With annual attendance reaching 150, and the 18th conference (1997) approaching, we realized our informal, non-organizational approach needed some tweaking. Paul Nelson, president of Mission Training International (MTI) in Colorado Springs agreed that MTI would sponsor the conference and handle all the logistical arrangements. We would continue as program co-coordinators, developing the program and arranging for presenters.

Paul provided magnificent direction and oversight in moving this to a truly professional level without sacrificing the informal atmosphere which marked its history. Karen Nelson, MTI registrar, brought her experience, sensitivity, and skills to the multiple tasks of getting us together in a smooth and delightful manner. This move seemed God-ordained and natural in the development of the conference.

Two additional changes were made. First, the format shifted to "menu style," with plenary sessions and concurrent workshops, allowing many more topics but preserving times when the entire group was together. The Potawatomi Inn had upgraded its facilities and offered ideal space for this new arrangement. Second, arrangements were made with the National Board of Certified Counselors to offer CEU's for at the conference, to help meet state continuing education re-certification requirements for some participants.

The four meetings under this new design (1998-2001) have received high marks from participants. The working relationship with MTI has been productive and enjoyable. Conference attendance topped 250 without losing the sense of informality and warm fellowship. Certainly this shows the grace of God. Having been retired from MSU for several years, John felt led to step out of leadership after the 22nd conference (2001). The program co-coordinators are now Dr. Dave Wickstrom, Dr. Rhonda Pruitt of Columbia International University and Dr. Duncan Westwood of Missionary Health Institute. Paul Nelson of MTI has recently moved into a new position as CEO of the Crowell Foundation, and Dr. Steve Sweatman, a veteran partic-ipant and presenter at the conference, is the new MTI president.

Further Observations

The conference focuses largely on North American mission agencies and those serving them. However, nearly every meeting has been blessed by international participants and sometimes international presenters. This has been important in keep-ing in touch with the broader member care movement around the world and sharing at a personal level as brothers and sisters in Christ.

At the 21st meeting (2000), through the assistance of the Narramore Christian Foundation and arrangements by co-chairs Dr. Kelly O'Donnell and Rev. David Pollock of the World Evangelism Alliance Member Care Committee (MemCa), some 25 member care workers from around the world, including several mental health professionals, attended. The interactions were rich. The group then stayed on for a post-conference meeting focused on international member care issues. A recent and excellent volume on member care around the world is *Doing Member Care Well: Perspectives and Practices from Around the World* (O'Donnell, 2002).

It has been important to relate to other areas of care in missions as well. One important bridge is with the Pastors-to-Missionaries Conference conducted each December by Barnabas International, held at the JAARS Headquarters in Waxhaw, N.C. This conference focuses largely on pastoral care for missionaries but overlaps somewhat with mental health care. Much of the broad contextual knowledge about missions presented at each is applicable to both; yet different foci are maintained and there is minimum overlap in participants. This relationship, and those with other organizations and conferences, shows the truth of "...all members of the Body work-ing together as one" (I Cor. 12:12, 14-27).

Concluding Comments

This book was written almost entirely by authors who have been a part of the conference, some almost since the beginning. These chapters represent many areas relative to mental health professionals serving missions, yet should be considered only an introduction to the complexity of mental health and missions.

With the rapid growth and increasing interest in mental health and missions in the context of member care, we need maintain a focus on helping missionaries within their calling. We are servants *to* them for their enhancement (their handmaidens!) and they are first and foremost servants to God in taking the Gospel cross-culturally.

Perhaps the fundamental beauty of this conference is that when Christians commit themselves and their vocations to God, he leads them in the pathways he desires. We seldom know in advance the final destination or the ultimate outcome; our task is to be faithful. With little organizational effort except for bringing people together, many new ideas have been spawned, ministries pursued, knowledge and experience shared, and relationships formed.

Each year we have been surprised and pleased at the way God has orchestrated the conference. The richness we and the participants have experienced is God's richness. May it be so for all the years yet to come.

References

Journal of Psychology and Theology. (1983). 11, 3. La Mirada, CA: Rosemead School of Psychology.

Journal of Psychology and Theology. (1987). 15, 4. La Mirada, CA: Rosemead School of Psychology.

Journal of Psychology and Theology. (1993). 21, 1. La Mirada, CA: Rosemead School of Psychology

Journal of Psychology and Theology. (1999). 27, 2. La Mirada, CA Rosemead School of Psychology

O'Donnell, K.S. and O'Donnell, M.L. (Eds.). (1988). *Helping missionaries grow: Readings in mental health and missions.* Pasadena, CA: William Carey Library.

O'Donnell, K. (Ed.). (2002). *Doing member care well: Perspectives and practices from around the world.* Pasadena, CA: William Carey Library.

Powell, J. (1992). Missionary care overview. In O'Donnell, K. (Ed.). *Missionary care: Counting the cost for world evangelization.* Pasadena, CA: William Carey Library (p 7-9)

Tucker, R. and Andrews, L. (1992). Historical notes on missionary care. In O'Donnell, K. (Ed.). *Missionary care: Counting the cost for world evangelization.* Pasadena, CA: William Carey Library. (p.24-36)

Part II

Professional Intervention Shaped by Context

2

Mental Health Professionals in Missions: An Overview

M. Elizabeth Lewis Hall and Judith L. Schram

*T*his chapter provides an overview of the diverse and significant ways in which mental health professionals have been involved in missions. We have seen a rapid growth in this specialty area over the last ten years, as reflected in attendance at the Mental Health and Missions Conference and in the number of quality publications synthesizing the state of the field. There are now a number of important resources to which new-comers to the field can be pointed, and a diversity of ways in which professionals can become involved.

Our hope is that this overview will serve as a road map for the many professionals interested in finding their place in the field, as well as providing mission administrators with a menu of options for enlisting the help of these professionals. In addition, we hope to challenge those already involved in the missions endeavor to consider some of the frontiers that lie ahead.

Many of the topics covered in this chapter are elaborated on in other chapters in this book, and in other books and articles cited throughout the article. With these goals in mind, the major themes characterizing the past and present mental health involvement in missions will be presented and some challenges for the future articulated.

Looking to the Past: Consolidating Gains

Psychology had a role in missions as early as the late 1920s, when mental health professionals first became involved in the process of missionary selection (Hunter & Mayers, 1987). In spite of this long history, the relationship between the behavioral sciences and the missions community has not been without tension. Reflecting the

Roles of mental health professionals in missions have expanded and diversified, especially in the last decade. In the past, primary areas were missionary assessment, care of missionary children, and providing counseling or therapy for missionaries. Current trends include networking, prevention, and crisis intervention. Looking to the future, gaps are noted: ethical standards, need for further research, and expanding the role of mental health professionals beyond member care to providing care for nationals.

attitude of the fundamentalist and evangelical churches in general, the missions community looked with suspicion at the "secular" field of psychology.

However, over the past 20 years psychology and the behavioral sciences have been able to move away from a defensive role as the contributions of mental health professionals to the missions movement have become clearer (Hunter & Mayers, 1987). During this time significant progress has been made on at least four fronts: (a) psychology has established a place for itself in missions, culminating in the creation of the new discipline of missionary member care; (b) pre-field psychological assessments have become increasingly sophisticated; (c) significant work has been done in promot-ing a greater understanding of the missionary family and in particular of missionary children; and (d) psychological care for missionaries has become increasingly available.

First, significant progress has been made in establishing a place for *mental health in missions*, particularly in North America. Psychologists and other mental health professionals have joined forces with pastors and human resource personnel to create the interdisciplinary area of member care. Furthermore, the need for member care is becoming widely acknowledged among mission agencies.

This movement is reflected in the increasing popularity of the Mental Health and Missions conference held annually in Indiana, in the increasing number of mis-sion agencies allocating resources to the care of missionaries, and in the well-established presence of centers for the care of missionaries such as Link Care in Fresno, California, and ALONGSIDE (formerly Tuscarora Resource Center) in Michigan. A more detailed overview of the area of member care can be found in O'Donnell, 1997 and 2002. While further work is needed to establish interdisciplinary connections at an international level, it is clear that member care is here to stay.

Second, the area of *missionary assessment* continues to build on its clinical and research foundations, and is an established area of mental health practitioners' in-volvement in missions. The task of candidate selection is indeed a specialty area, requiring the professional involved to move beyond the traditional role of assessment. In addition to taking into account suitability for the intended job, the candidate must be assessed for cross-cultural adaptability and for spiritual fitness. In addition, the candidate's family must be evaluated, all the while taking into account the limited financial resources of a mission's budget.

Assessment continues to be one of the primary ways in which mental health professionals contribute to member care, and a number of publications on the topic are available (e.g., Cureton, 1983; Ferguson, 1983; Ferguson, Kliewer, Lindquist, & Lindquist, 1988; Ferguson, Kliewer, Lindquist, Williams, & Heinrich, 1983; Lindquist, B., 1988; Lindquist, S.E., 1988; Shubert, 1992, 1999; Sweatman & Hall, this book; Wickstrom, this book; Williams, 1983).

Third, the *care of missionary children (MKs)* has received a great deal of attention, with research and networking providing important information that is being implemented to improve the lives of MKs. Excellent empirical and theoretical resources are available (e.g., Austin & Van Jones, 1987; Bowers, 1998; Bullock, 1993; O'Donnell & O'Donnell, 1988; Powell & Andrews, 1993; Sharp, 1985; Stringham, 1993; Wickstrom & Andrews, 1993; Wickstrom & Fleck, 1983), including a recent handbook by Pollock and Van Reken (1999) which reflects the accumulated wisdom in this area. As a body of knowledge in this area has grown, the focus has shifted from MKs to a broader concern with the well-being of the missionary family (e.g., Andrews, 1999; O'Donnell, 1987; Powell, 1999; Stringham, this book; Blomberg, this book; White, 1983).

Finally, resources for the *psychological care of missionaries* through therapy and counseling have become increasingly available. The openness of the evangelical community to therapy has contributed to this trend. The therapist now has a range of options available for providing treatment to missionaries and their families.   To illustrate the range of options, the therapist may function as an employee of the mission organization in order to treat the missionary, or as an independent practitioner, with advantages and disadvantages to either option.

Care can also be provided in the missionary's home country, perhaps during furlough, or, increasingly, in proximity to the missionary's host culture. For example, there are now counseling centers for missionaries in Nairobi and Abidjan. It is also becoming common for mental health professionals to fly out to field locations in order to provide services to missionaries. These and other options are further explored in the section of this book entitled "Models for Service Delivery."

Looking to the Present: Current Trends

The pioneering efforts of many professionals have provided a foundation for the current trends in mental health and missions. Three such trends will be discussed: a trend toward networking and partnering; a focus on prevention; and a mobilizing of resources for crisis intervention.

Trend One: Networking

The first trend is toward increasing networking and pooling of resources in the member care movement. This is taking place at three levels. The first level is *interdisciplinary*. Mental health professionals have joined with individuals trained in pastoral care and human resource development to form a specialized discipline within missions, known as member care (O'Donnell, 1992, 1997, 2002). The goal of member care is the overall nurture and development of missionary personnel. According to O'Donnell, member care consolidated as a movement in the late 1980s, and appears to be gaining impetus as more missions become aware of the importance of intentionally providing for members' needs throughout their lifespan.

The second level at which networking is taking place involves the *pooling of resources among mission agencies* and the active interchange of ideas between individuals involved in member care. The formation of RIMAs—Regional inter-agency member-care affiliations—is a prime example of what is taking place. Kelly and Michèle O'Donnell have been leaders in the movement to coordinate interagency member care efforts in an attempt to meet the myriad needs of missionaries (see O'Donnell, 1999 and 2002). Efforts like these, and the networking that takes place in groups such as the Mental Health and Missions Conference, the European Member Care Consultation, and a number of national interagency gatherings, are important for good stewardship of mental health resources, as we learn from each others' experience and avoid duplicating efforts. They also reflect the growing internationalization of this movement and its maturation in many countries.

The third level of networking involves *partnering with international mental health efforts* and drawing on resources outside of the missions movement. O'Donnell (1997) has documented the impact of the internationalization of the behavioral/health sciences on the member care movement and the consequent partnering with secular international health organizations for training and providing services.

Trend Two: Prevention

A second trend is the focus on prevention. Although the concept of prevention has been present since the first attempts to provide psychological screening for missionary candidates, in recent times the concern with prevention has found new momentum. This is reflected in the 1996 international conference on attrition sponsored by the World Evangelical Fellowship, with leaders from many missions joining forces to explore ways of preventing the unnecessary loss of missionaries (Taylor, 1997). As a result, mission agencies have strengthened pre-field training, and several resources are now available for providing missionaries with access to psychological skills and information to prevent excessive stress and burnout. A prime example of this is Interpersonal Skills Training, which is described in more detail in Chapter 30.

Trend Three: Crisis Intervention

The third trend is sobering and involves a concerted effort to provide crisis intervention to missionaries in an overseas context (Gardner, 1992; Jensma, 1999; Rosik & Kilbourne-Young, 1999). This trend reflects the realities of rising violence in the settings in which many missionaries live and work. The impact of economic chaos in many parts of the world also contributes to unrest and increases the chances of political uprisings, forced migrations, and violence.

It should be remembered that missionaries are impacted not only by major traumatic events such as political upheavals, natural disasters, or incidents of violence, but also by the accumulation of everyday stressors (e.g., Gish, 1983; Carter, 1999). The effects of these accumulated stressors may require intervention and, at the least, should be addressed in debriefings as a routine part of the homecoming experience.

Looking to the Future: Where Are the Gaps?

Mental health professionals have had a major impact on the field of missions and are attempting to mobilize their resources toward current missionary needs. However, certain important gaps remain to be filled. Many could be mentioned and explored, e.g., the need to develop long-term member care teams on the field, the need for cross-cultural applications for mental health resources, the need to focus on internationalization of member care, etc.

We will focus on three of these: the need for *more sophisticated ethical standards*, the need for *further research*, and the need to *expand the role* of mental health professionals in missions *beyond member care*. The maturation of the discipline of member care, and more specifically, of the mental health component of member care, brings with it certain responsibilities. These responsibilities are increased profession-alism, scholarship, ethical clarification, and perhaps the establishment of standards for training and competence.

Ethical Guidelines

The need for clearer ethical guidelines in working with missionaries and mission agencies is clear and constitutes the first major gap. Although all of the mental health professions have codes of ethics (e.g., American Psychological Association, 1992), tensions often arise when these are applied in cross-cultural situations and tight-knit communities such as those found in missions contexts.

A review of the published literature on missions and mental health reveals only three sources dealing primarily with ethical issues (Hall & Barber, 1996; O'Donnell, 1988; O'Donnell & O'Donnell, 1992). The chapters in Part VIII, Ethics and Professional Standards in this book represent important contributions to the area of ethics. How-ever, clear guidelines have yet to be articulated in such areas as the establishment of competence in providing services cross-culturally and the legal ramifications of pro-viding services to people in other countries.

Further Research

A second gap involves the need for a more sophisticated research foundation for clinical work in a missions context. With the exception of MK-CART/CORE, most published research in this area continues to be the result of dissertations or theses, which generally means that they are not part of an ongoing empirical exploration of a given area.

In addition, while descriptive research is a necessary first step in exploring uncharted areas, it is important to implement research projects that utilize increasingly sophisticated research methodologies and that build on previous studies to explore specific research hypotheses. Hunter's (1993) conclusion nine years ago continues to be valid: "What seems needed is greater chunks of time and long-term commitment from post-doctoral researchers with adequate funding for their work from evangelical sources" (p. 7).

The obstacles to these types of research efforts are great, including limited finan-cial and time resources and the difficulty of doing research with missionary partic-ipants (Jensma, Pike, Duerksen, & Strauss, 1997). One major obstacle to research appears to be a missions climate that, in the context of these limited resources, does not place a high priority on research. This is unfortunate, as good research could provide important information that would, in the long term, provide important benefits and enhance our stewardship of the human resources in missions.

Advocacy to key mission administrators might open doors and motivate participation in research, facilitating current efforts. Creative ways must be explored to provide an empirical basis for mental health member care and topics of research expanded to include all categories of people on the field – for example, single women.

Providing Care for Nationals

The third gap involves moving beyond the traditional role of mental health practitioners in member care to becoming providers of mental health care to nationals in the context of missions. Important as it is to take care of the needs of missionaries, the psychological needs of the millions of people subject to trauma-inducing stressors are pressing. While a few mental health professionals have been involved in crisis intervention with non-North Americans in overseas contexts, these have tended to be isolated efforts.

A legitimate concern is whether our Western psychological principles are cross-culturally valid. However, given the enormity of the needs, it seems that the best approach is to do what we can with humility, drawing on the recent advances in cross-cultural psychology, and becoming involved in the scholarship needed to context-ualize our interventions.

Conclusions

This review of the past, present, and future of mental health involvement in missions demonstrates the growth and development of this subdiscipline of mental health. It is an exciting time to be a part of what God is doing in missions. Mental health professionals can play an important part in the task that lies ahead. And in the broad spectrum of mental health services in missions, there is a place for every qualified professional willing to serve.

References

American Psychological Association. (1992). Ethical principles of psychologists and code of conduct. *American Psychologist, 51* (12).

Andrews, L. A. (1999). Spiritual, family, and ministry satisfaction among missionaries. *Journal of Psychology and Theology, 27* (2), 107-118.

Austin, C. N., & Van Jones, B. (1987). Reentry among missionary children: An overview of reentry research from 1934-1986. *Journal of Psychology and Theology, 15*(4), 315-325.

Bowers, J. M. (1998). *Raising resilient MKs: Resources for caregivers, parents, and teachers.* Colorado Springs, CO: Association of Christian Schools International.

Bullock, M.D. (1993). Separation anxiety disorder in a missionary child: Theoretical considerations and intervention strategies. *Journal of Psychology and Theology, 21*(1), 37-44.

Carter, J. (1999). Missionary stressors and implications for care. *Journal of Psychology and Theology, 27*(2), 171-180.

Cureton, C. B. (1983). Missionary fit: A criterion-related model. *Journal of Psychology and Theology, 11*(3), 196-202.

Cureton, C. B., & Kliewer, D. (1983). Service effectiveness at home and abroad: An annotated bibliography. *Journal of Psychology and Christianity, 2*(4), 45-51.

Ferguson, L. N. (1983). Issues in missionary assessment. *Journal of Psychology and Christianity, 2*(4), 25-29.

Ferguson, L. N., Kliewer, D., Lindquist, B., & Lindquist, S. E. (1988). Essentials and tools of psychological assessment. In K. S. O'Donnell & M. L. O'Donnell (Eds.), *Helping Missionaries Grow: Readings in Mental Health and Missions* (pp. 62-69). Pasadena, CA: William Carey Library.

Ferguson, L. N., Kliewer, D., Lindquist, S. E., Williams, D. E., & Heinrich, R. P. (1983). Candidate selection criteria: A survey. *Journal of Psychology and Theology, 11*(3), 243-251.

Gardner, L. M. (1992). Crisis intervention in the mission community. In K. O'Donnell (Ed.), *Missionary care: Counting the cost for world evangelization* (pp. 136-152). Pasadena, CA: William Carey Library.

Gish, D.J. (1983). Sources of missionary stress. *Journal of Psychology and Theology, 11,* 236-242.

Hall, M.E.L., & Barber, B. (1996). The therapist in a missions context: Avoiding dual role conflicts. *Journal of Psychology and Theology, 24*(3), 212-219.

Hunter, W.F. (1993). Missions and mental health: Introduction to a special issue. *Journal of Psychology and Theology, 21*(1), 5-8.

Hunter, W.F., & Mayers, M.K. (1987). Psychology and missions: Reflections and status and need. *Journal of Psychology and Theology, 14*(4), 269-273.

Jensma, J. L. (1999). Critical incident intervention with missionaries: A comprehensive approach. *Journal of Psychology and Theology, 27*(2), 130-138.

Jensma, J.L., Pike, P.L., Duerksen, C.L., & Strauss, G.H. (1997). The importance and the difficulty of doing research with a missionary population. *Journal of Psychology and Theology, 25,* 384.

Lindquist, B. (1988). Misuses of psychological assessment. In K. S. O'Donnell & M. L. O'Donnell (Eds.), *Helping Missionaries Grow: Readings in Mental Health and Missions* (pp. 70-74). Pasadena, CA: William Carey Library.

Lindquist, S. E. (1982). Prediction of success in overseas adjustment. *Journal of Psychology and Christianity, 1*(2), 22-25.

Lindquist, S. E. (1988). A rationale for psychological assessment of missionary candidates. In K. S. O'Donnell & M. L. O'Donnell (Eds.), *Helping Missionaries Grow: Readings in Mental Health and Missions* (pp. 55-61). Pasadena, CA: William Carey Library.

O'Donnell, K. (1987). Developmental tasks in the life cycle of mission families. *Journal of Psychology and Theology, 15*(4), 281-290.

O'Donnell, K. (1988). Some suggested ethical guidelines. In K. O'Donnell and M. O'Donnell (Eds.), *Helping missionaries grow: Readings in mental health and missions* (pp.). Pasadena, CA: William Carey Library.

O'Donnell, K. (1992). Perspectives on member care in missions. In K. O'Donnell (Ed.), *Missionary Care: Counting the Cost for World Evangelization* (pp. 10-23). Pasadena, CA: William Carey Library.

O'Donnell, K. (1997). Member care in missions: Global perspectives and future directions. *Journal of Psychology and Theology, 25*(1), 143-154.

O'Donnell, K. (1999). Developing member care affiliations: Personal reflections and community psychology contribution. *Journal of Psychology and Theology, 27*(2), 119-129.

O'Donnell, K. (2002). Doing member care well: Perspectives and practices from around the world. Pasadena, CA: William Carey Library.

O'Donnell, K., & O'Donnell, M.L. (1992). Ethical concerns in providing member care services. In K. O'Donnell (Ed.), *Missionary care: Counting the cost for world evangelization* (pp. 260-268). Pasadena, CA: William Carey Library.

Pollock, D. C., & Van Reken, R. E. (1999). *Third culture kids: The experience of growing up among worlds*. Yarmouth, ME: Intercultural Press.

Powell, J. R. (1999). Families in missions: A research context. *Journal of Psychology and Theology, 27*(2), 98-106.

Powell, J.R., & Andrews, L.A. (1993). Qualities desired in MK boarding school personnel: A preliminary study. *Journal of Psychology and Theology, 21*(1), 86-92.

Rosik, C. H., & Kilbourne-Young, K. L. (1999). Dissociative disorders in adult missionary kids: Report on five cases. *Journal of Psychology and Theology, 27*(2), 163-170.

Sharp, L. W. (1985). Toward a greater understanding of the real MK: A review. *Journal of Psychology and Christianity, 4*(1), 73-78.

Shubert, E. (1992). Current issues in screening and selection. In O'Donnell, K., *Missionary Care: Counting the Cost for World Evangelization* (pp. 74-88). Pasadena, CA: William Carey Library.

Shubert, E. (1999). A suggested prefield process for missionary candidates. *Journal of Psychology and Theology, 27*(2), 87-97.

Stringham, E.M. (1993). The reacculturation of missionary families: A dynamic theory. *Journal of Psychology and Theology, 21*(1), 66-73.

Taylor, W. D. (Ed.). (1997). *Too valuable to lose: Understanding the causes and cures of missionary attrition*. Pasadena, CA: William Carey Library.

White, F. J. (1983). Some reflections on the separation phenomenon idiosyncratic to the experience of missionaries and their children. *Journal of Psychology and Theology, 11*(3), 181-188.

Wickstrom, D.L., & Andrews, L.A. (1993). Personality characteristics of staff members at selected overseas missionary boarding schools. *Journal of Psychology and Theology, 21*(1), 74-85.

Wickstrom, D. L., & Fleck, J. R. (1983). Missionary children: Correlates of self-esteem and dependency. *Journal of Psychology and Theology, 11*(3), 226-235.

Williams, D. E. (1983). Assessment of cross-cultural adjustability in missionary candidates: Theoretical, biblical, and practical perspectives. *Journal of Psychology and Christianity, 2*(4), 18-24.

3

Mental Health Advances in Member Care

Frances J. White

*M*ember care is a broad term that encompasses many interdisciplinary facets of the care of mission personnel from the initial application process throughout the life span and into retirement.

Member care workers include all those who support and care for mission personnel—pastoral counselors, personnel directors, human resource specialists, field coaches, internal and external consultants, and psychologically trained therapists and educators.

This chapter traces the development of the role played by psychologically trained mental health professionals in facilitating the emotional well being of missionaries. Focusing this history of member care on the influence of psychologically trained professionals is not intended to suggest that those educated in other member care specialties have made a less important contribution.

What was behind the growing cry for psychological help? Prior to the mid-fifties it would have been considered superfluous and even suspect—holding onto God was considered to be the antidote to disturbing feelings. Missionaries would not even consider sharing openly lest they be seen as less than consecrated Christians. Yet authors like Ruth Tucker and Leslie Andrews in their chapter "Historical Notes on Missionary Care" (O'Donnell 24 – 36) give poignant examples of well-known missionaries who contributed immeasurably but suffered deeply emotionally.

The same spirit prevailed in our culture at large. This was not the age of openness. Yet, the Lord works according to the ethos of the historical moment and marvelous mission work was accomplished.

Mental health services have developed in numerous venues in the past half-century: pre-field screening, MK care, missionary support centers, use of outside consultants, conferences for mental health professionals and mission leaders, mission member care departments, on-field mental health centers, a large body of literature, formal training in member care, applied research, consideration of ethical standards, and finally internationalization and globalization of member care.

Missionaries could not escape the effects of what was occurring in the Western culture. The growing change and upheaval in social, political, and moral structures of society all over the world created an increasingly wounded populace. The spirit of the times affected Christians and non-Christians alike. Emotional dysfunction was in-creasingly widespread.

Questions started to arise. How could mission groups detect problems before candidates began service? How could they alleviate the struggles of those already serving? How could attrition due to emotional problems be reduced? How could those exposed to trauma be helped? Mission leaders began to realize that something had to be done.

Simultaneously God was raising up Christian professionals with the training and experience to provide answers. In the mid-fifties and early sixties, impetus for psychological help for missionaries was seen in the founding of Missionary Internship (later known as Mission Training International) in 1954 by R. E. and Ella Thompson, the Narramore Christian Foundation in 1956 by Dr. Clyde Narramore, and Link Care in 1965 by Dr. Stanley Lindquist. Each has expanded to include the developing aspects of psychological services for missionaries discussed below. In addition, pio-neers such as psychologist Dr. Henry Brandt motivated other professionals to minis-ter to the emotional needs of missionaries.

Pre-field Recruitment and Acceptance

As a result of increasing attrition among missionaries, one of the first major areas in which mental health professionals' help was sought was in the area of screening candidates. This generally has taken the form of a well-validated psychological bat-tery of tests, almost always including the MMPI or Millon plus two or three additional tests, hopefully an interview with the candidate, a written report synthesizing the results and giving recommendations, and a feedback meeting with the appropriate leaders. Although the process has greatly helped to redirect or refer for counseling those who were not prepared for the stress of cross-cultural living and has given some guidance to effective placement, the results are not foolproof.

Since most mission organizations are now doing some form of candidate evaluation to assess emotional stamina to function cross-culturally, study is needed to further determine: (1) the accuracy of specific tests in predicting success; (2) the value of test results for assignment decisions; (3) how best to share helpful information with field leaders; (4) ways to give maximally helpful feedback to candidates in an uplift-ing and honest way; (5) methods for safeguarding the integrity of the missionary in the entire process; (6) how to make the process cost effective for both the candidate and the mission.

A second role mental health professionals often play in the screening process is their involvement in candidate schools (the two to four weeks a candidate is at mission headquarters, prior to acceptance or before leaving for overseas). Conducting sem-inars, groups, interviews, counseling, and consultations are activities in which they participate.

MK Care

A second early and necessary emphasis was the well being of missionaries' children (MKs). Three organizations in particular—the Association of Christian Schools International (ACSI), Interaction Incorporated, and the Children's Education Department (CHED) of Wycliffe Bible Translators—provided the momentum for increasing interest in care for MKs through the International Conferences on Missionary Kids (ICMKs). The first was held in Manila in 1984, the second in Quito in 1987, and the third in Nairobi in 1989. Proceedings were published for the first two; contributions from the third are included in *Raising Resilient MKs* (Bowers 1998).

Many mental health professionals participated as facilitators, speakers, seminar and workshop leaders, and panel members. Mental health workers along with mis-sion leaders were sensitized to the special needs of MKs. Since then smaller but effec-tive regional conferences have taken place periodically.

In the eighties David Pollock founded Interaction, Inc. and began reentry seminars for MKs coming home for college. Third culture kids (TCKs, a term coined about fifty years ago by sociologist Dr. Ruth Useem from Michigan State University) whose parents work in foreign service and international business also have benefitted from his expertise. In 1999 Pollock co-authored with Ruth Van Reken the book *Third Culture Kids: The Experience of Growing Up Among Worlds*.

Mu Kappa is a fraternity organization designed to support MKs on college campuses. It provides a network for MKs to know each other and keep in touch. Counselors who work with missionary families often participate in Mu Kappa regional conferences. Barnabas International includes Mu Kappa among the many member care projects it has encouraged over the past fifteen years.

Today, an increasing number of MK schools have a counselor in residence. Preferred qualifications include a solid background in child/adolescent development, family education and therapy and child/adolescent counseling. Confidentiality policies for working with minors must be clearly understood and agreed upon.

Helpful literature and resources with mental health themes are increasingly available for MKs. Recommended readings and resources are listed in the appendices of the book Raising resilient MKs (Bowers 1998). See Chapter 15 by Janet Blomberg.

Missionary Support Centers

The first well-known residential center where missionaries could go for emotional restoration was Link Care in Fresno, California. Many other organizations have been established to meet the expressed need for residential centers. Like Link Care they work with multiple mission agencies. Many are expanding their offerings to include psycho-educative and preventive types of activities, screening of candidates, consultation when needed, and on-field assistance. Brent Lindquist, in his article, "Missionary Support Centers" (O'Donnell, 1992) discusses the subject of support cen-ters in depth. An interesting aspect he envisions is the establishment of on-field centers in accessible centralized areas to enable missionaries to obtain help without the need to return to their home country.

A unique variation of a support center is the Missionary Health Institute in Toronto (North York), Canada, directed by Kenneth Gamble, M.D., assisted by Glenn Taylor and Duncan Westwood, psychotherapists. It aims to provide a continuous flow of care for missionaries from their initial call to missions through their application, including screening, orientation, and assessment, to continuing care on the field, debriefing for home assignment, and assistance for transitions in ministry, including retirement.

Participation of Outside Consultants

Since the early seventies a growing number of mental health professionals have contributed time and often expenses to facilitate the emotional well being of missionaries. They contribute their skills in a focused, time-limited manner as needed. A relatively new phenomenon is the practice of Christian counseling centers, such as the one in Grand Rapids, Michigan, to provide training for clinicians who wish to be part of this ministry. Some centers enable one of their staff to serve for longer periods to give more long-term help. A helpful chapter on guidelines for short-term field consul-tants is in the book edited by O'Donnell (1992, 202-213). See also Chapter 21.

Conferences for Mental Health Professionals and Mission Leaders

In 1980, two psychologists already doing consultation work, Dr. John Powell and Dr. David Wickstrom, founded the Mental Health and Missions Conference where mental health professionals and mission leaders meet each November (see Chapter 1). This has proven to be an invaluable network to share what is being done, to glean new ideas, to meet resource people, to be updated on current needs, and to encourage one another. Several ongoing projects discussed below had their origins at one of these conferences (see Chapter 1).

Mission-focused organizations have devoted an increasing amount of time to mental health issues. The Interdenominational Foreign Missions Association (IFMA) and the Evangelical Fellowship of Mission Agencies (EFMA) continue to have conferences centered on member care topics. They invite mental health professionals to sug-gest topics, speak, lead workshops or seminars, and be panel members. These occa- sions have served to stimulate awareness and provide information on all areas of member care.

Some organizations also give specialized assistance in mental health areas. For example, Mission Training International in Palmer Springs, Colorado, directed by clinical psychologist Dr. Stephen Sweatman, conducts conferences for mission personnel and church mission committee members. Barnabas International sponsors the annual Pastors-to-Missionaries Conference to better equip pastors to counsel mission-aries.

Mission Member Care Departments

A more recent development is the inclusion of member care departments in mission agencies. The department's director often functions as a facilitator with an interdisciplinary social science background and networks to implement programs that meet the psycho-educative and psycho-remedial needs of the mission body. Every aspect of personnel care tends to be considered—candidate selection, preparation for cross-cultural stress, reentry seminars as well as the individual debriefing of returning missionaries, appropriate help with life span issues, trauma debriefing, and counseling on specific issues both in the home office and on the field. The counseling department of Wycliffe Bible Translators, developed by Dr. Phil Grossman, Dr. Laura Mae Gardner and Dr. Richard Gardner and others, has been a model program.

On-field Mental Health Centers

A more recent development is the formation of mental health centers centrally located in geographic areas where missionaries and nationals can receive both therapeutic and preventive on-field help. For example, the Tumaini Center in Nairobi, headed by psychiatrist Dr. Roger Brown and staffed by AIM and Wycliffe mental health professionals, serves Christian workers throughout central, eastern, and even more distant African areas. In Taiwan, Dr. Steve Spinella directs The Counseling Services Center of Taichung, a cooperative initiative by mission leaders since 1992. The staff includes expatriate members and trained Taiwanese counselors who care for the needs of Chinese speaking nationals and western expatriates.

Centers like these can handle the relatively immediate intervention so necessary in instances such as trauma. This often results in missionaries being able to remain on the field at least until home leave time. In addition to therapy, staff conduct seminars and workshops on needed subjects.

A variation which grew out of a Mental Health and Missions Conference is the model of mobile trauma intervention centers in strategic areas that would serve all the missions in that region. Dr. Karen Carr, a clinical psychologist, established the first team in Ivory Coast. She and her associates have assisted missionaries and admin-istrators through many crises in West Africa. It is hoped that similar centers will be established in many other areas. Qualified therapists willing to function on mission salaries would be needed.

The Development of Literature

Articles and books written by professionals experienced in cross-cultural counseling have increased in number since the mid-20th century. *The Evangelical Missions Quarterly, The Journal of Psychology and Theology, The Journal of Psychology and Christianity, Interact, World Report, Missiology,* and *The International Bulletin of Missionary Research* are among journals that publish articles pertinent to missionary care.

An increasing number of books have also been published during the latter part of the 20th century and into the 21st century.

Two that heightened awareness of mental health and missions are *Helping Missionaries Grow: Readings in Mental Health and Missions* (1988) and *Missionary Care: Counting the Cost for World Evangelization* (1992), both edited by Dr. Kelly O'Donnell. Many of the chapters in each were first presented at the Mental Health and Missions Conference.

Pastoral Counseling Across Cultures by David Augsburger (1986) gives a more scholarly theoretical approach.

Lianne Roembke's *Building Credible Multicultural Teams* (2000) incorporates many mental health principles in discussing cultural adjustment, trust factors, personal needs, conflict resolution, and communication.

Another specialized book is *Raising Resilient MKs (1998)* edited by Joyce M. Bowers, which draws on wisdom gathered through the International Conferences on Missionary Kids as well as many other resources.

A recent book dealing with the issues inherent in the experience of expatriate families is *Families On the Move* authored by Marion Knell (EMIS, 2001).

Most recently, the book edited by Kelly O'Donnell (2002), *Doing Member Care*

Well, includes chapters pertaining to mental health issues from an international perspective.

Formal Training in Member Care

With the increasing number of missionaries ministering among unreached people groups which are often located in frontier settings, or working in politically chaotic areas, the support and care given by mental health professionals has become a crucial component for the healthy emotional functioning of missionaries. Although the availability of clinically trained professionals does not fully meet the needs, clinicians are responding to the challenge in growing numbers.

There is a growing recognition of the necessity for cross-cultural training. Either during or after graduate programs qualifying them to be licensed clinically, many are taking courses in biblical studies, in the integration of psychological and biblical concepts, and in cross-cultural functioning, and are adding practicums giving field experience. Some Christian graduate programs have started to offer courses in the area of member care, often in conjunction with a Missions or Intercultural Studies Department.

Missionary support centers such as Heartstream, directed by Dr. Larry and Dr. Lois Dobbs, also offer short-term seminars for clinicians who want a broader awareness of member care ministry. These sessions are primarily staffed by professionals with cross-cultural as well as clinical experience.

A variation of available training is the Mid-West Member Care Network, which developed through the interest of the Christian Counseling Center in Grand Rapids, Michigan. Therapists meet on a regular basis to acquire a basic foundation for ministry to missionaries.

Another trend is to encourage members of a counseling center staff to spend a considerable span of time serving with a mission group, supported through prayer and often finances. Professionals with experience in a given culture are increasingly offering on-site member care training programs for both interested missionaries and nationals.

Research

There is a growing recognition of the need to subject methods used in the care of missionaries to objective evaluation. Dr. John Powell points out in his chapter "MK Research: Notes and Observations" (Bowers, 438-442) that in a search of entries relating to missionary families as catalogued in the Billy Graham Library at Wheaton College, prior to 1986 hard empirical research had been sparse.

Dr. Frances White looked at the entries relating to all aspects of missionary care at the same source up to 2000 and found that even this broader investigation revealed a small number of empirical studies compared with the greater number of controlled observations, surveys, and more objective anecdotal interpretations.

However, the increasing number of masters and doctoral candidates entering programs that provide training in member care skills (e.g., clinical or counseling psychology, social work, family and marital therapy, interpersonal programs) are doing more in-depth dissertations.

An impetus to more expansive research occurred in 1987 when the MK-CART/

CORE was founded by a group interested in mission families. CART, signifying the **C**onsultation **A**nd **R**esearch **T**eam, consists of mission representatives who identify the need of research topics. CORE, the **C**ommittee **O**n **R**esearch and **E**ndowment, is the group of member care professionals who volunteer their time and expertise to design and carry out the research. As several facets of the research progressed, the results were reported to missions representatives. This latter group also determined the ethical guidelines for recording and using the results, thereby developing an initial ethical code that can serve as a guide to other researchers. A description of the research and a bibliography of pertinent articles reporting results is authored by John Powell in *Raising Resilient MKs* (Bowers, 438-442). See also Chapter 56 in this volume.

MK-CART/CORE has highlighted the advantages afforded by team work in member care research, e.g., sharing of data for several hypotheses, accountability on methods in progress, a more comprehensive investigation, and sustaining motivation. A distinctive feature in this research is that it was driven by questions from a multi-mission group who worked in a coordinated way with one another and with the research team. Others spurred on by this research, particularly doctoral candidates, are investigating other aspects of member care.

The formation and continuance of research projects depends on financial provision and missionary cooperation in gathering data. An already overworked mission corps and constant need for finances to meet field needs pose a present challenge to much-needed research.

Financial Resources

As the MK-CART/CORE staff has realized, activities such as research, setting up counseling support and trauma centers can be cost prohibitive. E-mail, videotapes, printed material, and in-service educational materials generally require expensive equipment. To offer adequate help to missionaries, those responsible are realizing the dire need for grant writers who would work with them in writing proposals for financial backing.

For example, Dr. Roger Brown, a psychiatrist at the Tumaini Center in Nairobi, has recently spearheaded plans for a new building to house the counseling center in that city. He has had to spend considerable time making contacts for contributions, some in the form of matching grants. This plus the supervision of the construction has taken valuable time from the counseling services he offers, but the center is now completed and in operation.

Organizations like the Narramore Foundation, headed by Dr. Bruce Narramore, nephew of the founder, have provided funds for invaluable projects on mental health and missions. Other financial sponsors are sorely needed.

Ethical Considerations

Since emotional help for missionaries is becoming a necessity in today's world, mental health professionals are becoming keenly aware of the need to work with mission groups on a code of ethics that covers as many eventualities as possible. Some examples of issues to be addressed are confidentiality, credentials, competence, methods, dual relationships, and the many ambiguous areas that arise in varying cultural milieus.

The code of ethics developed by the professional organization with which mental health workers are affiliated (e.g., American Association of Pastoral Counselors, American Psychological Association, National Association of Social Workers) can serve as guidelines. See Chapters 51 and 52 by Richardson for a more complete discussion and excerpts from these guidelines.

The uniqueness of a mission context inevitably gives rise to ethical issues covered in no existing general code of ethics. Mental health professionals attempt to resolve confusing situations through consultation with colleagues and mission personnel. Reflection, Scripture, and prayer are essential ingredients.

Part of the concern is the increasing predominance of litigation all over the world. Insurance that includes the mission agency as well as the clinician has become an essential.

Internationalization and Globalization of Member Care

In this 21st century mental health practitioners are seeking a more global approach in member care. Kelly O'Donnell, a psychologist deeply dedicated to the care of missionaries, made the statement in 1992 that on an inter-agency and more global level, the field of member care is relatively unorganized. He advocated a macro-model that would be a more systemic, global, cooperative approach for member care (O'Donnell, 1992, p. 286).

Recently there has been an increasing response to the global need for mutually supportive interlinked networks among member care workers of many nationalities. In many cases the movement has accelerated through the intentional promotion of appropriate, comprehensive connections with the global missions community.

A particularly growing influence is the Task Force, also called Global Member Care Resources, under the auspices of the World Evangelical Alliance Mission Commission. Dr. Kelly O'Donnell and David Pollock are key coordinators of this commission with the aim of establishing cooperative interdependent initiatives to promote missionary care on the global level. (See O'Donnell 2002 for an in-depth view of member care worldwide.)

Harry Hoffmann began sending a networking newsletter via e-mail to inform practitioners of member care activities in world areas, particularly Asia, Europe, and North Africa. These briefings have recently been amalgamated into a newsletter titled *Global Member Care Briefing* as a service of the Member Care Task Force (MemCa), which is under the auspices of the World Evangelical Alliance Missions Commission.

Sent out three times a year to those known to be active in member care, the publication contains news of member care activities throughout the world, e.g., consultations, conferences, local meetings, training programs, updates, and analysis on the care and development of mission personnel, and relevant literature. Its purpose is to foster a flow of caretakers by enabling member care practitioners to develop appropriate, comprehensive connections with the global missions community. Requests for the e-mail newsletter may be directed to WEF-MCNB@yahoogroups.com.

The more international systemic approach is evident in member care activities, often including several countries, taking place in Thailand, Turkey, UK, the Philippines, Germany, North Africa, and the U.S.A. This international approach is more conducive to meeting the needs of an ever growing multi-cultural mission force. Member care workers would greatly benefit by affiliating with colleagues around the world who also have member care responsibilities. This can be done by becoming part of the e-info service dedicated to the information, networking and discussion of issues relating to member care. The contact address is member-care-europe@yahoogroups .com or member-care-asia@yahoogroups.com.

The global trend in mental health practice is timely for member care workers who face a rapidly changing world that allows no culture to live in isolation. The necessity for a global approach is even more acute as mental health professionals increasingly play a counseling role in newly developing Christian international schools that must consider the needs of diverse multi-cultural student bodies.

An excellent article by O'Donnell, "Going Global: A Member Care Model for Best Practice" in the April 2001 *Evangelical Missions Quarterly* presents challenges that encourage a more comprehensive and mutually supportive ethos for member care programs. Only as mental health professionals stay keenly alert to world trends can they be prepared to facilitate future movements to meet the emotional needs of missionaries of all cultures in this unpredictable world.

References

Augsburger, D. (1986). *Pastoral counseling across cultures*. Philadelphia: Westminister Press.

Bowers, J. M. (1998). (Ed.). *Raising resilient MKs: Resources for caregivers, parents, and teachers.* Colorado Springs: Association of Christian Schools International.

Knell, M. (2001). *Families on the move.* UK: Monarch Books. & USA: EMIS

O'Donnell, K. (1988). (Ed.). *Helping missionaries grow: Readings in mental health and missions.* Pasadena, CA: William Carey Library.

O'Donnell, K. (1992). (Ed.). *Missionary care: Counting the cost for world evangelization.* Pasadena, CA: William Carey Library.

O'Donnell, K. (2001). Going Global: A Member Care Model for Best Practice. *Evangelical Missions Quarterly.* 37, 212-222.

O'Donnell, K. (2002). (Ed.). *Doing member care well: Perspectives and practices from around the world.* Pasadena, CA: William Carey Library.

Pollock, D. C. & Van Reken, Ruth E. (1999). *Third culture kids: The experience of growing up among worlds.* Yarmouth, ME: Intercultural Press.

Roembke, L. (2000). *Building credible multicultural teams.* Pasadena, CA: William Carey Library.

4

Member Care in the Service of Missions: What Is In the Driver's Seat?

Brent Lindquist

Part I: Does Member Care Enhance Missionary Effectiveness?

This chapter reflects a number of my ruminations on member care and the degree to which it serves the ultimate goals of cross-cultural mission. I have had experience in cross-cultural training, prefield orientation, and CEO dialogues, and have participated around the edges of events such as missiological meetings and language and culture learning meetings, as well as making presentations in both. These experiences have given rise to discomfort in several ways regarding how member care is conceptualized and delivered.

For the last seven years I have consistently expressed my fear that member care may have become too heavily weighted toward counseling and related activities, and therefore may be in danger of drawing the missionary movement away from its true calling. This may sound alarming to people who are in close contact with the emotional, psychological, and spiritual pain that mission-aries experience during the "doing of mission." My intent is not to ignore that, but to suggest a multifaceted ap-proach which would meet emotional needs while promot-ing effectiveness in mission, which, I believe, is the ulti-mate calling of missions.

Counseling vs. Language & Culture Coaching

These concerns were confirmed at the International Congress on Language Learning 4, held in Colorado

What is the ultimate goal of member care? Is it primarily the well being of missionaries, or missionary effectiveness in fulfilling the Great Commission? Language and culture learning may seem to be at cross purposes with mental health care. Challenges are presented for the development of contextualized models for care and community-based member care. Provocative questions from diverse perspectives stimulate the reader to think about mental health services in new ways.

Springs. I engaged in dialogue with friends in the field of language and culture acquisition, who spend their lives helping missionaries become effective through communicative competence. I discovered that there is an increasing bifurcation between the roles of the member care provider and the language and culture coach.

In the best case scenario, these two people, would become aware of each other and talk to each other about their common goals and interests, even though they may not be connected through organizational structure *per se*. In certain cases, the language and culture coaches would be able to utilize the member care people and help the latter recognize issues that may need to be addressed before they become "clinical" issues—which is much more of a preventive focus. (This preventive model of encour-aging and enhancing health has been popularized in psychology through the new field of psychoneuroimmunology).

In the worst case scenario, the member care provider and language and culture coach do not talk to each other and actually work at cross purposes. For example, language learning is hard. It requires a certain degree of isolation with people of the target language, and it requires intense study and practice in the community. There is no way whatsoever to avoid this developmental learning process. However, in the midst of language learning, member care people give advice to new learners that is contrary to important aspects of language learning. They do not intend to confound the drive towards missionary effectiveness, but are simply ignorant of the developmental process of language and culture learning.

Language Learning: A Necessary Stressor

Language and culture learners become stressed out by language learning, they cannot isolate themselves from the host culture and work only with Americans. To do that prevents them from learning the language, which prevents them from developing communicative competence, which prevents them from developing opportunities to influence the people with whom they are called to serve.

If left uncorrected, this bifurcated approach could conceivably have more missionaries feeling better on the field, but would result in those missionaries being less effective in fulfilling their call. Unfortunately, the mission enterprise today is filled with scenarios and strategies which essentially do the above.

Some may question the importance I give this multifaceted approach in terms of missionary effectiveness. Some may even question "effectiveness" as a criterion for missions work. Some say that we are only there to "plant the seed" and the Holy Spirit does the rest. I won't dispute the role of the Holy Spirit, but I do dispute the assump-tion that whatever we do is OK, since we are not concerned with fruit, only planting.

Too many times, North Americans devise plans of ministry to respond to some need we see, and neglect a necessary viewpoint — the national viewpoint. I may have a great ministry idea, but if it doesn't scratch where "they" itch, I am not giving them what they need. We cannot assume that anything done in the Lord's name is good enough. I hope we would agree that doing wrong things in the Lord's name won't do him any good.

Joining the Target Group

When I approach the training of new missionaries, my goals include helping them to see the absolute necessity of connecting with and identifying with the target group. Missionaries who completed the program I once developed and operated came away understanding how essential it was for them to get into the culture, build networks and friendships, and see the target people and their context as a place the missionary needed to be part of. This incarnational mindset is based on communicative competence. Newcomers need to learn to communicate with the people around them, in their language. One's influence will always be limited without learning the context and how to communicate.

How does this relate to member care? Caring for missionaries needs to be multifaceted. It needs to take into account not just the personal/psychological, but the interpersonal/social/cultural as well. Any approach that ignores any of this will simply not help people in the long run. Helping new missionaries navigate the very difficult language learning period means having a balanced view of what cross-cultural development is and what it entails. Advice on such development needs to enhance the crossing of the cultural boundary, not protecting someone from it. Mental health thrives in such a balance.

Enhancing Effectiveness through Member Care

I choose the title of this article, "Member Care in the Service of Missions," very intentionally, as it expresses the key concept that I am trying to get across. Member care should mean providing a wide variety of services necessary for the development of effectiveness in cross-cultural ministry.

Member care is not about providing counseling services to missionaries on the field. It means coming alongside an organization, understanding the organization's culture and climate, the target culture and climate, and what missionaries are supposed to be doing, and developing strategies to bring workers to greater effectiveness. It might involve linguistic coaching, cultural coaching, emotional coaching, or administrative coaching—and, preferably, a combination of all of the above.

In so saying, I feel like I am placing myself outside the major flow of member care, which is dominated by counseling types who are focusing on alleviating symptoms and pain. Of course I am one of the counseling types myself, and see that as an incredibly noble and important call which needs to be continued. However, if the whole member care movement is driven by identification of symptoms and alleviation of pain, we will end up creating a member care system that is not complementary with the overall strategy of missions.

Need for Contextualized Models of Care

Another issue is that the member care system has thus far been developed almost exclusively by North Americans, or at least the major themes guiding member care are developed in the context of a North American model of therapy and care. Up to this point, there has been very little contextualization or indigenization by our international colleagues, to make caring for missionaries more relevant to their cultural contexts.

One notable movement towards internationalization of member care is the new book, *Doing Member Care Well*, edited by Kelly O'Donnell, which has many contributors who have an international perspective. It is unfortunate, however, that many of these international contributors quote from North Americans to provide rationale and support for their ideas. I long for the day when there is a body of literature with few exclusively North American references, as that will signify that we have moved beyond pedagogy to synergy in our arena of influence as Westerners.

For the rest of my professional life I expect to focus on mentoring, coaching and internationalizing. Space prevents me from articulating in detail what I will be doing, but I will sketch some of my major ideas and goals.

Member Care Subspecialties

First, member care of the future needs to be conceptualized as a number of subspecialties. Otherwise, we may increasingly work at cross purposes in our attempts to provide services.

Clinical Care

We need to define the role of psychotherapy and other intensely clinical forms of care provided by people with special training, and examine where those services should be provided. Assuming that a clinician can go in and provide intensive psychotherapy, even in brief form, in a context that may have a lot of question marks in it, does an injustice to the professional in terms of licensure and ethical practice issues in the home country.

Increasingly, licensing boards are asking questions about what professionals do —where, when, how, and why—and operating in the absence of a well-developed standard of care could cause professionals to risk their licenses. In an overseas setting, we can get sucked into relationships or situations that we would never approach in the United States. The long jet flight or the overseas trip will not keep us immune to any problems over the long haul. Situations may develop where work that we do overseas may follow us home and become an ethical dilemma or a professional practice issue, which can end up as a legal issue.

Standards of Care

At the same time, we need to continue to develop standards of care for our professional work, so that we can articulate models for providing intensive services in particular areas. A number of us are in dialogue about establishing regional centers for psychotherapy which will focus on the more difficult issues of emotional and psychological growth and well-being. While that may be a way to bring therapists closer to the field, I have significant concerns as to whether that is, in fact, the best way to utilize resources and funds. Sometimes people need to leave their place of ministry for more than a brief period to get help.

Community-based Member Care

We also need to define the role of another type of member care which I call community-based member care, in which member care resources are provided at the local community level. Unfortunately, North Americans tend to congregate together and like to have services, programs or seminars delivered in ways that are easier for them to grasp. I doubt that we will make significant changes in this area for several generations of missionaries. We do need to have Western-based seminars and models for the Westerners.

At the same time, seminar leaders need to have a more global view than in the past. The goal is not simply to provide stress management in Chiang Mai that is basically cut-and-paste from what we do in Fresno. Rather, the goal is understanding in detail what is going on in Chiang Mai among diverse Western missionary populations, and being able to speak to those issues, or at least point people in helpful directions, because of one's familiarity with the issues at the local level.

International Model of Member Care

There needs to be a much more well-defined and highly developed international model of member care, driven and developed by our international brothers and sisters. This is where I am choosing to put a lot of my time—coming alongside and helping people think through what they need to do for their personnel, involving much more than the mere adaptation of models we use in the West.

For example, I have been privileged to work with a number of folks in South Asia regarding two projects, one of which is the visioning of a retreat/pastoral care/counseling center for national missionaries. My concerns go beyond the standard, such as what topics need to be covered in retreats. My concerns flow from the context and environment. I want them to tell me about typical needs of the nationals—how various ethnic groups differ; how they eat, sleep, congregate, play, pray, etc. How do they learn and grow? If I assume they are more similar to us than different without understanding the differences, I will inadvertently help them create a resource the national missionaries don't recognize as their own. And, it will probably be less effective at meeting their needs.

Conclusion

We who are concerned with member care need to be relentless in pursuing the development of programs, resources, and strategies which keep the real purpose of missions as the guiding light. This is not about just taking care of people. It is about taking care of people, *so that* they can be as effective as possible in their call in missions.

Part II: Self-Development Challenges

These brief vignettes are attempts to develop a growing body of discovery processes, to enable us to think through a variety of questions relative to a particular case. At first glance, they may not all seem directly relevant to missionary care, but my purpose is to challenge readers to think "outside the box" by presenting situations and questions that are quite radically different from what is usually discussed in the context of member care.

A.   *Stomach Pain in Liberia*

Some years ago I stood with Pastor Imojahostin on a gravelly street in West Africa. He described his work with street orphans who had recently been combatants in a civil war action. We stood in front of a building that he had been given by the government in order to take these boys off the street and try to reintroduce them into society. Typically, he would ask boys if they had been in the "troubles" and if they said yes, he asked them if they felt sorry for what they had done. If they expressed a sense of guilt about their actions, he felt they possessed enough of a conscience to be rehabilitated, and he would bring them into his program.

They had removed fifty bodies from the building that he had been given, and we stood in the street where the bodies had been buried. There is a community well in front of the school. Standing on those graves, he shared with me one particular vignette which has haunted me ever since.

Pastor Imojahostin had picked a boy we will call Samuel off the street. Samuel was making great progress. One morning they were standing near the well and Samuel said, "Pastor, see this woman coming with her water can on her head?" As she walked by, they exchanged greetings with her. The pastor acknowledged that he had seen the woman. Samuel said, "When I was a rebel I raped that woman while holding a gun to her chin. I don't think she recognizes or remembers me. But, Pastor, every time I see her, I have this pain in my stomach. When will this pain go away?"

At that point I felt an incredible sense of hopelessness and helplessness based on my Western mindset about dealing with problems. Here was a street orphan with no money and little prospect for help other than the pastor who was reaching out to him. What could I, a psychologist, possibly give him? That incident, almost ten years ago, created one of the incredible paradigm shifting processes that brought me to where I am today. Everyone who works effectively cross-culturally has at least one of these painful shifts. What is yours? Using either yours or mine, answer the following questions:

- What sort of care is Samuel receiving in working with the pastor?
- What kinds of care might Samuel need besides counseling?
- What would be a possible diagnosis of someone like Samuel in a Western model, and what would be the standard treatment regimen? What factors might be used in diagnosis and treatment in that part of the world?
- How relevant is your treatment modality for Samuel? By whose standards? How would you determine this?
- How might we assist the pastor, helping him process his strategies and become more effective in helping street children?
- What do we look for in the pastor that would indicate problems in his own life, and how do we address them?
- What resources are available in the surrounding community to help the pastor with his task?
- How or where can you get information to help you with this?
- How does your Western training create difficulties for you in evaluating this problem?

B.   *Anything Is Better than Nothing*

We have to ask if what we are providing is, in fact, going to be useful in the long haul. Member care counselors or consultants sometimes offer advice and input which go against standards of best practice for language and culture learning. For example, a young family who are stressed by language learning may be told that it is okay for them to cut back on language learning and spend more time with their expatriate friends. Is this really for the long range good?

This is a very difficult question, because it seems like we are asking people to suffer, knowing that they need to get through a process. But life is like that anyway. My daughter suffered learning to play the flute. While this is certainly not the same as potentially becoming clinically depressed, I had to allow her to continue to have the pain in order to learn the skill. We must not try to make ministry too easy, because we may block learning and insight.

- Can you think of specific member care "solutions" which might create cross-cultural problems? Who could help you understand this better?
- How do you define a normal growth process in cross-cultural devel-opment? How is "normal" defined from the perspective of the local culture vs. Western models of growth?

C. *Pursuing Health Versus Pursuing Effectiveness*

Can we accept the idea that pursuing effectiveness might even be more impor-tant than pursuing health? As you work with missionary clients it is so easy to see, from your limited perspective in talking with them, what appear to be very unhealthy environments and situations. While we should not intentionally allow unhealthy situ-ations to continue, sometimes our interventions or comments serve to fracture the en-vironment and ruin the ministry as opposed to helping the missionary pursue health.

We may need to develop a strategy for communicating with a mission that will help the missionary develop a more healthy pace, but at the same time guard against doing violence to what the mission needs to accomplish. That is not to say that all mission policy is appropriate and good, or that all mission leaders are the picture of mental health. But too often we inadvertently create more tension than if we were to step back and look at the bigger picture.

- How do you feel about authority and chains of command?
- How do you explain confidentiality to your client and their organization?
- How do you meet the needs of both sides?

D. *What We Look For Is What We Find*

It is interesting that, if I am looking for something, I am going to find it (except if it is my hammer or tape measure, both of which are currently missing, and as my wife says, if I had put them back where they belong, I would have them now...). We all need to pay attention to this.

If we look for instances of organizations missing the mark, we will find them. Everyone is trying to do too much with too little. Instead of looking for what is mis-sing, we could start looking for what is there, and build on that. Building on strengths would be much better received by mission organizations than if we are perceived as somebody who is going to make the missionaries angry. This is a central organizing principle in the new field of psychoneuroimmunology—enhancing already existing health.

- "If something is worth doing, it is worth doing well." What about: If something is worth doing, it is worth doing poorly. Or, If something is worth doing, it is worth doing. How do you respond to these?
- How can you be an ombudsman between the organization and your client?

E.   *How Come Stable People Fall Apart Overseas?*

Too often, people who do well in their home culture and pass all the candidacy requirements, crash and burn in the field. Missions have historically asked psychologists to screen out people with problematic backgrounds. This is a problematic line of reasoning. Certainly, there are diagnostic categories that are quite problematic for cross-cultural ministry, and maybe these should be screened out.

However, with advances in care and medicine, some of these people can function well and be effective. The issue is not screening; it is what we do with the people we find, and what we find out about the people that we evaluate. This is not something that is easily caught, but I will use the concept of stability versus ultrastability as an example. I learned this from one of my mentors, Don Larson. Don was a linguist and anthropologist who co-led a pre-field orientation program with me for almost 20 years, and was a wonderful mentor.

We typically evaluate people by looking for evidence of stability in their home culture. I'll define stability as the ability to remain stable in a stable environment—not a very fancy definition. We look for people with victory testimonies, who have held good jobs and been effective, without major crises in their lives. And that is well and good. There are some people who pass through that grid who do come from problem-atic backgrounds, and they seem to be doing well and have victory testimonies. But their testimonies are in their own culture. They know the rules and they have learned to live accordingly.

Consider instead the concept of ultrastability—the ability to maintain or regain stability in a changing environment. I look for missionary candidates who have experienced difficulty, and then examine how they have managed it. If they have a victory testimony, that's wonderful. But I want to know if they had adversity in the same area, and explore how they manage harmful situations and still come out okay.

In addition, I look for people who have been outsiders on an insiders' turf, as that is the nature of cross-cultural ministry. If we focus on those kinds of issues in the candidacy process, and look for evidence of ultrastability (and if we do not find it, look for ways to build ultrastability), we may be able to develop more hardy and resilient missionaries.

- Should the mission be a hospital for dysfunctional missionaries? Or, a coaching or fitness training center?

Conclusion

This has been a somewhat random discussion of member care in the service of missions. I hope that I have caused the reader to think. These issues encompass more than one discipline or one theory. This is an incredibly complex field which needs input from many perspectives in order to produce what is needed—and that is producing people, encouraging people, or enhancing people, to do what God has called them to do. We can have no greater opportunity and no greater challenge.

5

Missionary Care and Counseling: A Brief History and Challenge

Laura Mae Gardner

*A*s the modern missionary movement continues to grow and develop, so also has the recognition that providing specific care for missionaries constitutes a needful activity. The modern movement essentially dates from the mid-1800s. In the first hundred years much of the care was focused on logistics, financial needs, housing, transportation, the care and education of children, and medical issues. Prayer was a basic part of this care and is always crucial to effective care. In the past 60 years or so there has been increasing development in the personal care of missionaries. Counseling and other services provided by Christian mental health professionals have become an important part of this care.

Missionary care is founded in Biblical principles and examples. When Jesus entrusted the Great Commission to the disciples whom he had just called (Mt. 10:5–15), he expected them to utilize local hospitality. When Paul wrote his masterpiece donor letter, Philippians, he acknowledged care given by the church at Philippi (Phil. 4:15–17) and the church's representative, Epaphroditus (4:18). In II Timothy (4:9–13) and Titus (3:12–14), Paul the writer expects God's emissaries to extend mutual care to one another in meeting practical needs. So missionary care is not new; it is expected and required.

During the modern missionary movement, missionary care can be seen as having moved through six stages, each having a different focus, each adding something new without minimizing or dismissing the focus of the past.

Stage One: *Self Care, pre-1940*

Missionaries of this time period were expected to make a lifetime commitment, to be extremely hardy physically and psychologically, and to be spiritual giants. In-

The mental health movement has made growing contributions to missions. Missionary care can be seen as moving through six stages, each building on and including the previous one: Self Care, pre-1940; Shared Care, c. 1940-1960; Structured Care, 1960-1970; Specialized Care, 1970-1985, Pervasive Care, 1985-1995, and Globally Shared Care, 1995-present. The current trend is toward providing adequate care for all.

41

cluded in their ranks are Amy Carmichael, Adoniram Judson, the Serampore Trio, Mary Slessor, Hudson Taylor, and many, many more. We acknowledge this heritage and applaud these "heroes of the faith."

But these missionaries' personal flaws and vulnerabilities were often overlooked. James Beck's book, *Dorothy Carey*, reminds us that even during those days mental illness existed among missionaries. The story of Felix Carey reminds us that children of missionaries were not automatically extensions of their parents' vision and commitment. However, there was little acknowledgment of these needs, and no provision beforehand, during, or after a tragedy to serve, care for and strengthen the missionary or his family.

Stage Two: *Shared Care, c. 1940–1960*

As missionaries began to realize the effect of field stresses on workers and their children in a given field or in a particular location, they rallied to meet one another's needs by establishing boarding schools such as Kent Academy (Jos, Nigeria), Morrison Academy (Taiwan), and Woodstock (India).

Other kinds of one-another care were demonstrated in the assignment of personnel in support roles, e.g., government relations, buyer services, and in-house medical services. Needed care was given on site and usually delivered by a rotating staff of missionaries who were generally untrained to meet this specialized need, but responded in a spirit of mutual care and Christian responsibility.

Stage Three: *Structured Care, c. 1960–1970*

Mission agencies accepted the responsibility of providing care for their workers. They developed systems such as Wycliffe's Children's Education Department (CHED) and correspondence courses adapted to meet needs of children from many countries. As the need for emotional care became more apparent, Wycliffe established a formal Counseling Department under the leadership of Dr. Philip W. Grossman. This was probably the first in-house counseling department within missions.

During this decade a number of missions also began utilizing outside psychologists, psychiatrists and counselors for pre-field assessments, treatment, consultation to mission leaders both on-field and in furlough seminars, and in other training sessions. Among other organizations, Link Care Center in California was established, offering both restorative and developmental care for missionaries. The efficacy of counseling and the usefulness of many features in the whole modern missionary mental health care movement developed firm roots in this period, but was yet to blossom more fully.

Stage Four: *Specialized Care, 1970–1985*

The Counseling Department in Wycliffe continued to grow under the leadership of Kenneth Williams, who had obtained a Ph.D. in Human Behavior after successfully serving as a Bible translator. Career guidance became a legitimate service in Wycliffe under the pioneering foresight of Mr. Joel Warkentin. Learning disabilities in children were acknowledged as part of a need that could be met by specially trained professionals and other special needs were addressed by trained professionals both within and outside mission organizations.

As psychiatrists began to be seen as valid contributors to missionary mental health, the services of such fine practitioners as Drs. Marjory Foyle, James Stringham, Esther Schubert, and others were sought. Screening of mission applicants became more specialized as experience was gained in the use of psychological instruments such as the MMPI, the Millon, and others. More sophisticated interview and question-naire procedures were developed for mission application.

Stage Five: *Pervasive Care, 1985–1995*

Mission agencies began to examine their structures for responsiveness to human need. Kelly O'Donnell's 1996 article "Member Care Eleven" gave a bold, broad vision of desirable manifestations of support for mission workers. Management training for mission leaders was accepted as an integral part of missionary care, and the intro-duction of job descriptions, position results descriptions, and annual work reviews became an expected part of the leadership role.

As the mission world became less safe and predictable, crisis planning and response increased in importance, legitimizing contingency planning and risk assess-ment. Those who had undergone traumatic events, or even those who were making major moves, were obviously helped by structured debriefings. Thus, training in debriefing became popular. Insurance for medical evacuations began to be viewed as necessary.

As danger and stress increased, a number of retreat centers were developed, staffed by counselors and mental health professionals: La Rucher in France near Geneva, Switzerland, other locations in Europe, and across the United States. MK schools such as Faith Academy in the Philippines and Morrison Academy in Taiwan began counseling services and made them available to missionaries whether directly related to the school or not. Tumaini Counseling Centre in Nairobi developed ser-vices for a large segment of missionaries in East Africa.

Residential therapy centers, such as Link Care, ALONGSIDE (formerly Tusca-rora Resource Center), Pilgrim's Rest, the Chalet Retreat, Fairhaven, Heartstream and others began anew or deepened their sophistication of services to missions. Marble Retreat in Marble, Colorado, led by Dr. Louis McBurney, extended their program of care for pastors to include missionaries as well, and many more mental health profes-sionals dedicated their time and expertise to serving missions.

Debate among students of world trends was stimulated by considering such issues as:

- Are missionaries becoming less hardy and more needy?
- Are we recruiting the right people?
- Is it fair to offer these services only to North Americans? Or to have an American flavor to education, counseling, management, crisis care and debriefing? Or do workers from other countries need equal care, care that is equally culturally sensitive?
- Might missionary care offerings become so specialized that they displace mutual care?

- How can missionary care be a handmaiden to world evangelization, rather than becoming a competitive industry?
- Given the global movement away from colonialism toward inter-cultural work teams and short-term service, and fierce nationalism (even among Christians), what should missionary care look like in the future?

Examining these issues led us to the next stage of missionary care.

Stage Six: *Globally-Shared Care, 1995 to the present*

To be effective, missionary care must be delivered in a culturally sensitive manner. It must be owned by all sending countries and all receptor agencies. It must not be exclusive, serving only one country or one mission agency. Some recent developments include:

- The Tumaini Counseling Center in Nairobi, Kenya, established in the late 1980s through the vision of Dave Dunkerton, continues to thrive under the leadership of psychiatrist Dr. Roger Brown from Africa Inland Mission. Psychiatrist Dr. Richard Baggé from Summer Institute of Linguistics has joined Dr. Brown, and credentialed therapists from other agencies have enlarged the staff.
- The Mobile Member Care Team under the visionary leadership of Dr. Karen Carr and Darlene Jerome has been established in Abidjan, Cote d'Ivoire, West Africa.
- MemCa, under the leadership of Dr. Kelly O'Donnell and Rev. David Pollock, is an international organization composed of care-givers from around the world.
- The annual Mental Health and Missions Conference, begun in 1980 by Dr. John Powell and Dr. David Wickstrom, brings mission-minded counselors and mental health professionals together to discuss pertinent issues. More than 200 participants now attend each year. In 2000, some 25 member care personnel were brought from around the world to this conference, giving it a greater international face.
- Link Care, serving the California community of San Jose as well missionaries who participate in the restoration program, has extended its vision to the possibility of setting up a care center in Chiang Mai, Thailand.
- Heartstream Resources offers both mobile and on-site preventive, developmental and intensive care to missionaries.
- As missionary care becomes more highly specialized, very international in scope, and increasing in cultural sensitivity, it is also becoming more mobile and less exclusive.
- Mission agencies are increasingly setting up structures for member care and assigning responsible persons to fill member care roles. Some member care units include all aspects of care: personal, professional (including medical and pschological), developmental, marriage enrichment, children's education, development of prayer and financial partners, crisis care, spiritual oversight and sustenance, physical well-being, conflict management and team-building for teams, couples and groups.

Looking back over these stages, it is obvious that each stage builds on and includes the previous one, rather than supplanting it. For example, personal hardiness and self-care as well as responsibility for self and family will always be needed. The same is true for mutual care, structured and specialized care, pervasive and globally shared care. All aspects must move forward together, with no aspect of care superior to another. Spiritual vitality and pastoral care has always been and always will be needed.

Where do mental health professionals fit into all of this? They have entered the picture gradually; recognition of their valid contributions has grown along with credibility among the mission population. Now they are generally received with increasing gratitude and respect.

The mission force has moved beyond ignoring or being embarrassed by mental health needs. Most agencies no longer simply send persons with such needs back home under the stigma of failure. The current trend is toward accepting responsibility for providing adequate care for all.

The mental health movement has entered significantly into the realm of missions by:

- Identifying elements of health in general and in the context of ministry goals
- Screening for mental health using psychological instruments, such as the MMPI, biographical interviews, and personal observations delivered by trained professionals
- Focusing attention on developmentally appropriate structures, resources, and responses
- Specialized therapeutic responses to a wide range of mental health needs by therapists who are missions-aware, Biblically and professionally sound, available and accessible
- Serving as consultants to administrators who are struggling with behavioral or mental health challenges within their areas of responsibility
- Evaluation and consultation regarding policies and procedures which affect health

In order for mental health professionals to be effective contributors to world mission, they must first choose their avenue of contact:

- Internally, i.e., from within a given organization. Phil and Barbara Grossman, Ken Williams, Dick and Laura Mae Gardner, Richard Baggé, Bill Hoppe, Roger Brown, Kelly and Michelle O'Donnell, Steve Edlin, and Bill Hayes have all served as members of mission agencies.
- Externally, on invitation. Marjory Foyle, John Powell, Dave Wickstrom, Esther Schubert, Frances J. White, Link Care staff, and many others serve missions but are not members of mission agencies.

Both avenues are legitimate; see the discussion by O'Ann Steere in Chapter 22 of this book. To be effective in serving missionaries, both internal and external mental health practitioners need the following essential factors:

- Useful skills with documented successful experience and competence

- Attitude of service (as opposed to professional expectations for a sound-proof office or an 8 to 5 workday)
- Objectivity and neutrality; willingness to understand agency policies and requirements as opposed to taking sides or condemning agencies, policies, etc.
- Biblical integration in life and word
- Avoidance of psychological or professional jargon
- Willingness to listen and learn; humility rather than professional arrogance

In conclusion, let's look at the future of counseling and mental health professionals in missions.

The needs will always exist, and will continue to include developmental issues, crisis care, stress tolerance, uncertainty, ambiguity, interpersonal conflicts, emotional breakdowns, various disabilities, poorly managed anger, cultural differences, competitive attitudes, competition for resources, isolation, loneliness, grief, and loss. These are human needs, exacerbated by spiritual attacks and spiritual oppression as well as by distance from the known and familiar.

Mental health professionals must be hardy and whole people. They must be people who have resolved their own issues as much as possible so they have a full array of emotional resources from which to serve. Otherwise they risk becoming defensive and self-protective, wanting to refer out the more troubling issues, and focusing on issues which bring them satisfaction and peer approval.

Missions will continue to need experienced, professionally trained mental health professionals to deliver sound psychological help based on tested principles and Biblical concepts. To be effective, they must have personal experience in mission settings and the ability to put Biblical truths and concepts above psychological theory and offerings.

There is a legitimate concern that increasing reliance on specialists will mean moving away from mutual care. We must not abdicate our responsibility to be brothers and sisters to one another. Friendship will continue to be important. Often the help given by a wise and godly friend is more beneficial and effective than that delivered by a well-qualified stranger who comes to visit.

Because of the emotional cost of providing therapy, practitioners may be tempted to move away from their primary specialized services toward more satisfying activities of consulting, educating, writing and debriefing, thus denying needy missionaries access to what only mental health practitioners can provide – therapy. Their primary service is too important to be lost in this way. Good and sturdy, whole and godly, well trained mental health professionals must be supported by respect, by structures, by policies, by adequate funding and facilities to do what only they can do, with God's help.

There is an additional dimension we must move toward if we are to serve the "the borderless church of Christ" well. Bill Taylor (1997, p. 549) reflects on the challenge in this way:

> As we gaze out over our vast unreached and under-reached world, we commit ourselves anew to the proclamation and incarnation of the fullness of the Great Commission. Inasmuch as it is in our power, we

want to provide a genuine and appropriate opportunity for all people in the world to consider and respond to the claims of Christ. Nevertheless, the fact is that the unreached worlds (primarily due to historical, geograph-ical, cultural, and spiritual factors) are tough to reach. . . . We must establish and nourish an incarnational Christian presence in the multiple and overlapping worldview of our globe, whether pre-modern or post-modern.

In order to reach this goal, those of us who are committed to caring for God's workers must be keen students of trends, cultures, and issues. Let us aim to be reflective practitioners who can function within a multi-cultural community of faith as a part of diverse teams. Unless we learn to do this well, we will continue to serve a small segment of the mission work force, and probably do it well, and be appreciated by those few. The tragedy will be that we will never know what we might have done!

Recommended Readings

Beck, J. R. (2000). *Dorothy Carey: The Tragic & Untold Story of Mrs. William Carey*. Wipf & Stock Publishers.

Jones, M. (Ed.). (1993). *Caring for the Missionary into the 21st Century*. Care For Mission.

O'Donnell, K. S., & O'Donnell, M. L. (Eds.). (1988). *Helping Missionaries Grow: Readings in Mental Health and Missions*. Pasadena, CA: William Carey Library.

O'Donnell, K. (Ed.) (1992). *Missionary Care: Counting the Cost for World Evangelization*. Pasadena, CA: William Carey Library.

O'Donnell, K.S. (January 1996). "The Member Care Eleven." *Evangelical Missions Quarterly*.

O'Donnell, K.S. (Ed.). (2002) *Doing Member Care Well*. Pasadena, CA: William Carey Library.

Taylor, W. D. (Ed.). (1997). *Too Valuable to Lose: Exploring the Causes and Cures of Missionary Attrition*. Pasadena, CA: William Carey Library.

6

Pastoral and Psychological Caregivers Working Together

Lareau Lindquist

*E*arly in his first letter to Timothy, Paul wrote, *I thank Christ Jesus our Lord that he appointed me to his service.* With that same spirit of gratitude, I thank God for calling me into His ministry as a young man. I am especially happy for my present calling to be a caregiver.

One Man's Pilgrimage

I will never forget the Lord's call to me. I was a collegian with no specific vocational direction, spending the Christmas break at my parent's home in Minneapolis. While alone in the house studying, I suddenly sensed God calling me to preach. It was very real and very unexpected. I took a piece of paper and wrote a note to God, giving five reasons why it was not a good idea.

God persisted and I began preparation for the pastorate that very day. I never doubted the call and never considered any other options. The call was specific—*feed my children*—a call to the ministry of feeding and building believers. Most of my ministry has been as a pastor-teacher to Christians during five pastorates in the United States.

My wife Evie and I received another call from the Lord in the spring of 1986. We were on assignment visiting mission friends at a Wycliffe Bible Translators center in Colombia. After ministering there, we went by plane to Cona Colorado and spent several days with Joel and Nancy Stolte. The JAARS plane came to take us back to Bogota but because of inclement weather we were turned back to spend another night in the jungle.

Both pastoral care and psychological care are concerned with helping people live more effectively before God. The mission community needs the ministries and services of both. This chapter considers biblical sources of care and surveys the growth of pastoral and psychological care. It describes the author's call to begin Barnabas, International, a ministry of pastoral care and encouragement.

49

That evening, Evie and I took a short walk on the airstrip which turned into a very long walk—back and forth, we walked and talked. God spoke with us about the next chapter in our lives, adding to the earlier call and making it specific to caring for pastors and missionaries. Three words loomed large: *encouragement, edification,* and *enrichment.* Evie and I committed ourselves to this new direction. When we arrived back in the U.S. I sought counsel from three friends who were leaders in world ministry: Bernie May, Ralph Winter, and Don Richardson. Each of them affirmed that the time was right to begin a ministry of care to missionaries and each invited Evie and me to join them in beginning such a ministry.

After considerable prayer and thought, we decided to not join an already established mission but to begin a ministry that had one purpose: encouragement for missionaries and other Christian expatriates. We started Barnabas International, a ministry of pastoral care. That was almost seventeen years ago; it has been our greatest chapter yet. Now I say, paraphrasing Paul, "I thank Christ Jesus, my Lord, who appointed me to be a caregiver."

Who started the ministry of care?

That's not a hard question. God started it. God has always been interested in the care of His children.

Zephaniah 2:7 *The Lord will take care of them.*

Zechariah 10:3 *The Lord Almighty will care for his flock*

In Psalm 55, David shares the heaviness of his heart in the most thorough manner in Psalms. After dumping his concerns on the Lord, he speaks to the rest of us, *Cast your cares on the Lord and he will sustain you* (Psalm 55:22). Hundreds of years later, Peter says the same thing in I Peter 5:7, *Cast all your anxiety on him, because he cares for you.* The Old Testament and the New Testament concur that he cares. As we begin a new century, we have the same confidence—God cares for each of us.

- Each of the members of the Godhead indicate God's care which is forever intrinsic to His nature. The Father is called the God of compassion and the God of comfort.

- The Lord Jesus is not only referred to as the shepherd, but as the *good shepherd* and the *chief shepherd.* He is also called *the wonderful counselor* (Isaiah 9:6)—forever setting him apart from the rest of us counselors!

- The Holy Spirit is named the *paraclete,* which tenderly describes him as the *One who comes along side, the comforter, and the encourager.*

God's comprehensive *care plan* for Christians includes the following:

- Godhead Care, administered to us by the members of the Godhead.
- Care through the ministry of pastor-teachers, who are called to shepherd God's people (Ephesians 4:11).
- Care given by individuals who are appointed to care for believers. When Paul met with the elders of the Ephesian church, his farewell address included this charge: *Keep watch over yourselves and all the flock of which the Holy Spirit has made you overseers. Be shepherd of the church of God* (Acts 20:28).
- Care, commissioned by Jesus to Peter in John 21:16, *Take care of my sheep.* Peter passed that commission on to the rest of us in I Peter 5:2, *Be shepherds*

of God's flock that is under your care.
- Care that is spontaneously given by believers to each other, *to care for one another* (I Cor. 12:25).

New Testament Case Studies

Peter learned his care ministry by watching Jesus. Peter was with Jesus for three years, observing Jesus' care for people. Perhaps Peter's most precious memory of the Christ's for him was immediately after the Last Supper, when Jesus and Peter had an amazing discussion, recorded in Luke 22:31-34.

Jesus said, *'Simon, Simon, Satan has asked to sift you as wheat. But I have prayed for you, Simon, that your faith may not fail. And when you have turned back, strengthen your brothers.'* But Peter replied, *'Lord, I am ready to go with you to prison and to death.'* Jesus answered, *'I tell you, Peter, before the rooster crows today, you will deny three times that you know me.'* Later, Peter does deny Jesus three times, after which *Peter remembered the word the Lord had spoken to him . . . and Peter went outside and wept bitterly* (Luke 22:61-62).

Jesus knew what Peter was going to do, and even before the triple denial took place, gave two promises to Peter (vs. 32). First, the invitation to return quickly to Jesus; His arms were still open, ready to receive Peter. Second, the promise of ministry, *strengthen your brothers.* Peter couldn't believe the depth to which he fell, *but* he also remembered Jesus' promises pertaining to forgiveness and future ministry. Through God's overflowing grace, just seven weeks later Peter was the preacher on the day of Pentecost. He was also the key person in the first half of the book of Acts. Peter's care ministry was powerfully credible after his experience of the Jesus' grace and mercy.

Timothy, who was mentored by Paul. Paul singled him out as an outstanding caregiver, saying, *I have no one else like him, who takes a genuine interest in your welfare. For everyone looks out for his own interests, not those of Jesus Christ* (Philippians 2:20-21). Other translations use the word "care" in referring to Paul's relationship with Christ and in his relationship with people. Paul said there is *no one else like him.* True caregivers evidently were hard to find then. The same is still true.

Timothy's secret? Perhaps this is it. Timothy really cared for people. The text also says he really cared deeply for Christ. There is a relationship. Imagine Jesus coming physically to visit a group of twenty of us. As he stands in the middle of the room, we form a circle around him. Visualize this. As each of us takes a step closer to him, we get closer to each other in the circle. The closer we get to Jesus, the closer we are to each other. And conversely, when we take a step away from him, the distance also grows greater between us and Christ, and between us and each other. The more we care for him, the greater will be our care for each other.

Indeed, God has set up a network to extend care to each of us. He is the Chief Caregiver, as stated in both the Old and the New Testaments.

God wants to touch lives through today's Peters and Timothys. That's you and me. Isn't it amazing that God has called you and me to partner with him in providing care to God's chosen ministers serving around the world? God, the Chief Caregiver, has chosen you and me to work with him in bringing healing and wholeness to his people. The Chief Shepherd has called us to be his under-shepherds.

Some years ago, Bruce Larson penned these words, "Because God cares for people, it is expected that I, too, will care for people. As His follower, I will mirror His care to others." As individuals and as Christian organizations, we ought to consistently and creatively evaluate the quality of care that we extend to each other and to others.

Is Care-awareness Growing?

Troubles and trials are common to all of us. Christians in ministry are not excluded from tough times. It is my belief that missionaries have more, not fewer, tough times. They have the typical stresses and pressures of life, and they also have additional stresses that often include language barriers, cultural barriers, financial uncertainties, schooling pressures with their children, unrelenting heat, distance from families, and many other challenges unique to mission communities.

Often they serve Christ in countries that are politically or religiously antagonistic to them. Terrorism has become another factor that increases stress. When these are added together, there is an intensification and multiplication factor.

Thank God, there is a growing interest in member care. Mission leaders have a growing conviction that member care is important. Many missions have departments of member care in place, and others are moving in that direction. Organizations with care as their primary purpose have been started. We can be thankful for men like Clyde Narramore and Henry Brandt who did early trail-blazing in Christian psychol-ogy. Today there are many leaders in the field.

Link Care Center in Fresno, California, has provided psychological care for over 20 years, with an excellent staff of Christian therapists and pastoral counselors. They have facilities for individuals, couples, and families to live on campus for extended care when that is needed.

Barnabas International in Rockford, Illinois was started in 1986. It essentially provides pastoral care with a staff composed of pastor-teachers, counselors, MK specialists and caregivers with other specialties such as marriage, women, worship, and leadership development. Most of the staff are based in the United States and travel extensively. We have had a presence in Vienna, Austria for several years, and several other overseas offices are scheduled to open.

There are also a number of *care forums*. Perhaps the two best known in the U.S. are the Mental Health and Missions Conference and the Pastors to Missionaries Conference.

The *Mental Health and Missions Conference* was begun by Dr. John Powell and Dr. David Wickstrom in 1980. See Chapter 1 for its history. While caregivers at different academic levels attend the conference, psychologists and psychiatrists find it to be challenging and rewarding. In the past few years there has been unprecedented growth in participants.

The *Pastors-to-Missionaries Conference* was started by Mission Training Inter-national about thirteen years ago, and its sponsorship was passed to Barnabas Interna-tional about five years ago. The program is planned by representatives of several mission organizations, and the thrust of the conference is pastoral care. It meets annually at the JAARS Center in Waxhaw, North Carolina. In the last two years it has also showed unprecedented growth.

Space does not allow me to mention the many other individuals, forums, and agencies that are involved in providing care for missionaries. Each of the examples cited, however, illustrates the desirability of those in pastoral care and psychological care working together.

Psychological Care and Pastoral Care: Why the Distinction?

In Matthew 22:37-40 Jesus says, *Love the Lord your God with all your heart and with all your soul and with all your mind. This is the first and greatest commandment. And the second is like it. Love your neighbor as yourself. All the Law and Prophets hang on these two commandments.* Mark 12:30 also adds *with all your strength.*

We acknowledge that there are physical, mental, and spiritual dimensions of humanity. Medical care is expected. Spiritual and pastoral care is well accepted. Unfortunately, some Christians have been slow in embracing the legitimacy of Christian psychological care. Yet, it is proving to be critical in many mission situations.

Psychological care (provided by mental health professionals) and pastoral care are both concerned with helping people live more effectively before God. There is some overlap, but each has expertise for working within different spheres of human experience and interaction.

Pastoral care has its primary interest in the spiritual realm and may touch upon the emotional and psychological. Tom Eckblad has coined the phrase, *spiritual cardiologists*: pastoral care majors on heart issues, drawing from the word and heart of God in helping with heart and soul issues of the missionary. This may involve teaching, pastoral counseling, encouragement and other caregiving activities.

Psychological care utilizes knowledge of personality and behavior, an understanding of human development and the processes of change, and applies theories and techniques of counseling and therapy in helping relationships. Psychological care may assist missionaries to enhance their vitality, overcome tensions and conflict, and/or resolve psychological disorders. Helping overcome bruised backgrounds, inner and interpersonal conflicts, trauma and stress, and responding to other issues often involves psychological care.

Both pastoral caregivers and psychological caregivers may engage in teaching and consultation, and as Christian caregivers, both draw on the love and strength of the Lord. Both are needed; neither is better than the other. I find the Biblical teaching on the Body and its members in I Corinthians 12 to be helpful. Just as no single part ought to feel that it is the most important, neither should any discipline think that it is superior to other disciplines. Each is important and each needs the others.

The mission community needs the ministries and services of both pastoral care and psychological care. Most of us would benefit greatly from spending personal time under the mentoring and tutorage of both pastoral care specialists and mental health professionals.

Which will better bring healing to the client? When I was a collegian, our president, Dr. T. B. Madsen, was involved in a severe automobile accident that almost killed him, and was hospitalized for months. When he came back to the college and spoke in chapel, he started out saying, "Praise God! He healed me." As an immature young man, I wanted to ask, "What do you mean, God healed you? Didn't you have surgeries, drugs, and rehabilitation therapy?"

Imagine going to the Scriptures with the question, "What is God's preferred method of healing?" As we start digging through the Bible, we would read of Naaman dunking himself in the River Jordan seven times (II Kings 5). Later we read of Jesus making mudballs and putting them on the blind boy's eyes. Then we discover the lady who touched the hem of Christ's garment and was healed. In each of these cases, a healing took place.

But we can't conclude that God's method is dunking in the river or using mudballs or whatever else. The chief point is this: *God is the Healer*. In the Bible, God sometimes used the river, or mudballs, or a touch, and sometimes nothing at all. Today, sometimes God uses surgery, medication, radiation, or nothing at all. He is still the healer.

Within the mission community, God uses clinical care for the road to wholeness. Sometimes, he uses pastoral care, and sometimes a combination, or neither. God may bypass our expectations and do his own thing in his own way. The good news is this: God is the Healer, the Restorer and people can be healed, restored, forgiven, mended, and rehabilitated. And God might use us in the process.

The Call to Partnership in Caregiving Ministries

Some seven years ago, Dr. John Powell and his wife Beverly attended our Pastors-to-Missionaries Conference. They have been back every year since. John invited me to speak at the Mental Health and Missions Conference, and Evie and I attended together. It was helpful and very stimulating. I have since attended several more. As we travel the bridge from one to the other, we are growing from our area of preference, training, and strength to see the value of what is on the other side of the bridge. We are complementary, not competitive.

Dr. Laura Mae Gardner has been useful in building respect in both fields. She is truly a bridge-builder. Each of us has much to contribute to the other and much to learn from the other.

Recently, my friend Dr. Brent Lindquist and I were co-leaders of several sessions at a caregivers' conference in London, England, sponsored by Global Connections. Something beautiful happened as we led the sessions together. Let me paint the picture.

Here we were, two Lindquists working together in workshops geared to caregivers. These two Lindquists were not brothers and not even relatives, except we are spiritually related as brothers in Christ. Both of us come from families that founded care-giving ministries to Christian workers. Brent's father, Stanley, started Link Care. It continues to be one of the finest Christian centers providing excellence in psychological care. I, together with my wife, founded Barnabas International, which is essentially a pastoral care ministry.

As Brent and I stood together at the seminar, we stated and modeled these truths. Total care for the mission community is not a choice between psychological care or pastoral care. We do not see ourselves as competitors but as partners. Neither of us is trying to take the place of the other or trying to be the other. We are hoping to forge a more meaningful understanding and participation among caregivers as to the continuing need of partnership within the Body of Christ.

7

A Theological Perspective on Missionary Care

Glenn C. Taylor

*T*he care of missionaries must be imbedded in a theological perspective. It is incumbent upon us to articulate care within the Christian theological perspective so we can respond appropriately to people involved in ministry from a Christian orientation. A Biblical theology of care can inform and infuse the other dimensions of care that are so necessary in a comprehensive approach.

An understanding of traditional systematic theology is important, but we must go beyond that to a theology dealing with the realities of life. If we engage in the prac-tice of psychology, particularly counseling psychology that encounters people in the raw experiences of life, we need a theology that does more than present doctrine or dogmatics. We must move from a theoretical under-standing of the Christian faith to a practical application in the stresses and strains of interfacing a world of need and the opposition encountered in that world.

Let me suggest we define theology as *an expression of our encounter with God in the realities of life.* Propositional truth, doctrinal exposition and statements may be important to clarify our understanding of God's revelation to us, but these must not be substituted for our encounter with God in the issues of life. God longs to be incarnated into the harsh realities of our flesh and blood.

Theology is discovering the relevance of God—His grace and revelation—in the context of life's pain, uncertainty, frustration, joys, celebrations and decisions. When God meets us in our deepest struggles with sin in our lives or in the lives of others, we are doing theology. Out of the

Theology may be defined as an expression of our encounter with God in the realities of life. A theology of care brings the grace and freedom of God into the experience of those who serve in harsh circumstances as Christians care for one another. Biblical caring includes fellowship, edification, comfort, confrontation, strengthening, compassion, leadership, and authority.

pit of despair and dependency, if we meet God there (and surely he is there), a theology emerges for life that is full of grace and freedom.

The Source of a Theology of Care

A theology of care reflects the relationship between the members of the Trinity, the care of God for us, and the expectation that we will care for one another.

God is at the source of all care. Paul brought this to our attention when he described God (2 Corinthians 1:3) as *the Father of compassion and the God of all comfort.* Additionally, he adds (7:6) that when he was in the depths of depression that *God, who comforts the downcast, comforted us by the coming of Titus.* Thus, God as the source of care is seen to use others as the means of his action toward us. An added dimension is given to us later (7:13) when it is pointed out that the community of faith in Corinth, finding Titus burnt out, *refreshed* him. God is the source but individuals or faith communities may be the means by which care is offered.

Some focus on the ministry of the Holy Spirit in comforting believers and transforming them into maturity. The danger is that we let ourselves off the hook by doing so. God is the source of care, but in almost all circumstances, we are the means of such ministry to one another. We have a dramatic and crucial role in each other's lives, as God not only works directly through the Holy Spirit in us, but indirectly through our being touched by the lives of others. As Luther put it, we are priests to each other in our growth toward Christlikeness. The experience of Paul and of Titus mentioned above illustrates that clearly.

Paul elaborates this in Colossians (3:10-17) where he urges us to be *renewed in knowledge in the image of the Creator* which is accomplished as we fulfill the exhortation, *Clothe yourselves with compassion, kindness, humility, gentleness and patience. Bear with each other and forgive whatever grievances you may have against one another. Forgive as the Lord forgave you. And over all these virtues put on love, which binds them all together in perfect unity... Let the word of Christ dwell in you richly as you teach and admonish one another.*

Indeed, in our care of one another we put a face on God for each other as Titus did for Paul. That is what Paul so carefully outlined (2 Corinthians 1:3-7) as he spoke of *...the Father of compassion and the God of all comfort, who comforts us in all our troubles, so that we can comfort those in any trouble with the comfort we ourselves received from God...*

Mutuality of Care in New Testament Communities

The culture of Christianity has as its central pillar the mutual nurturing of its members through gifts distributed by the Holy Spirit and freely shared. Thus, we are *built together to become a dwelling in which God lives by his Spirit...that the body of Christ may be built up until we all reach unity in the faith and in the knowledge of the Son of God and become mature, attaining to the whole measure of the fullness of Christ* (Ephesians 2:22; 4:12-13).

Community, where all stand on equal ground before the cross of Christ, is the essence of Christianity. We have differing roles as defined by the gifts sovereignly distributed by the Spirit of God. But, differing roles do not speak of differing value, and there is no room for elitism.

Individualism, with its interest in rights, privileges, egoism and self-actualization, conflicts with the selfless pursuit of others' interests which is modeled by Jesus Christ and intended to be replicated in the lives of His followers. Only individualism that exists in tension with interdependence is compatible with Christianity.

We live the life of Christ in our mortal bodies as we do the theology of care. In 2 Corinthians 4, Paul indicates that although we are but *jars of clay*, we bear a *treasure* showing that the *all-surpassing power* is *from God and not from us. We are hard pressed on every side, but not crushed; perplexed, but not in despair; persecuted, but not abandoned; struck down, but not destroyed... the life of Jesus may also be revealed in our body... so that his life may be revealed in our mortal body.... Therefore we do not lose heart. Though outwardly we are wasting away, yet inwardly we are being renewed day by day.*

It is this reality and this hope that a theology of care must bring as we minister to one another and to those who serve in the hard places of the world. Our theology must enable us to discover God in the raw experiences of life and enable those to whom we minister to find the reality of our God of compassion at the crossroads of their life's experiences. Neither an intellectual understanding of propositional truth nor a head knowledge of the attributes of God is adequate to incarnate the reality of His presence with us in the streets and highways of life.

Patterns of Care in the New Testament

If the intention of ministry in the New Testament was to **bring people from immaturity to maturity in Christ**, to convert people from "instruments of wickedness" to "instruments of righteousness," then we may ask, "How did the disciples of Christ seek to accomplish this?" New Testament believers encountered not only the challenge of their paganism but the stressors which came from evangelizing in a hostile environment. Many of the challenges they faced were similar to issues faced today by those for whom we provide care.

If one begins in the Acts of the Apostles and continues through the Epistles in chronological order, one can see a development in the patterns of ministry the apostles carried out. There is a movement from apostle-centered ministry to ministry focused in the mutual relationship of believers as well as the ministry of pastor-teachers and cross-cultural workers. The apostles came to grips with their finitude and knew they would not be around forever, so they transitioned from a single person focused ministry to a focus on the mutual ministry of believers.

Space does not allow me to take you through the Acts and the Epistles in detail, but I will present a summary and focus on a few terms which they used to describe their ministry. The terminology used to describe the ministry of the apostles in earlier writing is rather general and not clearly focused. They speak of teaching, preaching, exhorting to continue in the faith or of establishing the souls of the disciples. In the Epistles the process is more carefully defined as encouraging, comforting, strengthening, edifying and confronting, and there is a distinct shift to the mutual responsibility of believers to exercise this ministry in relation to each other.

There is also clearer definition of different approaches in ministry as being indicated by different situations. For example, *"Therefore, encourage one another and build each other up, just as in fact you are doing. Now we ask you, brothers, to respect those who work hard among you, who are over you in the Lord and who admonish you... And we urge* *you, brothers, **warn** those who are idle, **encourage** the timid, **help** the weak, **be patient** with everyone."* (1 Thessalonians 5:11-14) By the time we get to Ephesians, there is a very strong emphasis upon the responsibility of the believers to build each other up as interdependent members of the body. Ministry is diffused among the believers. This is perhaps best summarized by the "one another" passages in the New Testament.

A Spiritual House Built for "One Another" *(VanVonderen, 1995)*

I.   **How not to treat our spiritual brothers and sisters:**
  - Don't bite and devour one another (Galatians 5:15)
  - Don't lie to one another (Colossians 3:9)
  - Don't speak evil of one another (James 4:11)
  - Don't grumble against one another (James 5:9)
  - Don't judge one another (Romans 14:3)

  If I go against these "one anothers," someone inevitably gets hurt.

II.   **Where we can count on help when we need it:**
  - Accept one another (Romans 15:7)
  - Bear one another's burdens (Galatians 6:2)
  - Bear with one another, with all humility, gentleness, patience (Eph. 4:2)
  - Be kind to one another, tender-hearted, forgiving one another (Eph. 4:32)
  - Confess your sins to one another, and pray for one another (James 5:16)

  If I actively do these "one anothers", someone will always be helped.

III. **Interactions with other Christians that build us up:**
  - Pursue what makes for peace, building up one another (Romans 14:19)
  - Have the same kind of care for one another (1Corintians 12:25)
  - Admonish (gently warn) one another (Romans 15:14)
  - Be devoted to one another, prefer one another, giving credit (Rom. 12:10)
  - Serve one another (Galatians 5:13)
  - Submit to one another (Ephesians 5:21)
  - Regard one another as more important than yourself (Philippians 2:3)
  - Be hospitable to one another (1 Peter 4:9)

The Greek word translated "one another" is a part of speech called a "reciprocal pronoun," which means that both parties will experience the action being done. If the action is positive—love, support, comfort—*both parties will benefit.* And in the case of negative actions—speaking evil, consuming—*both parties lose.*

Fellowship

One of the most foundational ideas is expressed by the word "fellowship" in its various uses. In Hebrews 2:14-18, because the children of men were "fellowshippers" in flesh and blood, Christ came to participate in the same that he might redeem mankind. In Galatians 2:6-10, the right hand of partnership is extended between Paul and the Jerusalem leaders. Fellowship reaches across all racial and cultural boundaries in Ephesians 3:1-12 and Romans 11:11-18. It describes the offering taken by Gentiles to meet the need of poor saints in Jerusalem in Romans 15:26. It describes our participation in the efficacy of Christ's shed blood in 1 Corinthians 10:16.

Let me offer a definition: *Fellowship is entering into another's circumstance or condition in such a manner that your resources in Christ become theirs.*

Edification

The outcome of edification is the controlling standard for relationships and the expression of gifts. In 1 Corinthians 14:5, 12, and 26, gifts are to be exercised to this end and, indeed, the principle is, *Let all things be done for edification.* The image is that of building. I would change the image slightly by suggesting that we are to invite each other to live rather than to die. *Let your conversation be always full of grace, seasoned with salt, so that you may know how to answer everyone.*

The way believers speak to one another is important. Proverbs 18:20 says, *Death and Life are in the power of the tongue.* The Psalmist speaks of those *who have sharpened their tongues like a sword, they aim bitter speech as an arrow* (64:3). Proverbs 12:18 adds, *There is one who speaks rashly like thrusts of a sword.* It is so easy for us to invite each other to die, but edifying is inviting each other to live. *The tongue of the wise brings healing. A soothing tongue is a tree of life. Pleasant words are a honeycomb, sweet to the soul and healing to the bones.* (Proverbs 12:18; 15:4; 16:24)

My definition: *Edification is being to another person what that person needs for their good and resultant growth.*

Encourage/Comfort

The word translated comfort or encourage may be used more frequently than any other word to describe the growth-facilitating relationship we are to have with each other. It can be traced to a word in the Old Testament which means *to cause to breathe again.* The word is often translated "rest" as in Ruth 1:9; Deuteronomy 12:9; Psalm 119:49-50, 76 and Isaiah 51:12; Ps. 23:4; 71:19-21. In the New Testament it is used of the Holy Spirit's ministry in John (14-17), of Christ's present ministry in 1 John (2:1), and of God the Father's ministry to us in 2 Corinthians (1:3ff). It is the most common word used to describe our responsibility to come alongside each other. A related idea is that of bearing one another's burdens (Romans. 15:10; Gal. 6:2; Rev. 2:20).

There are five different terms in the Old Testament for the word comfort. These words mean to brighten or encourage; to refresh (as with food); to support; to rest in quietness; or to comfort as to give vent to one's sighs or to sigh with another. The image is what we call resuscitation, which in our context means to restore breathing. This word is used in a variety of contexts such as Genesis 5:29; 37:35; 50:21; Ruth 1:13; 1 Chronicles 7:22; 19:2; Job 2:11; 7:13; 29:25; Psalm 13:4; 71:21; 86:15-17; Ezekiel 31:1-13; and Isaiah 40:1; 49:23; 52:9; 66:12-13. The word is used both of God's response to people and peoples' response to each other. The rich imagery of "causing to breathe again" is an apt description of the care we are to provide for each other.

Comfort is coming alongside another to bear him or her and their need that they might be encouraged and strengthened or resuscitated.

Strengthen/Cleave/Endure With

Another group of words captures the imagery of supporting another by coming alongside so that the weaker may lean on, be supported by or be strengthened by the other. (1 Peter 1:12; Luke 9:15; 16:26; Romans 1:11; Acts 3:7, 16; 16:5) Another word may be translated, *to keep oneself directly opposite to any one, to hold to him firmly, or to cleave to him paying him heed.* (Luke 16:13; 1 Thessalonians 5:14; Titus 1:9). Another means *to be slow in developing anger or passion toward another* or to put it positively, *to be long suffering, enduring or patient with another* (Mt. 18:26,29; 1 Corinthians. 13:4; 1 Thessalonians. 5:14; Hebrews. 6:15; James 5:7,8; 2 Peter 3:9).

To strengthen another is to hold tightly and enduringly to another in support in times of stress or testing.

Confrontation

Another group of words brings into focus our responsibility to confront one another with a view to bringing our lives into line with God's revealed will. The word *"nouthesis"* is often translated "admonish" and was used by Jay Adams as descriptive of his understanding of counseling. Other words such as "rebuke" or "reprove" fit into this group.

Confrontation is to kindly, but firmly, bring one another to the awareness of discrepancies or incongruity between our lives and the will of God.

Biblical Relationships For Growth *(G.C. Taylor, November, 1995)*

Fellowship (Koinonia): entering into another's condition in such a manner that your resources in Christ becomes theirs.

Edification: being to another person what that person needs you to be for his good and resultant growth.

Comfort: coming alongside others to bear them and their needs that they might be encouraged and strengthened.

Confrontation: kindly, but firmly, bringing one another to the awareness of discrepancies or incongruity between our lives and the will of God.

Strengthen/cleave/endure with: to strengthen another and to hold tightly and enduringly to another in support in times of stress or testing.

Compassion and good will: to foster tender, compassionate, kind and sympathetic emotions toward one another.

Leadership: the right to serve others through identifying and exercising stewardship over the gifts and talents they have by grace for the accomplishment of mutual goals.

Authority: authority is for building, not controlling - 2 Corinthians 10:8; 13:10
Authority is for serving, not commanding - 2 Corinthians 12:14-16
Authority is exercised as power in the face of conflict - 1 Cor. 5:4f

Compassion and Good Will

There is a whole group of words that focus on issues of attitude and quality of relationship and relating. These include kindheartedness, brotherliness, sympathy, harmony, loving affection and being knit together in our relationships. (1 Peter 3:8; Romans 12:10, 16; Philippians 2:2; 4:2; 1 Corinthians 12:25f; Romans 12:15; Hebrews 4:15, 10:32-34; Romans 8:17; Ephesians 4:32; Philemon 12; Matthew 9:36)

We are to foster tender, compassionate, kind and sympathetic emotions toward one another.

The Relevance of a Theology of Care among Mission Personnel

As Christian care givers responding to the needs of missionary personnel, we need a theology of care. The ability to respond with psychometric, diagnostic, clinical and counseling skills is not enough. When our approach is perceived as secular it is frequently rejected in the missions community.

It is important for us to be able to articulate what we do within the cultural and linguistic milieu of the missions community. For someone thoroughly trained in the culture of psychology, counseling within the missions community involves crossing cultural barriers in a manner similar to the experience of missionaries.

My training and ministry experience have provided me with opportunities to work in several cultures, including church, correctional, psychiatric, educational, seminary, medical and mission cultures. These are quite diverse and require an understanding and ability to function within each culture with all its unique aspects of language, expectations, values and patterns of relationship.

How effectively do we cross cultures as we enter a missions environment? Do we insist they learn to communicate in our language or are we prepared to learn their language? The negative reaction of missionaries toward psychologists may have much to do with the different language with which we understand and communicate.

Some may see my suggestion as inviting role conflict. Am I functioning as psychologist or a person delivering pastoral care? Will this confuse the client and/or the counselor? Is it possible to function as a professional counselor in a manner that befits a Christian delivering services in a Christian context? I would argue that we must honor the culture and the belief systems of those to whom we offer services. If we share the same belief system, it is to their advantage and to ours. This might profitably be discussed in terms of our philosophy of integration.

Concluding Comments

If we would speak with maximum relevance in our care for mission personnel, we must develop a theology of care which brings the grace of God into the hard experience of those who serve in harsh circumstances. An intellectual, propositional expression of truth is not enough. We must incarnate the relevance of God in our lives and find him in the pain and pleasure of the lives of others.

In the words of Paul, *The God and Father of our Lord Jesus Christ, the Father of compassion and the God of all comfort [that is 'coming alongside'], comes alongside us in all our tribulation, so that we may come alongside others in any trouble with the same coming alongside by which he came alongside us...* To do so is to invite others to breath again, to live in the grace of God. This alone is sufficient to assist those who choose the hard road of cross-cultural ministry.

The ministry of those such as Paul, who cared with a burdened heart for those he served, models patterns of relationship and ministry that may be emulated by mental health professionals without in any way minimizing the use of their professional skills.

Part III

*Complexities
of Cross-cultural
Service*

8

Whirling Teacups: A Bi-cycle Analysis of Missionary Growth

Bruce Swanson

*A*t least once in your life you climbed on board. The ride begins calmly enough; each set of four teacups begins to rotate while the whole ride begins to spin. The rotation alone or spinning alone would be interesting, but the fun comes as the two actions combine their effects. One second the forces cancel out and you're calmly thinking "this is lame"; the next moment the whole world is spinning out of control.

Missionary personal growth is a lot like a whirling teacup. The missionary life cycle presents rather predictable developmental tasks; so does the missionary's family life cycle (or personal, psychosocial life cycle for singles). The ride can get wild, though, as these cycles interact, combining their challenges and tasks.

This chapter will consider the interaction of the missionary life cycle and the family life cycle and its implications for missionary growth in meeting the many com-binations of developmental tasks that are generated. We will look at the basic life cycle, which is more foundational, and impose on it the special issues of the missionary life cycle.

The model of family life cycle is based on one developed by Monica McGoldrick and Elizabeth Carter (1982), with some additions. Individual developmental tasks are incorporated into the family model. This model must be used with care, since it is bound to "typical" white, Anglo, middle class, traditional families in the USA. Given the increasing internationalization of missions, this model applies to a shrinking percentage of the global missionary population.

Missionary Life Cycle

We will use a missionary life cycle that reflects long-

All of us move through life cycles as individuals and families, and there are key issues and developmental tasks for each stage. The missionary life cycle is imposed on and interacts with the family life cycle, bringing its own issues and tasks. Implications and complications of the overlap are described. A critical key for coping with multiple changes is being grounded in one's identity in Christ.

term cross-cultural service with a "faith mission." There is a detailed breakdown of the early years of missionary experience—appointment through first furlough—because of the magnitude of the changes and challenges faced during those years.

The stages I identify are:

- Recruitment and appointment
- Deputation
- First term: language and culture learning
- First term: beginning ministry
- First furlough
- Mid-career terms and furloughs
- End-career terms and furloughs
- Retirement and aging

An additional category is included for unexpected events that can break into a missionary's experience at any time.

Detailed charts of the family life cycle and missionary life cycle are found in Table I and Table II. Most of the following discussion relates to the typical alignment of the two life cycles in which the recruitment and appointment phase begins with young adults. Very different issues arise when the two charts are aligned at different points, as is the case with the increasing number of second-career missionaries.

Young Adult Tasks

Tasks of the unattached young adult overlap with some of the tasks in the recruitment and appointment phase of the typical missionary life cycle. Unattached young adults work consciously or unconsciously to establish their own identity as distinct from their families of origin. If their own sense of identity is underdeveloped, it is much more of a challenge to imagine going overseas, leaving family or groups they identify with. Other issues are family expectations about marriage prospects ("How will you find someone overseas?") and parents' approval or disapproval of potential mates ("What if my daughter marries a national?").

In our screening process for young adults, we look for a healthy sense of identity in relation to parents. People sometimes think going overseas will solve problems of relationship, communication or maturity. Unhealthy patterns need to be discussed during the candidate process, or preferably, prior to it during discipleship and leadership development in the local church. Unresolved issues with parental authority often get transferred to local church leadership and then to mission agency authority.

When a newly married couple is in the deputation stage, major tasks in adaptation stack up: personal, career, financial, etc. A new family system is being established despite chaotic work, personal, and deputation schedules.

Peer Relationships

Ability to establish intimate peer relationships is critical as a young missionary moves into deputation and then language and culture learning. We look for that in the autobiography and in references and secondary references. Past behavior is the best predictor of future behavior, even in a new culture, and we want to see a person who

Table I: Family Life Cycle
with a Sampling of Issues and Tasks

Key Issues	Developmental Tasks
Unattached young adult Parent-offspring separation Identity Intimacy	Differentiate self from family of origin: values, faith, etc. Establish personal "dream" Establish intimate peer relationships Establish self in work
Newly married couple Commitment to new person & system Flexibility & change Conflict & Communication Influence/support of older generations	Adapt to spouse and in-laws Negotiate change to myriad of personal issues Realignment of relationships to include spouse
Family with young children New generation enters family system Marital satisfaction Care & protection of young Spiritual legacy	Adjust to new priorities, commitments, finances, etc. Shift from couple- to child-centered Assume parenting roles with help of previous generations
Family with adolescents Increasing children's independence & identity System flexibility Parents entering mid-life: identity, life purpose, physical changes	Redefining parent-child relationship Child makes forays out of system Resolve mid-life and career issues Begin shift to concern for older generations
Launching children and moving on Exits from and entrances to family system Concerns for both younger and older gen.s Identity of mother/wife Marital satisfaction	Shift from child- to couple-centered Mother/wife establish new, productive role Establish adult-adult relationship with kids Changing relationship with older gen.s
Family in later life Shifting generational roles Retirement Life review Physical limitations/death	Adjust to death of loved ones & peers Renegotiate family role with children
Unexpected events Difficulties/traumas: handicapped child, divorce premature death of family member violent crime, natural disaster	Adapt family system to new reality Grieve losses; work through trauma Reconcile losses and trauma with faith

Table II: Missionary Life Cycle
with a Sampling of Issues and Tasks

Key Issues	Developmental Tasks
Recruitment and appointment God's will & family attitudes Future separations from family Career implications Submission to authority	Come to a sense of "calling" Satisfy agency's requirements Work through family & career expectations

Deputation
Role change
Patience & trust in God
General life upheaval
Flexibility
	Adjust to new role: career, finances,
	    on-stage
	Adapt personal and family structures
	Deal with discouragement; maintain
	    dream

Language and culture learning
Transition & culture shock
Role & identity loss
Humility & learner posture
Flexibility & patience
Mentorship
	Adapt personal and family system to
	    new setting
	Establish identity in new culture
	Learn language; find cultural mentor
	Include missionaries & nationals in
	    family system

First term: beginning ministry
Relationships with nationals
Work/life balance
Mentorship
Humility & learner posture
Prolonged separation from family
	Establish appropriate role for sensitive
	    foreigner
	Find work mentor
	Enter long-term relationships with
	    nationals
	Establish good working relationships
	    with missionaries

First furlough Transition Re-entry shock Role change General life upheaval Renewed contact with family	Adapt personal and family system to new situation Re-establish identity in changed old culture Establish meaningful role Re-establish place in extended family system

Mid-career terms and furloughs
Transitions
Personal and ministry maturation
Career evaluation & redeployment
"Professionalization" of spiritual task
MK concerns: education, coping,
    separation
	Adapt personal and family system to
	    cycle of moves
	Adopt model of completion of present
	    work
	Consider and act on career options
	Exercise appropriate leadership
	Maintain spiritual vitality

Continued on next page

Table II *(continued)*: Missionary Life Cycle
with a Sampling of Issues and Tasks

Key Issues	Developmental Tasks

End-career terms and furloughs
Transitions
Finishing well
Transfer to next generation
Control
Distance from older & two younger
    generations
	Cope with rigors of missionary life and
	    physical limitations
	Release control to next generation
	Plan for retirement

Retirement & aging Return to "home" culture Change in roles Limited income Renewed contact with older & younger generations	Re-establish identity in "home" culture Adapt personal and family system Adapt to increasing limitations Establish meaningful role

Unexpected events
Difficulties & traumas:
    civil unrest,
    kidnapping/shooting
    loss of support, inflation
    disease, medical leave
	Adapt to new reality: family system,
	    career, calling, etc.
	Grieve losses; work through trauma
	Reconcile losses and trauma with faith

has been able to establish healthy intimate relationships, with peers and with other age groups, including people in authority over them and people with whom they have done ministry.

For candidates in their 20s or early 30s, peer relationships are more important than they were to boomers. Often the family of origin is less stable, and peer relationships and a sense of Christian community are more of a stabilizing factor for an unattached young adult. A sense of community and team is very significant to younger candidates considering working overseas.

Young married couples are more aware of relational issues than people of their parents' generation, but one gap in people in their thirties and younger is skill and knowledge in parenting. Because they lacked good models, many need to learn the basics such as setting boundaries, providing an emotionally stable and supportive environment, punishment, and encouragement.

New Missionaries, New Parents
Newly married couples and families with young children need mentoring, both as new missionaries and as new parents. In the typical juxtaposition of family life

cycle and missionary life cycle, young missionary parents have tasks both of establishing a new family and their first term heading overseas, which is incredibly exhausting. When entering new culture, even the most basic, rudimentary details of life take energy and attention. At the same time, having young children is demanding even in the home culture. There is a huge need for older, seasoned colleagues to give counsel and encouragement and to give young parents breaks from child care.

People from difficult backgrounds may pick up maladaptive patterns in the new setting. When the pressure is on in a new culture, some men will retreat into ministry and become workaholics; husbands and wives may become distant because they just trying to survive. When couples have very young children, marital satisfaction dips because both parents are focusing on the needs of the children and survival. These issues are exacerbated by being overseas.

Being Grounded: A Key Spiritual Task

A key spiritual task for anyone who wants to integrate with a new culture at a deep level is "regrounding" their worth in their connection with God and their identity in Christ. In a new culture and language, people feel useless, incompetent, off balance—and that is a blow to people who are highly educated and competent professionals, and good communicators. Suddenly they feel like a zero. It's normal to derive worth from what we can accomplish; heading overseas strips that away. If they can reground themselves, they don't need to look for significance in other things, like finding an internet community or doing ministry in English and short-circuiting language learning.

Language and Culture Learning

First-term language and culture learning requires humility and the posture of a learner. If we ground our identity in Christ, knowing God's acceptance of us and pleasure over us, that is the foundation for humility—an accurate assessment of the self. Then it's OK to be incompetent because it doesn't mean you are deficient; you can learn from the people around you.

Some first-term missionaries have a turbulent period of struggle, but given time they learn the culture and eventually become who they were in their home culture—competent, attractive people with a valuable ministry. As an individual learns language and culture and can once again do basic things on autopilot, a whole new person emerges who has energy for ministry.

One of the developmental tasks for the first term language and culture learner is to include other missionaries and nationals in their family system. In the midst of being broadsided with stress, it is tempting to retreat and withdraw. The family may isolate itself to find comfort and satisfaction in each other—a healthy coping mechanism if not done to extremes. They need to allow the new community to come into their life, such as allowing a national "grandma" to care for the children.

There are inevitable tensions in marriage, if one partner is more outgoing and the other less comfortable relating to nationals. Conflicts need to be worked through —a challenge in a time of high stress. In a new culture, the family's style of doing things has to be negotiated in many arenas, much more than in the home culture.

First Furlough/Home Assignment

By the time new missionaries begin to have some comfort and success, it's time for the first furlough, which can be helpful on the developmental path. There is time to rest, regroup, reconnect with family and friends, and get their feet back under them in the home culture—though it isn't quite their home culture any more. A lot of pressure is off, though they may be off balance because they are trying to catch up with changes. There is time to consolidate gains and gain perspective on the overseas work.

There is wisdom in having down time for reflection. Early missionaries traveled by boat, which gave time for integrative reflection spiritually, psychologically, and relationally. Today, some people stop in a third country en route to their home country, or find some other way to gain transition time.

The home culture is no longer completely their home culture, but intentionally using adaptive culture-learning skills helps reduce reverse culture shock. That may be more of an issue after several terms, as missionaries adopt another culture and are out of touch with the home culture. This can be a huge issue after spending a whole career overseas.

Mid-Career

If a family is young when they go overseas, by mid-career they have adolescent children and are in full stride in ministry. If they have successfully negotiated earlier stages, by mid-career many details of living can be done on autopilot, freeing the missionary to be more engaged in ministry. However, they need new tools to meet new challenges which may threaten to overload them.

As competency increases, so does responsibility; and they accumulate ministry tasks and get very busy. There are new challenges of parenting adolescents or separating from young adult children, and at the same time their own parents may be getting sick and needing them at home. These challenges can be just as difficult as earlier years.

As missionaries take on more responsibilities, it easy for their devotional and prayer life to get crowded out. Getting grounded in one's spiritual life is critical, and maintaining it through various stages of missionary life is often the difference between making it well and barely making it. In any ministry, the needs are infinite and demands on your time and energy never cease. Those who care about the kingdom risk short-circuiting their own personal growth and spiritual vitality, because the needs are so overwhelming. Also, it is easy to slip into doing ministry activities as a professional, confident in one's ability to minister and not consciously nurturing spiritual dependence on God.

Children Launched

In the life cycle, people move from being couple-centered to child-centered through their children's adolescence, then couple-centered again when children leave home. However, professional endeavors may crowd out the nurturing and enjoyment of a couple's own relationship as well as the intimacy of other relationships. Relationships may become hard and professional rather than tender and relational.

Another challenge in more traditional families (not unique to missionaries) is that the wife focuses on kids and management of the family, and the husband focuses on ministry outside the home, and they can lose sight of maintaining and building their own relationship. Then when the nest is empty, the mother's source of identity, fulfillment, and enjoyment is suddenly gone. The couple relationship has deteriorated, there is no child focus to keep the family system going, and the mother hasn't developed interests or abilities in outside ministry activities. It's more healthy for both husband and wife to be involved in parenting, in ministry activities and in each other's lives.

As young adult children are "released," they still need their parents. It can be agonizing to be halfway around the world while one's child launches out into college or work. At times, issues of delayed adolescence can complicate the child/young adult's transition. Always, there is a healthy need for the parents' counsel and support, more as a friend than a parent.

Families that anticipate this developmental task can prepare for it by encouraging the child to settle close to extended family or close friends. Furlough can be timed to coincide with the first year back in the home country. A sense of family with the local church can be cultivated. Basic living skills can be taught during prior furloughs and teenage years—using checking accounts, handling credit wisely, doing laundry, and the like.

End of Career: Releasing

At the end of the career, there is the new challenge of releasing responsibilities to national leadership. It is a bit like first term, with the threat of low self-image as people must leave an arena where they have carved out true significance, with meaning, joy, passion, and purpose. People who are happily and profoundly engaged nevertheless have to think about leaving and returning to their home culture that really doesn't fit any more. At "home," people don't know them and what they can do, and once again people can feel ignored and insignificant. The key task, once again, is to ground oneself in identity in Christ, not so much as a learner but as a releaser. Experienced, more competent missionaries need to allow nationals and younger missionaries to take over leadership and do things differently.

It is important to remember that God will continue His work in new ways through different people. Keeping the big picture mentality helps the experienced missionary be humble, release when they need to release, and more graciously make a transition and start over in retirement in a new culture. There they can find a new niche and earn their wings all over again as capable people. Once again, issues of maintaining spiritual vitality, continuing deeply meaningful and intimate relationships and establishing new relationships are critically important.

Unexpected Events

Unexpected events can intersect with both life cycles at any time. Each situation is unique, but the critical elements are habits of having solid relationships with people around you, being connected to the Lord, and being busy and stretched but still remaining grounded. Then, whatever the life stage, one has resources and tools to face and respond to difficulty or trauma.

At any stage of life there are enough tasks and challenges to overload people. It is always necessary to make choices to build into one's life the relationships, the rest and refreshment, and the discipline needed to absorb a new hit when it comes along. The unexpected event may be a newcomer's child picking up some tropical disease, a carjacking, or any number of crises in our increasingly dangerous world.

There is always the potential for overload in life and in ministry. If people are already in overload, they are in trouble when the inevitable crises hit. If they have factors of stability in their lives—relationships, spiritual vitality, eating well, exercise, relaxing, taking time off—there is a margin to draw on for a while during a crisis, and then they can go back to balanced living when the crisis is over. If they have been balanced, they have the strength to be unbalanced for a time without crashing and burning.

Other Life Cycle Alignments

We have tracked through the two life cycles with the typical pattern of young people going overseas for the first time, and the family and career developing more or less together. It is more and more common to have different combinations of the life cycles as people begin mission service later in life, when there are radically different issues and tasks to be concerned with.

The alignment of *launching children and moving on* and *recruitment and appointment* presents the need to work through family reactions from both generational sides. Young adult children may be struggling to establish themselves; if healthy differentiation from children has taken place, a healthy overseas transition is more likely. Prospective mid-career missionaries also need to prepare for separation from aging parents. Another challenge is resolving intensified career and financial considerations.

The alignment of *family with adolescents* and *first term language and culture learning* presents such overwhelming tasks such that many missions are extremely reluctant to send such families overseas. Adolescent issues of identity combine with cross-cultural identity loss and the desire for family to stick together in face of new culture. The family system faces flexing for adolescents and re-definition in new culture, in addition to issues of appropriate social relationships and possible boarding school. For the parents, the normal mid-life evaluation of role and meaning combines with loss of role and status experienced in a new culture—and this comes on the heels of the role change and upheaval of deputation.

Recruiting of a family with adolescents has to involve the youth in an authentic way. Parents need to adapt to their children's new capacities and needs. It helps if the local church and the mission organization can coach the family on how to involve adolescents in decision-making regarding overseas service.

Summary: Themes

Understanding developmental tasks of the life cycle is a useful construct to apply to understanding people in missions. It includes development in spiritual vitality and in relationships: with family, with God, with churches, with the sending agency, with fellow missionaries, with nationals, and with extended family. Spiritual vitality is also relational, having to do with an underlying sense of self-understanding. In Romans 12 we are told to think about ourselves soberly so as to have sound judgement, on one hand valuing our gifts but also being aware of weaknesses.

The foundational theme is our identity and our grounding in Christ. Owning and reaffirming that gives the strength, humility and flexibility to absorb most of the hits that come along and to tackle the challenges.

Obviously there will be pain and we will not react well all the time; there is also permission to be human and to be weak. Latching onto our identity in Christ and the character of God, we can weather just about anything—including trying to learn a new language and feeling like an incom-petent fool, or a plane going down with my colleagues in it, or sending kids off to college in another country.

Along the way, assumptions about the fairness of life and our concept of God get shaken. But whatever comes through crisis, the life cycle, or missionary life cycle, being grounded in who we are in Christ helps us to calm down, understand what's going on, see the bigger picture, and be able to absorb it or work with it.

Key References

McGoldrick, M., & Carter, E. (1982). The stages of the family life cycle. In F. Walsh (Ed.), *Normal family processes*. New York: Guilford.

O'Donnell, K. (1987). Developmental tasks in the life cycle of mission families. *Journal of Psychology and Theology, 15,* 281-290.

9

Spiritual Dimensions in Mental Health

Glenn Taylor

*S*pirituality and mental health are dynamic, evolving concepts which vary dramatically among cultures. They are also elusive terms, with meanings which have changed many times throughout history. To find a point of conjunction between the two may be a difficult task unless we first deal with the matter of definitions.

Mental Health

In this chapter, we will use a functional approach to mental health which emphasizes both the relational dimensions of a person's existence and the personal experience of the self. This definition seeks to balance the need for attachment as well as differentiation, while acknowledging biologically determined features and environmentally influenced patterns. The dimension of well-being experienced by the person in relation to self, others and the life context is essential.

Mental health must be understood in all of these dimensions. Personal evaluation of one's experience is coupled with the feedback from significant others who provide input that greatly impact the individual's subjective experience. Although biological or genetic contributions are of major importance, they are not beyond the influence of the subjective or relational dimensions of the person's experience. We do not clearly understand this dynamic synergism.

Elements of Mental Health
1. Attitudes toward self: acceptance, esteem, accurate perception
2. Actualization of potential
3. Integration and focus of personality

The spiritual life expresses itself in all we do, think, and feel, and spiritual health is an integral aspect of well-being. There are spiritual dimensions in our understanding and pursuit of mental health as well as physical health. Biblical foundations of spirituality, historical perspectives, the relationship between spirituality and mental health, and recent research into the power of belief are explored.

75

4. Consistent and dependable sense of identity and values
5. Perception of reality; accurate, not distorted by subjective needs
6. Ability to cope; master environment with satisfaction
7. Ability to experience relational fulfillment
8. Community experience where one is valued for being and function

Our understanding of mental health commonly includes these elements. A more clinical perspective might focus on the absence of symptoms or syndromes defined by psychology or psychiatry.

An area worth exploring is the relationship between mental health and physical health and the degree to which there is an interplay between the two. The term "well-being" may be used as a bridge when we look at physical and mental states. An emphasis on the reciprocal effects of physical and mental health, for good or for ill, would be helpful for our discussion. This dynamic has gained increasing attention in many circles.

The Spiritual Dimension

There has been a strong drive within our Western culture to keep the psychological and spiritual dimensions of our being divorced from each other. The passion of psychology to distance itself from both philosophy and religion early in its history has left us with a bifurcation in understanding the human being. Theology as the "queen of the sciences" was dethroned and supplanted by a humanistic understanding that defined itself as adequate to explain human experience. More recently, there has been an increased openness to explore spirituality.

The terms "spiritual" and "spirituality" have a wide range of meanings. Some limit these terms to references in Scripture related to the Holy Spirit, such as spiritual life or spiritual gifts. Others approach the issue from the much broader concept of creation itself. From this perspective, human beings are spiritual creatures in that they were created in the image and likeness of God, who "breathed into [their] nostrils the breath of life." In this discussion of the spiritual dimension in humans, I will use the term "spirituality" in this broader manner, as defining the essence of the human being.

Biblical Foundations

Some basic theological presuppositions are essential to understanding spirituality from a Biblical perspective:

1.   Human beings are creatures in whom resides the image of God and this speaks to the essence of their spirituality. Being differentiated from the animal kingdom in the creative action of God, humanity is higher than and responsible for creation while being less than God. Thus, obedience, humility, and acknowledgment of place in the order of things are expected.

2.   Human beings were created for relationship with God and experience full humanity only in that relationship. This relationship is one of both dependence and intimate friendship. Many older theologians emphasized this point.

3.   The capacity of human beings for self-consciousness is crucial to the concept of spirituality.

4.   Fourthly, human beings were created for and experience self in relation to others in community. People are only truly human in relation to other people and in

relation to God.   Older theologians used the term "corporate personality," empha-sizing the close relationship and even identity of the individual with the community of which he was a part and by which he was shaped.

In George MacDonald's adult fantasy, *Lilith,* the lead character awakens to this truth:

> I saw now that man alone is but a being that may become a man – that he is but a need, and therefore a possibility… He rises from and stands upon such a pedestal of lower physical organisms and spiritual structures, that no atmosphere will comfort or nourish his life, less divine than that offered by other souls; nowhere but in other lives can he breathe. Only by the reflex of other lives can he ripen his specialty, develop the idea of himself, the individuality that distinguishes him from every other. (1969, pp. 109f)

5.   Well-being from a Biblical perspective grows out of the synergism between physical, emotional, spiritual and relational dynamics that are actualized in a holy or God-defined pattern of living. Well-being cannot be separated from moral-ity or from creative expression through the meaningful engagement of one's abilities.

Biblical Foundations of Spirituality – Summary

Human beings are:
1.   Created by God and spiritual in essence
2.   Created for relationship and intimacy with God
3.   Self-conscious – inward and outward looking
4.   Created for and realized in relationships
5.   Well-being experienced holistically in morality and creative expression of abilities

The Spiritual Dimension in Historical Perspective

Spirituality has been pursued and understood in a great variety of ways down through the centuries. Cultural variables have significantly impacted the under-standing of spirituality. To acknowledge this may lead us to be critical of our own cultural biases and to question whether it is appropriate to seek to duplicate spiritual practices in another culture.

It is not possible to explore the rich literature available, but only to acknowledge the reality of the historical development of our understanding of spirituality. David G. Benner (1988) provides very useful insight, and I urge the careful study of his book. His discussion of the ways of experiencing God and his summary of Desert Spirituality, Eastern Orthodox spirituality, Roman Catholic spirituality, Reformation spirituality, Pietistic spirituality, and Puritan spirituality are foundational to our discussion.

There is no single approach that may be defined as a Christian understanding of spirituality, but rather a plethora of approaches. Each approach offers distinctive foci along with means that are emphasized and practiced. All of the approaches address the elements identified in the Biblical Foundations above but in different degrees and priorities. The pursuit of or welcoming of God in one's life for the end of experiencing intimacy with God is foundational. In this relationship, a peace, quietness and joy enlivens one's personal life and experience. Freedom from undesirable or controlling passions and an experience of love for others is sought and expressed in holy living, variously defined.

Where Spiritual Dimensions and Mental Health Meet

Space does not permit an adequate survey of psychologists and their views of the spiritual dimension of life. In the Western world, until recently, the critical approach of Freud in projecting religion as an illusory crutch has had a profound influence. Others such as Jung have not only tolerated but seen the spiritual dimension in an entirely different light, if not from a Biblical perspective. Adler and Kunkel explored the social dimensions of being and the need for self-transcendence and self-surrender. Kierkegaard saw man's existence as being determined by a relationship with God whether he knew it or not. Menninger, Mowrer, Frankl, Paul Tournier, and many others have focused on the role of the spiritual dimension in their therapeutic interventions. Whether one is struggling with the profound issues of sin or the pursuit of meaning, it becomes apparent that spiritual dimensions play a significant role.

Sydney Jourard (1964) wrote:

There is increasing scientific evidence that man's physical and psychological health are profoundly affected by the degree to which he has found meaning, direction, and purpose in his existence. Some at least of this purpose arises in man's relationship with his fellows... 'Spirit' is a term which scientists view with a certain suspicion, as a matter which does not lend itself to scientific study. I acknowledge the legitimacy of this reluctance to study the phenomena of 'spirit,' yet there is more to man than the structures and drives he shares with animals.

Many acknowledge this "more to man than" dimension and have tried to comprehend it. The history of attempts to integrate psychological and theological perspectives is rich and varied, and integration continues to be a very live issue today. Recent issues of the *Journal of Psychology and Theology* (Volume 28, Numbers 1-4) have assisted in this exploration, as well as the recent book, *Psychology and Christianity: Four Views* edited by Johnson and Jones (2000).

Research into the Power of Belief

In recent years, there has been much focus on the relationship between religion and well-being. Norman Cousins focused on the benefits of positive thoughts on one's experience of health and recovery from illness. A great deal of research has focused on the impact of mental processes on one's experience of well-being.

Earlier the pioneer work of Hans Selye established the relationship between illness as a consequence of stress in response to life events. Subsequent research led to identification of life events as stressors and differentiated between the impact of different events.

Researchers typically differentiate between religion and spirituality. Usually religion is defined in terms of institutional beliefs and practices and a personal commitment to the belief system of a church or similar organization. Spirituality is defined more broadly as seeking a relationship to something divine, transcendent, or ultimate which may or may not lead to one's involvement with formal religion.

Two research approaches are particularly relevant to this discussion. The first is best represented by the work of Dr. Herbert Benson, Associate Professor of Medicine at Harvard Medical School and the Deaconess Hospital. The work of Hans Selye on stress led to Benson's exploration of one's ability to impact the parasympathetic function of the autonomic nervous system. In *The Relaxation Response* (1975) he addressed the role of relaxation and its impact of stress. In his later books, he added the concept of the "Faith Factor" and its role in facilitating healing through focusing on one's faith.

Benson (1984) states, "Scientific research has shown that electrical activity between the left and right sides of the brain becomes coordinated during certain kinds of meditation and prayer." (p. 9) He speaks of the intensity of our personal belief system and the changes in the brain when deep personal belief and conviction take hold in our lives. When the mind is filled with faith, psychophysiological benefits are translated into the power and biology of belief (1987).

This effect is related in his thinking to the placebo effect, the reduction of stress and the positive chemical activity of the brain fostered by the mind/body relationship. "We've examined how influential faith can be when cultivated by an individual, by someone caring for an individual, or by the relationship between the two. We've demonstrated that beliefs have physical repercussions..." (1987, p. 197)

Inasmuch as we are "wired for God," belief in God is natural to humanity and, Benson would insist, is basic to every culture. Faith quiets the mind, generates hope and expectancy, and short-circuits troublesome reasoning and thus activates the body's neurosignature messages of healing resources.

Another research group that works in this area is the *National Institute for Healthcare Research*. They are "bridging the gap between spirituality and health" through an extensive research and reporting system investigating the relationship between spirituality/religion and mental health. Their work may be accessed through a web site at www.nihr.org for further information. The central question they address from a scientific point of view is "What are the effects of different belief and practices on human health and well-being?" Their research explores the relationship between three types of variables: *Faith variables* – spirituality and religious beliefs and practices; *psychosocial variables* – humility, love, kindness, forgiveness, gratitude, hope, revenge, and wisdom, and *health variables* – mental health, physical health, and social well-being.

It is not possible to elaborate or cite all of their research in this brief chapter. Two books are very relevant: *The Faith Factor: An Annotated Bibliography of Clinical Research on Spiritual Subjects* (1994) and the *Handbook of Religion and Health* (2000). Research articles cover such diverse topics as the impact of religion and spirituality on forgiveness, grief, disability, patient desire, crime, patient-physician relationships, longevity, depression, blood pressure, well-being in older adults and broad categories of mental and physical well-being.

Conclusion

Over the centuries, many have sought to explore and understand the impact of religion and spirituality on well-being. Whether one begins with theological or scientific presuppositions, the accumulated data demonstrate a correlation spirituality and mental health. The "Elements of Mental Health," "Biblical Foundations," historical attempts to see relationships between mental health and spirituality, and the research approaches of Benson and NIHR all indicate a clear place for spiritual dimensions in our understanding of and pursuit of mental health as well as physical well-being.

Whether one chooses to define spirituality as a non-religious phenomenon or to place spirituality in a clearly Christian context, this dimension of being is foundational to well-being, both mentally and physically. One of the differences between a religious and non-religious understanding of spirituality is that the former acknowledges the need for values—definitions of reality and truth that are objectively differentiated from one's self. Embracing such truth is the path to freedom which includes freedom from self through a redemptive encounter and enabling by God.

Spiritual health is an integral aspect of well-being. Spiritual maturity and well-being in all its dimensions are impacted by and dramatically impact our relational functioning. Social and relational experience impact our well-being spiritually, emotionally and physically. Jean Vanier (1998, p. 114) observes, "Maturity is precisely the acceptance of yourself with your own flaws, as well as others with their flaws."

The redemptive role of Christian community is a significant part of God's redemptive plan to free a person from the tyranny of the sinful dimensions of self and from all falsehood. The spiritual life is not something ethereal but rather substantive, expressing itself in all we do, think or feel. This impacts both brain function and the physiological functions of the body through the autonomic nervous system.

An area of concern to some mental health professionals is that of role confusion which may create confusion for the client. This is an important consideration which can be addressed first by being explicit about one's faith perspective and understanding of the role of the spiritual in well-being, and secondly by intentionally and with integrity entering into the life and world view of the client. When these issues are handled with integrity, openness, sensitivity and candor, one does not need to abandon either professionalism or the responsibility to function in a Christian manner.

In recognizing the relationship between the spiritual dimension and mental health, we seek to understand the gentle power of God in the earthly relationships and experiences of life. We acknowledge the work of Him who works in the deep places of our lives whether we know it or not.

References

Benner, D. G. (1988) *Psychotherapy and the spiritual quest.* Grand Rapids, MI: Baker Books.

Benson, H. (1975) *The relaxation response.* New York: Avon Books, Inc.

Benson, H. (1984) *Beyond the relaxation response: How to harness the healing power of your personal beliefs.* New York: Times Books

Benson, H. (1987) *Your maximum mind.* New York: Times Books

Johnson, E. L. & Jones, S. J. (2000) *Psychology and Christianity: Four views.* Downers Grove, Illinois: InterVarsity Press.

Jourard, S. (1964) *The transparent self.* Princeton, N.J.: Van Nostrand.

Koenig, H. G., McCullough, M. E. & Larson, D. B. (2000) *Handbook of religion and health.* Oxford: Oxford University Press.

MacDonald, G. (1969). *Lilith.* New York: Ballantine.

Matthews, D., Larson, D. B., & Barry, C., Eds. (1994) *The faith factor: An annotated bibliography of clinical research on spiritual subjects.* Rockville, MD: National Institute for Healthcare Research.

Vanier, Jean Vanier. (1998) *Becoming human.* Toronto, Ontario: House of Anansi Press

10

Maintaining Spiritual Vitality: Spiritual Resources for Tough Times

Lareau Lindquist

Everyone experiences tough times and needs resources to cope. How can missionaries maintain a strong, vital spiritual life in the midst of tough times? Answers are found in a Biblical theology of suffering, examples of Biblical characters, and the author's experience and testimony. Practical tips from missionaries suggest ways to keep one's spiritual life fresh and vigorous.

*S*eptember 11, 2001, will be remembered as an emergency "9-1-1" of enormous proportion—the horrendous day when the United States of America was attacked by terrorists. Four hijacked commercial air-liners, piloted by terrorists, became flying missiles of death and destruction that brought havoc to our nation. The damages were massive. Nearly 3,000 individuals were killed. Financial losses ran into the billions. The im-pact of the day was felt throughout our nation and around the world, and the aftershocks will have long-term conse-quences.

That 9-1-1 was colossal. It was a MAJOR 9-1-1 and it triggered other 9-1-1's in many families and lives.

Does everyone experience tough times?

All of us have experienced our own personal 9-1-1's. They come to us in a variety of sizes, shapes and severities. We have experienced them in the past and we will see new ones in the future. J. B. Phillips once said, "Sooner or later, we will all travel through a dark tunnel." The shock often is how long the tunnel may be and how dark and lonely it might be.

The entirety of Scripture addresses the certainty of such times in our lives.

• In John 16:33, Jesus said, *In this world, you will have trouble.* Trouble is not a possibility but a certainty.
• Peter added these words in his first epistle: *Dear friends, do not be surprised at the painful trial you are suffering, as though something strange were happening to you* (I Peter 4:12). Trials are neither strange nor surprising, but expected.

• Paul, in Romans 8:35, gives a brief catalog of tough times: *trouble, hardship, persecution, famine, nakedness, danger, and sword.* The phrase, *all things,* is found three times in chapter eight (8:28, 32, 37). In each case, the phrase refers to the description in 8:35. While 8:35 is neither comprehensive nor exhaustive, it clarifies the certainty and variety of tough times.

The Scriptures are clear in telling us to be prepared for these tough times, yet most of us are surprised when trouble tumbles into our lives. In spite of all the Biblical warnings, we often say to ourselves, *I can't believe this is happening to me.*

Tough times have been the common experience of all people, from the beginning of history. It has been true for the rich and poor, for men and women, for stone-age and sophisticated individuals, for believers and unbelievers. It has also been true for pastors, missionaries, and other Christian workers.

My experience with tough times confirms the truth of II Corinthians 1:3-4. I am more effective in ministering to hurting people when I have been there and especially when I have personally received comfort from the Lord. Then I become a first-person testimonial of his sufficiency. In our world travels, Evie and I have been impressed with the universality of tough times and often the enduring intensity of such times.

Personally, Evie and I have also traveled through some of our own tough times, including family heartaches, health challenges, ministerial disappointments, mission pressures and the extended trauma of an automobile accident that brought me close to death, followed by eleven weeks of hospitalization. I will say more about the accident later.

A brief sampling of a wide variety of tough times in the Bible include the following:

David experienced times of questions as seen in Psalm 10, 13, and 77. He used these descriptive words about his troubles: *distraught; suffering; anguish; the terrors of death; fear and trembling have beset me; horror has overwhelmed me; if I had the wings of a dove, I would fly away and be at rest; I see violence and strife; I cry out in distress* (all from Psalm 55). In Psalm 57, David speaks of a *disaster* in his life.

Job speaks very clearly of his losses, pain, grief, and perplexity in these words: *darkness, deep shadow, misery, bitterness of soul, groans, fear and dread, turmoil, unrelenting pain* — a partial listing.

Paul often uses his own plights to address the trouble of others. His longest recital of personal troubles in found in II Corinthians 11.

Where can we find strength?

As caregivers, we often talk with individuals who are experiencing a variety of troubles and hardships. We need to point them to a Power that is beyond themselves, described in the Bible.

God is the Source of our strength.

All three Persons of the Godhead are involved in giving us strength. God's strength is available to us, not to fulfill our own agendas but to make us to <u>be</u> what he wants us to be, to <u>become</u> what he wants us to become, and to <u>do</u> what he wants us to do. In Ephesians 1:19-20, God gives a sweeping promise. Paul prays that we will understand *his incomparably great power that is in us who believe. That power is like the working of his mighty strength, which he exerted in Christ when he raised him from the dead and seated him at his right hand in the heavenly realms.*

Paul introduces us to the dynamic principle of Resurrection Power—the *very same power* that the Father used in raising Jesus from the dead. And this power is available to us, to help us through the tough times of life. I have found that God is totally involved in our tough times, sometimes directly and at other times indirectly. This Resurrection Power is not only a truth to be understood; it is a principle to be utilized. What an overwhelming possibility!—but too often ignored.

The Scriptures are a source of strength.

So often, when traveling through a dark valley of shadows, the Word has been used by God to energize Christians. Perhaps the Psalms are most helpful and encouraging in the toughest times of life. This was true in Biblical times and still is today.

People can be a source of strength to each other.

When David was pursued by Saul who wanted to kill him, David hid in the Desert of Ziph. In his loneliness and fear, Jonathan came to minister to him. The text says . . . *Jonathan came to David at Horesh and **helped him find strength in God*** (I Samuel 23:16). What an amazing ministry—helping one another find strength in the Lord. David was a close follower of the Lord but when life became intolerably difficult, he apparently forgot that the Lord was the Source of his strength. He needed someone to come and remind him; to *help him find strength in the Lord.*

This could be a good summary of what caregiving ministries are all about. We are "on the road" and "on assignment" to help fellow-travelers in ministry—*to help them find strength in the Lord.* That's what all of us need when we face tough times.

We can strengthen ourselves.

Ultimately we must learn how to strengthen ourselves. David often faced a myriad of troubles piled one on top of the other. One such event is recorded in I Samuel 30. David and his warriors, after an enormous battle, returned to Ziklag, hoping to meet with their wives and families. But instead of a happy reunion, they encountered overwhelming troubles. Their families had been kidnapped. Their homes had been destroyed. When his private world unraveled, the Bible says that David and his men *wept aloud until they had no strength left to weep* (30:4). His men were so angry with David, that they *talked of stoning him* (30:5). What a scene!

As David's private world was collapsing around him, what did he do? He *found strength in the Lord his God,* or as many translations put it, *he strengthened himself in the Lord* (I Samuel 30:6). David discovered that the reservoir of God's strength was unlimited. He learned how to tap into that strength. That discovery allowed him to write and experience *I love you, O Lord, my strength. The Lord is my rock, my fortress, and my deliverer; my God is my rock, in whom I take refuge. He is my shield and the horn of my salvation, my stronghold.* (Psalm 18:1-2) and *The Lord is the strength of my life* (Psalm 27:1).

The Apostle Paul also discovered the reality of knowing God as his Energizer, as stated in Philippians 4:13, *I **can do** all things through Christ, who **strengthens** me.* In that short phrase, there are two power words in the Greek language to strongly state that

God's power is available *to* us and *through* us.

The testimonies of David and Paul demonstrate that we can have powerful testimonies to the strength of God in our own experiences of tough times. We, too, can go from *strength to strength* as stated in Psalm 84:7.

What steps can I take to aid in maintaining spiritual vitality for the tough times of life? Are there continuing disciplines that I can regularly pursue?

• *Seek the Lord as your primary Source of Strength.* Look to God as your primary Caregiver. Everyone else is secondary. Everything else is supplemental to this primary relationship. As caregivers, we are at our best when we are pointing others to him and helping them to lean on him, not on us. Nothing and no one can take the place of your intimate relationship with your Creator. Everything else is an inadequate substitute.

• *Build a Biblical theology of suffering.* Earlier I mentioned the bad news of the universality of difficulty. The good news is that the Bible is filled with a lot of help for hurting people. Major biblical books are dominated by this theme: the Book of Job, II Corinthians, and I Peter. Many other chapters, paragraphs, verses, and phrases are helpful.

Many Biblical authors also experienced exceedingly tough times and wrote of their woes within the wider context of the sufficiency of God. Many of these authors had a well-defined theology of suffering. Each of us needs to do the same. Without a sturdy foundation of Biblical truth on suffering, we run the risk of being consumed by our problems and pressures. In sharp contrast to that, we can grow stronger through the tough times of life if we have taken the time to build a theology of suffering.

• *Commit yourself to trusting God,* not once but again and again. Trust is a life-long commitment. We never get graduate degrees in trust. We never outgrow the persistent need of trusting God. Shortly before the death of Henrietta Mears, she said, "If I could start life all over again, I would trust God more." She was a pioneer developer of Christian education in America and founded many ministries that are still being used of God today. Henrietta was dynamic, and her life story continues to impact women around the world. Yet, she wished she had trusted God more.

• *Become a first-person testimonial of God's care.* Most of us have heard rich testimonials as to the sufficiency of God. We have heard preachers speak of God's sufficient grace, his unlimited power, his promised presence. But these stories are second-hand to us—true but not yet personally experienced.

The story of Job's losses and understandable pain is well known. His pain is well chronicled, and his tough questions persist. But when he quit complaining and questioning, God spoke and revealed himself to Job in some of the most profound and majestic language found in the Bible. After God's self-revelation to Job, Job was in awe. All of a sudden his losses and pain were diminished in the light of his new knowledge of God.

In the last chapter of Job, he proclaims in 42:5, *Once my ears heard you but now my eyes have seen you.* Here's what Job was saying (my translation) "O God, once I knew you with my ears. I had heard a lot about you. I knew you . . . but much of it was second-hand. Now it is so different. I have seen you with my own eyes; I have had a first-hand encounter with you. I have a profound personal story to tell."

My Testimony and Some Closing Thoughts

On January 22, 1999, I was involved in an automobile accident that appeared to many as the final chapter of my earthly life. That day I had returned from a ministry trip to Kenya, taking two ten-hour flights from Nairobi to Frankfurt to Chicago. That evening I officiated at our youngest daughter's wedding. After the wedding dinner, I traveled alone in my car to my home in Rockford, Illinois, a 3-4 mile trip.

I fell asleep at the wheel and crossed four lanes of traffic. My car hit a snowdrift that hurled the car into the air at high speed. The car hit a tree five feet off the ground. My face was smashed into the steering column. Immediately I was unconscious, and I still have no recollection of the accident or anything else for the next month.

At the scene of the accident, I was given less than a one percent chance of survival, as I was severely injured. I spent the next three weeks on a ventilator in the intensive care unit, and then another eight weeks in the hospital for reconstruction and rehabilitation. It was a long and a difficult ordeal, and recovery expectations were dismal.

For a long time we thought it was the worst thing for all of us. Now, nearly four years later, Evie and I see it as a gift. God took a bad thing, touched it with his remarkable hands, and continues to make something beautiful out of it. Only God can do such a thing.

Shortly after being released from the hospital, I had lunch at one of my favorite restaurants. I created a buzz when I entered. As I checked out, the receptionist welcomed me back and asked me, "How is the miracle man?" I said, "Let me tell you about the miracle man." She said, "Oh good. We are all curious for more details." I said, "I am not the miracle man. I am the miracle-receiver. God is the Miracle Man." I told her some of the incredible things that God had done. I had many doctors but only one Great Physician.

I often state these texts. . .

* *I can do all things through Christ who strengthens me* (Philippians 4:13).
* *I am more than a conqueror through Christ* (Romans 8:37).

I know who the Conqueror is. I know who the real Victor is. I know Christ, the Miracle Man. As long as I live I will speak of him to every counselee and to every audience.

Practical Tips for a Vital Spiritual Life

Rev. Ron McLain, pastoral counselor at Link Care Center, Fresno, California, shares these ideas collected from missionaries he has counseled:

☐ Enter a new culture as a disciple and a learner of spiritual things, and in particular learn how to receive from nationals. If you go as the "white theologian and spiritual guru" you will dry up and blow away!

☐ Find creative new approaches for your devotional time. Perhaps one day you will read a passage of scripture and meditate on it. Another day you may take a verse or two with you and go on a prayer walk. And yet another day you may play a tape of praise songs and sing along, worshiping the Lord. Using different methods helps to keep your devotional time vital and fresh.

☐ Pray informally throughout the day as if Jesus were right there—he is! This is a good way to maintain an active relationship. Read *Practicing the Presence of God* by Brother Lawrence, a monk who spent his time working in a monastery kitchen, to learn more.

☐ Have a spiritual accountability partner back home who can and will e-mail you regularly (weekly or monthly). This person should be someone with whom you can be totally honest and share the "good, the bad, the ugly." Like David, the psalmist, you need to be able to share your crying out of the depths of your despair to the Lord as well as your praises unto God and everything in between. Having a real person you can communicate with is a release and a relief—just knowing someone else knows, cares and is praying along with you.

☐ Write letters to God daily or weekly that describe "where you are at." Say whatever is in your heart, including struggles, joys, disappointments, unmet expectations, anger, etc. After writing, read the letter aloud to God as a prayer. Thinking, writing, and speaking involves more of your senses and helps you get in touch with things you might otherwise ignore.

☐ Be open to hear God speaking to you. Sometimes just being quiet in the presence of God is the best way to hear his voice. You might want use a lighted candle or a favorite picture as a visual focus, and invite God to join you as you relax with a cup of tea.

☐ Keep a fresh devotional book handy to read at night or in the morning. It could be a book that challenges your view of God, increases your understanding of his continual working in your life, and draws you into God's love and grace. Hebrews 13 states, "It is good for the heart to be strengthened by grace." If you don't have any good devotional books, perhaps someone back home can look for new releases and send you books.

☐ Tape series of sermons can bring fresh inspiration and knowledge and can be used on a weekly basis to hear good teaching and preaching—especially helpful if you attend worship services in a language in which you are not fluent.

☐ Read a different translation or paraphrase of the Bible. For instance, *The Message* by Eugene Peterson is very stimulating in the way it presents Scripture in descriptive, colloquial language. While you may not use such a version for detailed Bible study, it can be refreshing for reading and devotional time.

☐ Realize that your relationship with God is about more than reading the Bible, praying, going to church, and trying to do what's right. Challenge yourself with such questions and quests as:

☐ A. How can I draw into a more intimate relationship with my Abba, Father? Do I spend time just listening to his voice and letting him love me or am I always eager to get on to the next thing?

☐ B. Read the gospels as if they were totally new to you, and look for all the emotions that Jesus exhibited. Ask yourself, "Do I experience those? Are they appropriate?" The same can be done with the Psalms, noticing the emotions David expressed to God.

☐ C. How can I allow the indwelling life of Jesus to flow through me more to bring Him glory? What does it mean to live and let others "taste and see that the Lord is good?"

☐ If possible, develop prayer and worship times with missionaries from other missions.

☐ Find a list of the characteristics of God and pray them back to God (out loud is good) with gratefulness. God inhabits the praises of his people, and this will transform you into his image.

11

A Practical Approach to Missionary Transitions

Laura Mae Gardner

I ntroduction
Transition stress has been the subject of increasing concern in missions. In the 1980s Wycliffe Bible Translators conducted a descriptive preliminary research project, focusing on career transitions and their accompanying stresses. As a result of this and other evaluations, adjustments have been made to the Member Care services offered to Wycliffe's personnel. These will be discussed later in this chapter.

Major change is an integral part of mission work. Table I, a chronological listing of the major transitions points in the life of a Wycliffe member, shows change (transition points) falling into two categories—expected and unexpected.

Each of these points has its own stressors and the potential to produce feelings of grief, shock, loss, anger, depression and anxiety in those making the adjustment. Table II delineates the pressures attending each transition point.

Extreme change, including that of location, language, safety, health and career, are the norm in missions. Acceptance of this reality, while helping to keep expectations under control, does not obviate the need for advance preparation when facing sudden or planned transition. Nor does it lessen the need for expressions of concern by the missionary's constituency and the employing agency.

On the contrary, given the impact of change on all aspects of individual and family life, including the "environmental linkages"—hospitals, day care, peer group, school, social networks, the world of work, and other neighborhood and community relationships, both internal

Missionary life is exceedingly stressful, and much of the stress is caused by transition and change. This chapter looks at major transition points in the lives of missionaries, both expected and unexpected. Programs and resources which communicate care and aid in coping with transition stress are described. Responsibilities as well as needs of mission administrators are noted.

TABLE I
Major Transition Points in the Life of a Wycliffe Member

EXPECTED

Entrance into the organization

one-month screening/application program
linguistic/technical training
field training
assignment
establishing financial partnerships
travel to place of assignment
assignment begins
encountering the culture
language learning

Furlough

returning to sending churches – visiting constituency
constant travel
reconnecting with family

Change of assignment or change of career

linguist to administrator
mechanic assigned to field training staff
field worker asked to lead a new advance
field worker becomes a home representative – health or children's education needs
translation finished – translator given an administrative or public relations assignment
translator leaves agency; becomes a pastor

Winding down - end of career

finishing up on the field
finding retirement housing/activities
adjusting to limited income, limited health

UNEXPECTED

(Unrelated to the chronological missionary experience; can happen at almost any point.)

Trauma

natural disasters
ideological resistance
civil unrest
field work terminated for political reasons
kidnapping
burglary; assault
guerrilla activity; warfare
moral lapse among colleagues
corrupt local government/systems

Personal disaster

sudden death of family member
chronic or terminal illness
birth defect/disabling learning disorder
personal moral

Disillusionment

asked to do things they're not trained for
strongest gift not used
personal sacrifices met with little understanding or gratitude
chronic distrust and conflict – individuals and teams don't work effectively together
lack of organizational support when disagreements occur

Grief

agony of the final good-bye to ministry
out of step with things in the home country
loneliness

Table II
Pressures Accompanying Missionary Transitions

Intake: Evaluations
personal and technical evaluation
group living
child care
academic expectations

Intake: Fears
of the unknown
of primitive living
of cross-cultural implications
of raising support

Intake: Decisions
regarding choice of field
regarding area of contribution
regarding ministry and/or house
    partner (if single)

First Term on Field
new language
new food
new colleagues
new experiences

Furlough
need to defend one's work
how many souls have been won?
how many churches have been
    planted?
how much translation has been done?

Reentry stress
one's home country has changed
upheaval
travel
finances

Change of Assignment
new field or area
new supervisor
new task
new associates
loss of the old and familiar

Change of Career at Midlife
less energy
possible loss of life goals
midlife crisis

Point of Closure
regrets
feeling useless when facing retirement
financial stress
major adjustments

TIMES OF TRAUMA

Straightforward
tension, fear, and anxiety
production blocked
new responsibilities added
loss of the old and familiar

Complicated
moral lapse among one's colleagues –
    adds pressure, undermines morale,
    increases suspicion or cynicism.
kidnapping
hostile government forces – civil unrest;
    low-profile living

---

preparation and external support are essential to continued health throughout the transitions of missionary life.

For the missionary, the normal life changes, e.g., midlife, with corresponding career adjustments, impending menopause, children leaving home, etc., often coincide with other transitions particular to the mission community, with the potential of exponentially increased stress.

The latter part of the chapter discusses career transition. In the study above, one of the questions asked: "What has the organization done, or what could it have done to make your transition easier?" Wycliffe's organizational response to this input, as well as to the continued research into member needs, is summarized in a presentation of programs and resources currently available to the membership.

Career Transition Issues

Career change brings many areas of internal conflict, including:

1.   **Roots/place** – serious disruption of routine and stability, of both relationships and activities.

2.   **Responsibility for family** – materially, spiritually, and emotionally. Every change impacts all family members. Adults in the family must mitigate that impact.

3.   **Use of gifts**. Workers asked to meet a need for which they do not feel gifted, or take on a task which will not utilize their greatest gifts, may have difficulty justifying this to themselves and/or God.

4.   **Lack of preparation for the task**. Some things just need any willing, available person to do them. Inadequate training often increases a person's stress level.

5.   **Personal tolerance for change**. While some personalities thrive on change, challenge and new experiences, others crave a settled, predictable, routine and adjust slowly to any change.

6.   **Attitude to Christ's call**. How does one reconcile the tension between a call to do Bible translation and a request to serve in administration? How do we know when the request is a legitimate call to be obeyed and when it is a temptation or hindrance to be resisted?

7.   **Self-esteem**. How does one live with the knowledge that they have not finished the task to which they felt called; the feeling of inadequacy for the job they are being asked to fill; the fear of failure? Grief is deep and strong at times of loss and displacement.

8.   **Relationship with authority**. Wycliffe has long encouraged independence as an essential trait for field workers. A recent push toward partnership has shown the skill of being a team player to be equally important. Response to authority is a significant variable in missionary success. How much say should the individual have in making career decisions?

Symptoms of Transition Stress

Anyone making a career transition will struggle with the foregoing issues to some degree. Success in dealing with them depends on a number of factors, beginning with administrative response to their situation. Effective administrators of individuals who are not coping adequately with their transition experience must know the symptoms of transition stress and be able to assess their magnitude.

Symptoms include loss of, or failure to demonstrate, the positive aspects of the Christian life – joy, peace, harmony, and contentment. In their place, one is likely to see tension, irritability, fear, lethargy, criticism, anxiety, clinging to the old and familiar, clustering or consolidating rather than venturing, indecisiveness, withdrawal and anger (often unfocused, but sometimes expressed toward God as well as toward the administration or the system requiring the change).

The administrator will need to decide which of these characteristics are normal for this person and which are not, whether the member is able to move through these reactions on their own or will need external intervention, what will constitute this intervention, and when and how it will be offered.

Available Programs and Resources

Over the past 15 years, mission agencies have become increasingly aware of the effect good member care can have on the productiveness, longevity and satisfaction of their workers. Programs and resources are constantly being developed and evaluated, modified and expanded. These offerings are both intra-mission, i.e., by a mission for its workers alone, and inter-mission, e.g., Barnabas International, offering pastoral care; and the Mobile Member Care Team, providing crisis care in Africa.

Acknowledging that many missions are developing resources and programs to assist their members with transition issues, we have attempted to include inter-mission offerings in the following list of resources and programs. The bulk of the information, however, comes from services developed and offered by Wycliffe Bible Translators to its membership.

In 1990 member care was declared to be an organizational priority for Wycliffe. In 1998 the office of International Member Care was established. Four vital functions fall under that umbrella: 1) Children's Education and Family Services, 2) Counseling, 3) Health, and 4) Pastoral Care. Career planning, financial consulting, elder care and post-high school shepherding also are important services.

For anticipated transitions:
CHED-FS (Children's Education and Family Services)

Mission organizations have grown in their awareness that transition affects children as well as its adult members, and have established programs providing resources to help them through these stressful times. Studies by MK CART/CORE and others have documented the impact upon MKs (missionary "kids") of the quality of organizational care received by their families (Adult MK Study, MK CART/CORE).

Third Culture Kid/Missionary Kid reentry programs include The MK Connection, co-sponsored by The Narramore Christian Foundation and Barnabas International, "an enriching, informative, fun-filled, twelve-day reentry program" and Interaction Transition Seminars, "designed to provide ideas, activities and materials that will enable you to understand yourself and your reactions as you adjust to your new life setting" (E-mail: Interaction@compuserve.com). Both programs are geared to helping MKs transition to life in North America.

Wycliffe's Children's Education Department offerings to member MKs include career assessment and college advice, resources for job searches, internships and MK websites as well as counseling resources. Transition Packets are provided for parents.

Management Development and Orientation Course, in their training package, offers help in developing interpersonal, transition and other skills.

Career Counseling is a vocational guidance service staffed by trained counselors. When a translation project is completed or prematurely terminated for various reasons, or the complexities of Vision 2025 and the specialized nature of much of Wycliffe's work complicate the search for a "fit," there is a need for a specialized response from the organization. Having "in-house" career counseling enables the organization to tailor the content to meet the specialized gifts and needs of evangelical mission workers, male and female alike.

Personnel Administrators (PAs) are experienced members who offer seamless care to members beginning with their first contact with the organization and continuing through their final home assignment. PAs must be informed and caring good communicators who find satisfaction in making others successful.

The International Pastoral Care Facilitator focuses on strengthening both individuals and groups in their spiritual vitality, conflict management and peace-making skills, and resilience and spiritual health. Pastors Beyond and Barnabas International both offer pastoral services to the mission population overseas.

Local-level Wycliffe organizations address issues of re-entry and renewal.

Therapeutic Counseling: Wycliffe and SIL's International Counseling Ministries Coordinator oversees and provides resources for our counselors around the world. Wycliffe U.S. has established a counseling department to meet the needs of the membership, including those in transition. It identifies potential and established counselors and facilitates their entrance into and orientation to the organization. Extra-organizational therapeutic intervention is sought when appropriate, e.g., Link Care, Alongside, Heartstream, etc.

The strength of networking is seen in the recent development of inter-mission-staffed counseling centers on the field, e.g. Tumaini Counseling Centre in Nairobi, Kenya.

Financial Counseling and Aid is a recognized area of need. Financially insightful retired members have responded as consultants in this area and legislation has been developed to establish guidelines for members' retirement needs. Similar steps are being considered to meet members' financial needs in other areas.

For the unexpected transitions:

Crisis Care offerings are increasing to meet felt need. Risk assessment, formation of crisis management teams, debriefing workshops, etc. are now expected parts of overseas operations. Wycliffe's International Crisis Management office monitors situations world-wide and leads workshops in pre-crisis preparation. Its International Member Care office focuses on proactive preparation of personnel, leading various debriefing and member care workshops around the world. It also responds promptly to evacuations and other crises.

The Mobile Member Care Team and others are also "on call" for crisis situations.

Administrative Attitudes Toward Members in Transition

An administrator can enhance the work atmosphere by:

- Awareness of the high stress attending transition points in people's lives.

- Consideration of the entire family and the effect this change will have on each of them.
- Willingness to discuss all aspects of assignment change thoroughly with all the team members, making sure all understand and are in agreement. People deal better with a change they have had some control over.
- Realizing the effect differences in people's perspective has on their ability to accept changes of assignment.
- Valuing people over production. Though an administrator's main task is to make the product happen, he must give equal high value to maintaining the health and happiness of members and their families. Understanding and supportive administrators give their staffs time and help to replenish depleted resources.

Counseling Help

The counseling department provides certain specialized kinds of help for individuals and entities by:

- Promoting awareness of expected transition stress
- Providing help for members dealing with transition stress
- Giving input at the intake stage
- Encouraging counselors to visit the fields regularly, helping diffuse members' stress and teaching stress management skills.
- Promoting self-awareness by using tools such as the Myers-Briggs Type Indicator.
- Training administrators in people skills, e.g. the Sharpening Your Inter-personal Skills workshops under Ken Williams.
- Reviewing useful literature and suggesting titles for field libraries, writing and publishing bulletins of practical information to help promote health.
- Ministering to the leaders. Mission leaders give little attention to their own well-being. When helping the leader to meet the needs of the membership, the counselor also needs to be aware of the needs of the administrators, who may be losing heart or becoming overwhelmed.

All of these are much needed. But therapy must continue to be their primary service.

Self Care

The commitment to personal growth is crucial if the transition is a difficult one. Sometimes we are pushed into a change that is not of our choosing, e.g., adapting to illness. In that case it is obviously difficult to be committed to the change. It is at that point that our focus on the growth potential within the situation can be helpful. We can commit ourselves to the healthful things that will help us overcome the illness. (Even in terminal illness we read of people who are discovering the meaning of life and learn to see the transitions as a growth process.)

The single most important quality we can take to any situation is a strong personal commitment to growth! When that is a consistent pattern of focus we can speak of our commitment as a part of our growth identity. If we can activate our commitment both to the transition and to personal growth opportunities in that situation we have taken a major step in making the transition work for us. With that motivation behind us we are likely to build a strong support system.

Conclusions

Do these strategies implemented by Wycliffe members fit other missionary organizations? Other mission agencies have the same leadership shortage, the same overwhelming need and commensurate shortage of field personnel, the same flux of people. Therefore some of the above strategies should be found helpful by all mission organizations no matter how small or specialized.

In general:

- Missionary life is exceedingly stressful, whether recognized by missionaries and their administrators or not. Much of this stress is caused by transition and change.
- People vary in their tolerance of stress. Most have developed some way to coping with it. People need individual treatment at transition points in their lives.
- Stress is lessened when those undergoing it feel some semblance of control. Workers should be allowed to have as much voice as possible in career transitions that come into their lives.
- Families should be viewed as a unit and allowed to process the change together. Mission administration needs to acknowledge the skills and concerns of the wife, providing career counseling tailored to meet her needs and stage of life.
- Provision of tangible resources communicates care to the worker, aiding the transition process. Mission leaders can affirm God's provision and the mission's care for its members by considering the resource needs of their people and finding ways to provide these, e.g., counseling, financial, material or spiritual help.
- Administrators generally have more stress and less oversight and care than anyone else in the organization. They may find themselves more committed to achieving goals and caring for others than caring for themselves. Robbins (1984) suggests ways in which harried executives might help themselves. However, there is a need for formal encouragement of leaders to undergo periodic physical and emotional examinations and checkups.
- In-house counselors or other Christian professionals can train administrators in people-helping skills, provide training and preventive help to the membership of a mission agency and furnish therapeutic emotional and spiritual services during transition and other times of distress.

Transitions are an inherent part of missionary life. Coping well with them is made easier by informed administrators and skilled people-helpers.

Recommended Readings

Austin, C. (1986). *Cross-cultural reentry: A book of readings.* Abilene, TX: Abilene Christian University Press.

Bridges, W. (1980). *Transitions.* Addison Wesley.

Gardner, L.M. (1999). "Good manners in transition and change." Dallas: Wycliffe Bible Translators International.

Gardner, L.M. (2000). "How does a leader know when it's time to move on to a new assignment?" Dallas: Wycliffe Bible Translators International.

Gardner, L.M. (1999). "The making or breaking of missionaries: promoting resilience on the field." Dallas: Wycliffe Bible Translators International.

Gardner, L.M. (2001). "The morale curve in job transition: helping the administrator's wife." Dallas: Wycliffe Bible Translators International.

Grossman, Philip W. (1986). "Life changes." Dallas: Wycliffe Counseling Office.

Holmes, R. L. (1995). "Spiritual care for returning missionaries." Gordon-Conwell Theological Seminary, Charlotte.

Jones, M. (Ed.). (1993). *Caring for the missionary into the 21st century.* Care For Mission.

Jongeward, D., & Scott, D. (1992). *Re-entry.* Seattle, WA: YWAM Publishing.

Robbins, F.E. (1984). "Here's help for the harried executive." *Evangelical Missions Quarterly, 20,* 420-422.

12

Missionary Stressors and Implications for Care

Joan Carter

ote: The following was excerpted and adapted from an article by the same title published in Journal of Psychology and Theology 1999, Vol. 27, No. 2, pp. 171-180. See the original article for a fuller treatment. Used by permission.

Member care plays a crucial role in the personal adjustment and ministry effectiveness of missionaries. It is integral in both prefield and ongoing training in providing pastoral care and support, in team development, in personal or group counseling, in preventive and remedial medical care, and in crisis intervention. Mental health practitioners are increasingly involved in almost all of these aspects of missionary care. An understanding of the stressors missionaries face is crucial to all these tasks.

Research plays an important part in understanding the needs of missionaries and in shaping the role of the mental health practitioner in missionary care. Dorothy Gish's (1983) study on sources of missionary stress has made a valued contribution to missionary research and care. Gish identified as major stressors those items rated as causing moderate to great stress by at least 30% of the 549 missionaries who participated. Mission literature since that time has focused on recognizing stress factors. Few research studies, however, have been done since Gish's study, with most subsequent articles relying on Gish's landmark research.

The implications of Gish's findings for assessment, training, and ongoing member care paralleled concerns of the Christian & Missionary Alliance (C&MA), prompting them to initiate a study to identify the stressors for missionaries serving with them.

The classic early study of missionary stressors was done in 1983 by Dorothy Gish. Joan Carter updated and extended Gish's work in 1999. Stressors are identified which are consistently rated high by missionaries. Many of these can be alleviated by training, both pre-field and on-field, in areas such as interpersonal skills, conflict resolution, and basic management skills.

101

Procedure

Research was conducted by on-site visits. A missionary care and research package was designed to include the rating of stressors along with semistructured personal interviews and seminars dealing with stress management, self-care, personality (Myers-Briggs Type Indicator), and team building as appropriate to the needs of each field. The interviews included four questions directly related to stress. These questions were:

- What would you identify as areas causing stress for missionaries?
- What are major stress points for you?
- What are some culture-specific stressors affecting you?
- What kinds of external expectations cause you feelings of stress?

The qualitative data gathered during the interviews provided helpful perspectives for understanding and interpreting the quantitative data.

Respondents

Ratings were completed by 306 Christian & Missionary Alliance missionaries in 13 fields over an 8-year period. The respondents were all of the C&MA missionaries in a given country with the exception of those on home assignment at the time the survey was conducted and, in two African countries, two or three individuals in remote areas who were unable to attend any of the seminars. The majority of respondents were from the USA or Canada. The notable exception is Thailand which is highly multicultural, with only about half of the team from North America.

Stressors Identified

Below are items which were rated on the Stress Rating Form as causing moderate to great stress (3 to 5 on the scale). Stressors rated *moderate* to *great* by 40% or more of respondents on at least three fields are in bold print:

Seeing Needs I am Unable to Meet
Confronting Others When Necessary
Amount of Work
Communicating Across Language & Cultural Barriers
Work Priorities
Self Expectations
Conflicts Between My Values & Host Culture
Time for Personal Study of the Word & Prayer
Task Orientation vs. "Servant Attitude"
"Goldfish Bowl" Existence
Maintaining Relations with Home Churches/Friends
Travel Difficulties
Climate
Guilt Feelings Over Having Plenty in the Midst of Need
Relationships With Nationals
Making Decisions
Furlough Expectations & Schedule

Freedom to Take Time for Myself
Progress on My Work
Need for Pastoral Care
Need for Confidante
Self-Acceptance Including Self-Forgiveness
Uncertainty About My Future
Extended Family Concerns
Frequent Moving
Recreation & Exercise
Family Responsibility vs. Ministry
City Driving
Maintaining Relationships With Family at Home
Finances
Thievery
Inadequate Leadership & Support From Field Leaders
Children's Schooling
Type of Housing
Discouragement re: People's Lack of Response
Interpersonal Bruising (Marital or Team)
Lack of Forum to Talk About Personal Struggles
Sense of Demonic Oppression
Relationship With Spouse or Partner
Loneliness & Isolation

Differences

Two factors showed a statistically significant difference between male and female missionaries: "Extended Family Concerns" and "Relationship with Spouse or Partner." In both cases the stressors were rated higher by women.

Five factors emerged as significantly different for married individuals and single people. Of these, three were higher for married individuals and two were higher for single people. Married individuals scored higher on "Children's Schooling," "Family Responsibilities vs. Ministry," and "Communicating Across Language & Cultural Barriers." The stressors significantly higher for single people were "Grief at the Loss of Colleagues" and "Relationship With Spouse or Partner."

The fact that married individuals scored higher on "Children's Schooling" and "Family Responsibilities vs. Ministry" is easy to understand; that they scored higher on "Communicating Across Language & Cultural Barriers" is less so but is perhaps due to more limited time and exposure to the culture. All of the single people in this study were female.

Incongruencies

Stress levels reported in interviews and discussion of stressors often indicated considerable distress and pain, and yet these stressors would only be rated as a 2 or 3 on the scale. Does this indicate strength, resilience, and coping skills? Does it indicate a tendency to downplay the impact of stressors? Does it indicate that the missionaries want to appear adequate and able to handle the stressors in their lives? Or does it mean that 2 or 3 actually does indicate a high level of distress but not something the missionaries would rate as unmanageable or at crisis level and thus categorize as a 4 or 5?

Three hundred points of stress or above on the Holmes/Rahe stress scale is considered the danger zone for potential physical illness. Scores between 300 and 350 are considered to be very serious and scores of 351 and above as alarming. Dodds and Dodds (1997) pointed out that when they have used a modified version of this stress scale, the average cross-cultural worker has approximately 600 points of stress per year. They observed that "most missionaries do adapt and work effectively in spite of killing levels of stress. . . . [They] adapt and cope, becoming used to and remaining effective under loads of stress that would land more 'regular' people in the hospital. (p. 8)

Although many stressors were rated fairly consistently over time and location, some stressors rated fairly low on these forms would have increased dramatically a few weeks or months later, such as when political instability, violence, and missionary evacuation occurred shortly after the completion of the stress ratings. Others are more situation- and time-specific and are particularly unstable (e.g., "Pain re: Failings of Others").

Difficulties in Interpretation

Interpreting these data is difficult for a number of reasons. One is the limitations of the instrument and the analysis. As a case in point, consider the ratings for "Children's Schooling." The intensity of that stress for many parents is blurred by the fact that the ratings include single people and married individuals without children or whose children are grown. Another compounding factor is that in some fields the children are able to live at home, on other fields the only option is a distant boarding school, and still others have some of both. Further study is needed to sort out the effects of these various situations on stressor ratings.

A second reason interpretation is difficult is that stressors, by nature, are complex. Consider the stressor identified as "City Driving." The obvious interpretation of this is the stress produced by the driving itself – the safety, congestion, time involved, and pollution. Less obvious are implications like increased stress due to self expectations of high productivity that are sabotaged by "wasting time" sitting in traffic.

Another implication noted in the mega-cities is that fellow missionaries live scattered through the city, and although the distance may not be great, the driving time needed to get together often feels overwhelming or impossible, so it rarely happens. This impacts feelings of isolation, lack of community support, and diminished pastoral/mutual care.

A third difficulty in interpretation is that the blending of scores, helpful for overall trends, masks important differences. For example, "Guilt Feelings Over Having Plenty in the Midst of Need" was rated moderate to great by 42% of Cambodia missionaries and by only 3% of Thailand missionaries.

Conclusions and Implications

Stressors that are consistently rated high have been identified. In fact, on the whole, stressors were rated higher than they were in Gish's study (1983). This raises many questions such as: Are missionaries generally living at a higher level of stress than they did in the past? If so, is this trend expected to continue? Are multiple and potent stressors just part of being a missionary? What implications do the answers to these questions have for training, screening, and placement?

The 10 to 15 factors identified as top stressors are remarkably consistent over both time (8 years) and location (13 fields). Two major themes seem to emerge which encompass a number of these stressors, namely interpersonal relationships and management issues. These themes are certainly not unique to missionaries, but the cross-cultural situations in which missionaries live and minister can bring additional and/or stronger stressors and a less supportive environment.

Interestingly, these themes were identified by Gish (1983) in the 1980s, and now, near the end of the 1990s, the same themes and same individual stressors still top the list and are, in all cases, rated as more stress-producing than registered in Gish's initial study. Gish noted:

The most striking thing about these results is that those sources identified as producing the greatest amount of stress are all causes which can be to some degree alleviated by training. Many missionary organizations have orientation programs of some type. This study would suggest that conflict resolution and basic management skills should be included in such programs (or better yet be part of missionaries' basic training). However, it seems likely that preservice training is not enough. (p. 241)

More comprehensive, focused, ongoing training – both prefield and on-field – over a few years would be needed to ascertain its beneficial impact on missionary stress. Although it is never possible to control for all confounding variables in order to accurately assess the impact of training, it seems apparent that training which provides understanding and skills related to these stressors is an imperative component of missionary preparation and care.

Additional questions demanding further thought, research, and response are: What stressors can be addressed and lowered directly? What stress management tools and training can be given to missionaries to help them cope well in stressful situations? What kind of support is needed?

In considering which areas mental health practitioners could effectively address with an integration of psychology and theology, the following are readily identifiable: self expectations, time management, self-care, mutual care and community building, crisis management theory and skills, interpersonal skills and conflict management, and team building.

The wisdom of addressing the stressors identified as major and persistent seems evident, whether this is by education and skill development, administrative attention and possible restructuring, and/or pastoral care.

Recommended Readings

Dodds, L, & Dodds, L. (1997). *Stressed from core to cosmos: Issues and needs arising from cross-cultural ministry.* Paper presented at the American Association of Christian Counselors World Congress, Dallas, TX, November 1997.

Foyle, M. E (1987). *Overcoming missionary stress.* Wheaton, IL: Evangelical Missions Information Service.

Gish, D. J. (1983). Sources of missionary stress. *Journal of Psychology, and Theology, 11,* 236-242.

Miersma, P. (1993). Understanding missionary stress from the perspective of a combat-related stress theory. *Journal of Psychology and Theology, 21,* 93-101

O'Donnell, K.S. & O'Donnell, M. L. (1988) *Helping missionaries grow: Readings in mental health and missions.* See chapters by T. W. Dye, S. F. Dye, and K. L. Williams.

O'Donnell, K. S. & O'Donnell, M. L. (1991). Stress can be managed: One way is to do stress assessments at all levels of the organization. *Evangelical Missions Quarterly, 27,* 40-45.

O'Donnell, K. S., & O'Donnell, M. L. (1992). Understanding and managing stress. In K. O'Donnell (Ed.), *Missionary care: Counting the cost for world evangelization* (pp. 110-122). Pasadena, CA: William Carey Library. ·

O'Donnell, K. S. (1995). From rhetoric to reality: Assessing the needs and coping strategies of frontier mission personnel. *International Journal of Frontier Missions, 12,* 201-208.

13

Stress and Coping:
Learning How to Be Resilient

Jan Yeaman

Stress is an unavoidable and necessary part of life, but too much stress has consequences for physical, psychological, spiritual, and academic well-being. This chapter discusses sources of stress, explains physiological responses, and gives a model for understanding our reactions to stress. It also provides tools for assessing stress levels and developing better coping skills.

*T*his chapter will look at what stress is and why it is important in our lives. We live in a stress-inducing world but there are options for minimizing the impact of stress. Care providers can help missionaries become more resilient to stress.

What is stress? When I ask this question, people often respond with "It's when I feel tired and gritchy" or "It's when I feel totally overwhelmed." Such statements reflect what happens *when* we get stressed but they do not describe *what* stress is. Perhaps the single greatest way to help people deal with stress in their lives is to help them understand the true nature of the stress response.

Endocrinologist Hans Selye (1946) defined stress as "the nonspecific response of the body to any demand made upon it to adapt whether that demand produces pleasure or pain." Responses vary from person to person but are primarily physiological. The physical response, however, may have consequences that are psychological or spiritual. Often we are completely unaware of this initial step in the stress response.

According to Selye, our body responds "to any demand made upon it to adapt." Any time we face any kind of change, large or small, our bodies respond physiologically, whether we are aware of it or not, and whether the change represents something positive or something negative.

In his early work, Selye felt that both positive and negative situations generated equal physiological responses. For example, people decide to go to the mission field—the fulfillment of a life-long goal to serve God overseas. Although it is a positive choice, it is still stressful

to make this major move. Once overseas, people may have to deal with their home being broken into and their belongings being stolen; or perhaps their expectations about what it is like to work with other missionaries are not met—these are definitely negative situations which cause stress.

More recent research has shown that negative situations are more stress producing than positive situations, because usually we have less control and less predictability. As one's sense of control and sense of predictability go down, the intensity of stress goes up exponentially! This principle explains why missionaries' lives are highly stressful on an ongoing basis.

Physiological Responses

Whatever the stress, our bodies react with what Walter Cannon called the "fight or flight response." In the face of a perceived threat, our bodies quickly gear up either to fight the foe or to flee from it.   Almost instantly our bodies are flooded with epinephrine and norepinephrine. We perspire, mouths get dry, heart rate and breathing increases, and eyes get as big as saucers when the pupils dilate. Taking two to three seconds, other hormones are slower getting into our bloodstream but they are measurable six to eight weeks later!

These hormones include gluccocorticoids, mineralcorticoids, and vassopressin. An interesting one is thyroxine, which does not usually create noticeable symptoms until ten days after a stressful event—then we may feel paranoid, have nightmares, and thoughts race out of control. Someone experiencing the impact of thyroxine may have difficulty sleeping or may have digestive tract disturbances, such as diarrhea. It is interesting to note that every one of the stress hormones increases blood pressure, albeit by different mechanisms.

The same physiological reactions occur with emotions in general. While they may feel different, there is no difference in the physiological reaction to stress, happiness, anger, lust, or guilt. Negative emotions, however, tend to persist longer than positive emotions and are more damaging. Most North Americans have a diminished awareness of what is going on in our bodies until significant problems develop.

To sum up the contributions of Hans Selye and Walter Cannon, stress is what happens to your body whenever you are faced with change. The less able you are to predict and/or control those changes, the more your body will react.   These physiological reactions are consistent and inevitable, even when you are not aware of the changes. Everyone is exposed to sources of stress and everyone's body responds, but only some people become seriously vulnerable—why is that?

To get a quick, visual overview of what research can tell us about stress, Yeaman's (1994) model of stress and coping is helpful. The diagram provides a handle on the ever-increasing volume of studies on stress and coping. Our discussion of stress-proofing missionaries will start at the bottom of the diagram, with the consequences of chronic stress. It cannot be overemphasized that if our clients do not fully understand what can happen if they do not manage their stress, it is not likely that they will be motivated to make changes to minimize stress in their lives.

Consequences of Too Much Stress

How much stress is *too* much stress? The answer to that really depends on the

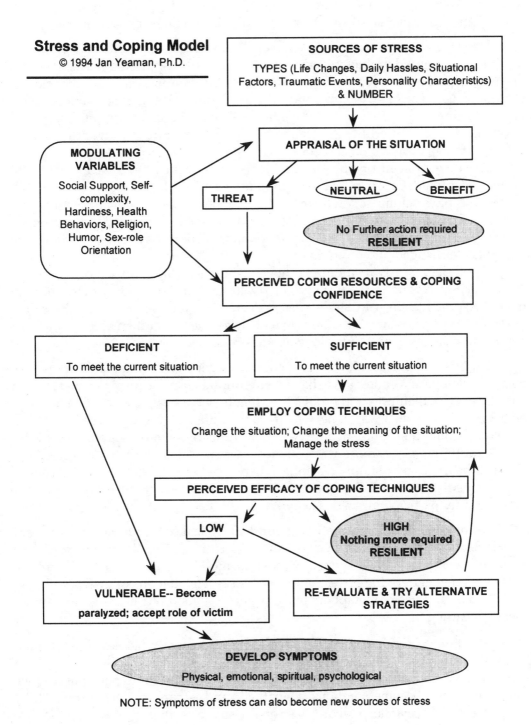

Stress and Coping Model
© 1994 Jan Yeaman, Ph.D.

NOTE: Symptoms of stress can also become new sources of stress

individual. Some people are biologically and psychologically predisposed to be more reactive. The key is to recognize the signs of overload, which may be physical, psychological, emotional, spiritual, or academic. Each will be presented briefly.

Physical consequences include ulcers; hypertension (systolic and diastolic); heart disease; thyroid problems; some cancers; tuberculosis; chronic yeast infections; respiratory problems; sleep disturbances; decreased immunocompetence; accident-proneness; use of alcohol, tobacco, and over-the-counter sleeping medications; allergies; autoimmune diseases (rheumatoid arthritis, lupus, etc); ammenorrhea, dysmenorrhea; and infertility in both males and females. Stress hormones also play a distinct role in weight gain and obesity.

The development of physical problems is frequently the first indication of untreated, chronic stress in missionary populations. How do our thoughts have such a profound physical impact on the body? It happens because we are fearfully and wonderfully made! Our minds and our bodies are intricately linked through a structure in the brain called the hypohypophoseal portal system—this is where thoughts get changed into physiology.

Our thoughts may result in psychogenic illnesses (those caused directly from stress, such as coronary disease) and/or psychomollitic conditions (those that are magnified or made worse by stress, such as decreased immune systems). Stress may also result in psychosanatic situations in which we take longer than necessary to heal because of changes in our physiology due to stress.

Try this: A great technique to get people to understand how quick and powerful these physiological responses is to have them count their pulse for six seconds. Then have them close their eyes and recall a time that they were angry. Ask them to focus on what was said, what was done, why it was so unfair. With their eyes still closed, have them count their pulse again. A 50 percent increase in pulse-rate is common; changes of 100 percent or more are frequent occurrences. They have just changed how fast their heart beats by simply recalling a memory—they did not have to feel angry to get immediate changes! Typically, people become more motivated to change their lifestyles after participating in this activity.

For more in-depth information about the physical consequences of stress, see Robert Sapolsky's book *"Why Zebras Don't Get Ulcers."* Sapolsky is masterful in presenting complex physiology in a "Reader's Digest" format. He gives a thorough presentation of underlying physiological processes related to major diseases. Sapolsky's humor and use of metaphors make his book a good one to assign for recommended reading.

Psychological consequences of stress include feelings of helplessness, despair, suicidal ideation, and suicide; depression; anxiety; anger; anorexia, bulimia, and compulsive eating; absentmindedness; worry; and increased interpersonal conflict. People may also become emotionally apathetic and lethargic. Recent research by Teicher (www.mcleanhospital.org/) strongly suggests that many psychological issues arise from changes in brain structures due to stress. Particularly impacted are the hippocampus and amygdala, key structures in the limbic system responsible for emotions.

Spiritual consequences are often unrecognized as stress-related. A sense of emptiness, loss of meaning, and doubt may be present. Other signs are being unforgiving; martyrdom; looking for magic; loss of direction; cynicism; apathy; and needing to "prove" oneself.

Academic consequences include decreased performance when performance is constantly monitored; a decrease in self-esteem; decrease in GPA, exam scores; increased cheating; increased absenteeism; and increased self-derogatory thinking. While missionaries may not be students, issues of decreased productivity and work performance are relevant.

The consequences of chronic stress can be far-reaching. In ancient days, people usually had time to recover from one stressful incident before being confronted by another. In the modern world, we are frequently bombarded with one fight-or-flight response after another, like waves pounding the shoreline. When today's stressors cause the release of more hormones, your body may still be dealing with those released in previous days or weeks.

Where Stress Comes From

Researchers have identified a number of different types of sources of stressors. Briefly, some of the major sources of stress are:

- *Life events* (Holmes & Rahe, 1967; Miller & Rahe, 1967)—These are major negative or positive events such as deaths, divorce, marriage, moving, and changes in sleeping habits. Scales have been developed in which each event is assigned a certain point value; the total score may an increased risk for poor health. Approximately nine percent of the variance in developing significant illness can be predicted by life experience.

- *Daily hassles* (Lazarus; Delongis, Folkman, & Lazarus)—While life events focus on major situations, daily hassles are about the grind of daily living. These are the 'little things' that bother and irk you, like the car not starting when you are already late or waiting for paperwork to be processed in some government office.

- *Situational factors* (Benjamin & Waltz, 1987; Holden, 1996)—These related to the situation you find yourself in, over which you have little control. An example is interpersonal conflict with coworkers that the missionary feels they "have to get along with" for the next three years. Other examples include a merger between two mission agencies with different ways of conducting business, trying to accomplish goals with limited resources, or having children away at a boarding school.

- *Traumatic events* (Pennebaker & Beal, 1986; Pennebaker, Hughes & O'Heeron, 1987)—Traumatic events have their greatest impact when a person does not feel able to confront or to disclose the situation to others. Missionaries often feel they can't share their experiences on the field when they get home, sometimes out of fear of making their sending agency "look bad," or a feeling of shame that they are not "as spiritually mature" as others.

Or, they may fear that their concerns will be trivialized by stories of "the old days."

- *Personality* (Nelson, 1988; Brown, 1989; Myers-Briggs)—Each personality style has its own potential set of stressors and ways of coping with stress. For example, for an extrovert being isolated is stressful but for an introvert never having any privacy or alone time is stressful. Some personalities are comforted by structure and having every detail worked out in advance; others are most comfortable being spontaneous with whatever the situation hands them.

  When co-workers with different personalities get stressed, they often revert to what is most familiar—the high-structure person becomes controlling and the low-structure person becomes more laid back, and the stress response escalates for both. If we are unaware of this pattern, dealing with our own stress creates more stress for those around us.

- *Total number of stressors*—Life events, daily hassles, situational factors, traumatic events, and personality are all potential sources of stress. If we are lucky, we are only dealing with one of these sources at a time. However, in mission work it is much more common to be dealing with issues in several categories simultaneously.

Consider this example: A missionary family moves overseas (a positive life event for some members of the family and perhaps a negative event for others). While overseas, a family member back home dies suddenly and they are unable to attend the funeral (a negative life event). In the first few months they live with a national family and work on language training while waiting for their lost containers to arrive (situational factors). The host family is in a remote rural area without running water or indoor plumbing and the mission family has never been "outdoorsy types" (personality). After completing language training, they move to a city where they will do church planting. Within months, they are robbed at gunpoint as they return from a Bible study and unlock the gate to their house (traumatic event).

It is little wonder that missionaries come home early due to illness or have less energy to give to their primary roles while on the field! When multiple sources of stress pile up, it is natural to feel overwhelmed.

Appraising the Situation

Being exposed to different sources of stress does not necessarily mean we will feel stressed out. Different people react differently to the same situation. Some people will appraise a new situation as neutral ("yeah, okay—no big deal"). Others may see it as a benefit or a challenge ("I can do this and if I can't, God can do it through me"). Those who see it as a challenge may convey hope, eagerness, and confidence. In either of these situations, a person would be considered resilient to stressors; they are keenly aware of the circumstances but do not feel threatened. Thus their bodies are not flooded with stress hormones.

Sometimes, however, we do feel threatened. Tell-tale signs of appraising a situation as a threat are feelings of worry, fear, and/or anxiety. Numbers 13 gives an account of twelve men who explored the Promised Land. When the men reported to Moses and Aaron about the land flowing with milk and honey they rebutted Caleb's declaration to go in and claim the land by saying it was impossible—the inhabitants were too big and strong. Those who appraised the situation as a threat said, "We seemed like grasshoppers in our own eyes, and we looked the same to them" (Numbers 13:33, NIV).

We may not start out with a "grasshopper mentality"; but our perspective can change in the midst of a situation. A dramatic example was given by a survivor of a plane crash. As a trained emergency medical technician (EMT), he calmly assisted others in getting out of the wreck. He was confident in this role. It then came time for him to leave the plane. As he slid down the chute he was still confident—and then his feet hit water. He panicked because he did not know the plane had landed in water and he did not know how to swim! His appraisal had originally made him resilient in the face of a crisis; but as his perception of circumstances altered, his appraisal quickly changed to that of a threat.

Coping Resources

People may be exposed to stressors and appraise them as threats, yet they may not be vulnerable. When we evaluate a situation we do a quick inventory of coping resources, often unawares. If our final tally says "I don't have enough resources to meet this situation" then we quickly become vulnerable to developing consequences of stress discussed earlier. Individuals may become emotionally or spiritually paralyzed; they may find themselves accepting the role of being a victim.

Sometimes when people take inventory of their coping resources they feel reasonably confident to meet the challenges of the current situation. Research suggests that they then employ a variety of coping techniques. Before considering major coping techniques, we will look at variables that can modulate the appraisal of both the situation and coping resources.

Modulating Variables

A number of variables can lessen the impact of stressors on us. As the name suggests, they are not a once-and-for-all immunization; rather they are insulators in given situations. Sometimes the modulating variables eliminate the sense of stress; other times they simply lessen the intensity.

While there are many modulating variables, some of the key ones identified by researchers are social support, self-complexity, hardiness, health behaviors, religion, and humor:

- *Social support*—One of the best predictors of quality of life across the age span is social support. The wisdom of Solomon states "Two are better than one, because they have a good return for their work; if one falls down his friend can pick him up. Pity the one who falls and has no one to help him up" (Ecclesiastes 4:9, 10). Social support is one of the best predictors of quality of life across the life span.

- *Self-complexity* (Linn, 1985, 1987)—Patricia Linn's work suggests that we should not put all our eggs in one basket. When individuals invest all their emotional energy in one direction, they become more vulnerable. For example, their sole focus might be on their children or their job. If life does not turn out the way they expected it to, it can be much more stressful than if they had multiple areas of investment.

- *Hardiness* (Maddi & Kobasa)—Maddi and Kobasa tried to determine why, when faced with the same situation, some people develop physical and/or mental illness and others do not. They concluded that those who did not become ill were "hardy." These people had a sense of *commitment* to the tasks of life; a sense of *control*—they did not perceive themselves as victims of circumstance; and viewed change as *challenging*, not as a threat.

- *Health behaviors*—These are behaviors we choose to engage in that promote our physical and mental health. Some of the key ones would include getting regular sleep; regular exercise; eating regularly; limiting refined sugars and red meat, and limiting caffeine.

- *Religion*—Having a faith commitment is a key modulating factor. Gartner, Larson, and Allen (1991) did a meta-analysis of 200 published studies. They found that religious commitment was associated with longevity of life, decreased drug and alcohol use, decreased rates of suicide, decreased incidence of clinical depression, and improved coping and protection from problems. Those with a faith commitment did not have fewer problems, but they responded to them differently.

- *Humor*—a good belly laugh actually changes our physiology, decreasing levels of the stress hormones epinephrine and cortisol (Berk, 1988). Our heart rate decreases (Scheff & Schule, 1979) and both systolic and diastolic blood pressure drops (Fry & Savin, 1982). Laughter also increases endorphins, our natural painkillers (Cogan et al, 1987) and increases our killer-T cells (Wise, 1987). King Solomon said that "a merry heart doeth good like a medicine" (Proverbs 17:22) and modern medicine verifies that!

Summary

A person is exposed to various stressors and each is appraised as either neutral, a benefit, or as a threat. There is a potential for a stress response to threats. The person does an inventory of coping resources and decides how well they can deal with the situation. Both the appraisal of the situation and the appraisal of coping resources are impacted by such factors as social support, humor, hardiness, religion, and health behaviors. If they do not feel confident, they may become a victim and develop physical, mental, or spiritual symptoms. If they feel able to rise to the occasion, they employ one or more coping techniques.

Coping Techniques

In 1978, a couple of sociologists by the names of Pearlin and Schooler did the first epidemiological study on coping styles. They conducted extensive interviews with 2,300 adults between the ages of 18 and 65. Pearlin and Schooler concluded that there are three major coping responses that people successfully employ: those that change the situation; those that change the meaning of the situation; and those that manage the stress.

Techniques that change the situation:

- Seek advice, brainstorm, identify resources
- Take optimistic action, assuming the best
- Learn to assert yourself and say "No." Ability can never keep up with the demand for ability.
- Develop better time management skills
- Choose not to worry
- Get better organized
- Plan ahead
- Make decisions about toxic relationships
- Change the environment. This may mean getting more organized or surrounding yourself with calming pictures or music. It may mean shaking the dust from your sandals and moving on.

Techniques that change the meaning of the situation:

- Relabel or redefine your situation. For example, you may be in a difficult work situation. By telling yourself you only have to be there for two more years, it puts a different perspective on your circumstances—you no longer are trapped indefinitely.
- Selective ignoring (play down the bad, focus on the good). Follow the tenets of the Scarlett O'Hara School of Coping and say "Fiddle-de-dee, I'll worry about this tomorrow!"
- Count your blessings. Develop an attitude of gratitude.
- Sleep on it.
- See the humorous side of the situation.
- Have faith. Trust that even in a confusing situation God is in control of the universe and God cares about you personally.

Techniques that manage the stress:

- Get regular sleep
- Get regular exercise
- Eat three meals per day
- Take time to play
- Take hot baths
- Learn and use relaxation techniques, like diaphragmatic breathing
- Develop support groups

Help! Where do I even begin? When faced with such a lengthy list, the options offered may seem like just one more source of stress. There are two principles to remember: the first is that to make a difference in your life, you only need to implement a few of the options.

The second principle is that coping is an acquired skill; the more we practice coping skills, the better we get at doing them successfully. However, the more we avoid coping, the more likely we are to become hypervigilant and to develop an exaggerated stress response. Coping skills do not remain static; they either improve or deteriorate.

The Top Six Coping Techniques

Sleep. Sleep deprivation has been associated with numerous disorders including high blood pressure, heart problems, obesity, and diabetes. Cognitively, sleep deprived individuals function like those who are intoxicated. Regular sleep also helps us gain perspective on life: "I will praise the Lord, who counsels me; even at night my heart instructs me" (Proverbs 16:6, NIV).

Hot baths. Part of the stress response is vasoconstriction—blood vessels contract and squeeze most of our blood into our body cavity and brain where our vital organs are. Vasoconstriction increases our blood pressure during the fight or flight. Hot baths have the opposite effect of vasodilation. Blood vessels, which are hard and rigid with stress, become soft noodles and blood pressure drops.

Humor, discussed above.

Eating. Eating regularly helps to stabilize our blood sugars and that helps all of our physiological functioning. Limit intake of caffeine (which mimics stress hormones), refined sugars, and red meat.

Exercise. Exercise allows us to burn off the stress hormones. Regular aerobic exercise is important to physical health and crucial to mental health. Aerobic exercise can reduce stress, depression, and anxiety, and is also associated with an increased sense of well-being. McCann and Holmes' (1984) work with mildly depressed women showed more improvement with exercise than either the control group or the relaxation-training group.

Prayer and meditation. A significant way to stop the flow of stress hormones is to engage in diaphragmatic breathing while praying or meditating on positive thoughts. Breathing from the diaphragm not only brings more oxygen into our lungs, but it also counteracts the fight or flight response.

Physiologically, the fight or flight response is due to the sympathetic nervous system, part of our autonomic nervous system. When we are stressed, the sympathetic nervous system arouses all of our physiological systems except for digestion and reproductive functioning (these two are not considered essential for fight or flight so they are turned off). The sympathetic nervous system is our body's gas pedal. There is a corresponding part, the parasympathetic nervous system, that acts as a brake and slows us down. When we breathe slowly and deeply from our diaphragms, we stimulate the parasympathetic response which shuts off the flow of stress hormones.

Try this: To breathe diaphragmatically, get in a relaxed position. Put your hands on your abdomen, with the thumbs resting on your navel. As you inhale through your nose, pretend that under your hands is a pouch that is filling with air; feel your hands rise. As you exhale through your mouth, feel the pouch empty and your hands fall. When first starting, continue to inhale on each cycle for a few seconds. With practice you can learn to inhale and exhale in longer, slower, rhythmic cycles. This technique can drop both heart rate and blood pressure.

There is no cure for stress. Stress is a vital part of our survival. The trick is to keep stress in check and not let the negative effects accumulate like compound interest. Trying some coping techniques, even our favorites, does not automatically mean that the stress is alleviated. We need to go back and try different techniques. Having others in our lives who can point out new alternatives is very helpful.

Summary

Stress is a fact of life; we need to acknowledge this fact and be proactive. Potential stressors can be from negative or positive events, from our situations or our personality styles. Each of us appraises these in different ways, but whenever we appraise any situation we have the possibility of releasing stress hormones into our bloodstream.

Having social support, faith commitment, or health behaviors are some of the ways that we can limit the impact of stressful events. Ways of successfully dealing with stress are to change the situation, change the meaning of the situation, and/or engage in coping techniques. The top six coping strategies presented in this chapter were sleep, hot baths, humor, eating, exercise, and prayer. While many alternatives were suggested, the important detail to remember is that even doing one or two will make a significant difference.

Key References

Brown, J. D., & McGill, K. L. (1989). The cost of good fortune: When positive life events produce negative health consequences. *Journal of Personality and Social Psychology, 57,* 1103-1110.

Gartner, J., Larson, D., & Allen, G. (1991). Religious commitment and mental health: A review of the empirical literature. *Journal of Psychology and Theology, 19,* 6-25.

Holmes, T. H., & Rahe, R. H. (1967). The social readjustment rating scale. *Journal of Psychosomatic Research, 11,* 203-218.

McCann, I. L., & Holmes, D. S. (1984) Influence of aerobic exercise on depression. *Journal of Personality and Social Psychology, 46,* 1142-1147.

Miller, M. A., & Rahe, R. H. (1997). Life changes scaling for the 1990's. *Journal of Psychosomatic Research, 43,* 279-292.

Pennebaker, J. W., & Beall, S. K. (1986). Confronting a traumatic event: Toward an understanding of inhibition and disease. *Journal of Abnormal Psychology, 95,* 274-281.

Pennebaker, J. W., Hughes, C. F., & O'Heeron, R. C. (1987). The psychophysiology of confession: Linking inhibitory and psychosomatic processes. *Journal of Personality and Social Psychology, 52,* 782-793.

Sailers, M. R. (1987). *Personal factors related to working as a missionary in another culture.* Unpublished doctoral dissertation, University of Toronto, Toronto, Ontario, Canada.

Selye, H. (1946). General adaptation syndrome and diseases of adaptation. *Journal of Clinical Endocrinology, 6,* 117-230.

Key Resources

Sapolsky, R. M. (1998). *Why zebras don't get ulcers: A guide to stress, stress-related diseases, and coping* (2e). New York, NY: W. H. Freeman and Company.

Schiraldi, G. R. (1996). Facts to relax by: A guide to relaxation and stress reduction. Provo, UT: Utah Valley Regional Medical Center [Education Dept., 1034 N. 500 West, Provo, UT 84603 (801) 371-7176]

Tubesing, N. L., & Tubesing, D. A. (1994). *Structured exercises in stress management: Handbooks for trainers, educators, & group leaders (5 volumes)*. Duluth, MN: Whole Person Associates. [210 West Michigan, Duluth, MN 55802 (800) 247-6789]

14

Forgiveness in Healing Wounded Servants

Dale H. Schumm

In this chapter, war in Liberia is the crucible for understanding, teaching about, and experiencing forgiveness. The development of a five-day workshop on healing and reconciliation in Liberia is described. The Biblical meaning of forgiveness, criteria for authentic repentance and forgiveness, benefits of forgiveness, and ways to facilitate the process of forgiveness are explained.

*I*ntroduction

"In your anger do not sin. . ." (Eph. 4:26a) are the words of the Apostle Paul in writing to the believers in Ephesus. I grew up with the impression that to be angry was to sin; it was not all right for Christians to be angry. The emphasis was on "do not sin"; it was not assumed that anger is a part of life.

The second part of the verse tells us how not to sin: "Do not let the sun go down while you are still angry." The writer is telling his readers not to harbor or "gunnysack" their anger. He finishes by saying, "do not give the devil a foothold." Paul says that it is all right to feel deeply, including feeling anger, but don't carry it around for long; do something about it. For if you don't, it will give the devil a foothold.

Anger, when it is retained, turns into hate. In *Getting Bitter Or Getting Better,* Dr. David W. Schell states, "hate poisons, forgiveness heals." Bitterness easily turns into hatred, and hatred, in its ultimate expression, kills.

Background

I witnessed hatred and its devastating effects on individuals, a whole population, indeed on the total country, as I worked with the trauma of civil war in Liberia in October and November 1991.

Liberia had a population of two and a half million prior to the war which had been going on for three years at the time. Over 300,000 refugees had fled the country and another quarter of a million were displaced within the country. Over 30-40,000 were killed during the course of the fighting.

After the initial part of the war was brought to a stalemate by the West African peacekeeping force, the Christian Health Association of Liberia (CHAL) invited me as consultant to help assess the psychological and spiritual needs of the people. Everyone had been traumatized. The physical needs were readily evident, but the deeper personal trauma was what concerned the Health Association.

Practically every family had experienced death, loss of possessions, and loss of dignity. The trauma was so widespread and so profound that the question was what to do and where to start. During consultations in Danane (a border town in Cote d'Ivoire) with representatives of CHAL, it was decided that we would focus first on people in the helping professions, which included teachers, health workers and religious leaders.

We developed a five-day workshop to help these professionals begin to get in touch with and work through their own trauma in order to be more available to help those who kept coming to them with their emotional and physical needs.

People in Liberia were shot at close range as they tried to make their way through check points to safer grounds. Their homes were looted and burned, and many experienced betrayal by neighbors and friends. They experienced tremendous personal devastation seeing family members being killed in front of their eyes. If persons dared to show any emotion in response to what was happening, they would get the next bullet. They were not allowed to take care of the bodies of loved ones that had just been killed. They were ordered to move on and let the bodies lie. Sometimes people saw family members mutilated, and even then did not dare show horror or any other emotion. Such was the trauma!

Seth (all names have been changed to protect their identity) was an ordained minister, translator and a radio speaker. While he was fleeing the capital city of Monrovia, the crowd was stopped at a check point. A 14-year-old fighter, with an AK 47 pointed towards Seth, commanded him to completely undress. The next event after a person was undressed usually was the fatal shot. As Seth undressed in embarrassment in front of hundreds of his fellow countrymen, the soldier was distracted by a commotion in another direction and Seth's life was spared. He went on, but could not forget his experience of humiliation.

Waldo and his wife owned and operated a pharmaceutical business in the capital city. When they were fleeing the city with their preschool son, a bullet from one of the AK 47s hit his wife in the spine and paralyzed her from the waist down. Waldo picked her up and carried her on his shoulders for the next several days until they reached a hospital that had been spared looting and destruction. Waldo's wife is permanently paralyzed and confined to a wheelchair.

Yolanda was a woman of obvious means in the past. She came to the workshop angry and bitter and would not do any exercises or engage in any interaction for four days. Her story unfolded bit by bit over the course of the week. Yolanda's three brothers and a sister were in the Lutheran church on July 26, 1990, when the government-supported soldiers killed 600 women and children who had taken refuge in the church.

Yolanda also had to flee from her home and entrusted the keys to her house to neighbors who stayed since they were from the "right" tribe. Upon return after the fierce fighting had subsided, she discovered that her trusted neighbors had looted and torched her house. So the stories went on day after day and week after week.

How does one deal with such inhumane treatment? What do you do with the unforgivable? This is the context for this chapter. This situation drove me to the Bible to search for words of hope and peace in the midst of evil and destruction. In this context I reworked my understanding of forgiveness and the relationship of forgiveness, healing and mental health.

Healing and Reconciliation Workshops

We structured the Liberian Healing and Reconciliation Workshops around a rhythm of teaching and therapy. The didactic and the therapeutic go hand in hand.

Day 1 we focused on getting in touch with the pain, the wrong, the tragedy, the injury and the woundedness. We encouraged the participants to name their loss and to grieve the losses and tragedy. We focused on helpful, healing listening rather than listening that reinforces hatred and revengeful feelings. We attempted to lead them to get in touch with that which they had not been allowed to be in touch with before and to grieve their losses.

Day 2 we focused on conflict and mediation—the causes of conflict and approaches to conflict resolution including the traditional tribal approach to conflict. We included an actual mediation experience.

Day 3's subject was an alternative to revenge: forgiveness and repentance. This turned out to be the most intense day of the week. It also became the turning point in the process.

Day 4 focused on healing and hope. Here we went through several healing rituals described later in this paper.

Day 5 projected a new Liberia. In this exercise we used all of the five senses in projectratory prayers. They also projected plans and activities of how to share the healing they had experienced when they returned home.

Pain and Healing

According to a January 1991 report from the Carter Center, which monitors wars and sometimes offers to mediate, in 1990 there were 112 wars fought in our world. 32 of them were major wars, defined as having 1,000 or more casualties as a result of the conflict. Most of these conflicts were within national boundaries. This is a macrocosm of the world we are living in and of the conflict and woundedness in it.

A microcosmic view focuses on the individual. James asks the question "What causes war and what causes fightings among you? Is it not your passions that are at war in your members? You desire and you do not have so you kill. You covet and cannot obtain so you fight and wage war" (James 4:1-2a).

We know all too well the bruising and pain that many missionaries experienced prior to beginning service. Many carry wounds of harsh words, beatings, unjust punishment and abuse. Others come from broken families and carry feelings of betrayal and bitterness. Where is their healing? How can we offer healing to a world when the healers have active, contagious infections?

Healing is taking place when the infection is neutralized and no longer contagious. The person who is experiencing healing can begin to offer healing. This is the concept behind the "wounded healer" of Henri Nouwen. He says the minister "must look after his own wounds but at the same time be prepared to heal the wounds of others"(Nouwen 1972, p. 84). The healing that is offered is not the removal of the pain; rather it is taking it to a level where it can be shared.

Healing and Nurture of Missionaries

How is forgiveness relevant to God's servants overseas? The nature of cross-cultural stress is such that whatever unfinished business a person may have gone overseas with tends to surface under stress and needs to be attended to. This unfinished business should be worked through in the pre-field preparation, but this is not always the case. It is far better to work through this "stuff" before going on assignment and be free to be more totally available to the people we go to serve. If it is not worked through prior to going overseas, then it tends to surface and interfere with field relationships. It then needs to be worked through either on the field or upon return.

The nature of the cross-cultural ministry is such that business cannot go on as usual within a person. What was manageable in relatively normal stable circumstances will surface and become issues in the cross-cultural setting. Part of our ministry to God's servants—those who have been called to preach forgiveness—is to help them experience forgiveness.

The Meaning of Forgiveness

Forgiveness is not forgetting, but is neutralizing the effects of the wrong. The Apostle Paul, in his writings to the churches, again and again reminded them not to forget their past and where they had come from. In Colossians 3:5, he exhorts them to "put to death . . . what is earthly in you, fornication, impurity, passion, evil desire, covetousness which is idolatry, in these you once walked when you lived in them...." Peter in his letter reminds his readers that, "Once you were no people but now you are God's people, once you had not received mercy but now you have received mercy" (1 Peter 2:10). The Bible exhorts us to remember the kind of life that we have come out of so that we do not return to the former life. He who does not know his history is liable to repeat it.

In order to get to the true meaning of forgiveness we need to go back to the original language of the New Testament. The Greek word translated forgiveness is "aphieme". This word is used 146 times in the New Testament but translated "forgive" only 47 times. We must examine the other 99 times when it is translated by some other English word to get the true meaning.

Meaning and usage of "Aphieme" in NT

leave	52	times
forgive	47	
suffer, let	14	
forsake	6	
let alone	6	
miscellaneous	13	(let have, send away, omit, let be, yield up, lay aside, let go, cry, remit, put away)
Total	**146**	

The central idea of "aphieme"is "to let go."

Forgiveness: A Process

God's forgiveness is an act. God forgives and it is finished. But for us to incorporate forgiveness into our life and practice is usually a process. The deeper the hurt and the more profound the injury, the more of a process is needed. Forgiveness is not simple or easy; it is profound.

Criteria for Authentic Forgiveness

1.   The wrong must be named and the pain and its consequences acknowledged. The flip phrase, "Oh, it doesn't matter" is not evidence of authentic forgiveness. It does matter what has been done; that I hurt and carry the conse-quences. It does matter that my reputation was destroyed. It does matter that I'm messed up psychologically as a result of childhood abuse and cannot handle intimacy. It does matter that my brother was killed by a rebel or that my wife is paralyzed for life. It does matter that you never gave me affirmation or that you were not at my games. The first step in the process of forgiveness is to name the wrong.

2.   The second step is to refuse to exact a penalty from the wrongdoer in the proportion to the wrong committed. Before Waldo had processed his wife's injury and the loss of his business and his personal goods, he said, "I had such hatred that whenever I saw one of the fighters on the street I would turn around and walk the other way." After having been through one of the workshops where he had a chance to process and to own the depth of his loss and of his anger and to grieve his loss he was able to say, "Rather than wanting revenge I can walk right past the fighters." The process of forgiveness was happening.

3.   The third criterion is to begin to have some empathy for the humanity of the wrongdoer. Waldo is now saying that the fighters also should have the opportunity to attend one of these seminars. He also said "I now want to talk to the fighter who looted my house and is wearing my coat in the marketplace, whereas before I hated him." Hate for Waldo turned to pity which in turn became concern and eventually compassion. On the fifth day of the seminar Seth said, "I had vowed to not talk with anyone from 'so and so' tribe ever again. Now I have been with them for five days and I have been talking with them and we have become friends. They also have been wronged. Seth was beginning to have some feeling of empathy for the wrongdoer. This is a mark of authentic forgiveness happening.

4.   The fourth mark of authentic forgiveness is the ultimate aim to restore the community relationship of all the parties involved.

It is not always possible to accomplish all four. There is forgiveness when one and two are present, and more complete forgiveness if three or four are reached.

The Meaning of Repentance

Forgiveness in the healing process is independent of repentance. Repentance, on the other hand, is also independent of forgiveness. One tends to encourage the other, but neither is dependent on the other. The Greek word for repentance is "metanoia" which means "to turn," "to change one's view and purpose," "to change one's mind," "to feel sorry for or regret."

Criteria for Authentic Repentance
1. Name and acknowledge the wrong perpetrated.
2. Be willing to make restitution. Restitution is not always possible, but willingness to restore what is possible is an important criterion.
3. Begin to have some empathy for the victim's suffering.
4. The ultimate aim of repentance is to restore the community relationship of all parties involved. Again, number four may not be possible.

The Goal of Repentance and Forgiveness
The purposes of repentance and forgiveness are the same.

The Purpose of Repentance and the Purpose of Forgiveness:
- To effect change
- To seek freedom
- To heal broken relationships
- To acknowledge the wrong done
- To seek justice

Both Repentance and Forgiveness:
- Attempt to heal old wounds
- Break the cycle of violence and hatred
- Require the same mindset
- Look to renewed future
- Tend to inspire the other
- Either of them can come first

The main difference between repentance and forgiveness is whether you are the offender or the offended, the victimizer or the victim. Forgiveness in its judging, empathizing, revenge-refusing and renewing makes a new community possible. (Shirver 1991)

Application
How does this fit into our ministry with missionaries? The question is how do we concretize the experience of forgiveness when it happens. Evangelicals often do not have rituals to concretize the experience, in contrast to Catholics who have the ritual of confession and absolution. The development of a ritual to seal and concretize the experience is helpful and important.

Developing Rituals
1. Naming the wrong. I often invite people to write the wrong that has wounded and pained them on a piece of paper or 3 x 5 card.
2. The second ritual is a "letting go" ritual. Here I ask them to write on another card what he or she is ready to let go.
3. Then I will invite them to bring it to a fire, if we can have a fire, and burn the card.

If having a fire is not possible I have used a waste can with a garbage bag to dispose of the old hurts. I then ceremoniously take the sealed garbage bag out to the dumpster.

Recently I was with a missionary team where we worked a whole weekend on what the hurts in the group were and how they had hurt each other. I invited them to list their issues, injuries or grievances on a 3 x 5 card at the beginning of the session. This became the agenda for the weekend. At the end of our time together I invited them to look over their cards and to write on another card what they were ready to let go, and burn them in the fire in a ritual of letting go. If they were finished with all of the items they had written at the beginning of the weekend, they could burn that card.

I did the same kind of ritual with another missionary group where everyone in the group of 30-40 people had things that they needed to finish and "let go." One young person was going overseas for the second time. His parents were divorced while he was overseas the first time. He carried a great deal of anger and hurt from that experience. In this session he let it go; he finished it. He decided he could not be responsible for his parents' actions and let go of his anger and sense of betrayal.

Another group was a group of church planters in a screening pre-appointment process. In a session on forgiveness of the past, one person realized that church planting was not for him. He could not let go of past hurts and so did not proceed on to an assignment.

4. After the naming of the wrong and the letting go ritual, I offer prayer and laying on of hands for healing to come in a fuller sense.

5. Fifthly, we offer anointing with oil for anyone who desires it. In the biblical context, oil was used for medicinal purposes and for a symbol of commitment. Combining both of these in the same ritual has proven meaningful to many. I use a simple prayer for anointing, such as "I anoint you in the name of God who blesses, the Son who heals, and the Holy Spirit, who inspires and empowers."

Rituals are helpful in concretizing the experience and should not be neglected.

Benefits of Forgiveness

The benefits of forgiveness are first and foremost to oneself and secondly to the community. The forgiven one may not know or even care, though it is rewarding if they do.

Forgiveness is not indicative of moral or spiritual superiority. It is merely a means towards good emotional and spiritual health.

To live as a forgiving person requires practice and energy. This is also true for being hateful and bitter. The difference? Forgiveness is constructive and builds strength. Bitterness, on the other hand, is an emotional disease which weakens." (Schell 95)

Forgiveness does not demand trust or respect. We do not need to allow ourselves to be subjected to abusive behavior after forgiveness has taken place. It does not mean trust when the person is not trustworthy. Forgiveness requires giving up our right to hate. The right to forgive, love and exercise compassion is much more productive, assuring, healing and growthful than hate.

Pseudoforgiveness

1. Pseudoforgiveness is defined as "I will forgive but...." Any qualifier to

forgiveness is pseudoforgiveness. "I'll forgive but make sure it doesn't happen again" or, "I'll forgive, but I pray God will make him suffer as much as I have." Other forms of pseudoforgiveness are: "Don't worry about it, I'll get over it." "I don't let it bother any more."

Pseudoforgiveness restricts healing and growth and contributes to a false appearance of piety. It disguises bitterness. Ironically, it masks hostility to make it look like a virtue. Pseudoforgiveness is an attempt to short circuit dealing with the depths of the hurt and the anger.

2.   Conditional forgiveness. "I'll forgive if she says she is sorry." "I'll forgive if he pays for it." "I'll forgive when I get even." Conditional forgiveness allows inner peace to be at the mercy of the offender. True forgiveness has nothing to do with the behavior of anyone else. (Schell, p. 115)

Unconditional Forgiveness

"...while we were yet sinners Christ died for us."(Rom 5:8b) Unconditional forgiveness is "I forgive; it's over." "I forgive totally." "I forgive."

For most of us humans, however, forgiveness is not easy. Our sense of fairness tells us that people should pay for the wrong they do. However, vengeance ties both the injured and the injurer to an endless cycle of violence and retaliation. Forgiving can bring a miraculous kind of healing – even at times reconciliation.

Unconditional forgiveness is a personal choice. With this choice we regain control of our inner lives. The alternative is to continue in bitterness.

Summary

Forgiveness offers no guarantees other than inner peace. "Forgiving is only for the brave—for those willing to confront their pain and accept themselves as permanently changed." (Flanigan, p. 39) Forgiveness frees you from the quagmire of hatred and the control of the one who injured you. Forgiveness leads to personal healing and growth.

Recommended Reading

Augsburger, D. (1981). *Caring enough to forgive.* Scottsdale, PA & Kitchener, Ont.: Herald Press.

Flanigan, B. (1992). The unforgiveable war crimes of the heart. *Psychology Today,* September/October, pp. 36-92.

Nouwen, H. (1972). *The wounded healer.* Garden City, NY: Image Books, Doubleday & Company.

Schell, D. W. (1990). *Getting bitter or getting better.* St. Meinrad, IN: Abbey Press.

Shirver, D. W. Jr. (1991). *The politics of peace.* B. Frost, Ed. London: Darton, Longman and Todd Ltd.

Smedes, L. B. (1984). *Forgive & forget.* New York: Pocket Books.

15

Families in Mission:
Issues and Resources

Janet R. Blomberg

*R*aising children is a creative endeavor, an art rather than a science, according to Dr. Bruno Bettelheim. This is especially true for parents raising their children overseas. Their children are third culture kids (TCKs) and their experiences are very different from those of mom and dad who grew up in one culture and have entered a new culture as adults. The lives of their children are being shaped by the highly mobile, cross-cultural environment in which they are being raised.

Many resources within missions go into the care, education, and development of children in this context. Member care providers, including mental health professionals, are often called upon to provide assistance in child and family matters.

This chapter focuses on the family in mission and discusses a number of factors which affect healthy family and child development in mission settings.

Parents love their children and want good things for them. Sometimes they fear that obeying God's call to serve overseas may hurt their children. Parents must remember there are no guarantees in raising children in any culture.

People in overseas ministry face additional challenges in parenting.

- How do they balance the competing priorities of family and ministry?

- How do they cope with the transitions that are routinely part of life?

- How do they help their children develop meaningful connections to their home and host cultures?

Parenting is challenging, especially for missionaries. Basic issues for raising healthy missionary children are keeping marriage strong, loving children in ways that make them feel unconditionally loved, affirming individual strengths and needs, planning for transitions, involving children in family decisions, including them in ministry, and maintaining ties to the home culture. Educational questions bring all of the above into focus. A variety of resources are recommended.

- How do they provide for the educational and peer needs of their children in areas where educational options are limited?

- How do they equip their children to reenter their passport culture as independent young adults who are discerning, obedient followers of the Lord Jesus Christ?

C. S. Lewis said, "Never knowing where they're going they can never go astray." Parents need to think through their goals and values for their family. So what's the goal? *Being a family in ministry.*

Family vs. Ministry?

In recent decades the pendulum has swung back and forth between an emphasis on the demands of ministry and the needs of the family. There was a time when it was ministry over family, and commitment was measured in terms of sacrifice. Commitment to Jesus Christ and to ministry does require sacrifice, but not the sacrifice of one's children. That's what many pagan gods required.

In reaction against this attitude, the pendulum swung to the other extreme and the goal became family over ministry. Parents would not make any move (whether geographic or in ministry) that would require stretches and sacrifices by the family. The goal seemed to be safety and freedom from hardship and pain.

Yet sometimes these experiences are the very things the Lord uses to teach important lessons that could not have been learned in any other way. Tears and grieving as well as joy are all part of life. Isaiah describes Christ as "a man of sorrows and acquainted with grief." So can we expect we won't experience sorrow and grief if we are truly following him?

Family in Ministry

Family and ministry are not mutually exclusive options as if one must choose between the two. Rather, the commitment is to *both* family and ministry. This means caring for the needs of each family member while carrying out the Great Commission work to which they have been called. It is not a matter of simply giving mental assent or lip service to these as goals and values for the family. The question is, "When push comes to shove, are these truly the values that drive all other family decisions?"

Commitment to being a family in ministry affects every area of life and ministry. It affects use of time, children's education, location of ministry, timing of home assignment, and much more. It requires a genuine commitment by parents to prayerfully consider each family decision before the Lord with open hearts and minds and a willingness to obey. It also requires building a prayer team who will uphold not only the ministry needs, but the family needs.

How does a family function well overseas? There is no right answer or formula, but here is a checklist that parents can use in evaluating their own family situation. It may also be a helpful tool for those who work in a sending agency, counseling or care-giving capacity to help flesh out what it means to be a healthy family in ministry.

Healthy Marriage

First, what is the status and health of mom and dad's relationship to each other? Is their marriage loving, healthy, and growing? Since TCKs do not have geographic roots in one location, their sense of rootedness and belonging comes from the relation-ship between mom and dad. When that relationship is alive and well, it provides the foundation and security that children need to grow and develop in healthy ways.

Parents need to be partners who are working together toward the same goals in terms of their work and family. Are the parents promoting each other's personal, emotional and spiritual growth? How do they make decisions? What is the style and substance of their communication?

In evaluating the health of their marriage, couples need to be honest with one another. Couples shouldn't wait until problems develop to work on the health of their marriage. Denying problems solves nothing. Instead, couples need to consider what will keep their marriage growing. What has to be sown, pruned or cultivated? Scheduling time for regular "dates" or for meaningful communication, attending seminars on marriage enrichment or communication, or being mentored by an older couple are all tools couples can use to maintain a healthy, growing relationship with one another.

It is crucial that both husband and wife share a sense of call to overseas ministry. Neither spouse should go reluctantly or simply to please the other person. Both the husband and wife must be certain that this is God's will for their lives—the foundation needed to weather tough times.

Balance of Roles and Responsibilities

It is also important that the father learn to balance the competing demands that he faces. While ministering to others, he must not neglect spiritual leadership within his family. His wife and children must not get whatever time and attention is left over in his busy schedule, nor can he expect his wife to carry all of the parenting and educa-tional responsibilities for their children. His roles as husband, father and spiritual leadership within the family cannot be abdicated to others.

There must also be clarity and agreement regarding the wife's roles. Given the many hats she wears (wife, mother, ministry, educator, team member, etc.), the de-mands and expectations placed on her may be very unrealistic, whether they are of her choosing or imposed by others. It is critical that these roles be clearly defined and that there be agreement not only between the husband and wife, but also between the agency, team and the couple.

Sometimes it is assumed or expected that a woman can fulfill all of these roles simultaneously with equal time and attention given to each. This is not possible. The resulting stress, pressure, frustration and guilt when these expectations aren't met can be destructive to the entire family.

Loved Unconditionally

Second, does the child feel loved and valued unconditionally? The question is not whether or not the child is loved, but does he or she *feel* loved. Often parents say the right words, but their actions and decisions send another message. For example, if family night is always being replaced with ministry responsibilities week after week, children quickly conclude they are not important. If a child at boarding school rarely receives an e-mail or phone call from his parents, or when he comes home there is no special time set aside for the family, the child quickly concludes he is not valued, no matter what words the parents may say.

Balance Family and Ministry

Balancing work and family is a challenge for anyone in ministry. However, striking the balance is important not only because of its long-term impact on the parent-child relationship, but also because of its impact on the child's attitude toward God. Usually the term "absentee father" is used to describe someone who has physically separated from his family. In a mission context, a father may be physically present, but functionally unavailable to his children and removed from their lives and from parenting them in meaningful ways.

Obviously, ministry requires travel and separation from the family. Children can understand this. However, when father is never home or is home but always working, it takes a toll. Because of father's pivotal role in the family, this functional absence creates many problems. It adds stress to mom's life because she must handle more household and parenting duties. It creates anger and resentment in the children, not only at dad, but ultimately at God who called him into ministry. Many adult MKs who have walked away from their family or from God would say of their father, "He had time for everyone else, but not for us."

Understanding Parental Love

Parents must discern what communicates love to their children, recognizing that it may be different for each child. Time is an obvious one. Gary Chapman's book, *Love Languages of Children,* can help parents determine what will communicate love to their children. Parents' love must also be unconditional, clearly reflecting the type of love God has lavished on us.

Some types of parental love can be emotionally crippling for children. For example, authoritarian love can cripple a child's developing healthy independence and decision-making abilities. On the other hand, some parents and extended family indulge their children because they feel guilty over what they perceive their children have missed out on while growing up overseas. It is important to educate people regarding who TCKs are and to help them understand the benefits of growing up overseas. Mom and dad need to be clear as to what love is and is not. It's not indulging children out of guilt whether by parents, extended family and friends.

Sometimes parents confuse love with permissiveness. Discipline and boundaries are crucial to a child's healthy development. However, it is not a harsh or cruel love. We parent the way we were parented, and a growing number of those serving overseas did not grow up in homes that modeled healthy, loving, Christ-centered parenting. Once these families go overseas, their access to help and to the tools, models, etc., needed to reshape the patterns they've been exposed to may be more limited. Thus, sending agencies and churches need to provide the training and support these parents need.

Individuality Affirmed and Individual Needs Considered

Third, is the individuality of each child affirmed? Are their needs considered in family decisions? This obviously means cooperating with the God-given bent of each child, recognizing his or her unique needs and nurturing his or her unique abilities.

There are seasons of ministry in which changes in assignment are made to meet the needs of the children. An adolescent child's need for a peer group may require a family moving from an isolated village setting into a major city or using boarding school as an educational option. A child with a severe learning disability may require returning to the home country because the school options available may not be able to meet the child's needs. Sometimes the educational or personal needs of children may require relocating to another area.

Seasons of ministry, however, does not necessarily mean leaving the field. Rather it may involve moving to another ministry assignment and/or location where the needs of the children can better be met. This requires openness to and awareness of these needs on the part of agencies and churches as well as creativity in programs and policies.

Parents need to recognize that each of their children will respond to their TCK experiences in very different ways. One child may say, "Thank you for raising me overseas." Another child may say, "You ruined my life." Whether processing transition experiences or using a particular educational option, each child will respond differently to the same experiences. Children must be allowed to process things at their own speed and respond in their own way without being compared to their siblings.

Planning for Transitions

Fourth, are the children's transition experiences planned for? People often ask TCKs, "Where are you from?" Although the question sounds simple, it is a complicated one for TCKs. Home assignments often brings these issues to the surface. Parents say, "We're going home." Their son or daughter says, "I'm leaving home." Mom and dad call their passport culture home, but for their children, where they are living overseas is home and their passport culture is a place they visit periodically. This is sometimes difficult for parents and extended family to understand and can often lead to hurtful comments.

Saying Goodbye and Grieving

A related issue involves whether or not children are given opportunities to grieve and say goodbye. Parents must understand that how one leaves a culture shapes how he enters a new culture. The concept of building a RAFT provides good closure for both children and adults. RAFT refers to **R**econciliation, **A**ffirmation, saying **F**arewell, and **T**hinking destination (developing realistic, positive expectations). An excellent, detailed explanation of RAFT is presented by Pollock and Van Reken in their book *Growing Up Among Worlds: The Third Culture Kid Experience.*

TCKs are always saying good-bye to someone. Usually it is not just to one person, but to whole groups of people at a time. Thus they face multiple, simul-taneous grief experiences. Without permission, people to assist, and time to process their grief, children will "stuff" their pain into invisible knapsacks that they carry with them into each new culture.

Parents often view transitions and home assignments in a short-term context. Their minds are filled with practical questions regarding housing, schools, church visits, transportation needs and finding time for visits with family and friends. For children, however, these experiences have enormous long-term implications as each home assignment paves the way for future ones. If it is a good experience, it builds the child's confidence about their ability to cope with transition and builds positive expectations for future reentry experiences. If it is a difficult experience, then it creates doubt and anxiety about future transitions and fear for future home assignments.

Need for Sense of Rootedness

Physical rootedness produces emotional rootedness. Parents can use their home assignments to pave the way for their children's future reentry into their home culture. If possible, it is helpful for families to return to the same area to give children a sense of rootedness in their passport culture as well as allow them to maintain relationships. As children get older (junior high and high school), they need peer relationships, a sense of belonging, and the spiritual nurturing that can come with belonging to a church youth group.

However, the mobility home assignment requires and the expectations of supporting churches sometimes work against these needs. Parents must carefully consider how many deputation trips their children will make. Is it necessary for them to go on every trip? Will they have quality time with their extended family as well as supporting churches? Have parents given their children enough time with these people during home assignments to allow these relationships to become significant for their children? If not, these connections will remain mom and dad's, and the relationships will not transfer to the children.

Preparing for College

Parents and schools often focus on preparing students for returning for college in the months prior to their departure. While important closure experiences can be provided at that time, many other things can be done along the way to prepare them. Children need to be given age-appropriate decision-making opportunities. Parents need to discuss with their children how to choose a church to attend. Families should begin visiting colleges on any home assignment once their children reach junior high so they can return to their home country before having to choose a college. Home assignments can be used to help students develop basic life skills such as obtaining a driver's license, obtaining work experience, developing a budget, handling a checkbook, and much more.

Given a Voice in Family Decisions

Fifth, are the children given a voice in major family decisions? As children become older they need to have a voice in the decisions that are made which affect them. It gives them a sense of control and independence and also models the decision-making process. Children respond to a lack of control in many different ways, including acting-out behavior and developing eating disorders.

The anger that some MKs experience as adults regarding their childhood experiences often stems not from the decisions that were made but from their lack of voice or input in those decisions. Children recognize that not every decision will go their way and can accept that. However, they will accept any decision more easily if they know their parents have heard their feelings. What often compounds children and adolescents' anger over family decisions is that they are cast in spiritual terms as God's will.

Individuation, the process of separating from their parents and forming their own identity, is also a normal, necessary and important developmental step for all adolescents. While parents may not like the questions raised, it is important that children learn how to raise these issues in appropriate ways. Often parents are thankful if their children don't face normal adolescent challenges or never raise these issues. However, sometimes TCKs simply face normal adolescent struggles and rebellion at a delayed time when parents and caregivers aren't present to guide and to support.

Involved in Ministry

Sixth, are the children given opportunities to become involved in ministry and to internalize their faith? Parents minister to many groups of people, but their first and primary spiritual ministry must be to their own children and nurturing their spiritual growth. They can't assume that someone else will fill this role or that this will automatically happen.

My fear is that many children are growing up as spectators to ministry rather than having opportunities to be involved in ministry themselves. Whether it is through their school or a supporting church, they need to have opportunities to be involved in short-term ministry trips. These experiences can be crucial in their developing deep spiritual roots for themselves and in learning how they can be useful in ministry.

A related question is whether the parents give their children the freedom to fail and to ask questions spiritually. Many MKs feel pressured to be perfect because their parents' ministry may be affected if they aren't. They are expected to behave perfectly, to be spiritual giants, to know the right answers in Sunday school or youth group, and to behave properly for the sake of their parents' ministry. Consequently, they may not ever have opportunities to internalize and personalize their faith.

Strong Ties Nurtured to Home and Host Culture

Lastly, have significant ties been nurtured to both the local culture and the home host culture?

TCKs need rootedness in and meaningful connections to both their passport and the host culture in which they are being raised. They cannot be isolated in a bubble-like existence from the culture in which they are being raised, but need to know its language, history, culture and people.

On the other hand, TCKs need to know their passport culture and its language, history, culture and values. Some adult TCKs feel that they have missed out on the rich cross-cultural opportunities that were available to them because of choices their parents made. Some TCKs recall the pain and embarrassment they experienced because they did not have an adequate knowledge of their home culture's history and values. TCKs need help to understand that enjoying their current culture is not disloyalty to the previous culture.

Looking at the Educational Maze

In closing, we will take a brief look at one area of the family's life that pulls all these issues together—the area of education. How the children will be educated encompasses many of these questions. Parents must reach these decisions together; they can't simply be dropped in mom's lap or made unilaterally by dad. Mom should not homeschool the children just because dad thinks it best.

While parents may each play a different role in the day-to-day education of their children, they must be in agreement about these decisions. If they aren't and problems develop, finger pointing and blaming will begin which puts a divisive, destructive wedge into their marriage.

Whether the child knows that he is loved unconditionally has important implications for their education. Children must know that no matter what option is chosen, they are more important to their parents than any educational option. They need to know that if it truly is not working, they can honestly share this with their parents who will do their best to find another option. Parents need to recognize that there is no a perfect educational option, but benefits and trade-offs to each.

Boarding School Option

Some parents today are reluctant to consider boarding school as an educational option. They may have heard stories from adult MKs regarding their painful boarding experiences. While these stories exist, there are also many stories of MKs who are grateful for their experiences including boarding.

Many things shape the MKs perspective on educational options including how the decision was reached, whether or not they had a voice in it, how it was implemented, the teachers or caregivers involved, etc. Much has changed as training is now provided for boarding home parents and programs can now be accredited. Boarding is not the *only* option or a mandatory option. It is simply one of a range of options that must be prayerfully considered by parents.

Sometimes parents face the boarding school question because their son or daughter has asked to go. Adolescents may want peers or more social, academic and extracurricular opportunities than are available where the family is serving.

At this point parents must carefully examine whose needs are being met by the decision that is made. Sometimes, saying "no" is meeting the parents' need to have the child remain at home, but not the child's needs as a developing adolescent. Loving the child unconditionally may lead parents to make educational decisions that create feelings of grief and loss for themselves.

Nurturing Each Child's Gifts

Affirming the individuality of each child is crucial in planning for his or her education. It involves nurturing each child's God-given gifts and abilities. It also means cooperating with their God-given bent and God's creative purposes for their children's lives rather than molding them based on their own likeness or dreams.

Because each child is different, the same educational option may not be appropriate for each child or used at the same age. Mom may discover that the homeschooling curriculum that worked wonderfully for her first child does not work as well for her second child.

Evaluating Options

Both parents must honestly, open-handedly and prayerfully consider all of their options. They must think through: (1) the range of options available to them, (2) each of their children individually—his or her age, personality, maturity, strengths and weaknesses, etc., (3) their goals and values for their family, (4) practical issues such as cost, physical accessibility, etc., and (5) the future—who do they want this child to be at age eighteen, what skills and experiences do they want him to have had and where do they envision that he will go to college (country, not specific schools).

This may mean that parents may use several different educational options at the same time or in the course of their children's education. In addition, parents must regularly re-evaluate the educational decisions that they make for their families and not treat them as once-for-all-time decisions.

Planning for home assignment and transition also impacts education. Where will the family locate for home assignment? How far in advance does the family arrive where the children will attend school? When parents arrive at the last minute, it deprives children of the opportunity to adequately prepare for what comes next by visiting the school, meeting the teacher and other children, or other things that will pave the way for a successful transition.

Conclusions

We began by identifying being a family in ministry as an important goal for parents. They will face many challenges as they seek to balance many competing demands as they live out this goal. Couples will encounter challenges as they strive to build a strong, growing and supportive marriage. Parents will face many complex decisions as they raise and educate their TCKs in the area where they serve.

There will be times when they will fail to do what they desire, when there are hurts and struggles or things are not working as had been hoped. These are the times when honest, prayerful reflection and reevaluation are needed, and when they must rely on the grace and wisdom God has promised.

Parents know that they cannot live out this goal perfectly. However, they must not abandon the goal of being an effective family in ministry, but must pursue it for the good of each family member, for God's glory and for the advancement of his kingdom.

Helpful Resources

Books

Bowers, J. M. (Ed.). (1998). *Raising resilient MKs: Resources for caregivers, parents and teachers.* Colorado Springs, CO: Association of Christian Schools International.

Blomberg, J. R. and Brooks, D. F. (2001). *Fitted pieces.* SHARE Education Services.

Chapman, Gary, *Love languages of children.* Chicago, IL: Moody Press, 1997.

Knell, M. (2001). *Families on the move.* Grand Rapid, MI: Monarch Books.

O'Donnell, K. (Ed.). (2002). *Doing member care well: Perspectives and practices from around the world.* Pasadena, CA: William Carey Library.

Pollock, D. C. and Van Reken, R. E. (2001). *Growing up among worlds: The third culture kid experience.* Yarmouth, ME: Intercultural Press.

Sanford, T. L. (1998). *You don't have to be perfect.* Colorado Springs, CO: Llama Press.

Periodicals

Interact published by Interaction International (interact@tckinteract.net)

Among Worlds published by Interaction International (amongworlds@tckinteract.net)

Parents Teaching Overseas produced by SIL's International Children's Education Department (www.educatingourkids.org)

Other Resources

Educational Planning Seminar

This seminar helps parents working in areas with limited educational options to develop and implement workable, appropriate educational plans for their children (prefield@tckinteract.net).

Sponsored by Interaction and SHARE Education Services).

Home Assignment Goals

This excellent resource, developed by Karen Wrobbel and Beth Wyse from TEAM, helps parents develop goals for their home assignments that will pave the way for their children's long-term reentry into their home culture. (www.teamworld.org/goals.pdf)

Transition Seminars

These seminars for returning high school students prepare them to reenter their North American culture and to build positively on their experiences as third-culture kids

Interaction International Website (www.tckinteract.net)
Barnabas International (mkreentry@barnabas.org)

Educational Help and Support

For families who are homeschooling and using national schools to educate their children.

Asia Education Resource Consortium (AERC) in Asia
(janetblomberg@compuserve.com)
SHARE Education Services in Europe and the former Soviet Union
(www.Share-Ed-Services.org)

16

Missionary Women Speak

Nancy Crawford

*I*f *Mama ain't happy, ain't nobody happy.* This saying is no less true for missionary families. The translocation of the entire family into a new culture, often to a remote location of a developing nation, thus living on a less comfortable level than previously, taxes the whole family. However, often male missionaries appear to be invigorated by the challenges of the missionary lifestyle, while many missionary wives appear to be less charmed.

During my first seven years in Kenya, I worked primarily with "missionary kids" (MKs), but had opportunities to counsel adult missionary women. Typically, and ironically, they were struggling with depression while their husbands appeared to be feeling happy and fulfilled in ministry!

I also observed that several of the MKs who struggled had mothers who were also struggling. These observations raised the question which became the basis of my dissertation research: Are there measurable and discrete factors that influence the quality of a missionary woman's experience, and if so what can be done to enhance their experience?

The answer to this question has great relevance not only for missionary women as precious individuals, but also for the goal of world missions. Its answer may contain the seeds of answers to these pertinent questions:

• What can be done to help missionary women enjoy the same satisfaction that male missionaries appear to have, so that both spouses have a longer and more fruitful ministry?

• How can mission leadership ensure that the years of training (college, seminary, language school) and the thousands of dollars of investment (deputation, shipping of household goods, support) reach their full potential?

Making the best use of women's contributions is critical for meeting goals in world missions. Missionary wives often experience more struggles than their husbands. This research looks at various roles of married women and positive and negative factors reported by both married and single women. Implications are stated for the ethos (values and expectations) of mission agencies, placement of personnel, and pre-field and on-field training.

137

- How can we as a community help women attain a sense of well-being that is resilient in the face of material inconveniences, cultural exclusion or demeaning of women, and social isolation?

In order to answer the question "are there measurable and discrete factors which influence the quality of a missionary woman's experience" I first turned to the research literature to search for models to guide me in determining which factors to explore. I then turned to missionary women, themselves, to hear what they had to say.

Literature

Unfortunately, there is a dearth of psychological research literature available on missionary women. However, three other bodies of literature are available which are critical to an understanding of issues pertaining to missionary women:

International Service Personnel (ISP, role theory, and job satisfaction/organizational commitment issues. In brief, the ISP literature gives strong evidence that spousal satisfaction and cultural adjustment are important variables in expatriate success (Brett, Stroh, & Reilly, 1993; Briody & Chrisman, 1991; Stroh, Dennis, and Crammer, 1994).

Role theory literature suggests that multiple-roled women, e.g. a missionary woman who has some ministry in addition to her homemaker role, have a higher level of well-being than single-roled women (Adelmann, 1993, Gove, 1972; Greenberger and O'Neil, 1993; Sieber, 1974; Thoirts, 1983).

Women in direct achievement roles versus supportive roles are more likely to have job satisfaction, and thus organizational commitment (Burke, 1996; Dodd-McCue and Wright, 1996). This is important news to mission agencies.

Turning to published empirical research in regard to women in missions, five studies informed the structure of my study. Adams and Clopton (1990) concluded that while both men and women may express equal satisfaction with their ministry role, missionary women actually have lower levels of self-esteem than men. Beck (1986) in comparing 1950s research with that done in the 1980s, found that the educational level of missionary women has not increased to meet the demands of cross-cultural missions. This is surprising, in light of increased educational preparedness of missionaries in general. Wilcox (1995) discovered that spousal work/role satisfaction is a primary reason why MK educators remain in their schools for longer terms.

A fourth study which greatly informed the structure of my study, Bowers (1984), became the typology that I used as my independent variable. Bowers' key issue in her typology was *not* what the missionary wife actually does but how she perceives herself. Bowers' helpful typology is as follows:

1. **Homemaker**. She is primarily a full-time wife and mother. Her main focus is on the home and the support of her family. She manages household and family affairs, thus enabling her husband to pursue his career single-mindedly. The husband is the missionary; the wife is a homemaker.

2. **Background Supporter**. She actively supports her husband and his work. She may occasionally "help" her husband minister publicly, but her focus is on contributions she can make from the home such as hospitality and writing supporters. The husband is still the missionary; the wife is his assistant.

3. **Team Worker**. She works alongside her husband on a full-time basis, but her position is inseparable from the man's. Both husband and wife are missionaries, but the wife's role derives from the man's.

4. **Parallel Worker**. She fills a full-time position with the same mission agency, and possesses her own job description. Both husband and wife are missionaries in their own right.

The fifth study informing my research was Strickland (1990). Strickland added a fifth category of Non-parallel Worker to Bowers' four in his study of achievement roles and career wives. This wife actively pursues her own career outside the mission organization.

Because my study was drawn from a mission that does not allow outside employment for members on the field, this **Non-parallel Worker** category was not used. But it is of interest to notice how Strickland integrated Lipman-Blumen's concepts of *vicarious, relational, and direct achievement* styles on the same scale as Bower's augmented typology.

Figure 1

Homemaker	Background Supporter	Teamworker	Parallel Worker	Non-parallel Worker
Vicarious Achievement	Relational Achievement		Direct Achievement	

Based on the findings of the above listed published literature about the importance of spousal satisfaction in expatriate family success, and the link between a woman's role perception and her sense of well-being, my study asked five questions:

- How do women in a mission organization actually perceive their roles?
- What is the overall well-being of those women missionaries?
- Is there a relationship between how a missionary woman perceives her ministry role and her sense of well-being?
- What do missionary women wish they had known ahead of time?
- What have been the positive and negative factors in being an overseas missionary woman?

Method

Participants: Voluntary, confidential data was collected from 185 career missionary women of the Africa Inland Mission (AIM), a 100-year-old conservative evangelical mission with members from nine sending countries. In an attempt to rule out various confounding factors, questionnaires were only sent to career status AIM missionaries from the USA and Canada who have Africa-based ministries. Amazingly, there was a 69.5 % return rate. The questionnaire included both quantitative and qualitative measures regarding their experiences and perceptions as missionary women serving in Africa.

Quantitative measures: using Bowers' 1984 typology as the independent variable, the participants' well-being became the dependent variable. The women's overall well-being was assessed using four measures: Life Satisfaction Index (Neugarten, Navinghurst, and Tobin, 1961), Rosenberg's Self-esteem Scale (1965), Health Scale (developed for this study), and Center for Epidemiological Studies Depression Scale (CES-D; Radloff, 1977). The responses on the four scales were averaged to yield an overall score of well-being.

Qualitative measures: There were three open-ended questions: 1) "What do you wish you had known before becoming an overseas missionary woman?" 2) "What have been the positive factors involved with being a missionary woman?" and 3) "What have been the negative factors involved with being a missionary woman?".

Results

Quantitative results: As a whole, the participants expressed good life satis-faction, health, self-esteem, and experience low levels of emotional distress.

Of the married women, the highest percentage perceived themselves as Background Workers (36%), followed by Parallel Workers (29%), Team Workers (24%), and last were Homemakers (11%). When these results were recoded to fit Strickland's (1990) typology, we see that 11% of the women perceive themselves as Vicarious Achievers, the large majority of 60% as Relational Achievers, and 20% as Direct Achievers.

After I examined how the participants perceived their ministry role, a new simplified typology seemed both helpful and appropriate. In this new division, the main distinction between missionary women is those who perceive their husband as "the missionary" (Homemakers and Background Supporters combined), and those who see themselves as having an acknowledged ministry of their own (Team Workers and Parallel Workers).

An analysis was run to ascertain the relationship between perceived ministry role and measures of well-being using the new typology (after ruling out potentially confounding factors, for example, time on the field, marital status, level of education, etc.). Married Direct Workers had lower levels of emotional distress than Support Workers.

When Singles were added to the Direct Workers category, the whole category was found to have not only lower levels of emotional distress but also higher levels of overall well-being than the other group.

Finally, I compared the relationship between the participants sense of well-being and their plans to remain an overseas missionary. Women planning to return for at least another term had a greater sense of well-being. Further analysis showed depressive symptoms go along with plans to not return to the field.

Qualitative Results: The participants' free responses fell into four categories:

1.   *Interpersonal relationships* – children, spouse, parents, friends and family in the sending country, missionary coworkers, Africans, and the frequency of

having to say hello or good-bye to all of the above.

2. *Issues pertaining to oneself* – spiritual growth, world view, intra-personal growth, sense of purpose, obedience to God's perceived will, singleness, and finances.

3. *Issues pertaining to ministry* – negotiating a dual role, dealing with missionaries' view of women, home assignment, number of transitions, time management, direct ministry, and singleness.

4. *Issues pertaining to Africa* – how Africans view women, lack of privacy, cross-cultural adjustment, day to day living in a Third World country, health and safety, language acquisition, lifestyle perks.

Positive Aspects: In the open-ended section, the largest number of responses came in the area of Interpersonal Relationships, with more positives offered than negatives. The lowest level of response came in the category of issues related to Africa.

The most striking findings were the responses recording positive aspects about direct ministry experiences (88 responses). One woman saw a strong positive in her ability "to constantly expand my roles and projects to reach out to more people and see the spiritual growth as a result." The second highest response had to do with positive effect's on one's spiritual growth (72 responses). A representative comment in this area was "I have learned (and am continuing to learn) more about God through the eyes of other cultures."

The next most frequent positive factor concerned the advantages for their children (64 responses). Some examples follow: "Although our children went to boarding school, I feel it made us a closer family." "It has been a thrill to see God teach our children about trusting Him in a global setting." "Raising children in an accepting, nonperformance environment."

Negative Aspects: The number one subsection that received the most negative responses had to do with the loss of involvement with friends and family in the sending country. Two representative comments are "Missed brother's wedding and grandparents' funerals! Missed birth of first grandchild!" and "Lack of extended family presence to give advice and be with children."

Another striking result was the difference in responses between the Direct Workers and the Support Workers. The Direct Workers found both Africans' view of women and other missionaries' view of women to be a negative factor. Likewise, the Direct Workers reported positively on issues pertaining to Ministry and Mission Board, they felt better prepared for Africa, and conversely, Support Workers more often responded that they wish they had known more about Ministry Issues and had more cultural training before coming overseas.

Overall, Support Workers felt more concerned about Interpersonal issues: Direct Workers were more concerned about Issues Pertaining to Africa.

Singles: Finally, the responses of single participants were analyzed separately. Their primary areas of concern were loneliness and the way that missionaries and Africans view them. Interestingly, their singleness was reported mostly as a negative in the areas of Interpersonal Relationships and also the category of Oneself, but it was mentioned as a positive aspect in the area of Ministry! Two representative responses were "As a single, I was included almost as an 'honorary man' and involved in many interesting and forward thinking ministry activities," and "Single woman are chosen for committees, but married women rarely are."

Implications

The U.S. director of Africa Inland Mission asked me, "How can missions improve in their encouragement and positioning of women to enable women to be all that God has created them to be and do in cross-cultural missions?" Based on the results of my study, I offer three sets of implications. The first relates to the ethos or subculture of the mission. The second concerns job placement or assignment of personnel. The third set offers suggestions for pre-field training and on-field in-service training.

Ethos

Every mission agency has a certain ethos or unwritten set of values and expectations which has evolved over the years. This ethos changes slowly as society changes, but generally lags behind the home country culture by quite a few years. Leadership should deliberately foster an ethos moving in the following directions.

A.   It is foundational that mission leadership promote **a spirit of mutual respect, value and expressed appreciation for the contributions of both spouses**. A problem arises when the wife's ministry is perceived to be less important or necessary than that of the husband. (Philpot, et al, 1997, p. 27). One study participant wrote that a negative part of being a missionary woman is that she would "be overshadowed by the husband; if both are capable, he will be chosen." Another who had previously served as a single missionary, reported that after she was married she found out "my personnel record (at mission headquarters) totally ignored me—my ministry, language education, etc....it was only for my husband. I felt like a nobody after being a somebody in my own right."

B.   **Ministering to one's children, supporting the spouse from the home, and offering hospitality** *are* **all direct ministry and should be promoted as such**. We need to publicly affirm such ministry as well as encourage husbands to encourage their wives in these areas, particularly in the early years of a marriage when women are most tied down with small children. The Bible clearly teaches that all roles in the Kingdom work are important (Romans 12, I Corinthians 12, Ephesians 4). As one woman wrote, "Ministering to Kenyans from a home base is fulfilling the Great Commission."

C.   **True freedom and flexibility in choosing a healthy balance of time commitments for married missionary women should be accepted**. Every family will need constant adjustment as the number of children increase and the wife's health, energy, and age varies. The balance will look different for each couple and in each stage of life. Unfortunately, there is often silent censure of wives who don't contribute enough to mission objectives due to family needs; conversely, the same woman may be judged for neglecting her children or her husband if she does get involved in weekly ministry outside the home. We missionaries can be a very parochial bunch. As one said, "It seems in the setting I am involved in, being a 'stay at home mom' is not enough. Even when I'm involved in 'behind the scene' events and commitments, people still do not feel that I'm pulling my weight. Many leave their children with their workers (house servants), but I have never felt that is fulfilling my role as their mother. I certainly feel fulfilled, but when others criticize me, that hurts."

D.   We should **sensitize mission members, old and young, to both subtle and obvious "women bashing" comments and actions**. Misogyny is not a Christian value. Additionally, the mission community has a wonderful opportunity to model treatment of women as beings of equal worth and equal ministry partners to the African church.

Direct Workers mentioned a negative attitude toward women by Africans, but also by other missionaries, as a negative factor in their experience as missionary women. Christian love does not tolerate "women bashing" comments, actions, or criticism of those who are single or those who choose to work either inside or outside their home as missionaries.

Placement of Personnel

A.   It is important for mission leadership to deliberate carefully and **place missionary couples in positions based on gifts, desires, and abilities of both spouses**. Missionary wives, as well as husbands, need to be consulted. (Incidentally, this does not mean asking the husband what his wife thinks!) Giving women a voice indicates to them that their contribution is seen as important by leadership, and that their work, whether at home or outside the home, is perceived by leadership to be valid ministry.

B.   **Careful placement of single missionaries is also important**. It is important to offer independent housing for those who desire it and to allow for stability of assignment for singles just as much as for families. Many participants noted the difficulty they face from frequent losses of relationships. The single missionary does not have the relational stability of a spouse and children in her life. One participant wrote that she wished she had known ahead of time that "my field supervisor would not be taking my needs as a single woman into consideration for my placement, i.e. companions, others my age, the need for peaceful and quiet time, and safety factors in my immediate surroundings."

Pre-Field and On-Field Training

These recommendations are based on responses of participants concerning what they wish they had known before becoming overseas missionaries as well as negative factors.

A.   **Training in conflict resolution skills and interpersonal communication should be recommended, if not required**. Disappointment in inter-missionary conflicts came up frequently in responses. Normalizing conflict as part of human experience and providing a process and skills for resolution would greatly enhance missionary well-being. As one woman wrote, "It takes more emotional energy to deal with the interpersonal conflicts among the missionaries than with the cross cultural issues!"

B.   **Training in self-care, especially in proactively dealing with loneliness and multiple, frequent losses of relationships in both their sending countries and host countries, is also recommended**. This was the number one negative factor for most women missionaries, especially Support Workers, who perhaps need such training the most. One woman poignantly responded, "Even though you may be with other missionaries, you find yourself without a good friend. Some people stay at a distance because they don't want to say good-bye to a close friend." Another wrote, "All missionaries are moving; as I develop friendships, those friends may move or I may move. We know many, many people but have few close friends."

C.   **Language learning and cross-cultural learning should be required of all missionaries, both men and women**. Such training would underscore that the woman is a missionary in her own right, as well as better equipping her to work with Africans, to understand them, and to communicate with them. Surprisingly, many Support Workers wrote of their desire to have more cross-cultural, ministry and language learning opportunities.

Though costly in terms of time and money, it is important not to excuse or shortcut Support Workers when designing pre-field training. Because such training lowers fear and feelings of alienation, giving Support Workers such training might result in more confidence and understanding and hence a longer term commitment to the field. This suggestion mirrors the research about retention of International Service Personnel.

D.   **Add training in both African and North American gender issues for all missionaries**. Preparing missionaries to understand and thoughtfully anticipate traditional African gender views may help them interact respectfully rather than offensively. One participant wrote, "We live in a very male dominated culture, and I often feel like I'm viewed more as a 'baby machine' (which I'm not and often get questioned about) and also as a servant with no brain."

At the same time, we need to probe our own culture's understanding of gender issues, exposing some unconsidered misogyny and fears which underlie our put-downs of others' views. Some of the negative factors from fellow missionaries included, "being given a job without authority," "the continual censoring by male leadership to be the wife-at-home-serving-tea model," "experiencing a sense that my opinions were not taken as seriously as those of my male counterparts, even those who were also single and young," and "many missionary men (and some women) expect a woman to be silent—or nearly so all times. Silence = godliness. Luckily, my husband doesn't think so."

Because of the critical importance of interpersonal issues to the participants of this study and the finding in the difference in well-being between Direct Workers and Support Workers, every effort should be made in these four areas of training.

Conclusion

In summary, we need to promote a mission subculture of mutual respect, of consultative placement, and more thorough training both before and after arrival on the field of service. The women have spoken. *Bas.* (Swahili, may be used for "there you have it.")

Note: The author expresses great appreciation to Helen M. DeVries, Ph.D. of Wheaton College, Wheaton, Illinois, for her assistance in the design and implementation of this study, and to Sue B. DeVries, M.A. of OC International for her editorial guidance for this chapter.

References/Recommended Reading

Adams, W.E. & Clopton, J.R. (1990). Personality and dissonance among Mormon missionaries. *Journal of Personality Assessment, 54*, 684-693.

Adelmann, P.K. (1993). Psychological well-being and homemaker vs. retiree identity among older women. *Sex Roles, 29*, 195-211.

Beck, J.R., (1986). Women in missions: A pilot study. *Journal of Psychology and Theology, 14*, 224-232.

Bowers, J.M. (1984). Roles of married women missionaries: A case study. *International Bulletin of Missionary Research, 8*, 4-7.

Brett, J.M. Stroh, L.K., Reilly, A.H. (1993). Pulling up roots in the 1990s: Who's willing to relocate? *Journal of Organizational Behavior, 14*, 49-60.

Briody, E.K. and Chrisman, J.B. (1991). Cultural adaptation on overseas assignments. *Human Organization, 50*, 264-282.

Burke, R.J.(1996). Sources of job satisfaction among employees of a professional services firm. *Psychological Report, 78*, 1251-1234.

Dodd-McCue, D. and Wright, G.B. (1996). Men, women, and attitudinal commitment: The effects of workplace experiences and socialization. *Human Relations, 49*, 1065-1091.

Gove, W.R. (1972). The relationship between sex roles, mental illness, and marital status. *Social Forces, 51* 34-44.

Greenberger, E. and O'Neil, R. (1993) Spouse, parent, worker: Role commitments and role-related experiences in the construction of adults' well-being. *Developmental Psychology, 29*, 181-197.

Neugarten, B.L., Havighurst, R.J., & Tobin, S. (1961). The measurement of life satisfaction. *Journal of Gerontology, 16*, 134-143.

Philpot, C.L., *et al.* (1997). *Bridging separate gender worlds: Why men and women clash and how therapists can bring them together.* Washington, D.C.: APA.

Radloff, L.S. (1977). The CES-D Scale: A new self-report depression scale for research in the general population. *Applied Psychological Measurement, 1*, 385-401.

Rosenberg, M. (1965). *Society and the adolescent self-image.* Princeton, NJ: Princeton University Press.

Sieber, S. (1974). Toward a theory of role accumulation. *American Sociological Review, 39,* 567-578.

Strickland, W.J. (1990). A typology of career wife roles. *Human Relations, 45,* 797-811.

Stroh, L.K., Dennis, L.E. & Cramer, T.C. (1994). Predictors of expatriate adjustment. *The International Journal of Organizational Analysis, 2*, 176-192.

Thoits, P.A. (1983). Multiple identities and psychological well-being: A reformulation and test of the social isolation hypothesis. *American Sociological Review, 48*, 174-187.

Wilcox, D.K. (1995). Who perseveres? A discriminant analysis of missionary school personnel by intention to extend service. *Journal of Psychology and Theology, 23,* 101-114.

17

Serving Single

Ruth Ann Graybill

A significant segment of the entire missionary work force is comprised of single missionaries, with women by far the majority. Serving single as a missionary has its own distinct joys and blessings, advantages and disadvantages, struggles and difficulties.

The Blessings of Serving Single

Missionaries who have served the Lord as singles for many years speak freely of the joys and blessings that come with their single state.

Singles typically experience a greater degree of freedom than their married friends. Freedom from marital and family responsibilities gives them more time to develop a close relationship with the Lord and to minister to others. They can have uninterrupted devotional times and can come home to a quiet place in the evening. They can visit friends without having to hurry home to prepare dinner or watch the children. They are spared the pain of sending children to far-away boarding schools or colleges.

Local Culture

Typically, single women have more opportunities to integrate into the local culture, to develop friendships with national women, and to learn the native language, privileges often envied by married women. Singles can more easily change work assignments or locations. They have more freedom to travel, to pursue other interests. They are often able to live with a greater degree of spontaneity in their lives. In short, serving single as a missionary clearly has distinct advantages.

Challenges

While the single missionary typically has much in common with her married counterpart, yet the unique

Much of mission work is carried out by single women, but their specific contributions and needs are often overlooked. This chapter considers both blessings and challenges of single missionaries, particularly women. Challenges include finding validation, missionary subculture, healthy relationships with men, and living arrangements. The goal is for single missionaries to give their best in faithful, effective, fulfilling, and joyful service.

challenges of singleness are rarely given much attention in the mission community. These challenges are addressed here with the hope of bringing an increased understanding of singles in mission service. The following issues generally apply to both genders, but because most single missionaries and certainly most long-term single missionaries are female, the focus will be on women.

Learning to "Go It Alone"

Some of the challenges facing single women missionaries include:

Functioning as a "solo." As one veteran single missionary wryly states, "The hardest part of singleness on the mission field is being single!"

Emotional needs. Whether single or married, every woman is ultimately responsible for getting her emotional needs met. A single person may need to be more intentional and assertive in order to thrive in a mission setting. She can draw on a close, intimate relationship with God for emotional sustenance, reach out to others, and nurture herself in healthy ways.

Loneliness. Singles are likely to have more alone time, which needs to be turned into restorative, creative solitude. A good balance between "alone time" and "people time" will enhance well-being in many ways. While they are lonely at times, singles need to enjoy and value their own company as well as friendships with others.

Functioning independently. The single person has responsibility for basic house and car repairs, conducting business affairs in a foreign language, interfacing with local authorities, and possibly dealing with government "red tape," without the support of a life partner.

Restrictions on activities. In many countries, it is unsafe for a woman to travel alone, especially after dark. In some locales, a single woman may need to stay indoors after dark or find a companion with whom she can travel without raising suspicion.

Developing Close Friendships

Both single and married women express the need for an intimate, close friend. Single women especially often long for a kindred spirit with whom they can confidentially share thoughts and feelings, knowing they are loved and accepted.

Developing such a friendship in a mission setting can present a real challenge. Hindrances to close friendships include isolation and geographical distance, a high degree of mobility in the missionary community, and the resulting sense of uprootedness created by numerous moves and transitions.

An additional factor is the busyness of women's lives as they struggle with unending demands on their time. Missionary women may be continually faced with the needs of nationals, with a steady stream of needy people coming to their door. Establishing limits and boundaries is a key issue which is often more difficult for women than men; it is critical to see that women's needs do not simply get lost.

Single missionaries can get caught up in the busyness of work, as expectations of them may be greater in the absence of marital and family responsibilities. In some settings, there is the unspoken assumption that singles have more discretionary time and should be willing to work longer hours, take fewer vacations, or even be on call around the clock.

In order to enjoy effectiveness and a sense of well being, singles need to move beyond these barriers to reach out and develop relationships, building a sense of community. Single women need to actively and intentionally cultivate friendships with other Christian women, even if long-distance. If they broaden their circle of friends beyond the mission community, the variety of friendships can be enriching and gratifying. Nationals and the larger expatriate community can provide rich sources for additional friendships.

Finding Validation and Affirmation

Singles want to be accepted as full members of their team, with equal recognition given to their ideas, skills, and leadership potential. Some mission organizations appear to grant a greater status of adulthood and maturity to married couples, though in other settings singles may have more leadership opportunities than wives. A single woman may feel like an appendage to a larger ministry team if most of the decision-making and general direction is handled by men, or she may feel that she is viewed as "helper" even though carrying a major ministry responsibility.

All missionaries need to guard against drawing an inordinate sense of identity from their work. Single missionaries, especially, must be careful not to overextend themselves in their work, given the deep sense of purpose and significance their work provides.

Host Culture

In some host cultures there is no social category for a single adult woman unless she is physically or mentally handicapped, and the single woman may be seen as an anomaly. While this may work to the single missionary's advantage in freeing her from cultural restrictions experienced by married women, in other situations the unmarried woman may lack respect in society.

Sexual harassment may be a problem, a delicate issue for the single missionary to deal with in the absence of a husband. One woman describes the challenge this way: "In the country where I serve, you're open to every conceivable lewd comment from the national men. When you go to the market, you simply learn to expect sexual harassment. I often wish I had someone to stand up for me." Affirming her worth and specialness to God in these discriminating settings can present a challenging assignment.

Missionary Subculture

Fitting into the missionary subculture may also be a challenge for single missionaries. When mission communities are comprised primarily of couples and families, singles may feel like a social peculiarity. They may feel excluded from mission social events or even looked down on due to their marital status, and may struggle with self-doubt or shame. They mention the unfairness of raised eyebrows if two singles spend considerable time together and a lack of understanding of the dynamics of long-term same-sex friendships.

The Possibility of Never Marrying

A missionary single often has little opportunity to develop a relationship leading to marriage. If a woman embraces or at least accepts her singleness, she will experience less frustration. For some, this issue is a recurring one, rather than one that gets settled once and for all. The biological clock ticking away may all too loudly remind one of the passing of childbearing years. Singles may struggle with God, wondering, "Is this my reward for serving you faithfully! What happened to your promises to fulfill my deep desires?"

Whenever the issue re-surfaces, the single missionary needs to pour out her heart to God, once again committing her singleness to him, and find someone with whom she can freely share her feelings. Ultimately, she needs to recognize that she does not need a husband in order to be happy, fulfilled, complete, or whole.

Developing Healthy Relationships with Men

The single missionary needs opportunities to relate to men, both single and married, missionaries and nationals. Naturally, she needs to exercise caution as she relates to men. Wives are often less directly involved in mission work than are single women who typically work alongside the men. Single women must exercise discretion in relating to their missionary male co-workers to prevent misunderstanding. In relating to national men, the single missionary must be especially sensitive to cultural cues concerning decorum in male-female relationships. She needs to decide whether or not she will date national men and be aware of possible implications of doing so.

Healthy Sexuality

Questions are often raised such as, "Can one honestly and truly be sexually fulfilled as a single? What are appropriate ways to meet sexual needs?" Sexuality rarely gets addressed on the mission field or in pre-field training, whether for singles or marrieds.

It is important that single missionaries honestly acknowledge and address their God-given sexual needs and feelings. They need to find healthy, creative ways of expressing these needs and feelings, recognizing that, if properly channeled, sexual energy can become a source of tremendously productive, creative energy. Singles need to learn to relate comfortably to their sexuality and to fully embrace it, being careful neither to deny nor suppress it. They need opportunity to dialogue about this issue with appropriate persons.

Missionaries, whether single or married, need to carefully guard against involvement in any form of pornography or attempting to find "pseudo-intimacy" through such avenues as an unbridled fantasy life, excessive reading of romance novels, or inappropriate Internet "chat rooms." They need to be attentive to their vulnerabilities, especially when feeling emotionally needy. The lonely, hurting missionary who is not handling his or her emotional needs well is unfortunately a prime target for a moral failure, whether heterosexually or homosexually.

Physical Touch

All people have a God-given need for touch. The single missionary can meet this need by developing close, healthy relationships with missionary and national children whom she can hug freely, taking advantage of physical touch that may come naturally with greetings or farewells in certain cultures, asking her married female friends for hugs, or even taking on a loveable pet. When she has physical contact with another adult, she needs to be aware of her needs and motives and be sensitive to cultural and mission norms concerning the propriety of such behavior.

Good Living Arrangements

Single missionaries often feel that their living situations are assigned a lesser priority than those for families and couples. There is sometimes the misconception that any two singles should be able to live together and adapt to each other, despite different personalities, temperaments, or personal habits. Unfortunately, this may have disastrous consequences.

Singles may feel that considerably more flexibility is expected of them in living situations than of their married co-workers. One single missionary woman told of having 16 different roommates in 18 years! With a multitude of changes in living arrangements, it is difficult to make home feel like a stable refuge or a place to build long-lasting relationships with roommates.

Even if a living arrangement is relatively temporary, the single woman can decorate or add simple personal touches. Favorite photos or decorative objects help make any residence feel like home. While flexibility and adaptability are positive values, excessive change can lead to a sense of chaos. Being aware of one's needs for stability and finding ways to meet those needs is helpful.

Aging Parents

Another challenge concerns the care of aging parents. Married siblings may assume that a single daughter is in a better position to provide care for aging parents, regardless of the emotional or financial cost to her or the proximity of other family members to the parents. Even if she lives on the other side of the world, the single missionary may be expected to interrupt or terminate her work and return home to care for parents.

Security in Later Life

Recognizing that she may never marry raises issues of security for the single missionary. She asks, "If I stay single, who will take care of me when I'm older and possibly unable to take care of myself? Will I have adequate resources in my later years?" These questions can begin to hit hard, especially in mid-life. It is the rare missionary who is comfortably situated to handle financial needs in later life.

Learning to Live with Unmet Needs

The single missionary, not unlike her married counterpart, must come to terms with the reality that some needs may simply go unmet for periods of time—and, with God's grace, learn to be content in the process. Like the apostle Paul, she must learn to say, "I have learned to be content whatever the circumstances. I know what it is to be in need, and I know what it is to have plenty. I can do everything through him who gives me strength."

Ultimately, while experiencing both the blessings and the challenges of single-ness, the task of the single missionary is to give her best in faithful, effective, fulfilling, and joyful service for as many years as God calls her to mission work.

Recommended Readings

Foyle, M. (2001). *Honorably wounded*. Grand Rapids, MI: Monarch Books.

Graybill, R. A.(2001).   The emotional needs of women on the mission field. Unpublished manuscript.

Hansel. Tim (1991).   *Through the wilderness of loneliness*. Elgin, IL: David C. Cook Publishing Co.

Jeremiah, David (1983).   *Overcoming loneliness*. San Bernardino, CA: Here's Life Publishers, Inc.

Koons, Carolyn and Anthony, Michael (1991).   *Single adult passages: Uncharted territories*. Grand Rapids, MI: Baker Book House.

Lewis, A. and Gardner, L. M. (2001). Women in missions revisited. Paper in process.

18

Married Women in Missions: The Effects of Role Expectations on Well-Being, Stress, and Self-Esteem

M. Elizabeth Lewis Hall and Nancy S. Duvall

N ote: the following is excerpted and condensed from a much longer paper which will be published by the Journal of Psychology and Theology, Vol. 31 (4), Winter 2003. Used by permission.

Missionaries are subject to a great number of stressors, many of which are unique to living cross-culturally. The resulting burnout may be more of a problem with missionary wives than with their husbands because of the roles into which they feel they must fit in addition to the isolation and confinement (both cultural and social) that they often experience.

Among the variables Gish (1983) identified as more stressful for women were co-worker's attitudes toward their job, loneliness and isolation, self-acceptance, and communicating across the cultural and language barriers —all of which are related in some way to role issues. Carter (1999) found that extended family concerns and relationship with spouse or partner were reported as more significant sources of stress for women than for men. These findings highlight the role tensions between family de-mands and work that women experience.

Married women missionaries may face more stress than their husbands because of the multiplicity of roles that they assume, as well as frequent role changes. O'Donnell (1987) presented a family life cycle approach to understanding the missionary family. In almost every stage, the woman must face major role renegotiations.

Initially, this involves balancing the responsibilities of child rearing with mission-related work and domestic duties. Later, as midlife career issues come to the fore-

Married women missionaries may face more stress than their husbands because of the multiplicity of roles they assume, frequent role changes, and conflicting role expectations. Research findings note the importance of self-expectations in the well-being of married women. Freedom in choosing a role emerged as a key factor for well-being, fulfillment, satisfaction, and self-esteem. The homemaker role is a satisfying one for many mothers of young children.

front, she may want to develop herself beyond the roles of child rearing and home-making. When the children leave the home, her marital role will need to adjust, and she will be free to become more active outside of the home. This last transition can be particularly difficult for women who have found their main role identity as a mother.

Bowers (1984) further explored role-related issues of concern for women missionaries. She defined a role as "a cluster of behavior patterns that carries with it expectations on the part of the person filling the role, and also expectations on the part of others who are related to a person in the performance of the role" (p. 6). In an attempt to investigate role-related issues of concern among women missionaries, the present study focuses on role expectations, those of the missionary herself as well as those of the host culture.

Sources of Role Conflict for Women Missionaries

In a cross-cultural setting, the surrounding societal expectations vary from those in the women's culture of origin. Sources of conflict can be grouped into societal and self-related sources of expectations.

Societal expectations. Role expectations may be complicated for women overseas. Cultural factors may limit the extent of roles, or in some instances expand them. For example, in Islamic countries female missionaries may be limited to a ministry among females. Foyle (1987) suggested that single women working in cultures that hold very traditional views of women may find it easier to adapt to the situation than married women. Their singleness is an anomaly, and consequently they are considered social enigmas. In contrast, married women have very strong role expectations imposed on them.

Self expectations. A second source of role conflicts is the tension between women's own expectations of what they could or should be doing, and the role they are in. Many of the women who come to the mission field are highly trained, very intelligent, and committed to the task they are to fulfill. They may feel a sense of responsibility regarding their stewardship of gifts and abilities. Yet often they are placed in roles on the basis of their sex rather than their abilities. Severe discrepancies between ideals and reality can easily lead to burnout and discouragement.

Conflicts between role expectations and the actual role may be intensified by women's status as missionaries. Bowers (1984) stated that "the missionary role is a representative role; the missionary represents the Christian faith, the sending church, and his or her home country to the people of the country in which he or she serves. Generally speaking, the more representative a role is, the more pressure there is to fulfill role expectations." (p. 6)

Hypotheses

Three hypotheses were examined in the present study. The first two are related to congruence with societal role expectations, and the third is relevant to congruence with self expectations.

Hypothesis 1. Sex-role congruence theory, made relevant by the large sex-role differences often experienced by women overseas, was tested by the hypothesis that stress will increase, and well-being and self-esteem decrease, as congruence decreases between role and host culture expectations.

Hypothesis 2. Sex-role congruence theory suggests that incongruence from the role ideal endorsed by the culture of origin may result in decreased well-being. It was hypothesized that women who are exclusively homemakers will experience more stress than those who are more actively involved in the cross-cultural missions task, while women who have positions of authority outside the home will experience less stress and greater well-being and self-esteem. This hypothesis is supported by Bowers' (1985) observation that women who are overseas primarily because of their husband's call have a harder time enduring the vicissitudes of missionary life, as well as the pertinent research on women's roles in society.

Hypothesis 3. The role of self-expectations was examined by two hypotheses: (a) Stress will increase, and well-being and self-esteem decrease, as congruence decreases between role and self-expectations; and (b) Lower levels of role satisfaction and freedom in choosing a role will lead to greater stress and lower levels of well-being and self-esteem.

Method and Results

Participants consisted of 41 married missionary women who were currently serving overseas (in Latin America or Muslim countries) or had returned to their home culture within the past two months, and had served overseas for a minimum of one year. A questionnaire was mailed or hand-delivered covering personal background information, missions experience, role information, and cultural information.

The actual roles in which women were functioning were assessed utilizing Bowers' (1984, 1985; see Appendix A) description of four categories in which women in missions can be classified: homemaker, background supporter, teamworker, or parallel worker. Stress was measured with the General Well-Being Schedule (GWB; Fazio, 1977); self-esteem with The Self-Esteem Scale (SES; Rosenberg, 1965); and well-being with the Index of Well-Being (IWB; Campbell, Converse, & Rodgers, 1976).

The hypotheses were evaluated through correlations between the women's role congruence scores and the outcome variables, with ANOVAs comparing women in each of the four categories on the outcome variables, and with t-tests comparing women whose role was congruent with self gender-role expectations with those whose role was not congruent. Further details on the statistical results can be found in the longer version of the article.

Discussion

The study assumes that expectations are central to an understanding of role-related issues—that self-expectations and the expectations of others interact with the roles that women assume, and can be sources of stress or satisfaction. The study explored the effects of multiple expectations on the well-being of married missionary women. The focus was on the expectations regarding a role, including both self-expectations and the expectations of the host culture. Hypotheses stemmed both from the largely anecdotal material related to women in mission and from research in women's roles.

Hypothesis 1. The first hypothesis was that stress would increase, and well-being and self-esteem decrease, as congruence decreased between role and host culture expectations. The results of the study did not support this hypothesis; there are several possible reasons. First, women missionaries may be prepared to expect a discrepancy between their role and the expectations of the surrounding culture. Second, women missionaries may tend, in general, to assume roles that are acceptable within the framework of their host culture, thus avoiding conflict in that area.

An alternative explanation is that, while the gender-role expectations of the host culture are occasional irritants and make good missionary stories, they really have little impact on women's overall sense of well-being.

Hypothesis 2. The second hypothesis was that women who were exclusively homemakers would experience more stress than those who were more actively involved in the cross-cultural missions task, while women who had positions of authority outside the home would experience greater self-esteem. This hypothesis was not supported by the data.

On the contrary, the data indicated that the Homemaker group appeared to be more relaxed and to experience life as more satisfying and interesting than other groups who had more out-of-the-home involvement. It should be noted that many of the women in the Homemaker group indicated that they considered involvement in this role temporary, and looked forward to moving into other roles as soon as their children became older.

The additional finding that freedom in choosing roles appeared to be an important determinant in well-being and self-esteem is relevant here; the Homemakers in this study apparently chose this role, and did not feel constrained by it because they felt that other options were open to them at a later time. Freedom in choosing a role and women's attitudes toward working exclusively in the home may have a greater impact on well-being and self-esteem than the role behavior itself.

These findings, which contradict a stable pattern of research findings in the secular literature, also suggest the importance of subcultural factors in the area of sex-role expectations. The results of the present study may reflect sex-role values of a conservative Christian population that encourage mothers of young children to remain at home.

Hypothesis 3. The third hypothesis, examining the role of self-expectations, was supported by the data. The key findings were that higher congruence between self-expectations and actual role leads to greater feelings of well-being and lower reported distress. In particular, higher congruence of role with self-expectations was correlated with reports of finding life satisfying and interesting, and with feelings of relaxation and absence of anxiety. Role satisfaction and freedom in choosing a role likewise contributed to greater well-being and self-esteem, and decreased stress.

These findings suggest that congruence with self-expectations may be more important than congruence with the expectations of the host culture. While missionary women may find sex-role limitations a source of occasional frustration, it appears that these societal sources of tension have a minimal impact on long-term well-being and self-esteem. Discrepancy from self-expectations, in contrast, appears to be detrimental to well-being.

Implications for Mission Organizations

The results of this study have some implications for mission organizations. On a very basic level, mission agencies can provide women with the role guidance and an opportunity to examine their self-expectations that is ordinarily given to men entering the mission field, in order to enhance their options and thus their freedom in choosing a role. This might be particularly important at developmental transition points, such as when children start school or leave the home. For example, a woman whose children are leaving the home may need assistance in locating suitable work or training for new responsibilities.

A second implication is that, to maximize well-being and effectiveness, mission agencies should allow women to make their own decision regarding their work involvement outside of the home. Self-expectations, which vary significantly from one person to another, are an important determinant of well-being among women.

The present study is limited in size and does not empirically demonstrate cause and effect, and should be considered preliminary. However, it contributes in several important ways to an understanding of role issues for women missionaries. Freedom in choosing a role emerged as a key factor for well-being, fulfillment, satisfaction, and self-esteem. Fulfillment in exercising a role was also important. Congruence between the actual role and the women's self-expectations appears to be important, while congruence with the expectations of the host culture was not crucial. The actual role involvement of women does not seem to be as important as freedom of choice, fulfillment, and congruence with self-expectations.

The unexpected finding of better outcomes for homemakers is important in that it contradicts a large body of research and suggests the importance of subcultural factors such as religious values as mediating variables.

This issue is of more than simply academic interest. The oft-repeated finding that homemakers are more depressed than employed women has led some to strongly advocate that this role be discouraged by career counselors. The finding of the present study that homemakers in a conservative Christian group are, in fact, better off in some ways than employed women suggests that congruence with strongly held values and the freedom to make choices consistent with those values are more important than employment status.

References

Bowers, J. M. (1984). Roles of married women missionaries: A case study. *International Bulletin of Missionary Research, 8*(1), 4-7.

Bowers, J. M. (1985). Women's roles in mission: Where are we now? *Evangelical Missions Quarterly, 21*(4), 352-360.

Carter, J. (1999). Missionary stressors and implications for care. *Journal of Psychology and Theology, 27*(2), 171-180.

Foyle, M. (1987). Stress factors in missionary marriages. *Evangelical Missions Quarterly, 23*, 20-31.

Gish, D. (1983). Sources of missionary stress. *Journal of Psychology and Theology, 11*(3), 236-242.

O'Donnell, K. (1987). Developmental tasks in the life cycle of mission families. *Journal of Psychology and Theology, 15*(4), 281-290.

Appendix A

Bowers' (1984) Classification of Married Women Missionaries' Roles

Homemaker: This woman is primarily a full-time wife and mother. Her main focus is on the home and the support and nurture of her family. She is the enabler of her husband in his work. She may have very young children and/or may teach her own school-age children.

Background Supporter: She actively supports her husband and his work. She is moderately involved in outside activities, many of which relate to her husband's assignment. Her main focus may be on work that can be carried out within the home, such as entertaining, listening/counseling, home classes, or language classes.

Teamworker: Her main focus is on a team work with her husband, and on helping to reach the goals of their combined ministry, whether working side-by-side or separately. She may be involved in a variety of activities, some of which relate directly to her husband's work. She may have part-time paid employment, but it does not detract from her sense of teamwork with her husband.

Parallel Worker: She sees her role as distinct from her husband's role. She may work within the same organizational structure as her husband's assignment. Both husband and wife are involved in the childrearing.

19

Re-entry: An Introduction

Dorris M. Schulz

*D*r. Clyde Austin edited the first books on the challenges faced by returning missionaries and repatriates of other sponsorship groups. Kohls wrote in Austin's 1986 book, "The uncovering of culture shock, and then of reverse culture shock, have been two of the most monumental milestones in the development of the intercultural field." Before Austin's and others' pioneering work in the study of reentry, a certain vagueness surrounded the reentry process. Naming and understanding the process has made all the difference.

Missionaries work hard to adapt to the host culture, and are usually successful. However, missionaries who form close, empathic relationships with nationals and other missionaries may experience reentry as one of the greatest challenges of their lives. They discover that patterns of personal expectations and values have changed in ways more profound than they were aware. Adler (1981) believed that the more pleasant the experiences in the host nation, the more difficult the return "home."

The Reentry Experience

The difficulties associated with returning home are less often anticipated and, perhaps because of that, can be more challenging than those of leaving home and entering a new culture. Asuncion-Lande (1980) states that re-entry shock is "aggravated by a feeling of anger or alienation at the discovery that one has become a stranger in one's own culture." Missionaries know they have changed as a result of their experiences, but often fail to recognize the consequences of these changes as it relates to their home culture.

Nida (1967) observed that the most grievous readjustment confronting returning missionaries was dealing with "departmentalized religion." Missionaries returning

In the past two decades, the mission community has become aware of re-entry (returning to one's passport country) as one of the most difficult aspects of the missionary sojourn. This chapter describes typical stages of the re-entry experience and special considerations for missionary children and other "third culture kids" (TCKs). Coping strategies and the role of mental health professionals are discussed.

to a religion that is systematized and where externals appear to be more important than internals, think back to their experiences on the field with yearning. The difficult things seem to be forgotten and the freedom to think and act out their faith are remembered fondly. Returned missionaries find that the issues that concerned them before going to the mission field were different than what concerned them upon return. Majors become minors, and minors become majors.

Stages of Reentry

The experience of reentry is similar to the shock of entering a culture for the first time, and for this reason is called "reverse culture shock" or "reentry shock." According to Ascuncion-Lande (1980), there are four distinctive patterns of response:

- Excitement
- Re-establishment/frustrations
- Sense of control
- Re-adaptation

Excitement: At first, there is a great deal of excitement. Missionaries and their families receive a lot of attention and embrace their loved ones and good friends once again. Stage one is wonderful, like a honeymoon, and like a honeymoon, may be brief.

Re-establishment/frustrations: The missionary begins the task of becoming reestablished in the home environment. Missionaries note changing prices and ways of doing business, observe affluence and waste of Americans (e.g. people go through buffet lines, pile their plates high and leave half of it to be discarded); and are confused by so many decisions (e.g. 50 choices of toothpaste in different brands and sizes). Personal, internal changes are also affirmed. The missionary's world-view has changed, including values, customs, and behaviors. "Home" really doesn't feel like home anymore. This leads to frustration and irritation and feelings of ambivalence about the wisdom of "returning home."

Sense of control: In order to rid oneself of the dissonance, the sojourner plunges into the third stage, trying to manipulate the environment so that a sense of control is reestablished.

When missionaries have been through the process of cultural immersion, psychological acculturation and acceptance of the culture of their host nation, two alternative outcomes for one's original cultural identity are possible. In the first, assimilation, the individual essentially switches cultural identities, becoming a member of the new culture and losing his or her original cultural identity. The second alternative is "additive bi-culturalism" or "alternation." (La-Frambois, Coleman, & Gerton, 1993)

A missionary who has become assimilated or absorbed into the host culture may have more reentry stress than the missionary who has been able to maintain a status of alternation. When re-encountering one's home culture, the host culture will be seen as more positive than one's home culture.

Alternation allows an individual to maintain two separate cultural identities. It implies that a person can experience two cultures and maintain separate cultural beliefs and attitudes with bicultural efficacy. One is able to communicate in either culture, understand one's role and place in either culture, and is stable and grounded in both.

Readaptation: In the fourth stage missionaries relearn their own culture, and accept changes that have taken place in the environment and within themselves. Ideally, they learn how to alternate between cultures, so they are "at home" in both.

These stages may not be experienced in sequence or with equal intensity. Reentry is a process, and is complicated by stress, a sense of loss and grief, feelings of impotence, and ethnocentrism. Other complications include maladaptive behavior patterns, temperament, the availability of social support, expectations of others around them, emotional and spiritual security (or lack thereof), and the availability of resources. Individuals, even members of the same family, may have very different experiences.

Missionary Kids (MKs)

It is important to note that missionary children experience reentry differently from their parents. If the children were born overseas or were very young when the family moved to the host country, their cultural orientation may be predominantly that of the host culture. When they come "home" with their families or to attend college, they enter a strange environment which they have never experienced in the same way as their parents.

To state the obvious, missionary children are reared in missionary homes. The implications may be less obvious. Missionary home environments are typically counter-cultural in comparison with U.S. homes. Characteristics are likely to include the following:

- Finely honed sense of mission; everyday expressions of dependence on God
- Living on the local economy without noticeable consumption of material goods
- Greater degree of autonomy than in the U.S.
- Higher tolerance for cultural, linguistic, and political differences; less rigid
- Able to identify with a greater spectrum of socioeconomic levels of society
- Sense of divided loyalty between the host country and the home country
- (In some cases) social constriction because of geographic isolation
- MKs may attend a boarding school or national school

All of these characteristics make missionary children different from their mono-cultural U.S. peers.

MKs are TCKs

Missionary Kids (MKs) are Third Culture Kids (TCKs). Pollock and Van Reken (1999) in their excellent book, *Third Culture Kids: The Experience of Growing Up Among Worlds*, use the following definition:

> A Third Culture Kid (TCK) is a person who has spent a significant part of his or her developmental years outside the parents' culture. The TCK builds relationships to all of the cultures, while not having full ownership in any. Although elements from each culture are assimilated into the TCK's life experience, the sense of belonging is in relationship to others of similar background.

The TCK designation applies to children in a variety of overseas sponsorships, including military, federally employed civilians, business personnel, and missionaries. TCKs usually recognize each other immediately and gravitate to other TCKs, those of other cultures, and minority groups. The TCK experience greatly affects the reentering missionary young person.

An MK from Africa who graduated from a Christian university with a 4.0 grade point average said, "Our family came back to the States when I was 16. It took me about two years before I felt normal. My main problem is I don't know what I want to do with my life. I want to go back, but I don't want to be a missionary, but that's all I know . . . I feel stuck." (Schulz, 1986)

Navigating Reentry

Though reentry stress cannot be avoided, it can be ameliorated by education and understanding. Austin (1986) suggested the following:

Prior to departure:
- Begin preparation at least six to twelve months in advance.
- Review reentry materials as a family.
- Develop a tentative USA family budget.
- Consider and/or discuss difficulties you might encounter in the areas of verbal and nonverbal behavior.
- Read home culture magazines, journals or newspapers. Talk to recent on-the-field arrivals about current events. Ask for a "refresher course" on slang.
- Bring back special belongings of children.
- As much as possible, prepare young people for the world of employment.
- If possible, allow time for a gradual "decompression period" on the homeward trip in order to relax and mentally prepare for reentry.

In homeland setting:
- Be aware that you may experience depression, loneliness, fatigue, and illness as symptoms of stress. It is normal to go through a grief process.
- Be alert to your own expectations and the expectations of others. Value conflicts are inevitable.
- Be open to a new discovery of self. Seek hobbies and community/church activities that fit new interests.
- Reevaluate parenting procedures and talk with other parents.
- Remember that reintegration will take time. Be resilient and keep a positive outlook.

Schulz' (1986) respondents reported better reentry adjustment if the decision to return included children in the decision making process. Missionary families who made decisions together reported a greater feeling of closeness.

Closure is critical. One mother said, "I wish I had known how important it was to say good-bye. I denied myself any sad feelings before we left. If only I could go back and say 'good-bye' to the marketplace, to the flower vendor, to the street cars, and to Olah. She died last year."

Without closure there is unfinished business. Reentry programs offered on the field and at home help missionaries process this transition in their lives and realize the implications of giving up the missionary lifestyle.

Reentry Workshops

Reentry programs ease transitions into life in the home culture and are helpful to returning missionaries and their families. It is important to normalize the reentry experience. Guides and mentors are helpful to returning missionary families. On Christian college campuses, returned missionary kids can act as mentors to new arrivals. Sponsoring congregations and mission boards can provide support for returning missionaries. They may need to furnish career, personal and/or financial counseling, or financial support.

The Role of the Mental Health Practitioner

The mental health practitioner's role may be one of educator. Interpersonal relationships are influenced by the norms of our culture, but American social roles may not be understood. Rules concerning relationships can be very specific, yet unspoken — and those who persistently violate social rules incur sanctions. The practitioner needs to make the rules explicit. The therapist-educator can point people to sources of information, and when necessary, give "recipes of behavior" to help missionaries and MKs cope more effectively.

Day-in and day-out negative confrontation with the home culture makes the host culture look increasingly better, so that it is imagined to be a panacea. Austin recommends a "Journey of Clarification," in which an MK returns to the country of service so the bubble of perfection can be burst. For MKs whose parents remain on the field, Andrews (1995) ascertained that "the more frequently AMKs returned to their parents' place of service after graduating from high school, the greater their sense of existential, religious, and spiritual well-being." Upon return to the home culture, cognitive-behavior therapy may be helpful for those MKs who are still struggling. Processing the reentry experience with a therapist may be easier after a trip back to the host country.

Many missionaries have lived in communal environments or in boarding school dormitories, and loneliness is sometimes a critical issue in their "home" environment. One respondent stated, "Christians were not bonded together so much in the U.S. Christian brothers and sisters surrounded me, but I was never so lonely. I do not feel the close family ties among the Lord's people here that I felt overseas." (Schulz, 1986)

In group therapy or other gatherings, returning missionaries and/or MKs can explore their confusion, loneliness and adjustment difficulties and share how they are learning to cope and adapt. Sculpting, role-plays and group-written skits are useful activities. Life-changing decisions can be hammered out together, and life-long friendships can be forged in a group.

Existential therapy is particularly useful for those who are suffering. If the suffering has meaning, one can endure and grow spiritually. Reframing is particularly useful in this situation. Learning to live with incongruity and ambiguity is part of Christian growth.

The following web sites offer some excellent tips for churches on how to support returning missionaries:

www.mislinks.org/practical/membercare,
www.membercare.org/cross_cultural_reentry and
www.mrnet.org.

Note: This chapter is dedicated to Dr. Clyde Austin, with grateful appreciation for all that he and his wife Sheila have done for missionary families, mission board executives and mental health practitioners. Dr. Austin freely shares his research on re-entry, and he and his wife have provided incomparable hospitality to many people.

References

Adler, N. (1981).   Reentry: managing cross-cultural transitions. *Group and Organizational Studies, 6,* 3 (Sept.): 341-356.

Andrews, L. (1995). The measurement of adult MKs' well-being. *Evangelical Missions Quarterly,* October.

Austin, C. (1986) *Cross-cultural re-entry: A book of readings.* Abilene, TX: Abilene Christian University Press.

Asuncion-Lande, N. C. & Casmir, F. I. (1990). Intercultural communication revisited: Conceptualization, paradigm building, and methodological approaches. In J. A. Anderson (Ed.), *Communication Yearbook 12,* pp. 278-309. Newbury Park, CA: Sage.

LaFramboise, T., H.L.K. Coleman, and J. Gerton (1993).   Psychological impact of biculturalism: evidence and theory. *Psychological Bulletin, 114,* 395-412.

Nida, Eugene A. 1967. Readjustment—an even greater problem. Practical Anthropology, 14: 117.

Pollock, D. & Van Reken, R. (1999). *Third culture kids: The experience of growing up among worlds.* Yarmouth, ME: Intercultural Press, Inc.

Schulz, Dorris M. (1986). *A study of third culture experience in relation to the psycho-social adjustment of returning Church of Christ missionary families.* PhD dissertation, Univ. of Nebraska at Lincoln.

20

The Reacculturation of Missionary Families: A Dynamic Theory

Edward M. Stringham

Successfully returning from overseas and adapting to life in the passport country is a complicated process for missionary families, especially if they have spent significant time overseas. This study takes a careful look at dynamics of early stage, mid-stage, and late-stage returnees. Re-entry variables which emerge relate to home vs. host cultures, concurrent life transitions, extra-family social support, and marital power structure.

*N**ote: The following was excerpted and adapted from an article by the same title published in Journal of Psychology and Theology 1993, Vol. 21, No. 1, pp. 66-73. See the original article for a fuller treatment, including extensive references.*

Reentry is the phenomenon of returning to one's home culture after a sojourn abroad. Reacculturation, or the reentry transition, is the long-term process of readaptation after the return home, and is widely considered by researchers to be the most difficult aspect of sojourning.

In existing literature on reentry, there is little that focuses on missionaries. In addition, there is a lack of research on repatriating families. Although most missionaries sojourn in family groups, the bulk of the research focuses on individuals and fails to examine the reciprocal, interpersonal influences exerted by members of family systems.

Method

This study investigated the experiences of three families who had repatriated to the United States for different durations of time. Originally completed as a doctoral dissertation (Stringham, 1990/1991), the inquiry was guided by the following research questions:

- How did individual participants experience reacculturation?
- How did reacculturation affect family dynamics?
- What factors influenced the patterns of cultural readjustment?

Participants in the study were three families of returned missionaries, totaling six adults and five children, who had lived abroad for eleven to sixteen years and who were in various stages of repatriation.

Individual experience

Individuals' experiences during reacculturation were characterized by
- Grief for the loss of reinforcing events
- Awareness of changes in values and attitudes
- Time management stresses

Grief for loss of reinforcing events. All of the adults and all except one of the children expressed longings for various aspects of life overseas. They suffered emotionally during the reentry transition and many expended considerable energies attempting to transfer reinforcers to their home culture.

Early stage returnees acutely missed such things as foods, music, and smells. Others lamented the loss of house servants and small, neighborhood grocery stores which supported a flexible life style and afforded many opportunities for spontaneous social contacts.

The loss of social reinforcers was the most profound grief for the adults. In addition to longings for contact with friends abroad, each reported emotional turmoil because they lost their missionary role and identity (role shock). Feeling a lack of purpose and personal value, they looked for ways to use their missionary skills and experience in the home culture.

Awareness of changes in values and attitudes. Personal values and attitudes undergo subtle changes during an international sojourn, and the impact of these changes is suddenly thrust into conscious awareness during reentry. Many react strongly to the values of American society, especially regarding material possessions and tangible marks of success.

The early stage returnees expressed the revulsion to American riches, and also mourned what they perceived as self-centered motivations in academics, friendship development, and concern for the poor. Individuals engaged in ongoing internal dialogues attempting to preserve cross-cultural perspectives and reduce apprehension and guilt.

Similarly, the mid-stage returnees reported internal dialogues and parallel value conflicts, although with milder emotional reactions. They, however, reported more efforts to persuade other Americans to adopt a cross-cultural viewpoint than the family in the early stage. On the other hand, the late stage repatriates made few comments that suggested significant value conflicts with the home culture.

Cultural frames of reference were gradually transformed during the reentry transition. During the first two years, returnees may be overwhelmed by disparate cultural values. Trying to conform to the dominant home culture may stimulate apprehension or panic.

By about four years, the dissonance may abate and, while still keenly aware of value differences with monoculturals, returnees may seek to implement practical strategies to increase interpersonal influence. After six years, the distinctions in values may decrease further, and the former missionaries may be less likely to see themselves as change agents. For adolescents, this process occurs more rapidly and is discussed in a later section.

Time management stresses. Adults reported chronic preoccupation with time management stress since their return home, but experienced in different ways. Adults who had all of their children at home reported excessive busyness while those with adult children described a lack of activity. None felt they understood very well why time was such an issue.

Perceived time management stress seemed to be closely tied to other factors of re-entry. For example, a mid-stage mother concluded that her sense of being chronically overscheduled arose in part from her children's increased activities outside the family – a normal development in the family life cycle. A decrease in the relatively satisfying time she spent with her children led her to believe she was too busy.

By contrast, a late stage repatriate, who felt ineffective in her current ministry and longed for closer ties with her adult children and friends she knew abroad, expressed the desire "to be busy again." Overall, reentry transitions heightened the sensitivity of all participants to developmental tasks of the family life cycle and/or to vocational adjustments, which in turn contributed to their experience of time management stress.

Family Dynamics

Reacculturation affected family dynamics in the following ways:

- Decline in family cohesiveness
- Increased dependence of wives upon their husbands for emotional support
- Interpersonal tensions consequent to children's adaptations to the home culture

Decline in family cohesiveness. Cohesiveness may be defines as "the degree of commitment, help and support family members provide for one another." Reentering missionary families, including the subjects of this study, often have above average family cohesiveness.

However, there were a variety of complaints relating to an unwanted decline in family cohesiveness during reentry. A major concern was the reduced availability of mothers due to employment outside the home. Cohesiveness also seemed to be reduced by more rigid boundaries between home and work. For example, a child who frequently traveled with his father during ministry activities overseas felt cut off from his father's work environment in the United States.

Ironically, positive factors were also seen as reducing cohesiveness. Increased evening activities, especially for children, were prominently reported by the mid-stage returnees as reducing family time.

The adults in the late stage reentry reported having experienced this problem in the early years following reentry, but it was not a current concern. They may have become accustomed over time to a reduction in family cohesiveness.

Increased dependence of wives. Some studies have found that reentry is more problematic for women than for men, but others have not. In the present study, the three adult women all experienced greater reentry stress than their husbands.

In all three families, the wives became more dependent on their husbands as primary sources of social support and, as a result, marital power shifted in each case toward the husbands. The three families had three different patterns marital power: (a) husband-dominated, (b) symmetrical, and (c) wife-dominated. In the first case, reacculturation magnified the marital asymmetry by increasing the husband's importance to his wife. In the latter two situations, repatriation involved a strengthening of symmetry or a shift toward more symmetrical roles.

Adjusting to the dual roles involved in home and work place, often following a period of full-time homemaking overseas, exerts unique stresses upon women. This also affects husbands and impacts the dynamics of marital power distribution.

Interpersonal tensions. Marginal social identity is a major readjustment issue for missionary children (MKs). Four of the five children in this study reported that they felt culturally "different" and that they often concealed their background of living overseas from peers and teachers. The only child not reporting social adjustment problems reentered at age seven, and was at least two years younger than the other children at reentry.

These difficulties contributed to interpersonal tensions in each home. In the early stage family, the children demanded popular brands of clothing the parents viewed as extravagant. The mid-stage children wanted their parents to attend all of their school functions, a practice that their parents thought was more practical in the overseas setting with limited social activities than in the hectic American environment. A late stage child concealed the satisfaction she experienced with her peer-aided cultural adjustment, perhaps because she thought her parents would view such contentment as disloyal.

The normal developmental crisis of adolescence is intensified for MKs because of the additional psychosocial challenge of cross-cultural adjustment, and the children's efforts to adapt to their peers caused relational strains with parents. The overtness of these tensions decreased over time as families adapted to their new environments.

Readjustment pattern influences

The following factors influenced the patterns of cross-cultural readjustment:

- Cognitive processes
- Background variables
- Sojourn outcome
- Reentry variables

Cognitive processes

Nancy Adler (1976, 1981) identified four distinct coping styles returnees use to create internal consistency when confronted with the transition to the home culture. The differing strategies of readaptation used by adults in this study correspond to three of Adler's coping styles. Early stage adults clearly responded to reacculturation with alienation, described by Adler as the passive rejection of the home culture. The proactive pattern describes the mid-stage adults as they recognized both advantages and disadvantages of living in the host culture and attempted to maximize the benefits of bicultural experience. The late stage couple appeared to use resocialization, coping by blind acceptance of the home culture with failure to benefit from cross-cultural exposure. The data suggest that the alienation may be normative for early stage returnees, and that proactive and resocialization styles may develop after the first two years.

Background variables

Background variables include a variety of demographic and other factors related to pre-sojourn experiences. Those that exerted significant influence were gender, age and family-of-origin relationships.

Gender and age.   The reentry transition was relatively more difficult for the women. An age effect was observed in that the children appeared to adopt American values more rapidly than their parents.

Family-of-origin relationships.   Family background influenced the pattern of cross-cultural readjustment for the women in study. Disruptive relationships experienced during childhood by two of the women were thought to create psychological deficits, limiting their ability to cope with life's challenges. In addition, they lacked meaningful social support from their families of origin after reentry. The study's only adult female who used a proactive coping style credited the nurturing environment she experienced during childhood for helping her gain psychological and spiritual resources needed for effective cross-cultural adaptation.

Variables related to families-of-origin have previously been described in the reentry literature. As novelist Helen Hooven Santmyer (1982) said: "The greatest gift you can ever give is the gift of a happy childhood."

Sojourn outcome

The sojourn variables relate to experiences overseas.   The present study indicates that the sojourn outcome may have affected the participants' experiences after reentry. Two of the families reported successful sojourn experiences, with the projects they established continuing under the leadership of the host nationals. Awareness of the enduring nature of their work may have provided a focus for their grief, and for one the adults, a sense of purpose in the United States.

The third family witnessed the closing of mission work as a result of their expulsion by a hostile host government. This result appeared contribute to a profound feeling of failure and consequent obfuscation of their grief that seemed painful for them to contemplate.

Reentry variables

Reentry variables are contextual factors associated with the physical, cultural and relational dimensions of the repatriate's environment. Four of these emerged from the analysis of the data:

- Degree of similarity between home and host cultures
- Concurrent life transitions
- Connectedness with extra-family social support
- Marital power structure

Similarity between home and host cultures. Cross-cultural similarity facilitates the readjustment process. The adults who coped proactively had sojourned as missionaries in an environment that more closely resembled the conditions they experienced at home than was the case with the other two families.

Concurrent life transitions. Major psychological changes such as geographical moves or transitions in the family life cycle were more stressful when they occurred during reacculturation, especially during the first two years. The demands of making these adjustments added complications and distracted the returnees from a focus upon the tasks of cross-cultural readjustment.

Connectedness with extra-family social support. Social support is a critical reentry variable. The relative abundance or lack of social support was reported by all of the adults as affecting their perceptions of the home culture. The couple using proactive coping described diverse sources of support at their church and workplaces. The other adults expressed disappointment in the dearth of friendships and opportunities for developing close friendships since their return home. It appears that returnees' perceptions of connectedness with sources of social support are associated with adaptive or maladaptive coping styles.

Marital power structure. Power structure is an important element in understanding marital functioning. One conclusion from the present study concerns the influence of power structure upon reacculturation, in that marital symmetry seems to facilitate proactive coping, whereas marital asymmetry may contribute to maladaptive coping styles.

Cross-cultural reentry helped to crystallize the proactive couple's view of their relationship as symmetrical and secure. By contrast, the husband-dominated marriage used a coping style of alienation, and the wife-dominated marriage used a coping style of resocialization. The optimal social support provided in symmetrical marriages seems especially important for families during reacculturation.

Summary

A grounded theory of missionary reacculturation was generated incorporating the perspectives of individual members as well as the dynamics of three missionary family systems. The theoretical propositions are dynamic and interactive, and provide answers to the three research questions that addressed individual experiences, family dynamics, and influences upon the patterns of cross-cultural readjustment.

Both adults and children reported grieving over loss of reinforcing events and relationships they enjoyed overseas and changed values and attitudes. Adults reported a greater awareness of management stresses that accentuated problems related to vocational adjustment and family life cycle changes. Families experienced a decline in family cohesiveness, greater dependence of wives on husbands' emotional support, and interpersonal tensions resulting from children's readaptation to the home culture.

Four points are reported for the first time in the literature on missionary reacculturation:

- A history of dysfunctional family of origin relationships is predictive of reentry transition difficulties for women
- Concurrent transitions in other life dimensions after reentry are complicated by stresses associated with completing the intercultural cycle.
- Favorable sojourn outcomes facilitate adaptive grieving processes.
- Couples whose marriages develop symmetrical power distributions following repatriation benefit to a greater extent from mutual support than couples whose relationships assume more asymmetrical distributions.

The grounded theory presented here does not purport to describe every case of missionary reacculturation. Applicability to other families depends on their similarities with the participants of this study and to the circumstances experienced.

References

Adler, N. J. (1976). *Growthful re-entry theory.* Unpublished manuscript, University of California, Los Angeles

Adler, N. J. (1981). Re-entry: Managing cross-cultural transitions. *Group and Organization Studies, 6,* 341-356.

Santmyer, H. H. (1982). *And ladies of the club.* Columbus: Ohio State University.

Stringham, Edward M. (1991). The reacculturation of American missionary families (Doctoral dissertation, University of Nebraska. Lincoln, 1990). *Dissertation Abstracts International, 51,* 2416A.

Part IV

Interfaces with Sending Agencies

21

A Tripartite Model for Missions Consultations

John R. Powell and Frances J. White

*M*any missions have incorporated consultation by mental health professionals as an important part of their care for those on the front lines of missions. Planned and carried out in close collaboration with field leaders, on-site visits by mental health professionals play an important role in the development and effectiveness of Great Commission workers. Fruitful interactions which combine the resources and perspectives of missionaries, field leaders and visiting mental health professionals demonstrate the Body of Christ in action (I Cor. 12).

Prior to a field visit, mission personnel may ask:

- What issues and concerns would we like the consultant to address?
- What are the best ways of using his or her time and expertise?
- How can we collaborate?

Questions from the consultant's standpoint:

- How can I fully understand the situation I am being asked to address?
- What needs and issues are being expressed, explicitly or implicitly?
- How can I best be of help?
- With whom do I need to collaborate?

Questions for both mission personnel and consultants:

- What are the objectives of this visit?
- How can we work together to bring about the best results?
- How can Christ be honored and missions be advanced through these activities?

Mental health professionals often serve missions by making visits overseas. This chapter presents a comprehensive plan for making the best use of such visits. Three core activities are workshops and seminars; brief counseling and therapy; and consultation with field leadership. Consultation is a collaborative process in which relationships are central and critical. Maintaining consulting relationships over time enhances the effectiveness of brief visits.

Such questions imply a cooperative partnership between the mental health professional and those within missions, an important undergirding principle in field consultation.

Each mission, field, situation, and consulting visit has unique characteristics. Yet, in the authors' combined decades of work as psychologists consulting with missions, an approach has emerged which provides helpful parameters and definitions. This tripartite model includes:

> I. **Workshops and seminars addressing topics pertaining to current interests and needs**
>
> II. **Individual, marital and family counseling**
>
> III. **Consultation with field leadership on personnel issues and related matters**

While any number of other matters utilizing the consultant's expertise may spin off from these, the above three activities constitute a reliable and consistent focus for field visits. This chapter gives some background for work in these three areas, then touches on other areas where mental health consultation is often requested. It is written from the standpoint of outside consultants, but much of the content applies to those working from inside mission structures.

Foundational Principles

This tripartite model provides a constellation of services and activities which involve definite parameters, maximum exposure to consultant expertise by those on the field, and a core from which other activities can be pursued as desired. The following foundational principles undergird it.

- *Prayer* is essential. It should precede and be an ongoing part of consultations, and continue on through follow-up. Communication between field leadership and consultants is important in identifying specific areas for prayer. Participation in prayer by those in the mission and those in the home community of the consultant is crucial.

- Everyone involved has something to contribute, making consultation a truly *collaborative process*. Workshop participants, providers of services, field leaders, recipients of services, and others all have important parts to play. As each does his or her part, God "gives the increase" (I Cor. 3:4-9)

- *Two consultants working together* bring a level of expertise and help that is greater than the sum of one plus one. Their interaction, consultation and prayer with one another, complementary skills and experience, and different personalities add depth to the consultation.

- *Sensitivity to and respect for the mission and the host culture* are important to success. The consultant's professional training is no guarantee of these qualities; they must be developed over time through experience, compassion and understanding. Crucial aspects of sensitivity include remembering that an outside consultant is never a formal part of the mission structure and that the learning curve never ends. Humility is a byword.

- As a matter of ethics and personal integrity, consultants must confine their activities to areas in which they have *competency*, and neither imply competency which is nonexistent nor promise results which cannot be demonstrated.

- *Consultation is a process.* It unfolds as data are gathered, knowledge is shared, relationships are built, plans are made, activities are carried out, and change occurs.

- *Consultation is relational.* It takes into account the relationship the consultant has with him/herself (e.g. sense of core identity, awareness of strengths and weaknesses, knowledge of one's effect on others, personal identity in Christ), relationships with those in the mission, and the relationships all have with and before God.

Mission/Consultant Relationships

The hallmark of effective mission consultation is healthy relationships. The first contact between mission and consultant sets the tone for the myriad relationships which develop as consultation unfolds. Continuing relationships are built and maintained over time through repeated visits. These provide a continuity of care with greater power and efficiency than is possible in one-time or short-term consultation.

Some keys to effectiveness are:
- Observance of boundaries and structure
- Capacity for closeness without violating boundaries
- Concern about and sensitivity to context

Boundaries and Structure

At the outset it is important for the consultant to learn the structure of the mission organization and formal and informal aspects of field operations. In an interactive data-gathering process, the consultant shares information about him/herself and learns of the concerns and needs of the mission. Both the manner of this interaction and the information exchanged begin to establish important interpersonal and organizational boundaries for the consultation. These pave the way for understanding and observing other boundaries germane to the visit.

Boundaries and structure include logistical details, responsibilities for travel and accommodations, time expectations for seminars, who is responsible for what, ethical considerations regarding personal counseling or therapy, and structures governing consultation with field leaders on personnel issues. A healthy relationship has proper and known boundaries and structure, whether or not formally articulated. A healthy consulting structure needs to include rest and reflection time for the consultants—essentials which are too often ignored.

Capacity for Closeness

Healthy and effective relationships, especially those in a counseling/therapy relationship, involve degrees of closeness. The capacity for intimacy, one's awareness and understanding of it in such relationships, and the degree of psychological exposure are significant variables in effective helping relationships. The intensity of certain mission situations and the need for closeness, disclosure and/or understanding on the part of clients underline the need for heightened understanding of oneself and maintaining the necessary boundaries on the dimension of intimacy.

In order to be most effective, one must manifest a sense of vulnerability, compassion, empathy and being truly present with others, while being absolutely clear about one's own boundaries and respectful of those of the client and others in the mission.

Concern for Context

While each part of this model creates a certain context in and of itself, as the consultation progresses it also relates in dynamic ways to the larger context of the mission community and host culture. It is important for the consultant always to be aware of this larger context, and to utilize this knowledge in the work being done. Cultural sensitivity, respect for differences, knowledge of the mission organization and its history, and information about the roles of those with whom relationships are built are important.

Continuity of Care

Repeated and regular field visits over time provide many dividends in the life and development of missionaries. Time and energy are saved since one visit builds on another. When crises or emergencies arise requiring e-mail or phone consultation, the consultant already has contextual information and understanding. Missionaries can anticipate follow-up from previous counseling or seminar situations without repeating their history. Field leaders can pick up a consulting relationship from where it ended with the last visit.

Establishing a long-term consulting relationship involves more initial logistical details and agreement of purpose, role and function, but the end point is that the same consultants are available over a period of time. This ongoing relationship can be utilized for problem-oriented situations requiring intervention and for preventive, and developmental activities.

Integrating Medical and Pre-service Assessments

A close relationship between medical and mental health consultants has excellent potential for continuity of care. At the candidate stage, baselines for both physical and mental health are gathered, risks (including psychological risks) are assessed for different situations, and interconnections are explained to the missionary in order to enhance self-care. Appropriate mission staff are also involved in this process.

In this way, pre-service assessment findings can be integrated into a long-range plan for continuity of care, rather than merely serving as a "pass-fail" evaluation which overlooks the potential for ongoing care and growth. The missionary is given responsibility for understanding of risk factors and self care through educational seminars and individual interpretation, and is encouraged to participate in periodic reviews. An integrated approach can be incorporated into the tripartite model; doing so brings focus to prevention, development and enhancement. For a more complete discussion, see Chapter 33 by Dr. Ken Gamble.

Preparation for Partnership

It is crucial to attend to matters of logistics in detail prior to the visit. Logistical arrangements include agreement on time and place, who makes airline arrangements, who bears the cost of what, fees and how they will be paid, accommodations, books and materials, reports needed or expected, taping of sessions, space arrangements for seminars and counseling appointments, scheduling, workshop design, expected participation (e.g. optional or required), how appointments are made available, and confidentiality and ethical issues.

It is essential that these and other matters attendant to the visit be discussed and determined as much as possible in advance. In all this, it is crucial that the consultant maintain a learner's attitude and a humble spirit and be consciously aware of the interplay of spiritual, physical, emotional and contextual aspects of the potential visit. If one senses unspoken assumptions or expectations, it is important to surface and clarify them during the preparation stage.

It is important to be clear as to the reasons for the visit, its purpose and objectives, the activities envisioned and potential plans for follow-up. One feature of this tripartite model is that each visit, whether new or in a continuing series, is designed to meet a specific purpose or address particular issues as identified by field leadership. It is designed collaboratively and may be modified by consultant and field leaders for a specific issue or need. Each program, individual intervention and consultation with field leaders is done with "customization" in mind.

Again, one key to preparing for and building this partnership is to understand that consulting is a relational process, that each participant has something to contribute, and that it is God who brings things together as each part of the body does its work.

Part I: Workshops and Seminars

Great creativity is required in the design and conduct of seminars and workshops. Unlike the standard college class, these usually work best with a tailor-made non-formal or adult educational approach with continual practical applications of the topic. The task is to understand the needs, interests and potential of participants in order to bring information, learning experiences and applications relevant to the issues which called for the consultant's visit.

Some workshops are of almost universal applicability in missions, but they can be adapted to the *specific* needs and issues in a given field at a given time. Examples are the widely embraced "Sharpening Your Interpersonal Skills" developed by Dr. Ken Williams (see Chapter 30) and training in crisis response done by Mobile Member Care Team/West Africa (See Chapter 47).

Other workshop topics with wide appeal include coping with stress, conflict management, understanding emotions, and family and marriage relationships.

Giving a relevant and effective workshop or seminar requires preliminary information gathering about the group, their needs and motivation. A cardinal principle for brief visits is assuring that participants have ownership or at least a sense how the subject relates to their own interests. Following this principle requires careful thought on the part of both consultant and field leader as to how best to involve the participants. One is reminded of the proverb which states "He who answers a matter before he hears it, it is folly and a shame unto him" (Prov. 18:13). Having prior information about the group and knowing their questions, concerns and potential is crucial.

Research on stresses in missionary life have consistently shown that two areas high on the list are lack of time for individual spiritual and devotional life, and interpersonal conflict. (Gish, 1983; Carter, 1999). With respect to the first, participants welcome having a clear Biblical basis for the workshop with time for peaceful reflection, prayer and quiet opportunities for spiritual renewal at the beginning of the workshop.

Interactive exercises which put people together in a team-building or problem-solving manner often pave the way for affirmation of relationships, or even confession, forgiveness and reconciliation, as needed.

One of the authors was a consultant in a challenging conflict resolution situation some years ago. Nearly half of the week-long process was spent in reviewing scriptures on who we are in Christ, considering anew God's many promises and Biblical truths about relationships, and working in small groups on tasks relating to these truths and the work of the mission. By the time we reached the point of doing the hard work of digging in to some longstanding conflicts in the group, the participants had already begun working on those themselves.

Seminars as Entry Points

Workshops or seminars are a desirable entry point for on-site consultation because they provide opportunities to establish a commonality of Christian faith and practice between the consultants and participants. In a seminar context, participants are able to see the consultants as sisters and brothers in Christ without risking anything. In earlier years, the authors did not escape suspicions about the co-existence of their profession as psychologists and their Christian commitment. Misgivings were sometimes expressed quite blatantly and even with rancor.

Seminars also allow missionaries to observe and get to know the consultants. If there is more than one consultant, a missionary can choose the person he or she feels most comfortable with for individual counseling.

Starting with seminars also allows field leadership to provide immediate feedback on the topic, direction and style and how both the topics and the consultant are being received by the group. This is helpful to the consultants and part of the collaborative relationship and joint ownership of the visit. If possible, arrangements should be made for daily review and prayer with mission personnel who are central to the planning and conduct of the visit.

Part II: Brief Counseling and Therapy

Direct service interventions are pivotal to the consultant's visit. Yet, they cannot occur as effectively without the context provided by the model's other parts, or apart from the overall context of the mission.

Individual needs vary widely. At one end of a continuum are issues which are fairly common and are usually helped by effective listening, compassionate understanding, godly guidance, and knowledgeable counseling. They include:

- Encouragement to take normal developmental steps in personal and spiritual growth
- Gaining insight into spiritual or ministry growth needs
- Re-affirming a sense of call or working through on-the-job conflicts
- Making important decisions
- Issues of ministry change or transitions
- Understanding children and aspects of parent-child relationships
- Removing barriers to deeper marital satisfaction
- Understanding family of origin issues
- Finding ways to manage stress
- Handling interpersonal tensions

At the other end of the continuum are a variety of symptomatic manifestations fitting various diagnostic categories. Among these are:

- Adjustment disorders
- Anxiety disorders
- Depression and other mood disorders

Successful treatment of these on the field, particularly during a brief visit, is less likely, although uncomplicated depression may be amenable to on-field treatment through counseling and appropriate use of medication. See Chapter 35 by Dr. Esther Schubert on mood disorders.

The combination of readiness on the part of the missionary, rapid and accurate assessment by the consultant, and creative, intense work under the guidance of the Holy Spirit may well take one beyond anything expected in regular office practice at home. Timely assessment and referral for follow-up, in cases where on-going help may be available, can be of significant help.

Missionaries with personality disorders present a challenge to both consultants and field leaders (not to mention fellow missionaries). In such instances, consultation with field leadership about options for handling the situation is usually the best course of action. See Chapter 40 by Dr. Esther Schubert.

The availability of an empathic, competent outside counselor often serves to prevent the further development of distressing changes a person is undergoing, and often helps the individual regain balance and perspective in a short time. Utilizing short term or brief approaches developed in recent years is often prudent. One approach which is adaptable for brief counseling overseas is Budman and Gurman's *Theory and Practice of Brief Therapy* (1988).

Concerns amenable to brief interventions include some types of marital issues, working relationships, parent-child concerns, unresolved grief and loss, guilt over past behaviors, and certain problems from the past that are kicked up by the stresses of missionary life.

Sometimes addictive problems such as Internet addiction, pornography, eating disorders, other types of acting out, and more serious emotional problems or disorders can be assessed and identified, and recommendations made for further treatment and/or administrative action. Although there are more services now available on the field, being sent home for care is sometimes the best course of action, so that limited on-field resources are not absorbed by a few difficult or complicated cases.

Many times field leadership will have identified issues prior to the visit and made plans for immediate assessment and interventions, or at least consultation. In providing brief counseling or therapy, it is important to make rapid assessments and accurate evaluations, and to use one's strengths for the intervention. It is also important to go no further in the work than will allow for adequate closure during the visit, and in many cases to work with the client to ensure on-going support and accountability.

Part III: Consultation with Field Leadership

Consultation on personnel concerns and perhaps other field issues is another important part of the tripartite model. This activity can be thought of as the third leg of a three-legged stool. It helps make the overall visit more secure and solid, rather than relying on two legs, or even one leg, for balance.

To be successful, such consultation must have the integrity of sound ethics, respecting the bounds and rules of relationships, confidentiality and communication. A written memorandum of understanding which includes the ethical guidelines pertaining to missionaries as clients is often quite helpful. In ongoing consulting relationships these understandings become threads in the fabric of on-going work. Ethical practices are then an integral part of the process. It is important for the consultant to be aware of, communicate about and be certain of informed consent for treatment of missionaries as clients.

In individual counseling, matters pertaining to the mission, missionary responsibilities, or relationships with field supervisors are often brought up. Within the counseling relationship, options can be developed which involve communication with relevant others in order to achieve the best outcome. In our experience, missionaries are often willing to permit the release of information sufficient for discussion with field leadership if needed to resolve a problem. How this is done may be a therapeutic issue. Common examples are changes in work responsibilities, resolution of a conflict with a fellow missionary, or further consultation regarding medical or mental health issues.

One of the consultant's major contributions is to help the leader understand situations more fully and develop options with recommendations. This may entail facilitating a discussion between the leader and a missionary or helping the leader gain insight into his or her own dynamics and how they affect the situation. In one's eagerness to help a field leader gain *understanding about* a given situation, person or family, the personal needs of the leader for encouragement, discussion and sharing may be overlooked. Again, the nurture of relationships is important. Consultants may be asked to conduct workshops just for field leaders in which their personal concerns, tensions and needs are addressed.

Other Areas of Consultation

The tripartite model is an important core for work done by consultants. However, as the world changes, missions adjust and the characteristics of new missionaries change, mental health consultants also need to make changes and adaptations.

In recent years, there has been an increased need for professionals who are qualified to help in the *aftermath of traumatic events* such as sudden evacuations, kidnapings, robbery, assault, political upheavals, natural disasters, murders and other traumatic events. Needs for debriefing of those directly involved, those who have lost dear ones, crisis managers who have had to make decisions as events unfold, and many others have created what is essentially a sub-speciality in mental health services to missions. See Chapter 37 by Karen Carr on crisis intervention and debriefing.

Another arena where mental health professionals are increasingly used is in *conflict resolution* procedures. There are useful strategies and approaches for this work, and both authors have experienced an increased number of invitations to serve as consultants in such situations. See Chapter 32 by Dr. Barney Davis on conflict resolution and Chapters 14 and 43 on forgiveness and reconciliation.

The move toward more international teams makes *team development* more of a challenge. Team building is another arena where mental health consultants can work in both preventive and remedial modes. Dr. Lianne Roembke's book *Building Credible Multicultural Teams* (2000) is a good example of work in this area, as is her chapter 31 in this volume.

Missionary children's issues continue to be an area of much concern on the part of missionary parents, where mental health consultants can be helpful. Many resources have been developed in recent years; see Chapter 15 by Janet Blomberg for a summary of issues and resources.

The area of MK concerns is an excellent example of persons representing various disciplines, professions, experiences and perspectives coming together to provide a picture of the whole. Mental health professions represent only one type of resource. Help is often sought for these concerns from consultants on field visits, and it is incumbent upon them to learn about the broader field so they can give assistance or direct parents to helpful resources.

Another important area for compatible and complementary work is the interface between *pastoral care and mental health care*. Both cover crucial aspects of missionary life and development, and in many instances they directly collaborate in seminars, and field consultations.

Many missions now have regular pastoral visits on the field for spiritual refreshment, counseling, and encouragement. Barnabas International, based in Rockford, Ill., provides staff who make multiple field visits with many missions, bringing pastoral training, experience and expertise. Some are credentialed mental health professionals. Just as the Annual Conference on Mental Health and Missions is oriented to mental health professionals (and others!), the Pastors-To-Missionaries Conference, held each December at JAARS in Waxhaw, NC is oriented to pastors (and others!). See Chapter 6 by Dr. Lareau Lindquist for more discussion on this partnership.

Concluding Comments

The tripartite model has been demonstrated to be a core model for much of what mental health professionals do overseas. In its actual operation, many spin-offs develop for service in other areas; the consultant has the flexibility to pursue these as well. Consultation in any of its many forms depends on the collaboration of many others in mission organizations as well as the broad array of member care workers who work for the development and well-being of missionaries.

Working in this arena is truly a labor of love. It increases one's dependence on the Lord and provides opportunities for wonderful relationships and learning. It brings joy as missionaries grow, change, build their lives, and help expand God's reign on earth; it also brings tears as we see hurts, difficulties, loss and discouragement. May we never lose these God-created human abilities, and may we live out the Great Commandment as we seek to faithfully serve those on the front lines of the Great Commission.

References

Budman, S. H. and Gurman, A. S. (1988). *Theory and practice of brief psychotherapy.* New York: Guilford Press.

Carter, J. (1999). Missionary stressors and implications for care. In *Journal of Psychology and Theology, 27,* 2, p. 171-180.

Gish, D. J. (1982). Sources of missionary stress. In *Journal of Psychology and Theology, 11,* 3, p. 137-142.

Roembke, L. (2000) *Building multicultural teams.* Pasadena, CA: William Carey Library.

22

In-house Staff vs. Outside Consultants: A Comparison

O'Ann Steere

*A*s a mission organization moves to support its missionaries and their families through the services of a member care or mental health professional, a natural question is, "How do we find and deply such persons?"

Traditionally, there have been two approaches to this question—some mission agencies identify and train selected members who have natural gifts for mental health services, and others look toward outside consultants. Both approaches have their strengths, and each has inherent weaknesses.

Many missions utilize both approaches, depending partly on member needs, though they may lean predominantly one way or the other in structure and practice. Many factors require consideration in determining which is best for a given mission agency.

Advantages of Using In-house Staff for Mental Health Care

A member shares the mission's goals, culture and values.

While progress has been made, some agencies are still uncomfortable with the outside "shrink." Even those who are comfortable with psychological professionals wonder if the outsider really shares a common agenda with the mission agency.

The world of missions is more like a stir fry than a homogeneous gruel. By using members of their own agency, administrators and missionaries alike can be sure

Mental health professionals may serve missions as in-house members of the sending agency or as outside consultants. This chapter looks at the advantages and disadvantages, strengths and weaknesses of each model from the point of view of the missionaries served as well mission administration. Often, it is advantageous to use a combination of both in-house and outside consultants.

that there is a good fit between themselves and the member care provider, as they share common experiences within the agency.

A member can be seen as less threatening. He or she carries the same commitment as all of the other members of the team.

Agency administrators have control over the quality, training, and approach of inside staff.

As the idea of providing member care to missionaries has gained credence, a greater variety of individuals are available for services. Some charge a fee and others provide services *pro bono*. How is the mission to judge who is and who is not competent to serve their staff?

Large missions, such as Wycliffe Bible Translators, now design their own training programs, intended to produce a staff of caregivers whose training is a known quantity and whose values and approach are compatible with the sending agency. Even those who join Wycliffe already having credentials and experience are required to have an internship in this training program.

As these large agencies send their own personnel into member care situations, they are able to judge who is effective. Once a track record has been established, the agency can rely on its own observations as to who is best suited to work in a particular situation.

A member usually has a sense of history in the given situation.

They know the players without a scorecard. They understand the unique "language" of the mission. They know background, personnel, and policies. This lets them "cut to the chase" without spending valuable time getting oriented to what is going on.

A member knows what resources exist within the mission to address the missionaries' needs.

When adjustments need to be made, an insider is more likely to know who and how to push for change. According to Dave Brown, Director of Pastoral Care and Counseling for TEAM, "Staff often perceive systemic issues within the organization. While they may admittedly not always be objective (or at least as not as objective as an outside consultant), they may know better how to communicate appropriately and effectively to mission leaders and other staff."

A member often has had experiences similar to the client's situation.

Many in-house caregivers have come "up through the ranks." They have "been there and done that," and are often seen as having the interest and potential for training in a member care specialty. That is beneficial both to the caregiver and care recipient.

That experience, plus relevant training, provides the caregiver with confidence in his or her capacity to understand and the receiver with a sense of being understood within the context of the mission. Dr. Laura Mae Gardner has said that having completed Bible translation in a previously unwritten language gave her and her husband immediate respect within Wycliffe Bible Translators; they had proved themselves in the arena most significant to their colleagues.

Dr. Gardner writes, "A member care professional, both for personal credibility and a sense of adequacy, would greatly benefit from time overseas in a mission's apprenticeship or from working with an experienced missionary or missionary team. There is no substitute for going through the same experiences—the joys and the sorrows, the challenges and the victories—as those to whom one intends to minister." (1992)

It makes financial sense to fully utilize in-house caregivers; doing so can lead to proactive care.

When there are staff members on salary or full support, it is reasonable to keep them fully active. In the absence of urgent, critical needs, in-house staff can monitor the staff and look for areas to shore up. They can attend to glitches before they become crises.

As Director of Member Care for World Relief, I often observed staff members peek through my door and then enter saying "since you aren't busy. . ." Most of them would not have asked for help if they hadn't perceived (correctly or incorrectly) that I was available and my time unfilled.

When resources are limited—and they always are in the mission enterprise—there is a tendency to avoid bringing in outside help until it is clear that the problem is severe enough to warrant the expense. When that is combined with the classic missionary spirit of "somehow, Jesus and I can get through this," needs often are not reported to someone in a position to respond until they are chronic or severe. Even reported needs don't get addressed until funds are available, which can be an unreasonably long delay, based on budget and giving cycles.

There is a perception of longevity regarding in-house caregivers.

There are no actual studies known to the author that support this common assumption; turnover among consultants may actually be lower than among in-house staff. But, the belief persists.

If in-house caregivers do indeed have an advantage in longevity, we can also assume some advantage in effectiveness. While some needs can be addressed in a single set of sessions, other issues demand input over the long haul. "Sustained contribution is key. There is value in short-term contributions in the areas of training, crisis intervention, and consultation. However, significant changes in people's lives (and agency health) by means of therapy, coaching, organizational development or preventive ministries normally take place over longer periods of time." (Gardner 1992)

Missionaries may have more confidence that an in-house caregiver will be available over the long haul than an outside consultant will be. This confidence can be translated into a commitment to the good of the individual and inspire a willingness to risk that an outsider would not enjoy.

On the other hand, some missionaries may be more willing to work with an outsider because they trust that the consultant will disappear after the help has been given. There is no fear of meeting the caregiver again years down the road and feeling pigeonholed by a past difficulty.

Advantages of Using Outside Consultants

Even small agencies can access a wide variety of servants and services.

Many mission organizations are simply too small to support a full range of services if they must be provided by mission members. By using outside consultants, the smallest mission can provide a full range of services to its members.

Specialized care can be provided.

Many sending agencies have one or two generalists who are interested in and oversee the area of member care. These in-house staff bring in consultants as needed.

There are two trends in specialized consultants. First is specialization by function, in which professionals concentrate on issues such as crisis intervention, orientation, reentry, family dynamics in cross cultural adjustment, trauma debriefing, conflict resolution, team building, etc. They are able to bring this strong background to whatever location or situation needs assistance.

A more recent trend is for the consultant to concentrate on one geographical area. Consultants return to one area again and again, providing service to a variety of missionaries and agencies living there. This type of specialization lets caregivers develop an understanding of the culture and unique stresses of the location, as well as to build long term relationships with individuals stationed there. (See Chapter 46 for a model for on-site and rotating services by outside consultants.)

The care provider is seen as committed to the individual missionary, not as an agent of the institution or the agency.

Missionaries and consultants see this as a huge plus. Several of the consultants and nearly all of the missionaries who were interviewed in preparation for writing this chapter cited this first when asked about the advantages of outside consultants.

Missionaries see it as an advantage: "I like knowing that the counselor isn't going to 'report' on me to headquarters. They are here to help me!"

If boundaries have been set properly, the therapist knows what responsibilities he or she has to give feedback to the agency, and except for that, can concentrate on the welfare of the missionary.

Therapy is streamlined because the client doesn't waste time trying to get the therapist to solve agency problems. Cheri Auman, a psychotherapist who has worked with numerous agencies over the past twelve years, said "I never wonder if the client is trying to pitch me. They know I can only work with them and their responsibilities. The *only* issue is their emotional health."

However, agencies sometimes see this as a minus. "Outside providers often focus on the missionary as the client and ignore the mission. . . They can actually put themselves and/or the missionary in an adversarial position with the mission. . . When the mission is brought into the healing process, the welfare of the missionary is enhanced. However, if the mission is left out or ignored in the process, the welfare of the missionary often suffers." (Steve Edlin, Pastoral Care and Counseling, TEAM)

Consultants are likely to be impartial and to see things objectively.

And even when they aren't impartial and objective, they tend to be perceived that way! Those needing help don't think that the deck has been stacked against them before help arrives. Therapists arriving fresh from the outside world are assumed to have arrived without bias.

Consultants have "nothing to lose."

Since their friends, reputation, and orientation are all outside the particular organization, outsiders can take whatever action or position seems best to them, without reference to "political correctness" within the organization or fear of negative personal or career consequences. However, most also are sensitive to their responsibilities within the mission, and wish to work in collaborative ways.

Perhaps because they are not personally invested either in the past or in a model for the future in the same way an in-house consultant may be, outsiders can push hard for needed changes.

Outside consultants can develop a broader frame of reference.

By knowing different agencies and many missionaries, consultants develop a sense of what is "normal" rather than just what is the pattern within one mission. Having been exposed to the broad spectrum of approaches to a particular area or difficulty, the outside consultant can suggest options that may not occur to an insider. They see the forest as well as the individual trees.

Dr. Lois Dodds of Heartstream Resources puts it this way: "We have the advantage of knowing situations from over 200 agencies, therefore we are able to recognize meta-level, or system level, problems which are typical to mission agencies. This provides perspective on an individual's situation, especially when we know the same kind of problem exists across the spectrum of agencies or in a given country or region of the globe. This kind of perspective is not possible when working only in one agency."

Because they will be "moving on," outsiders feel safe to hurting staff.

Those coming for assistance probably have less fear of information being shared with other people in their organization.

A consultant usually has access to a wider network of resources.

Because they work with a variety of agencies and in a variety of settings, consultants tend to be more aware of who and what is available. They can suggest resources outside the scope of one particular mission.

Consultants are cost effective.

Specific types of expertise are contracted for only when needed, so agencies may have lower ongoing overhead costs. The professional is already trained, and additional or ongoing training is their responsibility.

There is a limit to this efficiency. If the mission community is to be committed to member care, someone has to be committed to expanding the pool of resources. Every agency would prefer to work with consultants who have years of experience in working with the unique stressors of missions. New professionals need to be included in some type of mentoring process in order to provide the experienced staff needed to serve the next generation of missionaries.

Some experienced outside consultants now invite interested but less experienced mental health professionals to accompany them on field visits. The Midwest

Member Care Netword (MMCN) has arranged several such experiences.

Consultants have a stronger record for keeping missionaries on the field.
Mental health professionals who are established and experienced in their profession do not need to work with missionaries as a way to earn money or ensure job security. On the contrary, they often have to make special arrangements and sometimes professional sacrifices in order to serve missionaries. Their motivation is to help keep missionaries healthy so the objectives of the mission can be accomplished. Consultants go "there" so missionaries don't have to come back "here." Inside staff are more likely to move toward calling a missionary back to their home country.

Which Is Best?

Which will be best for your organization? Inside staff or outside consultants? Be wary of a simplistic answer; there are many factors to consider. Many organizations find their best approach is a "both/and" one. Inside staff, committed to the mental health care of all members, can call on outside consultants for specific assistance as needed and also make use of a variety of programs offered by independent organizations when appropriate. Conversely, even "regular" outside consultants usually collaborate with in-house member care staff or other mission representatives for the most effective approach to service. Many types of programs and approaches are described in this book.

As the field of missionary care continues to grow and mature, new models of service delivery are emerging. (See Section VI of this book for some examples.) It is good to be open to new possibilities which may not fit into current categories. Wisdom and flexibility will help guide choices for how best to serve the mission community.

Recommended Readings

Gardner, L. M. (1992). Training and Using Member Care Workers. In O'Donnell (Ed.), *Missionary Care, Counting the Cost for World Evangelism.* Pasadena, CA: William Carey Library.

23

Organizational Consultation with Mission Agencies

John R. Powell

The best way to enhance the effectiveness of missionaries may be to work with sending agencies. In this chapter, a definition of consultation and essential characteristics of the consultant are presented. A systems approach to consulting looks at different parts of mission organizations and how they interact with and affect each other. Strategies for and modes of consulting present a wide variety of interventions.

*M*ike was in a quagmire. His workload as a key technical administrator in the field headquarters of his mission had increased exponentially, and he experienced the familiar symptoms of depression which sometimes accompanies overwork and fatigue. With great effort he was able to keep up with demands, but he was surprised by deep angry feelings. Mike believed (correctly or incorrectly) that the changing ethos of his mission didn't allow any pity for "slackers," as he felt he was. He accepted the support of his wife, but felt there was little he could do. Mike suspected that his field leader was increasingly aware of his difficulty. He was beginning to fear that he wouldn't "make it." Perhaps it would even be a relief if he were sent home.

This fictional situation has many elements which are not uncommon. Not only could Mike use help, but it would be clear to an observer that the mission, his immediate co-workers, his field supervisor and others were all being affected and might themselves benefit from assistance.

Is this situation due solely to Mike's dynamics and personality? Does the organizational system contribute to it? Do organizational dynamics work to maintain the situation or prevent its resolution? If Mike should leave the field, what are the implications for the mission, his co-workers, himself, and his family? If he is successfully treated and recovers, what can he do to prevent the recurrence of depression? What could the mission do?

This situation and the questions it raises form an example of what can sometimes be successfully addressed by a mental health professional providing consultation from a systems or organizational viewpoint in collaboration with mission leadership. This consulting approach would involve not only Mike, whose mental health is on a downward slide, but also the missionaries, national workers and leadership who form the community in which he lives and works. The approach would be sensitive to the context in which the situation has developed.

With concurrence and collaboration of appropriate mission leadership, this approach would not only include providing help to Mike, but would look at the organizational systems involved. Is there some change or improvement that might prevent similar situations from occurring? Would a timely consulting visit be likely to help? What questions should be asked to determine whether a consultant would be appropriate? Is this more than just an individual issue? Are there contributing factors in the organization?

This chapter will address what is meant by consulting, some observations regarding consultation, and key elements to consider including aspects of the consultant, the organization, and approaches in working collaboratively to help find solutions to the problem(s) for which the consulting services were engaged.

What is Consulting?

In the interface between mental health professionals and missions the terms *consultation* and *consultant* are now widely used. Different meanings and usage of the terms evoke differing reactions. In some instances *consultation* is played down because of an assumed status difference between consultant and consultee. The terms may be used comfortably with the understanding that what actually matters is the quality of relationship, the competencies of those involved and the usefulness of outcome.

This chapter is written from the point of view of an outside consultant, though principles apply equally to professionals who are part of a mission agency staff.

What goes on is not defined by the terms, but by the relationship, process, sharing of information and expertise and, yes, by results. Ideally, these terms take on precise meaning and help establish parameters for the consultation.

Over the past quarter century the broad field of consulting has rapidly expanded and developed an impressive literature. The theory and practice of managerial, educational, psychological and mental health consultation have been prominent. Many books reflect the growth and effectiveness of consulting.

One example is *Psychological Consultation: Introduction to Theory and Practice* (Brown, Pryzwansky and Schulte, 1999), which provides a detailed introduction to and excellent overview of the field. Others are by Caplan (1970) and Caplan and Caplan (1993), which along with others by the same author(s) are seminal in the field's development.

There are several on process consultation by Schein (1969; 1999) which have been especially adaptable to mental health professionals. An early landmark work by Blake and Mouton (1976) is foundational, coming from the approach of industrial/organizational psychology. Many more could be cited; the resource on psychological consultation, above, is a good first choice for study.

Definition of Consultation

Consultation with missions has distinctive features. Here is a broad and flexible definition:

Consultation with missions is a collaborative, respectful process utilizing the skills and expertise of both consultant and mission personnel to effect a remedy or improvement which enhances effectiveness in fulfilling mission objectives.

Characteristics of consultation include:

- A respectful and mutual relationship between the consultant and those in the mission
- Use of valuable and complementary skills
- Desire to serve Christ through consultation activities
- Utilizing relevant expertise in a respectful and understanding manner
- Complementing the skills, expertise and responsibilities of those within the mission
- Directed toward fruitful and fulfilling growth, effectiveness and satisfaction
- Assists missionaries to live out their calling before God

Some Fundamental Observations

The essence of consultation in missions is mission personnel and mental health professionals working together in a process of defining need, formulating objectives and developing desired approaches. The consultant provides expertise and services complementary to that provided from within the mission in order to move the needs, problems, or issues toward fulfillment or remedy. The consultant also learns from the consultee; the obtained results come from collaboration.

The consultant must communicate and build relationships with those who can provide the information necessary to understanding the situation both in specifics and in context. Common ground for assessment and addressing the situation comes both from our common commitments to Christ and from the uniqueness of individual relationships. Although there is different expertise and responsibility, there is equality of persons before God which allows each to contribute to the whole. Paul, in discussing the meaning of Body in I Corinthians 12, affirms respect for all and valuing of the contributions of each person.

Taking a broader view and utilizing knowledge of systems can be complex, but usually results in more effective outcomes both for the individual at risk and for others not yet affected. As the example shows, concurrent work in several areas is a good approach, though in some situations working in a singular mode may be the most desirable (e.g. providing only individual services, or only personnel consultation, or only systemic interventions).

Most consultations requiring this multi-modal approach are best handled by having two consultants rather than one, but one sometimes works well. In the initial stages, a very important part of determining the approach is establishing the proper relationship with key mission personnel, and *always* having prayerful and thoughtful reflection before the Lord before embarking beyond the initial exploratory stage. For example, "Am I the right person for this situation at this time?" "Can what may be needed be done with full concurrence from mission officials?" "Am I clearly hearing the 'still, small voice' about moving ahead before doing so?"

When the consultant has not sufficiently explored and assessed the situation requiring consultation, he or she may agree too quickly to a particular approach—an error soon regretted! For example, it is tempting to say yes to doing a week's seminar with availability between sessions for counseling, because families are not getting along with one another, morale is dropping and effectiveness is slipping.

Further inquiry might suggest reasons for this situation, and with more thorough consideration, the consultant and consultee may discover an approach to the problem which allows a fuller use of the consultant's expertise and results in a better solution.

Before planning a consultation, the wise consultant studies and seeks to understand the history of the organization, its leadership philosophy and the background and style of relevant personnel. When this accomplished up front, there is more economy of time and effort and usually better outcomes. It avoids disrupting the intervention process to understand these variables. Having established categories for in-process understanding without needing to go back for basic information makes the process go more smoothly.

The Person of the Consultant

A key to effective consulting resides in the *person* of the consultant. Personal integrity, reflected in both inward and outward qualities, the ability to relate well to a variety of persons in a range of levels within the organization, and expertise relative to the situation on which the consultation focuses are hallmarks of this person. Characteristics desirable for a consultant are summarized by the following:

Committed

- Deep and abiding faith in and commitment to Christ, demonstrated through professional understanding and practice, relationships, and servanthood in life and work
- Committed to the cause of missions expressed by a commitment to learning from those within the mission, from the host culture, and from other consultants
- Committed to seeking, learning and pursuing the direction God has for each situation

Competent

- Background, training and experience for addressing the situation in question
- Relevant degrees and licensure or certification consistent with representations made
- Awareness of limitations as well as realistic confidence in abilities
- Confine services to areas in which training and experience demonstrate competency, and avoid attempts to work beyond those areas. In mission situations some try to "help" outside their competency, but dedicated incompetency is still incompetency.

Caring

- Both the ability to care and the practical demonstration of the love we have in Christ

- An inward understanding and outward expressions of the teachings of Christ in Chapters 13-16 of the Gospel of John
- Listening, really listening, is a key to caring. Often, to be heard is to be healed.

Clarity

- Clarity about one's identity and a good sense of interpersonal boundaries
- Ability to provide clarity in relationships
- Understanding cross-cultural behaviors and dynamics, and clear respect for the boundaries and prerogatives of others
- Understanding the mission structure, its history and organizational culture
- Ability to work toward clarity where it is lacking
- Clarity about one's own strengths and weaknesses and reasonable *ownership* of these qualities. Romans 12:3, "...not to think more highly of himself than he ought to think, but to think so as to have sound judgement, as God has allotted to each a measure of faith." (NAS)

Communicative

- Able to communicate concepts, feelings and, ideas in a relational manner
- Awareness of consistencies as well as conflicts between verbal and non-verbal communication
- Sensitivity in hearing others; able to listen in such a way as to *really* understand what is said
- Skills in spoken and written communication

Connected

- To others through sound and healthy relationships in all areas of life
- Through prayer, especially during travel and consultation
- With prayer supporters through reports of how God answered
- With those on the field receiving consultant services
- With God through prayer, spiritual disciplines and fellowship with other believers

Accountable

- Welcomes and has appropriate relationships for professional, personal, relational and spiritual accountability
- Openness to suggestions, encouragement, correction and learning from others
- Accountability relationships within the mission where consultation takes place

This list is not exhaustive, and it is unlikely that any consultant has all to an optimal degree. These characteristics are offered for guidance in the growth and development of consultants and for missions in their selection of or ongoing relationship with a consultant.

The attitudes and behaviors of consultant from outside the organization and in a culture not one's own, are very important to the success of a consultation and may be predictive of its outcome. Karen Carr (2002), in a sensitive article entitled "A Guest in Their World," discusses the importance of attitude and sensitivity as a clinical psychologist "guest" in the world of missions. She concludes, "We have a lot to learn. And many from the missions community are willing and able to teach us and welcome us as guests in their world." (p.328).

A Look at Systems

Any mission organization is a complex system, containing many sub-systems. Many sets of relationships, characteristics and behaviors combine to create a whole greater than the sum of its parts. Within the overall ethos of a mission, each set of relationships has its own characteristics but all relate to the whole. A change in one part of the system affects other parts; when changes occur, the whole becomes different and in turn has further effects on the sub-systems and the individuals within them.

Characteristics of systems are determined by many factors such as formal and informal policies and procedures, influence from outside the system (e.g. working in a country with hostility toward Christians, missionaries and/or outsiders), individual personalities, team dynamics, work groups and living areas, and not least, the style, manner, activities and philosophy of leaders, from the top down.

Fran White (1992) has developed an analysis of dimensions and patterns which exist in mission organizations. From a systems point of view, she describes patterns as they relate to the dimensions of *cohesion, boundaries, adaptation, regulation* and *communication* (p. 235-246). The central point on each dimension, where the extremes are counterbalanced, is the healthiest place for a mission organization to be. While all the dimensions are important and work together to constitute a healthy whole, in my experience the dimension of *regulation* often provides an entry point to a fuller understanding of the other dimensions.

The healthy center of the *regulation* dimension is *structured flexibility*, with the extremes being *rigid regulation* at one end and *chaotic regulation* at the other. Factors influencing regulation are leadership, discipline, negotiation, degree of organization and values. White discusses the points and details of each dimension and relates them to mission organizations. (p 239-240).

Concepts such as these provide tools with which the consultant can assess and understand aspects of a mission organization and, in collaboration with appropriate mission personnel, develop remedies, suggest more healthy features and work toward enhancement. A number of models from the field of organizational consulting are available, though White's is particularly useful in that it was developed for missions.

The role of mental health consultants in missions has largely been providing mental health services, including pre-field testing and psychological assessments, on-field and homeside counseling and therapy, and leading seminars and workshops. Other services are consultation with mission leadership on personnel issues and, more recently, crisis intervention and debriefing. The mental health consultant with a systems viewpoint usually brings expertise in these basic areas with an eye on the broader context, and may see characteristics in the mission which, if addressed, would serve the well being of missionaries and possibly reduce the need for some mental health services.

In an expanded understanding of mental health consultation, concern with personnel issues, leader/missionary relationships, organizational and systems dynamics, program planning, assessments of leadership style and characteristics and even mission policy, become areas where mental health consultants can have useful input. Other areas include intersections between mental and physical health, intra-mission relationships, conflict resolution, team building, family life, and satisfaction and effectiveness.

Research on mission-related issues is also within the expertise of some mental health consultants. This is an area which could profit from more activity, especially in cooperative, multi-mission endeavors. The research on attrition reported in the book *Too Valuable to Lose* (Taylor 1997) is an example. Another is that of MK CART/CORE projects discussed in Chapter 56 of this volume.

The consultant with this broader view tries to be aware of how the process and results of consultation in one area of the mission affect other areas (subsystems), and tailors services accordingly. More missions are beginning to utilize this broader expertise, and mental health professionals are appearing by invitation at the policy making and executive levels in missions. While this type of organizational consulting is often *indirect* in that it may not involve direct services *to* missionaries, it nonetheless is *for* their welfare, care and effectiveness.

Many field consultations involve both. A psychologist colleague who recently became director of his mission's member care department says a significant part of his time is requested for consultation with other leaders in the mission regarding how their decisions and departmental operations affect the work and well being of missionaries.

A Consultation Strategy - Stages

Effective consultation has five important and interlocking parts:

1. **Initial Contact** – a preliminary exploration, gathering information about the situation, and if there is agreement, discussion of preliminary contract arrangements and movement to the next step.

2. **Tentative Problem/Issue/Need Identification** – More data are gathered, further discussion with relevant mission personnel regarding the situation, development of objectives, type of services and establishment of parameters of responsibility for both parties. Joint decision to move forward and contract is made pending further information gathering regarding the specific program, process or interventions which may be desirable. Time frame, expenses, and other details are solidified. Final details follow the administration of a questionnaire or a needs assessment.

3. **Consultant's Assessment** – Utilizing information to date, the consultant, in collaboration with consultee, shares views on the issue and how it can be addressed. Recommends specific activities or actions.

4. **Actual Consultation.** This may be direct and/or indirect or in other modes discussed below. Anticipation of in-process changes is discussed and arrangements are made for regular communication and feedback during the specific consulting activities.

5.   **Action Plan and Follow-up.** Though often overlooked, it is important to develop an action plan and follow-up procedures with the consultee with some later point of accountability. This might include both at-completion and delayed evaluation of the process by those involved, periodic communication regarding defined areas, or a further visit by the consultant.

A Consultation Strategy - Modes

As the initial contact is made and assessment is completed, decisions need to be made regarding the particular mode of the consultation. Basically, the modes are:

1.   **Provisional.** Both parties agree that the best approach is for the consultant to provide direct services to missionaries regarding identified issues. This may involve individual counseling, seminars, team building, conflict resolution, debriefing, or crisis intervention, to mention a few. Preventive or enhancement services are valuable in maintaining a healthy missionary corps. Whatever is provided, moving through each of the above stages is important.

2.   **Prescriptive.** Following the assessment, it is agreed that the best approach to the issue is for the consultant to recommend certain actions or steps which the mission can take to remedy the situation. This may require further study or research on the part of the consultant, and perhaps coaching or mentoring, but it is usually something that can be carried out by mission personnel with input from the consultant.

One example would be for area directors to make more frequent field visits following a protocol developed by the consultant in conjunction with area directors. Another might be a regular ministry review, periodic de-briefing, or spiritual restoration time for missionaries. At the systems level, it might be changes in personnel policies or practices which help to maintain balance in missionaries' work, family and spiritual life. A more extreme example is changes or dismissal of personnel or leadership following appropriate assessment and understanding.

3.   **Combination.** An integrated approach to the situation uses a combination of the above. The case study is a good example of this and demonstrates the value of continuity of care or consultation which relies on relationships built over time with mission leaders as a foundation for other strategies.

4.   **Collaborative.** While the above modes are all collaborative in the sense of the consultant and mission working closely together and each contributing their expertise and understanding, this focuses on mission representatives directly sharing in the services provided. For example, a person in the member care department might work together with the consultant in providing team building exercises, a seminar on conflict management or in crisis debriefing. Or, as in the above case, an administrator might join some individual counseling sessions with the consultant (with appropriate release of information considerations) as a missionary or couple work toward changes in work and/or family responsibilities in order to function more fully.

Conclusion

This chapter has touched on several aspects of mental health professionals consulting in areas beyond the provision of mental health services, especially in organizational consulting. The field of possibilities here is large. They are still in the stages of infancy, however, given the rapid development of the field of consulting and the present state of knowledge in this area.

As mission leaders and mental health professionals come together, an important beginning point is the affirmation of the relationship with Christ which binds them together and mutual respect and appreciation for one another's gifts, skills and calling.

For the outside consultant, it is always important to enter the mission organization at a level where the leaders have power to make changes which may be recommended as a result of the consultation. For the mission leaders, it is important to ascertain that the consultant has the competency required for the consultation and the personal qualities and values that allow him or her to relate to a range of people within the mission.

It is important to note that the outside consultant has no structural power within the mission organization. Any power is the power of influence and the relevance and helpfulness of suggestions and recommendations which may be made. Relationships play a key role in this.

As relationships continue to develop between mission agencies and mental health professionals new opportunities for collaboration will no doubt develop. May they enhance the vitality of missionaries, affirm one another's gifts and bring glory to God.

References

Blake, R. R. & Mouton, J.S. (1976). *Consultation.* Reading, MA. Addison-Wesley

Brown, D., Pryzwansky, W.B. & Schulte, A.C. (1999). *Psychological consultation: introduction to theory and practice.* Needham Heights, MA: Allyn Bacon

Caplan, G. (1970). *The theory and practice of mental health consultation.* New York: Basic Books.

Caplan, G. and Caplan, R. B. (1993). *Mental health consultation and collaboration.* San Francisco, CA: Jossey-Bass.

Carr, K. F. (2002). A guest in their world. In O'Donnell, K. (Ed.) *Doing member care well: Perspectives and practices from around the world.* Pasadena, CA: William Carey Library.

Schein, E. H. (1969). *Process consultation.* Reading, MA: Addison-Wesley

Schein, E. H. (1999). *Process consultation revisited: building the helping relationship.* Reading, MA: Addison-Wesley.

White, F. (1992). The dynamics of healthy missions. In O'Donnell, K. *(ed.). Missionary care: Counting the cost of world evangelization.* Pasadena, CA: William Carey Press.

24

What Mission CEOs Want from Mental Health Professionals

Paul McKaughan

*F*orty years ago, when I began working in missions, virtually no mental health professionals were involved at any point. There was little psychological screening of candidates, and very few mental health professionals were familiar with the unique issues involved in cross-cultural ministry.

Today mental health care for missionaries is a veritable industry. The expansion of mental health services for missionaries parallels the growth of pastoral care for Christians in the U.S. The profession of mental health in missions has its own sub-specialties of pastoral care, cross-cultural adaptation, crisis intervention, and even organizational development.

In order to address the topic of what mission CEOs want from mental health professionals, I sent a simple, informal survey to some 100 member agencies of the Evangelical Fellowship of Mission Agencies (EFMA), which I serve as president. 25% of the agencies responded. The survey was a quick-and-dirty sort of inquiry and did not meet the requirements for academic research. However, the results give a good sampling of what mission CEOs are thinking about the area of mental health and missions.

Common Uses of Mental Health Professionals

Most of the mental health professionals used by EFMA agencies which responded to the survey are not part of the mission staff, but are outside consultants. The most common use of mental health professionals is in candidate screening; 90% of respondents said they use such professionals regularly in candidate processes. Their degree of satisfaction was surprising to me—about a third

Mental health professionals typically work with personnel staff and field leadership of mission agencies and have little contact with the CEOs. This chapter reports on an informal survey of mission CEOs who were asked about mental health services given to their agencies. The number one issue for CEOs is the need for more communication in a language the CEO can understand. Thinking corporately is a key to effective consultation.

of those who use mental health professionals say they are always or marginally satisfied.

The use of mental health professionals in candidate screening grew out of the realization that mission organizations needed help as they tried to determine whether candidates would be effective and successful missionaries when they got to the field, and whether they would withstand the stresses and demands of missionary life and serve more than a few years. It was assumed that tests and interviews by professionals would be better predictors than interviews by mission personnel executives or board member who were not trained in assessment but had responsibility for interviewing and decision making.

It would be interesting if research could demonstrate whether or not missionary effectiveness has increased as a result of more thorough screening, and whether the quality of life of missionaries has improved. It would be difficult to determine, because so many other factors have changed in the last few decades.

Most respondents to the survey said their agencies consult with mental health professionals frequently; only a few said it was once in a while. No one said they never consulted with mental health professionals.

Long-term Relationships

The majority of respondents have long-term relationships with their mental health consultants—three to five years or more. 40% of respondents have used the same mental health professionals as consultants for over six years, and have developed good relationships over time. In that amount of time, the consultants and executives become "known quantities" to each other and there is a development of confidence and comfort. The mental health professional also becomes more familiar with the ethos and unique characteristics of the mission organization.

None of the respondents said they were very or somewhat dissatisfied with the consultants they used. The majority said they were very satisfied or marginally satisfied with mental health professionals.

Knowledge and Support of the Agency

Of the respondents, 70% of CEO's said the consultants they were using knew, agreed with and supported the mission of the agency. However, a majority revealed that there has been tension between the mental health professional and the agency caused by the interventions of the consultant. About a third said mental health professionals are much more supportive of individuals whom they counsel than of the agency. About two thirds of respondents feel that the mental health professionals they work with have a balanced view of the mission agency and the individual candidate or missionary.

Areas for Intervention

Apart from candidate screening, the most common areas for which mission agencies request help from mental health professionals are:

- First tier, most common by far: marriage and family, including children's issues
- Second tier: team dynamics, depression and burnout

- Third tier, far less frequent than first two tiers: crisis intervention, candidate issues, cross-cultural adaptation

The frequency of needing mental health professionals to deal with marriage and family issues reflects that many of these problems are arising, and the mission personnel departments or other executives don't feel competent to handle them. Common issues are relationships between husbands and wives and a variety of concerns related to children.

Mission organizations and systems have become very professional, with specialists in many different areas. Many of these specialists are on the staff of mission agencies; others are outside consultants. Mission executives don't feel they have the competency or expertise in-house to work through problems in interpersonal areas. They do not feel they can maintain mental health professionals on staff, so they prefer to outsource these services rather than bringing mental health professionals into their system.

Top Issues for Mission CEOs

The survey asked mission CEOs what was the one issue they would like brought to mental health professionals. By far, the first issue was a need for better communication, discussed below. Other issues were not even close in rank. Their comments highlight the need to build trust between mental health professionals and executives.

Two other issues were distant seconds: better candidate screening and the cost of counseling. Regarding candidate screening—CEO's would like better candidate screening; they would like the magic process that would identify and screen out every candidate who is going to have a problem later, so the mission doesn't have to spend its human and financial resources dealing with them.

The cost of follow-up counseling is becoming a burden for agencies. Many times needs are identified when missionaries are overseas and a recommendation is made that they return to the U.S. for counseling or get counseling during their next home assignment. Unlike medical treatment, costs for counseling have not traditionally been part of missionary care. Such costs can create a significant hardship for some agencies in spite of the willingness of mental health professionals, in some instances, to see missionaries at reduced rates.

The Number One Issue: Communication

Communication is the #1 issue for CEOs, starting with building a relationship and a climate of trust between the organization and its top management and the mental health professional. Relationships must be built with agency management and not just the personnel people. Usually mental health professionals have their closest working relationships with staff who are on the third administrative level in the organization, and there has been little direct communication and development of trust at the very top, where policies are formulated and decisions are made.

Mission CEOs deal with at least two groups of professionals who have their own language and talk about their area of expertise in ways the executive does not understand. Those two groups are mental health professionals and technology "gurus." The CEO really doesn't understand what they are talking about. He reads a report which says something very meaningful to the counselor, but it doesn't mean anything to the CEO. *Mental health professionals need to communicate in language executives can understand.* There is no way to serve the agency and its missions well without clear, straightforward communication, both with personnel or member care staff and with top executives and management teams.

A second communication issue is ambiguity about who the client is—who is the mental health professional serving? Is it God and God's mission in the world, to glorify Jesus among all people? Or is the client the individual missionary, so the counselor's primary concern is serving that individual? Or is it the agency and its particular mission? Are mental health professionals part of the mission team, or are they isolated "fixers"? These questions place a high priority on clarification of goals and the need for closer collaboration in determining the role and function of the consultant.

Mental health professionals need to be able to articulate a balance between these top three concerns to the senior executive or management team so that they know very clearly where the consultant is coming from. Otherwise executives are surprised and confused when they feel that the mental health professional supports the mission, but the recommendations which are made seem skewed completely toward individual needs, including continued therapy for the missionary. Mental health professionals need to have a good understanding of the organization and a sensitivity to the impact of their recommendations on those within it.

Expectations of CEOs

It's important to remember when talking to top executives that CEOs consult resource people because they want things or people fixed. They want issues resolved. They don't want long, drawn-out, inarticulate or confusing discussions of possible outcomes. If they refer someone it's because they want the situation resolved.

However, CEOs may not have a realistic view of how long and what it will take to get resolution. Someone has said we don't have personality conflicts, we have conflicts of expectation. Many times the senior executive team has very unrealistic expectations of what mental health professionals can do for the organization as well as for the individuals they refer. It's very important that consultants are clear in the communication process, setting up expectations so unmet expectations don't surface.

If a mental health professional works with an organization for three or six or ten years, it's his or her responsibility to build expectations appropriately. They can't let the agency put some kind of "infallibility trip" on them. They must be honest about what they can and can't do and very frank about their limitations. To do that, it is necessary to know themselves and their own limitations, and to know the realistic needs of the mission.

Thinking Corporately

It would be helpful for mental health professionals as they interface with senior executives to develop the skill of thinking corporately. Most mental health professional skills have been developed primarily for working with individuals, but corporate culture and structure impact individual lives and the whole mission of the organization. There seem to be positive changes occurring in this arena.

Become familiar with the agency structures and its constraints. There are things the agency can and can't do. For example, if they are a part of a denomination, there may be constraints on them by the organizational entity to which the mission is responsible. Consultants need to know what those limits are so they can operate within the system.

Keep the big picture in mind – it's all about God's mission, not merely the well-being of the individual or the family. Mental health professionals need the perspective of participation in God's mission in the world, as well as a sense of partnership with the specific mission of the agency they serve. Consultants should think in terms of "our mission" not "their mission."

At the same time, prescriptive behaviors are sometimes necessary. Sick cultures exist in mission agencies. It can be demonstrated historically that there are mission subcultures that abuse people, and that people are constantly destroyed by these sick cultures. In such cases, even when individual players are changed, the results seem to be the same. Mental health professionals need to become involved with organizational development issues and to help the organization find solutions, both for individuals and systemically.

Prophetic intervention in the life of the organization is essential. Consultants can't deal with individuals in isolation. After gathering the facts, they must begin to speak to the issues of abuses of power and position, but to do it to the people involved in a Biblical fashion. Too often a counselor takes the side of the individual who is hurt by the organization, and doesn't help the organization resolve the issues that may have caused the problem. Professionals working with agencies have a responsibility to be engaged in this. Given an understanding and sensitive approach, mission leaders generally welcome an outside perspective.

"Chaortic" Structures and the Last Days

We are in a new age. The world has changed and continues to change constantly. We live in a day of what has been called "chaortic" structures—structures that look a lot like chaos but have a modicum of organization that keeps them from sliding over the edge. Cross-cultural adjustments are constantly in flux. There are pastoral necessities that we all face constantly. Crisis intervention is much more commonly needed in this stressful and unpredictable environment.

St. Peter encountered some of these things. We read in II Peter, chapter 3:

> Dear friends, this is now my second letter to you. I've written both of them as reminders to stimulate you to wholesome thinking. I want you to recall the words spoken in the past by the holy prophets and the command given by our Lord and Savior through the apostles. First of all, you must understand that in the last days scoffers will come, scoffing and following in their own evil desires. . . .
>
> The Lord is not slow in keeping his promises, as some understand slowness. He is patient with you, not wanting anyone to perish, but that everyone should come to repentance. But the Day of the Lord will come like a thief. The heavens will disappear with a roar. The elements will be destroyed by fire, and the earth and everything in it be laid bare. Since everyone will be destroyed in this way, what kind of people ought we to

be? You ought to live holy and godly lives as you look forward to the Day of God and speed its coming.

Peter the apostle was in the mental health business. He wrote two books of the Bible so that his readers would be stimulated to wholesome thinking. Consulting the original Greek language for the meaning of that, the main idea is the faculty for understanding, feeling and desiring—Peter wanted it to be wholesome. The image for wholesome is that of something unfolding and exposed to the sun.

Peter wanted his readers to be wholesome thinking people amidst the confusion and destruction of the last days. As they lived holy and godly lives and looked forward to the day of Christ's coming, they speeded its coming. How can we speed Christ's coming? That is a question many have wrestled with. In Matthew 24 Jesus said, "This gospel of the kingdom shall be preached in the whole world as a testimony to all nations, and then the end will come."

Let us be about that task: making the Gospel known, participating in God's mission by enhancing the effectiveness of the servants of God, and hastening the coming of Christ.

Part V

Models for Preventive Services

25

Dimensions of Care in the Missions Community

Glenn C. Taylor

*M*issionary care has received increasing attention in recent years. This may be a result of increasing pressure on missionaries in today's world or of seeing more clearly the relationship between the care of personnel and their endurance and effectiveness. On the other hand, we may be more aware that the quality of our care for each other within the Christian community dramatically impacts the effectiveness of our witness.

David Pollock (1997) emphasizes the relationship between the **Great Commandment** (*...that you love one another as I have loved you*) and the **Great Commission** (*Go into all the world...*). If we would be effective in evangelism, we must learn the art of caring for each other, for that is the most effective witness we have to draw people to Jesus Christ. Pollock asks whether our obedience to the Great Commission has preempted obedience to the Great Commandment, from which missionary care flows.

Care for one another, including missionaries, is one result of experiencing and putting into practice Paul's prayer in Ephesians 3:14-21:

> *For this reason I kneel before the Father...I pray that out his glorious riches he may strengthen you with power through his Spirit in your inner being, so that Christ may dwell in your hearts through faith. And I pray that you, being rooted and established in love, may have power, together with all the saints, to grasp how wide and long and high and deep is the love of Christ, and to know this love that surpasses knowledge – that you may be filled to the measure of all the fullness of God.*

The term care has many meanings, and care is expressed in many ways. Caring for one another is an effective means of Christian witness. This chapter looks at a comprehensive definition of care and different ways care may be received in terms of the experience of the person. Elements in a concert of care are identified as divine care, self care, mutual care, organizational care, church care, and professional care.

The source of all care is Divine Care, modeled in the relationships within the Godhead, demonstrated in the Father sending the Son, the Son redeeming humankind, and the coming of the Spirit to indwell and enable believers. Such Divine Care is expressed in our love and care for each other and, in our context, the missionary community. When we are "rooted and established in love" we are enabled to express that love in dimensions of care which reflect love's Source.

In this chapter, we will consider missionary care as *a response to the person in terms of their experience, at the place they are along their career path, beginning at the access point they provide but going beyond as indicated and responding with a concert of care appropriate to the individual.* We will consider each element of that definition, beginning with the concept of care itself.

A Definition of Care

Care is defined in this chapter as *the actions of one person intentionally responding to conscious or unconscious needs of another for their well-being, protection or enhancement.* Care may be proactive, preventive, or remedial; it may be direct or indirect. "Care" is a broader concept than "counseling" or "therapy." It includes a wide range of interventions which may or may not be professional in nature, and may be provided by professionals, family, friends, or colleagues. Neither professional nor non-professional care is given priority in importance over the other; both are important.

Individual needs for care, whether conscious or unconscious, are experienced in many different ways at different times and are expressed with great variety. The presenting problem as identified by the individual or mission leadership (in the case of referral) may not be the most significant issue but may represent the most painful part of the person's immediate experience, or the part of their experience they are able to acknowledge at that time. The problem may be defined by the culture of the organization or community of which the person is a part. On the other hand, different professional care givers will define the need for care differently, depending on their orientation, training or biases.

The Continuum of Care Along the Career Path

One dimension of missionary care is related to the missionary life cycle, from family of origin through preparation, overseas service, home ministry, and repatriation or retirement. There are very different needs for care depending on the individual's or family's developmental stage as well as their place on a missionary career path. See Chapter 8, "Whirling Teacups: A Bi-cycle Analysis of Missionary Growth" by Bruce Swanson for a fuller treatment of this dimension. Care through the life cycle of the missionary, if practiced, would provide a seamless flow of care resulting in more effective and enduring service and the fulfillment of Christ's command that we love one another deeply.

Care along the career path has far-reaching implications for the understanding of the dimensions of care necessary and appropriate in the missions community. Such care will require the involvement of many individuals, non-professional and professional, in the life of the prospective candidate and the missionary at various points in their career. Parents, siblings, pastors, youth workers, psychologists, medical doctors, administrators, fellow-missionaries, spouses, and sometimes other specialists will be involved. It is important for the mental health professional to remember that his or her interventions are only one aspect, albeit a significant one, of the whole continuum of care. Integration and/or cooperation with other caregivers enhances the contributions of each.

Care Defined by the Experience of the Person

It is useful to see care from the perspective of the *experience of the person* rather than from the formulations of various professional disciplines. Exposure to the work of psychiatrist Roberto Assagioli (1985) provided the impetus for me to develop this perspective. I believe that people respond to their world of experience through an interactive process involving six pathways. Since I have not shared the concepts in this section widely, I invite creative and corrective input from readers.

Six Pathways to the World of Experience

- Senses
- Emotions
- Desires
- Cognitions
- Intuition
- Imagination

The self interacts with the world of experience through each of these six pathways, but individuals place greater emphasis on some of these pathways and less

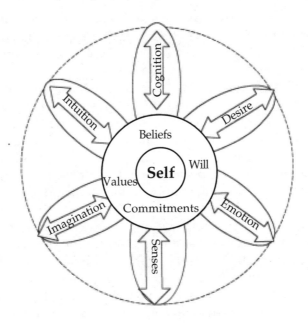

World of Experience

on others. For example, some people are very "sense" oriented and find sensual input to be a much clearer definition of reality than others who emphasize "emotion" or "imagination."

Professional training may predispose care-givers to a greater emphasis on one dimension than on another. Also, in some periods of history greater emphasis has been placed on one or another of these pathways. The twentieth century may be seen as the period when emotions and desires became the significant measure of the Self and its understanding of reality.

People tend to define or experience fulfillment in selected pathways. For example, if I define the well-being of my self in terms of my emotional experience, I may place an inappropriate emphasis upon that dimension of my experience. Or, I may define my well-being in terms of my desires, and experience discontent or "dis-ease" if my desires are not fulfilled.

Placing an undue emphasis on any one of these pathways and defining one's well-being in terms of the experiences of that pathway may lead to significant problems, as listed below.

Pathway:	Distorted emphasis may produce:
Senses	Materialistic understanding
Emotion	Neurotic perspective
Desire	Hedonistic pursuits
Cognition	Rationalistic explanations
Intuition	Mystical definitions
Imagination	Psychotic experiences

How does one avoid (or help others to avoid) the potential distortions that are present in an exaggerated focus on each pathway? It appears that the self is in need of some defense or protection; this may be provided by circling the self with Beliefs, values, commitments and a strong will (see diagram).

This may be illustrated with Biblical examples: Moses responded with emotional pain, which he personalized, when his God-given leadership was rejected. God reframed the matter in terms of rebellion against himself (Numbers 13-17). Elijah focused on his fear of Jezebel, separated himself from others of faith, and became suicidal in his aloneness (1 Kings 19). On the other hand, Joseph saw his dreams as well as his abuse in Egypt from a perspective outside of himself by asking, "What is God doing here?" rather than focusing simply on his own emotional or rational understanding of his experience. In the end he declared, "God intended it for good" (Genesis 37-50). We all interpret experience through these pathways and identify the well-being of the self in terms of that interpretive response.

Five domains in which resources for coping with stress can be defined have been outlined by Allen L. Hammer and M. Susan Marting in their *Coping Resource Inventory* (Form D, 1987). One is the "Spiritual/Philosophical Domain," which measures the degree to which actions of individuals are guided by stable and consistent values derived from religious, familial, or cultural tradition or from personal philosophy. Such values serve to define the meaning of potentially stressful events and prescribe strategies for responding effectively. The person who defines and protects the self in terms of beliefs, values and commitments is not only able to cope more effectively but also has a more accurate and helpful definition of self and reality than the person who defines self in terms of the pathways of experience.

Therapeutically it is often effective to differentiate a person's self from their feelings in response to an experience. Similarly, differentiating one's self from desires, imagination, thoughts, etc., distancing one's self and controlling one's self by an exercise of the will so that one functions in a manner consistent with one's commitment may lead to more healthy and productive functioning. Assagioli places great emphasis upon strengthening the will. I would choose to assist the person in defining the content of the belief system—the values and the commitments that one would choose to be the foci of one's life.

What are the implications of such an approach for care? It is helpful to identify which pathway may be most emphasized by the person, and/or which pathway may be used to define the well-being of the self. People tend to reveal their use of different pathways by their selection of professional assistance. That is, if I experience physical pain I may seek a doctor. If I define the pain as emotional, I may seek psychological help. If I define the problem as one of desire, I may realize the need for moral guidance and seek out a pastor.

My bias is to focus on the internal dimensions of beliefs, values and commitments which lead into the spiritual dimensions of one's being. This leads us into the areas of morality, virtue, or goodness and their impact on well-being. Although historically the behavioral sciences have largely removed morality and value discussions from the scope of therapeutic interventions, I believe a Christian professional helper must address these issues. Nicholas of the Yale Department of Psychiatry has opened this discussion in *The Mystery of Goodness* (1994).

This model helps clarify the need for care as a response to the person *as they experience life* and forges an integration of the disciplines which respond. Over time, all of the professional disciplines as well as the responses of administrators, fellow travelers, etc. are needed to respond to the multi-faceted experiences of individuals.

Accessing the Person

What is my *access point* as a professional engaging with a person? By access point, I mean the entrance by which the person invites or permits me to enter their life. When individuals invite intervention, they do so in terms of their experience or understanding of the discomfort, pain, dis-ease or need for healing of which they are aware. At Missionary Health Institute (MHI), people may arrive defining their need in terms of physical pain or disease. However, after they invite the doctor into their lives at that access point, the physician may discover other areas of need that the patient had little or no awareness of.

The multiplicity of access points and the degree to which they may diffuse, cover or obfuscate issues necessitates the care giver having an acute awareness of access points. We need to realize that an access point is only a place to enter the person's life and may have little to do with the real issues that need to be addressed.

Let me suggest six points of access. The reader may wish to define others as well.

1. **Physical**: The focus is on health concerns, nutritional concerns, or well-

being issues. In our culture there is more freedom to focus on medical concerns because they entail less embarrassment or disgrace.

2. **Intellectual**: The symptoms usually focused on are confused thinking, difficulty in recall, irrationality, "crazy thoughts," sad thoughts or disturbing thought content.

3. **Emotional**: People request care because of depressive, sad feelings, anger, phobias or other concerns about their emotional experience.

4. **Interpersonal**: People define their problems in terms that involve or implicate others with whom they experience conflict or discomfort.

5. **Contextual**: Individuals see their physical, social or organizational environment as the issue needing to be addressed.

6. **Spiritual**: Individuals focus on loss of faith, doubt, changes in values, beliefs or commitment. Some express fear or experience of abandonment by God, tensions in their faith community, guilt, loss of meaning or loss of hope.

There are many factors that influence an individual's definition of their problems, which in turn determines the access point. Culture, family, the pain threshold, the availability of help, or the degree of insight or analytical skills of the person may influence the access point they offer to the care giver. Shame and guilt either from within the person or from the social or organizational context will often determine the access point.

We must honor the access point at which people invite us into their lives and take seriously their identification of symptoms. That does not mean that we accept the person's definition or diagnosis of their problem. It is only a place to begin. We frequently have to expand the contract to lead them into a deeper and wider understanding of their experience, exploring other areas which may be more difficult or painful.

Identifying Primary Issues and Creating a Concert of Care

Once the care giver has engaged the person by honoring their identified issue, it may be necessary to bring a microscopic view or a wide-angle view to the situation and in doing so redefine or reframe the problem. The care giver may shift the focus by providing other perspectives, thus identifying issues that may be more foundational or clarifying the sequence most helpful in dealing with multiple issues.

For example, a person may need to have their depression eased via chemical intervention before they can benefit from other interventions dealing with underlying issues which generate the depression. It is often necessary to understand the context in which the individual experienced their symptoms or tensions. Often systemic factors contribute to the problem at least as significantly as individual factors.

Providing adequate and effective care may necessitate activating caregivers at various levels of the environment of the individual. Sometimes a co-ordination of various dimensions of care provided by many potential care givers (including self-care) is necessary. Individual therapeutic or medical intervention may be foundational, but frequently issues related to marriage, children, or co-workers must be addressed. This often requires the effective engagement of teachers, house-parents, administrators or peers in the process of care. Consultants may be most effective in influencing the organizational structures of the mission. Both home and national churches may also play significant roles in care.

Joe was urged by a friend to seek counseling for his depression. He agreed to a medical/psychiatric assessment which revealed that he was moderately suicidal, but he refused to take the medication prescribed and discontinued counseling. A few days later he met with his regular prayer/support group. When they asked about his progress, he said the counselor had refused to see him because he refused to take medication. The group would not let him get away with that. If he did not take his medication voluntarily, they would visit each day to see that he did. They cared too much to let him continue as he was.

Joe then took his medication and requested continuance of the counseling. In a relatively short period of counseling, he resolved many issues, began to function well, went off medication and has functioned well for many years. Counseling, medical intervention and, especially, Joe's peer group provided a concert of care that was more effective than any caregiver would have been alone.

The concert of care will include as many persons, professional or non-professional, as it takes to respond to the physical, intellectual, emotional, interpersonal, contextual or spiritual dimensions of the person. Thus, we have defined care as *a response to the person in terms of their experience, at the place they are along their career path, beginning at the access point they provide but going beyond as indicated and responding with a concert of care appropriate to the individual.*

A concert of care requires multi-disciplinary intervention. This, in turn, requires awareness of the contribution of other care givers, an honoring of their intervention and the humility to invite or recommend such. Each care giver must function within the parameters and limits of their expertise whether they are professionals or non-professionals.

Care: A Multi-dimensional Perspective

To provide effective care requires an acknowledgment of the multi-dimensional aspects of care and the breadth of care. Briefly, the foundation of all care is *Divine Care*. The model of care provided by Father, Son, and Holy Spirit in their relation to each other and their response to humankind is basic. One cannot read the Scripture without being aware of the care of the Father for the Son. The role of the Comforter is clearly defined in Scripture and is experience by believers.

Another essential element in the concert of care is *Self Care*. The disciplines of the Christian life need to be learned and practiced by anyone entering ministry. Self care also involves caring for one's physical, emotional, mental and relational well-being. People in ministry often fail to practice self care, avoiding adequate recreation, rest, or pacing of their expenditure of energy. This leads to over-extension that is motivated by the heart of the person rather than by the real needs of the ministry.

One of the strong emphases of Scripture is *Mutual Care* of believers for one another. The "one another" passages and those that focus on encouraging or comforting each other in the Christian community demonstrate that this is a primary dimension of care. Paul became discouraged when he tried to stand alone and learned to depend upon the mutual care he received from his fellow-workers. My observation over many years is that missionaries are not trained, nor do most have the vision, for

MISSIONARY CARE
(Glenn C. Taylor)

I. **Divine Care**
- Redemption
- Healing
- Holy Spirit Ministry

II. **Self Care**
- Spiritual
- Emotional
- Physical
- Recreational
- Social

III. **Mutual Care**
- Family
- Team
- Friendships
- Peers

IV. **Organizational Care**
- Administrative
- Systemic Issues
- Affirmative Supervision
- Accountability

V. **Church Care**
- Prayer
- Support
- Communication
- National Church

VI. **Professional Care**
- Medical/Psychiatric
- Pastoral
- Psychological
- Trauma Response

mutual care. Our tendency to focus our attention and energy on "the lost" frequently closes us off from the mutual ministry we could give to and receive from each other.

Mission organizations often fail entirely to recognize the responsibility of *Organizational Care.* Understanding of the systemic nature of organizations and their impact on the well-being and productivity of employees or members has developed over many decades. Christian organizations, above all others, must be concerned about the impact of systemic variables upon the well-being of their members and the impact of these factors on the effectiveness and endurance in ministry of their workers.

There has been and will continue to be a need for *Professional Care* in many different forms. Medicine, psychiatry, psychology, social work, organizational consultation, conflict resolution specialists and many others can contribute effectively to the completion of the task of missions. It is my conviction that if we trained missionaries in self-care and mutual care, and enhanced the organizational care provided by missions, we would reduce dramatically the need for professional care.

Those who offer services to mission organizations have a primary responsibility to understand the contribution of the individual to personal self care, the role of mutual care in Christian community, the impact of organizational variables and the roles of a variety of professionals who may be effectively involved. It is incumbent on all to integrate these contributions into a meaningful and effective concert of care. We must seek to achieve a synergism among the dimensions of care that will enhance the effectiveness of our God-given work in missions.

The Scripture indicates that the laborer is worthy of his hire. We may rephrase that statement, with due respect, to read that the laborer is worthy of a concert of care that will increase effectiveness in achieving the divinely commissioned task of missions. Missionary care is an activity with many dimensions, and many participants are required to do it well.

Recommended Readings

Assagioli, R. (1985). *The Act of Will*. New York: Penguin.

Hammer, A.L. & Marting, M.S. (1987) *Coping Resource Inventory-Form D*. Palo Alto, CA: Consulting Psychologists Press.

Nicholas, M. (1994). *The Mystery of Goodness*. N.Y.: W.W. Norton & Co., Inc.

Pollock, D. (1997). Developing a Flow of Care. *Interact*, Vol. 7, No. 1.

26

Choosing the Right People: Factors to Consider in Pre-field Assessment

David L. Wickstrom

A young husband and wife just out of Bible college felt called to work among primitive tribal folk in an unevangelized area. The husband was an outgoing, spontaneous and non-scheduled person who loved interacting and sharing the Gospel with people. He often spent hours getting to know people in his neighborhood and had an easy-going "we'll deal with it as it comes" outlook on life. He rarely noticed when things were out of order, and if he did notice he figured, "I'll get to it later."

His wife, on the other hand, was reserved and needed a great deal of time alone. She was shy and unsure of herself when interacting with people, especially about sharing the Gospel, preferring one-on-one in teaching situations. She discipled people with in-depth Bible studies and liked to have structure and a plan for each day. When things were in disarray she usually became stressed and irritable—frequently at her easy-going husband— and she did not like unexpected changes in her daily schedule.

The mission placed this couple in a remote area where villagers were extremely relational and curious and valued an "open-door policy." They felt free to walk into one another's homes uninvited, day or night. To refuse such a visitor would be rude. This placement worked well for the husband, as he liked having nationals walk into the house unannounced to finger and examine objects in the house and/or to peer in through the windows. He cared little about personal possessions and valued opportunities to interact with new people, invite them for a meal or pay a return visit, providing more opportunities to share

Much of the early service provided by mental health professionals in missions was pre-field assessment. It is widely practiced today and makes an important contribution to the well-being and effectiveness of missionaries. This chapter gives a brief history, assessment criteria, a rationale for psychological tests, benefits of well-done professional evaluations, and pitfalls which can cause assessments to be misleading and potentially harmful.

the Gospel.

The wife, however, felt constantly violated, resented the intrusions, feared for her safety and worried that precious keepsakes would be broken or stolen. Things were constantly being misplaced, she had little sense of privacy, and she became more and more irritated. She took her anger out on her husband, who tried to encourage and reassure his wife, reminding her that God had called them to these people and that things would get better. At times he tried to listen to her and comfort her. When exasperated he admonished her to "stop being so self-centered; just buck up and accept the culture as it is." He alternated between resenting his wife and resenting the people who caused her considerable pain.

Eventually, he withdrew from his wife and worked with the nationals to avoid his wife's anger and unhappiness. He became discouraged, doubted his call and wondered why they had ever come to this place. When he verbalized these feelings, his wife felt anger that her husband would "even think of leaving the mission field," and guilt because, "my husband is a really nice guy, so his unhappiness must be my fault. And we were called to reach these people for Christ, so I'm letting God down." She began to doubt her own call, became lethargic, and eventually her anxiety, anger and depression increased until she withdrew from everyone—husband, co-workers and nationals.

At that point the mission asked the family to return home and not come back. With deep feelings of guilt and failure the family complied. What went wrong?

Many factors contributed: goals of the mission, initial zeal of the young couple, lack of understanding of personal factors, inadequate knowledge of the culture, inappropriate placement, and other factors likely interacted. What *is* apparent is that a complete pre-field assessment of the couple, including a psychological assessment, could have helped prevent this tragedy.

History of Pre-Service Assessments

It is helpful to review some of the history of pre-service assessments and the factors which are addressed.

In 1980 and 1981, at the first Missions and Mental Health conferences held in Indiana, "hot" topics of discussion involved the use of pre-field psychological evaluations to select missionaries. In 1981, Stan Skarsten pointed out that "both the mission organization and the missionary are aware of the need to spend the Lord's money responsibly. If a missionary quits her job, raises $10,000 for travel as well as monthly support, goes to the field for three or four months, finds that she is totally unsuitable for the job and returns home, it is assumed that the Lord's money has been unwisely spent. Thus, many mission organizations have started an assessment program for candidates." (Skarsten, 1981).

Skarsten noted a variety of perspectives on the need for psychological assessments. Some agencies stated that they have been sending out missionaries for nearly one hundred years and they don't need any help, thank you! Others were more progressive, and wanted a thorough assessment of candidates. However, they tended not to know what critical factors to assess. A third group made new attempts to assess candi-dates, partly through outside consultation from people who share their spiritual convictions as well as having adequate professional training and knowledge.

However, when asked what they wanted to have tested, they were at a loss. They began to consider their past experience in terms of missionary performance as well as some of the practical and clinical knowledge which the professionals had.

Assessment Criteria

Stan and his colleagues ferreted out some of the critical factors involved in predicting the performance of a missionary candidate, including work performance, interpersonal relations and general emotional stability. Four criteria were identified as significant areas to assess:

- Personality
- Mental Health
- Vocational Interests
- Marriage and Family (Skarsten, 1981)

Others provided assessments with slightly different emphases. In Peabody, Massachusetts, a multi-disciplinary group known as Health Integration Services (H.I.S.) assessed candidates for psychological variables and also provided physical exams. The variables H.I.S. measured included the following:

- Interests and preferences
- Skill areas
- General personality, adaptation and integration
- Inter-personal and self-esteem issues
- Other significant areas including temperament, theological issues and Christian maturity (Ensworth, 1981)

Although H.I.S. is no longer functioning as a group, they provided comprehensive guidelines which are used by many missions today.

Perry Draper, who provided services in the early 1980s, believed there were eight different factors or traits which could be considered vital to successful missionary experience (Draper, 1980). Not all were measurable by using standardized tests, but they could be identified through tests combined with interviews. They were:

- **A teachable attitude**—the ability to receive instruction, learn by it, and profit from experience.
- **Adaptability**—the ability to adjust to new situations and people and to have a fairly high tolerance for ambiguity.
- **Interpersonal relationships**—the ability to get along with most people, work out problem areas, and to readjust one's own position when necessary.
- **Authority relationships**—the ability to work under authority without either undue resentment or over-dependence on authority.
- **Personal autonomy**—the ability to begin a task, see it through, and to work toward realistic goals on a reasonably consistent basis. Motivation comes from within and is not dependent on someone else.
- **Personal stability**—being able to maintain reasonable self-control under stress, not be given to extremes of reaction, distortion of perception, or over-impulsiveness.

- **Single or married adjustment**—to demonstrate that one has worked through relationships with the opposite sex, whether single or married, and is able to handle oneself in the present state reasonably well. Married couples need to demonstrate their ability to communicate openly and share themselves freely in all aspects of marriage.

Since the early 1980's the dimensions of personal functioning focused on in assessment have remained fairly constant, though different styles and emphases are used. Specific tests and measures used also vary among individuals and mission boards.

Effective pre-field assessment involves much more than the use of standardized psychological tests. This chapter will explore issues related to pre-field assessment:
- the rationale for using extensive psychological test batteries
- the benefits and potential liabilities associated with psychological evaluations
- the extent and type of psychological assessments used to improve selection and reduce attrition
- other factors which need to be considered

Rationale, or "Why use psychological tests to assess missionaries?"

Opponents of psychological testing often present the following arguments: "Psychological tests are expensive and unnecessary." "The apostle Paul and the early church spread the Gospel quite effectively without using them. In fact, if Paul had gone through a psychological assessment, he likely would not have been appointed." "For hundreds of years, missions appointed people primarily on the basis of being *called by God* to be a missionary. Isn't that enough?"

These comments can cause mental health professionals to squirm, for they imply that the professional is not needed in missions, is presumptuous in assuming that he or she has more to contribute than God himself, and must not be a Christian or at least not very spiritual. Without a well-defined personal understanding of psychological assessments, the professional is likely to feel confused about the issue.

Space does not allow a discussion of all the questions and objections. The simple answer to the question, "Why use psychological evaluations?" is "Because they are helpful."

Benefits of Psychological Evaluations

Pre-field evaluations are helpful in a number of ways. First, they help identify people who would be ineffective or detrimental to the work. We would not send a person who is wheelchair-bound and has other serious physical limitations to the African bush. They could not live independently, and would require so much care that other missionaries would be limited in fulfilling their own responsibilities.

In the same way, a person who is mentally, emotionally or interpersonally handicapped will likely not be able to handle the realities of many mission placements. The time and energy required to care for this person would drain the personal resources and lower the effectiveness of other missionaries.

Second, pre-field evaluations can help prepare missionary candidates by identifying personal issues and areas in which they need to grow in order to be most effective. By working on these issues *prior* to going overseas, candidates or new appointees can overcome them or reduce their impact when they arrive on the field.

Third, pre-field evaluations can help mission organizations make placement decisions. By identifying gifts, talents, strengths and weaknesses, new missionaries can be placed where they will be most fulfilled and most useful. The Scripture is very clear that all believers are gifted in specific ways, and when these gifts are used properly the Body of Christ is built up and edified (Eph. 4). But when believers do not use their gifts, or when there are divisions in the body because of personality traits and sins exhibited by individuals, the work of Christ suffers, and his Body is affected and suffers also (I Cor. 12).

Fourth, pre-field evaluations are helpful in identifying core areas for candidates and new missionaries to work on in the process of ongoing sanctification *after* they have reached their assignment. Both God and the individual bear responsibility for growth and sanctification (Philippians 2:12, 13), and pre-field evaluations are a means of identifying areas for growth.

Finally, with the growing emphasis on *teams* in missions, pre-field evaluations can help team members to understand one another better, rely on each other to use identified gifts in appropriate places and roles, and help one another in areas in which they are weak. Mutual accountability, better communication, greater respect and enjoyment of one another on the team can thus be enhanced, resulting in more effective individuals *and* teams.

When Psychological Evaluations Are Detrimental

While it is clear that psychological evaluations can be beneficial, are there also ways in which they can be detrimental? The answer is yes, in at least five ways.

Untrained Administrator or Interpreter

The first and perhaps most obvious is when a an untrained person is asked to administer tests and evaluate the candidate from the data obtained. Erroneous, unethical and illegal judgments will be made. A variation of this is when a trained professional evaluates the candidate but provides decision makers an inadequate or incomplete explanation of the results in a written report. Mission leadership, including personnel directors and team leaders, some of whom may have a little familiarity with the tests but no training, can draw erroneous conclusions.

It is vital that professionals communicate test results as completely and accurately as possible in their findings and recommendations. It is also vital that untrained personnel neither administer nor interpret tests for mission organizations and that professionals warn missions against such practices.

Lack of Psychological Interview

Second, tests can be detrimental when candidates are evaluated without an accompanying psychological interview. Candidates often answer questions based on a misunderstanding of the question or a test-taking bias, and often take the tests in less than desirable circumstances. If overly tired, highly stressed, or in a hurry, candidates may make mistakes which will not accurately reflect their general functioning. The professional must review the test results with the candidate and draw on other data such as references and life history questionnaires. The professional needs to ask definitive, appropriate and probing questions in order to ascertain the accuracy of the test results and gain a clearer perspective regarding the candidate's previous and present functioning.

Candidate Draws Erroneous Conclusions

Third, psychological evaluations can be detrimental when the candidate is given test results and concludes *erroneously* that, good or bad, "This is the way I am, and I'll always be this way. A professional has told me this is true, and who am I to argue? I will have to accept it, and other people will too."

This conclusion can lead candidates either to a fatalistic belief that they are bad and cannot change, thus setting them up for negative behavior and relationships, or it may lead to an inflated view of self. With an inflated view, individuals may be unwilling to listen to or learn from constructive criticism because, "I couldn't have done such a thing. I'm above that. A professional said so." While a professional may not have said exactly what the individual heard, misconstruing the test results can lead to serious problems later. It is wise for professionals conducting pre-field evaluations to ascertain, if possible, the interpretations that candidates may have drawn from the evaluation and feedback.

Erroneous Expectations

Fourth—and a variation of the previous paragraph—is when leadership either in the sending office or on the field draws erroneous conclusions, expecting someone either to be a problem or a "shining star" because of statements made in a report. The leader may "set up" the new missionary to behave in certain ways. If the leaders have been forewarned about potential problems, they may *look for* problems which may not really be there and create an atmosphere of mistrust and suspicion. Or if the leadership has been told that the new missionaries are of a high caliber, expectations may be so high that they cannot be reached, or the missionaries may work so hard that they "burn out." Or they may gain a reputation of being superior to co-workers, thus alienating those with whom they work.

If a missionary becomes a "problem" after a few years of service, leaders may want to know the results of pre-field testing in order to look for causes or precedents of the negative behavior rather than dealing with what may be a situational difficulty. Sometimes leaders blame the professional who did the testing for not picking up subtle nuances which might have given a warning of potential problems. The professional then risks being ignored on future evaluations, losing his or her reputation with the mission or others who need services, and may lose the job of conducting pre-field evaluations.

To prevent these eventualities, professionals need to educate mission agencies regarding issues which may need investigation, rather than just give the results of pre-field assessments. This may open other opportunities for the professional to become involved with and knowledgeable about the mission agency. The professional will likely become more intimately acquainted with and may be asked to intervene in situations missionaries face. Professionals may be asked to advise leadership, helping resolve interpersonal conflicts, helping leaders make more informed decisions in emergencies, or guiding decision makers in placement issues. Thus the mission agency, the missionaries, and the professionals involved can all benefit.

Need to Evaluate the Whole Family

A fifth and often-overlooked issue relates to the need to evaluate the whole family. The husband and wife only may be evaluated on an individual basis since they are identified as the missionaries. This can be a mistake in several ways. First, while it is important to evaluate both adults individually, the functioning of the marriage and family system also needs to be assessed. Numerous studies, including the extensive one cited in *Too Valuable To Lose,* indicate that a primary reason for missionary attrition is "family issues." Often marital issues cause early departure, for these conflicts often have reverberating effects on the couple, their children, and coworkers, both nationals and missionaries.

Children who are uprooted and separated from their homes, schools and friends, especially teenagers, may be extremely resistant to moving overseas. An angry teenager may act out and cause considerable damage to the work and reputation of parents and mission alike. To exclude teens from pre-field evaluation can be extremely risky. Younger children are often more pliable and may look forward to a "great adventure," but they also can represent a risk if they are not included. It is vital that both the family system and various subsystems be evaluated.

The Old Testament states that young men should not go to war in the first year of marriage, but should remain at home to pleasure their wives. Similarly, newlywed candidates wishing to do battle with the forces of evil should not become "involved in the battle" for at least a year, but should focus on necessary adjustments so that both husband and wife can serve more effectively. Prior to going overseas, there should be follow-up interviews with the couple, both individually and together. A standardized test measuring marital satisfaction can be used and reviewed with the couple.

Couples who are not newlyweds but who are without children should have their relationship evaluated, both in individual sessions and together. Standardized tests may be used to identify potential difficulties, and guidelines and advice may be given to help couples maintain a healthy relationship.

Families should have the above evaluations but also evaluations of the children. Observing how the parents and children relate with each other and interviewing the children individually and together without the parents present provides significant information. Areas of potential unrest or conflict can be explored and recommendations made.

Finally, professionals need to investigate issues of the family of origin. Dave Pollock of Interaction points out that unresolved issues with family and friends can create considerable distress on the field. A wise husband and wife will resolve these issues or reconcile relationships with parents prior to missionary service.

Couples often say that they battled with *each other* because one or both sets of parents wanted them to stay home where their parents could see them and the grandchildren on a regular basis. Some missionaries' parents have either disowned or threatened to disown their children if they became missionaries. These issues need to be resolved prior to overseas placement. Otherwise, there is great potential for early attrition or diminished effectiveness. It is vital that marriage and family issues be addressed prior to candidates being appointed and serving overseas.

27

Tools Used to Assess Missionaries

David Wickstrom

*T*his chapter will discuss tests which are most frequently used by mission agencies, including the value and applications of each test, following Skarsten (1981) regarding critical factors to assess.

Personality, Temperament and Preferences

A candidate's personal style or temperament greatly impacts potential effectiveness overseas, as well as interpersonal relationships with co-workers, both national and expatriate. It can help guide decisions about placement and type of work. For the couple described at the beginning of Chapter 26, a pre-field assessment of personal style would have helped administrators avoid a poor placement and would have prevented considerable pain and reduction of effectiveness.

Tools used to assess *personal style* include the following:

Myers-Briggs Type Indicator (MBTI)

The MBTI is a self-report inventory in which the test-taker states a preference between one of two or three choices. Results are given in four dimensions, each of which is a continuum indicating the strength of preference. The MBTI indicates

- Where test-takers prefer to focus their attention (Extraversion or Introversion)
- The way they prefer to take in information (Sensing or Intuition)
- The way they prefer to make decisions (Thinking or Feeling)
- How they orient themselves to the external world (Judging or Perceiving)

Pre-service assessment typically involves paper-and-pencil tests as well as interviews and other methods of assessment. This chapter presents brief descriptions of the most commonly used tests for missionary candidates. This information is useful for the non-professional who seeks to understand options for pre-service assessment.

There is no right or wrong to these preferences. The MBTI can help candidates understand themselves, identify how their styles are expressed in interactions with people and the world in general, and learn the strengths and the weaknesses their "Type." It is useful in building teams, as each "type" demonstrates unique gifts, and people can be placed in positions appropriate to their natural ways of thinking and doing. The missionary couple in the remote village setting was moved to a placement which provided a good fit for both husband and wife, where they flourished. The MBTI identifies interactional patterns and styles of problem-solving and communication which can enhance the effectiveness of teams.

Personal Preference System, known as the DISC

The DISC has been widely used in business, and many find it to be a more reliable indicator of personal style and functioning than the MBTI. Test takers indicate one preference in each group of four words and develop a four-scale profile. The test provides narrative descriptions of each profile: "D" for "Dominant" style, "I" for "Influencing," "S" for "Steady," and "C" for "Cautious." The DISC is useful in building teams, especially when team members are given the chance to demonstrate their unique gifts and understand the personal style of each of the team members. Assignment and placement decisions can also be based on personal profiles.

Taylor-Johnson Temperament Analysis (TJTA)

The TJTA is best known for marital and pre-marital counseling. Perry Draper describes the TJTA as useful "for assessing the more surface level temperaments and attitudes . . . and how these might affect interpersonal relationships. These characteristics are more subject to change over time and do not have the accuracy of the MMPI, but are effective in assessing present and potential interpersonal relationships, particularly within a marriage."

Test-takers first answer the True-False questions about themselves and then answer the questions regarding their partners. Comparing scale scores shows discrepancies between self-perception and how others perceive an individual. Discussion of discrepancies may explain blind spots, potential and actual conflicts, and potential solutions for conflicts.

16 Personality Factors Test (16PF)

This test defines sixteen different scales. It is widely used to assess personal style, and provides a rough measure of potential areas of pathology. The 16PF also indicates whether questions were answered in a defensive, "faking good" manner or in a self-deprecating, "faking bad" manner. Combining scores from the 16 scales provides information on more "global" factors such as introversion/extraversion, tough-mindedness, independence, anxiety and self-control.

The 16PF is relatively easy to explain to candidates; the profile is quite readable (especially in the 5th edition version); and it tends to be non-threatening for candidates to read and interpret. The 16PF can act as a backup to more complex tests such as the MMPI.

Test of Attentional and Interpersonal Style (TAIS)

The TAIS can be used for employment decisions. It was designed to measure processes which determine a person's decision-making abilities, ability to function in a crisis or under pressure, and ability to analyze environmental situations and to integrate information. Besides identifying areas of greatest effectiveness, the TAIS performs well in identifying potential problems, including lack of discipline, performance anxiety, depression and unhappiness, tendencies to become overloaded and confused, and difficulty getting along with others.

Skarsten used the TAIS as part of his battery of tests, and reported that the majority of candidates found it to be more helpful than almost any other test. Skarsten and his associates are the only ones known by this author to use the TAIS routinely with missionary candidates.

Mental Health

Trying to identify what constitutes good mental health of missionaries is a real challenge, somewhat like "trying to nail Jello to a wall," but factors which contribute to a person's effective functioning as a missionary have been identified. Perry Draper listed several qualities associated with mental health, including "a teachable attitude, adaptability, interpersonal relationships, authority relationships, personal autonomy and personal stability." (Draper, 1980) The following are the most commonly used instruments for assessing mental health.

Minnesota Multiphasic Personality Inventory-2 (MMPI)

Sales of the first version of the MMPI were discontinued in 2000, but some professionals still prefer to use it because it contains subscales which are helpful in assessing missionary candidates and which are not included on the MMPI-2.

The MMPI's primary purpose is to *assess problem and potential problem* areas in personality functioning. It identifies symptoms of depression, anxiety, psychosis, impulsiveness, social avoidance, impaired judgment and areas of interpersonal difficulties, as well as test-taking attitudes and defensive structures. Numerous content scales and experimental scales provide extensive information about such useful factors as stress-resistance, how people handle anger, relationships with families of origin and response to authority.

Some professionals utilize *only* the MMPI along with an extensive life history questionnaire, and the MMPI is the only instrument with extensive research history regarding its efficacy in predicting missionary functioning. The 16PF is frequently used in conjunction with the MMPI.

Personality Research Form-E

This instrument is more effectively used as a measure of personal style and provides a range of behaviors and attitudes which fall in the "normal" range. However, there is also a measure of test-taking attitude and defensiveness which can be useful. When the factors measured fall at either extreme of a continuum, it provides clues to potential dysfunction.

Vocational Interests and Abilities

Given the wide variety of roles and positions available in missions, it is important to assess personal interest and aptitude. This has become increasingly important in the last decade, as many missionary candidates express their desire to use their unique talents and interests in specific ways rather filling in wherever needed. In the past twenty years, some missions have used interest inventories to assess candidates, but it seems rare that organizations actually make use of the results.

References

Draper, P. L. (1980) Evaluating Candidates for Missionary Service. Paper presented at Mental Health and Missions Conference, Angola, IN.

Skarsten, S. & Morehouse, M. (1981). Critical Factors in Missionary Assessment and Placement. Paper presented at Mental Health and Missions Conference, Angola, IN.

28

The Call: Psychological, Cultural and Spiritual

Leslie Andrews, Carl Miller, and
Esther Schubert

For centuries, people have become missionaries in response to God's call. A call was the primary motivator and qualifier for mission service. Today, a sense of call is still important, but it is understood in the context of mental and emotional health. This chapter describes true calls and counterfeit calls. Nine unhealthy patterns which may masquerade as calls are identified, in addition to psychological and cultural factors which may lead to a false sense of call.

*T*he concept of "call" has been discussed from many viewpoints for generations. Marjory Foyle suggests that it is a "distinct, personal experience of God's leading, supported by Scriptures and confirmed by other people."

The concept of "call" has several meanings, including our calling to be Christians, "followers of the Way," and the concept of being called to be a missionary, pastor, or to another particular vocation. When a missionary candidate tells us "I am called" we can easily ignore the possibility that what he perceives to be a call might be mere cultural proddings or psychological agendas.

We must distinguish between the calling (cf. "called out ones" or *ecclesia*) inherent in our salvation and the definition of call which includes God's calling in our lives to vocation and vision. In the first we are called to know him, but in the second, we are called to service. That is, first we are called to Someone, and secondly, we are called to vocations and places. In either one, the calling must not supercede the Caller.

God normally calls us along the lines of our giftedness, but the purpose of giftedness is stewardship and service, not selfishness. Following this, our calling should lead to a choice of career or vocation.

In the context of Western individualism, it is easy to believe that individual callings take precedence over corporate callings. The entire goal of the prefield process is to match the individual's sense of calling with the overall needs of the *ecclesia*, in this case represented by mission sending organization. If the individual call contradicts the guidance of those in authority over us (corporate call),

then the genuineness of that call should be questioned. Discernment is necessary by the sending organization, mental health care professionals who are involved in the selection process, the candidate himself, and supporters.

Common Characteristics of Call

There are six common characteristics in the Evangelical understanding of call.

1.   There is often a struggle in the individual's life which leads to a *crisis experience* and culminates in obedience. Depending on the theological background of the individual, this may be called consecration, dedication, or the baptism of the Holy Spirit.

2.   Call also requires *confirmation from external sources*. These may be mentors, church leaders, or mission leaders as well as Scripture, prayer, and the leading of the Holy Spirit.

3.   The call *endures over time*. It may not be limited to just one job or location; the vision and vocation often endure for a lifetime.

4.   Individuals who have answered their call develop a *desire to prepare* both educationally and with ministry experience. Paul, immediately after his Damascus Road conversion and call, went to Arabia for 3 years of preparation prior to his active ministry.

5.   Individuals who answer a genuine call usually find that their *eyes are opened* to the lostness of others. This leads to empathy and a servant's heart.

6.   A genuine call must be *Christ-centered*; the call never takes precedence over the Caller.

Some missionary candidates present with narcissistic or conceited personalities. In contrast, although a person with a genuine call may be chosen, gifted, and special, his sense of call includes the awareness that being chosen is a miracle of God's love. According to Os Guinness, "One of the most common, subtle, and manipulative distortions of call is in religious empire building . . . the call of God is enlisted in this setting to camouflage ego, stifle disagreement, excuse failure, decry opposition, and guild the commemorative plaque of success."

Accountability and humility are the opposites of narcissism and serve as the great antidotes to counterfeit call. The way a missionary candidate approaches the prefield process is almost as important as how he scores on the tests. Is the candidate so convinced of his call that he is not teachable or willing to submit to authority? If so, there may be psychological or cultural agendas masquerading as call.

Guinness comments "consideration of calling always has to precede consider-ations of career, and we can seek the deepest satisfaction of work only within the perspectives ... of calling. Calling is the supreme motivation, the ultimate 'why'" (p. 149). MK CART/CORE research indicates that missionary perseverance correlates positively with a specific call or vision in contrast to a general sense of going because of needs overseas.

Successfully answering an individual call requires readiness in four areas:

1.   Spiritual maturity
2.   Educational training for the task at hand

3. Physical health for the location considered
4. Psychological wholeness

Psychological Counterfeits

To understand the psychological counterfeits of call in the context of missions, it is helpful to understand the dilemma that personnel departments face. In many agencies, the recruitment department is separate from the personnel or selection department. While working with a large number of potential recruits, it may be difficult for personnel directors to discern the difference between an individual who has a psychological agenda that makes him feel called to missions, and the genuine calling of God. Until a mission has been "burned" by sending someone overseas who is obviously not fit, the personnel department may ignore a negative psychiatric evaluation and send a person overseas who feels called.

However, as mental health care professionals are involved in educating mission sending agencies, the agencies are becoming more aware of unconscious defense mechanisms or psychological agendas and how these can masquerade as calls.

Nine Unhealthy Patterns

Here are nine unhealthy patterns sometimes seen in missionary candidates.

1. *Making God love me.* This is very much like winning Dad's approval. Candidates who come from abusive backgrounds usually feel that they are not worthwhile, and may transfer that sense of worthlessness into their relationship with God. Thus sacrificing to become a missionary may be an unconscious effort to win God's approval.

2. *Need for family, identity, security, or belonging.* Christians represent the family of God and there is strong approval for individuals who become missionaries, ministers, or find other vocations in full-time Christian service. Missionary candidates from dysfunctional families who did not feel they belonged or who were neglected in childhood may be unconsciously motivated to apply for missionary service in an effort to win approval from their new Christian family, or to belong to a caring, secure organization.

3. *Penance.* Candidates with unconscious, unresolved issues, especially sexual abuse, previous sexual behavior, abortion, or even criminal behavior may apply to missions in an effort to deal with unconscious false guilt. This is demonstrated in the movie, *The Mission.*

4. *Rash promise.* Although this tends to be a more conscious issue, there may be unconscious underpinnings. "Foxhole religion" may have to be addressed to understand underlying motives.

5. *Family pressure.* This is most commonly seen in candidates whose parents felt called to a Christian vocation but did not or could not answer that call, so they try to vicariously relive their lives through their child. Occasionally, family pressure can occur due to the parents' need for prestige within their Christian culture.

6. *The Hero.* Often specific roles are taken or demanded within dysfunctional families. The ne'er-do-well, clown, pet, or lost child is less likely to become a missionary than the hero. The hero in the dysfunctional family of origin fulfills his role by succeeding in life, overachieving, and always being good. If the unconscious

agenda of the dysfunctional family role is not addressed, the hero will likely carry that role into his Christian experience. What could be more heroic or successful than going to the mission field and living in an overseas or primitive setting?

7.   *The Rescuer.* This role may overlap with that of the hero. The rescuer may become a co-dependent missionary, social worker, pastor, or pastor's wife. This individual sets out to rescue the perishing, but can become extremely disillusioned if the perishing do not want to be rescued.

8.   *Going home.* This is most likely to occur for the MK or Third-culture kid who consciously wants to be a missionary, but on an unconscious level may be want to "go home" without a genuine personal call to missionary work. In evaluating MK or TCK candidates, it is important to find out if they are maladjusted in the U.S. (or passport country) and trying to escape by going overseas. Have they been productive while in their home country, or are they just marking time until they can get back overseas?

9.   *Personality disordered.* A small number of individuals with personality disorders apply to missions. Narcissistic candidates may look very good on the platform and may be able to raise support quickly. However, they don't wear well in the mission setting. Their unconscious issues can be quite harmful overseas. Occasionally, persons with antisocial personality disorders may apply for missionary service. Many of them tend to be rather predatory and may not be aware of their own unconscious motivations.

Cultural Counterfeits

Cultural background can also mask the calling that a person has. Family culture, local culture, and church culture can mask the call when it is not viewed through a clear, unbiased Scriptural lens. Calls may be missed because of family prejudice, racism, or bigotry. Local culture can certainly impact one's perception of call if it is strongly biased or xenophobic. Even church culture can limit interest in missions if the church is strongly monocultural and provincial.

Another significant cultural counterfeit of call occurs when an adult TCK or MK feels called to go back to the country in which he or she was raised and misinterprets that as a true spiritual call when it is actually the comfort of returning to a familiar culture.

In some small denominations individuals may feel called to ministry, but there is no emphasis on education or preparation for ministry. Such individuals rarely survive with effective ministry over time, they may not have valid confirmation from others, and in many cases, a servant's heart is not developed.

Another cultural counterfeit can be pressure by a particular church or pastor who feels a need to produce missionaries from the congregation. Individuals may feel pushed within that context to consider missions when perhaps they do not have a personal call.

A final type of cultural counterfeit can stem from a multicultural background in which the individual may feel that since he or she is comfortable with different cultures, fluent in more than one language, and experienced in travel, therefore he or she must be "called" to missions.

Conclusions

With the concept and experience of call such an important component in selection and planning for cross-cultural ministry, it becomes critical that those assessing candidates' readiness for missionary service be aware of characteristics in both genuing and counterfeit calls.

For married couples, ascertaining that each have a genuine call prior to field service may eliminate considerable stress later on for the couple as well as strife for the missionary community in which they live and/or work.

The spiritual certainty of a genuine call helps missionaries move ahead successfully, even with vitality, in difficult times. Those experiencing a counterfeit call may show some success over a short period of time after arriving on the field, but usually end up as casualties, either for themselves or someone else.

In summary, a spiritual call to ministry can sometimes be the central motivator for missionary or other full time Christian service. A genuine call can decrease the likelihood of attrition in missionaries and tentmakers. Nevertheless, there can be counterfeits to spiritual calling. These counterfeits may be unconscious, and they can occur in both psychological and cultural realms. The current emphasis on careful pre-field evaluation and testing of candidates for cross-cultural work is an effort to place persons with genuine spiritual calls in appropriate locations.

Reference

Guinness, O. (1998). *The call: Finding and fulfilling the central purpose of your life.* Nashville, TN: Word Publishing.

29

Affective Domain Training: A Critical Ingredient in Missionary Preparation

Tom Eckblad

One aspect of training for effective cross-cultural ministry that receives little attention is the "training of the heart" – training in the affective domain which includes the spiritual component of grace. "Heart" factors are more critical for early terminations than either knowledge or skill factors. This chapter gives guidance for effective training, based on the SPLICE program of Mission Training International.

*W*hat characteristics are needed to make an effective cross-cultural missionary? This question has been asked since the time of Paul and Barnabas. They argued over this issue concerning John Mark (Acts 15). Their different perspectives on this question led to the formation of a new mission agency. Paul said that John Mark was not ready to be a missionary, while Barnabas saw the future potential in this young man and was determined to give him another chance.

Though the area of incompetence in John Mark was evident both to Paul and Barnabas, for Barnabas it meant more time was needed to invest in John Mark's training, not that he should be ruled out as a missionary. Paul wanted to say, "Come back when you are ready." The outcome was that Paul and Barnabas went their separate ways.

John Mark did receive training from Barnabas. Later, Paul wrote to Timothy, saying, "Send John Mark; I have need for him." (II Tim. 4:11) Even when failure occurs or competencies are lacking, they can often be learned through adequate training and nurture.

An Essential Ingredient

Today we ask the same question. What are the characteristics of an effective cross-cultural missionary and how do we make sure those ingredients are included in the training process? When we don't the find the proper ingredients, do we provide intervention?

Missionary trainers have developed charts and lists of desirable competencies which give us a good framework for discussing issues of missionary preparation.

Examples of competencies include such things as Bible knowledge; early family formation; formal education, both secular and in ministry areas; functioning in the local church; and the sharpening of specific skills that will be used in that individual's ministry. All of these are part of the preparation process.

Another part of the preparation process is looking at how God has been active in preparing and directing the pilgrimage of individuals who will become cross-cultural ambassadors. The Holy Spirit's involvement has generally been evident long before they move into their cross-cultural ministry. Some of this preparation is acquired through formal, systematic training and other parts are ingredients which are blended in through the serendipity of God's wondrous working in people's lives. A chance meeting with a missionary that gives one person a vision for a specific country, a missionary biography that stirs another person's heart to serve, or a quiet call to missions in a church service all can contribute to the preparation of a potential missionary.

In this article we explore one aspect of training that is critical to missionary training but often lacks attention. It can take place outside a formal training setting as the Lord brings certain circumstances and insights into individuals' lives. It can also be done through intentional, informal, reflective training programs. This aspect of training is what Mission Training International programs call the area of "training of the heart." We will describe this training and look at the methodology and outcomes involved.

Understanding the Concept of "Training for the Issues of the Heart"

Much of the Western world has lost the true concept of the "heart." In American culture we have narrowed the image of heart essentially to the highs and lows of emotion. In "pop" culture, emotions are out of control either on the "high" of a newly found love or in the depths of despair over some great loss. "Heart" has become defined as surface emotions rather than the seat of our deepest thoughts and longings, its basic Biblical meaning.

From the Biblical perspective, heart is that focal point in God's creation of humankind where mind and emotions blend together to give direction to our thoughts, feelings, will, and actions. It is defined as the core of who we are.

Attending to "issues of the heart," then, becomes an important part of missionary preparation. The Scriptures say "Keep your heart with all diligence, for out of it are the issues of life." (Prov. 4:23) They also warn "The heart is deceitful above all things, and desperately wicked; who can know it? (Jer. 17:9) Vine (1966) points out that in Scripture, "...the word heart came to stand for humans' entire mental and moral activity, both rational and emotional elements. In other words, the heart is used figuratively for the hidden springs of the personal life." (Pp. 206-207) Old and New Testaments contain hundreds of references to heart, showing it as a place both of Divine influence and of base desires and spiritual blindness.

Dealing with issues of the heart does not rule out thorough study in the cognitive areas of missionary preparation, i.e. missiology, anthropology, church-planting, world religions, cross-cultural adaptation, etc. But a person with a Ph.D. in cross-cultural communication may in some cases return from overseas service more quickly than the high school educated tradesman, not because of a lack in cognitive preparation and skills training, but because he has received no training in the issues of the heart.

Training in the affective domain is one way of approaching such training. This has become an increasingly utilized area of focus and good resources are available. But training for the issues of the heart goes well beyond affective domain training because it also includes the spiritual component of grace and godly insight operating in an individual's life. This type of training brings to light incompetencies in a person's life but at the same time provides a framework in which they learn how to live with these incompetencies by finding grace which is bigger than weaknesses (II Cor. 3:4-6 and II Cor. 12:7-10).

Affective domain training focuses on the discovery and acknowledgement of attitudes, values and emotions. It provides opportunities for understanding issues of the heart more clearly and adapting or changing them as needed.

It is not unusual to find inconsistencies between values and behavior, or values and projected mission service. In such training these can often be better understood, accepted, and through God's grace, overcome or changed. A variety of instructional strategies are used with attention to experiential and interactive modalities including role playing, group tasks, and case studies. Important relationships are formed which lead to further discovery and enjoyment of learning.

Here is an example: In the context of the training program, Carol realizes that one of her highest values in life is cleanliness and order. Hygiene and putting things in their proper place are very important to her. However, she is headed for a culture where people eat out of a common bowl, share a common cup and spit on the floor. During the process of training, Carol needs to think through how she will face the issue of cleanliness and order in her new world of non-hygiene and chaos.

Is Carol disqualified from overseas service unless we can somehow reach into her affective domain and change the values of her heart, or do we say, "Carol, we perceive that cleanliness and order are very important to you. The culture into which you are moving does not have these values. How do you intend to find the grace sufficient to live in that situation?" We would love to say that we can do training that will change each of these critical areas in each person's life, but it is more realistic to say that we can explore areas of conflict and help people find means of grace to adjust.

This area of training for the issues of the heart is much more difficult to quantify and evaluate than either knowledge or skills training. But it is a more critical factor in early terminations of missionaries than either of the two other areas. We may be able to evaluate Bible knowledge and skill in preaching, but it is difficult to assess all of the areas of the heart. Reports from participants, however, point to the effectiveness of this training.

Elements of Training for Issues of the Heart

Training in the affective domain reaches into issues of the heart, though by no means touches them entirely. As missionaries in preparation participate, they are provided various means for drawing from their own hearts in practical ways that allow for personal discovery and the work of God's grace.

Work by Knowles (1984) on adult learning, written with missionaries in mind, includes many useful methodologies. Martin (1989) in a paper entitled, "A Checklist for Designing Instruction in the Affective Domain" provides a sample of eleven principles instructors should include when training in the affective domain. These are listed, followed by comments on ways they may be practiced based on experience at Mission Training International (MTI).

1. *Provide cognitive information that is new to learners, or is presented in a new way.*

In a missionary training program one of the participants may have a Ph.D. in cultural anthropology while the person sitting next to him has no clear understanding of the concept of "culture." One way to approach this situation is to have the Ph.D. define culture; this would be new for the other person. Another way would be to emphasize that a culture involves a group of people who have shared values, and that one cultural practice is to eat out of common utensils. By asking participants to drink out of the same glass, they are presented with an affective domain challenge. It is the same concept but presented in a different way.

2. *Use successive approximations either to break a task into smaller units so success can be achieved, or to gradually increase the learner's cognitive base or tolerance for an idea.*

Participants are urged to look at the values of the culture in which they will be serving and compare them to their own personal values. They are asked, "Where will the clash between your personal values and the values of your adopted country take place? The first step is to have the participants express their personal values in small groups. Through the weeks of training they are introduced to conflicting values they will face in their adopted culture. At the same time they are making friends with people outside their usual range of contacts and learning to adapt to cultural and personality differences.

3. *Model attitudes, values, emotions, etc. that are consistent with the desired behavior.*

The facilitator's responses to differences presented by the participants will provide the atmosphere for the participants to be open to change. A rigid, closed facilitator will produce a closed atmosphere. Openness and flexibility are bywords in good modeling.

4. *Use group discussions or social interactions (one-to-one, small groups, role plays, etc.) to assist learners to (a) see another position, (b) take another's perspective, (c) verbalize their own position, and/or (d) solve problems.*

The program is built around social interaction and personal reflection times. Participants also have opportunities to spend time with facilitators on an individual basis or as a couple. In the safe environment of one-on-one interaction, they can explore the application of the general principles that are being talked about in the larger group to issues in their own life. No two days of the class time in the program are identical. Role-plays, field trips, video clips, and case studies all form part of the exploration process.

5. *Use direct reinforcement to (a) establish attitudes, emotions, and values when there is consensus on the desired attitude, emotion, or value and (b) reward cooperation, participation, independence, and success.*

Applications of principles to the present situation are difficult but part of the real learning process. If we talk about eating the food in other cultures in the classroom and there a number of people who are "picky" about what is served in the dining room, we need to make the connection. If we are talking in the classroom about in-depth relationships on the field and two mothers will not let their children play together after class we must talk about it. As they deal with these issues we can see the life situations as opportunities to grow rather than reprimanding people for bad behavior.

6. *Match the learner's task to their abilities; strive for a moderate level of difficulty.*

Determine which of the individual's core values needs to be addressed during the program. Not everything can be dealt with. Show them that some of the future obstacles that seem impossible to overcome now will be eventually be surmounted in small steps. Stories of actual people doing this are helpful.

7. *Provide opportunities for the learner to take overt action.*

Keep the participants moving around the classroom doing different things: a 15 minute presentation, followed by a 30 minute case study in small groups, followed by a role play explaining what they have decided about their case study.

8. *Use the principle of contiguity to help learners associate learning in general (school, training sessions), and specific learning (affective or cognitive knowledge and skills) with a pleasant and stimulating environment.*

Creating a pleasant, safe environment is a critical issue in this type of training. We are asking the participants to look inside themselves; in order to do this they need to lower their defensive posture and relax. A well-designed conference center in the mountains is very conducive to this type of learning and exploration.

9. *Relate learner success to his or her ability and effort. Relate failure to lack of effort.*

We seek to: 1) give participants an overview of what they will face in a new culture and 2) help them determine what will be the greatest areas of difficulty. How will they find grace to succeed in these areas is a crucial element.

10. *Encourage learners to set goals for themselves, and provide opportunities for learners to work toward those goals.*

In the discovery of areas of concern for the future life and ministry there is a time when participants are encouraged to focus on finding grace in that specific area. There are a number of approaches to dealing with potential areas of difficulty: God may take away the obstacle in one's life and value system or direct the person to another location where it is not a problem. God may not take it away but give sufficient daily grace to find strength to overcome, or God may change the individual. The worst approach is to deny it is a difficulty. That is why this type of training involves some aspects of intervention.

11. Use a variety of instructional strategies, and use a variety of external conditions to facilitate affective and cognitive development.

Though the training program focuses on the affective domain, we need to provide cognitive "pegs" with which to connect the other areas. The areas of cognitive learning are outlined below, but we must realize that mastery of cognitive information does not guarantee a successful outcome in mission service.

Affective domain training requires a different setting and conditions than a cognitive seminar. One reason is that in life-changing affective domain training a person needs to reveal to the facilitator/trainer or to someone else in the community what is going on inside of them. In order for them to reveal this private, personal information, the learning community needs to develop a great deal of trust and security. Annette Simmons' book, *A Safe Place for Dangerous Truths: Using Dialogue to Overcome Fear and Distrust at Work* (available on the Internet) describes what we are trying to achieve.

This title also reflects one of the key roles of the facilitator/trainer in this type of program; to create an atmosphere of openness and learning beneath the surface, instead of just having the right answer. The learning environment becomes a place where the expression of doubts, questions, paradoxes, joys, expectations, and hopes is invited. It is a place where someone who will be in a mission setting next month can openly say, "I am not sure my marriage will survive the coming transitions." Or "This is the first time I have ever thought about how much being a missionary is going to cost me." It is a place where there is the deepest possible level of engagement. The heart issues that are dealt with vary as greatly as the participants who attend the programs.

This exploration of key heart issues is done in the context of both the sufficiency of the grace of God and the purpose of extending God's reign. Thus, the backdrop of the program is not a therapy group where wellness in individual development is the only goal. Instead, the program focuses on wholeness for the purpose of effective cross-cultural ministry. It emphasizes the glory and grace of God shining through earthen vessels who in turn have the privilege of sharing this glory and grace with others in cross-cultural settings.

We have looked at some aspects of methodology for affective domain training, but the question remains whether there are both content and objectives that can be measured and evaluated. The desire of the staff is that each participant interact with all of the different content areas. At the same time there is a desire that each participant will engage "with a burning heart" a few specific areas that are important to them.

In the biblical example of Jesus with the two disciples on the road to Emmaus, Jesus began with Moses and all the prophets and explained his death and resurrection in a systematic way. Discussing this encounter, the disciples asked, "Were not our hearts burning within us while He talked with us . . . ?" (Luke 24).

Curriculum Content

At Mission Training International, work on "issues of the heart" is done in a three-week training program known by the acronym SPLICE. Below are some of the basic areas of the curriculum.

Spiritual vitality and spiritual conflict

Lifestyle choices that will enhance your ministry and help you adapt to your new culture

Personal values and stressors that you will need to engage

Interpersonal skills that are critical for working with both colleagues and nationals

Cultural and language learning skills

Enduring the difficulties on the field (or developing a theology of suffering) and

Enjoyment of your new surroundings (or making the new culture your home)

While the classroom provides the framework for discussion about these issues, it is during meals, evenings, and weekends that the participants can personalize and apply the issues to their own lives. Thus, the program is not rushed and participants are encouraged to spend a lot of time in reflection.

Open sharing with each other of what participants are dealing with in their personal reflection times crystallizes the learning process. Sometimes the issue being dealt with by an individual seems not to be mission related, i.e. a father who abandoned the family when the participant was a little child. But we realize that the loneliness they feel now as they move into new settings is the same feeling they were overwhelmed by when their father left. Through the process of dealing with the issues of the heart, this person might explore the past loneliness they experienced as a child in the context of learning new ways to deal with the loneliness they are beginning to feel as a missionary preparing to move into a new culture. The facilitator/trainer can help bridge that gap.

How can this kind of program be evaluated? One step is to make sure participants can discuss the various issues they face in areas of SPLICE. They can recall the material later when they are overseas. But one of the basic evaluations that the staff use in evaluating the effectiveness of each of the programs is, "Did each participant engage in at least one area of the heart where they dealt honestly and openly with an area that will affect their missionary effectiveness in both their life and ministry?" If we can say that about the great percentage of participants in each program, we feel we have contributed a significant ingredient in preparing them for missionary effectiveness. At the same time, we have also helped them move toward greater wholeness wherever God leads them.

Recommended   Readings

Apps, J.W. (1966). *Teaching from the heart*. Malabar, FL: Krieger.

Goleman, Daniel (1995). *Emotional intelligence: Why it can matter more than IQ*. New York: Bantam.

Martin, B. L. (1989).   *A Checklist for designing instruction in the affective domain*. http://plaza.powersurfr.com/kegj/mar.html

Knowles, M. (1984). *The adult learner*. 3rd ed. Houston, TX: Gulf.

Simmons, A. (1999). *A safe place for dangerous truths: Using dialogue to overcome fear and distrust at work*. American Management Association.

Vine, W. E. (1966).   *Expository dictionary of New Testament words*. Westwood, NJ: Fleming H. Revell Co.

30

Training Missionaries in How to Relate Well: Pay A Little Now or A Lot Later

Ken Williams

Good interpersonal skills are critical to missionary effectiveness and longevity. Missionary candidates may have good knowledge and technical skills, but without interpersonal skills they are handicapped in relating to others, especially in cross-cultural settings. This chapter describes a training program which has been widely used, including key components of content as well as process and practical issues.

Introduction

Linda and Ian had been married for less than a year and were on their way to mission service overseas. As the time approached for leaving, serious marriage problems began to surface. They asked if I would help. As a graduate student preparing to become a counselor to Wycliffe missionaries, I told them of my lack of experience, but they wanted to give it a try. We met a couple of hours a week for a year. That was in 1971. They are still serving in missions today, and thriving in their marriage and ministry.

Looking back on those many hours together, most of our time was spent helping them learn how to relate to each other. That experience helped mold my view and model of counseling over the following 21 years. It is true that intensive psychotherapy was required in many cases. However, much of my time was spent just helping people learn how to relate well to each other—in families, teams, with friends and enemies—indeed in every relationship. Of course, a foundational aspect of healthy relating had to be their relationships with God and themselves.

Informal research on the long-term results of my counseling turned up something surprising and humbling. Generally, counseling involving more than one person at a time was reported to be more helpful than individual counseling. This included growth groups, group therapy, family therapy, and couple therapy. Apparently, clients were developing skills of how to relate to each other, and that was what many of them needed most.

Many studies on missionary attrition have found poor relationships at or near the top of lists of reasons for leaving. Recently one large mission asked all their personnel what they needed help in most. The greatest need, reported by 78%, was for help in relationships. This may be representative of missionaries in general—yet we do so little to train them how to thrive in their relationships!

Informal follow-up queries on the results of interpersonal skills training for missionaries reveals an unexpected benefit. Organizations in which a significant percentage of their staff have been trained discover that people not only relate better to each other, but the organization itself is being transformed in the way it does business, e.g., in relating to staff, in conducting committee meetings, in seeing trust as an imperative, and in providing care for its members.

Some Missionary Myths About Interpersonal Skills

In order to make changes needed in providing effective training in interpersonal skills, each mission must recognize and confront any myths they hold. Here are a few myths that have surfaced among missions:

1. *New missionaries come with the necessary interpersonal skills.*

The corollary to this is that we do not need to train them in this area. However, at least for those from western cultures, the breakdown of society, the failure of families to model healthy relationships, and the lack of biblically based interpersonal skills training at every level of education has ill prepared them for life, and particularly for the intense relationships they will encounter in most mission situations.

2. *Technical skills and/or theological knowledge are more important for success than interpersonal skills.*

Few mission agencies would admit to believing this myth, but their priorities in training demonstrate it.

3. *If people are committed Christians and called to missions, they will relate well to others of like mind.*

This needs no commentary.

4. *Our work and ministry are largely unrelated to how we relate to each other.*

Jesus' view of this is, "By this all men will know that you are my disciples, if you love one another" (John 13:34-35). While translating the N.T. for a remote language group in Guatemala, we discovered that the host people knew the intimate details of the lives of every missionary in the other four surrounding language groups! By far the most important issue was how they treated other people – their spouses, their children, other missionaries and the local people.

5. *Some people have rough edges, but they will naturally grow out of them as they mature.*

This passive, do-nothing response to missionary development has caused great harm in missions.

6. *If a missionary is needed and doing well in his or her work, treating others poorly can be tolerated.*

If you have been in field situations, you already know how one destructive person will cause immense harm across a very broad spectrum.

7. *Giving information in this area develops and improves people's skills and attitudes.*

Those who hold this myth are apt to provide lectures, books and other knowledge-based materials to their missionaries, assuming that this brings about change. As far as I can determine, receiving more facts about relating does nothing to improve skills and attitudes in this area.

There are other myths, but these are sufficient to demonstrate much of the current thinking. All this is quite negative, so let's look at the positive side: People *can* grow in their relationship skills and attitudes, and training can be effective in enhancing their development.

Since 1970 I have been involved with others in a process of helping missionaries grow in relating effectively. Granted, our first efforts were not very effective, but we have continued to improve through experience and continual evaluations by those in the learning process. Although we have not yet conducted formal research on the effectiveness of the training, informal follow-up with individuals and organizations indicate significant long-term improvement for many.

Characteristics of Effective Interpersonal Skills Training

Effective training for missionaries in interpersonal skills will have the following characteristics:

1. *Biblically-based.* My conviction is that we must base our training on Scripture, with a core belief that God has given us the teaching we need to be able to relate well – to God, to ourselves and to others. My personal goal has been to try to discover everything the Bible says about each particular issue before training others in that area. Words cannot express how much insight ensues from this process.

A very practical advantage of basing our training in Scripture is that it works extremely well cross-culturally. Mission teams and organizations are increasingly multicultural, and our training must reflect that diversity. In training experiences where as many as a dozen different cultures are represented, participants respond incredibly positively as they go through a simple process of exploring two simple questions: 1) What does God say about this aspect of relating, e.g., confronting. 2) How can we in our culture live out God's word in this area?

2. *Focused on core beliefs.* Core beliefs are firmly-held convictions that consistently motivate our behavior. We may or may not be aware of them. Core beliefs are *lived* out but not many are *thought* out; they are not reflected in what we say we believe, but in how we live. Core beliefs may be true or false, healthy or destructive. Destructive behavior patterns will only be changed as the underlying false core beliefs are examined, consciously rejected, and replaced by core beliefs that reflect the truth of God's word. Unless destructive core beliefs are addressed, people tend to give mental assent to new ways of relating, but their long-term behavior remains the same.

Core beliefs are changed not by teaching but by learning, through a sometimes painful process of confronting them by looking at consistent behavior, comparing it with what we say we believe, and discovering the core beliefs that motivate it.

Effective training in interpersonal skills gives examples of effective core beliefs, and invites participants to examine their behavior in light of them. Then participants are encouraged to wrestle with any inconsistencies between the example and what they truly believe.

It often helps to present core beliefs in somewhat extreme forms, in order to incite reactions from the participants. For example, "Everything we accomplish for God is through relationships." Rather than an absolute truth that participants are expected to passively accept, this statement is intended to cause them to wrestle with it and come up with what they truly believe, as demonstrated in their lives. They don't have to agree with the core beliefs presented!

One caveat about core beliefs: they are not the only motivator of behavior. For example, unresolved anger or fear can override one's core beliefs and cause behavior that is inconsistent with what one truly believes. Obviously when this is the case, more than a course in relationship skills is required for change.

3. *Based on a Wellness Model.* Training in interpersonal skills should be clearly separated from therapy. This training works well with basically healthy people, but it is ineffective in addressing pathology. A tendency in missions is for administrators to send dysfunctional members to interpersonal skills workshops, with the hope that pathological behavior will be corrected. This is not only ineffective, but significantly dysfunctional participants usually damage the experience for everyone else.

4. *Interactive.* Lecturing about relating is fruitless in bringing about growth in skills and attitudes. Participants must interact with the concepts in small groups, pairs, triads, and in the whole group. They need to wrestle with new ideas and attitudes, and this happens best in relationships. Sometimes this wrestling comes in the form of looking together at Scripture in new ways, and discussing how to apply it. Other times it comes from looking at one's self in new ways, being vulnerable to share with others what one sees, and struggling with what and how to change.

5. *Demonstrative.* Learners need to actually observe skills demonstrated. For example, watching demonstrations of how to manage conflict and how not to mange it provides far more transferrable insight than merely hearing or reading how to do it. As participants observe, they learn more as they actively participate by writing their observations, insights and questions, and then discussing them with others.

6. *Active.* The next stage of learning new skills is to actually practice them. To state the obvious, people learn new skills by doing them. After learning what God says about issues, and observing some ways of applying scripture, true growth in developing skills begins with the process of trying them out.

Obviously, practicing a skill once or twice does not make it a part of one's life, but it is an essential step in the process. There are four stages of developing new skills:

    a.   Awareness
    b.   Awkward stage
    c.   Do it by the numbers
    d.   Integration

Participants gain awareness through studying, discussing and observing. Most experience awkwardness as they try a new skill for the first time. But as they do it a few times, most get through this stage, and can utilize the skill by concentrating on the process. Eventually, with enough practice, the skill becomes integrated. It is a part of who they are, and they do it without consciously trying. With most skills the best we can hope for is to lead participants through the awkward stage and far enough into stage 3 so that they are able to practice the skills on their own if they choose to do so.

7.   *Reflective.* How many times have you been given time to quietly reflect during a learning session? This is usually a missing but important ingredient in developing new skills and attitudes. Learners need some time to consider what they have learned, observed and practiced, and to prayerfully contemplate what they want to do about it when they leave the learning experience.

8.   *Relevant.* The specific issues addressed must be relevant and experienced as a felt need by the participants. In many situations, this information can be best determined by conducting well-designed needs assessments before the training. In other situations, ongoing experience will determine the needs of missionaries, based on feedback from each group.

9.   *Safe and respectful.* The first tasks of trainers are to build safety and demonstrate respect for the learners. These can be done in many ways, and depend on the cultures of the participants. Interactive learning experiences can be very threatening for some people, as they are asked to share their lives with others, to try new skills or old skills in new ways, and to be vulnerable to one another.

We have found that for seasoned missionaries to experience safety and respect, participation in the learning experience must be completely voluntary, with no pressure whatever. This can be a very difficult change for missions in which personnel are routinely required to all go through the same training. An exception to this rule is in pre-field training programs, where everyone expects to go through a pre-determined process. However, safety and respect are especially needed in these situations. One very effective way to build safety and respect is for trainers to be appropriately vulnerable, especially in acknowledging their own struggles and need to keep growing.

10.   *Co-facilitative.* A team of two trainers co-facilitating each session is very effective for providing interpersonal skills training. Participants learn about relating as they observe the trainers relate to each other. Two trainers can demonstrate the skills well. In interactive learning, so much is going on that it helps to have one trainer actively involved with the group, and the other observing what is going on in the process. Having a variety of people up front also helps to prevent boredom.

An Example of Interpersonal Skills Training for Missionaries

International Training Partners (ITP) has provided this training for ten years, by making four and a half day *Sharpening Your Interpersonal Skills Workshops* available to missionaries. ITP is a partnership of missions committed to providing this training, not only to their own staff but to members of other missions. Currently, over one hundred fifty facilitators from 40 organizations live in many different countries.

These facilitators have other ministries, and do this part time. The majority of the facilitators are "ordinary" missionaries, without graduate degrees in the mental health professions.

1.   *The curriculum.* The curriculum is modified from time to time, based on ongoing needs assessments and evaluations from participants. Currently, the following issues are addressed. The reader can no doubt think of other important issues in relating. A description of each module is provided on the ITP Web site at www.RelationshipSkills.com.

- How to Kill Your Relationships. (The workshop begins on a light note, with a humorous demonstration of as many ways to harm relationships as possible.)
- Loving Listening
- How to Draw People Out
- Helping Others Solve Problems
- Confronting Well
- Receiving Confrontation Well
- Managing Conflicts Well
- Helping Others Manage Conflicts Well
- Building Personal Trust (When the participants are in leadership, an additional session on Building Organizational Trust is added.)
- Living in Community in Ways that Glorify God
- Managing our Grief and Helping Others Manage Grief
- Managing Stress and Helping Others Manage Stress
- Maintaining Margin. This includes helping others maintain margin
- The Battle for Moral Purity, including helping others maintain moral purity
- Being an Encourager
- Integrating the Workshop

2. *Key components of the workshop.* As you read these, compare them with the more traditional method of lecture only. They are built on several core beliefs, one of which is: "People take away what they have processed."

- Lecture: Very little lecture is given, and that is done in dialog with the participants.
- Reading assignments: A 215-page workbook is provided, and participants are asked to read selected parts before and during the workshop. The rest is for personal study later, for those who desire to do so.
- Bible studies in small groups
- Whole group discussion
- Demonstrations of skills: Sixteen demonstrations are used in the training. These are done by facilitators, facilitators with participants, participants with participants, and shown on video. In multicultural workshops, participants of different cultures are often invited to demonstrate how they live out God's word in relation to specific skills.
- Practice: Each skill is practiced in pairs or triads.

- Reflection: Times are provided often for reflecting on how to improve in the skills, on examining core beliefs, and on ways to grow.
- Self-assessment: In each session participants are asked to assess how they are doing are in regard to the issue at hand, using an instrument provided. When couples participate, they are sometimes encouraged to assess each other, and discuss their perceptions.
- Scripture memory: At the beginning of the training, participants are given a label with Colossians 3:12-14 written out. They learn it together throughout the week, and are often asked to consider the qualities and behaviors in the passage, in light of what is going on in the learning process.
- "Snapshots." At the end of each session participants are invited to prayerfully consider what they want to take away from the session, and write their thoughts on a "Snapshot Page."
- Sharing and prayer: At appropriate times, participants are given the opportunity to share in pairs or in small groups on a variety of issues, and pray for each other.
- Opportunities for growth: Each session has a page designed to lead participants through a process of applying what they are learning in their relationships.
- Personal consultation: Participants are invited to consult with facilitators during breaks and meal times. Facilitators avoid counseling participants during the workshop. The focus of consultations is on application of the skills.
- Integration of the workshop: Significant time is provided during the last session to reflect back over the workshop, using various helps provided, and prayerfully begin writing a growth plan.

3. *Some Practical Facets of the Training.* Often insufficient attention is given to practical issues in training, but especially in interpersonal skills training, these become critical. Here are some that are addressed in ITP workshops.

- *Venue.* Whenever possible, the workshops are held in locations where distractions are at a minimum. For example, mission headquarters or offices are avoided. Facilities should be as comfortable and quiet as possible, away from work and home, with areas where people can naturally interact during breaks and meals.
- *Meeting room.* The meeting room should be comfortable, with good acoustics, and sufficient room without crowding. More room per person is needed than in typical training contexts because of interacting in smalls groups and pairs. Participants sit at tables rather than in rows; this provides natural and comfortable settings for group discussions. Round tables are preferable to rectangular tables. Facilitators do not stand behind a podium. They use a table and sometimes stools, so they can walk around the room as needed. Obviously, compromises in the venue and meeting room must be made in some overseas settings.
- *Schedule.* The normal schedule is from 8:30 to 5:00, with one and one-half hour sessions, half hour breaks, and a one and one-half hour lunch time.

However, the schedule is flexible, depending on local conditions and culture.

- *Size of workshop.* The number of participants is normally between twelve and twenty-four. This provides safety and works well for whole group discussions. Workshops can accommodate larger numbers, but the quality and character of the experience is affected.
- *Number of facilitators.* Two to four facilitators is best. However, only two of them facilitate any one session. Facilitating interactive learning of this kind can be much more exhausting than lecturing, so it helps to have more than two.
- *Length of training.* A little training in this area may be better than none. However, ITP has found that in order to bring about lasting change in attitudes and skills, four or five days of experiential learning are a minimum. We in missions have deceived ourselves into thinking that we can bring about significant, ongoing development in people by giving them a few hours here and there. We must give adequate time to this issue if we want results that endure.

Conclusion

Every missionary and every mission leader knows that relationships are important. But that knowledge alone is clearly not sufficient. In the judgment of this writer, missionaries must receive effective training in how to relate well. Effective training in relationships cannot be accomplished by our traditional methods of education. We must employ the very best methods of adult education, in safe environments that are conducive to interactive, reflective learning.

Missions leaders and organizations have a difficult choice: Ignore this area and pay the terrible price of high attrition, distrust, dysfunctional and destructive relationships, and more. Or pay the seemingly high price of providing their missionaries with the best possible training in how to relate, with the obvious rewards.

Recommended Reading

Cohen, N. (1995). *Mentoring Adult Learners: A Guide for Educators and Trainers.* Malabar, Florida: Krieger Publishing.

Powers, B. (1992). *Instructor Excellence: Mastering the Delivery of Training.* San Francisco: Jossey-Bass Publishers.

Vella, J. (1994). *Learning to Listen, Learning to Teach: The Power of Dialogue in Educating Adults.* San Francisco: Jossey-Bass Publishers, 1994.

Vella, J. (1995). *Training Through Dialogue: Promoting Effective Learning and Change with Adults.* San Francisco: Jossey-Bass Publishers, 1995.

Williams, K. (2000). *Sharpening Your Interpersonal Skills.* Colorado Springs: International Training Partners. *Note:* this workbook and related materials are available through the ITP web site at www.RelationshipSkills.com.

31

Team Building

Lianne Roembke

More and more mission teams are international, and members of teams must make cultural adjustments to each other as well as to the host culture. The normative culture to which all team members should adapt is the host culture. Adaptation is defined as removing cultural obstacles which hinder the clear, credible communication of the Gospel. This chapter provides tools for understanding and training multicultural teams.

*T*he Achilles heel of mission work is in the arena of personal relationships, and the team situation is usually the crucible. For this reason I will emphasize a proactive approach to team building. It may also be necessary to facilitate the healing and rebuilding of broken relationships of disillusioned team members.

All mission workers come to their teams with certain expectations and assumptions. Today, the majority of teams are multicultural. For example, I have trained Europeans who went to Africa expecting to adapt to an African culture. But because of the majority of Americans on some teams, the overriding culture felt more American than African. Straddling the two cultures was indeed confusing and sometimes frustrating! Often the consequences were even more severe.

Most of what happens on teams is due to our default settings—our tendency to revert back to our own cultural patterns. Many hardships created on teams are not intentional; they just happen because we are not sensitized to one another's cultural backgrounds.

A few years ago at a large conference for workers in a limited access country, I greeted the workers at my breakfast table. Most were very happy to be at the conference and were enjoying a relaxing time. One worker, however, was quite solemn and despondent. "There's a story behind that," I thought.

Later, after my first seminar on multicultural teams, she came running up to me and said, "That's it! That's why I haven't been able to define what's going on." She then related her story. She had served for seven years in this country and been sure of her call to missions since childhood. She had even begun learning this difficult language as a teenager. She loved her ministry and the students

with whom she was working. But her team relationships were frustrating, a puzzle to her. She was even beginning to question her call.

Cultural Norms for Multicultural Teams

What was happening in her team and in most others I've encountered? No one had defined the cultural goal of the team adaptation. The culture of the team was happening by default and was unwittingly injuring people in the process. The question no one is asking on multicultural teams is: **What are the cultural norms on a multicultural team?** Which culture should be normative? To which culture are we all adapting? This is perhaps the most neglected question and *therefore part of the problem.*

What usually happens? The culture of the majority on the team often dominates the culture of the team. Perhaps this is because it is so well represented, because the majority is so powerful that the one in the minority dares not bring up the issue of culture. But *should* the majority rule? And if the majority culture happens to be the same culture as that of country of origin of the mission or the leadership, it is doubly difficult. Often this is not an intentional or conscious decision; it just happens and is not questioned.

The question deserves to be asked in each team: **Which culture should be the norm in our team?** There is a precedent which has been set for us. In I Corinthians 9:19-23, the apostle Paul makes his great mission statement. He, the apostle, the "sent one," the mission worker, is also Paul, the expatriate missionary—the short-termer in some cases.

In verse 19 he confirms his choice, *though I am free…I choose to become like a Jew, to win the Jews…to become like those under the law…in order to win [them], and to become like those not having the law…in order to win [them]. To the weak, I became weak in order to win the weak.* Paul's summary statement is in verse 22: *I have become **all** things to **all** people so that by **all possible means** I might save some. I do this for the sake of the gospel, that I may share in its blessings.* (NIVI)

Culturally speaking, what is Paul's assumption? He, as the expatriate long-termer or short-termer, moves culturally in the direction of those of the host culture.

Paul rarely traveled alone; he was mostly in a small multicultural team, either with Barnabas or Silas or even John Mark. He did not impose his culture on the team; neither did he let their culture become normative. The conclusion of Paul—stated repeatedly—is that the norm culture for him and his team is the culture in which they lived and worked. This answers the question regarding which culture deserves to be the norm culture for the team.

Does this imply that the mission workers are to throw their own cultures overboard, to "go native"? Not at all. Earlier in verse 12, Paul writes of setting aside his rights for this one purpose: *we put up with anything rather than hinder the gospel of Christ.* Those parts of our cultural background which prove a **hindrance** to the credible communication of the gospel of Christ are areas in which we should change. Change is certainly not necessary in every area. This was borne out in my surveys of national missionaries and their expectations of expatriate missionaries.

In summary, two conclusions emerge for us as major guidelines for multicultural teams:

> **1.** The normative culture to which all team members adapt is the host culture, not the cultures of one another. (Roembke 2000, p. 70)
>
> **2.** The definition of adaptation is removing cultural obstacles which hinder the clear, credible communication of the Gospel. (Roembke 2000, p. 83)

Credibility means those around us can embrace the message because it is believable. Not only are our words are credible; we also live a life congruent with what we say.

Granted, it may seem easier and less stressful for the majority of the team to let their culture dominate, but let us consider briefly what happens when a culture other than the host culture is allowed to dominate. First, when the majority culture (other than the host culture) dominates, it presents a barrier to the clear, credible communication of the message. Why would we require those we are trying to reach to jump cultural hurdles to understand the message of Christ on our cultural terms? It adds useless baggage to the message.

Paul confronted even Peter about adding cultural conditions to the gospel. Peter had wanted the Gentiles to refrain from eating meat that was considered unclean by the Jews. God had to give him a special revelation to convince him otherwise. Paul said, in effect, the Gentiles did not have to become Jews in order to become Christians.

If the team lacks credibility, so does the message—and it will not be embraced, particularly over time. The message may be initially attractive because of the thrill or status of associating with exotic people, but it will not transfer long-term into an indigenous church.

Second, when the majority culture (other than the host culture) dominates, it raises barriers for those in the minority cultures on the team. These persons then often suffer alone because of this effect. This creates extra stress for them, which is not necessary and also is not wise, helpful, healthy, or loving. It can cause deep hurts and an unnecessary split in their personal identity.

Does this mean we have to accept the host culture purely, even with its ungodly biases? Not any more than we should accept our own culture at home with all of its ungodly biases. No culture is pure. No culture should be embraced without first letting God's Word filter out the dross—those things which are specifically against God and His Word. This is what happened to us, particularly if we became Christians as adults. God's Spirit began pointing out things in our lives which, although culturally appropriate, were not in line with God's core values and which we then began to change. Most things in culture, however, are culturally neutral. Some things in the new culture may go against our cultural bias, but they are not necessarily against God's Word and are therefore neutral. We need to let them stand. And we need to ask the question: are there things I need to change that present a barrier to them?

What actually happens if a multicultural team is adapting properly? The team forms a culture that more and more approximates the host culture, purified. (See diagram on following page.)

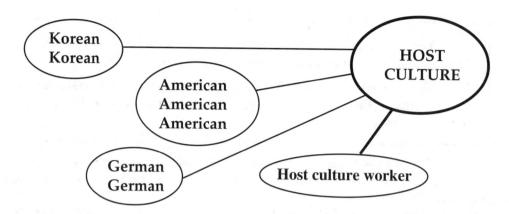

Such multicultural teams, though not without problems, are blessed with many advantages. For one, because the message is "filtered" through a team of many cultures, it keeps the gospel purer. The cultural taint is often offensive and can lead to rejection of the message. Such teams reflect the Body of Christ more fully, offering a richness and depth of experience. There are many different kinds of Christians with whom new believers can identify. They can provide a foretaste of that day when all peoples will praise God together.

Where are the potential problems likely to surface? Frankly, in almost every area of life, some with graver consequences than others. Finances and lifestyle as well as other areas that can be morally interpreted, including men-women relationships, dress, and demeanor are some of the hot spots of difference and misunderstanding. In some areas we can't afford to make mistakes first and change later, despite the "honeymoon phase" usually allowed newcomers.

Personal Values

Why are some areas harder to change than others? One can view one's person-ality as a set of concentric circles, with the innermost circle of values being those held most dearly and therefore, the values hardest to give up or change. A good team exercise is to have the team members evaluate their personal values according to the resistance to change they sense. Circle A represents values one can change without feeling any loss or struggle. Circle B represents values one sees the need to change and intends to as one can. There may be felt resistance but it is mostly related to the comfort of habit, not real conviction about the inherent worth of the value. Circle C represents values one struggles with greatly to change; the need to change may or may not be clear, or the values themselves are closely linked to one's self-perception. Circle D represents values one holds so dearly it would be very difficult, if not impossible, to change. The estimation of these values will be different from person to person.

The list of values to be considered is endless. One can start with the more obvious: food, eating habits, dress, courtesy and manners, concept of time, concept of personal space, modes of transportation, form of housing, language, pronunciation, methods of hospitality, planning and scheduling of time, lifestyle, use of finances, view of property, concept of privacy, sanitary facilities, cleanliness, orderliness, punctuality, egalitarianism, health care, how to raise children, views of dating and marriage, men's and women's issues, concept of freedom, methods of discussion, decision-making and leadership style, pattern of logic, measures of success, etc. (One can add to the list as one becomes more aware of one's own values or those of the new culture.)

And then the less academic but most important part of the exercise: Have the team members evaluate with *national* friends and colleagues which areas are necessary for credibility, which add to credibility, which are relatively neutral, which would detract from credibility (with the changes implied, of course). These should all be validated by several other members of the culture as well. Not all things need to be changed. This validation process will help determine if a particular value has a bearing on the reception of your message in the host culture or on your team members. Is this cultural difference perceived as neutral? Or is it a barrier? If so, what am I going to do about it? What would Paul have done about it? And what would Jesus do?

In Philippians 2, we read how Jesus gave up his rights and privileges as God's Son to be enculturated as a human being. In chapter 3, Paul talks about what he did with his credentials and rights – he gave them up as well. In fact, he moved them from the credit side to the debit side of his account, knowing well that they might get in the way of the credible communication of the message.

Team members should take a good look at those things in circles C and D and ask themselves: Am I willing to give up my rights to anything that might hinder a credible communication of the message? At this point it is a spiritual issue. There seems to be no limit to change as long as it is willing change. "Identity means, not

Values Categorized in Concentric Circles

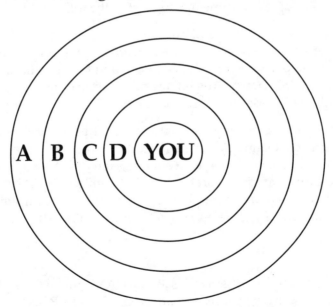

being someone else, but being more than oneself." (Eugene Nida, *Message and Mission*, 162.) Am I willing to be made willing? Underlying this process one will sense either resistance and tension and/or the moving of the Spirit to be willing to be made willing to change in crucial areas.

Direct vs. Indirect Communication

The differences between **direct** and **indirect communication** often trip up mission workers from Western countries. I remember how I, as an American, was initially shocked at the directness of my German colleagues. The bluntness felt abrasive to me; I tended more towards tactfulness and diplomacy. What were they probably thinking about me?

A person who is accustomed to direct communication will view indirect communication as dishonest, suspicious and untruthful. A person who has been enculturated in the art of indirect communication will view direct communication as very impolite, blunt and offensive. This is probably the dynamic of what is happening when someone from an indirect culture can't bear to say "no." For the direct communicators the issue of truth is at stake. For the indirect communicators the issues of love and respect are of highest value. Therefore, "yes" as an answer does not always equal the "yes" direct communicators are used to. "Yes" may mean: "I understand" or "I'll think about it." Direct communicators need to learn to formulate their questions wisely and appropriately, not bluntly, in such situations.

Both of these values, truth and love, are godly and we hold them dearly. Can we not emphasize them both? *Neither cultural pattern is inherently wrong.* But to follow the cultural practices of one in a country where the other is valued can very well cause offense. It's a matter of learning the cultural rules. Using the appropriate method is important to gain a hearing, but we need to do so without neglecting either truth or love. This applies to the team as well.

My Chinese friend, when asked how she would deal with a team situation in which a difference of opinions came up, suggested the following:

- Make a private appointment rather than discussing it in the team.
- Creating an atmosphere of acceptance and presenting the issue without accusing help to open up the discussion and facilitate finding a solution
- Involving a third party, trusted by both, is appropriate if the issue is a "hot" one or if the foundation of trust is shaky.

Many more such areas are dealt with in detail in the book *Building Credible Multicultural Teams* by Lianne Roembke (Pasadena: William Carey Library, 2000). Working together on a team is not an academic exercise, although such training is necessary to increase awareness – preferably before mission workers are sent out.

Learning how to communicate love in terms the other can understand is an exercise in *agape* love. This, as we all know, takes a lot of work.

References

Nida, E. (1960). *Message and Mission.* Pasadena, CA: William Carey Library.
Roembke, L. (2000). *Building Credible Multicultural Teams.* Pasadena, CA: William Carey Library.

32

Conflict Resolution

Barney Davis

Relationships are at the core of mission work, but interpersonal conflict is ubiquitous and occurs normally in any relationship. Skills of managing and resolving conflict make an important contribution to mission work. Consultants are often asked to help missionaries deal with marital, organizational, and cultural conflict. This chapter provides insight into sources of conflict and gives guidelines for understanding and resolving conflict.

*B*arnabas wanted to take John, called Mark, along with them also. But Paul kept insisting that they should not take him along who had deserted them in Pamphylia and had not gone with them to the work. (Acts 15:37-38)

Only Luke is with me. Pick up Mark and bring him with you, for he is useful to me for service. (2 Tim 4:11)

One can only surmise what took place in the years between the events recorded above. The first, recorded by Luke, is a familiar passage, often used as an example that Christians, even the founders of the faith, can have interpersonal conflict. The second, penned by Paul during his final imprisonment, gives us hope that conflict properly resolved can lead to fellowship restored.

The intervening events, however, which allowed such major conflict to evolve into trust and respect, are not recorded. Did Paul "forget" his disappointment with Mark's decision to leave Paul and his companions in Perga, and return to Jerusalem? Did John Mark have to do something to "re-earn" Paul's favor? How did they deal with their conflicted relationship?

Interpersonal conflict is ubiquitous, and occurs normally in any relationship. Those who work in Christian service are not spared, and Biblical examples of conflict abound, yet there is still the occasional voice (either individual or organizational) which is heard to cling to the belief that Christians should not experience disharmony with others.

This has historically been the case in missions, where missionaries were seen as "special," chosen by God, and more righteous than others. Mission organizations have been known to ignore potential personal conflict situations. In recent years, however, there has been a growing awareness of the practical stewardship of recognizing the

reality of conflict, to proactively find ways to reduce it, and to address it appropriately when present.

It is assumed that the reader is involved in missionary care, and is reading this chapter because they anticipate or find themselves seeing missionaries on home assignment or on field assignment. As one involved in missionary work or member care, you will encounter conflict occurring between two or more individuals, between individuals and organizations, and individuals and other cultures.

Sometimes, the conflict is characterized by easily understood, simple differences in perspective occurring between two people. Other times, conflict may present as a complex, convoluted intertwining of missed communications, hidden agendas, or organizational traditions that involve many individuals. Our task as mission consultants is to do whatever is appropriate to make sure conflict is handled in a way that is biblically appropriate, recognizes the context of the mission purpose, and is consistent with the philosophy and mission of the organizations involved.

Areas of Conflict

Relationship is at the very core of mission work. This includes not just the opportunity for someone to have a personal relationship with Jesus Christ, but also relationships that exist within missionary families, relationships among team members, relationships that develop with nationals, and the relationship between the missionary and his mission organization. Paul, writing to the church at Rome, suggests that it is each Christian's responsibility to pursue conflict-free relationships: "*if possible*, so far as it depends on you, be at peace with all men" (Romans 12:18, NASB, italics added). Yet, biblical evidence and practical experience both attest to the fact that sometimes it seems impossible.

The most likely place of functional difficulty in missionary life is disturbance in relationship, and change in the mission candidate population over recent years has increased the likelihood of conflict occurrence. More and more missionary candidates are entering mission service on a short-term basis; these may be older individuals with greater life and relationship history, who are being deployed onto more volatile and dangerous fields. Less time for pre-field evaluation and preparation further elevates the potential for interpersonal difficulty.

Conflicts in Marriage

One of the frequently seen areas of conflict is in the marriage relationship:

> A married couple enters mission service for the first time at his age 53, hers 50. Their children are grown and no longer live at home. He was a successful executive with an international industrial firm and was able to retire at an early age with no financial obligations. During the last twenty years of their marriage, he spent most of his time in work, she in raising the children.
>
> They felt called to mission service, and have been assigned to a two-thirds world country. They find themselves living in a two-bedroom flat, working together ten hours each day, and with few others of their own home culture with whom they can relate. Her contacts in the local com-

munity soon lead to a more effective involvement and potential ministry advancement than he has been able to establish.

His response is to work harder, and to complain that she has not been able to provide a comfortable home environment. Their communication has deteriorated, and he is spending more and more time with a younger female national team member who often functions as his interpreter. His wife becomes more upset and depressed.

Organizational Conflict

Also seen are conflicts between mission organizations and their members:

A family of five joins a conservative mission organization, and is sent to a poor African nation to begin church planting work. The husband is very relational, creative, and unconventional in his approach to work and family roles. As his ministry becomes more and more successful, his supervisor expresses discomfort with his style and method. One of their children has behavioral problems, which the mission organization insists will require the return of the family to their home country for attention.

Communication between the leadership of the organization and the husband and wife continues to deteriorate, and although the family does return to the field for a brief time, they eventually resign from their mission organization and leave mission work.

Cultural Conflicts

Problems can arise between the missionary and the culture in which they work:

A young missionary, Western in his ethnicity, is the son of missionary parents, and was born in a South American country. Now, after several years of training in church planting, he is shepherding a new church in the worst section of a large city, where crime, drugs, political unrest, and kidnaping are daily occurrences. He marries a young woman from the U.S. who has minimal cross-cultural experience. Although committed to her husband, she is uncomfortable with living in circumstances of such threat. His parents, still living and working as missionaries in the same country, insist that the couple should trust God more and worry less. Others have advised the husband that he needs to provide a more safe and secure environment for his wife. She is expecting their first child in three months, and is beginning to experience symptoms of anxiety and increasing fear.

Conflict between a missionary and their field culture is common, yet will not be addressed in this chapter, as this is typically seen more as the effect of cultural stress on the missionary. Traditionally, conflict resolution addresses difficulties that develop between individuals or between individuals and organizations, and it is those situations we will further explore.

Management of conflict

Assuming that all involved parties are followers of Christ, the core strategies for managing conflict are outlined in the Bible. While many passages may pertain to relationship management, Matthew chapters 7 and 18 specifically give instruction about self-assessment and confrontation with others:

Self assessment

Why do you look at the speck that is in your brother's eye, but do not notice the log that is in your own eye? Or how can you say to your brother, 'Let me take the speck out of your eye,' and behold, the log is in your own eye? You hypocrite, first take the log out of your own eye, and then you will see clearly to take the speck out of your brother's eye. Matthew 7:5-7

Before attempting to resolve conflict with another person, it is prudent to spend time alone with the Lord to ask Him to reveal one's own contribution to and issues in the conflict situation. A useful question in all situations of conflict is, "Why is God allowing this to happen in my life at this time? What is He trying to tell me or teach me in this situation?" God allows conflict in our lives to bring us closer to Him, and to make us more like Him.

It may be that a situation of conflict will best be resolved by the simple recognition of one's own issues involved in the conflict. We are also called to forgive others, and to place the needs of others ahead of our own. One must be careful to examine each situation of conflict carefully, to determine if the degree of conflict is such that it requires confronting the other person. Sometimes, effective resolution is accomplished by choosing to forgive and forget the issues that led to the conflict.

One-on-one confrontation

...if your brother sins, go and show his fault in private [lit: "between you and him alone"]... Matthew 18:15 NASB

Whenever possible, resolution of conflict between two individuals should first be dealt with between the two (or if the conflict includes an organizational entity, then with an appropriate leader or supervisor). As a potential facilitator of conflict resolution, it is important for the member care specialist to not circumvent this biblical dictate, or attempt to act as a third party communicator until a one to one meeting has been attempted.

This is not say that you cannot educate and give help about the process of conflict resolution. You may be in a situation where you become aware of the conflict in your working with one of the parties involved, and if so, it is biblically appropriate to encourage that person to directly deal with the other(s) involved, and you may provide instruction on ways that can best be done.

Should the one to one confrontation fail to reach adequate resolution of the conflict, then another person or persons should be brought in ("...but if he does not listen to you, take one or two more with you..." Matt 7:16); this is where the member care specialist often is asked to intervene. Particularly where individuals are in conflict with their own mission organization, attention to issues of confidentiality are to be acknowledged, while trying to work within the authority structure of the particular organization.

Specific techniques of communication and listening are well known; many mission agencies include teaching in these areas in their preparation for missionary service. Whether you find yourself in the role of advisor to someone in conflict who needs to understand these basic techniques, or (when a direct one-on-one meeting has failed or is not possible) in the role of mediator or facilitator, the use of such techniques will greatly increase the likelihood of successful resolution of the conflict.

Setting

Care must be taken to pick a "right time and right place" to resolve the conflict. The Bible teaches that we should be timely in reconciliation. *Therefore if you are presenting your offering at the altar, and there remember that your brother has something against you, leave your offering there before the altar and go; first be reconciled to your brother, and then come and present your offering.* (Matthew 5:23-24); *...do not let the sun go down on your anger...* (Ephesians 4:26). Such meetings should be private and should take into consideration the freedom of both parties to give proper attention to the matter at hand. In addition, cultural norms may dictate a particular protocol, which if ignored might further increase the conflict.

If possible, choose a time and place where noise and interruption are less likely.

Body language speaks loudly. Two people trying to resolve conflict should be facing each other, and eye contact should be maintained particularly when important and emotionally charged points are being made.

Communicating

Feelings should be expressed in such a way that there is no attack on the other person. "I" language statements, as opposed to "you" language statements, are most important. Example: "I often feel left out of decisions that you reach for the team," rather than "You leave me out of team decisions."

Keep the focus on one issue, rather than on many; concentrate on specifics rather than generalizations. Particularly avoid use of "always" and "never" terminology.

The focus should be on describing behaviors, not on attacking or assuming motivation. ["I was hurt when you said that" rather than "You were just trying to hurt me by saying that"].

Listening

Listen without interruption. As one speaks, the other listens. The person listening should be careful to concentrate on what is being said, and not use this time to plan a "counter attack."

Focus on content, not style; as one listens, try to hear the emotional content, the what is being said, rather than reacting to the how it is being said.

Reflect what you heard. When the person speaking is done, the listener should reflect back what they have heard the person say.

Resolution

Once both have had an opportunity to express their thoughts and feelings, then a solution to the conflict should be proposed. This may simply be the offering of an apology, or a clarification of meaning; the focus should also include addressing how to avoid similar conflict in future interactions.

Forgiveness should be offered and received by both parties; if one or both are not able to do this at the time, then there should be at least an agreement to work toward that in the near future.

General guidelines

We have found the following general guidelines useful for the mediator in a conflict situation:

1.   As much information as possible about the individuals and organizations involved should be obtained. Conflict has both manifest and latent components; manifest issues are the more obvious circumstantial elements that are usually evident to the examiner. Latent issues are less obvious, and usually are tied to "old baggage," events and circumstances of earlier experience that may predispose one to conflict or distort one's reactions to it.

Having an opportunity to listen to each person's personal history, looking for such events in the past that may be contributing to current conflict, is most desirable. Similarly, each mission organization has its own "personality," and often has events and circumstances of the past which may dictate how the organization responds to situations.

2.   The presence of underlying personality disorder (see chapter on this topic by Esther Schubert) may dictate a different approach to dealing with conflict. These disorders, pervasive and entrenched, do not respond well to short term resolution, and patterns of conflict occur repetitively.

3.   Likewise, the presence of a major affective disorder such as depression can sometimes better explain conflicted behaviors. In such cases, identification and treatment of the underlying disorder is necessary to prevent the development of further conflict.

4.   There may be other medical problems that predispose or contribute to conflict. Often, access to medical care is either difficult or delayed on the mission field, and there may be environmental risks that are unique to specific mission fields. Thyroid imbalances, exhaustion stemming from chronic infection, and intolerance of extremes in day/night duration and temperature change can all lead to altered mood, which in turn can predispose to a greater likelihood of interpersonal conflict.

5.   The level of general environmental stress should be taken into account when conflict is being assessed. The effect of living under constant threat of kidnaping or other violence, frequent moves being necessitated by political unrest and national unrest, exposure to extremes of poverty and hunger, and witness of atrocities can all increase the likelihood of conflict between individuals, or between an individual and an organization.

6.   It may be difficult to see that, even when properly approached, conflict has been resolved. For instance, a missionary in conflict with their agency may choose to leave the mission field (or may be sent home by the agency), when an apparently desirable outcome would be that the missionary would be able to continue in their work.

Yet, we have seen times when God apparently allowed such conflict to develop, so that issues in the person's life that they had not previously been aware of or willing to deal with are brought to light in the context of such conflict. While this can take place on either overseas or when removed from the place of assignment, repatriation might allow time and opportunity to deal with such issues and afford the missionary another opportunity to serve.

33

Intersections of Physical and Mental Health

Kenneth Gamble

*M*issionary vitality is enhanced through effective care in spiritual, physical and mental health areas. The development of coordinated care approaches in these areas recognizes that God created us as unified beings and allows treatment to be given with the understanding that difficulty in one area usually affects another.

Assessment for missionary service, particularly in physical and mental health areas, is too often seen as a one-time event with a pass/fail outcome. Such a view leaves little room for utilizing models which could serve the missionary over a span of time, viewing this as an entry point and allowing incorporation of base-line data to be utilized effectively in on-going care, assignment adjustments and/or emergency and crisis situations.

A multi-disciplinary approach, utilizing base-line data, risk assessment and knowledge of the intersections between physical and mental health within a context of spiritual understanding, forms the basis for a promising approach to continuous health care management in missionary life. This chapter discusses considerations and issues in such a model.

Two Situations

George, age 84, was born to pioneer missionaries and raised among aboriginals in the hills of Vietnam. Prior to the development of antibiotics he relied on remedies used by traditional healers, and many were incorporated into his repertoire of self-care strategies. Legends abound of his forays into territories riddled with Vietcong guerillas. He says, "When I was commissioned as a missionary I claimed

Medical and psychological assessments of missionary candidates are done with care, but the information gleaned is not always used to inform decisions in later stages of the missionary career. A systemic, multidisciplinary, "continuous care" model for health care enhances physical and psychological health and encourages self care and mutual care. Risk assessment and the concept of a continuum of risk provide a framework for health care management.

the protection of Psalm 91 and I never looked back."

David was a missionary from an earlier era. As a pioneer to an unreached continent, he ventured into regions of tropical Africa that were nicknamed "the white man's grave." There he witnessed the death of many colleagues and almost succumbed to complications of malaria himself. Intrigued by reports of the therapeutic effects of a tea brewed with bark from the Chincona tree, Dr. David Livingston managed to successfully treat malaria and is credited with being the first to use quinine for preventive therapy.

George represents the philosophy of those who dismiss health care management, exhorting their followers that "there is no safer place than in the will of God." David represents the emergence of preventive care and early intervention. Both illustrate the importance of the self-care component of member care—a factor which has not changed in the increasingly technological milieu of health care.

The capacity for appropriate self-care is an essential attribute of people chosen for inter-cultural assignments, and a strong sense of God's provision sustains many through the dark passages of their international assignments. Appropriate preventive health strategies are generally accepted by missionaries (though not always practiced). Psychological testing is now widely used in the selection process, ensuring as much as possible that expariate workers enjoy good basic mental health. Nevertheless, health crises erupt and result in many tensions.

Tom Smith's Story

Tom Smith's story illustrates the tensions that can emerge. We invite the reader to reflect on how a systemic, multidisciplinary response could be provided to work toward a better outcome.

Tom and his family enjoyed a two-year assignment working with refugees in Southern Ethiopia. Tom's family seemed well adjusted and the famine relief efforts that he initiated were a model for others. Tom was reassigned to another region for his second assignment because someone with his ability "to get things started" was needed.

Though Tom had taken malaria medication faithfully during the first assignment, on two occasions he had contracted malaria. That undermined his confidence in the effectiveness of the medication. During his second term, Tom began to experience some adverse side effects and colleagues told him the drug was dangerous. Tom discontinued taking the medication; he believed that by now he knew exactly how to recognize the disease and could treat it when symptoms developed.

Unfortunately, his next bout of malaria presented like the flu and his initial management was delayed. He became very ill. Though he recovered, Tom experienced a protracted period of profound fatigue that limited his capacity to fulfill his duties as project manager.

A colleague implemented some of his own ideas during Tom's lengthy absence from the project. That was problematic for Tom, who thought the project would suffer. He became disillusioned and angry when his colleagues failed to follow his suggestions, and these conflicts had an adverse effect on his marriage. Halfway through the second term

Tom had to be repatriated because of chronic fatigue. He arrived "home" sick, disillusioned, angry with God and on the verge of a divorce.

The agency's personnel director, Carl, knew there were conflicts on the project because Tom's behavior was so disruptive. He hoped that encouraging Tom to return for medical reasons would help to defuse some of the problems. Carl was upset with the earlier psychological test results. Carl had been told that Tom had a "strong personality," but the psychologist had thought that Tom's profile would be an asset for pioneering relief and development efforts. In retrospect, Carl could identify signs of a personality disorder in Tom; he felt that the psychologist should have been more direct in stating that prior to the assignment.

Physicians also disappointed Carl because they couldn't find anything wrong and could not treat Tom's chronic fatigue. Doctors blamed the patient, noting that he would have remained healthy had he listened to their advice. The mission committee felt that Tom's chronic illness was related to a spiritual issue, and asserted that God could not bless Tom while he was angry and bitter toward God.

By the time Tom Smith returned home, the adverse impact was considerable. Seemingly, a single bout of malaria had impacted Tom's relationship with his personnel manager, the personnel manager's relationship with the psychologist who did pre-service assessment, relationships on the project, Tom's faith, his family, and his supporting church.

Though fictitious, the above scenario is not rare. In a recent survey using a self-reporting health assessment questionnaire, 20% of missionary personnel who reported health concerns signified that they had either lost or were questioning their faith, compared with 4% of their colleagues who did not report any health concerns. They also complained of more fatigue, headaches, and stressful work schedules.

In Tom's case, blame was flying in many directions. Blame often does erupt, even on the part of professionals who are attempting to solve a problem. Tom's story illustrates turmoil affecting many people and the work to which they have been called. Some of this turmoil might be avoided if we developed multi-disciplinary teams that are philosophically committed to the concept of continuous care. Granted, implementation is difficult with limited resources and a globally mobile community.

Goals for Medical and Psychological Assessments

Medical and psychological assessments are the most universally accepted practices in the area of missionary care. We may begin a consideration of a more comprehensive view of physical and mental health by looking at a broader use of assessments.

Psychological assessments have come to be widely accepted among mission agencies, although to what degree psychological assessment prevents early attrition is not clear. The majority of personnel managers focus on the *Yes/No* outcome of health and psychological assessments, as they are responsible for putting together solid and effective teams.

From a cost : benefit perspective, psychological testing could well be justified even if the sole objective were to identify personality disorders. Borderline personality disorders occur in 2% to 10% of the general population, and many people with those traits apply for international posting. Redirecting one candidate with a personality disorder can save sufficient disruption and wasted resources to warrant the cost of the whole program.

Costs for medical assessments could not be justified if a pass/fail outcome were the sole purpose. Generally, only healthy people apply for mission service; those with health problems know that their impediment would impact their effectiveness and perhaps endanger their well-being in a location with few medical resources. The Missionary Health Institute eliminates very few candidates for medical reasons. On the other hand, the value of medical assessments would be greatly enhanced by including education and coaching on such things as stress management and prevention of malaria, hepatitis, and other threats to missionary health instead of focusing on a pass/fail outcome.

Assessment should have a multi-disciplinary focus. We should enlarge the boundaries and encourage more depth so that the benefits of pre-service assessment do not end with deployment. Outcomes from the assessments can flow into the beginning of a "continuous care" cycle. When the assessment process is complete the outcomes should:

- Establish a risk profile for each individual
- Enable appropriate management and deployment (organizational responsibility)
- Encourage the adoption of appropriate preventive measures and preparation (individual and organizational responsibility)
- Empower the individual to effect meaningful self-care
- Engage the community to participate in mutual care
- Enhance the expression of care between the individual and the organization

The last three points in particular have the potential of opening the missionary community to a nurturing and caring process that will become an integral part of their life journey. The philosophical undergirding for this is best articulated in the *Code of Best Practice* developed by People in Aid.

Assessing Risk

According to Marjory Foyle, psychiatrist and medical consultant, there are "factors in the personal and family histories of those who struggled in international settings which could have been identified during the selection process as likely to increase the in-service risk to mental health." (MD Thesis, 1999 *Expatriate Mental Health*)

Assessment professionals recognize the gravity of the recommendations they make, especially when identifying personality disorders. Psychologists are conscious of the legal implications of their assessments, a topic treated in detail in Chapter 53. When the conclusion is drawn that the applicant should not be given an international assignment, the weight of evidence is usually very compelling.

Tom Smith was said to have a "strong personality". Perhaps he was like David Livingston—blessed with vision, a clear view of what needs to be done and a willingness to overcome obstacles to achieve his goals. To disqualify Tom on those grounds would be a disservice to the sending organization.

Results from the assessments are often used to augment personal interviews and when appropriate, the results can be used in group sessions and team building. The group and personal interactions can inspire candidates to pursue life-long and continuous development, and enable the professionals involved in pre-service work to be seen as resources for problems which may occur later. This can be an effective aspect of continuity of care.

Appropriate Deployment

The group that is ultimately hired following assessment enters with a lower risk for mental or physical health challenges, but not a zero risk. The concept of "passing" the assessment process is dangerous, as it implies completion. Rather, the transition from applicant to candidate marks a critical juncture in the candidate's career path— his or her desire to serve internationally and the agency's decision to invest in him or her. The assessment process then can be an entry point for continuous care, not a completed event.

As new missionaries face the challenges of intercultural assignments, some will struggle, including those who had no identified risk factors. According to Marjorie Foyle, many of "those developing adjustment disorders overseas have little evidence of concern in personal and family histories, and vulnerability to such disorders could not have been predicted during selection."

Tom Smith's personnel manager concluded that a faulty assessment (failure to identify a personality disorder) led to premature attrition. However, a host of other factors played significant roles. For example, relief and development work has an inherently high risk of compassion fatigue. Debbie Lovell found that 46% of aid workers reported depression occurring either during or after service. The vast majority reported that they had never had psychological problems before they became aid workers; they would have been considered low risk candidates.

Of the personnel who have had routine medical debriefing at Missionary Health Institute, 20% noted that they were experiencing fatigue. A recent assessment of the wellness of 200 missionaries disclosed that 49% had experienced a change in worship activities, 30% had a change in their daily routines, 30% had a significant change in their assignment, 14% a change in finances and 12% faced the challenge of a major health problem in someone close to them. Any of these factors could have an adverse impact on their health, physical and mental.

Corporate and Personal Responsibility

The first two points listed above relate to our expectations of the assessment process. The third addresses the expectations of members of the international organizations. How open is that relationship? In her thesis entitled *Psychological Adjustment Among Returned Overseas Aid Workers* Lovell (1997) noted, "Sending agencies were only aware of about one in six of the cases of psychological difficulties among their workers."

Lovell asserts that there is an iceberg effect and the identified problems are only a small fraction of the whole. Many of the hidden, subtle problems will continue to mature. Given sustained stress and additional contributing factors, a crisis is sure to erupt. Perhaps Tom was experiencing compassion fatigue during his first assignment but was healthy enough to appear unscathed.

Lovell cites other factors that contributed to agencies' lack of awareness: aid workers did not know where help was available; some believed that seeking help would be seen as a sign of weakness; others felt that they would not be understood by people who had no experience of aid work. One participant wrote, "My organization offered no help when I returned. I felt I needed help from people who understand the pressures of re-entry and the symptoms of burnout."

A couple working as managers for a relief and development team came for a routine medical assessment. The only identified medical risk factor was that the husband had resumed smoking. His wife had insomnia, in part related to menopause. There were no overt clinical signs of depression and the clinical evaluation was void of clues that would disclose the magnitude of the psychosocial trauma and compassion fatigue that both were experiencing. When asked why they had not reported that to the mission or scheduled an appointment for debriefing they both asserted, "It came on so gradually we were not aware of how we felt until we answered the debriefing questionnaire."

We have the capacity to "screen out" some undesirable candidates, but the assignment will prove to be the ultimate assessment tool. What will emerge are "people with problems"—often those who were judged to be at lowest risk. When problems do emerge, it is likely that the agency will not know of their existence unless the relationship is secure enough, the steps to help are clear enough, the intention to discover is deliberate enough and the ensuing support is sincere enough.

Attempts to help can be seen as intrusive or as an extension of care. Two families experienced the same debriefing. The first responded, "How many ways will the agency develop to spy on us?" The second exulted, "I have had access to medical care for 20 years but I have not been cared for so well as I have since I joined this mission."

Viewing the patient as a member of the health management team provides another possibility. In a successful program of continuous care, there will only be one provider that has the capacity to remain connected at all times—the patient. Tom Smith could have identified symptoms but may not have known which were likely to resolve spontaneously and which would lead to an illness requiring professional assistance. Had he been included as a member of his health management team, he likely would have learned about this and the outcome could have been different.

David Sobel, director of patient education and health promotion at Kaiser Permanente, calculated that more than 80% of all medical symptoms are self-diagnosed and self-treated without any contact with a professional health care provider. Sobel and his colleagues determined that chronic diseases such as diabetes and arthritis can be managed more effectively and with less cost if the patient is included and coached as a member of the health management team. The same is very likely true for mental health issues.

Meaningful Self Care

The fourth goal stated earlier is to empower the individual to effect meaningful self care. Sharon Heid states, "Patient empowerment is the promotion and development of the skill and knowledge necessary to make informed medical decisions and relevant self-care and lifestyle modifications."

Tom Smith is a perfect example of one who was not fully informed and made the wrong decision. However, rather than blaming him for failing to use malaria prophylaxis, we should view his capacity for self care as part of our solution.

Futurists assert that the emerging postmodern culture will be characterized by persons who will openly challenge protocols, even if deemed to be effective by the experts, and will determine for themselves what risks they are going to take. The next generation will be more inclined to develop their own information networks and use the input to enable them to make the right decision. Here is an example to illustrate the point.

Natalie (an alias) is an intelligent, non-medical, independent thinker who wants to make the right decisions to protect her health. She works in a region where malaria still reigns supreme. She was comfortable with her choice of prophylaxis until she became pregnant and received conflicting counsel from colleagues. In an e-mail message, she said:

> I wrote that I was pregnant and asked you some questions about continuing to take Mefloquine. I took it throughout the pregnancy, didn't get malaria and am happy to report that our son is a healthy and peaceful boy, and we like him! I confess that I am resistant to taking a regular drug for a long period of time. On the other hand I enjoy being protected from malaria.
>
> I have three other questions related to Mefloquine and newborns...

E-mails such as this one are becoming more common. As communication networks improve, the Internet will help to bridge skill and knowledge gaps. However, there are serious legal and ethical risks involved in providing medical or psychological advice or treatment via e-mail. See chapter 54 for a discussion of these issues.

Continuum of Health Risks and Continuum of Care

Tom Smith needed care. The challenges he faced were far too complex for him to handle without tangible care: a critical incident debriefing session, psychological care that would help Tom and his family understand the interrelationship between his faith, stress and marriage relationship, medical care that would be of value even if it did not offer a cure for his chronic fatigue, and spiritual support that would sustain him during the dark days of despair.

Varying levels of care may be provided in response to a continuum of health risks. At one end of the continuum is minimal risk: robust health, giving the individual the capacity to endure high levels of stress and to resist disease processes. At the other end of the continuum is high risk: severe illness and ultimately death. Throughout their lives, people move back and forth on the continuum. They may experience serious injury or illness which is nearly fatal, then recover and move toward the minimal risk end of the scale.

In the conventional medical model, care providers usually operate on autopilot until red lights start to flash in the symptom zone; they are only engaged when the patient is in the higher risk area of the continuum. Health care providers typically expend relatively little time and effort to coach patients regarding preventive or health-promoting behaviors. It is far more exciting to treat a case of malaria and save someone's life than to reinforce preventive principles to dozens of persons at risk, especially when many are resistant to your counsel!

The caring process should not stop when a battle with illness is over but should move with the patient toward the lower risk end of the continuum. Though not formally recognized as health care providers, the community becomes the primary provider when health risks are lower, as stated in the fifth outcome goal noted earlier: Engage the community to participate in mutual care. The importance of supportive social relationships in the maintenance of physical and mental health has been documented in many studies. Though not a direct member of the health management team as such, the community is a crucial partner.

The mission agency has the lead role in enhancing the expression of care between the individual and the organization. At the pre-departure stage the agency must lead with the health plan. Later, if the missionary moves toward the higher risk end of the spectrum, care must be mobilized, often from trained professionals.

Once health care has been activated and health improves, the emphasis changes from care to support. The health continuum shows why a continuous flow of care is so vital and supports the need for a multi-disciplinary team. Different parts of the team are utilized as a missionary moves up and down on the risk spectrum, and base-line data from the pre-field assessments (and perhaps subsequent contacts) provide helpful and more immediate possibilities for optimum response and care.

The challenge is to determine when movement toward the high-risk end of the continuum is taking place, and how to connect with the continuum of care as needed. Similarly, the task also is to maintain connections with the necessary maintenance and support to stay at the low risk area of the continuum as much as possible.

A Model for Improved Health Care

The following observations are adapted from "Ten Rules to Guide Redesign of the Health Care System" recommended by the Institute of Medicine (2001), published in *Crossing the Quality Chasm*. See Appendix A.

Had a system of continuous care with the above noted features been in place in Tom's case a better result would almost certainly have taken place. There would have been the anticipation of needs by both Tom and the organization, based on data gathered earlier, and the knowledge that in his move Tom was susceptible to a greater risk for depression.

Based on the earlier assessment, and the knowledge that de-briefing would be useful in this situation, the personnel director could have acted in a supportive and preventive mode by seeing that it was provided.

Extensive pre-field interviews and testing, if carefully weighed in the context of continuous care needs during change in job assignments (a known stressor), might have alerted the personnel officer that any change in assignment should be custom-ized (as much as possible) to fit Tom's needs, values and dynamics.

A better attempt by the organization in sharing knowledge and information, based on available data about Tom and the risk of malaria, might have prevented its development.

In such a model or system trust between the member and the organization is important to its success. Had there perhaps been more transparency between them earlier on, the information flow may have been smoother. Further, if the overall health plan, taking into account features of the model, had been made clear and the information reinforced periodically, Tom might have confidently moved toward care much earlier. However, the patient as a source of control is critical to the success of this model; Tom has the data that will inform the understanding of those who can provide care. But also, care in this approach is based on continuous healing relationships, and health managers must take initiative in sustaining these relationships so that the missionary is not alone.

This brief outline of a model care draws from the important intersections of physical and mental health sees the initial assessment in these areas as an entry point for continuous care. It places responsibility on health care providers, the mission organization and the missionary, all members of a team working together to provide the best care to enhance missionary vitality. Its underlying success rests ultimately on our reliance upon the Great Physician as each member of the team utilizes gifts and skills, takes individual responsibility, and participates in relationship.

References

Foyle, M. F. (1999). *Expatriate Mental Health*. M.D. Thesis.

Institute of Medicine. (2001). *Crossing the Quality Chasm: A New Health System for the 21st Century*. Washington, D.C.: National Academy Press.

Lovell, D. (1997). *Psychological Adjustment Among Returned Overseas Workers*. Bangor, Wales: D. Clin. Psyc. Thesis, University of Wales.

People in Aid. (1997). *Code of Best Practice*. London: People in Aid. www.peopleinaid.org

Appendix A

New Rules to Redesign and Improve Care
Reprinted from *Crossing the Quality Chasm*

Private and public purchasers, health care organizations, clinicians, and patients should work together to redesign health care processes in accordance with the following rules:

1. Care based on continuous healing relationships. Patients should receive care whenever they need it and in many forms, not just face-to-face visits. This rule implies that the health care system should be responsive at all times (24 hours a day, every day) and that access to care should be provided over the Internet, by telephone, and by other means in addition to face-to-face visits.

2. Customization based on patient needs and values. The system of care should be designed to meet the most common types of needs, but have the capability to respond to individual patient choices and preferences.

3. The patient as the source of control. Patients should be given the necessary information and the opportunity to exercise the degree of control they choose over health care decisions that affect them. The health system should be able to accommodate differences in patient preferences and encourage shared decision-making.

4. Shared knowledge and the free flow of information. Patients should have unfettered access to their own medical information and to clinical knowledge. Clinicians and patients should communicate effectively and share information.

5. Evidence-based decision-making. Patients should receive care based on the best available scientific knowledge. Care should not vary illogically from clinician to clinician or from place to place.

6. Safety as a system property. Patients should be safe from injury caused by the care system. Reducing risk and ensuring safety require greater attention to systems that help prevent and mitigate errors.

7. The need for transparency. The health care system should make information available to patients and their families that allows them to make informed decisions when selecting a health plan, hospital, or clinical practice, or when choosing among alternative treatments. This should include information describing the system's performance on safety, evidence-based practice, and patient satisfaction.

8. Anticipation of needs. The health system should anticipate patient needs, rather than simply reacting to events.

9. Continuous decrease in waste. The health system should not waste resources or patient time.

10. Cooperation among clinicians. Clinicians and institutions should actively collaborate and communicate to ensure an appropriate exchange of information and coordination of care.

Part VI

Clinical Interventions

34

Brief Counseling and Therapy During Overseas Visits

John R. Powell

One of the main activities for mental health consultants on field visits is counseling. But not all problems are amenable to brief counseling or therapy. This chapter defines brief counseling/therapy and gives guidance for practice, including issues of assessment, treatment plan, and use of limited time. A discussion of areas often dealt with in brief counseling, and a look at levels of intervention help determine how best to use one's time.

*P*roviding brief counseling or therapy to missionaries overseas presents interesting challenges, opportunities and complexities. The overseas context often requires new levels of skill, understanding and creativity. The privilege of providing such services far outweighs the challenges as one has opportunities to enhance the vitality of those on the front lines of cross-cultural missions. Successful brief counseling/therapy is Kingdom work in the spirit of being "one in Christ."

The needs or concerns which can be helped through effective counseling/therapy approaches are not wholly different from many encountered at home. However, they are shaped by the context—the demands, experiences and ethos of missionary life.

Some years ago, in the final meeting of a week-long counseling/discussion group which had worked on carefully circumscribed issues, we had summarized some of the gains and insights realized and were moving toward closure and some difficult good-byes. I asked the group, "If you could send a message with me to people at home, what would it be?" Here is a summary of their answers:

> First of all, that we're just like them. We hurt sometimes and we rejoice sometimes. We struggle a lot but by God's grace we overcome.
>
> We worry about our spouses, our children, our families at home, and we sometimes wonder if we really heard God's call right.
>
> At times we feel angry, have conflicts, get depressed. We even doubt our faith sometimes.

When awful things happen, we have to find ways to go on. Sometimes we greatly need help.

Tell them we need and appreciate their prayers. We like it when someone lets us know they *really* understand our situation, and acknowledge something that is uniquely plain old individual "me."

Though we live in very different circumstances, we are all members of the body of Christ. Keep sending people to encourage us.

A basic truth is embedded in these answers: each of us is "like all others, like some others and like no others." (An old psychological adage, and Biblically true!) One of the tasks in providing brief counseling/therapy on the field is to be keenly aware of likenesses, acknowledging the desire of the Father for Christlikeness in all of us, but concentrating on the uniqueness of each person and his or her experiences, needs, resources and possibilities.

The complexities multiply when we also need to understand the history, strengths, weaknesses and current struggles of the person seeking help, to develop a reasonable intervention plan which can be accomplished in a brief counseling/therapy format, and plan for adequate closure. Such is the challenge! And such is the clear need to rely not on our own strength, but God's.

What is Brief Counseling/Therapy?

The terms *counseling* and *therapy* (short for psychotherapy) are often used inter-changeably, but in this discussion we will distinguish between them.

Counseling is a relationship and process directed toward improvement. It utilizes skills ranging from educational, advice-giving, providing support, clarifying decision-making and encouraging, to helping an individual gain insight about self and others, handle interpersonal tensions, achieve more happiness in marriage, be a better parent or overcome inner tensions or anxieties.

Therapy is a relationship and process directed toward achieving relief from intra- or interpersonal tensions, overcoming psychological disorders or problems, gaining insight into self, others and problematic interactions, and changing harmful patterns of thought, feelings or behavior.

There is obvious overlap. *Counseling* is broader than *therapy*, is used by a wider range of professionals, and focuses largely on normal problems of normal people. Therapy focuses more on change within individuals and usually has more circumscribed parameters.

The *brief* aspect of interventions makes time an important variable. In mission settings, the duration of therapy is often controlled externally and helps determine just *what* problems are addressed, *how* they are approached and *when* (duration and intensity) they are treated.

The literature on brief, time limited counseling and therapy has blossomed over the past three decades, spurred by theoretical and conceptual development, successful practice and the necessity for greater efficiency. For an understanding of these developments in historical context see Strupp and Binder (1984) *Psychotherapy in a New Key* and Budman and Gurman (1988) *Theory and Practice of Brief Therapy*.

For the purposes of brevity the term *therapy* will be used here to encompass the broader spectrum of counseling and therapy. Counseling, while not always therapy, almost always has therapeutic qualities.

Approach to the Process

In providing brief therapy, the therapist bears a heavy responsibility for clear, accurate professional work taking into account a complex set of variables. Process is important, and the parameters which surround it in a mission setting can both facilitate and limit it. An effective approach to brief therapy involves a three-fold task:

1. *Knowing the What*

A rapid, accurate assessment includes the strengths and weaknesses of the person, their capacity to effectively utilize treatment, a contextual and historical understanding of issues and persons, and sound judgement in making a *therapeutic contract*.

Judgement might involve choosing some aspects of the problem which can reasonably be expected to be resolved or have closure in the allotted time, with acknowledgment of larger issues but no plans to work with them in the current therapeutic relationship.

Another option is simply to work on the solution of a situation created by a deeper problem, but not get into the deeper problem. Work would thus be oriented to problem solving. Suggestions for later work or referral might be made in reference to deeper needs.

2. *Knowing the How*

Developing a treatment plan takes into account the reality of time, the assessment, the strengths of the person(s) involved, and the larger context. This involves clarifying issues with the client, agreement on a goal, awareness on the therapist's part of a reasonable outcome, and choosing a relevant approach within the time-defined relationship.

Therapy is a process and often involves change or adjustment as it unfolds. A key to its success is continual integration and relating the approach to the identified goal. In very short work, such as a session or two, it is important that the therapist be aware of the issues and goal, but it may be unnecessary to articulate those in detail to the client.

3. *Knowing the When*

Here the variable of time becomes a capstone for creativity. Given the need, assessment, goal and therapeutic strategies, how can time be optimally utilized to bring about the best possible results? A quick good-bye to the weekly fifty-minute hour, still used in most time-limited or time-defined brief therapies Stateside, is usually a requirement.

Options are governed by the optimum balance of: 1) client needs, 2) what he or she can tolerate in intensity, 3) the understanding and skills of the therapist, and 4) always, the necessity of an orderly closure within the defined time limit.

A missionary whom a therapist had seen on previous visits for tensions in an unhappy marriage (his wife refused to be seen) said to the therapist upon arrival, "I'd like to spend an afternoon with you on the beach." The meaning was clear without further elaboration. The next afternoon they spent four hours together discussing fears about his impending retirement and his wife's insistence that they live in a rather isolated spot so she could care for her aged father. This intense closeness, he feared, would not allow him to use coping skills he had developed to tolerate the marriage.

In these hours several options were developed, a plan suggested for consideration and development over the next two days, and two additional two-hour sessions were scheduled. These were effectively used and a satisfactory closure was obtained, part of which included referral to a Christian counselor within a two-hour drive of the retirement location.

While balancing of the *why, what* and *when* variables focuses almost solely on the client-therapist relationship, the therapist must always be aware of the context, relationships with and responsibilities to field leadership, other resources such as prayer, support, and follow-up, and the needs and concerns of other missionaries. Attention to self-care for the therapist (especially exercise, rest and reflective/prayer/devotional time) is also important.

Distinguishing Features

The following features distinguish brief counseling/therapy in comparison to open-ended therapy (Powell, 1992, p.125).

- Utilization of time as a treatment variable
- Limited number of sessions .
- Concentration on one issue or goal
- Rapid, early assessment
- High level of therapist activity
- Ventilation of emotional tension
- High therapist flexibility, pragmatism and creativity
- Formation of a quick therapeutic alliance
- Careful attention to the selection of clients
- High client motivation for change

Budman and Gurman (1988) point out that "many changes will take place following therapy and be unobservable to the therapist," and that it is important to see the client "as being in the world rather than being in therapy" (p. 11). The therapist is never alone in helping to bring about improvement. Many others play both subtle and obvious parts in the resolution, decision, understanding and/or action of the person as improvement takes place.

A bedrock truth is in Christ's statement "I will never leave you nor forsake you." In the midst of difficulties, the experience of this truth is sometimes diminished or lost. The therapist can remind the client of this truth—not so much in words, perhaps, but in listening, understanding and a compassionate presence.

The wise therapist is also aware that brief therapy, while usually helpful, can also be harmful, especially in the time-limited circumstances of mission settings. Thus, a heavy burden is placed on the therapist for the best possible understanding of the client, his or her situation, and the relevance of the approach undertaken. The features listed above allow flexibility for adaptation, balance and applicability to a particular situation.

Two important considerations

First is the key concept of **humble collaboration**. As noted above, one must embrace and rely on many factors affecting the client and his or her understanding, growth and change. A fundamental reliance on God's guidance and strength, and communication with him in prayer throughout the process, is a must.

Collaboration with field leadership and others with responsibilities relating to the field visit, and communication with those in the client's life as necessary while observing professional ethics, are also important. For example, pastoral care and counseling is often very helpful. Family members, friends or co-workers may be able to provide support, encouragement and accountability. Collaboration with medical personnel may be indicated when medication is an issue or the problem is related to a physical condition. It's important for the outside therapist to remember that he or she is a guest in the mission world, is always on a learning curve, and that humility is the watchword. (See Dr. Karen Carr's (2002) article, "A Guest in Their World," for a meaningful discussion.)

Second is the awareness that **brief therapy may be contraindicated**. The therapist may be very useful to the person and situation by taking the role of consultant rather than therapist. Meeting with the person to explore and/or assess the problem or concern can result in a referral, a recommended course of action, or a treatment approach outside the purview of brief therapy. See Chapter 45 on long-term therapy for a good example of this type of consultation.

Leaving the field is sometimes the best course of action, unless on-going services are available while on the field at a location such as Tumaini Counseling Center in Nairobi. Some missionaries report excellent success in seeing nationals who are English-speaking mental health professionals.

Areas of Focus

We now turn to potential areas of focus. Some overlap with others, while others clearly stand alone. In practice it is important to define a clear area of focus and to set a definite goal.

Crises

Crises seem to be part of the fabric of missionary life. *A crisis is any event or situation which interrupts the normal flow of life and diverts attention away from usual concerns.* While crises have objective differences in severity, the existence of a crisis is determined in part by the individual's interpretation of the event and its effect, subtle or obvious, upon the person.

Much attention has been given in recent years to having mental health professionals available as soon as possible following a crisis. Brief therapy can often help restore equilibrium by processing the event and working to alleviate unwanted feelings or patterns which emanate from the experience. One helpful aspect is helping the victim normalize reactions to the event, often important to a process of healing and overcoming its effects.

Traumatic Events

These events constitute crises but also imply a wound to the physical, psychic, spiritual or relational structure in an individual. Brief interventions following such events can be quite helpful, though sometimes more than brief therapy is indicated, especially if post-traumatic stress disorder develops.

In some cases the residuals from a traumatic event will kick up problematic responses to an immediate situation. A carefully discerned brief therapy approach is often helpful in such cases. The focus would likely be on the current event and how to respond to it, with understanding achieved as the client sees how his or her reaction to it may have been overdetermined, as it were, by the previous trauma.

Transitions

Transitions are also part of the fabric of missionary life. These may involve geographical moves, changes in work or ministry responsibilities, sending a child to boarding school, illness, change in a relationship, and a host of others which seem routine in missionary experience. (See chapter 11 by Dr. Laura Mae Gardner for a discussion of transitions in missionary life.) Brief therapy can often be helpful by focusing on the unfinished business of transitions, helping an individual or couple prepare for a known transition to come, or process one which may have some traumatic feelings associated with it.

Losses

In missionary life, losses are often experienced which are not fully recognized or adequately grieved. The demands of missionary life too often mitigate against the quiet reflection needed to process and accept losses. Unrecognized, they can result in feelings that "something isn't right" but the person isn't aware of the source.

Examples of losses are health changes, difficulties in relationships without resolution, a long-anticipated hope being dashed, or reassignment that takes one away from satisfying work and ministry. Brief therapy can help reveal losses, allow the person to relate the loss to their current malaise, and find freedom from the effects of not having processed the loss.

Developmental Hurdles

Sometimes missionaries are stuck in achieving a new level of development. Examples are a single woman who is convinced that God wants her to be married and have children but is finding neither, failure to mature in tolerance of others in relationships, difficulty in taking on new responsibility, and failure to grow in normally accepted ways.

New responsibilities in the family life cycle can also create challenges for which help is needed. The chapter titled Developmental Tasks in the Life Cycle of Mission Families (O'Donnell, 1988) provides a helpful backdrop for assessing these issues.

Interpersonal Conflict

This is an area of high frequency in missionary service, and shows up among the top causes of stress in two studies on missionary stress. (Gish, 1983; Carter, 1999; see Chapter 12.) This area is sometimes the sole cause for inviting a mental health professional to the field. Despite the clear directions in Matthew 18 and other places in Scripture for handling this, it remains a problem of some frequency.

Interpersonal conflict can be handled successfully through a short term intervention in a number of cases, though where there is long-standing group conflict much more is required. Forgiveness sometimes becomes the point of focus in such cases. Chapter 43 by Rebecca Leverington and Chapter 14 by Dr. Dale Schumm in this volume deal helpfully with forgiveness, and Chapter 32 by Dr. Barney Davis discusses conflict resolution in more detail.

Stress

Many situations, events and relationships can account for stress in a missionary's life. The focus for brief therapy in this area is not just the stress itself, but causes and means of coping. Chapter 13 by Dr. Jan Yeaman deals helpfully with aspects of stress.

The task for the therapist doing brief therapy here, as in most areas, is an accurate assessment and the development of therapeutic strategies which take into account the level of stress, its causes and ways of preventing and/or coping with it. Adequately dealing with situations involving stress may require interventions well beyond brief therapy and may involve consultation at an organizational level within the mission.

Marital and Family Tensions

This common area of concern may cut across the areas of stress, transitions, interpersonal conflict and developmental hurdles, thus making it difficult to find a specific focus for short term work. However, when a couple is ready and has a high motivation for change, or find a common bonding in parental concerns, brief interventions can often help in ways beyond that normally expected.

Work- or Ministry-Related Situations

These can often be successfully addressed in brief therapy, though direct collaboration with field leadership may be necessary for resolution. A misfitting assignment, inadequate use of gifts, skills or competencies, too much or not enough work or responsibility, lack of clear expectations, lack of supervisory support and understanding, and missionary/leader conflicts are examples of this area.

The primary therapeutic focus may need to be the participation of the missionary in allowing situations to continue, given a readiness to project onto mission leadership issues which are primarily those of the missionary.

Symptomatic Manifestations

Some requests in a brief field visit have to do with long-standing symptoms such as sleep disorders, sexual dysfunction, phobias, bipolar disorders and others. Budman and Gurman (1988) point out that in brief therapy it is important to attend to these at the symptom level, not at the level of underlying causes, and to develop a strategy directed at symptom removal rather than structural change. In short visits even this may be more than can reasonably be accomplished, although thorough assessment may produce options which can be helpful. Providing some instant relief and understanding while looking to referral and possibly treatment during home assignment may be the best course of action.

Spiritual Concerns

These may permeate many of the other topics and yet be the essential point of focus. Chronic busyness as an avoidance of spiritual disciplines, relationships or reflective time before God are not uncommon foci for brief therapeutic work on the field. Failure to adequately integrate one's faith with his or her work or sense of call may be another area. Even the growing recognition that the sense of call one has may be a pseudo call is sometimes a point of focus (See Chapter 28 on the call for more discussion of this).

Moral Failure

Such things as sexual acting out, child abuse or molestation, thievery or dishonesty with management of funds, internet addiction, pornography and other behaviors constitute moral failure on the part of missionaries. Mental health consultants are often asked to assist in determining the best administrative course of action in such circumstances, although brief therapy is usually not the treatment of choice. The therapist can sometimes be helpful in assisting the person to see the results of what they have done, understand the consequences and begin some important internal processing.

These are only a few of the possible focal points for brief therapy. Some almost automatically involve others, some are highly internal and others have features not always amenable to this treatment modality. Again, the responsibility of the brief therapist is to make rapid and accurate assessments, develop a treatment strategy in which time is an important variable and which has a reasonable chance for a positive result and, always, to be guided through prayer.

Levels of Intervention

The therapist is responsible for developing an approach which is optimum for the situation, given an understanding of the person and his or her needs. It is helpful to consider what level of intervention is most relevant to the need. Here is a simple model of levels of approach.

Level 1: Strengthening – a relationship, process or interaction strengthens or builds up the person. Present strengths are affirmed, potential strengths are developed, and visions, hopes or goals are brought into sharper focus.

Level 2: Permitting – the individual is helped to move into areas of greater growth, fruitfulness, satisfaction and/or spiritual depth through a relationship and interaction that permits, encourages or motivates that movement. It allows the person to move forward, overcoming internal or external barriers to doing so.

Level 3: Facilitating – the person needs active facilitation for change, initiative in a relationship or ministry, resolving a conflict or making personal changes.

Level 4: Clarifying – removal of blockages due to inner tension, conflicting goals or values, or uncertainty in relationships. Work at this level is designed to clarify aspects of life, self, work or relationship with God which may be clouded. Some examples are lack of clear knowledge about the self or lack of clarity of mission, purpose, strategy, or definition of one's work.

Level 5: Resolving – active interventions are designed to identify underlying conflicts or tensions which show themselves in patterned behavior. A fear of closeness and the wish for it, the desire for responsibility and the avoidance of it, the making of commitments and the failure to follow through are examples of need at this level. Presentation often comes in terms of a situational experience, but gentle questioning can usually surface and identify the issue requiring work.

Level 6: Remedying – remediation of self-defeating or destructive patterns of behavior and movement toward or restoration of more healthful patterns. This is a level of more serious need and usually not appropriate for brief therapy. At times, one particular pattern may be identified and worked on, with adequate closure and without a lot of psychological uncovering.

Level 7: Extensive/Intensive Intervening – more serious and long-standing problems need to be assessed and treated. This level is seldom appropriate for brief work. The therapist may be helpful by providing consultation and referral.

Encouragement is an important part of successful work at all levels. Although the strategy and technique may sometimes be confrontational and anxiety-producing, when the desired result is achieved it is usually experienced as encouraging.

In the span of brief therapy—an hour or two or several—the therapist may work at most of these levels. He or she may see need at deeper levels but consciously avoid doing so in order to stay with the defined focus and goal. This minimizes the risk of opening up an area where adequate closure cannot be obtained.

Complementary Care

The effective therapist never works alone. Complementary care facilitates the work of brief therapy, and brief therapy complements the ongoing care of others. Collaboration with mission administrators, medical doctors, pastoral caregivers and counselors as well as the broad array member care workers enhances the lives and work of missionaries. It is important to acknowledge others and to work effectively, relationally and cooperatively with them, utilizing one another's resources and working toward the common goal of enhancing those who carry the Gospel into far away and often difficult places.

Concluding Comments

This chapter has focused on brief counseling and therapy during overseas visits by mental health professionals. It is written from the perspective of an outside consultant, though much applies to in-house mental health professionals as well. In many situations, those from within and outside mission agencies often work together, each bringing a valuable perspective. This is particularly true during crises, traumatic events and other unusual circumstances. Even in "normal" situations, collaboration, cross referral and consultation with one another demonstrate being members of Christ's body, working for the same purpose.

Chapter 21 in this volume gives a tripartite model of consultation relevant to this discussion. An extensive treatment of issues in field counseling, including common errors, can be found in Cerny and Smith (2002).

The privilege of working with and serving those on the front lines of missions is unparalleled for the Christian mental health professional, but not without its demands. Someone has said "It's a great life if you don't weaken." The truth is, we all weaken, and before God we all need one another to be strengthened and built up again—which God provides. That's a great life indeed!

References

Bauer, G., & Kobos, J. (1988). *Brief therapy: Short-term psychodynamic intervention.* Northvale, NJ: Jason Aaronson.

Budman, S. H., & Gurman, A.S. (1988). *Theory and practice of brief therapy.* New York: Guilford Press.

Carr, K. (2002). A guest in their world. In O'Donnell, K. (Ed.). *Doing member care well: Perspectives and practices from around the world.* (pp. 323-329). Pasadena, CA: William Carey Library.

Carter, J. (1999). Missionary stressors and implications for care. *Journal of Psychology and Theology 27,* 2, 171-180. (Summarized in Chapter 12 of this volume.)

Cerny, L. J., & Smith, D. S. (2002). Field counseling: separating the wheat from the chaff. In O'Donnell, K. (Ed.). *Doing member care well: Perspectives and practices from around the world.* (pp. 489-499). Pasadena, CA: William Carey Library

Gish, D. J. (1983). Sources of missionary stress. *Journal of Psychology and Theology 11,* (3), 236-242.

O'Donnell, K. S. (1988). Developmental tasks in the life cycle of mission families. In O'Donnell, K.S. and O'Donnell, M. L. (Eds.). *Helping missionaries grow: Readings in mental health and missions.* (pp. 148-163). Pasadena, CA: William Carey Library.

Powell, J. (1992). Short-term missionary counseling. In O'Donnell, K. *Missionary care: Counting the cost for world evangelization.* (pp. 123-135). Pasadena, CA: William Carey Library.

Strupp, H., & Binder, J. (1984). *Psychotherapy in a new key.* New York: Basic Books.

35

Missionaries and Moods

Esther Schubert

I ntroduction
For many years the topic of depression or mood disorders in missionaries or Christian workers has been addressed as if mood disorders were a character flaw or a moral failing. This has caused the delivery of poor care to genuinely ill people and has also saddled people with incredible false guilt at times when they may not have been able to think clearly or rationally.

Fortunately, as psycho-biochemistry has become more sophisticated, we have seen that clinical depression and other mood disorders are true medical illnesses rather than character issues.

To understand depression or any mood disorder, one first has to be cognizant of the term *euthymia*. By definition, euthymia is a relatively even-keel mood that could be characterized visually as a horizontal line lasting the length of a person's life. Although most people who are euthymic have mild, brief mood changes, the overall pattern is a more or less straight line. Any mood disorder is a significant (by amplitude) and lengthy deviation from the horizontal line.

Mood disorders or episodes can deviate above the line looking much like a bell-shaped curve (or other shape). These are defined as manic episodes. A reversed bell-shaped curve below the line would be defined as a depressive episode.

By definition, an episode of mania has to last at least one week, or it could be a bit shorter than one week if hospitalization is necessary. A manic episode is a specific period of unusual and persistent elevated, expansive, or irritable mood lasting for a week or more. During the time of this elevated or irritable mood, the individual must have three or more of the following symptoms:

Depression has been called the "common cold" of psychological problems. Clinical depression and other mood disorders are treatable medical ilnesses. Missionaries can be successfully treated for depression and returned to effective service. This chapter explains common mood disorders and helps non-medical people identify when depression needs medical treatment and in some cases crisis intervention.

- Inflated self-esteem
- Decreased need for sleep
- Talkativeness
- Rapid thoughts, often quickly switching from topic to topic
- Distractibility
- Increased activity or agitation
- Excessive involvement in pleasurable activities even though they have a high possibility of painful consequences.

A depressive episode must last for two weeks and include five out of nine symptoms:
- Depressed mood
- Lack of interest in usual pleasures
- Feelings of guilt or worthlessness
- Change in energy
- Decreased concentration
- Change in appetite
- Psycho-motor slowing
- Death preoccupation
- Suicidal thoughts

Most mood disorders are recurrent; the use of a horizontal timeline depicting a person's life can be valuable in revealing the long-term pattern of a mood disorder for a particular person.

Unipolar depression defines a type of mood disorder where all of the mood episodes are in one direction, that is, an inverted curve below the horizontal line. (See Figure 1)

Figure 1: Unipolar Depression

Bipolar mood disorders, as suggested by the name, include mood changes with episodes that may be either mania or depression. (See Figure 2)

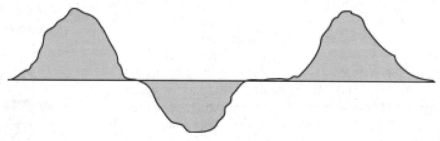

Figure 2: Bipolar Depression

The time span of episodes for both unipolar and bipolar illnesses can vary in length, but the minimum for diagnosis is one week for a manic episode and two weeks for a depressive episode.

Occasionally, individuals may be seen who exhibit "rapid cycling" of their bipolar illness. This does not imply mood changes within a day or several days, but four or more mood episodes (either manic or depressive) within a year.

Another type of mood disorder is Seasonal Affective Disorder, which is thought by some to be a subtype of Bipolar Disorder. Individuals with this illness are most likely to have an elevated mood during the summertime and a depressed mood during the winter. It is believed that, through the optic pathways, the length of days specifically affects areas of the brain that are related to mood.

For instance, the incidence of Seasonal Affective Disorder in Florida, where the days are relatively similar in length between winter and summer, is just one percent. At the U.S.-Canadian border, the incidence of Seasonal Affective Disorder is closer to ten percent. In Alaska, with its marked seasonal changes of very short days in the winter and very long days in the summer, the incidence of Seasonal Affective Disorder is approximately 17%.

Another type of mood disorder is Bipolar II, which has the cyclic components of Bipolar Disorder but the amplitude for the elevated moods is significantly less in a vertical direction. If an individual has an elevated mood but it does not quite meet the intensity criteria for mania, it is called a hypomanic episode. Individuals with Bipolar II Disorder still have some episodes of elevated mood and significant depressive episodes. However, their elevated moods tend to be hypomanic and their depressive moods are full-fledged depressions. (See Figure 3)

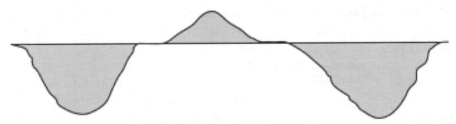

Figure 3: Bipolar II Depression

There are individuals with Bipolar Disorder who have characteristics of depression and mania at the same time. These are called mixed episodes and are usually characterized by a high energy level similar to the manic episodes, but at the same time the person may be experiencing significant dysphoria. People who are in a mixed episode of Bipolar Disorder are at high risk for suicide since they have the depressive mood, often with a preoccupation with death, and they also have the energy to act on their desire to die.

One other type of mood disorder is Cyclothymia. By definition this is an illness where, for at least two years, there may be numerous periods of hypomanic symptoms as well as numerous periods of depressive symptoms but they do not quite meet the criteria for a major depressive episode. In children these symptoms need to be present for at least a year.

Other mood disorders can include depression due to a medical illness, due to drug abuse, or precipitated by hormonal changes or certain types of medications.

Since unipolar depression is the most common type of depression, and has been referred to as the "common cold of psychology in missions," I will devote more space to it, starting with treatment.

To address treatment for depression in missionaries, we will look at the pre-field process, on-field episodes of depression, and after-care.

Pre-field Process

In the pre-field process, it is sometimes difficult to identify individuals who have a tendency toward depression. Since the psychological testing is essentially a snapshot in time, and since the illness tends to be episodic, the individual may not give indications of depression at the time of pre-field testing. For that reason, I include many questions in the life history questionnaire to rule out tendencies in this direction. These include: personal episodes of depression, previous counseling or need for medication; family history of mood disorders or other psychiatric family history; and matters of childhood environment such as dysfunctional families, alcoholism in the family, absent parents, abuse and neglect, sexual abuse or assaults, and incest. This allows the mission committee or personnel department to identify tendencies that might surface under the stress of cross-cultural living even if the individual at the time of testing is very healthy.

On-field Episodes of Depression

The on-field evaluation of a missionary or tentmaker who might be depressed can be quite complicated. This evaluation needs to address the seriousness of the person's depression, and whether there is any suicidality. Many mission locations have limited availability for psychiatric hospitalization (if the person is suicidal) and there may not be sophisticated medical personnel to prescribe medication or to arrange for psychotherapy when the person is able to engage in it.

In my opinion, a missionary who becomes depressed enough to be suicidal probably needs to be brought back to the home country for the care that is needed. This also frees up other missionaries to do mission work rather than attempt psychological or psychiatric care in an environment that may not be conducive to quality wraparound services.

There are locations where a missionary doctor or a national psychiatrist could provide medication and there may be a western or national psychologist available to do psychotherapy. Although medication can be prescribed by someone who is not a Christian (in the same way that a non-Christian doctor can prescribe an antibiotic for a strep throat), lengthy psychotherapy needs to be done by a qualified professional who is both a Christian and is cognizant of the patient's cultural context.

Occasionally individuals who become depressed or manic are also psychotic. The vast majority of mission locations overseas are not able to address an illness that is this severe. In addition, psychosis often involves religious delusions which can be very confusing, are obviously not scriptural, and therefore can cause difficulties for the mission and the national church.

Whether a depressed missionary is treated on the field or in the home country, in most cases medication needs to be prescribed for as much as a year or longer. In addition, if the patient has had a previous episode of depression, the possibilities of other episodes in the future are increased to the degree that the individual may need to stay on anti-depressant medications indefinitely. After one episode of depression, there is about a 50% chance of a second episode. After a second episode, the recurrence rate is closer to 70%, and after a third episode, the rate approaches 90% or more.

Missionaries and their sending organizations are sometimes guilty of wanting a "quick fix" for mood disorders. Part of this is due to the expense of long-term psychotherapy and also because some people are still hesitant to acknowledge depression as a biochemical illness rather a personal flaw. However, if a patient with depression has the opportunity for good psychotherapy, this should be done as long as necessary (often weekly for six months to a year or even longer), because depression often decreases defense mechanisms so that long-hidden unresolved issues can be addressed effectively.

After-care

After-care involves appropriate continuation of medication depending upon (a) the severity of the episode, (b) whether the individual is psychotic or not, and (c) whether the individual can be maintained appropriately on field or needs to return to the home country. Mission organizations need to provide whatever long-term psychotherapy is necessary rather than expecting a quick turnaround in treatment. A need for long-term medication for depression should be seen as similar to needing ongoing medication for diabetes or high blood pressure, not as a factor which disqualifies the individual for further mission service.

Although this discussion of depression emphasizes unipolar depression, it is important to remember that overseas personnel with a personal history or a family history of bipolar disorder must be managed very carefully. Placing a person who is bipolar on anti-depressants when he is depressed may actually change the polarity into a manic episode which is very difficult to deal with overseas.

Obviously, if a person is in the process of becoming bipolar and the first episode is a depressive episode which occurs overseas, the diagnosis of bipolarity may be inadvertently made when the individual is started on an anti-depressant without a mood stabilizer and becomes manic. Obviously, people who are psychotic with their mood disorder will need anti-psychotic medication. Those who are bipolar need to have their treatment centered around a mood stabilizer with anti-depressants added only as a second-line treatment.

One final caveat has to do with a type of depression not mentioned in the article so far. People with deep-seated personality disorders may appear to be depressed, but many of them have been referred for psychological or psychiatric help because their personality problems have created so much discomfort that they *feel* depressed.

Unfortunately, people with personality disorders need a very lengthy course of treatment which often takes years and is best accomplished in one's own country. Many of us who are involved in pre-field testing feel quite strongly that individuals with personality disorders should, in most cases, be steered in a direction other than overseas missionary service, since the cost of lengthy treatment is likely to divert too many mission resources into mental health care.

Crisis Intervention

Field leaders need the following in order to provide crisis intervention for mood disorders:

- Understanding of different types of depression
- Ability to detect and diagnose depression
- Clarification of the potential for suicide
- Arrangements for disposition (deciding on location and type of treatment)
- Ensuring the safety of everyone involved

Fortunately, as we better understand the biochemistry of mood disorders, we can increase the number of missionaries who can be successfully treated for mood disorders and returned to effective missionary service after treatment.

36

Psychosomatic Disorders

Barney Davis

Stress and emotional pressure often produce physical symptoms. Many factors in mission service make development of symptoms more likely or problematic. This chapter looks at physical symptoms which are a normal response to stress, are aggravated by stress, or are abnormal responses to stress. Proper assessment and intervention for psychosomatic illness is discussed, including spiritual factors and therapeutic relationships.

*T*hen the king's face grew pale and his thoughts alarmed him, and his hip joints went slack and his knees began knocking together. Daniel 5:6 NASB
I will give thanks to you, for I am fearfully and wonderfully made. Psalm 139:14 NASB

From the very first time that someone experiences embarrassment and feels a hot flushing sensation in their face as they blush, the connection between emotion and physical symptoms is evident. Every person at one time or another has experienced physical symptoms related to stress and emotional pressure.

Between 60 and 80% of people in the general population experience physical complaints during any one week, and physicians can find a physical cause of these complaints in less than 70%. Missionaries are no less susceptible, but there are unique factors in mission service that can make such symptoms even more likely or problematic:

Inadequate utilization of medical care

Money – unfortunately, money (or the lack thereof) still exerts a major impact on the accessibility to and utilization of medical resources. This is particularly the case with missionaries, who often find themselves chronically underfunded for even the most basic of life activities. Even when medical consultation is donated or provided for minimal cost, the expense of diagnostic testing and medications may still prohibit adequate evaluation.

Time – one of the most frequently heard complaints from missionaries is that they do not have enough time to address the needs of their ministry, their family, and their own personal spiritual growth. To take even a little time to

attend to preventive health activities or early medical evaluation of symptoms is problematic.

Attitude – the nature of many Christians is to believe that because of their faith, they should be able to handle any stress, anywhere, anytime with no adverse consequences. As a result, they may tend to ignore early warning signs of escalating stressful situations, and begin to experience physical symptoms.

Poor availability of medical care

Distance – missionaries serving on distant fields may find that medical and counseling care, if available at all, may be so far geographically removed that efforts to access it are reserved for only the most obvious and serious of medical or emotional conditions. Therefore, stress-related physical symptoms may be allowed to develop to levels of significant duration and severity before receiving any attention.

Inconsistency of medical expertise – those who are accustomed to "Western-style" medical care are used to finding medical personnel who share a common body of knowledge, similar evaluation and therapeutic philosophies, and have access to a plethora of laboratory and diagnostic tools.

While similar levels of care can be found in developed countries (and large urban sites in less well developed countries), that found in remote areas may be inconsistent, highly variable in approach, and limited to the personal skill of the clinician, who may have little or no useful diagnostic equipment. Physical symptoms that may arise from stress might be misdiagnosed, overlooked, or approached with ineffective treatment.

Unique aspects of stress in mission settings

Some unique aspects of stress in mission settings are likely to lead to physical symptoms.

Extremes of heat, cold, or diminished sunlight – these can cause emotional stress, which can present primarily as physical symptoms.

Parasitic disease – climate and poor sanitation techniques lead to a greater risk of infection with parasitic organisms. Often these will cause subtle, gradually progressive symptoms such as weakness, lethargy, and loss of initiative.

Dangerous circumstances – living in areas with the threat of kidnapping, physical attack, or political upheaval can lead to "campaign stress," which may manifest by vague, generalized physical symptoms.

Dietary issues – maintenance of healthy dietary habits may not be possible in many parts of the world; anemia and vitamin deficiencies can result, leading to both emotional and diffuse physical symptoms.

Exposure to others in dire need (compassion fatigue) – many missionaries serve in situations where they are witness to extremes of poverty, famine, and displacement. Emotional numbness and somatic discomfort are frequently felt as a result of constant exposure to such circumstances.

Inadequate medical intervention by uninformed medical personnel – as noted above, financial need might motivate the missionary to seek care from the most affordable resource. Many health care providers are willing to provide such care without charge or at minimal cost, but they themselves may have little if any awareness of the special circumstances of missionary service, and may tend to over- or under-evaluate somatic symptoms caused by stress.

Poor communication between missionary and agency concerning health care - often it is not clear whose responsibility it is to insure the health care of the missionary, whether it might be the missionary's personal physician or health care personnel provided by the mission agency. As a result, symptom clusters may be overlooked, or evaluation of symptoms to determine their origins may not be appropriately pursued.

Pressure to accept missionary candidates – with decreasing numbers of missionary candidates and ever-problematic attrition issues, there is an automatic tendency to minimize characteristics of the candidates that might predispose them to stress-related physical disorders.

Spiritual attack – one should never forget that physical complaints as well as emotional symptoms could be the direct result of attacks of Satan.

Physical symptoms that are related to stress can take many different forms. Once thought to be a nonspecific bodily response to any excessive demand or unpleasant condition, stress-induced physical symptoms and disease are now known to be a very complex adaptational reaction to a situation that is perceived as stressful.

The individual's emotional response to the stress has more bearing on the development of symptoms than does the actual degree of the stress itself. Three people working together in the same stressful circumstance might exhibit totally different reactions; one may have little adverse reaction to the situation, another might have primarily an emotional reaction with or without secondary physical symptoms which they attribute to the stress, and the third might have physical symptom or malfunction which they do not recognize as connected to the situation.

The differences in response are due to the wide range of genetic, developmental, and experiential circumstances that make each of us unique. Some stress related physical symptoms and conditions are more likely to occur "normally" in anyone who experiences such stress. In such cases, both the person experiencing the symptoms and the person who may be called to evaluate them see and accept the cause-and-effect connection between the stress and the physical symptoms.

However, stress can, in a way not fully understood, create physical symptoms that may not be so obvious in terms of cause and effect, and in such situations the person experiencing the symptom may avoid or resent any explanation that the underlying cause may be due to stress.

Missionaries are perhaps more prone than many to have difficulty accepting that they may be having an adverse reaction to stress, if they belief that such a reaction indicates a deficiency of faith. The member care specialist has a daunting task: not only to make a correct connection between the stress and the symptoms, but also to assist the missionary in understanding and accepting such a connection, so that a more successful approach to the stressful situation can be sought.

Table 1:   Physical Manifestations of Anxiety and Stress

Chest pain	Muscle aches
Choking sensation	Muscle tension
Diarrhea	Nausea
Dizziness	Numbness and tingling
Dry mouth	Sexual dysfunction
Easily startled	Shakiness
Faintness	Shortness of breath
Fatigability	Smothering sensation
Fidgetiness	Stomach pain
Flushing	Sweating
Headache	Tachycardia (rapid heart beat)
Hot or cold flashes	Trembling
Hyperventilation	Unsteady feeling
Jumpiness	Urinary frequency
Lightheadedness	Vertigo
Lump in throat	Vomiting

The interface between emotions and physical symptoms can be grouped into four different general categories:

I.   *Physical symptoms that are a normal response to stressful circumstances or psychological conditions*

These are readily recognizable and expected physical symptom clusters that occur in the face of acute or prolonged situations of significant external stress. There are no specific diagnostic tests which would confirm such patterns, nor do any tests reveal obvious damage or malfunction of any particular part of the body.

Any organ system may be affected, but the most common are the cardio-vascular, gastrointestinal, and musculoskeletal systems. Cardiovascular symptoms would include rapid heartbeat, a sensation of the heart skipping beats, light-headedness, and shortness of breath. Gastrointestinal symptoms can include queasiness, nausea, diarrhea, and loss of appetite. Tension headaches, backache, and generalized muscle aches can come from involvement of the musculoskeletal system. Table 1 lists some of the many physical manifestations of psychic stress.

This is certainly not a complete list, as stress has been known to cause or mimic almost any medical symptom with the possible exception of fever. These symptom clusters tend to be seen with any of the anxiety disorders, and with some of the mood disorders. The Diagnostic and Statistical Manual Fourth Edition (DSM-IV) lists a number of diagnoses that would be expected to have such symptoms:

Adjustment Disorder – these are the emotional reactions that occur in response to life events such as marital problems, job insecurity, disruption or termination of a relationship. While significant in their own right, these life events do not pose an immediate threat to the life or physical integrity of a person.

Such stressors usually are recognized by the individual as causative of the physical symptoms that may accom-pany the emotional distress, and the duration of symptoms usually are less than six months if the person can be removed from the stress or its consequences. Sustained stress, however, can cause ongoing symptoms. Overall, this category is the most common diagnosis made for missionaries suffering emotional and physical symptoms from their circumstances.

Acute Stress Disorder – this can occur when a person is exposed to a traumatic event in which they experienced, witnessed, or were confronted by a situation that involved actual or threatened death or injury, or threat to their physical integrity. In addition to the physical symptoms noted above, feelings of emotional detachment, altered awareness of one's environment, and recurrent thoughts and dreams of the event may also be seen. The actual stress event should have occurred within the preceding four weeks, and the symptom picture should clear within four weeks.

Post Traumatic Stress Disorder (PTSD) – similar in cause and symptom presentation to Acute Stress Disorder, PTSD may occur months or years after the stress event (such a delayed physical symptoms in adulthood that can be traced back to episodes of childhood sexual abuse), and may last longer than four weeks. Physical symptoms associated with PTSD typically include markedly increased startle response with increased muscular tension, headaches, chest tightness and shortness of breath, all which are more likely in situations which may resemble or recall the original stress event. In mission settings, PTSD often results from witnessing or experiencing life disrupting or threatening events caused by political upheavals, unexpected abrupt removal from the field, and mass casualties seen in famine and natural disasters.

Generalized Anxiety Disorder (GAD) – similar to Acute Stress Disorder, GAD is characterized more by its duration (more than 6 months). The psychosomatic symptoms tend to be more diffuse and vague, particularly easy fatigability and muscle tension.

Panic disorder – a discrete, sudden onset of intense fear or discomfort which is accompanied by multiple symptoms such as pounding, racing heart beat, sweating, trembling, sensations of choking, chest pain or tightness, numbness and tingling, and a feeling of impending death or fear of losing control. The circumstances which trigger such an attack may not be obvious, or may be appear minimal and inconsequential. The person who has had a panic attack will often spend much time and effort subsequently trying to avoid any circumstance that might trigger another.

Depression – people suffering from clinical depression experience an increase in somatic symptoms, often vague and indistinct (fatigue, dizziness, loss of appetite) but frequently involving the gastrointestinal tract (pain, constipation, bloating, multiple food intolerance). While the cardinal symptom of depression is an alteration in mood, on occasion the disease will present primarily as physical complaints (more common in elderly and in children).

II. *Physical illnesses that are initiated or aggravated by stressful circumstances*

Where the previous conditions with somatic symptoms usually do not show any obvious tissue pathology (damage or illness of any particular organ), nor do they accompany a recognized physiological change (such a migraine headache or asthma attack), stress can trigger or worsen the course of some general medical conditions. The person with the symptoms (or the member care specialist) may not be aware of the underlying medical problem, and thus the discomfort of the symptoms themselves creates more stress and subsequently more symptoms.

The correct diagnostic terminology for such a situation is "psychological factors affecting medical condition," with the subcategory of "stress-related physiological response affecting a medical condition." Common examples of such disorders include tension and migraine headaches, high blood pressure, peptic ulcers, ulcerative colitis, and asthma.

III.   *General medical conditions that can cause symptoms which mimic those seen in stress reaction*

There are classic medical disturbances which may present initially with what appear to be psychological symptoms. When these occur in the context of stressful circumstances, the underlying medical problem may not be recognized. While many medical conditions can cause such symptoms, the more frequently seen are thyroid dysfunction (particularly hyperthyroidism), adrenal gland dysfunction, neurological conditions such as multiple sclerosis and the early phases of some central nervous system infections, autoimmune disorders such as systemic lupus erythematosus, and the effects of medications.

The latter, side effects of medications, is particularly problematic for missionaries who may experience mood and anxiety symptoms from certain anti-malaria medications, or who may be given medications produced in countries where contents and quality of medications may be suspect.

IV.   *Somatic symptoms that arise from an abnormal response to stressful circumstances*

Whereas the previous categories have described either "normal" reactions to stressful situations, or the interaction between a defined medical problem and stress, this current category is characterized by an "abnormal" process of handling internal and external stress.

This process by definition is an unconscious one, and the person is not aware of the connection between the stressor and the somatic symptom. Usually, any efforts to attribute the physical symptom to an emotional or stress-related cause are met with disbelief and anger. Even though these individuals suffer significant distress from their disorders, the presence of a "physical" symptom may be more acceptable than a "psychological" explanation.

These disorders represent a more pathological handling of stress, and generally will require more formal psychological intervention than is usually available in mission settings. They are diagnostically grouped under the name "Somatoform Disorders."

Somatoform Disorders – the common feature of this group of disorders is the presence of physical symptoms that suggest a medical problem, are not under voluntary control, and for which no general medical condition can be found to account for the symptoms.

Somatization Disorder – this syndrome, formerly known as *hysteria* or *Briquet's syndrome*, is characterized by many physical complaints involving multiple organ systems, all of which develop before age 30 and persist for years. Necessary for the diagnosis are (1) a history of pain related to at least four different sites or functions, (2) at least two gastrointestinal symptoms other than pain, (3) history of at least one symptom involving sexual functioning or the reproductive system, other than pain, and (4) history of at least one "pseudoneurological" symptom or deficit such as weakness, paralysis, changes in vision, hearing, etc., for which no medical explanation can be found.

Differentiation between Somatization Disorder and the physical symptoms which can accompany Acute Stress and other Anxiety Disorders can be difficult, but the pervasive nature of and persistence of physical complaints is striking in Somatization Disorder.

Conversion Disorder – this condition presents as one or symptoms or deficits affecting voluntary motor or sensory function, for which no other medical cause can be found. Symptoms such as paralysis, localized weakness, numbness limited to one area or limb, double vision, blindness, deafness, and even seizure-like activity may be seen. The individual often seems surprisingly unconcerned with their symptoms (*la belle indifference*), and is totally unaware of any connection between stress in their lives and the physical symptoms which their reaction to such stress may manifest.

Hypochondriasis – preoccupation with fears of having, or the idea that one has, a serious disease, based on the person's misinterpretation of bodily symptoms. A person experiencing stress-related physical symptoms may misperceive those symptoms, and in spite of reassurance by appropriate medical evaluation, cling to a belief that they have a serious medical problem. For this diagnosis to be made, such feelings and symptoms must have a duration of at least six months.

Body Dysmorphic Disorder – this rather unusual condition is characterized by an imagined defect in one's appearance. Complaints commonly include exaggerated concerns about minor skin blemishes or scars, particularly on the face, or preoccupations with the size or shape of the nose, eyes, or other facial features. The person is greatly discomforted by this perception, and discounts others' attempts to reassure them about their appearance.

Pain Disorder – isolated, persistent pain in one area of the body, with no medical explanation. The pain is not voluntarily generated, and psychological or stress-related issues may not be seen as causative.

Proper Assessment and Intervention for Psychosomatic Symptoms

Spiritual Assessment – While the focus thus far has been on recognizing the more traditional categories of psychosomatic presentations and causes, one must consider that there will be times when the issues of unconfessed sin may underlie what appears to be a physical complaint: *When I kept silent about my sin, my body wasted away through my groaning all day long.* (Ps 32:3 NASB). Any assessment should begin with prayer, and include obtaining as much information as possible about any areas of conflict, past or present, that may be contributing to the current symptom picture.

Adequate medical evaluation – In the evaluation and management of psycho-somatic symptoms, it is imperative that medical disorders that might better account for the symptoms be ruled out. One of two mistakes is commonly made by health care personnel: prematurely attributing the somatic symptom to a psychological cause before adequate evaluation has been performed, or excessively pursuing diagnostic tests rather than addressing the probability of a psychological cause. The former leads to mistrust and potentially to worsening disease, the latter to prolongation and intensification of the symptoms.

Unfortunately, as noted in the first section of this chapter, access to qualified and competent medical care may be impractical, unaffordable, or flatly unobtainable on the field. Every effort should be made to make such an evaluation possible, but when impossible, it is important to not fall into the temptation to try to fit a psychological explanation to the symptom. To be able to assist with examination of possible stress and psychological etiologies, one must be able to assure that all medical factors that might contribute have been evaluated.

Establishment of trust in the therapeutic relationship – If a psychosomatic disorder is present, it is of little value to argue with the person about the origin of their symptoms. To be able to help the person understand the impact of stress and psychological factors in their symptoms, the clinician must first become an ally. The development of such a trusting relationship takes time, and cannot be rushed. This may pose a problem on the mission field, where access to care and time to develop it may be at a premium.

Appropriate and balanced intervention – Where external stress factors are con-tributing to the development of psychosomatic symptoms, a careful balance of inter-vention should be maintained. Depending on the nature of the stress, a primary intervention may be to remove the person from the stressful circumstance. This would certainly be true if there were evidence of ongoing physical or emotional threat. Yet, the focus is not just to remove the effect of the stress, but to have the individual develop more successful ways of dealing with it.

Psychological reactions during combat in World Wars I and II revealed that simple removal of the person from the conflict (such was the case in WW I and early in WW II) tended to make psychosomatic symptoms more resistant to treatment. Later techniques were more successful; short-term removal from conflict, adequate rest and basic emotional support, coupled with allowing a chance for emotional expression, allowed a return to action without residual dysfunction.

In much the same way, a balanced approach to the missionary experiencing stress-induced psychosomatic symptoms should be allowed a break from the action, with appropriate attention paid to issues of rest and restoration. The expectation, however, is return to the field wherever possible.

When internal psychological factors seem to be more causative than external ones, it may require more time to understand those factors and bring them to light, and therefore may lead to a longer period of removal from active missionary status being recommended.

While many different treatment philosophies and techniques have been attempted in approaching psychosomatic difficulties, a cognitively-based approach which teaches the individual to avoid catastrophizing their symptoms (the tendency to become so focused or preoccupied with the physical sensations that the stress and anxiety induced by the symptoms perpetuates the symptom) seems to have the most positive effect over time.

References

Diagnostic and Statistical Manual of Mental Disorders, Fourth Edition. Washington, DC, American Psychiatric Association, 1994.

Wise, Michael and Rundell, James: *Concise Guide to Consultation Psychiatry*, Washington, DC, American Psychiatric Press, Inc., 1988.

37

Crisis Intervention and Debriefing

Karen F. Carr

*T*he impact of trauma

When someone commits his or her life to God to serve as a missionary, there is an understanding and acceptance that this choice may involve suffering and trial. We accept this as part of the Christian life. Scripture tells us, *Dear friends, do not be surprised at the painful trial you are suffering, as though something strange were happening to you. But rejoice that you participate in the sufferings of Christ, so that you may be overjoyed when glory is revealed* (I Pet. 4:12).

We also know that God works good from suffering. James 1:2-7 tells us to *Consider it pure joy, my brothers, whenever you face trials of many kinds, because you know that the testing of your faith develops perseverance. Perseverance must finish its work so that you may be mature and complete, not lacking anything.*

So, suffering is predicted. In fact, it is guaranteed. But, does this knowledge prepare the missionary for its impact and consequences?

Many do not realize that the impact of trauma can go very deep, be far reaching, and last a long time. This lack of understanding often leads the victim to circumvent the healing process by denying the impact, speeding up the process, or using poor coping mechanisms. It also leads those around the victim to impede healing, often through well intentioned words that communicate an impatience with the process.

Normal reactions to a crisis or trauma include: intense levels of shock, anxiety, denial, guilt, anger, shame, and grief. Each person is unique in how he or she responds to a crisis and in how long the recovery phase takes. Comparison with others may set up unrealistic expectations, which can lead to discouragement and despair.

Trauma and crisis are often part of missionary experience. Critical incident stress debriefing (CISD) is a model for debriefing which helps reduce the impact of trauma. Factors of counselor availability, time frame, spiritual issues and resources, cross-cultural issues, confidentiality, systems issues, and follow-up are discussed, as well as the need to debrief the debriefers. A format for debriefing is included.

Some people may experience long-lasting complications, such as major depression or post-traumatic stress disorder following a trauma. Personal history, genetics, current coping mechanisms, and the nature of the trauma all affect the development of complications. Talking about the event in detail in a supportive context will not necessarily prevent complications, but it is a powerful tool for assisting in recovery.

I've heard many missionaries who went through trauma say things like, "No one ever asked me how I was doing with this," or "I have never talked about this with anyone." The impact of trauma goes much deeper than what is visible immediately after the event. But we can lessen the impact and facilitate the healing process. We can be part of the work of perseverance, which has as its goal that we be mature and complete, not lacking anything.

If we ignore missionaries who have suffered trauma, or fail to follow up with them, they may develop serious symptoms and experience a lack of fruitfulness, as the Scripture says happened with Tamar. She was raped, told to be quiet, and "lived in her brother Absalom's house, a desolate woman" (2 Sam. 13:20).

Some traumas missionaries experience on the field are life threatening, such as rape, armed robbery, shootings, evacuations, murders, kidnappings, torture, imprisonment, natural disasters (e.g., earthquakes), and medical emergencies. Other types of trauma, which aren't necessarily life threatening or dramatic, include government opposition, false accusations, betrayal of friends, saying multiple goodbyes, significant family events in the home country (death, marriage, illness), cancellation of a long-term project, serious team conflicts, and changes in roles.

All of these crises involve loss and result in grief. This grief may be compounded if there is unresolved grief from the past or if multiple losses occur in close proximity and time. The hardiest and most enduring of missionaries still has emotional limits and must have mechanisms for processing and coping with trauma. If these mechanisms are established on the field, the result will be increased endurance and longevity of service. I also believe that the result will be more joy, lightheartedness, and peace (Psalm 126:5-6).

Response to trauma, a model for missionaries

One mechanism for helping individuals process the impact of a trauma is the use of the Critical Incident Stress Debriefing (CISD) model, developed by Jeffrey Mitchell. It has been used successfully with emergency personnel, and has been adapted for missionaries. The essential components of this model are: (1) a trained de-briefer meets with the traumatized individual or group within 24 to 72 hours following the trauma; (2) the debriefers facilitate a discussion of the traumatic event in which they cover the facts, the mental and emotional reactions to the incident, and the symptoms experienced both during and after the event; and (3) the debriefers educate the victims on normal responses to crises in order to normalize their response and to give them increased understanding about what they are currently experiencing and what they might experience in the future.

A number of unique factors must be considered when applying this model to missionaries. These include time frame and availability of counselors, spiritual issues and resources, cross-cultural issues, confidentiality, systems issues, and follow-up.

Time frame and availability of counselors

The CISD model asserts that the ideal time for debriefing is 24 to 72 hours after the trauma. This allows enough time for the numbing and shock to wear off, but catches the person before the sealing over and distancing process begins. On the mission field, however, this may not be a reasonable time frame. Complications such as flight times, visas, finances, and availability may prevent a trained counselor from arriving on the field until a week or more has passed.

In some cases, administrators may decide that the benefit of bringing a counselor to the field will not outweigh the cost. This decision might be made on the basis of how many missionaries are involved or on some assessment of the visible emotional Impact on the affected missionary.

At other times, an administrator might want to bring a counselor on the field, but the missionary may insist It is not necessary. How does one decide when to bring a counselor to the field? The decision must be made on a case by case basis.

Field leaders can plan ahead by setting up guidelines or a flow chart of factors to consider. For example, certain events (i.e. life threatening ones) might always warrant an immediate CISD regardless of the apparent impact on the missionaries. The impact of such events on family members and colleagues is often overlooked as well, and we must consider what other missionaries on the field need.

If a person does not receive a debriefing In the 24 to 72 hours following the trauma, he or she may still benefit from debriefing later. As time passes, it becomes more difficult to access the memory and feelings related to the event. However, symptoms such as nightmares, depression, flashbacks, poor sleeping, impaired performance, and withdrawal indicate that the trauma is unresolved and the person could benefit from debriefing or therapy. Even without symptoms, certain types of trauma may not be resolved without some form of debriefing.

A young missionary woman was referred to me by her mission board one year after she experienced a significant trauma. While on furlough, she began experiencing nightmares regarding the event. She had never been debriefed. While on the field, she was interviewed by field administrators, but no attention was given to her emotional response.

During two counseling sessions, which lasted two hours each, she had the opportunity to talk in detail about the trauma, her emotional reactions to it, her symptoms, and her coping style. She worked through a plan for bringing some closure to her grief, and developed some additional coping resources.

A letter I received from her just before she returned to the field indicated she was feeling optimistic and positive about her return. A number of personal and spiritual resources made her adjustment prognosis very good. Although she may continue to have difficulties, she had the opportunity to talk about the event, and to gain deeper insight into its impact. She also gained a better understanding of her own reactions to trauma and of her ability to cope. She also knows there is someone she can talk to if she ever feels the need. Her experience and feelings were validated. She knows that she is not crazy or unusual. She feels she has the strength to continue in her service to the Lord.

Spiritual issues and resources

One of the key questions that comes up for missionaries who experience trauma is, "Why did God allow this to happen?" It is a difficult question that each believer must wrestle with. Certainly there are many examples where it seems the Lord miraculously delivered a person from a terrible tragedy. So, why do some suffer terribly? It is normal for a missionary who has suffered trauma to ask, "Where was God?"

Resolving this question will be different for each person. But each one will need support getting through it. Support involves allowing the person to ask questions and search God and Scripture for the answer, without giving him or her pat answers. It also involves the mission administration communicating a position of acceptance during this time of ambiguity.

There is something particularly terrible about suffering at the hands of another person. Perhaps it is the violation of a deeply held belief or conviction that compassion or decency is inherent to human beings. If so, this belief is shattered, or at least challenged, when one is the victim of another's choice to do evil.

Whatever our beliefs about what humans are capable of, one is rarely prepared to be the victim of evil. A new set of assumptions, which initially may feel like paranoia or extreme suspiciousness, will be developed. One becomes more cautious and less willing to trust, which may be counter to the original world view and self-image.

Missionaries do have a set of spiritual resources available to them. They have a body of believers who can support and pray for them. They have their own prayer life and the Bible. They have worship and praise. They have faith, a perspective on the world, and eternal truths that nonbelievers do not. All of these are invaluable in the healing process and can be encouraged and further developed.

Cross-cultural issues

Some traumas missionaries experience may be directly related to cultural norms. For example, the missionary may witness an infant being killed because of birth defects or a woman being beaten and mistreated by her husband. Feelings of helplessness, horror, or guilt may be pervasive and long-lasting.

The coping process is also affected by cultural norms. Grieving rituals, verbal expressions of pain and suffering, and social support networks are culturally defined coping mechanisms. Missionaries who have acculturated to their place of service may accept or adapt to these norms and face misunderstanding from those in the home country.

Other missionaries may attempt to cope using norms from their home country, which are not understood or accepted in the culture where they are serving. In the United States, when someone is robbed, the police are called, a report is filed, and the victim expects that the case will be investigated. It is hoped that the perpetrator will be arrested and held accountable for his action. There is an expectation of justice and fairness. However, in many countries, where the legal system is corrupt, or where there is apathy or lack of resources, one has little recourse in the face of victimization.

Confidentiality

Sometimes, certain aspects of a trauma remain secret or confidential, further complicating the debriefing process. This may happen for a number of reasons:

- A missionary who was held hostage and then released may have been instructed to keep parts of his release confidential so as not to further endanger those still in captivity. Yet some of those details may be painful for the victim to carry alone.
- A missionary may be advised by the mission agency that it would be detrimental to his or her ministry if the supporting church back home learned the details of the trauma. The missionary may be asked to reveal some aspects of the trauma, but not others.
- Someone may have been indirectly affected by another person's trauma, but unable to talk about it because he or she wants to honor the victim's privacy or confidentiality.
- Certain parts of a trauma, such as rape, might not be discussed by the victim because of a sense of shame and exposure.

While these reasons may be quite legitimate and understandable, it is more difficult to process and resolve a trauma when restrictions are placed on what can be discussed. When weighing the cost of allowing details to go public, the administration must carefully consider what impact the mandate for silence may have on the trauma victim.

Certain information may be detrimental to the organization's image and ultimately to the ministry. Therefore, it may be prudent to carefully control who has access to this Information. However, these things should not be considered apart from what might hinder the victim from adequately processing and resolving the trauma.

Systems issues

The relationship the trauma victim has with his or her family, colleagues, mission administration, nationals, and supporting church all have an impact on the recovery process. Ideally, each of these relationships will be supportive and empathic. Realistically, however, there may have been tension or problems in one or more of these relationships prior to the trauma, which can be exacerbated at, this time.

Follow-up

A victim receives the most attention and care immediately following a trauma. Friends, family, and colleagues are most likely to be sensitive and ask questions that allow the victim to process the event. Administrators are most likely to seek counseling assistance for their members. Furthermore, symptoms and visible distress are most likely to be linked to the trauma now.

However, many missionaries may experience the worst impact much later on-weeks, months, or even years later. It all depends on a number of factors, such as trigger events, other crises, and the personality of the victim. So a plan should be put into place following any missionary trauma and debriefing.

At the point of the CISD, the counselor can assess who might need further assistance. Counseling sessions may be recommended. These could be provided intensively on the field while the counselor is still there. Or, the counselor may recommend that the missionary leave the field to receive treatment. Some missionaries may chose to receive counseling when they go home on furlough. This decision can be made on the basis of the missionary's current ability to function, his or her future prognosis, and the available support systems.

Even those who appear to be doing very well at the debriefing should receive follow-up from a designated person, someone the individual sees as caring and competent. The follow-up can be through phone calls, letters, e-mail, or visits. This contact gives the individual an opportunity to talk about the impact of the trauma.

The timing and frequency of the follow-up contacts will vary depending on individual circumstances. Someone who experienced the death of a loved one may need particular attention on key dates such as holidays, birthdays, and the anniversary of the death. Others may need follow-up contact when they experience a trigger event. For example, those returning to where they were robbed or raped may need debriefing before and after their return. Sights, sounds, or smells similar to any aspect of the trauma may also trigger very intense feelings which need to be debriefed.

Debriefing the debriefers

Another important aspect of debriefing, often neglected or overlooked, is giving the debriefers supportive listening following a debriefing session. Debriefings are, by nature, intense. The debriefers cannot help but be emotionally impacted by what they have heard. They may experience sympathetic crisis reactions, such as numbing, depression, anxiety, nightmares, sleep loss, and appetite disturbance. To preserve the longevity and mental health of the debriefers, a system should be in place for them to talk through what they have heard and processed. This should be done within 24 to 72 hours of the debriefing. Failure to do this can result in cynicism and the depletion of compassion in the debriefers.

This doesn't have to be complex. Recently I was called out to assist in a police negotiation with a man who had just killed his wife. Before the negotiations began, the man killed himself. When I arrived at the police station, about 10 family members were gathered there. They had just gotten the news of the two deaths. I was asked to speak with them and help them. I spent about an hour just being present for them – listening, assisting them in making decisions about informing other family members, and setting up support for each other.

When I went back to the mental health center, several colleagues gathered around me and started asking me how I was doing. As I began talking about what I had heard and how it impacted me, I realized how deeply I had been affected. My colleagues' timely and simple questions of "How are you doing?" and their empathetic statements such as "That must have been awful" allowed me to debrief and process the experience in a way that felt very supportive and helpful.

Emotional and spiritual preparation is invaluable. First, debriefers should have several people pray for them consistently. Second, they should be well rested so they can be focused and enduring. The debriefer should avoid scheduling any emotionally draining or demanding events just before and after a debriefing. Third, if possible, the debriefer should have a partner or co-leader. Doing a debriefing alone should be the exception, even though it is more costly to do it in pairs.

Intensive debriefing

Counselors may also offer intensive debriefing for individuals, couples, or families following a trauma. This seems particularly useful for missionaries who have been through extreme trauma, multiple traumas, or for those who have experienced a trauma which triggered past unresolved memories. This intense debriefing may last several hours to several days, and may be done on or off the field.

It should be done only by a trained counselor who has experience with trauma, cross-cultural issues, and mission work. Individuals who do not have this training should not attempt to do an intensive debriefing, which may be more harmful than helpful.

The questions and interview process are not complex. The complexity lies in the interpretation of what is said and the subsequent recommendations made to the missionary and mission administration. Often, these recommendations dramatically affect a person's future. For example, should the missionary return to the field? The recommendations must be based on carefully gathered information incorporating the missionary's preferences and strengths.

Clearly define from the start what the missionary wants to keep confidential and what might be reported back to the administration. In general, the report should address the missionary's current coping and functioning level and the resources he or she will need to successfully adjust, such as further counseling, financial help, or decreased responsibilities. The report does not need to include personal details.

When debriefing missionary couples who have been referred to me following kidnappings and robberies, I have used a format which includes history taking, trauma processing, and planning for the future (see A Format for Debriefing). This format allows the counselor to develop a foundational understanding of thetrauma victim's baseline of coping and relating. It can then be used to develop a strategy for future coping.

Conclusion

Trauma is inevitable for many missionaries. But, by formulating a compassionate and comprehensive response plan, we can perhaps lessen its painful impact. The result will be missionaries who are strengthened and encouraged to continue their service on the field—a goal which is shared by missionaries, administrators, and counselors.

Author's Note

Since this article was published in *Evangelical Missions Quarterly* (October 1997) there has been some concern expressed in the literature regarding whether utilizing the CISD model prevents PTSD or whether it may even exacerbate symptoms associated with trauma in some cases. A comprehensive review of relevant literature reveals that research on these questions is inconclusive. Subjective reports from recipients of CISD indicate that it is helpful.

Caution should be observed in how the model is applied. It cannot take the place of trauma therapy, but it does provide normalizing of the symptoms and general education, and can decrease the sense of isolation felt by many who were affected by the crisis event. The Mobile Member Care Team (MMCT) largely utilizes this model. See Chapter 47 for a description of the MMCT.

References

Carr, K.F. (1994). Trauma and post-traumatic stress disorder among missionaries. *Evangelical Missions Quarterly,* July, pp. 246-255.

Mitchell, J., and Everly, G. (1993). *Critical incident stress debriefing: An operations manual for the prevention of traumatic stress among emergency services and disaster workers.* Ellicott City, Md.: Chevron Publishing Corporation.

Recommended Reading

Figley, C. R. (1995). *Compassion fatigue: Coping with secondary traumatic stress disorder in those who treat the traumatized.* New York, N.Y.: Brunner/Mazel Publishers.

Herman, J.L. (1992). *Trauma and recovery.* New York, N.Y.: Basic Books, 1992.

Matsakis, A. (1996). *I can't get over it: A handbook for trauma survivors.* Oakland. Calif.: New Harbinger Publications Inc.

Terr, L. *(1990). Too scared to cry.* New York, N.Y.: Basic Books.

Editor's Note

This chapter was first published in *Evangelical Missions Quarterly,* October 1997, with the title "Crisis Intervention for Missionaries." Used by permission.

A Format for Debriefing

1.   *Introduction*
   - Give an overview of the schedule and the purpose of time.
   - Discuss the parameters of confidentiality (particularly if there is going to be a report submitted to administration).
   - Give the opportunity to express expectations for the time.
   - Provide a scriptural basis for doing an intensive debriefing.
   - Pray with them.

2.   *History*
   - Have each person tell his or her testimony (this gives you very valuable information about their spiritual development and may also reveal current spiritual struggles).
   - Family history (look for patterns in relationships and communication style).
   - Education.
   - Work.
   - Marriage – what is the foundation of their love; what are their strengths and weaknesses as marriage partners; what was the state of the marriage before the crisis?
   - Kids – best and worst experiences.
   - Happiest times – time when doing best.
   - Most stressful time other than hostage situation.
   - How they handled stress in the past.

   - Friendships.
   - Strengths (personal, marital).
   - Weaknesses (personal, marital).

3.   *Debriefing of the trauma*
   - Facts of the event.
   - Thoughts about the event.
   - Reactions/worst part of the event.
   - Symptoms experienced during and after the event.
   - Spiritual struggles related to the event.

4.   *Education*
   - Stress – recognition of the symptoms.
   - Stress reduction techniques.
   - Effects of trauma – cover the normal reactions to a trauma.
   - Post-traumatic stress disorder.
   - Depression.
   - Anxiety.
   - Grief.

5.   *Plan for the future*
   - Plan for next 3 months – ideas for coping.
   - Long-term plan-build in stress reducers, communication, check-ups.
   - Recognition of triggers and plan for how to respond.
   - Dealing with expectations, questions, responses of others.

38

Caring for Mission Personnel in Crisis: A Matrix Approach

Miriam Kellogg

Personnel Care Matrices provide a system for analyzing and managing crisis so that important factors are not overlooked. Four matrices give a framework for considering the type of crisis and the people involved, areas of personal and community life affected and responses needed, handling communication, and reflecting on and learning from crisis. The matrices can be used for training, crisis intervention, and post-crisis debriefing.

Introduction

"Stay alert. This is hazardous work I'm assigning you. You're going to be like sheep running through a wolf pack, so don't call attention to yourselves. Be as cunning as a snake, inoffensive as a dove." (Matthew 10:16, *The Message*, Eugene Peterson, 1993, NavPress)

Crisis, by its very nature, happens suddenly and without warning. It's too late to begin thinking and planning once the crisis is upon you. Mission agencies and missionaries need to do some serious strategizing in order to be prepared for crisis events. The focus of this paper is the care of personnel in crisis rather than management of the crisis event itself.

The idea of using matrices to demonstrate various types of crises and responses came from original thinking by Dr. Laura Mae Gardner (currently the Vice President of Personnel for SIL) in March 1994. This author began with Gardner's original concept and changed and greatly expanded it into its present form of four distinct matrices dealing with various aspect of personnel care in the midst of crisis events.

The complete training package entitled *Personnel Care Matrices: Crisis Intervention in the Mission Community* includes an expanded version of this chapter explaining the use of the matrices; four simulation exercises with samples of completed matrices for two of the exercises; a complete set of the four matrices and accompanying supplemental pages; teaching notes and graphics to use as overheads; and finally, a set of all of the materials on computer disk (Microsoft Word 7.0) so that the user may reproduce any or all of the materials for personal or ministry use.   Order information is at the end of the chapter.

Personnel Care Matrices

Why matrices?   A matrix readily allows one to see the *interplay* between different factors involved in a crisis situation. Because the matrices proposed in this paper are generic in nature they can be used in a wide variety of circumstances and by different types of teams. That is, an international member care administrator, an on-site entity administrator, and a crisis response team may all use the same matrix but from a slightly different perspective.

Potential Usage

The four matrices proposed in this paper can be used in three distinctive ways: for training, for crisis intervention, and for post-crisis debriefing.

Training

The matrices provide a visual means of seeing the wide variety of things that must be considered in handling a crisis. This author suggests that these matrices can help in training for all three phases of crisis work.

Before — What kinds of resources and types of personnel are needed to handle the different categories of crisis events?

During — The matrices provide a visual reminder of the many details and concepts that one must keep track of in the midst of a very stressful time.

After — The matrices provide a way of looking back on a crisis event and determining what was done well, what areas need improvement, and what things are ongoing?

Crisis Intervention

The matrices may be used during an actual crisis in two ways: as a checklist for a response team and as a quick and simple record-keeping system.

Post-crisis Debriefing

Once the actual crisis situation is over, it is important to look back and determine what things were done well, where there is need for improvement, etc. This debriefing could include (1) residue still to be handled: What? Who will do it? How? and (2) What did we do right? What still needs improvement?

While no system can possibly cover every possibility or eventuality, the matrix system does cover the major issues that need to be considered. If nothing more, it will serve as a catalyst to stimulate thinking. The matrices provide a simple framework from which to consider various issues.

Each matrix is composed of cross-sections (cells). While it is not likely that every cell will be applicable to any given crisis situation, the beauty of this system is that it allows one to at least quickly consider every issue (illustrated by a cell) and then cross off those that do not apply.

Strive for simplicity. Check (T) only those cells that are applicable and/or write in a key word or short phrase as illustrated in the following examples.

Personnel Care Matrix 1

Personnel Care Matrix 1 allows us to look at the different categories of crisis (five rows) that may occur and the primary people (four columns) that may be involved. (See sample at end of chapter.) Having these arranged in matrix format allows one to quickly see the interplay between the *type* of crisis and *who* is involved.

Each matrix is accompanied by a supplementary sheet that explains more fully each of the categories of crises and also the personnel that may be involved in a crisis situation. (See sample at end of chapter; others are included in the training package.) *These lists are not exhaustive and the order given does not necessarily suggest priority.*

PERSONNEL CARE MATRIX 1	Primary Victim(s)	Secondary Victim(s)	Perpetrator/ Causative Agent	Others Affected
Ethical Shock (Domestic Violence)	*Susie (wife)*	*2 young children*	*John (husband)*	*Entity members*

Rows

The five broad categories listed below describe the kinds of crises most often encountered in mission settings. Some of the categories would require a full crisis management team to handle the event and its after-effects, while a single administrator may handle others. Some will necessitate involvement of home country and international mission staff and others will be primarily handled at a local level. Mission legislation and/or procedures may dictate the steps to be followed in cases of immorality.

No matter how extensive or how localized management of the crisis situation becomes, using the crisis matrices will assist responsible administrators to grasp the full picture of which issues must be considered in any given crisis situation.

- Natural disasters
- Human-induced acts of hostility
- Ethical shock
- Bizarre behavior
- Tragedy

Some types of crises are more complex to handle than others. Take the time to train mission personnel in at least one type of crisis from each of the five broad categories so all personnel will see the differing complexities. It is also important that crisis responders are knowledgeable of mission policies and practices with regard to various types of crises.

Columns

Teams or individuals handling any part of a crisis situation need to quickly identify persons for whom they are responsible and to what degree they are responsible for those persons. Depending on who is evaluating the crisis, the identity of the primary victim, secondary victim, etc. will be different. Furthermore, the identity of the primary person one is responsible for may change at various stages of the crisis intervention process. Consider the following example:

In a child-abuse situation occurring within the local school, the entity administrative team handling the crisis will initially consider the child as the primary victim and his/her family as secondary victims. However, if the victim and his/her family leaves (to return to their home country), the entity team now needs to consider the other school children and their families remaining on the site as the primary victims for whom they are responsible (for immediate care, needs, etc.) while remaining in touch with the abused child and his/her family which is now predominantly in the care of another team (home country member care staff). This is not to say that the entity no longer has any responsibility to the abused child or his/her family, but rather that they have relinquished temporal care to another entity.

Personnel affected by a crisis will usually fit into one of the following categories:

- *Primary victim(s)* — Those most directly affected
- *Secondary victim(s)* — Those indirectly affected by the crisis event(s) or directly affected, but to a lesser degree than is the primary victim.
- *Perpetrator(s) and/or causative agent(s)*
- *Others affected* — Crises in a mission community have a widespread effect because of our "family" atmosphere and our global lifestyle. Discernment must be used in considering how far afield to go in handling the effects of a given crisis event.

Personnel Care Matrix 2

Personnel Care Matrix 2 helps one to identify the areas of individual and community life that have been affected by the crisis event and the different types of responses possible for each area affected. The user of this matrix may be very general and look over the big picture or be very specific and look at how the crisis affects a specific person (primary or secondary victim). It may be helpful to fill out a new matrix for each perspective considered.

The *rows* indicate twelve different areas/aspects of individual and community life that may be affected by a crisis. The four *columns* are response-related issues that

PERSONNEL CARE MATRIX 2 (domestic violence)	Impact	In-house (mission) response		Response from external source
		Type	Level	
Emotional	✓✓	Admin. Team, Counselor	Local admin, Mission-assigned counselor	Local law enforcement

need to be considered in management of personnel care in a crisis situation. *These lists are not exhaustive and the order given does not necessarily suggest priority.*

Remember that normally not all of the cells will be used in any given crisis situation. Check (✓) or fill in with words or short phrases only those cells that are applicable. Looking at the entire matrix, however, forces one to at least briefly consider all of the possible combinations.

Rows

- Emotional issues
- Physical (biological) factors
- Spiritual issues
- Cultural issues
- Financial factors
- Environmental (geographical) aspects
- Socio-political factors
- Mission & its constituency — any related issues
- Relationships (family and others) issues
- Work/job/task issues
- Time factors
- Moral/ethical factors

Columns

- Extent of impact —
  - ✓ = average priority should be given to this aspect
  - ✓✓ = high priority should be given to this aspect
- Type of in-house response needed (internal to the mission)
- Level of in-house response needed (internal to the mission)
- Responses from external sources (external to the mission) — these services may be requested by the entity in crisis or some may be automatically imposed upon the entity in crisis

Personnel Care Matrix 3

Because handling communication during a crisis situation is extremely important and very complex, an entire matrix is devoted to it. The ten rows of this matrix list individuals and groups who will need some sort of communication during a crisis situation. The three columns address the questions, "What, How, Who?" with regard to communication.

We live in an age of rapidly developing communication technology. Electronic mail, cell and/or satellite phones, fax machines, and video cameras are now accessible even in remote areas of the globe. This makes it very important that those individuals assigned to handle communication work together with entity personnel to ensure that, as much as possible, only approved information be communicated. We believe it is important to get accurate information out as rapidly as possible, first of all to those who *need to know*, and then on to other appropriate audiences as well. During crisis events, it is also important to identify confidentiality issues and protect vulnerable people.

Communication is vital. Depending upon the magnitude of the crisis, it may require a person assigned full-time to this task. Mission legislation (or practice) may dictate that certain communication must take place. However, it is vital to think carefully about *how much* and *what kinds* of information are shared with various individuals or groups. In times of crisis, communication is a high priority emotional need. Communication is a way of feeling connected, of *maintaining the blood flow* through the Body. There is a need to consider:

- What will help to maintain information quality?
- How much and what kinds of information will be shared?
- Who should *not* receive communication and what kinds of things should *not* be communicated about the crisis at any given time?
- The pressure that can come from prayer chains that insist on information must be resisted. Prayer is indeed important but can also become a vehicle for mismanaging information.

It is important to be guided by the organization's existing legislation, policy, protocols, and personnel when managing communication regarding crisis situations. When in doubt about anything it is best to consult with appropriate individuals within the entity and/or mission administration. *These lists are not exhaustive and the order given does not necessarily suggest priority.*

Rows
- Victim(s) and their families
- Perpetrator(s) and their families
- Entity administration
- Entity membership (including those on furlough, retired, reassigned, etc.)
- Mission international administrators
- Home country offices and staff directly affected
- News media (home/host country)
- National personnel (employees, pastors, churches)
- Mission constituency
- Special interest group (i.e. high school peers if a teen is sexually assaulted; aviation personnel with a plane crash)

Columns
- What is appropriate to communicate?
- How will it be communicated?
- Who will handle this communication?

Personnel Care Matrix 4
The theme of Personnel Care Matrix 4 is looking back to see what we've learned while handling a crisis. Because others are likely encounter a similar situation in the future, it is important to pass on what has been learned in this situation.

The twelve *rows* in this fourth matrix are the same areas/aspects of individual and community life that are listed in Personnel Care Matrix 2. The three *columns* are components of post-crisis debriefing. *These lists are not exhaustive and the order given does not necessarily suggest priority.*

Rows (See rows for Matrix 2)

Columns
- Residue: What remains to be handled once we think the actual crisis period is over?
- Debriefing of crisis management: How well did we handle the crisis?
- Proactive thinking/preventive measures — planning ahead for next time:

Conclusion

We face an ever-increasing number of traumatic events occurring around the world. We must prepare wisely in order to care well for our personnel. These matrices provide a powerful tool to stimulate comprehensive thinking about personnel care in times of crisis. The matrices are general in nature and may readily be used in combination with a mission's legislative guidelines, crisis policies and protocols as a training tool, a crisis intervention checklist, or a post-crisis debriefing tool.

The matrices are a powerful tool, but they won't be very helpful if you have to figure them out in the midst of an actual crisis. It is much more efficient to practice with some simulated crisis situations before facing the real thing. The training package includes four simulated exercises designed with that in mind.

Please remember, that above all else, our trust in any crisis situation is in God, not in ourselves or in anything that we can do. God is our strength, our hope, and our protection.

> Have I not commanded you? Be strong and courageous. Do not be terrified; do not be discouraged, for the Lord your God will be with you wherever you go. *(Joshua 1:9, NIV)*

To order the complete training package entitled *Personnel Care Matrices: Crisis Intervention in the Mission Community*, please contact Miriam E. Kellogg. The cost of the package is $25.00 (US) and includes shipping.

Miriam E. Kellogg, M.A., NCC, LMHC
Counseling Ministries
Wycliffe USA
P. O. Box 628200
Orlando, FL 32862-8200
Phone: 407-852-3830
Fax: 407-852-3831
E-mail: miriam_kellogg@wycliffe.org

Personnel Care Matrix 1

Viewed from the perspective of _____ team
(local, entity, or international mission administration; counselor, etc.)

PERSONNEL CARE MATRIX 1	Primary Victim(s)	Secondary Victim(s)	Perpetrator or Causative Agent(s)	Others affected
Natural Disaster				
Human-induced Acts of Hostility				
Ethical Shock				
Bizarre Behavior				
Tragedy				

Note: Matrix 1 is reproduced above in reduced size as an illustration. All matrices and supplements are available in full size in the training package.

Personnel Care Matrix 1 Supplement

Rows - Types of Crises

Natural Disasters — earthquake, volcano, typhoon, flood, tornado, fire, famine, drought, landslide, epidemic, etc. [Become familiar with appropriate mission crisis management policies, procedures, protocols, and personnel regarding management of these issues.]

Human-induced Act of Hostility — murder, hostage, theft, armed robbery, physical assault, sexual assault/rape, war, revolution, coup, terrorism, bombs, dangerous living situation, any violence involving a member, etc. [Become familiar with appropriate mission crisis management policies, procedures, protocols, and personnel regarding management of these issues.]

Ethical Shock — child abuse, extra-marital affairs, sexual immorality, abortion, homosexuality, suicide/suicide attempt, divorce/separation, embezzlement, intense conflict, HIV/AIDS or exposure to these, sexual harassment, pornography, etc. [Read and follow appropriate mission policies, procedures and protocols regarding these issues.]

Bizarre Behavior — psychotic break, anorexia, bulimia, desertion, multiple personality (D.I.D.), effects of past satanic cult involvement, etc. [This area is less governed by organizational policy and therefore may be a more challenging administrative task.]

Tragedy — accidental death, plane crash, auto crash, severe accidental injury, sudden illness resulting in a rapid death, etc. [These, while tragic, may elicit resources from colleagues that need not be specialized.]

Columns — Principle Personnel

Primary Victim(s)	Secondary Victim(s)	Perpetrator/ Causative Agent(s)	Others Affected
– those most directly affected by the crisis situation	– those indirectly affected or directly affected to a lesser degree than the primary victim(s)	– person(s) or event(s) directly linked to cause of the crisis situation	– all others affected by the crisis situation (within reasonable judgment)

Note: this supplement to Matrix 1 is included as an illustration. All matrices and supplements are available in the training package.

39

Mobile Crisis Response: Responding in the Aftermath of Trauma

Karen F. Carr and Darlene Jerome

Most missionaries encounter some kind of trauma in the course of their career. A case study of a traumatic event illustrates the need for and usefulness of good crisis response. A model for responding to trauma includes initial assessment, the service contract, and resources. It deals with staffing, timing, goals, and strategic concepts of on site crisis intervention, attitudes of crisis responders, and leave-taking and follow-up.

Introduction

Trauma seems to have become part of the fabric of ordinary life experience. There was a time when a person could not be diagnosed with Post Traumatic Stress Disorder unless they had experienced "an event that is outside the usual human experience and that would be markedly distressing to almost anyone." (APA, 1987). The Diagnostic and Statistical Manual of Mental Disorders (DSM IV) modified this language and now states that "the person has been exposed to a traumatic event."

Exposure includes directly experiencing, witnessing, or being confronted with an event that involves actual or threatened death or injury in addition to feelings of intense fear, helplessness, or horror (APA, 1994). The language about "outside the usual human experience" is gone.

If trauma has become a usual experience for us as human beings, we must learn how to prepare ourselves, how to cope, and how to help one another if we are to follow in the steps of Christ who suffered for us, leaving us an example, that we should follow in his steps. (I Peter 2:21).

Most missionaries we have met have suffered some kind of trauma in the course of their missionary career. In Bagley's study of 31 missionaries who were working on 4 different continents, 94 percent had experienced trauma at least once on the field and 78 percent had experienced multiple traumas. The most common types of trauma reported were combat/civil unrest, violent crime, natural disaster, and life endangerment. (Bagley, 2002).

The Mobile Member Care Team is a multi-disciplinary, inter-mission team providing crisis training and response to missionaries in West Africa. This team has been in Abidjan, Cote d'Ivoire since May 2000. (For more information, see Chapter 47.)

The most frequent types of trauma that we have responded to through debriefing and consultation are armed robbery, civil unrest, carjacking, and death of a colleague. The most common problems addressed by brief therapy services have been depression, marital conflict, job stress, child behavior problems, team conflict, anxiety, and post-traumatic stress symptoms.

Case Study: The Trauma

The situation and people described in this case study have been disguised to protect confidentiality.

MMCT received a call that a missionary woman with three small children had been robbed at gunpoint in her home while her husband was away. This family lived in a West African city where there had been increased civil unrest and numerous incidents of violent robberies targeting expatriates. The family did not employ a day guard and it was one of the children who opened the gate, inadvertently allowing three gunmen to enter the house. They terrorized the woman for about 30 minutes, threatening to kill her and the children while demanding money. One of the gunmen pointed his gun at her head and pulled the trigger, but it appeared the gun had jammed. She was treated roughly, pushed around and punched.

The children were miraculously calm and quiet. After the robbers left, the woman cried to her neighbors for help. Some were very helpful, coming to be with her and help her with the children, while others kept their distance. The woman was fairly certain that some of her neighbors had heard the robbers and she wondered why they had not done something to help her. Her husband was contacted and was able to be with her within an hour. Together they went to the police but they did not get much cooperation or sympathy from them.

The director of the mission and his wife came to be with the couple for support. The family indicated to the director and his wife that this incident was just about the last straw in a series of events and they just wanted to go home. They had an older child living at boarding school who had been worried about the news she had been hearing of civil unrest, and they were unsure what they should tell her. They also wondered what they should communicate to their families in their home country.

The mission administration called MMCT to see if they could come to provide some assistance for this family. They also wanted help for others in the mission community who had been through difficult situations in the past six months including death of a colleague, theft, and serious illness. The administration indicated that the risk of violence had increased in their area and they were wondering what they could do in response to this.

The Response: Initial Assessment

The information above gives important clues as to the kind of response that will be needed. We know there were young children involved who may not be able to verbalize what happened to them. We know that the woman has ambivalent feelings toward her neighbors and may be experiencing feelings of anger or betrayal. The child who let the gunmen in may be feeling guilty. The parents may feel guilty for not having implemented better security measures. The child in boarding school is already feeling considerable anxiety, and it is likely she will hear about this attack on her family eventually.

The family has had previous stressors which affect their view of this situation, but we do not know what those stressors are. There have been other incidents of violence in the mission community, so a variety of issues including grief, depression, burnout, anxiety, and post-traumatic stress disorder may be present. The administration would like consultation regarding crisis contingency plans and we may be able to give them input regarding member care during times of crisis.

Questions we might ask before responding include:

- How long has this family been on the field?
- How have they coped with other difficult things?
- What kind of support system do they have?
- Who else is being affected by this event?
- As an administrator, what is your hope for what will ultimately happen with this family?
- What other needs do you have within your mission community?
- What member care resources do you already have?

The Response: Service Contract

The above questions relate to member care needs. There are also logistical details which need to be sorted out before making the decision about who will respond and how they will respond. For example, the issue of confidentiality should be clarified ahead of time. Is the administration expecting a report and what will this report include? Who has the authority within this particular mission to request this help—field leadership or the home office? Who will pay for the trip and what will be covered (i.e., travel, room and board, honorarium)? Finally, we need all relevant contact names, phone numbers, and e-mail addresses.

The Response: Preparation Before the Trip

The preparation for the mobile response includes developing a strategy for response, gathering relevant resources and materials, and preparing oneself physically and spiritually.

Developing the Strategy for Response

We need to decide who should go, how many should go, and how long they should stay. As we assess the skills that are needed in the above case study, it seems it would be good to have someone with crisis debriefing skills who can work with both children and adults. It would also be good to have someone who can serve as a consultant to administrators dealing with practical crisis contingency matters. Given the number of people who may need to be served in this scenario, we would ideally send two staff to stay for approximately one week.

The plan of action should include times set aside for debriefing and assessment of the family, counseling for others who express a need to see a counselor, and consultation times with the administration. Plans might be made for a group meeting where we present practical materials or help lead the group in discussion and prayer.

We could work with the administration ahead of time to write an e-mail or group announcement which will let members know who is coming and what they can provide while they are there. A system can be set up for individuals to anonymously sign up for appointment times ahead of time.

As we set up the time we will spend with the family, we want to know if someone is available to assist with child care so that we can have some uninterrupted time with the family. It's possible that the children will not tolerate being separated from their parents, depending on the impact of the trauma for them, so we will be flexible in this regard.

If possible, we will arrange ahead of time to have meeting space that is quiet, comfortable, and free from distractions. Someone other than the trauma victims should be designated to host and take care of practical needs such as housing, meals, and transportation. It's good to know ahead of time what the e-mail and phone access will be.

Gathering Relevant Resources and Materials

As we anticipate needs, we plan to take selected assessment tools, handouts, books, and contact information that will be helpful. Handouts can be left behind for those who do not choose to see a counselor but who would benefit from written materials.

The assessment tools that we have found helpful to include in our crisis packet include:

- Beck Depression Inventory (Beck, 1972)
- Post Traumatic Stress Diagnostic Scale (Foa, 1995)
- CHOPS 100 Stress Inventory (O'Donnell and Cerny, 1996)
- Burnout Inventory (Williams, 1998).

Some handouts in our crisis packet include debriefing handouts (found on our website at www.mmct.org), and the grief U curve (Greeson, et.al., 1990). See the reference list below for books and articles that can be helpful to take and/or leave behind. Other practical things to take include extra passport photos, information about counselors and centers available in the victim's home country, mobile phone, credit card, local currency or U.S. dollars, and appliances with the correct plugs and voltage.

Preparing Yourself Physically and Spiritually

For travel within West Africa, it is very important to stay up to date on all vaccinations. This includes yellow fever (mandatory), typhoid, meningococcol, Hepatitis B, and Hepatitis A. Malaria prophylaxis is also strongly advised. Given the intensity of this kind of intervention, the responders should be well rested and healthy for this trip. This means having a balanced life with margin built in before the crisis call comes!

Spiritual preparation is essential for the effectiveness of this kind of trip. Being covered in prayer by supporters before, during, and after these trips is a key part of the strategy. Also, we will be most effective if we have developed our own theology of suffering and are at peace with the difficult questions of why God allows evil things to happen and why there is so much suffering and pain (Romans 5:1-5). This is not for the purpose of sharing it with the victims, who will need to discover it for themselves, but rather so that we can abide with the trauma victims during their time of deep spiritual turmoil (2 Corinthians 1:3-11).

The Response: On site crisis intervention

Staffing

In the case study described above, MMCT would ideally send two staff to respond to this situation but, realistically, we are often only able to send one. Other types of staff may be used as adjunct to MMCT including associate staff (mental health professionals who are available part time to assist MMCT) and peer responders (missionary peers who have been trained by MMCT in basic crisis assessment and response skills including debriefing).

Given the number of missionaries in West Africa (over 5000), the frequency of trauma, and the limited number of staff on MMCT, part of our strategy is to train missionaries to become peer responders. This goal is achieved through a screening process, an intensive training program, and follow-up consultation and supervision provided by MMCT staff. In this way, we can multiply the crisis response efforts being made throughout the region. Our belief is that missionaries have been providing crisis care to one another for years and this program is just a means to enhance their existing skills.

Timing

On-site response should be as soon after the crisis event as possible, but must take into consideration factors such as availability of staff and needs of the victims. Adequate time must be given to prepare for the trip as described above. Logistical details may need to be completed before a psychological intervention can begin (i.e., legal requirements following a crime, funeral arrangements following a death, etc).

The total amount of time of the intervention will vary from situation to situation with a range of 3 to 10 days being the norm. Pacing is key in this kind of intensive response—it's a combination sprint and marathon, and building in rest time for both the responders and the victims is important.

Goals of the Crisis Intervention

A detailed description of crisis intervention objectives and strategies can be found in Slaikeu's BASIC model (Slaikeu, 1990). In most crisis situations, our primary goals of the intervention will be to:

- Assess the impact of the crisis on the primary and secondary victims (including children)

- Debrief the trauma and provide supportive care which stabilizes the victims and defuses post-Drauma symptoms
- Provide education which helps to normalize the post-trauma symptoms
- Identify and reinforce the coping mechanisms of the victims
- Mobilize support systems
- Develop a follow-up plan that maximizes successful adjustment and growth

Strategic Concepts for Crisis Intervention

It is important to develop rapport and effectively communicate with the victims and their support system. This rapport building includes the administration and necessitates clarity regarding the parameters of confidentiality at the very beginning.

In most cases, it is helpful if we establish from the beginning that we will be giving administration a general report of how each victim is doing and any recommendations for follow-up. This can be done without the person feeling that their privacy has been violated, especially if we agree to show them anything we will send to the administration before sending it.

Part of the rationale for this is that it is the administration that will often be providing the ongoing care after the crisis responders leave, and they are the ones who can facilitate support and further care being provided as needed.

The crisis responder must listen carefully and patiently and draw out the trauma victims so that they are able to talk about all details of the trauma at their pace and in stages. We modify our debriefing or therapy approach according to where they are in the grief or post-trauma process, sometimes being directive and sometimes non-directive. We may need to take initiative and be assertive when it comes to setting up the structures and times for meeting with members and yet low key and not intrusive as we listen to them.

We look for opportunities to provide gentle education and normalizing of the post-trauma symptoms. For more specific techniques of crisis intervention see *Crisis Intervention: A Handbook for Practice and Research* (Slaikeu, 1990). For more details on specific areas to cover in an intensive crisis intervention see Chapter 37.

One type of intervention which is often effective in post-crisis situations is the Mitchell model of Critical Incident Stress Debriefing (Mitchell & Everly, 1993). This seven-step model provides structure for the crisis victims to talk about the facts, thoughts, emotions, and symptoms related to the crisis. It also includes a psycho-educational component. While this intervention cannot take the place of trauma therapy and is not proven to prevent PTSD, it does provide normalizing of the symptoms, general education, and can decrease one's sense of isolation related to the event.

A key conceptual difference in mobile crisis response for missionaries is that it often does not fit the traditional therapy mode or rules. For example, we may be washing dishes together with the one we are providing supportive counseling to or we may spend eight hours in one day with one person. This requires flexibility as well as a strong sense of boundaries and self that allows for the phenomenon of dual (or multiple) relationships without compromising the integrity of the therapy relationship.

When in a position of providing crisis response on the mission field, as missionaries ourselves, we find ourselves in the multiple roles of therapist, friend, dinner mate, fellow worshiper at church, etc. This can feel and is awkward, but it is a reality of life in mission settings.

A key strategic concept in this kind of crisis intervention is to identify those who will be the ongoing supporters and caregivers and to heighten their understanding of what is helpful and what is not. When there have been child victims, it is helpful to spend time with the parents, teachers, dorm parents, and other significant adults. They can tell us about the child's pre-crisis functioning and we can give them handouts and coach them as to how to help the child walk through this crisis.

Parents can be coached to try to re-establish a safe and structured routine for the children that will enhance their ability to cope. To the extent that we help the adults to re-establish stability and peace, the children will be indirectly helped.

In this case study, the administration has asked for assistance in responding to a mission community that has dealt with a series of violent and traumatic events. Providing the administration with a listening ear and an opportunity to debrief can be very helpful. Often field administrators are carrying a number of burdens that they have not been able to share with others. It is helpful to provide them with practical, tangible resources related to risk assessment and contingency planning.

MMCT has developed a workshop that trains mission administrators in the skills of assessing and giving member care to crisis victims under their care. Crisis Consultants International (www.hostagerescue.org) provides training in risk assessment and crisis contingency planning as well as a video series available for purchase. Also, see Chapter 38 for a helpful method of planning crisis response.

Attitudes for Crisis Responders

The key attitude for us as crisis responders is to enter the situation as learners, not assuming that we are experts or that we have a full understanding of what has happened. We need to leave our egos at the door—not needing to be noticed, appreciated, valued, or esteemed; remembering that our presence there is not about us, it's about them. A related concept is that we cannot judge the success of our interventions by how people respond to us in the moment.

Another important attitude or belief in crisis intervention with missionaries is that most people we are working with are normal, strong and resilient and have what they need to work successfully through the traumatic aftermath. Many of us have been trained as mental health professionals to look for and find pathology as opposed to searching out and reinforcing strengths and coping skills.

Whenever possible, we need to avoid pathologizing and diagnosing the victims. At the same time, we can help them identify their liabilities as well as potential triggers of traumatic reactions so that they are better prepared for future stress or trauma situations.

Some attitudes that we look for in the missionaries we train as peer responders include: non-judgmental, humble, teachable, respectful, non-cynical, tolerant of ambiguity, and genuine.

General Concepts for Leaving and Follow-up

Sometimes we compare the crisis intervention model of the MMCT to that of a MASH unit in the war. We're out in the field and we work with people who have been wounded in the battle. Our job is to assess whether or not they can be helped on the field or if they need to go home away from the battle. If we can help them on the field, then we need to provide them with care that will equip them to return to the battle with the best functioning possible. We don't expect to see them again unless they are wounded again.

Generally, as we are leaving a scene, we ask the people we have helped to keep in touch and let us know how they are doing, but we do not foster a continued relationship of dependency or ongoing care. We will make referrals if ongoing care is needed. We do, however, try to work with their support system so that they understand and value the importance of follow-up and ongoing care. We try to help them understand that recovery can be a long and slow process and friends will be needed long after the intense memory of the trauma has passed.

Follow-up care is also important for the crisis responders. It's important to build in a plan for us to be debriefed when we return from the crisis scene. We also need some rest and recovery time. This should be scheduled in from the very beginning. As Elijah experienced after his victory over the prophets of Baal, sometimes the hardest spiritual battle comes after the crisis is over (I Kings 18-19). In the letdown and post-crisis fatigue, we are vulnerable to spiritual attack. If we are to persevere and thrive in this role of crisis responder, we need to be sure that our full armor is on and practice what we preach!

References

American Psychiatric Association. (1987). *DSM-II-R*. Washington, D.C.: American Psychiatric Association.

American Psychiatric Association. (1994). *DSM-IV*. Washington, D.C.: American Psychiatric Association.

Beck, A. T. (1972). Measurement of depression: The Depression Inventory. In A. T. Beck (Ed.), *Depression: Causes and treatment*. Philadelphia: University of Pennsylvania Press.

Bagley, R. (2002). Trauma and traumatic stress among missionaries. *Journal of Psychology and Theology, 30:2* (Summer, 2002).

Carr, K. (1994). Trauma and post-traumatic stress disorder among missionaries. *Evangelical Missions Quarterly, 30* (July), Wheaton, IL: Evangelical Missions Information Service.

Carr, K. (1997). Crisis intervention for missionaries. *Evangelical Missions Quarterly, 33* (October). Wheaton, IL: Evangelical Missions Information Service (Chapter 37 of this volume).

Doleski, T. (1983). *The hurt*. Mahwah, NJ: Paulist Press.

Foa, E. (1995). *Posttraumatic Stress Diagnostic Scale*. Minneapolis, MN: National Computer Systems.

Gardner, L. M. (1992). "Crisis intervention in the mission community." In O'Donnell (Ed.) *Missionary Care*. Pasadena, CA: William Carey Library.

Greeson, C., Hollingsworth, M., & Washburn, M. (1990). *The grief adjustment guide*. Sisters, OR: Questar Publishers.

Heegaard, M. E. (1992), *Facilitator guide for drawing out feelings.* Minneapolis, MN: Woodland Press.

Hicks, R. (1993). *Failure to scream.* Nashville, TN: Thomas Nelson Publishers.

Jerome, D. (2001). *Crisis Readiness: Putting essentials in place for member care while managing crises.* Member Care While Managing Crisis workshop notebook.

Jerome, D. (2002). "Mobile Member Care Team – West Africa: Our journey, vision, and strategies." In *Doing member care well: Perspectives and practices from around the world.* Kelly O'Donnell (Ed). Pasadena, CA: William Carey Library.

Matsakis, A. (1992). *I can't get over it: A handbook for trauma survivors.* Oakland, CA: New Harbinger Publications, Inc.

Mitchell, J.T. & Everly, G.S. (1993). *Critical Incident Stress Debriefing: CISD.* Ellicott City, MD: Chevron Publishing Corporation.

Mitchell, J.T. & Resnick, H.L.P. (1986). *Emergency response to crisis.* Ellicott City, MD: International Critical Incident Stress Foundation, Inc.

O'Donnell, K. & Cerny, L. (1996). CHOPS 100 Stress Inventory.

Slaikeu, Karl A. (1990). *Crisis intervention: A handbook for practice and research.* 2nd edition. Boston, MA: Allyn and Bacon.

Tada, J. E. and S. Estes. (1997). *When God weeps.* Grand Rapids, MI: Zondervan Publishing House.

Wangerin, W. Jr. (1992). *Mourning into dancing.* Grand Rapids, MI: Zondervan Publishing House.

Wright, H. N. (1993). *Recovering from the losses of life.* Grand Rapids, Michigan: Fleming H. Revell.

Yancey, P. (1980). *Where is God when it hurts?* Grand Rapids, Michigan: Zondervan Publishing House.

40

Personality Disorders and Overseas Missions: Guidelines for the Mental Health Professional

Esther Schubert

Personality disorders and the resulting emotional instability are destructive to mission work and communities. They are not usually treatable in a mission setting, and the best way to prevent disasters is to improve the selection process so that candidates with personality disorders are not sent overseas. A case study is presented along with a discussion of types of personality disorders, how they are manifested, and prevention strategies.

*S*ophisticated selection tools are available for missions, but not all sending organizations are utilizing these options. Occasionally missionaries are placed overseas who do not have the emotional stability to be there. Crises culminating in personal and organizational disasters have alerted many mental health professionals to deficiencies in the selection process of some mission agencies. These deficiencies are most apparent in the inadvertent placement of people with personality disorders.

In this chapter I will discuss the fact that some missionaries are personality disordered, investigate the selection process that allowed their overseas placement, discuss the unique aspects of overseas work that makes their presence untenable, and present what can be done by mental health professionals to prevent these catastrophes in the future.

Having devoted the last eighteen years to overseas consultations, preventive care, therapy, and medical treatment of depressed missionaries, I am seeing some patterns that deeply concern me. I strongly believe in treating unipolar major depressive disorders on the field, and I have been successfully doing so in most cases. I call these "healthy depressions" when talking with mission personnel. These illnesses respond well to counseling and medication, and clients can usually return to productive work wiser and more insightful.

In contrast, I have seen more characterological, or "unhealthy depressions," occurring in missionaries. These clients may initially respond to treatment, but an underlying personality pathology is uncovered that may preclude their continued missionary service. Individuals with personality disorders may have slipped through selection without adequate evaluation.

Their presence on the field is usually surrounded by contention, dissension, disagreements, and exhaustion on the part of other missionaries and field executives who try to support them emotionally and spiritually.

The following case study is an example:

Herb N., a thirty-four-year-old candidate, is sent to an African country with his wife and three children, aged 10, 8, and 5. His mission organization believes in pre-field testing, but due to the pressing needs on the field, Herb and Mary do not participate m the entire battery of tests, interviews, and follow-up. Herb does not seem to mind the limited evaluation.

Once overseas, in planning sessions and team meetings, Herb has periodic rages followed the next day by abject repentance, tears, and the promise never to get angry again. He has difficulty submitting to authority or being a team player. The field leader is at a loss to know how to manage the situation, since Herb is so obviously sincere in his Christian commitment. Complaints begin to pour in from the national church regarding Herb.

Mary makes efforts to keep things smooth at home, trying to avoid conflict, but periodically the two school-age children are seen with unexplained bruises on their faces and bodies. One child shows evidence of childhood depression associated with acting out; another has frequent medical complaints which cannot be documented by physical exams or laboratory testing.

The family is strongly advised to return to the U.S. for family therapy and treatment of the children. They refuse, withdraw further into the family unit, and eventually leave the mission, but remain on the field without accountability to anyone. The country in which they reside has no child abuse laws so that concerned missionaries there are unable to intervene in the obvious on-going abuse of the children.

Later investigation into Herb's past reveals that prior to application to the mission, he was in a series of brief jobs followed by three pastorates that ended in termination—none lasting longer than a year.

His childhood had been chaotic, with profound disruption occurring in his first five years of life. Once, while in college, he was seen by a psychologist who told him that lengthy counseling might help his problems with identity and emptiness, but Herb refused to return to the clinician, calling him an unqualified professional who did not know what he was doing.

As we recruit our missionary candidates from an enlarging pool of bruised individuals, mission board personnel departments may need more sophisticated selection tools to avoid placing well-meaning candidates in jobs beyond their emotional skills. The mental health care professional is an invaluable asset in preventing the overseas placement of personality disordered individuals.

Many large sending agencies utilize extensive pre-field testing, but smaller, newer organizations are often limited in experience, finances, and psychological expertise. The mental health professional can help in suggesting policy changes for these boards.

Currently I provide official consultations to several missions. I also frequently see individuals from other agencies both in the U.S. and overseas. All of the missions for which I consult use the MMPI in selection. In one mission that previously did not use the instrument, I discovered three individuals who met the criteria for personality disorders. All three needed to return to the U.S.; their families were disrupted, supporters disillusioned, field teams exhausted, and the mission financially stressed by the financial obligations of the emergencies.

Another self-insured mission that uses the MMPI accepted a missionary candidate against professional advice because of pressure from the sending church. The individual was never able to go overseas, could not find a job in the homeland office that he could adapt to, and ended up in a psychiatric hospital for months at mission expense. He was diagnosed with a personality disorder.

One other mission sent a couple overseas in spite of warning signs on the MMPI and from the psychological evaluation. After a difficult first term, the field recommended more intense homeland evaluation and review. Unfortunately the family was sent back to the field, the marriage failed, the field team was split, and repercussions were felt both overseas and in the homeland.

In spite of the anecdotal nature of the above comments, I have yet to find a missionary with a personality disorder who reached the field if the MMPI was done by experienced professionals, with interviews, and if the recommendations of professionals were heeded.

Clinical experience suggests some alarming trends that merit future quality statistical research. Unfortunately data is difficult to acquire from some organizations due to (a) issues of confidentiality, (b) embarrassment, (c) pastoral rather than psychological approach to selection, and, though this is rare, (d) a philosophy that spirituality surpasses all psychological problems.

Mental health professionals can occasionally be intimidated by the obvious spiritual qualifications of non-psychologist personnel directors. Nevertheless, we need to help educate toward the use of psychological tools in the selection process. At the same time, personnel directors must understand that candidates' own psychological agendas (Schubert, 1989; Sexton & Maddock, 1980) may be misinterpreted as a spiritual call to missions. Sending agencies cannot afford to be psychologically naive, especially now that our recruits often come from such varied and sometimes damaged backgrounds.

Uniqueness of Overseas Settings

Boundary issues are almost always problematic with persons having a personality disorder. North American professionals are protected from boundary violations by answering services, separate office and residential locations, and office staff. Overseas mental health care workers, field executives, fellow missionaries, and nationals are vulnerable to victimization in a setting where none of these protections exist. The assumption made overseas is that the missionaries are emotionally, as well as spiritually, mature. Since the personality disordered missionary has twenty-four hour access to others' homes, offices, and spheres of influence, his presence overseas resembles living day and night with a disordered family member. Naïve nationals and loving fellow missionaries are quickly exhausted and frustrated by the unmeetable needs and demands. Boundaries are almost impossible to establish and there is often false guilt for trying to set these limits.

Also, since the majority of missionaries go overseas with training in theology or other non-psychological fields, they are ill-prepared to deal with personality disordered individuals who may appear psychologically healthy, that is, not delusional or thought disordered, yet have deep-seated maladaptations.

Finally, the defense mechanisms employed by many people with personality disorders, especially splitting and projective identification, play havoc with team unity and individual relationships. I have seen field teams permanently split over these difficult personnel issues.

I believe that the deterioration of the family in Western society, the erosion of stable traditions, and the frequency of child abuse, sexual abuse, neglect, alcoholic families and other dysfunctional families contribute to the marked increase in personality disorders seen in missionary candidates and selected missionaries. Some of these individuals with emotional bruising can do a good job overseas if issues are worked through psychologically first (Schubert, 1989). However, if the damage is intense enough, and unhealthy traits are maladaptive and inflexible enough to be considered a true personality disorder, that individual should not be placed overseas.

Types of Personality Disorders

The Diagnostic and Statistical Manual (DSM-IVTR) classifies personality disorders in three clusters. We will briefly note clusters "A" and "C' and then concentrate attention on cluster "B."

Cluster A includes paranoid, schizoid, and schizotypal personality disorders. The Christian with paranoid personality disorder may be rigid, dogmatic, and suspicious. In mission settings this person's pathology may be focused on legalisms, divisive doctrines, and theological deficiencies of others. There is little humor in interactions and a great deal of sensitivity to power and rank.

The schizoid personality disorder manifests extreme shyness, aloofness, and insensitivity to others' feelings. When overseas, the individual may be reclusive, a loner, and have few, if any, friends within the mission group. The schizotypal person has a tenuous hold on reality, may have eccentric convictions and beliefs, and may have what they believe to be religious experiences that are actually the result of psychotic processes. (Oates, 1987).

Missionary candidates with cluster A disorders often appear so odd or eccentric that they are eliminated from selection by interview, along with close scrutiny of letters of recommendation and telephone calls to authors of the letters.

Cluster C includes avoidant, dependent, obsessive-compulsive, and passive aggressive personality disorders. Candidates with avoidant personality disorder who proceed through the selection process may be seen in missionary settings as loners who might function to some degree in a solo placement as independents or pioneers. Oates (1987) describes Christians with this disorder as "actively detached adults" with histories of rejection and a deep fear of being hurt (pp. 102-103).

Persons with dependent personality disorder place responsibility for life decisions on others, subordinate personal needs to others, have markedly low self esteem, and cannot tolerate being alone. They drain fellow missionaries emotionally in the overseas community where boundary setting is so difficult. They are particularly unable to deal with the separations that are an inherent part of missionary living.

Obsessive-compulsive personality disorder (ego-syntonic) must be distinguished from obsessive-compulsive disorder (ego-dystonic), (Gabbard, 1994). The ego-syntonic individual is comfortable with his or her symptoms while the ego-dystonic individual recognizes his or her symptoms as maladaptive or pathological. The personality disordered obsessive-compulsive individual may simply appear overly conscientious and scrupulous, but be so exacting that conflict arises over criticism of other missionaries. Though occasionally these people can function in a book work, laboratory, or isolated office setting, their rigid, controlling, lack of people orientation is destructive to the cohesive missionary team.

Finally, the individual with passive-aggressive personality disorder may appear to be a fine Christian who never gets angry. Unfortunately, in overseas situations which are already fraught with frustrations, this person's obstinacy and anger will be expressed indirectly with procrastination, delay, and discreet refusal to follow orders. Other missionaries are puzzled by their own angry reactions to such a nice person.

Candidates with avoidant and dependent personality disorders are often filtered out by interview and non-psychological evaluation, but those with obsessive-compulsive and passive-aggressive personality disorders may progress through the selection process if more sophisticated testing is neglected.

Cluster B Personality Disorders

Persons with cluster B personality disorders are particularly destructive if sent overseas. They may appear dramatic, suave, emotional, yet deceptively healthy. Their erratic, impulsive, disruptive, and splitting behaviors are not always apparent until they are stressed with the cultural adjustments of living overseas without their usual support systems. Each of these aspects will be discussed in more detail.

Millon and Everly (1987) have written extensively on personality disorders; Oates (1987) and Landorf (1982) provide Christian perspectives of these disorders.

I.   **Antisocial personality disorder** was formerly referred to as sociopathy or psychopathy (Magid & McKelvey, 1987). The newer title is deceptive in that these people are often smooth, good talkers, and sociable on a superficial level. In the mission setting they make wonderful deputation speakers, possibly raising their full support in a month when the rest of the mission candidates take six months to two years. In candidate school they are seen as manipulators and exploiters, usually lacking real empathy and compassion. They seem to be born with a social and moral learning disorder. Their sociopathic "swiss cheese" conscience predisposes to sexually immoral behavior even while they loudly proclaim moral purity from the mission pulpit.

Boundary violations for the sociopath revolve around the superego deficiencies. They include sexual morality, ethics, business dealings, money management, parenting, and work behavior. The obvious discrepancies between talk and walk are devastating to the mission setting as well as to the constituency.

Occasionally evangelicals find it hard to acknowledge that there can be a disorder that leaves the individual truly incapable of moral decision-making. They want scriptural documentation of this difficult concept. I have suggested they study Deuteronomy 21:18-21, which describes capital punishment applied to incorrigible teenagers prior to marriage and the potential genetic components of a disorder.

II.   Borderline personality disorder was not clearly defined until the past 20-25 years. It is characterized by instability of mood, interpersonal relationships, and self-image. Identity disturbance is almost always present especially in self view, sexual identity, long term goals, career, types of friends, and values. There are usually symptoms of emptiness and boredom (Gabbard, 1994).

Persons with this disorder have unstable and intense relationships, often alternating between the extremes of over-idealization and devaluation. They cannot tolerate being alone, and frequent outbursts of anger occur for which they may later be sorry, or they may deny that they were angry. Self-mutilation or suicide gestures may occur.

Individuals with borderline personality disorder are frequently involved in *splitting*. The outward behavior associated with this is seen in two settings overseas. The first occurs in one to one relationships, that is alternating between the extremes of idealizing a person, then suddenly devaluing the same person. This leaves missionary colleagues with no consistent frame of reference for interaction and relationships.

The second situation where splitting occurs is in group and team functioning where several team members will be strongly in favor of the borderline and easily manipulated by him or her, whereas others see the dysfunctional patterns of behavior and feel that the individual is a detriment to the team effort. With the passage of time and the onset of exhaustion most of the team will perceive the destructive impact of continued interaction.

People with this disorder have not completed important developmental milestones, some of which can never be reclaimed (Gabbard, 1994). Fear of abandonment is intense and may persist in spite of therapy. This is exacerbated by the frequent separations that characterize missionary living. Many borderlines were sexually abused as children (Gabbard, 1994). For this reason history taking in selection needs to include questions regarding childhood sexual abuse.

In orientation programs, these individuals may be observed in frequent anger-remorse-depression cycles. Once they arrive overseas their disruption to the field ministry team is almost as severe as that occurring with the antisocial personality. At times the borderline appears normal, therefore other missionaries are caught off guard when outbursts or decompensation occurs.

Identity establishment is so incomplete in people with this disorder that they find it almost impossible to successfully integrate into a new culture, hence the basic incompatibility of this personality disorder with overseas missionary service. They may look to the mission to provide their identity. Their identity is diffuse enough that they often do not know what boundaries are, and their limited capacity for empathy precludes understanding others' needs for privacy and time alone.

The borderline's inability to self soothe creates demands on other missionaries to be the sole source of a holding environment. Busy missionaries without the capacity to set limits are unable to provide this.

III. Narcissistic personality disorder is marked by a pervasive pattern of grandiosity, hypersensitivity to the evaluation of others, and lack of empathy (DSM-IVTR). People with this disorder think of themselves as special, but when faced with the normal disappointments of life, they may decompensate. They often feel that they are unique and entitled to special treatment. Their feelings of entitlement seldom have a corresponding sense of reciprocal responsibility. We live in a somewhat narcissistic society, therefore, cultural traits must be distinguished from a true personality disorder.

Gabbard (1994) distinguishes between the oblivious narcissist who "has a sender, but no receiver," and the hypervigilant, who is exquisitely sensitive to how others react. In either case, people with this disorder have a very fragile self-esteem. They have the exaggerated sense of self-importance of a small child. Becoming a star missionary may further feed this pathology, though the stardom is usually short-lived.

The developmental stages of learning to face gradual, limited disappointments with parental support may not have occurred. Consequently they do not develop the mature ability to withstand disappointment and failure that are a part of mission life, while retaining self-regard. They then alternate between feelings of grandiosity and inferiority. Often they appear to have individuated but not separated (Gabbard 1994).

In the selection process, individuals with this disorder may be detected by an inability to accept criticism, disappointment, or suggestions. They seem unable to love. On the field they may project a favorable image, but are unable to consider the needs of others. Because these individuals feel that they are special and entitled they do not maintain social distance. Consequently, their boundary violations tend to emotionally drain other missionaries.

They are also poor team players. In the face of disappointment they may respond with a brief reactive psychosis which can be very disruptive to the work of the mission. Treatment, if possible, often involves providing a holding environment that allows development to proceed. This is simply not feasible overseas.

IV. Histrionic personality disorder manifests itself with excessive emotionality and attention seeking. People with this disorder constantly seek and demand reassurance, praise, approval, and affirmation. They need to be the center of attention. Their emotions seem shallow and rapidly shifting. Loss and rejection, perceived or real, create severe distress. They may be creative and imaginative, but they lack analytical decision-making skills.

It is important to distinguish between the more healthy hysterical personality and the true histrionic personality disorder (Gabbard, 1994).

Causes of the disorder may be early life separations and disturbance in attachments, as well as poor bonding and limited role modeling. Self-esteem for the adult histrionic is centered on physical attractiveness, often to the point of seductiveness.

This person has a limited capacity to tolerate delayed gratification, which does not blend well with missionary service. The constant need for reassurance and affirmation wears down other missionaries and nationals, creating a level of exhaustion in the entire team.

In candidate school or orientation programs, histrionic individuals seem overly emotional, flighty, and seductive. They may be the center of every party, but in a very superficial way. Letters of recommendation often comment on these characteristics. These people are so desperate for attention that they may cross any boundary to get it. Their seductiveness can be either social, sexual, or both.

It is possible for a person to display mixed features of personality disorders, now titled "Personality disorder, NOS."

In advising mission boards one must distinguish between the healthy depression mentioned at the beginning of the article, and the unhealthy depression accompanying personality disorders. The former usually is clinically responsive to medication and counseling. In contrast, characterological depressions are only symptoms superimposed on fixed, maladaptive traits. These unhealthy depressions occur when the style of the personality disordered individual is not succeeding in day to day life.

Productivity in stressful settings is out of the question for these individuals. The mental health care professional is uniquely positioned to help mission boards gain sophistication and use appropriate tools in treatment (when possible), and in providing expertise in preventive selection procedures.

Mission personnel are sometimes uncomfortable with the fact that most descriptions of personality disorders include some characteristics that remind them of themselves. The key to overcoming this discomfort is to remember that to diagnose a personality disorder, the patterns must be lifelong, pervasive, inflexible, and maladaptive enough to cause either impairment in interpersonal or occupational functioning, or subjective distress.

Compassion for the Individual vs. Protection of the Overseas Team

One of the most difficult issues any mission has to face is what to do when a person with one of these personality disorders progresses through the selection process, arriving overseas with all of his or her emotional difficulties. The individual's behavior quickly results in credibility gaps with the nationals, exhaustion on the part of field executives, and frustration and sometimes resignations from other missionaries.

Compassion would suggest an extended effort to work with the person in the field environment. Unfortunately we are all aware that the statistical probability of success anywhere, much less in the heat of the battle overseas, is negligible. Meanwhile, the work, the other missionaries, the nationals, and the field leader suffer immense pain.

Can a Christian have a personality disorder? Yes. Is that emotional damage healed by a committed Christian experience? Not necessarily. We understand that a person with physical crippling such as polio is not necessarily made whole by salvation and growth. We must communicate that psychological crippling is not automatically healed with Christian commitment.

In talking with mission executives, the analogy I draw is that we would not send a physically wheelchair-bound individual to the battlefront in war. I contend that we must not send our psychological wheelchair cases to the spiritual battlefront overseas. When we do, we compromise the work and expose the individual to unnecessary failure. We also add frustration, anger, and decreased effectiveness and efficiency to the stresses with which coworkers are already dealing. We can use the mistakes made in the past to educate our missions to the need for quality prevention.

In many cases people with personality disorders are intelligent and educated. They may appear to be very spiritual, and their skills may seem to be just what a particular field needs. Too often, though, the mission has chosen people to fill the immediate needs overseas without selecting according to emotional qualifications.

The mental health professional may also need to remind his organization that a mission that accepts a candidate with a personality disorder who decompensates while in their employ may be responsible to provide hospitalization. The workman's compensation matters involved in these cases can bankrupt a self-insured mission board since the cost to the organization may reach as high as $1,000 per day.

Prevention

It would seem that the obvious long-term solution for missions resides in the selection process. Consulting professionals may help avoid inadvertent recruitment of personality disordered individuals by suggesting the following:

1.   All candidates and spouses should receive the MMPI. The MMPI is the gold standard of personality inventories, in my opinion. Mission groups need to understand that these tests must be interpreted by a seasoned professional who should also conduct an interview. The primary objection is the cost; however, this seems a small price to pay in comparison to the financial and human toll involved with sending personality disordered individuals overseas.

Missions need to understand the limitations of the MMPI; for instance it will not detect sexual deviancy. The three mistakes I see regarding the use of the MMPI in mission selection and personality disorders are (a) not doing it, (b) not doing it well, and (c) not listening to the professionals providing the assessments.

2.   In-depth personnel interviews must be conducted for all candidates. This should include separate interviews with the spouse and any older children. Delicate matters such as childhood sexual abuse, dysfunctional families of origin, and alcoholic backgrounds must be addressed.

3.   All recommendation letters should be followed up by a personal telephone call. Letter writers will often be more candid regarding problems if their opinions do not appear in print.

4.   All candidates should submit a detailed occupational and social history which has been verified by outside sources. My experience has been that many people with personality disorders have frequent job changes, though short term jobs related to schooling should be clarified.

5   If any questions surface, the candidate should be interviewed in several

additional sessions by a seasoned mental health professional with experience in diagnosing personality disorders and with awareness of the unique stresses of overseas living.

Summary

This article should not be considered a complete psychological handbook for the missionary selection process. Rather, it is intended to help avoid the overseas placement of individuals with personality disorders. There may be useful places of service for these people within the church at large, but not overseas.

Selection comniittees need to be especially careful in placement procedures. Prevention is the best cure, with heavy emphasis on psychological testing and wise use of interviews, job records, and personal histories.

Addendum

Although this article is geared to detection of adults with personality disorders, families with a child or adolescent with this type of problem may also not be able to serve overseas as long as the child is living in the home. Care needs to be exercised during the selection process and testing problem children prior to overseas placement is critical. Families who adopt troubled youngsters may find that those children are too damaged or identity disordered to adjust to overseas settings.

The titles of personality disorders listed here are applicable only to individuals aged eighteen and older. Comparable childhood disorders have different titles.

References

American Psychiatric Association. (2000). *Diagnostic and statistical manual of mental disorders* (IV TR.).Washington, D.C.

Gabbard, G. (1994). *Psychodynamic psychiatry.* Washington, DC: American Psychiatric Press.

Landorf, J. (1982). *Irregular people.* Waco: Word.

Magid, K., & McKelvey, C. A. (1987). *High risk — children without a conscience.* Golden, CO: M & M Publishing.

Millon, T., & Everly, G. (1987). *Personality and its disorders.* New York: John Wiley.

Oates, W. E. (1987). *Behind the masks.* Philadelphia: Westminster.

Schubert. E. (1989). Emotional bruising in missionaries. Paper presented at TMF conference, Taiwan. Tapes available through Dallas Theological Seminary tape library.

Sexton, R. & Maddock. R. (1980). The missionary syndrome. *Journal of Religion and Health, 19,* pp. 59-65.

Note: This chapter was first published in the *Journal of Psychology and Theology,* Vol. 21, No. 1, Spring 1993. Reprinted by permission.

41

Recognizing and Dealing With Demonic Involvement

Joyce M. Bowers and Clinton E. Arnold

Introduction (by Joyce M. Bowers)
Mental health professionals who work with missionaries may be faced with questions in the area known as "spiritual warfare" for which they have little or no background or training. This chapter provides an introduction and overview but not a prescriptive approach for the counselor's work.

Christians—and perhaps especially missionaries—may be targets of demonic forces, particularly when they are effectively communicating the Gospel in areas where forces of evil have long held sway. People who may not give much thought to demonic powers in their home environment are often confronted with that reality when they serve in other cultures. Opposition to the spread of the Gospel can take the form of attacks on the messengers. While Christians cannot be possessed by evil spirits in the sense of ownership, they can be harassed or oppressed in ways that are hard to identify clearly.

Spiritual gifts, easily recognized as coming from the Holy Spirit, are often enhancements of an individual's natural gifts, not something totally uncharacteristic. In a similar way, perhaps, forces of evil exploit existing natural weakness and sin in human beings, giving it extra power and impact. As explained later, "the devil" works in concert with the other enemies of the human soul, "the flesh" and "the world."

Mental health professionals who work with missionaries would do well to keep in mind that demonic forces may be at work, opposing and hindering the process of healing and growth. This may be suspected when "things don't add up"—when good interventions are

The Bible presents three forms of evil influence: the world, the flesh, and the devil. Christians, including missionaries, can be targets of demonic activity. This chapter presents a Biblical framework for understanding and dealing with demonic power. It is important to take evil power seriously, but maintain balance in using spiritual resources for protection and at times taking authority over an evil spirit.

ineffective or honest emotional and spiritual efforts on the part of the missionary seem inexplicably thwarted. It is advisable to ask missionaries if they have had any known contact or experience with evil forces or occult practices, while in their overseas assignment or at other times. A missionary may be hesitant to bring up the topic, fearing that the counselor will "really think I'm crazy."

If missionaries have not been raised in strong Christian homes and congregations, they may have dabbled in or even had considerable exposure to occult practices prior to making a firm commitment to the Christian faith. If those evil influences have not been identified and renounced, they may still be providing an entry point or "foothold" for the demonic.

This is an area for which it may be especially important to have a working relationship with a mature pastor. Just as counselors make referrals to other professionals when issues demand specialized expertise, they may need to refer a counselee to someone with experience and the gift of sensitive discernment in the area of demonic involvement.

A significant advantage of providing pastoral care alongside clinical care is that the pastoral counselor is encouraged to discuss and pray with the client regarding areas of spiritual warfare. In fact such an approach can be significantly helpful, especially if the pastoral care provider assists in the steps of confession and renunciation of any foothold of the evil one.

In contrast to the pastoral care approach, a caution for professional clinical counselors is that an accusation of "exorcism" on the part of a client toward the licensed clinical counselor may place one's state license in jeopardy. Confirming this caution, Gary Collins, (The Biblical Basis of Christian Counseling for People Helpers, p. 171), wisely urges professional clinical counselors to consider any impact on their state license for counseling in certain areas.

This concern should not in any way limit the reliance of a mental health professional upon spiritual resources, but rather provide increased sensitivity to professional boundaries and parameters in determining the best approach to any situation.

It is easy for a counselor who is inexperienced in this area to feel overwhelmed. It is important to remember that "greater is he that is in you than he that is in the world" (I John 4:4). Dr. Paul Hiebert makes the point that the battle between good and evil is between unequal combatants. Satan and other fallen angels who do evil are part of God's creation, as are the angels who do God's bidding. God continues to allow Satan to do evil, but God's power is as far superior to Satan's power as the Creator is superior to the creation. God has the final word.

With a great deal of focus on exorcism in popular culture and "spiritual warfare" in Christian circles, Satan and demons have received a great deal of attention in recent decades, much of it unbiblical and unhealthy. There are a host of ap-proaches to discerning and dealing with demonic activity in the lives of Christians; there has been a lot of controversy in Evangelical circles about various approaches.

The most balanced and helpful approach the editors of this volume have seen is that of Dr. Clinton E. Arnold, professor of New Testament at the Talbot School of Theology, which is part of Biola University in southern California. The rest of this chapter contains excerpts from his book, *3 Crucial Questions Regarding Spiritual*

Warfare, published by Baker Book House in 1997 (part of a series of "3 Crucial Questions" books). Excerpts are used by permission of Baker Book House.

We strongly recommend the whole book, particularly chapter 1, "What Is Spiritual Warfare?" and chapter 2, "Can a Christian Be Demon-Possessed?" from which these excerpts are taken. Space limitations allow only a taste of Arnold's book, but we hope it will whet the appetite of the reader for a fuller treatment of these often confusing issues.

Clinton E. Arnold, *3 Crucial Questions Regarding Spiritual Warfare*

Excerpted and condensed by Joyce M. Bowers

Maintaining the Balance: Our Three Enemies
The Bible teaches that there are three forms of evil influence that exert their power over the lives of people to lead them into transgression and away from God. These three enemies are simply described as the world, the flesh, and the devil. The Bible shows there to be a balance among these three, woven together as strands pulling us toward evil, as in Ephesians 2:1-3:

> As for you, you were dead in your transgressions and sins, in which you used to live when you followed
> *[The World] the ways of this world* and of
> *[The Devil] the ruler of the kingdom of the air, the spirit* who is now at work in those who are disobedient. All of us also lived among them at one time, gratifying
> *[The Flesh] the cravings of our sinful nature* and following its desires and thoughts. Like the rest, we were by nature objects of wrath.

The Bible takes all three seriously. The inner inclination to think and do evil (the flesh) and the external pressure to conform to ungodly social standards (the world) are seen as just as important as the supernaturally powerful beings who are hostile to God and his people. Each of these influences needs to be taken into account in equal measure to the other two and the nature of their interconnectedness must be considered.

The flesh is the inner propensity or inclination to do evil. Although we are new creatures in Christ, this inner compulsion continually seeks to reassert its claim and we can only resist it by the power of the Holy Spirit (see esp. Gal. 5:16-17).

The world is the unhealthy social environment in which we live. The world represents the prevailing worldview assumptions of the day that stand contrary to the biblical understanding of reality and biblical values.

The devil is an intelligent powerful spirit-being that is thoroughly evil and is directly involved in perpetrating evil in the lives of individuals as well as on a much larger scale. Paul describes him in Ephesians 2:2 as "the spirit who is at work in those who are disobedient." The devil, or Satan, is portrayed as powerfully at work in the lives of unbelievers.

Christians not only continue to struggle with the inner propensity to evil and the powerful impact of worldview and culture, but also with a personal, supernatural being that is also bent toward doing evil. It is crucial to recognize that these three influences work in concert. There is a large area of overlap, where all three influences converge, working in harmony and with the same intent. One of the influences may be more prominent in a given situation. Only through union with Jesus and experiencing his empowering presence do people have hope for escaping the compelling power of these influences.

Satan works in harmony with the flesh. For instance, if a person struggles with lustful thoughts, Satan will exploit this tendency. As the tempter (I Thess. 3:5), he will stimulate the natural inclination and introduce new ideas.

The activity of the devil is also closely connected to the world. His primary concern is people, but if he can focus his energies on people of status and power, he can thereby exert a significant impact on the course of culture.

This way of looking at the nature of evil influence has significant implications for life and ministry. This perspective would encourage deliverance ministry in conjunction with sound therapy and a solid mentoring discipleship relationship. If a person is troubled enough to see a deliverance counselor, it may also be advisable to have sound counsel from a Christian psychologist as well as a close mentoring relationship with a more mature Christian.

Ephesians 6:10-20: The Accessibility of Divine Power

The classic spiritual warfare passage is Ephesians 6:10-20. The emphasis is on the day-to-day struggle of every believer, a struggle that involves us as individuals and requires us to be individually prepared.

God bestows on his people divine power for the struggle. Paul urges the Ephesians, "be strong *in the Lord and in his mighty power*" (Eph. 6:10) and emphasizes the immediate access believers have to the power of God. God empowers us through his indwelling Spirit and on the basis of our relationship with the Lord Jesus Christ. We share in Christ's kingdom authority over the demonic realm and can resist demonically inspired temptation. We have power to command an evil spirit to flee if it manifests its presence.

Paul encourages the Ephesians to "be filled with the Spirit" (Eph. 5:18). We find our strength in the presence of the indwelling Lord, who empowers us to stand against the devil's schemes. Each of the weapons is crucial for preparing for the ongoing struggle that is part and parcel of living the Christian life. The following list provides a summary interpretation of the armor of God:

1.   ***Put On Your Trousers: Wear Truth***
Know the truth of who you are in Christ (for the powers of darkness will try to deceive you). Practice honesty and live with moral integrity.

2.   ***Put On the Breastplate of Righteousness***
Realize your status before God as one who has been acquitted of all guilt. Acquire personal holiness and develop good character.

3.   ***Put On Your Boots: Prepare to Share the Gospel of Peace***
Prepare yourself for sharing the gospel wherever God calls you.

4.   ***Take the Shield of Faith***
Do not doubt! Believe that God will help you overcome.

5 .   *Put On the Helmet of Salvation*

Be secure in your identity in Christ – as one who has been saved, united with Christ, made alive, co-resurrected, and co-exalted.

6 .   *Take the Sword of the Spirit, the Word of God*

Devote your life to aggressively spreading the gospel. Know Scripture and apply it to every difficult situation.

7 .   *The Bottom Line: Pray!*

Ask God to strengthen you and other believers to resist temptation and share the gospel effectively.

Prayer is the heart of spiritual warfare. It is the means of intimacy and communion with the almighty Lord and an expression of faith. Part of spiritual warfare is the recognition that you need God to hold you by the hand and fight on your behalf. Prayer is foundational to deploying all of the other weapons. Prayer is the essence and mode of spiritual warfare.

Do Demonic Spirits Affect Christians?

The believer has a new identity as a child of God, a citizen of heaven, and a saint. Yet the Christian still retains a structure of the present evil age: his or her body and the power of sin presenting itself as an inner propensity to do evil. Demonic spirits seek to exert their influence in the same way and in the same places that the evil impulse does. They attempt to reassert their control over the mind, will, and emotions of the individual in a variety of insidious ways.

The difference between a believer and a nonbeliever is at the core of their being. The believer has an entirely new nature, endowed with the Holy Spirit. Demonic spirits cannot penetrate to the core of this person's being and snatch away what belongs to God. A believer may, however, yield to the evil impulse or to a demonic spirit, allowing it to assert a dominating influence over mind, will, emotions, and even the body.

Because of the presence of the Spirit, the believer is no longer under the *compelling* sway of sin and the powers. He or she is energized by the dynamic and empowering presence of God to defeat these unholy influences at every turn. Nor is this struggle a battle of equals. God's power is incomparably greater than the power of sin or the power of Satan.

The biblical, theological, and historical evidence suggests that Christians can be profoundly influenced by evil spirits—even to the extent that it can be said that they are inhabited and controlled by demons. The passage in the Epistles that comes closest to the language of demonization is Ephesians 4:26-27: "In your anger do not sin; do not let the sun go down while you are still angry, and do not give the devil a foothold." Paul calls believers to vigilance and moral purity so that they do not relinquish a base of operations to demonic spirits.

As outlined earlier, evil asserts its influence in three ways: through the "flesh," through the "world," and directly through Satan and his demons. Demons can dominate and they can control. Their authority and control, however, are not absolute. By virtue of our union with Christ, we have the ability to offer every aspect of our lives to God and allow him to reign over us.

The Epistles show us a variety of ways that Satan often works to reassert his dominance over the lives of believers:

- Temptation
- False teaching
- Creating feelings of guilt, doubt, and fear
- Physical attack
- Persecution

Most of the ways that demons work against believers would not be described as symptoms of "demonization" or inhabitation. There is an immense variety of ways our enemy works to influence believers and thereby thwart the purposes of God in their lives. The most fruitful and accurate way of describing demonic influence is along a continuum:

1	2	3	4
Tempted or persecuted	Regularly yielding to a demonic temptation	"Devoured" "Taken captive" "Taken as plunder"	Demonized "Has a demon"

There is sufficient biblical, theological, and historical evidence to assert that a Christian can be inhabited and controlled by a demonic spirit, though they cannot be fully owned or "possessed." The evidence also supports the appropriateness for an afflicted believer (or someone ministering to him or her) to exercise authority in the name of Jesus and firmly command a spirit to leave.

A Biblical Framework for Dealing with Demons

If Christians can be inhabited and controlled by demons, what can they do to avoid and rid themselves of these unwelcome intruders? What can we do to help other believers who are deeply struggling? The following summary, based on some vital biblical concepts, suggests ways for Christians to deal with various forms of evil influence in their lives, particularly the demonic.

A.   **Draw Near to God** (James 4:7; Ps. 91:9)

The Book of James gives the most important way to deal with this problem: "Submit yourselves, then, to God. Resist the devil, and he will flee from you" (James 4:7). The most important first step for any struggling believers is to draw near to God. Turning to God involves prayer, worship, and exposing oneself to God's will through the Scriptures.

B.   **Resist the Devil and His Foul Spirits** (James 4:7; 1 Peter 5:9; Eph. 6:11-13)

The second part of the instruction from James is to "resist the devil." The command is so important, it is reiterated by both Paul and Peter. What does it look like for a person to resist the devil? Successful resistance entails a set of nine convictions and actions.

1.   Give attention to the area that has made you susceptible to demonic attack.

- Intentionally inviting their presence through false religions, witchcraft, sorcery, or channeling
- Residual influence from the past through false religions, witchcraft, sorcery, channeling or intergenerational ("familial") spirits
- Unintentionally inviting their presence by the habitual practice of sin (Eph. 4:27)
- Special attacks against Christians: deception, temptation, physical attack, or special periods of attack (Eph. 6:13)
- Demonic opposition to carrying out the mission of the church, especially in sharing the gospel

2. Determine to resist

3. Know who you are in Christ

4. Know your resources in Christ

5. Deal with their ground for attack

6. If necessary, deal directly and firmly with the demonic spirit

The strategy we have outlined for dealing with demonic spirits thus far has said nothing about "casting out" spirits. This is not always necessary. As a person draws near to Christ, renouncing sin and appropriating the resources in Christ, demonic spirits will often flee. James says, "Resist the devil, and *he will flee from you*" James 4:7). Resistance involves a set of actions that may or may not include a firm command to a spirit to depart.

There may be times when it is appropriate and necessary to exercise one's authority in Christ to command a spirit to leave. The basis for one's authority to issue such a command is derived from union with Christ. We are united to him and have been filled by him and thus share in his authority over the realm of the demonic (see Col. 2:9-10). Such a situation requires a firm verbal command addressed to a demonic spirit; this is not a prayer to God (although the whole confrontation is prepared for and supported in prayer).

There has been some controversy about whether it is appropriate to take authority in Christ and command a spirit in another person to leave. As we minister to an individual who is clearly troubled by a demonic spirit, should our goal be strictly to enable him or her to exercise authority in Christ to command any residing spirits to depart? Or, upon discerning their presence, should we intervene and demand that the spirits leave?

This issue is sometimes described as the difference between a "truth encounter" or a "power encounter" approach. Such labels oversimplify the issue, however, since both approaches rely on the power of God and encourage people to know and appropriate the truths of the Christian faith. The real distinction is what we might call "self-deliverance" vs. an intervention-based approach.

While I applaud the emphases of the truth encounter approach, I don't find substantiation for what it denies—that is, the advisability of a mature believer to act on behalf of another person to command a spirit to leave. The example of Jesus, the

Twelve, the Seventy, and Paul as well as numerous examples from the early church point to the propriety of an interventionist approach.

The early church recognized the need for Christian leaders to intervene in cases where people had recently professed faith in Christ and were just beginning their growth. Only rarely are demonic issues dealt with in the assimilation process of new Christians in contemporary churches. This may mean that there are more unresolved issues of sin and demonic influence among Christians today than among Christians in the early church.

One of the key issues is *when* is it appropriate to take authority in the name of Christ and demand a spirit to depart. And, closely related to this is the issue of *how one discerns* the presence of a demonic spirit and distinguishes it, for example, from simply the "lust of the flesh." Some have attempted to create a list of symptoms that point to the kind of demonic activity that would require direct confrontation. However, it is difficult to diagnose the presence of a spirit merely by a set of symptoms.

There are often legitimate psychological explanations for symptoms that were sometimes understood to be clear signs of a demonic spirit. Voices in the head, the presence of different personalities, bizarre behavior, hallucinatory experiences, seizures, all may have a medical or psychological explanation. On the other hand, however, they may point to demonic affliction.

Spiritual issues require spiritual discernment. We need to develop our sensitivity to the leading and impressions from the Holy Spirit as we minister to people. Empirical verification will often be difficult to come by as we seek to discern what is really going on. But the Holy Spirit is God's guiding and empowering presence in our lives who can lead us into ministering in the most appropriate way to people.

When there is evidence pointing to the presence of a spirit and the Holy Spirit confirms this conclusion to us, we can then exercise our authority in Christ to order the spirit(s) to depart. There may be occasions when it is appropriate simply to say, "If there is a demonic spirit causing this problem, I now command you in the name of the Lord Jesus Christ to depart!"

Much more can and needs to be said about the process of discernment and then directly confronting demonic spirits. Our purpose here is merely to assert the fact that we have the authority in Christ to take such direct action and that there may be occasions when it is appropriate.

7.   Be meaningfully attached to the Body of Christ

One Christian counseling center that understands the role of the demonic and will not hesitate to cast out demons if they are discerned also understands the vital role of the Christian community in the deliverance/healing process. They require every counselee to join a local church, have a spiritual mentor and several prayer partners. The professional counselor then is only one member of a larger team working together to help a person come to wholeness in Christ.

8.   Pray and solicit prayer support

9.   Expect Christ to give victory! (James 4:7)

Summary

1.   Christians cannot be demon-possessed if one means by that expression ownership of a believer by Satan or demons. Believers are the property of God and belong exclusively to him.

2.   Christians can be inhabited by demons, but only if they provide the spirits with the "space to occupy" through protracted sin or by inviting their presence.

3.   The behavior of Christians can be controlled by demons, but only if they have yielded that control to the spirits. Just as sin can "reign" over one's body, so a demon can assert a high level of control.

4.   Christians can yield so much control to a demon that they may even display an altered state of consciousness and manifest the presence of an intruding demon (with the demon speaking through the person, etc.).

5.   Christians can be delivered from evil spirits and that is what God wants for them. God does not want his people to live defeated lives, in bondage to sin and impurity or to unclean spirits. The power of God is infinitely greater than the power of the enemy and his realm. Believers can experience freedom and victory from the compelling influence of Satan and his forces.

6.   Resisting Satan and finding deliverance from the influence of evil spirits involves drawing near to God in faith and prayer, becoming immersed in the Scriptures, attaching oneself to other believers in meaningful relationships, and understanding and appropriating the work of Christ.

7.   Resisting a demonic spirit on some occasions may involve exercising authority on the basis of one's relationship to Christ as his disciple and firmly commanding an evil spirit to depart.

8.   It is important to recognize the wide variety of ways that demons seek to exert their unhealthy influence on the church. To become overly fixated on the dramatic symptoms of what has classically been called "possession behavior" could cause one to lose sight of the ways he works to harm relationships, thwart the evangelistic mission of the church, or distort what one thinks of Christ and his work.

Recommended Reading

Arnold, C. E. (1997). *3 crucial questions regarding spiritual warfare.* Grand Rapids, MI: Baker Book House

Collins, G. R. (1997). Biblical basis of Christian counseling for people helpers. Colorado Springs, CO: Navpress Publishing Group.

42

When Should They Leave: Retention and Referral of Personnel in Field Settings

Timothy R. Sieges

Sometimes the best way to deal with a personnel crisis is for a missionary individual, couple, or family to return to the home country. Analyzing a situation and making a good decision presents challenges for both leadership and missionaries. This chapter provides guidelines for dealing with personnel crises, examines the makeup of a management team, and suggests critical questions for decision-making processes.

*A*fter a brief prayer, the mission director began the meeting by asking the participants to introduce themselves. Around the circle sat the parents, the clinic physician, the high school counselor, the parent's work supervisor, and the mission mental health clinician. Following terse introductions, the director haltingly stated the purpose of the meeting, "In view of your daughter's recent and thankfully failed suicide attempt, we are here to consider the best place for her recovery."

Tears and frustration, opinion and fact, Scriptures and "common sense," prayers and protocol dominated the subsequent discussion. After everyone had his/her input, all eyes turned to the director. The moment of truth lingered in the tense silence. The director understood that whatever the decision, it would be unacceptable to more than one person in the room.

The above scenario, plus or minus some details, is played out nearly daily in mission environments around the world. Personnel crises usually lead mission leaders to make heart-wrenching decisions about who stays and who leaves. Even when these conclusions are shared among a variety of competent and informed participants, getting these interested parties "on the same page" is a major challenge.

This chapter provides guidelines for dealing with personnel crises, examines the makeup of a management team, and suggests critical questions for decision-making processes.

Crises of Personnel Conduct

Some of the greatest challenges in field settings involve things other than managing geopolitical crises, illness, natural disaster, or indigenous resistance to the gospel message. Often, administrators struggle most with issues involving "crises of personnel conduct"—situations involving disruptive behavior by an individual, group or family that (1) diminishes the effectiveness of the mission's ministry, (2) draws resources and energy from ministry goals, (3) negatively affects the mission's reputation in the national community and sending constituency, and/or (4) creates divisions and factions within working groups.

These personnel conflicts are usually acted out in *personal, group,* and *work* relationships. Personal concerns involve such destructive behaviors as domestic violence, child abuse or neglect, chronic marital discord, ongoing child oppositional-defiant behavior, marital infidelity, and addictive behaviors.

Group activities that may initiate a personnel crisis involve adherence to or insistence on non-orthodox religious beliefs, extreme sectarianism, unsafe and/or bizarre religious practices, polarized factions regarding mission focus or philosophy, and nationalism or racism that ostracizes part of the membership.

Vocationally focused conduct crises may include ongoing work conflicts, chronic insubordination, non-compliance with national and organizational regulations, sexual harassment, angry outbursts, and inability to complete assigned tasks.

A Collaborative Process

A team of *relevant, knowledgeable participants* is imperative when addressing crises of personnel conduct. Successful managers understand the wisdom of obtaining wise counsel in the time of a crisis. Proverbs 15:22 says, "Plans fail for lack of counsel but with many advisors they succeed." When making difficult personnel decisions, increasing input allows the administrator to view a complex situation from several different perspectives. This ensures a complete picture of the issues, since each team member offers an important piece of the crisis puzzle. However, inclusion on the crisis team needs to be limited to those with an *informed and pertinent relationship* to the situation.

A person's relevance to the crisis is determined by his/her relationship to the situation or event based on training, knowledge, or expertise. In the opening example, a medical doctor was included because the physician attending the young person following the suicide attempt was able to give pertinent information about the seriousness of the attempt, the child's demeanor in treatment, the need for subsequent intervention, and medical factors related to the case. In a case of someone with chronic, unresolved conflicts with colleagues, a physician would probably not be on the team. A good standard for inclusion on this kind of team could be "as few as possible, but as many as necessary."

"Too many cooks" can wreak havoc in an administrative kitchen. In personnel crises, well-meaning friends or advisers often want formal input in the decision making process. However, relevance means that each team member must have knowledge, training, experience or professional credentials that inform the decision. In the above example, parents were included because their knowledge and experience with the teenager were indispensable. For a more detailed examination of team inclusion see Miriam Kellogg's "Crisis Matrices: A Mission Training Package" (1996).

Critical Factors in Retaining or Referring Personnel

"Getting everyone on the same page" begins with assembling a team of informed and relevant participants. The next step involves the group asking goal-directed questions about the situation. Each member will answer the questions from his/her perspective with the intention of moving toward a plan that is beneficial to the person(s), mission, and national community. These *basic* (not exhaustive) questions facilitate discussion; they are not a checklist or a test to determine the outcome. For additional questions see Appendix A.

1. Is there a clear antecedent, precipitating event or condition, or onset to the crisis?
2. What is the duration of the problem?
3. How pervasive is the impact of the situation?
4. How intrusive on the person and mission's functioning is the situation?
5. What is the potential for harming self or others?

Question One: Onset

The first question involves factors initiating the personnel crisis. Each team member will reflect on any clear onset to the present crisis. For example, Kate had isolated herself from colleagues and friends and rarely came out of her home. After a month of seclusion, the administration was concerned about her ability to remain in the field setting. Asking about onset revealed that this behavior was uncharacteristic. Kate had formerly been outgoing and actively engaged in her work. There was a specific time when her behavior changed from gregarious to reclusive, following a robbery and assault at an in-country resort. Two other victims had progressed fairly quickly through post-trauma recovery, but Kate was unable to move on. Her withdrawal was primarily in response to unresolved victimization. An identifiable onset helped the team make plans for her retention or referral.

Identifying an antecedent usually *increases* the probability of successfully treating a problem in the field setting. For Kate, a clear antecedent allowed the team to consider the in-country resources for post-trauma counseling. The team would have an idea of the prognosis based on the literature on trauma recovery. They were also able to generate in-house solutions for this person's workload; physical, emotional, and spiritual support; and possible medical treatment.

Understanding a precipitating event or condition is helpful in decision making. Consider the following examples:

- A person is in ongoing conflict at work. The onset was apparently when the individual changed to a new, unfamiliar work role. The administrative team may strategize to solve job-related problems that can have impact in interpersonal relationships. The person doesn't necessarily have to be sent home for required counseling.

- A teenager is involved in numerous destructive activities on the mission station. The antecedent seems to be when he began making friends with local troublemakers known for drug use. The antecedent may cause the team to lean more toward referral than retention.

Knowing the antecedents for crisis behaviors is important but the *absence* of clear onset is also significant. No obvious precipitating event often *decreases* the chance of the situation being adequately treated in a field setting. Consider the following examples of a vague or no apparent antecedents:

- A husband and wife have had chronic marital discord since arriving in the country. Personnel records indicate questions about their problem-solving ability, communication and role understanding in the candidacy process. No specific antecedent increases the probability this couple may need to return to the sending country for marital counseling.

- An administrator whose staff refuses to work for him. Similar problems have been present in several positions over his entire career. No clear onset in this case indicates a long-term problem that may not be solved by adjustments on the field.

Some questions that aid in determining antecedents include: What changes have taken place recently in the person's vocational, physical, social economic, or spiritual world? Has this type of behavior characterized this person's conduct before? Under what circumstances has this person or others acted this way before?

Question Two: Duration

The next question is the length of time a problem has been present. If there is a clear onset, how much time has passed? If no obvious onset, how long has this characterized the person or family's functioning? In general terms, the shorter the duration of a problem, the better the prognosis for successful treatment. Longstanding, well-practiced maladaptive behaviors are more difficult to deal with in counseling and thus require longer-term treatment.

As duration *increases*, probability for treating the problem in the field setting *decreases*. Long-term problems do not remediate quickly or easily. The crisis team will have to consider the available resources needed, and whether it is wise to invest limited on-site resources for long-term treatment.

The following scenarios illustrate this dynamic:
- A program supervisor is sexist and racist. This person has long-term attitudes and beliefs about women and ethnicity. He persists in his bigotry in spite of cross-cultural training and decades of work in multicultural settings. His well-developed beliefs make it difficult for him to admit liability. He is not open to changing or accepting counseling. Successful treatment on the field is unlikely.

- A tribal worker is troubled with chronic angry outbursts. In his village allocation he is known as the "Angry One." The people in his language group often threaten their children that if they misbehave, they will be sent to the Angry One's home. His reputation among other expatriates is similar.

Retaining this worker during treatment seems unwise, and since duration is longstanding and without apparent onset, referral seems appropriate.

Obviously, problems that have a short duration often have a clear antecedent. The earlier examples illustrating apparent onsets are also of short duration. Problems with both of these characteristics can usually be handled successfully on the field through administrative, medical, counseling or pastoral interventions. However, longstanding patterns of troubling behavior often require resources and time unavailable in field settings.

Question Three: Pervasiveness

This question involves the extent of the problem's impact on several field domains. The influence of some crises of personnel conduct is confined, impacting only a single relationship or social setting. Other cases have pervasive impact because the significant issues are generalized over numerous settings, people and situations. As pervasiveness *increases*, the probability of treating the problem in the field setting *decreases*. Conversely, as the personnel crisis is more confined or less pervasive, the possibility of field remediation *increases*. The following illustrations demonstrate pervasiveness:

- A team of two single women missionaries have ongoing, unresolved conflicts. Certainly their inability to resolve conflicts hurts their productivity and Christian testimony among local national people. However, the impact in a larger sense of the mission's goals and personnel is not negatively affected, so there is not a wide and pervasive impact. Counseling, skills training, or reassignment may successfully address this problem, and could take place in the field setting.

- A missionary with a reputation as a "maverick" continues to defy his supervisors about guidelines for accountability and filing reports. He is required to attend counseling sessions and is relieved of his position in the group. He complains to colleagues about the administration's unfairness, spiritual blindness, vindictiveness, unforgiveness, lies, and impatience. The mission's membership is beginning to take sides in the issue: those for the troubled member and those for the administration. This case illustrates pervasive impact, and includes the added dimension of a long-term problem (defiance of authority) with no clear onset. The possibility for remediation in the field setting seems unlikely.

- A small group within the mission adopts the teaching of a captivating writer and speaker who emphasizes demon exorcism. The group unfortunately "finds a demon behind every bush" in the mission's activities and is quite vocal about this dynamic in the community, at committee meetings, and in the local school and church. The mission and national community polarize over the issue. Those who resist the emphasis on demonic influence feel pressured and judged as spiritually immature. Those who accept the teaching believe that Satan has a "stronghold" in the resistant community. Can this crisis be dealt with on the field? The pervasiveness of impact is high.

However, the duration is relatively short and has a clear onset (the teaching on demons). This situation may or may not be dealt with in a field setting.

Pervasive impact is always played out in terms of disruptiveness to the mission's goals. The greater influence of a personnel crisis on the organization's functioning, the more energy is required to contain and control the problem. Mission administrators refer to pervasiveness when talking about "putting out fires." If the fires are relatively small and isolated, resources may be available for immediate, local action. If the personnel fires are bigger, hotter and quickly spreading, local resources may not be adequate.

Question Four: Intrusiveness

How does the crisis affect the main participants? To what extent does the problem inhibit an individual, family, or other person's ability to contribute to the mission's objectives? Personnel administrators want to be sensitive to personal needs and not view staff simply as part of a production machine. However, mission organizations are in foreign countries to perform a service. If a member's impairment is so intrusive that they are unable to make a contribution to the mission's goals, referral may be necessary.

Intrusiveness exists on a continuum of least/slight to most/severe. At one end of the spectrum are those people with some interpersonal skill deficits who make occasional missteps but are able to cope with ongoing personal challenges and still remain productive. Crises sometimes appear like a blip on their life screen, but they quickly return to healthy baseline functioning. They are still productive during a crisis, and their colleagues are able to continue to function in their defined roles as well.

On the other end of the continuum is the person whose coping strategies and skill deficits have brought his/her vocational activities to a grinding halt. These people are managing personal problems or creating problems with such regularity that they have little energy left for their mission assignment. They drain energy from colleagues who must "pick up the slack" or provide emotional and practical support for a chronically struggling person. Intrusiveness reaches a peak when the member is making no viable contribution but is consuming resources designated for ministry.

The following example illustrates how intrusiveness on people's functioning affects the retention or referral decision:

- A wife experiences a major depressive episode that confines her to bed. The husband, who works in a key support role, is unable to keep regular hours at the office because of demands at home. He is home-schooling their four children, managing the house help and trying to meet needs of his work assignment. Colleagues double their work efforts to cover his responsibilities. Others provide supportive care to the family. This example shows a high level of intrusiveness. The depression has debilitated the wife, the husband's vocational activities are limited and mission resources are diverted to maintain the family. However, even though the intrusiveness level is high, sending this family home may not be indicated. If an antecedent is clear (e.g. postpartum depression or bereavement response), duration is short (e.g. three weeks), and pervasiveness is only moderate (e.g. confined to the husband's work department and local friends) then sending the family home may not be necessary. The wife's depression may be treatable on the field.

Pervasiveness is just one factor that contributes to the decision making process. However, in most cases, as pervasiveness of the personnel problem's impact *increases*, the possibility for retaining people on the field *decreases*.

Question Five: Harm

The final question involves the issue of harm or danger to the identified person or others. As the possibility of harm to self or others *increases*, it is less likely the person should be retained for treatment in the field setting. Mental health clinicians on the team can educate members regarding the safety, ethical, and legal issues involved with suicidal or homicidal clients. Self-harm includes such things as self-mutilation by cutting oneself and disorders like anorexia and bulimia nervosa. Harm to others includes issues of child abuse, spouse battery or statements involving revenge. Ques-tion five is the only item that is able to stand on its own. Significant potential harm supercedes all the factors in questions one through four above and moves cases toward the homeland for treatment.

Physical threat is a clear indicator for the need to refer to the sending country, but what about the threat of psychological or relational harm? These issues are harder to evaluate but need to be taken seriously. Cases with potential emotional harm would rarely be decided based on question five alone; other factors are needed to determine a course of action. For example, if retaining the individual or family will extend the normal duration of recovery (e.g. for treating PTSD or depression) because of a lack of appropriate field services, referral back to sending country is advisable.

However, antecedent, duration, pervasiveness, and intrusiveness are still key dynamics to consider. Relational impairment that causes harm in the missions community could be the result of prolonged conflict causing damage to the mission's reputation. In such cases, questions one through four would be important in determining the appropriateness of a referral to the sending country.

Sometimes consensus regarding the potential for physical harm is not possible, as when suicidal overtures are seen by some as empty threats. In such cases, it is best to err on the side of safety. Issues involving psychological or relational harm can usually be clarified using questions one through four.

Putting It Together

The five questions are designed to help the group conceptualize the personnel conduct problem. Using the introductory illustration, let's see how this model works for making an actual decision about retention or referral: The crisis involving the suicide attempt of a teenager.

1. Is there a clear antecedent, precipitating event or condition, or *onset* to the crisis? Answer: **No**. She had attended a youth retreat over the weekend but there was no apparent event that initiated an attempt on her life. By her own account, she had

Table One
Questions and Potential Actions

Questions	Retain in field setting	Refer to homeland
1. Onset?	Apparent onset increases retention	No apparent onset increases referral
2. Duration?	Shorter duration increases retention	Longer duration increases referral
3. Pervasiveness?	Lesser pervasiveness increases retention	Greater pervasiveness increases referral
4. Intrusiveness?	Lesser intrusiveness increases retention	Greater intrusiveness increases referral
5. Harm?	No potential harm increases retention	Harm potential **necessitates** referral

enjoyed the outing with friends. An inventory of possible traumas (e.g. situational, relational or environmental traumas, medical conditions, or physical difficulties) yielded no apparent precipitating circumstances: **Referral potential increases**.

2.   What is the *duration* of the significant contributing issues? Answer: **Long term duration**. There is a history of problems in several boarding homes, with each situation ending in conflict. Her school record shows noncompliance and antisocial behaviors. Her adjustment difficulties have been longstanding and well documented. Please note that questions aren't answered with vague, judgmental labels such as "longtime trouble maker" and "bad kid;" duration questions need specific answers. The group notes that acting out behavior has been long term. **Referral potential increases**.

3.   How *pervasive* is the impact? Answer: **Moderate**, affecting several mission domains. Her behaviors affect children living in the youth hostels and adults in the community, as numerous adults, teachers and peers have tried to "help" this student. The school counselor has seen her off and on for nearly two years. The parents are often called in from their work in a remote location to deal with their daughter's problem behaviors. **Referral potential increases**.

4.   How *intrusive* are the significant factors? Answer: **High**. The family, work, community and school are disrupted by her behavior. Retaining her in the setting would require ongoing vigilance to ensure her safety. Children's home staff are reluctant to take responsibility for her care. The parents cannot carry out tribal work at the mission center and the teenager can't accompany them to the village. Her behavior is significantly disruptive to several important organizational functions. **Referral potential increases**.

5.   What is the potential for *harm to self or others*? Answer: **High**. The method used in the suicide attempt could have ended her life. Only the children's home parents' quick action and subsequent medical care saved her. Even though she stated emphatically that it won't happen again, the attempt was extremely serious. **Referral is necessary**.

The above questions are guidelines for action, intended to direct the discussion in a structured, goal-oriented manner. They help sharpen the focus of the issues in the personnel crisis; they do not dictate what to do. An underlying concern regarding each question relates to services available on the field. In some instances, a person who has good potential for on-field treatment may have no appropriate services available, and this would need to be a consideration in the final decision of whether to retain or refer.

Beyond a Decision
The decision of whether to retain people on the field or return them to the sending country is only the first important step toward restoration. The next step involves a treatment strategy. If people leave the field, a statement outlining the team's expectations for remediation should accompany them. If they remain, a statement of expectations should give accountability to future conduct.   Planning beyond the decision to retain or refer demonstrates the team's commitment to mission goals and to the growth and future ministry of people who labor toward them.

References

Gardner, L. M. & Sieges, T. R. (1999) Considerations for staying on the field or returning to passport country. *International Member Care Bulletin*, Dallas: Wycliffe Bible Translators International.

Kellogg, M. E. (1996) *Crisis matrices: A mission training package*. Huntington Beach, CA: Wycliffe Bible Translators.

Appendix A

Additional questions from Gardner & Sieges (1999) "Considerations for Staying on the Field or Returning to Passport Country":

Questions for the Counselor to Ask:
1. How does the counselor's training, experience, and/or available supervision match the person's treatment needs?

2. Does the counselor's present schedule allow adequate time for treating this person?

3. Is more appropriate treatment available in the person's homeland?

4. What will treating this person cost the counselor in terms of other ministry opportunities or responsibilities?

5. Will attempting to treat this person on the field prolong his/her recovery in the long run?

Questions for the Administrator to Ask:

1. What are the potential benefits or liabilities to the organization of retaining the person or family on the field?

2. Does the behavior represent a threat to the organization's reputation or placement in the country?

3. What is the preference of the individual and/or family? How do they view the significant issues?

4. Are existing services able to meet the needs? Will serving this person or family stretch services beyond their intended, typical function? Will other potential consumers of services be excluded because of this person/family's unusual needs?

5. What is the *probable* impact of this person's presence on community morale? On community security and/or safety?

6. What is the *potential* impact of this person's presence?

7. Is harm being caused or experienced by anyone right now?

8. Is there a change in sight?

9. Is the member willing to work for change?

10. How much support service is needed?

11. How many people are being impacted by the presence of this person?

12. What are the costs (financial, emotional, etc.) to keep the person there?

43

Facilitating Confession, Forgiveness, and Reconciliation

Rebecca Leverington

*F*ictional Case Example
Missionaries Sam and Joan are told that their daughter Lisa has been molested by a missionary from another mission who is her piano teacher and also a friend. They are in shock. They learn that Lisa was uncomfortable, but the molester was "Uncle Butch," her teacher whom she respects and obeys. Lisa is too young to understand the seriousness of the act, and feels scared and bad with all the fuss. Soon Butch and his family are told to leave the field. Sam and Joan are strongly encouraged to return home to get their child counseling. There is no confession from Butch, in fact no contact at all. Sam and Joan are asked not to explain to others what has occurred in order to protect their child from the added trauma of the abuse becoming widespread knowledge. They return home and they and Lisa get counseling.

Sam, Joan and Lisa all use counseling well. After a year, Lisa begins to act like their normal little girl again. They have worked through their shock, questions of God, and anger at Butch, and have learned how to help Lisa in the future when effects of the abuse may surface again. However, pieces are missing. What happened to Butch? Was he required to get counseling? Has he owned his responsibility and overcome his problem? Did he abuse any other children? Will he be allowed to return to the field or have contact with other children? What explanation has he given when asked why he returned home?

Now let's consider Butch. He, too, has been sent home and used counseling well. However, he wonders if Lisa is OK. Does she hate him? Do Sam and Joan hate him? Why didn't he face them on the field and ask forgiveness

In the case of serious moral failure and injury, one way to provide accountability and bring healing and resolution is to facilitate a process of face to face confession, forgiveness, and reconciliation. Preparation includes counseling both the responsible party and the injured party. A structure for the face to face session protects the interests of all involved and helps ensure that the process will have a good outcome.

363

then? He's thought about writing or calling to say how sorry he is, but doesn't have any idea if that would be appropriate. Will they be able to return to the field?

Introduction

As counselors and administrators, we have all helped people work through wrongs done to them and counseled others to own their responsibility and begin to overcome problems that led to harmful actions. These are important interventions. Yet we live in community, and need to go further than working with individuals. We need to ask, "Is it possible and would it be helpful for the people involved to meet face to face to work through confession, possibly forgiveness, and if appropriate, reconciliation.

Matthew 5:23-24 commands us to be reconciled with our brothers, saying it's so important that if we are offering our gift at the altar and there remember that our brother has something against us, we are to leave our gift there and first go and be reconciled. Matthew 18:15 states that we should do this also when we remember that another has wronged us. An important part of counseling and personnel work should be facilitating confession and possible reconciliation.

The importance of face to face confession, forgiveness, and reconciliation

There are at least three reasons for facilitating this process within mission organizations. The first, of course, is the Biblical mandate. I believe McClanathan's statement (2000) regarding churches also applies to missions: "Perhaps through a misplaced understanding of peace, or a desire not to interfere, relational sin is often tolerated in missions that otherwise are biblically sound and effective in ministry. How much more might be achieved if mission leadership were to intentionally teach, model and enforce an atmosphere of reconciliation?"

Secondly, mission settings have more intense community than in our home countries. The opportunity for face to face confession, forgiveness, and reconciliation is greater, and the fallout when it doesn't occur can be greater, because of the importance and multiplicity of relationships.

The third reason is the proven effectiveness of this approach. The field of malpractice has recently documented the benefits of confession and accepting responsibility for wrongs. Apologies significantly reduce lawsuits. Research also demonstrates the powerful effect of restitution. In malpractice, this is shown in fair settlement offers.

A final powerful result is that where people can freely admit their errors and take responsibility for them, the organization becomes better at preventing errors. When missions deal quickly with wrong committed by one missionary toward another, or by the mission toward a missionary, much deeper healing takes place. It is clear that injustice will not be tolerated and people are given extra help to avoid committing wrongs.

The timing of the process

We will describe one method for facilitating a face to face meeting between the offending and injured parties. It provides a format aimed at proceeding as far as both parties are able to go toward acknowledgment of responsibility, confession, forgiveness, and reconciliation.

Several administrative steps must be taken before these counseling meetings can occur. Mission administrators investigate allegations and enforce mission policy regarding consequences. This often includes loss of mission membership or administrative discipline and return to the sending country for required counseling. Immediate care must be given to the victim and confidentiality maintained. The offending party is given guidance in writing an approved letter to supporters, or the mission administration sends such a letter. What is told to missionary colleagues is determined. These steps must be taken quickly and effectively to prevent more harm occurring through information or misinformation spreading in a way that breaches the victim's rights to confidentiality.

Because moral lapse frequently means return to the sending country, the best opportunity for a face to face meeting is often on the field. The desire to proceed quickly must be balanced by the cost/benefit analysis of taking the time for counseling, confession, and repentance while the two parties are still in the same location. Confession is best facilitated when the crisis and administrative actions encourage responsibility. The counselor in the home country lacks direct case facts and the missionary is tempted to minimize responsibility. If confession occurs on the field the counselee can make fuller use of counseling to overcome root problems that led to moral lapse.

At the same time, this confession must not be rushed. If it cannot occur before one or both parties leave the field, counselors and mission administration should facilitate it happening at a later date. It is never too late to facilitate these kinds of meetings.

Steps in the process

Although the length of time needed for the process varies, asking each participant to set aside two full days is optimum. Sessions are scheduled for two- to three-hour time frames, with breaks as needed for individual processing, individual meetings with the counselors to prepare for the next step, and for meals. The process requires full knowledge of what to expect, preparation for each step, and trust in the facilitators to keep the process on track and observe ground rules. Suggested steps in the process follow.

1.   Greetings

Prepare each party separately by telling them that the other party will be fearful of their response and that they are taking a courageous step just by agreeing to meet. Help them plan what greeting, verbally and physically, they can honestly make.

2.   Establish positive expectations

Thank them for taking this courageous step. What they are doing in these meetings is kingdom work — the hard work of reconciliation — demonstrating obedience, discipline and unconditional love.

3.   Agree on ground rules

Ground rules may include confidentiality, respect for one another, commitment to keep voices and emotions moderated, freedom to ask for clarification of the next step, and freedom to request a break at any point. Reassure both parties that the process will stop if either party moves outside the ground rules or when each party has gone as far as he is able to proceed at this time. Either party can request individual time with a facilitator to prepare for the next step.

4.   *Prayer*

Ask each person to consider praying for the day. This allows you to gauge the level of their preparation, as well as hearing concerns they have about the meetings. One counselor stated, "I always like to hear a man pray. It is almost as though the Holy Spirit is listening with me, giving me a second pair of ears."

Some may use prayer as a method of excusing their actions, or as an expression of anger or blame. If that happens, you need to confront it and deal with it. Such a prayer may hamper or destroy progress during the session if not dealt with.

5.   *Forgiveness and reconciliation*

Briefly review forgiveness and reconciliation— what they are and are not.

6.   *Review the steps and time frame.*

Listing them on a flip chart is very helpful.

7.   *Statement of responsibility*

The responsible party reads or shares his statement of responsibility and his willingness to hear the effects of his actions on the other party. It is helpful to have it written so that it is worded in a helpful way and can be reviewed later. The statement needs to state the offense explicitly. It must be sincere, and have no references to blame or responsibility of the other party. This step establishes taking responsibility and can be a powerful testimony to the person's spouse, who is asked to be present. It is also important to talk beyond the prepared statement, sharing more openly and in depth.

8.   *Statement of effects of the actions*

The injured party shares honestly and concretely but without excessive emotion the effects of the actions. For example, a parent of an abused child might share that he's had nightmares of not being able to protect her, had difficulty controlling his anger, developed an ulcer and spent a year in weekly counseling. The parent might explain that the abused child replayed the abuse over and over in play, demonstrated a strong fear of parents being gone, and had difficulty adjusting to a new school. The injured party expresses an ardent desire that the responsible party understand the hurt that was caused. The more empathy that the offender demonstrates, the easier it is for the other person to forgive. (McCullough et al., 1997 as quoted in DiBlasio, 1999).

The injured party may ask questions and/or the responsible party may explain in a non-defensive manner the reasons behind the behavior. It helps the injured party to have accurate information, rather than depending on imagination or assumptions. Emotional distance is reduced by the sharing of information.

Before step nine it is important to allow the responsible party time to prepare for the next step. Once he has written out what he intends to say, one counselor meets with him individually to assure he has done it in a healthy, complete way so there is no chance for failure.

9. *Specific request for forgiveness*

The responsible party now responds by sharing his understanding of the specific effects of his actions and asking for forgiveness for each of those effects. It must be individual and specific. Body language and positioning are important. It is helpful to assist the person in thinking this through; suggestions may include moving his chair closer, maintaining eye contact with the injured party, and taking a one-down stance. McCullough, Worthington, and Rachal (1997, as quoted in Sandage 1999) found that the degree of offender apology predicted the degree of victim forgiveness.

10. *Statement of change*

The responsible party shares honestly and concretely what he has done and plans to do to work through the causes of his wrong actions. This statement needs to include specific behavioral changes and a plan for ongoing accountability. McAllister (1983, as quoted by DiBlasio, 1999) stresses that this statement needs to demonstrate a precise plan that will eliminate the offensive behavior. The responsible party should practice this statement ahead of time with coaching so it does not include references to how hard the process has been or prior hurts that influenced him to cause hurt.

11. *Restitution*

Restitution is equally important for the responsible party and for the injured party. A concrete demonstration of responsibility costs the responsible party something and acknowledges that his actions cost the hurt party. After having completed steps 9 through 11, the responsible party makes a sincere and humble request for forgiveness.

12. *Extension of forgiveness*

Here the injured party extends forgiveness. Because this is a difficult step, it may be helpful to take a break before this step for a few hours or overnight, to give the injured party time to process the offending party's confession and acknowledgment of responsibility. The injured party has worked through the theology and process of forgiveness in individual meetings with the counselor to be sure he is prepared to do it in a healthy manner. This includes not minimizing the severity of the actions and understanding that forgiveness is a process, this being the first step. It is most effective if the injured party is able to relate his forgiveness to the forgiveness he has received in Christ.

13. *What others know*

In a close community it is important that both parties share how they have responded to others' questions about why they are leaving the field and about the incidents. This begins to rebuild trust as they learn how the other handled the aftermath.

14. *Filling in the work/family gaps*

Individuals may share a little about their lives, families, and jobs. The moral lapse often severs a previously close working relationship. They may not know the other party's plans regarding leaving the field, their mission status, how family members are doing, or where they will go.

15.   *Clarifying any future relationship*

The injured party takes the lead in discussing any future relationship, including realistic boundaries. The counselor can coach them to state only the positive, leaving the negative unsaid but implied. For example, "I now feel able to be in missions meetings together, but we'd appreciate it if you would join a different Bible study." If the responsible party has not done a good job of acknowledging responsibility, it will be necessary to work individually with the injured party to decide on clear boundaries and how to state them succinctly, with steps they will take in the future if the boundary is crossed.

16.   *Fitting conclusion*

After the intensity and hard work of these sessions, it is important to end well. The facilitators might ask permission to end with prayer and then bring the conversation back to a more informal level. If full reconciliation has occurred, the parties may agree to end with communion or a ceremonial act. The focus is on assessing the injured party's comfort level, helping him get his needs met, or ending the process when it is at a positive state.

Preparation for the sessions

Counseling and preparation needs to occur with each party separately beforehand. If time is limited, the counseling will focus on preparing the responsible party for a full confession and the injured party to understand the effects of the injury and a Biblical understanding of forgiveness. In depth counseling, including working through the causes of the behavior for the responsible party and the trauma for the injured party, would occur after the face to face meetings.

Preparation with the responsible party

There are at least seven areas that should be worked through with the responsible party before the face to face meeting is scheduled.

1.   Ownership of responsibility and understanding the specific effects of his actions on the victim. Narramore (1984) labels this constructive sorrow, identifying it as the godly sorrow that Paul commends in 11 Corinthians 7:9-10. It has been positively correlated with empathy, apology, and reparative strategies following interpersonal conflict (Tangney et al, 1996 as quoted in Sandage, 1999). Proverbs 28:13, I John 1:8, Psalm 51:3-5, Psalm 51:6, and II Corinthians 7:10 are verses that can assist the responsible party in reaching this point.

2.   Statement of responsibility. This involves helping the responsible party to write a statement to read in the session covering acknowledgment of responsibility, willingness to hear the specific effects of his actions on the injured party, asking for forgiveness for the specific effects, and offering restitution. This statement often needs to be reworked several times until it contains honest, complete, specific, responsible, and helpful wording. McClanathan (2000) states, "To be effective, confession must admit specific wrongs without excuse or qualification. It must recognize and express sorrow for the hurt inflicted. And it must demonstrate a willingness to change."

3.   Restitution. The responsible party can consider what might be the actual costs to the other party of his actions. Bible references include Exodus 22:1-17, Levit-

icus 6:2, Numbers 5:5-8, II Samuel 12:6, Psalm 79:12, Proverbs 6:30-31, and Luke 19:8. Restitution could include such things as paying for counseling for the injured party or paying a portion of the family's plane fare to their home country for counseling.

4.   Travel, flexibility. The responsible party should be prepared to travel to make the sessions happen and demonstrate flexibility in the timing of the sessions to meet the injured party's needs.

5.   Ground Rules. In discussing ground rules for the face to face meeting, the person may need to work through areas he struggles with. These might include such areas as raising his voice, wanting to clam up, feeling uncomfortable expressing more than surface level things, or focusing on self rather than others. Philippians 2:4 is a good basis for this area of preparation.

6.   Preparation for the process. Finally, discuss the steps of the process, preparing the responsible party for his work in each step.

7.   Review and reassurance. If the individual work has occurred over a period of time, a follow-up meeting is needed shortly before the face to face meeting. There will be a high level of anxiety over this first contact. Thus, a whole session should be devoted to reassurance of the value of the process, normalizing fears, and focusing on Biblical precedent. Reassurance is given that our actions are the right ones regardless of what we are feeling and that feelings will understandably go up and down.

Preparation with the injured party:

1.   Counseling to the point of resolution. The injured party needs to resolve false guilt and understand the effects of the offense. He or she needs to integrate these events into a theology of suffering, understand forgiveness, and see how reconciliation is different from forgiveness. Another priority is establishing healthy boundaries with the responsible party in the future. A healthy understanding of forgiveness is a key.

2.   Statement of the effects of the actions. Help the injured party to write a statement to read in the sessions sharing honestly but appropriately the specific effects of the actions.

3.   Statement of forgiveness. Help the injured party to write down a way to express forgiveness honestly. This may involve recognizing that feelings about the offense and the offender may not yet be resolved (Romans 5:8) but that he can cease keeping records of the wrongs (Psalm 130:3-4). Clarify that forgiveness does not excuse the offense or depend on forgetting. Encouraging empathy is the most solid intervention strategy in promoting forgiveness. McCullough, Worthington, & Rachal (1997) stress that when the negative behavior of others is attributed strictly to internal causes (e.g. "He's just a lazy person"), emotional empathy or compassion for that person will not follow.

Helping the injured party to see an opportunity to grow in the virtue of forgiveness facilitates this step. It helps gain control over hurtful, tragic events that now can be redeemed as part of growth in forgiveness or reversing painful legacies in the mission (Sandage, 1999).

Forgiveness involves the following elements. We surrender the right to get even with the person who wronged us, turning judgment over to God. Recognizing how much we are forgiven by God, we forgive the wrong done to us. We move toward reinterpreting the person who wronged us in a larger format, getting a picture of a needy, weak, complicated, fallible human being like ourselves. We develop a gradual desire for the welfare of the person who injured us (Smedes, 1984).

The injured party needs to understand what forgiveness is not. Thomas (2000), presents an excellent summary. Forgiveness is not dismissing. It involves taking the offense seriously, not condoning or passing it off as insignificant. It does not preclude the enforcement of consequences. Forgiveness does not automatically lead to reconciliation, as reconciliation takes two people, but an injured party can forgive an offender without reconciliation. Forgiveness doesn't necessarily mean forgetting. Forgiveness does not mean pardoning, a legal transaction releasing the offender from the consequences.

4.   Information. What information would be helpful to process the injury? This might include clarification about whether he has stopped hurting people in this way, whether he is in counseling, and whether he has an accountability partner.

5 through 7.   Ground rules, preparation for the process, and review and reassurance are the same as with the responsible party.

Who is present

It is best if two counselors co-facilitate the sessions, one for each party. It is recommended that both parties have an additional person present: an accountability partner for the responsible party and an advocate for the injured party.

This person should be the spouse only if they are able to serve effectively in the role needed. A major benefit is the opportunity of resolution for the spouse. If the spouse can see the responsible party owning responsibility, courageously facing the person he's hurt and asking forgiveness, this frees the spouse to begin taking the steps to forgive him for harm to the family. Witnessing the confession provides the spouse with concrete evidence of the responsible party's change in behavior, helping to rebuild trust. The spouse can also hear that the injured party doesn't hold the spouse responsible. Knowing the facts about effects on the injured party puts fears in perspective. Finally, it breaks the secrecy of the acts by letting the spouse in on the reconciliation. The healing that occurs for spouses is powerful.

If the injured party is a child, only the child's parents are present for the initial sessions. However, both parties have been prepared for the possibility of the responsible party also meeting with the child he has injured toward the end of the sessions. If the child is to be present, the prior step should be for the responsible party to demonstrate what he will say to the child to the parents first, with them having the right of making changes in what he says and/or choosing to prevent the step of meeting with the child.

Other possibilities are that the responsible party could make an audio tape for the child to be shared with the child when the child is ready to deal with that. There are real advantages in the child hearing he wasn't in any way responsible, that the adult's actions toward him were very wrong, that he is very sorry for the way he hurt the child, and that he is getting help so he won't hurt other children in the same way.

Most abused children even as adults struggle with this unless the responsible adult at some point takes responsibility for their actions. By making a tape, you have it available when the child is ready.

Follow-up

It is important to do follow-up with both parties two weeks after the session, and again at either one month or six months, if possible. Find out if further support, counseling, or follow-up is needed, and get feedback about the process.

Follow-up calls yield valuable feedback regarding the usefulness of this process. People often mention true reconciliation and significant life change. They can leave the past behind and move forward with a new freedom and intensity, free to go separate paths rather than be tied to the other party through the unresolved issue. They report a sense of release and closure.

Facilitating face to face confession, restitution, forgiveness, and when appropriate, reconciliation, is an underutilized area of counseling and administrative practice when dealing with moral lapse. This type of face to face session releases people to go forward much more quickly and more fully restored than working with individuals.

Recommended Readings

DiBlasio, Frederick A. (1999). Scripture and forgiveness: Interventions with Christian couples and families. *Marriage & Family (AACC)*, 2 (3), 247-258.

McClanathan, P. D. (2000). Honoring God, honoring each other. *EFCA Beacon*, September/October, pp. 8-9.

Sandage, S. J. (1999). An ego-humility model of forgiveness: theoretical foundations. *Marriage & Family (AACC)*, 2 (3), 259-276.

Smedes, L.B. (1984). *Forgive and forget: Healing the hurts we don't deserve*. New York: Pocket Books.

Thomas, G. (2000). The forgiveness factor. *Christianity Today*, January 10, pp. 38-45.

Web Sites

Campaign for Forgiveness Research: www.forgiving.org
International Forgiveness Institute: www.intl-forgive-inst.org
Peacemaker Ministries (EFCA Conciliation ministries): www.hispeace.org

44

The Why and How of Restorative Care

Christopher H. Rosik

*R*estore to me the joy of your salvation and grant me a willing spirit, to sustain me.
Ps. 51:12 (NIV)

There are times in the lives of most human beings when life events seem to go from bad to worse, often leading to the need for outside assistance. Despite what is sometimes portrayed in evangelical churches, missionaries are human beings who also may experience significant distress.

The difficulty is that, in an overseas context, when the "wheels come off" there are limited resources to assist the missionary in staying on the road. The purpose of this article is first to outline some common issues that result in a missionary's need for restorative care and then to highlight the continuum of member care that exists for missionary restoration.

The process of care at the Link Care Center, a residential treatment program for psychological and spiritual restoration, will be presented as a means of discussing treatment issues that likely apply to other care settings. Key elements in completing the restoration process successfully will be noted.

Common Ways Things Fall Apart

There is no single course of events that explains why missionaries come into need of restorative pastoral and psychological care. The reasons are, in fact, often complex. One study conducted at the Link Care Center (Olford, 1993), however, was able to identify the primary presenting concern for which restorative treatment was provided to missionaries between 1985 and 1992. Olford discovered that 36% of the cases were referred for treatment of

Sometimes things fall apart. Life events pile up and cause the need for restorative pastoral and psychological care. This chapter presents a continuum of options for restorative member care from furlough consultation to residential care. The three phases of the missionary restoration program at Link Care Center are described: initial orientation phase, working through phase, and transitional preparation phase.

depression. Another 17% were referred primarily due to marital distress, including problems with communication, problem solving, and infidelity.

It is this author's impression that missionaries referred to Link Care typically have comorbid conditions which also become a focus of their treatment. These conditions include ADHD, bipolar disorder, and trauma related symptoms and disorders. Characterological issues are also common, with cluster B personality disorders the predominant Axis II diagnoses.

The Continuum of Restorative Member Care

According to Williams (1992), "Restoration is the process of providing resources for missionaries and their families who are suffering or are unable to function adequately." Restorative member care occurs on a continuum of intensity with Link Care's program at the higher intensity end. Most missionary care occurs at less intensive levels, hopefully enabling the missionary to remain on the field even as the difficulties are addressed. While the continuum of restorative member care probably lends itself to many classifications, the categorization of levels of care noted below seems consistent with the types of interventions occurring currently.

1. *Furlough consultation.* At this least restrictive level, the missionary's difficulties are not so serious as to warrant immediate attention. The missionary may wait for months or even years to address the concern, utilizing resources in their home country upon the completion of their current term of overseas ministry. At this level, missionaries are not likely to report a feeling of things falling apart. It should be noted that it is not uncommon for missionaries to present to mission supervisors accepting only this least restrictive arrangement when a closer examination would reveal the need for a higher level of care.

2. *Episodic on-field pastoral care.* This level of care involves occasional on-field visitations by pastoral caregivers often affiliated with the missionary's sending organization. Such meetings are typically for the purposes of spiritual nourishment, encouragement, support, and pastoral counseling.

Another critical function of the pastoral caregiver at this level of care involves the identification of issues needing a higher level of intervention. Pastoral staff are often the member care personnel to whom distressed missionaries first disclosed their real concerns. Thus it is extremely valuable for pastoral caregivers to have a basic knowledge of psychopathology and the ability to identify potential signs of common problems such as depression, stress reactions, child abuse, domestic violence, and the like (O'Donnell, 1997).

3. *Episodic on-field psychological counseling.* Here a mental health professional, who may or may not be affiliated directly with the mission agency (Rosik, 1993) will have on-field contact with the missionary. Usually at this level of care a problem has been identified, such as coping with a traumatic experience, and the counselor comes to the field specifically to address the concern, as occurs with critical incident stress debriefing.

In a few instances, mental health workers may return regularly to one field and develop ongoing relationships with the missionary team there. This level of restorative member care may deal effectively with problems before they reach the point where a higher level of care is required. In ideal circumstances, pharmacological intervention is also available as needed. Issues such as mild depression, parenting skills, marital communication skills, stress management, and cultural adjustment difficulties may all respond significantly to intervention at this level.

4. *Regular on-field psychological counseling.* In instances where resources exist within the host country, outpatient psychological counseling can occur on a more regular basis for missionaries in need. Counseling may occur weekly, biweekly, or monthly depending on the severity of the presenting concerns.

Due to the demand for such resources, these providers may not enter into long-term therapeutic relationships with missionaries, especially those not affiliated with the counselor's mission organization. Restorative care at this level may be able to manage problems such as marital conflict, oppositional or defiant children, moderate depression, post-traumatic symptoms, and team conflicts, enabling the missionary to remain on the field. Problems not reaching a resolution within the time frame available to the on-field member care clinician can be managed through mental health and pastoral resources in the missionary's home country during furlough.

5. *Regular psychological counseling in the country of origin.* Provided mental health resources are available in the missionary's home country, problems that cannot be contained within the less restrictive on-field levels of care can be referred to clinicians in the missionary's country of origin familiar with the rigors of overseas service. This may or may not overlap with planned furlough times, as the severity of the issues mandates that the need for treatment take precedence over convenience of scheduling.

Missionaries at this level of care may relocate near the mission headquarters, their home church, or their extended family and seek outpatient counseling in that area. Some will take a leave of absence from the mission and join the civilian work-force if longer-term care is necessary. Pervasive marital distress, major depression, childhood trauma-related disorders, and acute character pathology are examples of problems that might be expected to result in this level of intervention.

6. *Residential outpatient counseling programs.* Link Care Center is an example of this level of care. In this setting, missionaries join with other missionaries needing intervention in the context of a community of care rather than the on-field community of service. Intensive (multiple hours per week) psychological and pastoral restorative care is available in contrast to the weekly sessions typical of other outpatient counseling settings. Pharmacological intervention is common.

Frequently, this level of care serves to stabilize the crisis situation and prepare the missionary for continued treatment and at a lower level of intervention. Recently disclosed marital infidelity, sexual addiction, intense suicidal ideation, pervasive interpersonal conflict, and abuse of a child are examples of the kinds of problems that result in referral to this level of care.

7. *Inpatient hospitalization.* As the most restrictive level of restorative care, inpatient hospitalization is reserved for the most acute and severe forms of mental

illness. In an age of managed care, such hospitalization typically does not last long in North America, with admissions averaging three to seven days. The emphasis is strictly on psychological restabilization and pharmacological intervention is nearly always undertaken.

Active and life-threatening substance abuse, profound depression with immediate suicidal risk, and thought disorders resulting in impaired reality testing are examples of problems requiring inpatient psychiatric care. Discharge will undoubtedly result in the need for the missionary to pursue continued care, most likely at the level of regular psychological counseling in the country of origin.

It is not uncommon for the continuum of restorative care to be seen in a one-way fashion. Namely, that the missionary proceeds "up the ladder" from a less restrictive level of care to a more restrictive degree of intervention until the level of care is sufficient to contain the problem.

However, it needs to be said that member care would be well served by being purposeful in guiding missionaries "down the ladder" of restorative care as well. Once a level of care is no longer deemed necessary for the missionary, a lower level of intervention should be brought into play in order for the missionary to solidify behavioral change and experience ongoing support so that serious relapse is prevented. This approach will, in the final analysis, be most restorative or the missionary and most cost effective for the mission.

The Process of Restoration at Link Care

Since this author has been affiliated with the Link Care Center for the past 15 years, this agency's restoration program will be examined as a window to understanding the restoration process for other levels of care. Link Care's program involves a team of from 2-5 pastors and therapists involved in providing to the missionary pastoral care, as well as individual, marital, family, and group psychotherapy. This adds up to approximately 5-7 hours of therapy and pastoral counseling per week.

Missionaries are also involved in formal weekly community meetings, one didactic and one for fellowship (a potluck), in order to facilitate the milieu dimension of the program. At any one time, about 20-25 individual and family units live in apartments on the Link Care campus. The length of stay varies, but usually ranges between two weeks to several months.

Once Link Care has been identified as a resource for the missionary, the process of restoration follows three broad phases: Initial orientation, working through, and transitional preparation. Some of the common issues encountered in each of these phases are described below.

Initial Orientation Phase

In this phase the missionary has recently arrived at Link Care and is orienting to the restoration program. The length of this phase depends on several factors. Missionaries who have had previous contact with pastoral and/or psychological counseling, have sought out the referral to Link Care, and lack character pathology tend to become oriented to the program and the associated expectations rather quickly. Usually this occurs between the first and second week.

By contrast, missionaries who lack psychological insight, are referred against their will, or overly spiritualize their difficulties will take a longer period of time to accept the program and begin looking at their issues. For them it may take weeks or, in some cases, even months before a working alliance can be established. Sadly, in some instances the missionary's defenses prevent him or her from moving beyond the orientation phase.

This consideration has implications for the referring organization. In practice, even in an intensive counseling modality, it is unusual that a missionary who is defended and resistant to treatment will progress past the orientation phase in a two-week window. It often seems that just as the guard begins to come down, the departure date comes into view and the missionary of necessity works hard to avoid examination of the deeper issues. The point is that for restorative member care to be most effective, the level and duration of care needs to be determined by the nature of the referral and not by the relative ease of scheduling.

In the orientation phase, while the presenting concerns are unlikely to be resolved, a fairly complete assessment can be achieved. Based on this clinician's experience, resistant and defended missionaries referred for less than a month will be unlikely to progress beyond the orientation phase, although they can still benefit from a thorough psychological and spiritual assessment which will guide the course of additional treatment. Under these conditions, referring agencies should not expect the presenting problems of their missionaries to be resolved upon their exiting of the restoration program.

By contrast, motivated and reasonably insightful missionaries may progress through the orientation phase by the end of the first week. It is not uncommon for these individuals to complete the assessment and additionally make significant progress toward resolution of their issues within the first month of intensive counseling. This has been achieved even in a two-week period with motivated and insightful missionaries, although the shorter the duration the less complete the resolution of issues is likely to be.

In general, it has been the consensus among Link Care staff that a minimum of one month in the restoration program will maximize the opportunity for significant progress to be made in understanding and healing the presenting concerns.

Working Through Phase

Once missionaries have become oriented to the program, they begin to settle into a working mode. In this phase an alliance with the counselors has been sufficiently achieved and attention is focused fully on addressing the presenting problems in an open and cooperative atmosphere. Missionaries begin to examine the issues and consider what they may be contributing to the problems. They begin to take the time to listen to the promptings of God as he reveals their woundedness and sin and, in the midst of this experience, his redeeming grace and love.

At the outset of the working through phase missionaries may begin to feel worse rather than better. Finally there is the safety and structure for personal and/or relational problems that have been avoided for months or even years to surface and be examined. The stress and discomfort typically associated with this process should not be underestimated. Normalizing this process and framing it positively as a sign of progress can ease missionaries' fears and help move them forward to a less distressful period of working toward the resolution of their issues.

It is also common for counselors and missionaries in the working through phase to discover that the presenting problem is actually a symptom of deeper issues. For example, undiagnosed ADHD may significantly explain a missionary's interpersonal conflicts, unrecognized bipolar disorder might have contributed to a spouse's infidelity, serious childhood abuse can be related to major depression, and unspoken resentments may underlie an aloofness from colleagues or spouse.

This author is aware of more than one instance where a male missionary dragged his family off to the most difficult field he could find in an effort, he later came to understand in counseling, to disprove his parent's statements that he was not tough enough to succeed. The assessment in the orientation phase, if conducted properly, identifies such potentially hidden issues and enables the period of working through to be focused and productive.

As the working through phase progresses toward its conclusion, missionaries experience a greater awareness of their problem, of themselves, and of God. They can relate less defensively and with more ownership of their contribution to the problems. Moreover, they have learned the requisite skills to help prevent them from returning to the old dysfunctional patterns. More healthy, effective, and Christian ways of thinking and behaving begin to gather momentum as change solidifies.

Transitional preparation phase

Although it is true that the working through phase may occur across multiple levels of care as the missionary becomes increasingly restored, each change of level that involves relocation will necessitate a time of transitional preparation. At Link Care this phase may take prominence about one to two weeks ahead of the departure date, although some degree of planning typically occurs earlier than this. This is the time when missionaries anticipate their upcoming change of surroundings and work to determine how best they can continue the restorative process in their new setting. Many return to overseas assignments while others relocate to an area in their home country where they can continue to receive less intensive restorative care.

The transitional preparation phase is not a time when new issues are to be addressed. Hopefully, any remaining issues are not so severe that they cannot be set aside temporarily until they receive due attention at a lower level of care. If the missionary is unable to emotionally contain these issues, this is a strong indicator of the need to continue the working through phase at the current level of intervention.

One important aspect of restoration that often comes into play near or during the transitional preparation phase is bringing meaning to the missionary's experience, often perceived to have been one of failure. This is regularly addressed in a theological context and thus the role of pastoral care may be primary. In one example, a missionary couple had to comprehend why they had spent years in preparing for overseas ministry only to have their first term cut short after six weeks due to the wife's serious depression.

While there are many prospective ways to make sense out of such a course of events, one that seems fairly common to the missionaries at Link Care can be summed up in the words of Stanley Lindquist: "God is just as interested in what he is doing in you as he is in what he is doing through you." In other words, missionaries not infrequently conclude that going overseas and having such struggles may have been the only way God could get their attention and engage them in a restorative process. Through this process, they come to know and experience Him in a much deeper way and are often prepared to re-engage in more effective ministry.

Missionary Restoration: Mission Possible

The prospect of entering into a restorative process that involves multiple phases and which may occur over multiple levels of care can seem daunting to missionaries contemplating or just beginning their own healing journey. The testimony of missionaries in the restoration program at Link Care indicates that the experience certainly can be emotionally and spiritually draining for a time. Yet God seems to be faithful in so many situations, renewing hope and creating a new vision for both missionary service and self-care. In fact, Link Care annually sees 65-70% of participants in the restoration program return to formal ministry.

Restorative member care is no longer just being talked about. It is now occurring throughout much of the global mission community. Missionaries who in past generations might well have been hidden casualties of their calling now have a real possibility of being restored to effective Christian service.

In spite of limited resources, the future looks bright as increasing numbers of member care pastoral and psychological counselors are engaging in restorative care at every level of intervention. There is a lot to rejoice about, and a lot left to accomplish in the service of missionaries needing restoration. May God grant us the wisdom, perseverance, and resources to more fully enable His restorative power to be experienced in the lives of missionaries worldwide.

References

O'Donnell, K. (1997). Member care in missions: Global perspectives and future directions. *Journal of Psychology and Theology, 25,* 143-154.

Olford, J. (1993).

Rosik, C. H. (1993). Mission-affiliated versus non-affiliated counselors: A brief research report on missionary preferences with implications for member care. *Journal of Psychology and Christianity, 12,* 159-164.

Williams, K. (1992). A model for mutual care in missions. In O'Donnell, K. (Ed.), *Missionary care: counting the cost for world evangelism* (pp. 46-59). Pasadena, CA: William Carey Library.

45

Long-term Therapy:
A Long Journey Towards
Deep Healing

Linda Leitsch Alford

Using a fictional story, this chapter looks at long-term therapy: when it is indicated, qualifications of a therapist, how to find a therapist, and nuts-and-bolts issues of time, cost, and support systems. Long-term therapy addresses issues that cause a deep unsettling in the soul, when problems from the past get mixed up with trauma and difficulties in the present to create a complex pattern of disturbance.

*N*ote: The following is a fictional account based on many real fragments of conversation.

The Invitation

Mark and Mary approached me, introduced themselves and asked if we might have lunch. I had dropped in on the conference they were attending and was delighted to have some company. They represented different missions but had served on the same field together and had become good friends.

As we looked for seats, they took a communal anxious deep breath and quietly asked if we might sit away from the main part of the room. That was my first clue that I had been invited to a serious dialogue about something important.

Anxious Questions and Studied Queries

As the lunch hour unfolded and flowed into the afternoon, the conversation was woven with gentle tears, some jovial laughter inspired by memories of happier days, and questions born out of serious intent.

The often intense discussion about the nature of long-term therapy was punctuated with myriad questions that sometimes came out as anxious fears and at other times seemed to be well-studied queries about the work of psychotherapy and their perceptions about the church, the missions community and my profession.

I was fascinated by the inquiry and felt deeply privileged that they had been pointed in my direction by trusted colleagues. They had shared a bit of their concerns with others at the conference and were told that a conver-

sation with me might be profitable. We began with basic introductions and moved quickly into deeper concerns that seemed to burst forth from deep places in their souls.

Getting Acquainted

They had been told that I did long-term psychotherapy, had done some work with missionary personnel, had some grasp of mission systems and had done extensive study of dynamics involved in acculturation and trauma recovery.

Mark was a college convert while Mary had been a Christian since childhood. Mark stated that his upbringing was "not pretty." Mary was frustrated by feeling significant inner turmoil even though by all measures her childhood was "very pretty." She figured she had no business feeling troubled about anything.

Mark and Mary had served different mission boards on the same field for some years. Mark had been the senior missionary when Mary came to the field for her first term "as green as they get." I was assured that they had a comfortable relationship by Mark's affirming nod, broad smile and gentle recognition that it had been a joy to watch Mary mature as a missionary and a privilege to count her an equal. Their mutually supportive relationship was the fruit of hard struggles experienced together in a very difficult location.

Personal Trauma

Mark shared that he had lost his wife and second child in a so-called "accident" on the field. He often wondered who were the real targets for the "accident." He believed that he and his national informant were the true targets, and this matter caused him great distress.

Mark had felt the support of his field community and his missions organization throughout his time on the field, particularly at the time of the "accident," but had taken a leave of absence shortly after the loss of his wife and child. Actually, the leave had been planned before the "accident" because Mark had begun to feel his task on the field was complete and wanted some time to regroup.

Faithful Servants in Great Distress

Mark was in his mid-fifties and had lived his whole adult life in rural third world settings. He had felt vital and full of purpose most days when he was on the field. Now he was at a loss as to how to move forward in life. He felt empty and lacking in purpose. The world had changed, his mission had changed, his goal of handing over tasks to nationals had been reached and he no longer really felt called to any specific mission or ministry.

Mark was, by his own description, worn out, used up, and lost. As we talked, I came to have great compassion for this man who had served God and his church so fully and faithfully, yet now felt empty, unsettled and useless.

Mary was still driven by the ideals that first called her to mission service. The difficulty for Mary was that while she was still full of vision and calling, she was also full of internal conflict. Her first term had been incredibly difficult and her second term was full of "third-world war, disease and famine stories." She was now on extended home leave to attend to her own physical concerns and obtain advanced medical training. Mary expressed creative ideas about how her new training could assist her in fuller service overseas. Her dream was to return to the field as faculty at a nursing school.

Problem: she believed that she, as a woman of faith, should not have so much internal conflict. Since childhood she had been taught that Jesus was sufficient for all her cares. She had understood the principles of Christian faith for decades, and she had been well schooled in the strongest of Bible-centered colleges. She had fought many spiritual battles in foreign lands and represented her Lord and her church over many years. Yet, as I listened to Mary, I heard deep distress and shame about her personal struggle.

The Agenda: Assessing Long-term Therapy

As the dining hall closed and afternoon sessions were about to begin, Mark and Mary politely asked if we could continue our conversation in the park across the way. I hesitated, and they assured me that they did not want to inconvenience me but had some questions about this long-term therapy they had heard I did. They were both eager to assess whether this was the course of treatment they should seek and how they might go about it.

I was now hooked; this was the piece I could sink my teeth into. They had a specific agenda and needed to know more about me and gain some trust in my ability to respond to their concerns before we could get to the bottom line.

It was a beautiful day and outside is always more appealing to me than inside on such days. I was drawn to these two and I have a real passion for my work. So, unable to resist the "missionary" in myself, I was off to the park to assist these two in unpacking their questions and their quest to journey to the deeper places in their souls.

A Flood of Questions

The questions rolled out with the power and thunder of Niagara Falls the minute we set foot in the park. At times they talked to each other with shortcut phrases and mutual understandings. At other times they filled me in about this or that history or concern. They asked questions that seemed simultaneously critical to future life fulfillment and dangerous to career and/or faith.

I listened in wonder at the depth of these two comrades on a journey of mission and life. There was wonderful refreshing laughter that I knew to be the saving grace for arduous inner struggles and cross-cultural movement.

The questions? Well, for starters: Tell us about the journey of long term therapy. And before I could answer: How does it work—how can I trust it—is there a specific path—is it a justifiable use of time and money and energy—can God be in the process—how do I find someone to do this work with—what do you think the mission will do, if they know—???

It seemed that with each of my statements attempting to answer some fragment of the questions, more questions were generated. Sometimes they seemed to come from fears of rejection by loved ones, the church, or the mission. Sometimes they reflected the pure joy of discovery and hope of freedom bubbling up from deep places within. At some points the hope turned to tears of relief, at others tears of remembered pain mixed up somewhere between hometown USA and the overseas culture.

I tried to lay out my answers in an ordered and careful manner. I suggested using the six words we often use in teaching interviewing skills to beginning coun-selors: who, what, why, where, when and how. We could start with the what, when and the why of long-term therapy, and later consider the nuts-and-bolts questions of who, where and how. I got about that far before they interrupted me and began to unload more information.

Previous Experience of Counseling and Therapy

Mark had been in therapy. He had also had some exposure to the therapeutic community once or twice on the field. After a crisis, counselors had come to do crisis intervention and he had found their assistance helpful. After one lengthy conver-sation with a crisis intervention counselor, he had been encouraged to consider further counseling. The counselor had felt that his responses indicated that the event might be tapping some difficulties from other places in his life. He acknowledged similar concerns and said he might look into it when he returned to the States.

When Mark returned to the States he did see a therapist who knew they had only a short time to work and insisted on keeping the focus on immediate events. The therapist indicated that Mark might want to look at other issues with a different therapist, as he didn't do that kind of work. While this seemed honest and ethical on the part of the therapist, Mark was disappointed. He had felt unrest for some time, and at various turns in his life the unrest was stirred up, ready to be addressed.

While in the states this time, he had encountered friends who had given him some clues about their own journeys in therapy. He was really curious about the process because it seemed that the work they were doing "over the long term" was making a big difference, bringing his friends to a point of deep internal peace. Mark had once believed peace would come automatically when he became a Christian, but it hadn't happened.

Characteristics of a Long-term Therapeutic Relationship

I told Mark and Mary that "over the long term" was a key phrase, because long-term work involves a therapeutic relationship that provides safety and invites a deeper look at oneself. It includes reflection on the part of the therapist who helps the client unpack the deeper pieces of their soul and come to hold them more peacefully. Sometimes a person knows they need long-term work and sometimes the process just evolves in the course of therapeutic insight.

Mary quickly inserted that she was currently in therapy with a counselor who had suggested she move into long-term therapy. She had been seeing a university counselor, but the counseling center rules stipulate a limit of one semester per student. Her therapist had stretched that to two terms, but was trying to move her to a more long-term situation. She was willing to make the change but she had already been in therapy for six months.

There were people in Mary's life with whom she had shared her journey. They had been very supportive but were no longer as comfortable with her process—it had taken too long. Mary was beginning to think that perhaps she had a faith issue, yet something inside her was pushing to be understood. She knew she needed to settle her unrest.

Why Extended Therapy?

Next we moved on to the why question. Why would you want or need to be in therapy for any more than a few sessions? Voices around us are sometimes critical and judging when the process extends over time.

There are justifiable concerns about long-term therapeutic processes. Some therapists see clients "forever" with no apparent progress. Some clients are disappointed with the therapeutic process; both the therapist and the client are contributing factors. Mary had to decide whether she wanted to go ahead with her own journey and let the world think what it will. She has the right to ask her therapist for a progress report as frequently as she desires.

When is Long-term Therapy Indicated?

How would they discern when long term therapy is indicated? I reflected that Mark seemed to have made up his mind and he simply needed to talk about it. Mary was more timid about entering a longer term process. What would happen if she opened up a lot of issues and it was time to go back to the field before she was done? What if she couldn't close it back up and became a babbling mess?

We talked about the fact that when you have a good therapist, she or he will help you know what work you need to do. Therapy does not have to be excruciating. Some therapists do their work like a hot knife running through butter, and while there is a place for such hard-hitting techniques, most therapy is gentle and ordered. Mary would have to decide what kind of therapist she wanted.

Setting Boundaries

Mary started to tell me more of her story. I reminded her that I wasn't her therapist but a mental health professional she was consulting about direction. I was doing a quick backyard consultation. Both Mark and Mary stopped the conversation and shared a new insight—good boundaries assist with gentle and ordered therapy. I encouraged them to look for someone who had the skill to set boundaries around the process and the relationship.

Mary had incurred some injuries while growing up, but before she entered mission service she had been able to keep them nicely tucked away. When she went overseas, she had put aside things which had troubled her most of her life—they would be "here," and she would be "there." However, throughout her missions service she had a keen sense that those things had come with her despite her best efforts. Situations would occur that stirred up the old stuff.

Deep and Complex Conflicts

Mary wondered if some of her concerns were related to what her therapist labeled gender identity and development issues. She shared a few specifics, and I concurred with her therapist that there was a valid need for long-term work.

Long-term therapy addresses issues that cause a deep unsettling in the soul. Things from the past get mixed up with traumas and difficulties in the present to create a complex pattern of disturbance. Questions of identity, development, complex and confounding patterns in relationships, and quandaries about deep-seated inner conflicts are not easily or quickly resolved.

We took a collective deep breath and said we had come to some consensus about what long-term therapy is and why one might engage in it. We hadn't covered all the nuances but we had done enough. We all sensed we could proceed to the nuts and bolts, but first we needed a break.

Taking a Break and Throwing Stones

We wandered down to the lake at the edge of the park, threw stones in the water, laughed, told some more stories and shouted at the ducks as we released the emotion of the past two hours. Mark threw his last stone and with an air of jest insisted he needed to know who his counselor would be. As we returned to our picnic table, I confessed that I didn't know, but I could give him some pointers in his search.

Issues of Reacculturation

They were both in the midst of reacculturation. Mark talked about being "lost" in his home culture. This also had to do with losing his wife, his child, and other valued people on both sides of the ocean. While throwing the rocks and in other parts of our conversations, many things told me they were both struggling with the church and culture in America.

There were many aspects of reacculturation they needed to address, and that needed to be taken into consideration when choosing a therapist. Their therapists must have some knowledge of the dynamics of acculturation. Understanding cross-cultural movement would be essential for hearing and reflecting the dynamics of Mark and Mary's stories.

A Therapist Who Understands Cross-Cultural Experience

If at all possible they both needed to find someone who could understand the world they had come from. This does not mean the individuals would have been to their villages overseas, or even traveled to the continent where they served. Cross-cultural experience (even a high school experience of rural teens working in the city), combined with training, personal work or knowledge of the dynamics of cross-cultural movement, would facilitate the process greatly.

The ideal person isn't always available, but at least they needed to find a therapist who was committed to growing in this area through study or supervision. They should ask if the potential therapist is willing hear stories of foreign places. Also they might inquire about the therapist's training in trauma recovery in a broader sense, not just sexual abuse recovery.

Credentialing

Mark and Mary needed to understand mental health professions and their credentialing. The field includes licensed marriage and family therapists, licensed professional counselors, licensed social workers, licensed clinical psychologists and psychiatrists. There are different types of credentials; all are valid. The license is important because it indicates a level of professional knowledge, experience and accountability.

Theories of Counseling

Sharing a bit about counselor theory also seemed important. I said there are various theories and as many applications of each theory as there are therapists who hold it. The therapist needs to be clear enough about theory to have a consistent style of intervention, in order for the process to move smoothly. The specific theory may not matter as much as the consistency of application, but the fit of therapist to theory and client to therapist are significant factors in therapeutic success.

Personal Preferences

At that point we discuss Mark and Mary's preferences for therapists, including gender and therapeutic style. I recommend that anyone considering long term therapy find someone who is not a candidate to be their counselor who can help them sort out options. I encouraged them to ask any potential counselor about their training, experience, style and theory. Ask what training and experience they have that qualifies them to do long term work. These questions may be asked by telephone or in a face-to-face interview.

Christian vs. Non-Christian Therapist

Mary wanted to know how important it is for the person to be a Christian. The counselor she was seeing was not a Christian, but she felt there was plenty of respect for her faith and room for her faith struggles. This woman had given Mary two or three names of therapists in their area who do long term therapy, but Mary sensed that she would feel better with a therapist who knew about Christian theology, culture, language and—most of all—Christian missions.

I agreed that it might be difficult for someone to fully understand the core of her inner struggle and/or the mission vision of her life without knowing Christ and the Christian community, but I wouldn't completely rule out a non-believer.

There is a limited pool of Christian therapists in every region of the US. It's always easier if you know someone shares your faith and at some level holds to the tenets of orthodox Christian theology. However, it is ultimately critical that the therapist be respectful of your faith journey and of your mission commitment, whether they be a believer or non-believer.

Some Christian therapists have wounds related to the Christian community which can lead to cynicism about Christianity, Christian missions and/or Christian disciplines. If they are unaware of their own issues, they may be less helpful than a non-believer who respects and honors faith. My words resonated with some experiences Mark and Mary had in the church, and they assured me they would keep this in mind.

Finding a Therapist

So we moved on to the next question. How does one find the desired person? To find a Christian therapist, a good place to start is a seminary or distinctly Christian graduate school which offers training programs for mental health professionals in counseling, psychology and/or social work. I encouraged Mark and Mary to call some of these academic departments and ask for recommendations of graduates.

They could also explore the web sites of Christian organizations which promote and network mental health professionals. It is important to understand that these would not be recommendations but just lists of member names which anyone with the required credentials can join for a fee. Generally professionals join organizations that they identify with, but that does not guarantee any level of counseling skill.

I also suggested that they might just look in the yellow pages and start calling. Many therapists are willing to say, "I am not the therapist for you but I know someone who might be of help in your search." Therapists are ethically bound to practice within the boundaries of their competence, and many are willing to work with callers on referrals.

Sometimes this process feels like picking through the haystack in search for the needle. I wanted Mark and Mary to hear that they, like most missionaries, presented as creative people who knew how to find their way along the twists and turns of life's pathways.

Other Practical Issues

Mary wanted to discuss nuts and bolts issues such as time, money, support systems and implications for change. They both had therapeutic needs for which it would be helpful to remain in the States for an extended time. Some people can do long term therapy with intermittent breaks, working in segments; others can't. It is impossible to say how long it will take, as every situation is different. I have been surprised both by people who need less time and others who need more.

Regarding costs: some therapists are willing to negotiate fees. In all the mental health professions, therapists do some portion of their work for reduced fees. It is acceptable to request a fee adjustment at the outset of treatment or at some later date if their financial picture should change.

Some health insurance companies help pick up the cost at some level for varying numbers of sessions per year. In some cases, churches or mission agencies have funds set aside to assist with therapy. I encouraged Mark and Mary to start the search process and include conversation about fee policies in the initial session.

Support Systems and Career Implications

Mark already had a support system that could take him a long way. Mary would need to carefully select people to share her journey who can "go the distance" with her. I have walked my own journey as well as walking with many others through the deeper work of the soul, and I know the hard work, the depths of pain and the new-found freedom it involves. I believe one has to protect the process so as to have the space needed to do the work. At times it is important to have safe places outside of the therapy room to give voice to new insights.

The implications for one's career are impossible to predict. As each of us becomes more healed and at peace, we have more to contribute to whatever career we choose, and missions is no exception. Mark and Mary were telling me this work needed to be done; I reminded them that the God they had trusted to walk with them through numerous difficult experiences would also walk with them through this phase of life.

Experiencing Real Change

Mark smiled and said he wanted to talk about change and becoming whole. He wondered if he or Mary would want to be a involved in missions when they finished. He was concerned about becoming self absorbed, a bit fearful about the nature of the changes ahead, and anxious about his ability to change.

Mary had said that she knew someone who has been in therapy "forever" and has never changed. Some people are invested in *not* changing. But most missionaries are accustomed to change—they can handle change and the outcome can be very good and very Christ centered.

Given the attitude and desires they had demonstrated that afternoon, I was fairly confident they would both see real positive change. I firmly believed that if they chose therapists who would honor faith, and if they intentionally kept themselves at the foot of the cross, they would become even more the people God had created them to be.

A Rich and Powerful Experience

With another collective sigh of relief, a sense of insight gained, and knowing it was time to call it a day, they thanked me for my time and I thanked them for the privilege of being part of their journey. We said good-bye, and I returned to my office where I had some "down time" to process this rich and powerful experience with two warriors of faith.

Linda Leitsch Alford
LakeSide Center
41 E. Main St., Suite 104
Lake Zurich, IL 60047
Tel: 847-540-9625
t.l.alford@worldnet.att.net

Addendum

This rich narrative points out a host of factors relative to long term psychotherapy for missionaries. Such treatment can address many issues which underlie emotional difficulties. The demands and stresses of mission service often trigger old unresolved issues, creating unidentified tensions and less effective patterns of feeling and thinking. The uneasy feelings and tensions experienced by Mary and the residuals of a "not pretty" childhood endured by Mark are good examples. Sometimes field experiences alone create deep wounds that make long-term therapy the treatment of choice.

With counseling and psychological services now available in a few on-field locations, receiving long-term therapy overseas is not out of the question, though it still is unavailable for most missionaries. The short windows of time in the same location during home assignment may make it difficult there as well. Many missionaries are able to arrange it during study leaves, or special home assignments, or have withdrawn from the field temporarily for the specific purpose of recovery and restoration.

An increasing number of practitioners in private practice or in Christian agencies are sensitive to and experienced in work in mission contexts. Link Care in California and ALONGSIDE in Michigan are able to provide long term therapy as part of their customized services. Excellent results can often be achieved in shorter term, more intensive therapy in conjunction with group or program activities.

Depending partly on the therapist, his or her experience, theoretical leanings and spiritual integration, long term therapy involves a distinct process which unfolds optimally over time. It usually involves a significant relationship between the client and therapist which is utilized for therapeutic movement. Important factors include the desire for and openness to change and a willingness to take psychological and spiritual risks. Both client and therapist often see God working in unexpected and freeing ways. In God's grace insights are realized, changes achieved, and healing occurs—and more satisfying and effective living is the result.

Evaluating Psychotherapies

In *Modern Psychotherapies*, Stanton L. Jones and Richard E. Butman provide an excellent survey of thirteen psychotherapies, evaluating each theory in terms of its compatibility with orthodox Christianity. Along with a critical, theologically informed evaluation of each therapy is a discussion of foundational concerns on the integration of psychology and theology.

John R. Powell

Reference

Jones, S. L. and Butman, R. E. (1991). *Modern Psychotherapies.* Downers Grove, IL: InterVarsity Press.

Part VII

Innovative Models for Providing Care

46

On-site and Rotating Professional Services

Timothy P. Friesen & Roni R. Pruitt

Background History

Berlin is a new field of service that has been targeted by mission organizations starting with the fall of the 'Berlin Wall' in 1989. Today the Berlin missionary community is comprised of 100 adult missionaries representing 30 mission organizations.

Since the 1880's Berlin has been known as a city of diversity. Today the nature of the city encompasses many contrasts, including both an eastern and western cultural focus. East Germany and West Germany had two different information systems. East Germany, based on a Communist political scheme, obtained their point of reference from Eastern Europe. West Germany developed concepts based on information resources from the West. There has been a political reunion of the two German governments, but the people communicate across a cultural divide.

Berlin is the largest city in Europe based on land mass. Travel within the city is very time consuming and regulates activity. The missionary community is dispersed to the various regions of the city where they live and minister, thus limiting contact with other missionaries.

Design of Berlin Member Care Team

Roni Pruitt, who trained in theology and psychology, has served as a missionary for 15 years. After the completion of seminary she served in China and Japan. During her field experience she saw the need for missionary care. From 1989 – 1994 she served in Hungary, then upon completion of her Ph.D. in Counseling, she moved to Berlin, Germany in 1995.

Her commission to Berlin was in the role of a traditional career missionary with World Mission Ministries,

The Berlin Member Care Team is a model for providing services to missionaries from many agencies who work in a large European city. Professional counseling is provided by rotating staff. This chapter describes the development of a team model, including its goals, structure, function, and constraints associated with the model. Implications for the model and plans for the future are discussed.

393

the board of the Pentecostal Holiness Church. She founded "Renew Counseling Services," a private practice to resource the missionary community in the former East German region.

The size of the missionary community did not warrant the presence of two full-time therapists. However, after becoming established after two years, there was a felt need to have professional consultation on case work with another therapist, and to broaden the areas of specialization another therapist could bring so a diversity of services could be offered.

Tim Friesen, Psy.D., trained in school and clinical psychology, has worked in outpatient psychological services since 1987. This included three years of living in central West Germany as an Air Force psychologist and ten years in the U.S. in the state of Michigan. While working at the Christian Counseling Center in Grand Rapids, Michigan, Tim began an outreach ministry to missionaries on the field called "Project Stephanas." The mission of Project Stephanas is to provide on-site psychological services in the form of education, consultation and short term intervention for missionaries.

The distinctives of Project Stephanas include

- preventive care
- provision of services on an itinerant basis (3-4 times per year)
- long term commitment to a specific field and or specific group of missionaries

The initial meeting of Tim and Roni occurred during the summer of 1998 when Tim came to Berlin to explore the development of Berlin as a first site for Project Stephanas. The outcome of the first meeting with representatives from the Berlin mission community resulted in the following: a) Berlin was identified as the first official site for Project Stephanas, and b) Roni validated the need for assistance in providing member and clinical care services to the Berlin mission community, particularly in the areas of marriage and child/family issues.

Since 1998 Tim and Roni have functioned as a team in providing a range of services to the Berlin community and in case consultation and planning for further development of member care.

Development of a Team Model

A. Goals of the Model

The following goals represent the development of a team model of member and clinical care in Berlin. These goals are also relevant to diverse models of member care in other parts of the world.

Professional Synergism

To function as a team it is necessary to know one another's professional strengths and develop ways of being collaborative and complementary. For example, Roni receives a request to assess a team and then recommends that one of the team members follow up individually to address inappropriate use of anger. Roni refers this individual to Tim, which allows Roni to remain available as a consultant to the team, while Tim provides counseling for the referred individual. The development of this "tag team" approach to treatment requires Tim and Roni to develop a professional working relationship which includes mutual understanding of clinical skills and agreement on ethical principles.

Specialized Services

To function as a team it is important to know one another's expertise related to specialty areas. Roni, because of her experience as a missionary living in other cultures, is knowledgeable and sensitive to the cross cultural issues of missions. Tim, with his experience related to psychoeducational evaluations of children, is a specialist in the areas of assessment and treatment of children. Knowing one another's areas of specialty is necessary in providing services as well as knowing when to include professionals with other specialities such as psychiatry or addictions.

Professionalism

The effectiveness of a team hinges upon maintaining professional standards. Although there are accommodations which are necessary when working cross-culturally, it is imperative that ethical principles such as confidentiality, risk management and use of effective treatment strategies be implemented. While working as a clinical team in Berlin, Tim and Roni have been intentional in discussing professional standards and how these standards fit into the context of providing services in Berlin. (See Chapter 51 by Richardson in this book for a more complete discussion of ethics and professional standards.)

B. Structure of the Model

Development of a structure for providing member/clinical services within the mission community of Berlin involves the following principles:

Credibility

Tim first arrived in Berlin the summer of 1998 to explore working with the mission community through Project Stephanas. At that time Roni was residing full time in Berlin and was established in the expatriate and German communities as a clinician. Because Roni had respect and credibility within the community, Tim was given a natural point of entry into working professionally. Tim's credibility into the community flowed because Roni had already established a positive presence.

Consistency

The success of providing member care and clinical services comes from building trust with those in the mission community. Trust is built through consistency over time. Initially, Roni built a framework for developing services by living in Berlin full time. Tim has developed stability through making 3-4 field visits per year, for three years so far.

Continuity

The Berlin model has flourished due to the long-term commitment to a particular field (missionaries serving in Berlin), as well as the commitment to the type of services provided.

- Commitment to Berlin as a field: Although Roni no longer resides full-time in Berlin she has maintained her commitment to serve this group of missionaries. Likewise, even though Tim resides in Thailand he has maintained his commitment to make field visits to Berlin.

- Commitment to services: Both Roni and Tim have been involved in team-building, consultation with leadership, training and workshops, and counseling. In most situations they have continued working with groups or individuals from previous contacts.

C. Function of the Model

Roni Pruitt, who was on-site all year, functioned as a communication agent. She organized a annual retreat for the missionaries in the region, which focused on fellowship, development of ministry skills and available resources. The member care team was presented at the retreat as a resource with up-dates on services and workshops that would be offered in the up-coming months.

One part of the communication system was to keep people informed of the dates Tim would be in Berlin and to notify Tim when missionaries expressed interest to meet with him. Roni engaged in short-term therapy in private practice and offered workshops. From her client base she made referrals to Tim and, as need arose, interfaced services with him.

One of the early functions for Tim occurred when he entered the Berlin community to do an informal needs assessment. A primary area of need surfaced through meeting with a cross-section of missionaries, which was identified as a high priority related to family life. This included the desire to maintain healthy marriages while serving on the field, educational and psychological needs of children, and balancing family life and ministry. Because Tim has expertise in child and family treatment this became the primary focus of his function within the team.

Tim was invited to share at the 1999 Berlin Mission Conference about maintaining healthy marriages on the field. This resulted in the formation of three marriage groups called "Marriage Link." These groups included couples who are all involved in ministry; the identified purpose of the group is to equip, encourage and challenge one another to grow as couples in the celebration of marriage. The couples involved in Marriage Link became the key families with whom Tim initially worked. Involvement with these families included clinical intervention, psychological evaluations for presenting issues such as ADD (Attention Deficit Disorder), marital counseling, trauma counseling and team building. Tim has expanded his involvement withe the mission community to be a available with teams and individuals, both single and married.

D. Constraints Associated with the Model

The ethos of the missionary community placed some constraints on member care/clinical services that had to be considered. Every missions community develops a personality that is derived from the local cultural influence and environmental factors.

The culture of Berlin places a high value on independence and self-sufficiency.

This creates a tendency for the missionaries to withdraw and not network or fellowship with other missionaries. Isolation is enforced by the 'hidden immigrant' status (Pollock & Van Reken, 1999). There are no outward visual characteristics that identify the missionaries as foreigners, so they blend into the society and thereby are cut off from contact with other missionaries.

These patterns are based on assumptions that the larger missionary community has no relation to their ministry role. The importance of developing a support system on the field is not recognized. As problems are encountered the missionaries do not have needed resources to be resilient.

Geographical distance and travel time serves as a barrier to member care events. Much time is invested in travel, so the average day would contain two meetings. The tendency is to have lengthy meetings that are planned well in advance and to meet less frequently. Having a good location for meetings is critical. Another time factor was related to meals, which placed enormous responsibility on the member care provider when organizing an event for a larger group.

Advance planning was a key factor. Most missionaries wanted to receive an invitation at least six months in advance, before they scheduled their calendar. Often missionaries complained their calendar was too full to attend, although they knew it would be a valuable meeting for them. These factors placed restraints on planning member care events.

Implications of the Berlin Team Model

1.   Member care providers, both pastors and clinicians, are greatly needed on site in locations where there are sufficient numbers of missionaries to form a community. Once there is an established presence of a member care provider, it is wise to develop a team approach of care. Ideally, this would include national and expatriate providers.

2.   Working as a team models the concept of "body life" to the mission community. This highlights the importance of mutual care, knowing one's gifts and struggles, and asking for help with areas of need.

3.   Living and working in isolation, particularly in cross-cultural settings, has strong implications for increasing the rate of burn out. There is mutual accountability in ministry and relationship when working as a team within a community.

4.   Member care providers need to know limitations related to treatment. In some situations, short-term intensive treatment is highly effective. There also are examples of growth occurring through meeting with an individual or couple every three months during a field visit. It is essential that intervention strategies consider the level of need, availability of resources and psychological health of the individuals involved.

5.   A long-term commitment by providers encourages the level of trust within a mission community. Several missionaries from Berlin have expressed their gratitude for being able to share from their heart about ministry and relationship issues, know that their sharing will remain confidential, and know that there is a potential for discussion in the future. This seems to provide a sense of comfort and

hope. Although there are favorable outcomes which occur when a trained professional comes to a group of missionaries for a one-time event such as a seminar, the consensus from missionaries is that a provider who has long-term involvement is preferred.

Future Developments of the Berlin Model

Training

The annual conference as well as special speakers coming to Berlin have made continuing education available to the missionaries. There is the potential to do a week-long or intensive weekend seminar with topics such as conflict resolution, working with multi-cultural teams, family transitions, and team building.

Building Community

There is the potential to create further opportunities to build community among Berlin missionaries. Currently there are quarterly meetings of the Christian Women's Group in Berlin and the annual conference as larger gatherings. On a smaller scale there are the "marriage link" groups and marriage retreats which have occurred. Building community encourages networking, support and fellowship, but also helps to draw from the body of Christ in evangelizing and discipling those who are searching for God.

Partnerships

Partnering with Christian clinicians living in proximity to Berlin would serve to expand the team and bring additional resources for referrals. This might include clinicians working with the expatriate community or German nationals with an interest in a Christian approach to treatment.

Application of the Berlin Model to Other Locations

The Berlin model of providing member/clinical care has been well received and has a positive momentum to grow and expand. It is possible that the framework and structure of this model can be birthed in other areas of the world. For this to occur there will need to be the melding of organizations, leaders and professionals working together to provide preventative care and intervention for workers on the field.

Conclusion

It has clearly been God's design for the work in Berlin to develop and bear fruit. The partnership between Roni and Tim, including each of their unique experiences and training, plus a desire to serve, has been a major factor in the success of the model. The Berlin model is a reminder of the principles found in Proverbs 19:21, "Many are the plans in a man's heart, but it is the Lord's purpose that prevails." Planning has purpose and encourages potential success, yet it is ultimately the "Lord's purpose that prevails." This the prayer of those involved and invested in bringing God's love and care to missionaries in Berlin.

47

Mobile Member Care Teams

Darlene Jerome and Karen F. Carr

When missionaries experience traumatic events, they need resources to help cope and heal. The Mobile Member Care Team - West Africa was established to provide consultation and crisis response. It serves 14 African countries and many mission agencies with a small staff and a great deal of wisdom and collaboration. Fundamental strategies described here include crisis response, staffing, training, and member care partnerships.

A Ministry Whose Time Has Come
Member care in missions has been practiced ever since the early church laid hands on Paul and Barnabas and sent them out with their support and prayers. In recent years member care has become a specialty involving the development of new modalities: one of these is a mobile member care team. This is the story of the Mobile Member Care Team - West Africa (MMCT-WA): a ministry whose time has come.

The Beginnings
Karen's Story: In 1993 I presented a paper on Critical Incident Stress Debriefing and its application to missionaries at the annual Mental Health and Missions Conference in Indiana. The response was overwhelming; there was a strong felt need for on-site crisis care for missionaries who were suffering the effects of trauma. The conference was an incredible time of fellowship and networking with people who shared the vision of caring for missionaries overseas.

My passion for missionaries and vision to work as a psychologist among them was birthed in 1983. For three months I worked alongside missionaries in Latin America who had suffered psychological trauma from coups, civil war, evacuation, death of colleagues, kidnapping of colleagues, earthquakes, and armed robberies.

There were no immediate, on-site services for early identification of symptoms or prevention of more serious post-trauma symptoms. Some missionaries suffered from suicidal thoughts, mood disorders, Post Traumatic Stress Disorder (PTSD), and severe relationship conflicts. It seemed to me that these things could have been prevented and that the Lord was asking me to be a part of his vision to provide preventative, proactive care for His servants overseas.

For the next ten years (1983-1993), as I worked on my Ph.D. in Clinical Psychology and started a career focusing on crisis management, I learned through many visits and conversations that the felt need of the field missionaries for on-site care was very high. In mission home offices, the understanding of the need for member care was rapidly developing.

However, the concept of a psychologist working on-site with missionaries in their place of service was novel idea. Some administrators were resistant to it, claiming that good recruitment and screening precluded the need for psychological care on the field. That attitude has shifted considerably as the benefits of member care and early intervention have become more evident.

In 1993, after presenting at Mental Health and Missions and writing an article entitled "Trauma and Post-traumatic Stress Disorder Among Missionaries" (*Evangelical Missions Quarterly*, July 1994), the doors began to open for my increased involvement in missions. At the time I was the program manager for an emergency services program in a community mental health center in Virginia. While gaining experience in crisis management, administration, and training, I was being prepared to work with missionaries in crisis. I began a private practice and worked with missionaries who had experienced trauma. I had opportunities to travel to Latin America, Asia, Africa, Europe, and the Middle East, leading workshops on interpersonal skills, crisis response, and grief management. With each trip, the vision was rekindled, intensified, and affirmed.

In 1996, at a Crisis Response Workshop for missionaries, I met and co-presented with Darlene Jerome, a missionary who also had a vision and heart for member care. It was the beginning of a partnership between a mental health professional and a mission administrator that continues today.

Darlene's Story: As a member of Wycliffe Bible Translators/SIL, I served for nine years in Africa as the Personnel Director of the Cameroon branch, working with an average of 200 adult members and 130 children. My preparation included training and experience as a physical therapist, a graduate degree in Intercultural Training and Management, two years of experience in primary health care and community development in a village in Liberia, the traditional SIL training to work in a language project, and some French study. Although I had experience in working with people and had read material for "people helpers," I had no formal training as a mental health professional.

Much of my job involved personnel management tasks, but many needs fit in the broad, newly developing category of "member care." During my tenure, our group experienced armed robberies, sexual assault, carjackings, political unrest, a coup, evacuations from neighboring countries due to civil wars, car accidents, depression, drug overdose, adolescent drug use, marital discord, teams in conflict, problems with anger, sexual immorality, several medical evacuations, deaths and the threat of suicide.

In the early 1990s, the Tumaini Counseling Center was established in Nairobi with some SIL counselors on staff. Their visits to our side of this huge continent were helpful, but were necessarily short and infrequent. Wycliffe/SIL has a well-staffed international counseling department in the U.S., but except for printed materials they provided, we were pretty much on our own. SIL counselors were very willing to consult from a distance, but when I first began the phone system was so bad it took 15 minutes to get a dial tone! Eventually that improved; we got a FAX machine and then the miracle of e-mail. This brought consultant help closer, but I needed training in crisis care that would make me a more effective caregiver.

Our branch developed a good response system in terms of logistics: the group would mobilize in prayer and help out in practical ways. We had a crisis committee, some wonderful nurses and an informal network of caregivers. But we did not have training or tools to assess how people were doing post-crisis and no training in debriefing—just an article from *Evangelical Missions Quarterly* written by Karen Carr that outlined the process. (See Chapter 37.)

During this time, neighboring countries were experiencing increasing political turmoil, war and crime. We received evacuation groups from Congo, CAR, Zaire— SIL and other missions as well—and though we cared for them in practical ways, it was clear that psychological needs were not being met. These were resilient people, but they needed help to process all that had happened and they often were not willing or able to return to their home countries to receive it.

Traumatic events contributed to the attrition rate of missionaries. My heart would sink when I learned that someone who was already struggling was the victim of an armed robbery or in the midst of a medical emergency. Some folks came out stronger after passing through deep waters; how could we help more victims become survivors or even celebrants?

In 1996 Laura Mae Gardner, Director of WBT/SIL's International Counseling Department, organized a workshop on Crisis Response for Mission Leaders. She invited me to co-present with Karen Carr, a psychologist whose specialty was crisis response, on the unique aspects of crisis for singles. That began a partnership between a mission administrator and a psychologist that contributed to the current multi-disciplinary MMCT model.

Mobile Member Care Team Begins

In 1997, several mission leaders gathered as a "think tank" to consider how to enhance the delivery of member care services. Primary concerns were the lack of access to care and the need to create a service that would be inter-mission, mobile, immediate, and crisis focused. Bruce Swanson of CBInternational asked Karen if she would give leadership to such a concept.

Later that year, at the Mental Health and Missions conference, the "think tank" brainstormed with a larger group about a possible team and strategies. This group became the Global Advisory Board for the Mobile Member Care Team and included Bruce Swanson as chair, Dick and Laura Mae Gardner, Kelly O'Donnell, John Powell, Erik and Jeltje Spruyt and Glenn Taylor.

Preparation for the Mobile Member Care Team spanned a two-year period from 1998 to 2000. With the blessing of Wycliffe administration, Darlene joined Karen in developing MMCT.

The Christian and Missionary Alliance provided MMCT's third team member, Marion Dicke, who joined the team in 2000. Marion had served in Zaire for over 15 years in midwifery, leadership training, mission administration, and member care, and now serves as the Member Care Services Director for MMCT.

We were advised to focus on one region so as to ensure our ability to respond and avoid setting up expectations for service that could not be met. We began in West Africa for several reasons: lack of member care resources in that area, increasing violence and crisis, mission infrastructure that could help launch a new ministry, and the fact that Darlene and Marion were already familiar with life in Africa and had natural connections there.

In 1998, Darlene and Karen explored the possibility of basing MMCT in Abidjan, Ivory Coast. Abidjan offers a well-developed communications system and is a transportation hub for West Africa. Several missions base regional personnel in Abidjan and the country has traditionally been politically stable.

In Abidjan, twenty-four mission leaders from fourteen mission organizations gathered to discuss this possibility. A needs survey had confirmed our impressions that traumatic events were very common and crisis response services were non-existent. This group welcomed the idea of a multi-disciplinary group based in Abidjan to provide missions in West Africa (14 countries from Senegal to Nigeria) with training, coaching and consultation for peer responders and administrators, debriefings, assessments, and referrals.

A group of eleven people representing eight missions became a Liaison Committee, providing confirmation from the Holy Spirit of our vision. We made plans with them over the next twenty months until we moved to Abidjan in May 2000. The Liaison Committee eventually gave birth to a regional Governing Board of nine people from six mission organizations that provides the MMCT-West Africa team leadership, advice, accountability, and networking within the mission community.

As the focus shifted to West Africa specific issues, the global advisory board passed its oversight role to the local governing board. During the 20 months of transition, the global advisory board continued to give wise counsel, support and strategic input as we fine-tuned the MMCT vision statement, spelled out our values, and developed strategy documents.

Core Values

Core values have been guiding principles in the development of our strategies. These values are common to many ministries but manifest themselves uniquely in the mobile member care team model.

Partnership

An African proverb speaks well to this ideal: "If you want to go fast, go alone. If you want to go far, go together." Inter-mission partnership is foundational; both the global advisory board and the regional governing board are inter-mission.

We are also committed to partnership across disciplines: we are a multi-disciplinary team with various backgrounds: mental health, mission administration, member care, medical, pastoral counseling, etc. Each role is vital for the care of missionaries.

We also work in partnership with mission organizations and their leaders, not in competition with them. Our desire is to come alongside and help them to do better what they already do. We encourage, equip and consult with mission leaders and caregivers in their roles as crisis managers and responders.

Accessibility

We can reach most places in West Africa within two days and can get visas in Abidjan within one or two days as well. Our proximity facilitates phone conversations and email correspondence turnaround times (same or one time zone away). One administrator said, "When I have a crisis situation, I feel more inclined to call you than I am to call someone off the continent."

Living in similar circumstances in West Africa may make us seem more accessible psychologically as well. Much less needs to be explained to a consultant who lives in a similar context and has visited the setting where the crisis occurred.

Proactive Care

Our desire is to see people trained and cared for in a proactive manner. In today's world, this means preparing missionaries for crisis situations. They need to be aware of the risks, know how to assess situations as they change, and get help if things around them deteriorate or they need to leave. If their colleagues become victims of generalized violence or targets of crime, they need to know how to be good friends to them. Mission leaders need to know how to assess victims and what their needs will be. Missionaries can be educated about how to address medical needs in remote areas, using books such as *Where There is No Doctor*; using a similar approach, we can train missionaries and their leaders for "where there is no mental health professional."

Fundamental Strategies

With the above core beliefs in mind and with the input of the MMCT Global Advisory Board, we have developed strategies that we will summarize here. (Complete strategy documents can be found at www.mmct.org.) These strategies have taken into consideration the logistical challenges of the 14-country region of West Africa.

Crisis Response Strategy

When a crisis occurs in the region and a mission asks for our assistance, we have three fundamental ways in which we can respond: directly, indirectly or by making a referral. We are a mobile team, so we go to the scene and respond directly when needed. Our presence in the region makes this much more possible than if we were in Europe or North America.

If the situation can be managed by those already there with coaching and consultation by phone or email, an indirect response is appropriate. If the victim needs to leave the situation, we can make referrals to resources where they are going by accessing the growing global member care network.

With any of these three response choices, we find that our ability to help is greatly enhanced if we have prior trust relationships established with the mission leaders concerned and the surrounding network of caregivers. These are made possible through our training workshops.

Crises we have responded to in West Africa include violent events such as armed robberies, civil unrest or coups, physical assaults, and carjackings; intra-personal crises such as stress reactions, burnout, depression, and anxiety in adults and children; interpersonal crises including team and family conflicts and difficulties; and some missionary kid issues including eating disorders, adjustment difficulties related to boarding school, separation anxiety, and depression.

An example of crisis intervention followed a situation in which a woman was taken hostage at gunpoint and used as leverage for an armed robbery. She was assaulted and verbally threatened throughout the ordeal, while other missionaries were victims of the robbery. Initially MMCT responded at the request of the mission by providing Critical Incident Debriefing for the entire group. Two MMCT members provided this group debriefing as well as individual follow-up.

A couple of months later the woman and her husband came to the MMCT office and received further care for continuing post-trauma symptoms; short-term counseling was provided and recommendations were made for lowering stress levels and improving coping skills. Consultation was given to the mission administration regarding supportive strategies. Ten months later, this missionary continues to heal from the trauma and has been able to remain in service on the field.

Some situations may not be related to violent trauma but are equally threatening to the integrity and longevity of field service. A couple in a neighboring country called MMCT and requested evaluation and counseling. The presenting problem was a feeling of severe burnout in the husband who was in a leadership role with numerous responsibilities. This couple felt that if they did not get help soon that they just might pack up and leave the field permanently.

Over a period of three intensive days, MMCT conducted a psychological evaluation and provided some brief therapy. It was recommended that the husband get treatment for major depression and that changes be made to his job assignment that would relieve the major sources of stress in his life. The regional administration supported these changes, a psychiatrist was consulted for medication, and two weeks of follow-up care was provided out of the country. The couple was then able to return to active service on the field in a different role.

We have many anecdotal stories of positive results of clinical intervention provided by MMCT, but we do not yet have research data to confirm our hypothesis that the provision of timely, competent crisis care on the field results in decreased post-trauma symptoms, more effective, healthy service, and less premature, preventable attrition. We have conducted two annual surveys of our consumers to ask questions related to satisfaction with services and perceived benefits. This feedback has been very positive so far. However, we hope to have systematic outcome research done in the future to determine the effectiveness of these interventions.

Personnel Strategy

Our team is not large: we have just four resident staff in Abidjan who are in the country under the sponsorship of their own sending mission and "loaned" to MMCT as their primary assignment. Currently, our fourth member is an invaluable administrative assistant, Janna Greenfield, who "holds the fort" while the rest of us are rather mobile. This leaves three of us, Karen Carr, Marion Dicke and Darlene Jerome, to staff workshops, provide consultation, relate to member caregivers and coach peer responders, and do debriefings.

Our capacity to do workshops and offer other services is greatly enhanced by about twenty associate staff in North America and Europe to whom we look for short-term involvement of two weeks to a few months at a time, depending on their availability. Many of the associates serve as workshop staff; some are available for direct crisis response work; others offer research and referral assistance. Associates who are counselors help Karen, our only resident mental health professional, provide brief counseling services.

MMCT serves as a student placement site for graduate students in mental health professional training and is glad to have their contribution while they are here.

We envision a team of six to eight resident staff in Abidjan serving all of West Africa. Our multi-disciplinary approach means that we seek mental health professionals as well as trainers, former mission administrators, member care specialists and pastoral counselors to join our team.

We also count as part of our personnel strategy the growing team of peer responders throughout the region. They are MMCT's "eyes and ears," making preliminary assessments, giving "emotional first aid," and connecting those in need with us when our involvement seems needed.

Training Strategy

Three workshops currently form the core of our training strategy:

- Sharpening Your Interpersonal Skills (SYIS)
- Peer Response Training (PRT)
- Member Care while Managing Crises (MCMC)

The SYIS is a four and a half day workshop developed over a period of nearly thirty years by Dr. Ken Williams, counselor with WBT/SIL. It provides training in key knowledge, attitudes and skills needed for developing and maintaining healthy relationships. Some of the topics are: listening, building trust, living in community, helping others manage grief, confrontation, conflict resolution, and managing stress. The workshop content is very Biblical in its orientation and meets with excellent response across mission cultures. We facilitate six to eight of these a year in the region, with about 24 participants from various mission organizations and countries of service in each workshop.

In addition to the personal growth that many experience through this workshop, there are other benefits: we as a team come to know many missionaries in the region and identify natural "people helpers" that are potential peer responders. We begin working relationships with mission leaders who take the workshop. Sometimes missionaries from organizations who have worked in the same area for decades are in a setting where they can build community and informal support networks across mission lines for the first time. This is crucial on the front lines of mission work.

Building on the interpersonal skills covered in the SYIS, Peer Response Training is a six-day workshop designed for those who already come alongside their peers as helpers. We give them tools so they can do an even better job. Participants learn about the impact and effects of crisis, potential pathological effects, how to make initial contact, and how to provide one-on-one peer debriefing. The workshop also includes personal assessment of attitudes towards suffering and a scriptural study of suffering and healing. Other topics include when and how to make referrals and ethical issues such as confidentiality and boundaries.

The last session of each day is a coaching group time when a group of four participants meets with the same staff person to share with one another what they have been learning and experiencing. These coaching relationships lend themselves to ongoing mentoring after the workshop through email, phone and occasional visits.

The Peer Response Training workshop requires an application process that includes recommendations from SYIS facilitators affirming basic interpersonal skills; from the mission leader confirming confidence in the applicant, the person's availability to serve and the mission's intention to use them once trained; and from a mission peer who expresses confidence in their interpersonal skills in crisis situations.

In the five-day Member Care while Managing Crises (MCMC) workshop, mission leaders learn what is a normal response to a crisis and how to walk alongside others through the necessary stages of grief after loss or trauma. We address the strategic role a mission administrator plays in member care while managing crisis situations.

Specific topics include: the impact of crisis; developing policies, procedures and protocols; the dynamic of trust for leaders in crisis situations; confidentiality and communication; information management; assessment of vulnerable members; unique needs in cases of suicide, sexual assault or evacuation; leadership styles in crisis; and the when, why and how of debriefings and crisis committees. Participants are also encouraged to further develop their own theologies of suffering and risk through Bible studies and times of reflection.

Two new workshops are under development addressing Missionary Kids and Crisis: one for MK caregivers and one for teenage MKs who want to be a better help to their friends in crisis situations.

Our training style is interactive and based on adult learning principles; these are indeed *work-shops* in that participants truly work during them. As one mission leader said at the end of the MCMC, "I didn't catch up on any of the reading that I usually carry with me to conferences and seminars to read when I get bored, but that's ok; I learned much more and had much more opportunity to apply what we were learning than I expected to in this workshop."

Member Care Partnerships

It has been a particular joy to see member care partnerships developing across the region of West Africa. As we travel from place to place we meet missionaries with a burden for member care who feel quite alone: the concept is new in their mission, they have few resources and their mission is too small to develop many more, they don't have enough time and the needs are so many. But through the SYIS workshops, these "kindred spirits" are finding one another and developing networks to resource and encourage one another in their member care ministries.

At this writing there are member care partnerships meeting regularly (every month or two) in four West African countries, sharing their concerns and resources, coordinating bringing in outside resources for the entire missions community and encouraging one another. We see the development and resourcing of member care partnerships as a priority and hope to see several more in the region.

Future Developments

Missionaries from Newer Sending Countries

About 10,000 missionaries serve in the 14-country region of West Africa; about half are from newer sending countries (NSC) such as Nigeria, Ghana and Brazil. We want to network more with NSC missionaries and their agencies and make our services and training more accessible to them. As the MMCT team grows, we hope to have staff from newer sending countries as well.

Africa

We often receive requests from missions in the neighboring regions of Central and North Africa; extending our services into those regions would be possible with more staff. Establishing similar teams in South and East Africa has also been proposed.

Global

Currently, the Global Advisory Board is considering where the next regional MMCT team might be launched and how different contexts might shape the strategies of future MMCT teams. The need is great in many places. We believe that Mobile Member Care Teams are a ministry whose time has come; we pray that God would give this vision to others who could join the team.

To contact MMCT: www.mmct.org
Clinical Director: Kfcarr@aol.com
Member Care Services Director: MarionDicke@cs.com
Personnel and Training Director: Darlene_Jerome@sil.org

48

Virtual Teams

Paul E. Nelson

*W*hen sparks ignited a grassfire recently near Mission Training International's new training center in the small town of Palmer Lake, Colorado, the alarm sounded and volunteer firefighters from all over the community dropped what they were doing and rushed to the scene to douse the fire.

These men and women take their responsibility seriously and invest a great deal of time and personal resources in making certain that they are prepared and available when the need arises. While it is true that a round-the-clock crew of well-resourced professional firefighters might be the town's preference, this team of competent volunteers is in scale with what the town can afford, and it has met most of Palmer Lake's emergency needs for generations.

The concept is simple. Identify and equip a team of qualified, motivated people in anticipation of the occasional crisis, develop a method to summon them, and then empower them to respond appropriately when the crisis occurs.

Virtual Fire Department

In a real sense, the community has developed a *virtual team* to provide for their common safety. These volunteer firefighters have complementary skills and are committed to a common purpose and approach for which they hold themselves mutually accountable. They go about their daily routines in different geographic locations but respond immediately whenever a crisis requires the team to act.

This model of a *virtual* fire department is one that both the mental health and missions communities might well consider emulating. Imminent threats of physical

Ever heard of a virtual team? Here is a challenge for the Great Commission Community to work cooperatively to assemble a virtual team of capable, motivated professionals to respond to crises. A case study shows how a virtual team might operate in practice. A model for a virtual team, how to make the vision operational, and characteristics of a team such as purpose, complementary skills, performance goals, strategies, and discipline are presented.

409

violence, destruction of property and loss of life are inevitable in the complex way of life inherent in today's missions community. The context and nature of cross-cultural ministry give rise to both real and potential dangers that often push missionaries into an emotional crisis.

In circumstances such as these, the skill, objectivity, and understanding of mental health professionals can make the difference between the continuation or termination of an effective ministry. Perhaps the Great Commission Community should work cooperatively to assemble a *virtual team* of capable, motivated mental health professionals who are available to serve the international missions community anywhere and any time a crisis warrants their intervention.

Example: Trauma in Colombia

In a scenario such as the following, a virtual crisis support team might function much like a volunteer fire department. A call comes from the director of a mission agency to the office of a veteran psychologist with a history of service within the missions community. He had just received a phone call from his field director in Colombia informing him of a traumatic event that occurred the previous night. They needed the assistance of the crisis support team.

A missionary husband, wife, and three children had been held for several hours by armed gunmen while their home was ransacked and their valuables stolen. The rebels, who were expecting to find more money and possibly guns, had beaten the husband several times before leaving in the mission's truck. The wife was extremely distraught, making it difficult to determine whether or not she had actually been physically abused or just repeatedly threatened. The children were being cared for by other members of the close missionary community.

As the gunmen entered the area they had injured two guards and threatened another missionary couple and their 10 and 12 year old children, without physical harm, before entering the more affected family's home.

Virtual Team in Action

The crisis team coordinator initiated their plan of action by sending an e-mail to the twenty-five counselors on the virtual team network telling them about the crisis in Colombia. Within an hour, the mental health professionals who were prepared and available to be part of the three-person crisis response team were making arrangements with their family and colleagues to be away. They were chosen partly because of immediate availability, but also because of the complementary skills required to respond to this situation.

The action plan continued with the team leader initiating a conference phone call with the crisis response team, and the Latin America field director to get an update on the crisis and confirmed travel and in-country logistics.

The interaction continued with all twenty-five members of the crisis support network and key field leaders in Colombia logging on to a secure internet chat room to get further details and make suggestions for immediate care, with a small group of five composing an "at home" monitoring team. The three members of the crisis team arranged their travel to meet at a pre-arranged departure city the following day and travel to Bogotá together.

Members of the small network monitoring team remained in contact with the people on site through the secure chat room and served as consultants to the field personnel as circumstances changed and decisions were needed. Once the crisis support team arrived in country, they planned their strategy to care for the victims, consult with the field leaders, and assist others in the community who were struggling with the heightened fears and uncertainties that resulted from the traumatic events. Attention was also given to mission-related nationals who were affected, and to the school which the children attended.

The crisis team remained on site for several days until the situation seemed stable and decisions were made concerning other interventions that might be needed. After seven days, the team returned home and continued consulting with the people involved via the internet as often as needed.

The Model of a Virtual Team

In this scenario, the responding crisis support team, along with the other therapists who served as consultants, might be commonly identified as a *virtual team* since they were dispersed geographically and communicated electronically. Businesses often refer to their national sales force as a virtual team and software companies may have virtual teams working on different parts of a program.

In a broader sense, the entire crisis support network makes up the *virtual team*. They represent an identifiable potential resource that is prepared and ready to function as an *actual* team any time and any place they are needed. The specific role each member will play during an incident is determined by the nature and location of the trauma, circumstances that may limit a team member's ability to be away at a given time, and the experience and expertise needed to assemble a team with complementary skills.

Making the Vision Operational

The model is relatively easy to describe and is actually operational, at some level, in several mission agencies. They have counselors upon whom they depend to come alongside when a traumatic event occurs. The challenge is not in describing such a team, it is in taking the steps necessary to make the vision operational. This is where things can get bogged down. Even the most committed and optimistic clinician can be overwhelmed by the sheer number of problems that have to be solved before the vision of a virtual crisis support team can become reality.

- Who would sponsor a crisis support team?
- How should the team be organized?
- What about training and preparation for the team?
- Who determines when there is a crisis?
- Who decides when to request the team's assistance and whom do they call?
- How will the expenses be covered?
- Could someone keep up a private practice and be part of a crisis team?
- Who decides when the team is ready?

There may appear to be so many practical obstacles to overcome that the vision can sound more like one of those workshop-generated "what ifs" than the basis for a working model. The key is to understand what the obstacles really are and focus the creative resources of the mental health and missions communities on overcoming the obstacles and creating a viable, sustainable, crisis response system. That requires discipline and teamwork.

Characteristics of a Team

In their 1990 book, *Wisdom of Teams,* (Harvard Business School Press, November 1992) John Kazenbach and Doug Smith point out that a compelling commonly held challenge is what creates a team, not the desire to be a team. When serving the missions community in such a critical and demanding way, the focus has to be on the higher purpose for which each person is drawn to the missionary enterprise. It cannot be on one's desire to share in a laudable venture with valued colleagues. The authors also draw some helpful differences between what it means to be a team as distinct from a group of people with similar interests and a common concern.

Purpose. First, each member of a team must own and commit to the purpose around which the team is organized. The specific purpose of a crisis response team might be expressed in terms of needs assessment, short-term intervention, peer resource development, or something as general as a listening ear. One of the first tasks a developing team should undertake is the shaping and articulation of the team's purpose.

Complementary Skills. It might become apparent through this process that the group is made up of people with similar interests, work styles, and competencies. Teams need complementary skills or the right mix of skills to accomplish their purpose. These requisite skills fall into three general categories: technical or functional expertise, problem-solving and decision-making skills, and interpersonal skills. Having people on the team with demonstrated aptitude in each of these categories is essential if the crisis support team is going to accomplish its purpose.

Performance Goals. Through the process of developing the purpose statement, this diverse group of people who are committed to its fulfillment will begin to articulate a set of performance goals. A team's purpose and its performance goals must go together. Both must be clear or confusion will likely prevent this group of people with a common vision from ever becoming a functional team. It will also prevent potential beneficiaries of this team' services from extending an invitation to assist or potential partners from becoming involved in funding the team's activities or sharing the load in other essential ways.

Strategies. Teams need to agree upon the strategies they will use to fulfill their purpose. This is where the hard work begins and where many teams get bogged down. Planning takes time and a lot of interaction. Most busy productive people have very limited time to spend in planning meetings and even less time for travel to participate in the meetings. This is where the term *virtual* has to be added to *team* if the model is going to be viable both in the planning stage as well as in its execution.

Discipline. The use of appropriate internet technology to facilitate continuity of planning, collaborative tasks, and accountability can make ongoing development and implementation of the team's plans possible. However, almost everyone has made well-intentioned commitments during a stimulating brainstorming session and then neglected those assumed obligations when the pressures of urgent demands consume the available time and energy.

In their recent book, *The Discipline of Teams,* (John Wiley & Sons, Inc. May 2001) Katzenbach and Smith point out that team performance is primarily about discipline —leader, peer, and self-imposed. Whether the task is participating in an on line training session or contributing to the development of agreed upon protocols for crisis intervention, the success or failure of crisis response teams will depend on personal and corporate discipline.

The Opportunity and Challenge

Perhaps there will be a day when the Great Commission Community will work cooperatively to assemble a *virtual team* of capable, motivated mental health professionals who are available to serve the international missions community anywhere and any time a crisis warrants their intervention. The distressing events from the Latin American scenario mentioned earlier, and literally dozens more like it, substantiate the need for such a team.

The capable, motivated, and godly mental health professionals who can meet that need are working in mission agencies, churches, and Christian counseling practices all over the world. All the required elements exist in the virtual world of untapped potential. Activating that potential will be the challenge of a visionary leader who is captivated by that potential and can enlist others to join him or her in this life-preserving venture.

49

Intensive Care Community: Moving Beyond Surviving to Thriving

Lois A. Dodds & Lawrence E. Dodds

The healing power of Christian community is a helpful Biblical model for care. Heartstream Resources is a loving, inter-disciplinary therapeutic community which provides a gracious setting for healing and growth for missionaries who suffer from crises, depression, stress disorders, burnout or other serious depletion. Its theoretical framework, approach, process, and program elements are explained.

*T*hroughout the history of missions the emphasis in missionary care has been on survival. We believe we should move beyond surviving to thriving. This implies the optimal functioning of the person—his or her best possible growth and development which maximizes potential in Christ for life and ministry. Growth is promoted through an enriching, nurturing, supportive and challenging environment, in contrast to a merely "adequate" provision of what is needed for survival.

Heartstream Resources is one of several ministries God has raised up for mental health care for cross-cultural workers, especially those who suffer from crises, depression, stress disorders, burnout and other serious depletion. We seek to be a loving, therapeutic community.

The ministry is inter-disciplinary. The staff includes a physician, counselors, pastoral counselors and others with extensive cross-cultural experience. Heartstream is the fulfillment of a vision to create a safe place for missionaries to receive assessment, care, and guidance in several life dimensions. Our homes offer relaxed, attractive accommodations and a sense of safety. Office, classes, meals and activities are centered there.

This chapter outlines principles relevant to caring for people whose lives are typified by chronic high stress —the hazardous occupation of serving Christ outside of one's own culture. These principles are based on a Biblical rationale for life in community as the locus for healing.

The Healing Power of Community

The health of the "body" is truly affected by the

health of each member. Healthy community provides mutual support and inter-woven lives, the power of prayer, and the humility of learning to love even when people disagree. Homes and families can be powerful allies in the healing arts. Beauty, color, and order in the environments of home and mission buildings is also healing.

Community can be created and fostered even in a few days. Attitudes and skills for community are transferable; once experienced they can be replicated to create community in other groups. "Life together" is not limited to long-term groups.

The healing power and growth potential of community has been demonstrated through Wycliffe's Quest program. In every group of candidates and staff, many people had deeply painful life stories which generated shame and depression. Most people had never told their stories; they discovered that in sharing with a loving small group they received healing, release, and new freedom.

Telling one's life story in a supportive environment has transformational power. Through telling their stories people see their whole lives, especially the work of God in them, from new perspectives. They find new meaning and healing.

Biblical Models of Healing: The Living Organism, The Family

It is not by accident that the models of relationship that Jesus gives the church are his body—the body of Christ—and the family. The body, as a living organism, exemplifies living together interdependently. Both "body" and family make possible true community. In intentional community people are drawn together in a web of relationship, committed to each other for the common good. (In contrast, accidental or unintentional community of non-commitment may lead to the common ill.)

Everyone is born into some kind of family. In family we are shaped for good or for ill. In family too we can best re-learn, be re-shaped, re-influenced, experience healing, love and be loved, and become whole. People don't learn and develop in a vacuum, devoid of close relationships. We learn better ways of thinking, behaving, relating through interactions with others. Today's unprecedented loss of extended family and community increases the need for caring, loving groups which nurture people, especially through their very difficult times of wounding.

The church is uniquely gifted and empowered to become the secure family—the functional one which provides re-birth and growth toward the optimum of the image of Christ. We need to enlarge our vision of "mission" to include the nurture which allows for thriving and longevity of its most precious resource—those who serve.

What is Community?

Community is rooted in God's essential being and our relationship to God. It means a shared, common life based on voluntary commitment to agreed-upon purposes, goals, and values. We are knit together by covenants which connect us, nourish health, foster healing and enable us to do the good work which God has prepared for us. (See Eph. 2:10.) Our model it includes small groups within the larger community.

1. In the Trinity, God's essence and nature as a relational being are reflected. The Trinity is a model of loving relationship; we are made in God's image.

2. Love is the greatest healer. Love is God personified, centered in and

springing from God. Relationship is essential for love to be enacted and experienced.

3. We are developmental beings created by God for growth. Becoming like Christ in all dimensions involves development.

4. Community is the optimal environment in which to foster loving personal relationships, to nurture growth and development, and to experience restoration and healing. Community provides a foundation for healthy service through affording both individuality and interdependence, the mutual valuing of persons and their gifts.

5. The word "restoration" implies that something has gone wrong. Deprivation of loving relationship in our original community (the family) wounds us. Things are not as they should be or as God intended for us. Community provides for the integration of relational, social, emotional and spiritual aspects of our lives.

6. Values of Christian community include

- Speaking the truth in love, honesty, immediacy, transparency and openness
- Time together, mutual availability
- Trust, respect and understanding
- Appropriate boundaries and safety
- Acceptance, affirmation, and nurturance
- Sense of family (place of belonging)
- Valuing each person as essential, gifted, and unique
- Mutuality, reciprocity and accountability
- Creativity

The Spiritual Foundation of Caring for Others

Our foundation for service is God as creator, restorer and healer. Jesus modeled this as the Servant Leader. Our divine resources include the Holy Spirit and his gifts, the healing Word, and prayer. God has already given us "everything we need for life and godliness" (II Peter 1:3 Phillips). Our challenge is to engage these resources daily. Restoring those who are wounded in the spiritual war is our high calling.

Intensive Care Community: Ambiance, Approach, Program and Process

Ambiance

All aspects of the physical and emotional environment are therapeutic. Beauty is a priority in the rooms, meals, and home environment. We consider that beauty is a NEED in our "care of souls." Our setting has refreshing, lovely views. Emotional safety is created by a sense of welcome, many small touches of concern, attentive listening, acceptance, respect, affirmation, and withholding of judgments and labels. People are invited to share things they cannot share with family or constituency.

Meal times (with crystal, linens, fresh flowers, and colorful table settings) reflect, reinforce and model what we teach about emotional and physical nurture. Conversations are rich in field stories, with much laughter. They relieve the heaviness generated by devotional and class discussions of life-threatening situations. We encourage guests to share in many informal ways. People discover they are not "the only one" who is depressed, exhausted in ministry, ready to give up, or having a crisis of faith.

Approach

We are very intentional in our interactions and programming, closely monitoring the flow and process. We are multi-disciplinary and multi-modal, assessing and treating in various life dimensions simultaneously. We are egalitarian, minimizing the usual hierarchy of doctor/patient and therapist/client.

We emphasize our oneness in Christ and our common need for growth and healing. This seems to us what Jesus modeled, consistent with being organism and family. This "natural life" context allows integration of life facets, rather than the fragmentation typical of today's western society.

Throughout the ages the church community has fulfilled multiple roles in the life of each person. It was the center of living, of participation in the sacraments and confession, discipleship, fellowship, teaching, comfort, celebrating birth and mourning death. We reclaim these important functions.

Our approach in counseling is eclectic, with a heavy emphasis on cognitive-behavioral therapy. We emphasize the need to change ways of thinking which lead to hurtful emotions and problem behaviors. We look at family of origin issues for the roots of problems, promote development of insight, and are solution oriented to promote more rapid change. We conceptualize a "therapeutic circle" in which the Holy Spirit brings insight, instructs, comforts and empowers change (Dodds, 1992, 1999). This model identifies what God gives to us through his Word and other resources:

- Motivation – a desire for something better than what we currently experience
- Model – the new ideas, persons, or ways of behaving which offer us an alternative
- Means – the energy of the Holy Spirit available to us and within us which empowers change towards Christ-likeness (health and wholeness)

This model, simplified, teaches:
- As a child of God, I have a right to a better life than the one I am living (depression, conflict, exhaustion, etc.)
- I can do something (choose to apply God's Word) to make it happen.
- God will empower me through His Spirit in me.

We normalize a great deal for our guests who have experienced trauma, hostile environments, the stresses of cross-cultural adjustment, and spiritual warfare—all of which can lead to adjustment disorders. Often people fear they are "going crazy." We help them to see that their symptoms and disorders are understandable and treatable.

Process

Our process is intense and personal, with a high degree of interaction. In our two-week program our staff works as a team, alternating formal and informal roles, moving from medical or counseling work to cooking, sharing meals and other activities. We try to model the loving interaction crucial to healing and well being.

The home environment provides excellent opportunities for interaction and observation of guests' habits of thinking, communicating, and behaving. It allows for immediate, appropriate feedback, frequent affirmation, and development of insight in natural contexts of daily interaction. The person cooking often listens to guests who feel at home in the kitchen (the central room). These are benefits beyond what traditional therapy offers.

Group process from arrival to departure is predictable. At first you can almost hear guests thinking, "Now why is he here? Why is she here? Am I an oddball? Can I trust these people?" By the third day, after hearing a brief version of each one's story, and sharing several meals and sessions, a palpable relaxation settles in. We move from the intake interviews to individual counseling, and guests feel that we care and listen attentively to their stories and needs.

As we move into the first week, and people go deeply into feelings, the atmosphere becomes heavy. We pray a great deal, asking God to reveal to us and to each guest the core need for healing. The second week feelings began to go up again as guests get perspective on their problems and needs and are learning tools and strategies to make changes. You can feel hope being born! The curve of this process is similar to what one sees in critical incident stress debriefing (Mitchell, 1995).

Living in community allows for speed and depth in addressing issues in the relatively brief span of two weeks. Guests feel safe, supported in the threat of going deeply into their past and present. Highly educated, committed and intelligent persons speed into the heart of issues which take weeks or months in other contexts. On one occasion in a family with rebellious teens we saw God work miraculously just in the first three days. Most people are ready for insight and change, having committed two weeks to getting help.

Program elements

Program components reflect the multi-disciplinary approach, integrating spiritual, physical, emotional, intellectual (actualization), and relational needs, including organizational relationship. This approach is implemented daily through devotions focusing on the life journey with God, interactive classes, guided journal writing, narrative and counseling (individual, couples and group), meals and other group activities.

1. Assessment: Taking into account the person's understanding of his or her own issues, the history, what the agency may have reported to us or requested of us, and our initial observations, differential diagnosis identifies core issues and resulting needs. There may be "spill over" from the original need or problem into other dimensions of life. Initial appraisals are modified as more knowledge is gained during the two weeks together. Several instruments augment the assessment.

2. Prayer: Prayer is crucial with both individuals and the group, in both assessment and therapy. Identifying the core issue requires the guidance and discernment of the Holy Spirit. Sorting out to what extent spiritual warfare may be involved and manifest in the person's needs is also crucial. We pray for deliverance and freedom in Christ when appropriate.

3. Classes: Each person is encouraged to assess his or her being (attitudes and approaches to life), to build knowledge (e.g., communication, child rearing, family of origin impact, life stage issues) and skills (conflict, communication, etc.). Flexible class topics and discussion are in tandem with counseling and devotions; often participants disclose attitudes or experiences which enlighten the counseling process. People continue discussing class topics during breaks, meals, or walks. The small group setting is unparalleled for integrating ideas and fostering sharing of experiences.

Topics build upon each other, beginning with helping guests assess, "Who am I? How did I get to be who I am? To what extent is my self-esteem and identity based on lies? What truth of God do I need to substitute for the lies? How do the lies lead me to wrong assumptions, projections, hurtful behaviors? How can I establish new patterns of thought, feeling and behavior using God's resources?" How we relate and have impact based on our functional, emotional foundations is considered, as well as the impact of the self on ministry effectiveness, and then we focus on tools and strategies for change.

4. Counseling: Each guest has an hour a day of counseling; couples and families are given counseling when warranted. Intelligent, committed, devoted, and productive people in the pain of crisis can progress at amazing speed. Another benefit of life together is identifying deep-seated problems never before diagnosed—underlying mental or physical conditions which contribute to problems, misjudgment, and misunderstanding. Often the subtle signs of mental illness or disorders are picked up through our daily interactions rather than in counseling sessions.

5. Journal writing and narrative: A daily, guided journaling class engages another modality for gaining self-understanding. Guests assess their lives in writing, later telling their stories. We model by sharing our own stories—pains, disappointments and hurts, major factors of formation. Our openness increases bonding and enhances development of trust. We take Henri Nouwen's stance as wounded healers (1972).

We also write the individual's story, inviting participation and feedback—a crucial step. This affirms we have heard deeply and accurately. It illustrates incongruities in the person's understanding of and owning of his or her own history (e.g., one person "sanitized" the written version of her life, unable to own what she herself had recounted).

6. Physical health: A thorough health history is essential in differential diagnosis. Patients can usually lead their physicians to the correct diagnosis. (The same seems true in counseling. People usually know at a very deep level the truth of hurtful experiences or attitudes which give rise to their dysfunctions.) Helping guests understand how the body is reacting to or generating stress is one of our goals in promoting health through life change. (See Dean Ornish, 1998.)

Health topics include how nutrition, sleep, fitness, and physical needs relate to stress hardiness, emotional well-being, longevity, and productivity. A health-risk profile pinpoints needed changes and reinforce positive behaviors. Meals served model healthy nutrition. Time is provided for exercise, and it is recommended for each person.

7. **Recommendations**: The final report includes comprehensive recommendations in each life dimension for each person (and the organization when relevant). Reports are completed only after the person has reviewed and approved every word. This encourages full honesty about needs, with nothing hidden. It allows the organization to foster healing and development and to correct any systems issues which have contributed to the problem. If a person is self-referred the report goes only to the guest.

8. **Library:** A library serves staff and guests, who are assigned readings based on individual needs.

Transferability of Intensive Care Program

For four years we have offered our program in France, in a cooperative venture with Narramore Christian Foundation and Greater Europe Mission. Born of the requests of missionaries in Europe, the Refresh! program brings together elements of our home programs, plus recreation and children's programs. This has allowed us to transfer the actual program, as well as the principles of care, into an international context.

With a trained staff who share the philosophy, the intensive care program is not "place dependent." Training is offered to persons who want to replicate this program or create similar ones. Our vision is to see a string of sites around the globe where cross-cultural workers can come for intensive care.

Future Programs

We have been offered a lovely mountainside site for the creation of a retreat center. As God provides funds, we anticipate building a center for six-week programs to allow more time to change habits of thoughts, behaviors and relationships and to recoup physical stamina. In this setting we expect to add physical therapy, a sports and fitness program, more music, art, drama and creativity, studios for painting, ceramics, and woodworking, and a garden for recreation and therapy. We would like to add personal appearance counseling and career development assistance.

Suggested Readings

Bonhoeffer, Dietrich. (1954). *Life together*. New York: Harper and Row.

Dodds, L. and Dodds, L. (1999). The role of the Holy Spirit in personality growth and development. *Journal of Psychology and Christianity*, Summer, pp. 129-139.

_____. Stressed from core to cosmos. *Women of the Harvest*, Jan/Feb/March 1998; April/May/June 1998; July/August/Sept. 1998.

_____. 1992. Doctoral dissertation: *The Role of supernatural, spiritual power in personality growth and change*. Dissertation Abstracts International.

Mitchell, J. and Everly, G. (1995). Class notebook for Critical Incident Stress Debriefing. Ellicott City, Maryland: International Critical Incident Stress Foundation, Inc.

Nouwen, H. (1972). *The wounded healer*. New York: Image Books, Doubleday.

Ornish, D. (1998). *Love and survival*. New York: Harper Collins.

Schaeffer, E. (1969). *L'Abri*. Wheaton, IL: Tyndale House.

Lois A. Dodds, Ph. D. and Lawrence E. Dodds, M. D., M. P. H.
Heartstream Resources
101 Herman Lee Circle
Liverpool, PA 17045
E-mail: Heartstream@compuserve.com
Telephone: 717-444-2374
www.heartstreamresources.org

50

Residential Care Facilities

Jeanne Jensma

One option for missionary care is a short or long stay in a residential care facility. A summary of information about seven ministries is presented in an easy-to-read format. It includes the population served, inclusion of family, professional staff, emphases, intensive short-term programs, ongoing programs, availability and length of stay, living arrangements, a summary of distinctives, and contact information.

*T*here are many variables involved in differing models of residential care, and different meanings to the word "residential" as that word is used in missionary-care circles. This chapter will look at definitions of the word "residential," delineate variables related to residential facilities, and give an overview of the distinctives of major North American residential facilities.

The author is clinical director of a residential care organization, ALONGSIDE. (*caps are part of the incorporated name*). ALONGSIDE, Inc., incorporated in 2000, was formerly known as Tuscarora Resource Center (TRC) located in Mt. Bethel, PA. It continues to offer programs and services developed over a number of years under the former organization and moved to Michigan in 2001.

This chapter utilizes survey data from seven organizations offering residential care to missionaries. The survey was not exhaustive but is believed to reflect characteristics of a majority of organizations offering such services. Other facilities located outside North America (some of which have similar characteristics) are not included here.

The Term "Residential"

The term "residential" is used in different ways. In a clinical sense, the word means 24/7 care (24 hours a day, 7 days a week) with a clinical program, constant supervision by professionals, relatively little personal freedom, prepared meals, and housing.

Philhaven Hospital in Mt. Gretna, PA, and Pine Rest Christian Mental Health Services in Grand Rapids, MI, are Christian residential mental health facilities that are available for residential care in the fullest, traditional meaning of the word. These facilities do not specialize in

missionary care, and most of the clinicians would not be familiar with cross-cultural issues, but 24/7 mental health care would be provided in a context friendly to the Christian faith.

Within member-care circles, the word "residential" means a place where counseling, lodging, and either meals or cooking facilities are available, and this is how the word will be used here. Within this understanding, there is much diversity. Below are some of the predominant variables.

Variables in Residential Care of Missionaries

Population Served

- Only or primarily missionaries
- Primarily pastors but also missionaries
- Christian leaders from a variety of contexts including missionaries

Many missionaries have expressed the importance of not having the "general public," even the Christian general public, as part of therapeutic community as it exists in residential facilities. To feel emotionally safe, many missionaries need to know that they will meet only pastors and others in full-time ministry in the therapeutic environment.

Another question is whether the member-care ministry offers services to singles, couples, half-couples (only one spouse comes) or families. Some serve only singles or couples, not accepting half-couples ("If couples do not grow together, they grow apart!"). Some have appropriate facilities and/or programming for children or adolescents. Some offer childcare but not children's programs.

Professional Staff

- No psychiatrists, psychologists or clinical social workers, but other caregivers
- One credentialed mental health professional who provides clinical supervision for unlicensed staff
- Several or all staff fully credentialed
- Mental health professionals complemented by health professional
- (Sometimes) pastor trained in pastoral counseling, spiritual formation, or spiritual direction

Variations in cross-cultural experience of staff:

- Short term visits (2-6 weeks) but no extended international experience
- Experience in another culture for several years, functioning in another language, learning a new way of thinking, values and approaches to life as daily experience
- Extensive cross-cultural experience prepares a mental health professional to minister more effectively to missionaries

Being mission-sensitive is also important. The experience of raising one's own support and living on the support that actually comes in sensitizes the professional to important elements of the missionary experience. Giving up a lucrative position and leaving family and friends contributes to fullness of empathy. Knowing the joys as well as the costs of being a missionary is important. Understanding the commitment that drives missionaries to face sacrifice and potential danger, and experiencing the grace of God that keeps missionaries there when many others would leave – these are at the heart of understanding the person of the missionary. Unless a mental health professional is mission-sensitive in this way, it is possible to mistake spiritual strengths and resources for defense mechanisms or psychopathology.

Another aspect of missions sensitivity is understanding "mission culture" as well as organizational culture. There is a larger "mission culture" which most missions would share, just as we talk about "Asian culture" or "Latin American culture"; but there is also the specific organizational culture of the sending agency to which the missionary belongs. A mental health professional can be of greater help if she or he understands mission culture in general and the specific systemic strengths and weaknesses of the sending agency.

Emphasis of different programs:

- Rest and relaxation, sometimes with counseling available
- Training to maximize effectiveness of missionary's ministry
- Preventive mental-health psychoeducation
- Counseling/therapy to resolve personal problems that have created difficulties: early- or middle-stage restorative work
- In-depth treatment and/or intensive care for missionaries with very serious problems

It is important to understand the needs of the missionary and match those needs to an organization with a corresponding emphasis.

Overall, very little attention is given to preventive mental-health psychoeducation in missionary training, yet a high percentage of avoidable missionary attrition is due to difficulties within the domain of mental, emotional, and relational hygiene. Dedicating several weeks to education and training in developing good mental-health practices and working out personal issues before they become truly problematic is a wise investment on the part of missions.

Programs

- All short-term preventive or restorative programs are nested in residential facilities
- Not all residential facilities offer training/educational or preventive/restorative therapy programs
- May specialize in individual care without offering a larger program
- Primarily preventive with focus on psychoeducation and training
- Primarily restorative with focus on dealing with troublesome issues
- Both restoration and prevention, focusing on current problems in therapy sessions, but providing education and training in other ways
- Emphasis on developing a sense of community (albeit short-lived) as the optimal context in which to foster healing;
- Allow community to spring up, but do not actively foster it

- Discourage fellowship outside of group therapy, so outside socializing does not interfere

The most common troublesome issues for missionaries are marital difficulties, depression and burnout, anger management, sexual addiction or pornography or extramarital affairs, anxiety problems, interpersonal problems, and systemic problems within the mission or between missionary and field leadership.

Where no program exists, the types of counseling offered are generally individual and/or couple therapy, group therapy, pastoral counseling, and bibliotherapy. Where a program exists, it may offer any combination of various therapeutic modalities: individual therapy (for adults, children, and/or adolescents), marital therapy, family therapy, group therapy, milieu therapy (targeting community as an important element of healing), bibliotherapy (utilizing reading materials and audio or videotapes), music/art/creativity therapy, psychoeducational seminars, directed or chosen personal work (such as journaling or aerobic exercise) and devotional and worship times.

Again, it is important to determine which of these factors are the most important for the needs of a given missionary or missionary family in choosing the best program for that person, couple, or family.

Length of Stay
- Longer-term therapy for months or a year or longer
- Short term, as little as a week
- Set programs with inflexible beginning and ending dates
- Set programs which can accommodate early arrivals, later departures, or the need for longer-term counseling after the intensive program ends

Living Arrangements and Meals
There is a wide variation in living arrangements, including
- Different rooms in the same house
- Separate cottages or motel-style units
- Clients/guests to reside in the home(s) of the counselors/staff
- Clients/guests in separate facilities (to maintain more traditional boundaries)
- Guest homes in the community at a nominal cost, but no organizational facilities available
- Arrangements for suitable place to rent in the community while engaging in longer-term therapy.
- Share all or some meals with other guests/clients
- Clients/guests prepare meals and eat alone or as couples or families
- Staff/counselors eat with the guests/clients
- All lodging, eating, and programming under one roof
- Walk or drive a distance from lodging to counseling offices and other program locations

Geographical Location and Physical Aspects of the Setting
- Within easy traveling distance of international airport

- Several hours "out in the boonies"
- Transportation to and from the airport may or may not be provided

Some facilities offer the beauty and serenity of nature, which can be a tremendously restorative element in itself; others exist in the bustle of urban life. Some facilities are attractive, maintaining many "niceties" to surround the missionary with beauty; others focus almost exclusively on functionality.

Overview of Existing North American Residential Restoration Facilities

The following overview of residential care facilities in North America seeks to emphasize the distinctives and salient features of each. Information is based on questionnaires sent to residential mental-health restoration centers for missionaries. Every effort was made to verify information through questionnaires, informational brochures, and e-mails. For ease of comparison, the descriptions are arranged topically.

Change is frequent in the still young field of member care as new developments take place and programs are improved. Thus, the information below may change not only in small facts and numbers, but in concept and structure as well.

A case in point is the ministry of ALONGSIDE, Inc. (ALONGSIDE was incorporated using capital letters, to make it clear that the word is used as a proper noun.)

The ministry was begun in 1984 as Mount Bethel Christian Ministries. Later, it became known as "Tuscarora Resource Center." It began as a ministry of rest and relaxation for pastors of one denomination. Early in its history, ALONGSIDE opened its doors to missionaries, became an interdenominational ministry, and added a strong counseling component. Within a few years, 70% of those served were missionaries.

Programming emphasizes a 3-week intensive counseling retreat in addition to longer-term counseling. In 2000 the ministry was restructured and named ALONGSIDE. In 2002 it moved to the Midwest in order to be closer geographically to the primary mission boards using its services.

Throughout the changes, there has been stability of core counseling personnel (mental health professionals with years of missions experience), programming (residential counseling with or without a 3-week intensive restoration program), and purpose (to provide spiritual, mental, and emotional caregiving services to missionaries, pastors, and their families, for personal wholeness and ministry effectiveness).

Though many changes occur in the relatively young field of member care, there is continuity at the core. God is at work, developing and honing residential services for missionaries.

Population Served

ALONGSIDE	Missionaries and pastors
Godspeed Missionary Care	Missionaries; pastors also welcome
Heartstream Resources	Cross-cultural workers, primarily missionaries
Link Care Center	Missionaries; pastors also welcome
Marble Retreat	Pastors; missionaries also welcome
Missionary Health Institute (MHI)	Missionaries
Mission Training International (MTI)	Missionaries

Inclusion of Family

ALONGSIDE	Children welcome; childcare available
Godspeed	Children welcome but no childcare provided
Heartstream	Adults only
Link Care	Children welcome; childcare available; some children's programming available (about an hour a day)
Marble	Adults only; if married, must attend as a couple
MHI	Children welcome but no childcare provided
MTI	Whole family required; full programming for children and adolescents, paralleling adult program

Professional staff

ALONGSIDE	Licensed psychologists; all personnel have extensive ministry and cross-cultural experience
Godspeed	Board-certified psychiatrist; nurse; counselors; pastoral counselor
Heartstream	Certified counselors; board-certified physician; all personnel have extensive ministry and cross-cultural experience
Link Care	Board-certified psychiatrist; licensed psychologists; pastoral counselor
Marble	Board-certified psychiatrist; licensed therapists
MHI	Physician with extensive ministry and cross-cultural experience; counselor
MTI	No mental health professionals providing direct service; CEO is a licensed psychologist

Emphases

ALONGSIDE	Psychological assessment; problem resolution via short- or long-term counseling and/or intensive program; (3-week "Restoration and Growth Sabbatical"); therapeutic community
Godspeed	Psychiatric assessment; problem resolution via short-term counseling
Heartstream	Cross-cultural training; problem resolution via 2-week intensive program ("Intensive Care Program"); therapeutic community
Link Care	Psychiatric and psychological assessment; Problem resolution via short- or long-term counseling as part of ongoing program ("Program of Restoration and Personal Growth"); pastoral counseling; therapeutic community
Marble	Psychiatric assessment; problem resolution via 2-week intensive program (Marble Retreat Program); therapeutic community
MHI	Physical and psychiatric assessment; problem resolution via short- or long-term counseling; psychoeducation via MK retreats

MTI   Psychoeducation via intensive 5-day program "Debriefing and Renewal" for furloughees; community (A variety of pre-field training programs and other special events for missionaries form the majority of emphases.)

Intensive Short-term Program

ALONGSIDE   "Restoration and Growth Sabbatical," a 3-week intensive program combining the following elements each day: 1 hour of individual/marital/family therapy; 2 hours of psychoeducation; 1 hour of group therapy; community devotional time; fellowship; bibliotherapy; directed or chosen personal work; milieu therapy. Each day offers 4-5 hours of structured therapeutic programming. Fees: Approximately $3700/family for first three weeks and $500/week thereafter. Price does not include meals.

Godspeed   No intensive short-term therapy program

Heartstream   "Intensive Care Program," a 2-week intensive program combining the following elements each day: 1 hour of individual counseling; several hours of psychoeducation; community devotional time; fellowship; creative arts therapies; bibliotherapy; directed or chosen personal work; milieu therapy. At least 6 hours of each day is structured with therapeutic programming. Cost: Approximately $1000/person for 12-day program. Includes meals.

Link Care   No intensive short-term therapy program, but missionaries may participate in the ongoing therapy program for the time they are on campus, even if only for a few weeks. Approximately 2 hours a day is structured with therapeutic programming. Cost: approximately $3700 - $4500 for a family for the first month and $1000 less per month thereafter. Price does not include meals.

Marble   The Marble Retreat program is a 2-week intensive program of 3 hours of group therapy each day and 2 individual sessions each week. Each day includes 3-4 hours of programming, almost all of it group therapy. Fees: $2500 per person for 12-day program; $700 discount for missionaries. Includes meals.

MHI   No short-term intensive therapy program, though regular office-based counseling is available

MTI   "Debriefing and Renewal," a 5-day intensive program of psychoeducation, devotional times, debriefing, and community. Intended for non-complicated re-entry (no trauma or major issues needing professional counseling). Fees: Approximately $1100/couple, $1300 - $1700/family for the 5-day program. Includes meals.

Ongoing Program

ALONGSIDE   No continuous ongoing program, but those staying long-term may repeat the short-term program as often as they choose, paying only for group and personal therapy Repeated psycho-educational seminars are at no charge, as are devotions, fellowship, milieu therapy, etc.

Godspeed	No ongoing program
Heartstream	No ongoing program

Link Care   "Program of Restoration and Personal Growth" offers individual/marital/family therapy 3-4 hours a week, group therapy once a week, and pastoral counseling once a week for adults, plus fellowship, bibliotherapy, directed or chosen personal work; offers kids' club 3 times a week (2-3 hours each time) for children; childcare can be arranged. Approximately 2 hours a day is structured with therapeutic programming. Cost: approximately $3700 - $4500 for a family for the first month and $1000 less per month thereafter. Price does not include meals.

Marble	No ongoing program
MHI	No ongoing program
MTI	No ongoing program

Availability; Length of stay

ALONGSIDE   Arrive/depart any time; participation in at least one 3-week short-term intensive program highly encouraged during stay. Length of stay usually 3-4 weeks but when necessary can extend to many months or even a year or longer.

Godspeed   Arrive/depart when personnel are available (often overseas) according to pre-arrangement. Length of stay usually a week or less.

Heartstream   Arrive/depart primarily around intensive program dates, but counselors are available at other times when Stateside. Length of stay usually twelve days or a bit longer.

Link Care   Arrive/depart any time to enter and exit ongoing program at missionary convenience. Length of stay sometimes only a month, often longer, occasionally a year or longer as necessary.

Marble	Arrive/depart according to intensive program dates. Length of stay twelve days.
MHI	Arrive/depart any time that is pre-arranged. Length of stay varies according to need.
MTI	Arrive/depart on program dates for DAR program. Length of stay five days.

Living arrangements/meals

ALONGSIDE	Individual cottages and efficiency motel units on campus, each with its own kitchen; meals on your own
Godspeed	Housing can be arranged off-campus; meals on your own
Heartstream	All meals together with staff
Link Care	Apartments with kitchens on campus, meals on your own
Marble	Suites in one house; all meals together
MHI	Bed and breakfast facility; breakfast together
MTI	Hotel-style rooms and suites; all meals together

Summary of Distinctives

ALONGSIDE Combines individual/marital/family therapy with group therapy and psychoeducational seminars on a daily basis for its 3-week intensive therapy program, all conducted by licensed mental health professionals, all of whom have had extensive ministry and cross-cultural experience.

Godspeed Primarily serves missionaries overseas. Available for consultation and services Stateside by pre-arrangement. Helps find community housing.

Heartstream Combines individual/marital counseling with psychoeducational seminars and creative therapies on a daily basis, all conducted by counselors who have had extensive ministry and cross-cultural experience. Special emphasis on physical health and environmental beauty.

Link Care Combines daily individual/marital/family therapy with weekly group therapy and weekly pastoral counseling, all conducted by licensed mental health professionals on an ongoing basis.

Marble Primarily offers group therapy, with four individual therapy sessions during the 2-week program; therapeutic community.

MHI Assesses missionaries from a medical and mental health perspective and provides medical treatment and counseling, conducted by physicians and counselors, most of whom have extensive ministry and cross-cultural experience.

MTI Debriefs missionaries upon re-entry in a 5-day program intended to help maximize the health and effectiveness of home assignment ministry. Is one program out of several designed for missionary training.

Contact Information

ALONGSIDE
P.O. Box 587
Richland, MI 49083-0587
(269)671-4809
info@alongsidecares.org
www.alongsidecares.org

Godspeed Missionary Care
P.O. Box 1754
Easton, MD 21601
(410)819-0497
info@missionarycare.org
www.missionarycare.org

Heartstream Resources
101 Herman Lee Circle
Liverpool, PA 17045
(717)444-2374
heartstream@compuserve.com

Link Care Center
1734 W. Shaw Ave.
Fresno, CA 93711-3416
(559)439-5920
KenRoyer@aol.com
www.linkcare.org

Marble Retreat
139 Bannockburn
Marble, CO 81623
(970)963-2499
mretreat@compuserve.com
www.marbleretreat.org

Missionary Health Institute
4000 Leslie St.
Willowdale, ON M2K 2R9
CANADA
(416)494-7512
mhiims@attglobal.net

Mission Training International   (800) 896-3710
P. O. Box 50110   info@mti.org
Palmer Lake, CO 80133   www.mti.org

Postscript: Overseas Residential Care Centers

There are differing opinions among mental health professionals regarding the appropriateness and feasibility of creating and maintaining overseas residential care centers. Those who expressed the strongest views regarding the need for such centers are care providers based in the United States but who spend significant time ministering to missionaries on host-culture soil.

North American mental health professionals based overseas were more cautious. They indicated a great need for preventive psychoeducational training, for dealing with marital and/or personal difficulties in the early stages, and for critical incident debriefing and counseling. These are their main priorities and do not require a residential restoration campus. Treating clients with major difficulties would require a disproportionate amount of time and preclude much of the preventive and early-stage restorative work which pays the greatest dividends. These veterans emphasized the importance of sending missionaries back to North America for in-depth help whenever the problem is fairly serious.

By our expanded definition of "residential care," however, the Tumaini Counseling Centre (sometimes referred to as AIM Care) in Nairobi, Kenya, could be considered residential. (Tumaini is the Swahili word for "Hope.") It is a cooperative ministry of AIM and SIL. Tumaini offers services to missionaries who come to Nairobi for mental health care—missionaries from 29 countries of Africa representing over 100 different mission agencies.

Some go to Tumaini for a one-time evaluation or consultation, others make repeat visits, and some relocate temporarily to Nairobi. Missionaries stay in mission guest houses or with friends. If they need to relocate for more than 2-3 weeks, the Tumaini staff assists them in locating homes in Nairobi that are temporarily available for house-sitting. Tumaini Counseling Centre's e-mail address is:

supervisor_aim-care@aimint.org

Conclusion

No single center is "right" for every person, couple, or mission board in all circumstances. It is also important to note that these centers are dynamic. What distinguishes each at the time of this writing might be different from what characterizes it later—such is the nature of this young and growing field of missionary care. It is incumbent upon mission administrators and missionaries themselves to identify the specific needs and the factors that will best contribute to meeting those needs and to choose a restoration center accordingly. Hopefully this chapter is of help in making these identifications and in serving as a springboard for further research, to the end of restoring many missionaries to personal wholeness and ministry effectiveness.

Part VIII

Ethics and Professional Standards

51

Ethical Principles for Mental Health Work with Missionaries

Jarrett Richardson

Mental health professionals working in missions often find themselves in situations where ethical boundaries and practice are unclear. This chapter presents general ethical principles which are common to all the helping professions. Origins of ethical standards based on the Ten Commandments of the Old Testament and the teachings of Jesus in the New Testament are discussed along with their application to work in missions.

Ethical Tasks for Mental Health Professionals Working with Missionaries

- Define accountability, responsibility, roles and boundaries
- Assure professional behavior with competence for providing standard of care
- Understand and implement the duties of beneficence, nonmaleficence, respect for contextual autonomy
- Commit to truth-telling and informed consent

Introduction

The above tasks provide a broad scope for setting excellent ethical boundaries. Yet, when working with missionaries and mission agencies, the mental health provider is faced with many situations that are unexpected and, realistically, could not have been anticipated. In spite of the best efforts at defining roles and limits and clarifying expectations, the person working with mental health issues in missions will be called upon to be as flexible and creative as are missionaries.

However, most of the ethical difficulties that arise can be anticipated and planned for, and a good faith effort to do so during the initial phases of establishing a relationship with missionaries and mission agencies usually leads to mutually acceptable resolutions.

A leading writer about consulting says that what happens at the beginning of a consulting relationship is often a hologram of how the whole experience will go.

"The personal interaction between the consultant and the client during the initial contracting meetings is an accurate predictor of how the project itself will proceed." (Peter Block in *Flawless Consulting: A guide to getting your expertise used*, p. 69).

Role Definition

Attention at the beginning of discussions to the many "hats" that a mental health worker may be asked to wear may save a significant amount of distress later. Defining as carefully as possible when each role is to be taken and who is responsible for deciding when various roles are taken can prepare all concerned for each stage of the relationship.

The mental health worker is often asked to operate as a consultant and therapist to individuals, couples, families, local teams, country teams, regional leadership, organizations and organizational leadership, churches and sending agencies. He or she may be asked to function in a role that is primarily identified as personnel, human resources, advisor, intervener, screener, troubleshooter, or therapist. While working, the roles may change imperceptibly from those of personnel representative to consultant to therapist, and this may be somewhat confusing for the "consumers" as well as the mental health worker.

Questions to help define roles and functions

- Who initiated the contact with the mental health professional?
- Who "owns" the process?
- Who controls the process and information?
- Who controls the confidentiality?
- What boundaries of confidentiality are needed and agreed upon?
- What are the limits of the contact?
- To whom is the mental health worker accountable for each part of the interaction?
- What ongoing commitment is each person making?
- Who has overall responsibility for maintaining the relationship?
- Who is able to terminate the relationship and under what circumstances?

Competence

The more complex the relationships and issues, the more important is the competence, experience, and ethical sensitivity of the mental health worker. Often skills are demanded that are not part of the usual practice and training of the mental health worker, and it should be made clear to all concerned when this happens. Basic skills common to all mental health work can often be applied to new and unexpected situations, but it is wise to acknowledge when the approaches and techniques applied are utilized as a pragmatic attempt to be helpful rather than as part of a proven approach or a professional standard of care.

One way to guarantee that recognition of the authenticity and effectiveness of mental health work will be undermined is for incompetent practitioners (however well intended) to provide services. A poor reputation developed by one mental health worker will affect the work of all others, as it is very hard to undo damage to the reputation of a profession. Although well-qualified providers do not always provide *successful* service, the presence of peer review, accountability to a certifying organization, and standards against which the practitioner can be measured for professional and ethical service will help preserve the trust of those we attempt to serve.

If ethical roots are kept in mind, and ethical codes to which we are accountable are readily available, mental health workers and those with whom we work will be better able to navigate the complexities that we will inevitably face.

Standard of Care

In order to partner with missionaries, sending agencies, and churches in the Great Commission, mental health professionals need guidelines regarding the standard of care to which they can be held accountable. Explicit definitions of their work and relationships will provide clarity of expectations for all involved.

Every professional will have participated in training and competency certification as part of their formal preparation. Most will have undergone supervised mentorship designed to assure that the practice and application of their knowledge and skills meets professional standards.

Although there are a wide variety of approaches to mental health assessment and care, every secular professional discipline has defined a core set of standards that has many similarities to standards of other disciplines. These standards carry the weight of commandments in that the privilege of practicing the profession is dependent on adherence, with little or no variance accepted. There are groups of peers (and at times consumers) who are responsible for interpreting and enforcing the standards and who hold the final authority when conflict arises over the professional's behavior and practice. Most of the standards are published and updated regularly by professional organizations and are part of the public domain, available to anyone who wants to know what they can expect from a professional practitioner.

General Ethical Principles for All Professionals

General ethical principles for all mental health professions include statements related to the following areas:

- **Competence**
- **Virtues** (such as integrity, compassion, courage and patience)
- Professional and scientific **responsibility**
- **Respect** for the rights and dignity of the client or patient
- Concern for the **welfare of others**
- The **social responsibility** of the practitioner as it relates to justice in the provision of professional service (resource allocation and distributive justice)

These principles are derived from the positive values of beneficence, nonmaleficence, and respect for the autonomy of the client/patient (which include rules for truth-telling and informed consent).

The primary environment in which ethical principles are applied is within relationships. The nature and definition of the specific relationship (or in some cases several relationships) is living and dynamic, and requires active participation by all parties involved. No relationship is one-sided, but the professional has the greater burden of responsibility for creating and maintaining the therapeutic relationship. Professionals hold each other to very high standards which honor the trust given to them by society and their clients or patients.

Origins of Ethical Standards

The history of the origins of ethical standards can in most cases be traced to ancient medical oaths and commitments, with some changes in emphasis as well as the adoption of new concepts as a particular profession has developed over many years. The cultural, philosophical, and religious underpinnings of ethics are complex and responsive to changes in society, but are also rooted in Biblical teachings.

Old Testament Principles

- Have no other gods before the One True God (First, Second, and Third Commandments)
- Keep balance (Fourth Commandment)
- Honor authority (Fifth Commandment)
- Avoid injury/do no harm (Sixth, Seventh, and Eighth commandments)
- Tell the truth (Ninth commandment)
- Avoid coveting power (Tenth commandment)

One set of core Biblical ethical teachings is the Ten Commandments (Exodus 20:1-17). For the Christian mental health practitioner, organizing ethical principles according to this God-given model may help to locate secular ethics within the faith context of the practitioner and client or patient.

First, Second, and Third Commandments: Exodus 20:1-7

The first three commandments emphasize that we are to have *no other gods* (including science and profession) before the One True God. Ultimately, we are *accountable* to God, and it is in that context that we build all other relationships. Our primary commitment in life is to love and be obedient to God. Therefore, if we find that our profession and its values come into conflict with God's values, we must be prepared to recognize and resolve those conflicts and communicate those issues clearly to those we serve.

God is the source of all truth, but humankind is capable of producing approximations of truth that can be misleading and destructive. Any discovered knowledge (knowledge discovered through research and theoretical investigation) that is *true* will not conflict with the nature of God as he has revealed himself, or the nature of humanity as God has revealed it in his Word. Although we are a little lower than the angels and crowned with glory and honor (Ps 8:5), we are never equal with God, and though we are redeemed we are still sinners and fallible. Trust in anything other than God's word for the final word of truth is folly.

At times there may be pressure to conform to human standards and behavior that do not call us to the highest good that God has revealed. At those times we need to be prepared to choose clearly whom we will serve, and to be able to articulate the reason we serve a higher commission than that of our secular profession. We must not stand behind our professional ethics if they conflict with obedience to God, but at the same time we should not use our service to God's cause as an excuse for exhibiting less than the highest professional behavior.

Fourth Commandment: Exodus 20:8-11

As we are true to our Maker in understanding the importance of *Sabbath*, we are accountable to keep *balance* between our professional, personal, and spiritual lives, and not to pridefully overvalue the work we do. The Sabbath principal, as modeled by God the Creator, affects the practitioner and everyone we serve. We need to model the Biblical guidance for righteous and healthy living in the way we live and work among those we serve. The same is true for the scientific guidance we have learned and recommend.

We may choose to behave in the relationships we undertake in ways that are *counter* to the missionary *culture* we serve. Even if we do this for good reason, we must be sensitive to the cross-cultural aspects of applying mental health principles to the mission and national cultures. It is important not to impose a psychological view of the world on people who do not share that view. Placing our mental health work in the context of Biblical revelation and making it subject to scriptural teaching is part of the balance we strive for when we take psychological thought into the context of missions.

Fifth Commandment: Exodus 20:12

The commandment to *honor* parents and others in *authority* reminds us that we owe what knowledge and skill we have to our teachers and mentors. It also validates the principle that we are subject to peer review and the standards of our professions. This commandment also reminds us that we serve at the pleasure of our client or the organization and that we need to be subject to their needs and principles as well as our own. We should not have an agenda that is counter to that of those whom we serve, and if such conflicts arise we must address the issues clearly and reach a mutually acceptable resolution before we proceed.

An unfortunate situation can arise when members of an organization attribute more power and influence to us than is authorized by or given to the rightful leadership. This can lead to covert and overt miscommunication and at times undermine the effectiveness of our work over the long term. We should define as clearly as possible the limits of our willingness to be subject to the mission authorities. This will not only make the "contract" a clear point of reference, but will allow us to know when we can no longer ethically work in a particular context.

Sixth, Seventh, and Eighth Commandments: Exodus 20:13-15

The commandments to *avoid injuring* or damaging those we serve is the root of the principle to *above all do no harm*, including the critical principle of preservation of confidentiality. This commandment also reminds us not to offer services for which we do not have expertise and experience. We must not misrepresent our knowledge and skill, and should defer to those who do have the requisite competencies when they can be made available.

This commandment also reminds us to be accountable for the nature and consequences of our service. When there is a scientific basis for what we know and the skills we have learned, we are to apply the state of the art or science to every possible situation. We are to maintain the highest level of professional expertise as the basis for what we do, and avoid the pressure to depart from appropriate standards. When we lack special expertise that is needed, we are to make that clear to the client or patient and offer to help obtain more appropriate assistance if possible.

Maintaining competency certification, licensure, appropriate supervision, and continuing education are a few of the ways we can minimize the risk that we will actually do harm when we set out to do good. It is easy to wander from the appropriate professional standard of care when we are out of our usual context. Peer accountability is often difficult to maintain when we serve missionaries and mission agencies in far-flung places, but this makes it all the more important to pursue excellence and avoid idiosyncratic ways of practice.

Ninth Commandment: Exodus 20:16

The commandment to **tell the truth** holds us to honesty and openness with our clients or patients about our abilities and limitations and guides us away from selfish ambition. It also helps us avoid becoming involved in deceitful relationships with individuals or organizations. We must disclose to those we serve what, if any, allegiance we have that may create a conflict of interest between our work with them and another client or patient.

We need to establish clear lines of authority and clear boundaries around the work we do. If we are responsible to an organization for the our work, we need to define how the information we are privileged to know will be managed, and to whom it will be available. We need to keep appropriate records of what we do and make certain that they meet the standards of our profession and any other authority involved, and that the appropriate confidentiality will be assured. The ownership of information usually belongs to the client or patient, though the actual records may belong to the professional or to an organization to which is delegated the responsibility for their preservation and utilization.

In our eagerness to serve, we may be vulnerable to laxity in these important guidelines of professional activity. The best interest of those we serve is seldom fostered by well-intentioned but ill-prepared or inexperienced efforts.

Tenth Commandment: Exodus 20:17

The commandment to **avoid coveting** applies to the importance of refraining from seeking power or influence that is not appropriate to the relationship in which we have engaged. We have particular responsibilities to the vulnerable, especially when our professional role places the client or patient in a dependent relationship with us. We are not to allow ourselves to exercise undue influence in the lives of individuals, families, or organizations that rely on us for professional expertise.

Professional jealousy or "turf wars" seldom help those we serve, rarely reflect well on our professions, and never honor God. The example that Jesus set for us in humility and selfless service should be our standard, and if we find ourselves caught up in personal ambition we should seek wise supervision and counsel to avoid harm to ourselves and those whom we seek to serve.

Ethical principles organized on the model of the Ten Commandments provide a reliable guide for the Christian mental health professional. In many other places the

Old Testament provides extensive, detailed further lists of behavioral standards for almost every aspect of life for the Israelites, though none surpassed the original dramatic revelation of God's will and guidance to Moses on Mt. Sinai.

In our effort to strictly keep to high ethical standards we may be prone to focus on the "do-nots" so much that we lose sight of the rest of the character of God. In Isaiah 55 God also provided a message of refreshment and replenishment for his people in their obedience. God invites all who are thirsty, hungry and poor to delight in the richest of fare in an everlasting covenant of God's fully satisfying and faithful love, mercy, and joy—freely offered to his obedient children for the asking.

New Testament Principles

We have *a higher set of standards* and guidelines from the New Testament that provide principles which can complete and expand the basic legal approach of the Old Testament.

Avoiding Externalism and Legalism

Our Lord Jesus spoke extensively about high standards based on the importance of avoiding externalism and legalism that are empty and meaningless if they do not reflect a genuine internal reality. He calls us to much more than meeting the minimal requirements of the law or behavioral standards.

Righteousness that surpasses that of the law

Jesus invites us to a righteousness that surpasses that of the law. In the accounts of the "Sermon on the Mount," recorded in Matthew 5, 6, and 7, Jesus emphasizes several admonitions to avoid meeting the letter of the law while ignoring the spirit of the law. He does not advise against observing the law, but insists that we avoid hypocritical legalism focused on gaining external praise (even the praise of God) while internally violating the meaning behind the rules.

Through these passages he moves from the most egregious behavior—murder, adultery, divorce, revenge, swearing and materialism—to more religious behaviors such as generosity, prayer, and fasting. In each case Jesus contrasts the obvious external sin with the reality he expects us to experience internally. As he admonishes us to fulfill the law with internal consistency, he recognizes that we cannot meet the requirements on our own power, and he promises the Spirit who will help and guide and comfort us.

New Testament Guiding Principles

In the Word of God's New Covenant there are guiding principles that can help us through the most perplexing circumstances that we face in serving God's missionaries.

Love is the foundation for righteousness. In the gospel of John, chapters 13-15, Jesus teaches us that love is the foundation for righteousness. Only in humility, dependence, and sacrificial service will we be able to successfully undertake a truly ethical practice. As we regard others as better than ourselves we will begin to treat them as Christ has treated us and be the channels of peace and healing that only come through him. As we are known as those who love one another, we will be able to enter into deep and trusting relationships with other children of God. Holding missionaries and mission agencies to this high standard is part of our service to them.

Conflict management. In Matthew 18 Jesus teaches us that we must honor the brothers and sisters with whom we have conflicts by working things out with them face to face before bringing in others to help find resolution. He teaches the power of several faithful people working as a group to reach conflict resolution, and he includes the church as a vital part of resolving differences. (Matthew 18:15-20) In this passage we are given a model of how to maintain our integrity and our commitment to ourselves, another individual, a smaller, more intimate group and the local congregation or group at large by managing conflict in a God-oriented context. There are no boundaries for God's involvement in every level of relationship, and we as Christian mental health workers have his ultimate truth and justice as our reference.

Mutuality in communication. Our Lord also modeled and taught the necessity of mutuality in communication and problem solving. He insisted that the Pharisees answer his questions as part of the dialogue that they intended for his harm. (Luke 20:1-8) He did not allow them to abdicate their part of the responsibility for effective, honest, and fruitful communication. Seldom did he answer a question with an answer that would "let them off the hook" of their need to be consistent with their own standards and their responsibility to seek and recognize truth.

Address point of need. Jesus dealt with people at their real point of need, not only with what was publicly manifest. In some cases he sought out and addressed those who had needs, as when he called to Zacchaeus and went into his "turf" in order to redeem his deepest need. (Luke 19:2) The woman with the chronic hemorrhage, the rich young ruler, and many others sought him out for what they *thought* were their greatest needs, but he identified and responded to deeper and more important needs.

Mutual responsibility. As Jesus addressed people's physical, emotional, relational, and spiritual needs, he expected sufferers to accept some degree of responsibility for their healing and their ongoing health. He asked for change within the person as well as in the individual's behavior, and related the present healing to eternal healing. As we seek to help those he has called to serve him in missions, it is easy to empathize with them as we recognize what they have sacrificed to serve. This empathy can tempt us to hold them less accountable for their behavior than we do others, but we actually devalue their human and divine nature if we do this. Insisting that each person accept responsibility for their part in healing is the highest complement we can pay them and their Creator.

Grace. Grace is the essential distinctive of all Christians. In all of our dealings, personal and professional, we are indebted to our Lord for his undeserved and boundless grace toward us. In humility we recognize that we and all other humans are equally in need of God's grace. Only as we recognize our identity in Christ and dependence on him for all things are we able to experience his grace in our lives and relationships. Our professional work has no less obligation to grace than our personal lives. Our expertise must be surrounded by and imbedded in our identity in Christ if we are to be true to his purposes.

Conclusion

When mental health professionals seek to serve the cause of Christ by serving missionaries and mission agencies, we are following in the steps of Dr. Luke and many others who were an essential part of the success of the earliest mission teams. Our role as servants to those who are on the front lines in Satan's territory make us vulnerable to Satan's attacks on a personal and professional level.

By pursuing consistency with the commandments that provide external guidelines for our behavior, and the teachings that provide internal guidelines for our hearts and minds, we can be equipped to behave ethically and effectively. If we neglect either the internal or external dimensions of our calling, we make ourselves and our professions vulnerable to losing our moral and ethical validity and with that our effectiveness. By being faithful to our Lord and his Word and seeking to follow the expectations of our calling as professionals, we are most likely to be able to do our part in fulfilling the Great Commission.

52

Professional Codes of Ethics

Jarrett Richardson

As a companion piece to the previous chapter on ethical principles, extensive excerpts from "Ethical Principles of Psychologists and Code of Conduct" are presented, as well as brief excerpts from codes of conduct for marriage and family therapists, pastoral counselors, social workers, and psychiatrists. The excerpts chosen highlight issues of particular importance to work with missionaries.

*T*he following are summaries of applicable codes of ethics for mental health professionals and may serve as useful references for those involved in clinical work, consulting, and employment testing.

> **Universal General Principles**
> * **Competence**
> * **Integrity**
> * **Professional and scientific responsibility**
> * **Respect for people's rights and dignity**
> * **Concern for others' welfare**
> * **Social responsibility**

Every profession that licenses practitioners has published codes of ethics that have developed from the tradition and history of the profession. Although each professional group has some values and commitments that are unique, there are principles and values common to all professions based on universally accepted understanding of the nature of the helper and the inherent value of the person being helped.

The author of this chapter reviewed the published codes of ethics of most professional organizations whose members would be represented among those who care for missionaries or consult with mission organizations. The principle used to select components of each code was to highlight the basic values and to provide detail where it applies to this particular professional practice.

The material presented here is not intended to be comprehensive or exhaustive. The excerpts are chosen by the author to highlight certain issues of particular importance to work with missionaries and do not represent the whole of the professional codes. They are to be used as general references, and the reader is referred to the original complete publications for the complete legal statements by each profession. Of particular note is the fact that most of these professional codes insist that adherents manage personal lives in a healthful fashion and seek appropriate assistance for their own personal problems or conflicts. This acceptance of fallibility and statement of humility underlines the fact that it is the persons involved in healing relationships that are of central importance.

Because the majority of those involved in the mental health care of missionaries are trained as psychologists, the **Psychologists' Code of Conduct** is most extensively excerpted. This code also is the most comprehensive and detailed with respect to the issues most likely to be considered in work with missionaries and mission agencies.

"Ethical Principles of Psychologists and Code of Conduct" published in *American Psychologist*, December 1992, outlines the **General Principles** of Competence, Integrity, Professional and Scientific Responsibility, Respect for People's Rights and Dignity, Concern for Others' Welfare, and Social Responsibility. There are several components that are of particular interest to those working with missionaries and missions agencies. Principles are abstracted and summarized here; numerical references will help interested readers find the original language.

1. General Standards

1.03 Professional and Scientific Relationships . . . Provide . . . services only in the context of a defined professional or scientific relationship or role.

1.04 Boundaries of Competence

(a) . . . provide services . . . within the boundaries of their competence based on their education, training, supervised experience, or appropriate professional experience.

(b) . . . provide services . . . in new areas or involving new techniques only after first undertaking appropriate study, training, supervision, and/or consultation from persons who are competent in those areas or techniques

(c) In those emerging areas in which generally recognized standards for preparatory training do not yet exist, psychologists nevertheless take reasonable steps to ensure the competence of their work and to protect . . . others from harm.

1.05 Maintaining Expertise . . . maintain a reasonable level of awareness of current scientific and professional information . . . and undertake ongoing efforts to maintain competence in the skills they use.

1.06 Basis for Scientific and Professional Judgements . . . rely on scientifically and professionally derived knowledge. . . .

1.07 Describing the Nature and Results of Psychological Services . . . using language that is reasonably understandable to the recipient of those services, appropriate information beforehand about the nature of such services and appropriate information later about results and conclusions.

1.08 Human Differences . . . Where differences . . . significantly affect psychologist's work concerning particular individuals or groups, psychologists obtain the training, experience, consultation, or supervision necessary to ensure the competence of their services or they make appropriate referrals.

1.09 Respecting Others. In work-related activities, psychologists respect the rights of others to hold values, attitudes, and opinions that differ from their own.

1.13 Personal Problems and Conflicts

(a) Psychologists recognize that their personal problems and conflicts may interfere with their effectiveness. . . . .refrain from undertaking an activity when they know or should know that their personal problems are likely to lead to harm to. . . .person to whom they may owe a professional or scientific obligation.

(b) . . . obligation to be alert . . . obtain assistance for their personal problems at an early stage, in order to prevent significantly impaired performance

(c) . . . take appropriate measures . . . and determine whether they should limit, suspend, or terminate their work-related duties.

1.14 Avoiding Harm . . . take reasonable steps to avoid harming those . . . with whom they work, and to minimize harm where it is foreseeable and unavoidable.

1.15 Misuse of Psychologists' Influence . . . be alert to and guard against personal, financial organizational, or political factors that might lead to misuse of their influence.

1.16 Misuse of Psychologists' Work . . . do not participate . . . likely that their skills or data will be misused by others. . . .

1.17 Multiple Relationships

(a) . . . refrains from entering into or promising another. . . relationship if it appears likely that such a relationship might impair . . . objectivity . . . effective(ness) . . . or exploit the other party.

(c) if . . . A potentially harmful multiple relationship has arisen . . . attempt to resolve . . . best interest of the affected person.

1.21 Third-Party Requests for Services

(a) . . . clarifies to the extent feasible, at the outset . . . the nature of the relationship with each party . . . includes the role of the psychologist (therapist, organizational consultant, diagnostician, or expert witness), the probable uses of the services . . . or information, and the fact that there may be limitations to confidentiality.

(b) If there is a foreseeable risk of the psychologist's being called upon to perform conflicting roles because of the involvement of a third party, the psychologist clarifies the nature and direction of his or her responsibilities, keeps all parties appropriately informed as matters develop, and resolves the situation in accordance with this Ethics Code.

1.23 Documentation of Professional and Scientific Work

(a) . . . appropriately document . . . work . . . in order to facilitate provision of services later . . . to ensure accountability, and to meet the requirements of institutions or the law.

2. *Evaluation, Assessment, or Intervention*

2.01 Evaluation, Diagnosis, and Interventions in Professional Context

(a) . . . perform evaluations, diagnostic services, or interventions only within the context of a defined professional relationship.

(b) . . . based on information and techniques (including personal interviews of the individual when appropriate) sufficient to provide appropriate substantiation for their findings.

2.02 Competence and Appropriate Use of Assessments and Interventions.

(a) . . . in a manner and for purposes that are appropriate in light of the research on or evidence of the usefulness and proper application of the techniques.

(b) . . . refrain from misuse of . . . and take reasonable steps to prevent others from misusing the information the information . . . includes refraining from releasing raw test results . . . to persons other than to patients of clients as appropriate, who are not qualified to use such information.

2.04 Use of Assessment in General and With Special Populations.

(a) . . . familiar with the reliability, validation, and related standardization . . . and proper applications and uses of, the techniques they use.

(b) . . . recognize limits to the certainty with which diagnoses, judgements, or predictions can be made about individuals.

(c) . . . attempt to identify situations in which particular interventions of assessment techniques or norms may not be applicable or may require adjustment in administration or interpretation because of factors such as individuals' gender, age, race, ethnicity, national origin, religion, sexual orientation, disability, language, or socioeconomic status.

2.05 Interpreting Assessment Results . . . taking into account the various test factors and characteristics of the person being assessed that might affect psychologists' judgement or reduce the accuracy of their interpretations. They indicate any significant reservations they have about the accuracy or limitations of their interpretations.

2.06 Unqualified Persons . . . do not promote the use of psychological assessment techniques by unqualified persons

2.07 Obsolete Tests and Outdated Test Results

(a) . . . Do not base . . . on data or test results that are outdated for the current purpose.

(b) . . . or on tests and measures that are obsolete and not useful for the current purpose.

2.09 Explaining Assessment Results. Unless the nature of the relationship is clearly explained to the person being assessed in advance and precludes provision of an explanation of results, . . . ensure that an explanation of the results is provided using language that is reasonably understandable to the person assessed or to another legally authorized person.

2.10 Maintaining Test Security . . . make reasonable efforts to maintain the integrity and security of tests and other assessment techniques consistent with the law, contractual obligations, and in a manner that permits compliance with the requirements of this Ethics Code.

4.　*Therapy*

4.01 Structuring the Relationship

4.02 Informed Consent to Therapy . . . implies that the person (1) has the capacity to consent, (2) has been informed of significant information concerning the procedure, (3) has freely and without undue influence expressed consent, and (4) consent has been appropriately documented, . . . and seek their assent, consider such persons' preferences and best interests.

4.03 Couple and Family Relationships

(a) . . . clarify at the outset (1) which of the individuals are patients or clients, and (2) the relationship the psychologist will have with each person.

(b) As soon as it becomes apparent that the psychologist may be called on to perform potentially conflicting roles, the psychologist attempts to clarify and adjust or withdraw from, roles appropriately.

4.09 Terminating the Professional Relationship . . . do not abandon patients or clients.

5. *Privacy and Confidentiality*
5.01 Discussing the Limits of Confidentiality

(a) . . . discuss . . . (1) the relevant limitations on confidentiality, including limitations where applicable in group, marital, and family therapy or in organizational consulting, and (2) the foreseeable uses of the information generated through their services.

(b) discussion of confidentiality occurs at the outset of the relationship. . .

5.02 Maintaining Confidentiality
5.03 Minimizing Intrusions on Privacy

(a) . . . include in written and oral reports, consultations, and the like, only information germane to the purpose for which the communication is made.

(b). . . discuss confidential information. . . only for appropriate scientific or professional purposes and only with persons clearly concerned with such matters.

5.04 Maintenance of Records . . . maintain appropriate confidentiality in creating, storing, accessing, transferring, an disposing of records under their control . . . in accordance with law and a manner that permits compliance with the requirements of this Ethics Code.

6.04 Limitations on Teaching. Psychologists do not teach the use of techniques or procedures that require specialized training, licensure, or expertise, including but not limited ot hypnosis, biofeedback, and projective techniques, to individuals who lack the prerequisite training, legal scope of practice, or expertise.

6.10 Research Responsibilities. Prior to conducting research (except research involving only anonymous surveys, naturalistic observations, or similar research), psychologists enter into an agreement with participants that clarifies the nature of the research and the responsibilities of each party.

The **American Association for Marriage and Family Therapy** (AAMFT) accredits individuals trained in several different professional disciplines. The code of ethics reflects commitments particular to work with marriage and family issues. This code is very similar to the psychologists' code of ethics and conduct in detail. The codes of the primary profession apply in addition to the codes specific to marriage and family therapy.

AAMFT Code of Ethics: Revised July 1, 1998

Contents:
- Responsibility to clients
- Confidentiality

- Professional competence and integrity
- Responsibility to students, employees, and supervisors
- Responsibility to the profession
- Financial arrangements
- Advertising

This code is published by:
American Association for Marriage and Family Therapy
1133 15th Street NW, Suite 300, Washington, DC 20005-2710
(202) 452-0109; www.aamft.org

The **American Association of Pastoral Counselors** (AAPC) is an accrediting association committed to maintaining high standards of professional conduct and competence. In addition to ethical principles very similar to those of other helping professions, the AAPC members covenant to maintain responsible association with the faith group in which members have ecclesiastical standing.

Code of Ethics: American Association of Pastoral Counselors (Amended April 28, 1994)

Table of Contents:

American Association of Pastoral Counselors
9504A Lee Highway
Fairfax, Virginia 22031-2303
Phone: 703-385-6967; FAX: 703-352-7725; E-Mail: info@aapc.org

The Code of Ethics of the **National Association of Social Workers** (NASW) is as comprehensive and detailed as that of psychologists, though focused more on the primary goal of social work to help people in need and to address social problems. The code emphasizes the importance of responsible choices within a moral community, and the rationale for the code is thoroughly presented.

Code of Ethics of the National Association of Social Workers Approved by the 1999 NASW Delegate Assembly

Table of Contents:

- to Colleagues
- to Practice Settings
- as Professionals
- to the Profession
- to the Broader Society

National Association of Social Workers
750 First Street NE, Suite 700,
Washington, DC 20002-4241
Tel: 202-408-8600 www.socialworkers.org/pubs/code/code.asp

The *Standards for Educational and Psychological Testing* reflect the opinion of several professional organizations whose members are involved in testing and formal assessment. Although the reader is referred to the entire book for excellent reference, the chapter on testing in employment and credentialing is of particular relevance to those who work in these areas with missionaries and mission agencies.

See **"Testing in Employment and Credentialing"** Chapter 14, pp 151-162, in *Standards for Educational and Psychological Testing*, 1999, published by the American Educational Research Association, American Psychological Association, and the National Council on Measurement in Education.

Psychiatrists' ethical responsibilities are based on those of the medical profession in which all are licensed before further training in psychiatry. The publication noted below states general ethical principles, discusses each in detail, and has an extensive section on procedures for dealing with ethical complaints. This publication builds on the foundation of the Code of Medical Ethics published by the American Medical Association Council on Ethical and Judicial Affairs.

The Principles of Medical Ethics: With Annotations Especially Applicable to Psychiatry.
2001 Edition American Psychiatric Association, Washington D.C.

Section 1:   A physician shall be dedicated to providing competent medical service with compassion and respect for human dignity.

Section 2:   A physician shall deal honestly with patients and colleagues, and strive to expose those physicians deficient in character or competence, or who engage in fraud or deception.

Section 3:   A physician shall respect the law and also recognize responsibility to seek changes in those requirements which are contrary to the best interests of the patient.

Section 4:   A physician shall respect the rights of patients, of colleagues, and of other health professionals, and shall safeguard patient confidences within the constraints of the law.

Section 5:   A physician shall continue to study, apply, and advance scientific knowledge, make relevant information available to patients, colleagues, and the public, obtain consultation, and use the talents of other health professionals when indicated.

Section 6:   A physician shall in the provision of appropriate patient care, except in emergencies, be free to choose whom to serve, with whom to associate, and the environment in which to provide medical services.

Section 7:   A physician shall recognize a responsibility to participate in activities contributing to an improved community.

American Psychiatric Association

1400 K Street N.W., Washington, DC 20005 Tel: (888) 357-7924; FAX: 202-682-6850

E-mail: apa@psych.org; www.appi.org

53

On the Use and Misuse of Psychological Assessment In Candidate Evaluations

M. Elizabeth Lewis Hall and
Stephen M. Sweatman

Pre-service psychological assessment of missionary candidates is widely practiced, but there is a lack of specific standards relevant to mission groups to guide practitioners. The implications of legal and ethical standards may not be carefully considered. This chapter presents the context, method, and goals of psychological assessment, five problem areas of misuse of assessment, and reasons why assessment may be misused.

*I*ntroduction
It has become common practice for mission boards to require a psychological assessment of all of their candidates. If you walked the halls of most sending agencies during orientation school, you might hear candidates saying "Did you see the shrink yet?" or "When is psych week?"

This chapter considers ethical issues in psychological assessment of missionary candidates. Although the primary audience is mental health professionals engaged in this task, these issues will also be of interest to mission organization administrators who interface with psychological consultants for the purpose of candidate selection.

This review is motivated by a desire to serve with excellence in the area of missionary assessment. Ethical principles and legal guidelines set standards for good practice and avoiding harm and injustice, and practicing according to these guidelines has a number of benefits. It raises the standard of excellence, increases the accuracy of assessment, and allows us to exercise our God-given stewardship of the human resources entrusted to us.

This review of ethics is particularly relevant because of the current lack of standards in the field of assessment in missions. Most missionary assessments are currently accomplished by independent consultants who may have little training in candidate screening and evaluation, and a wide variety of methods is employed. Some of these practices fall short of ethical and legal guidelines, provid-

ing the mission with weak or inaccurate information.

This was brought to our attention at the 2000 Mental Health and Missions Conference by R. P. Ascano, Ph.D. (2000), who said that many of our practices and methodologies are ill-informed and potentially illegal. We need to ask whether we are within the confines of the law, and more importantly, whether we could accomplish our task in a more virtuous and effective manner.

Applying ethical principles requires a thorough understanding of the role of psychological assessment in candidate evaluation. Our understanding of assessment will be briefly outlined, emphasizing psychological assessment in the context of the larger candidate selection process, and examining methods and goals.

The Context of Psychological Assessment

Psychological assessment is but one piece of a larger assessment strategy. Many variables are evaluated which are beyond the scope of a psychological assessment, including doctrine, biblical knowledge, the needs of the field, congruence with the vision of the agency, proven leadership and perceived authentic Christian living. It is important for consultants to recognize that the decision making responsibility regarding selection lies with the mission which is accomplishing a much broader assessment of the candidate.

The Method of Psychological Assessment

In conducting a comprehensive evaluation for overseas service, the psychologist should utilize a multi-source, multi-method approach. Information that is confirmed by multiple sources and methods is more likely to be valid and reliable. Psychological test results should be combined with other sources such as structured interviews, observations, simulations, work samples, and peer and supervisory references.

The Goals of Psychological Assessment

The first ethical problem we encounter in psychological assessment is a lack of clarity regarding its purpose. Assessment goals vary depending on the selection strategy and mission statement of the organization. Goals should be clarified between the mental health professional and the mission *before* beginning any assessment. Given that assessment and methodology are driven by purpose, the goals must be crystal clear and understood by both parties.

Without clear, mutually agreed upon goals, the professional may simply do what is familiar—screen for psychopathology, since most professionals in this ministry are clinicians with expertise in treating disorders. Depending on the administrator's view of psychology, the sending agency may downplay the findings or overestimate the power of the assessment to predict future behavior.

Common goals include screening for outcomes of missionary longevity, effectiveness and well-being by evaluating maturity, interpersonal health, stress-resilience and cross cultural adaptability. The information is typically used for screening and placement—and in the case of some mature organizations, for personal and team training both pre-field and on-field. Unfortunately, for some of these goals we currently have limited research and empirical studies that would allow us to make accurate predictions.

Whatever the ultimate goal, it is important to recognize that assessment starts as an employee selection or fit-for-placement process. In most cases, the assessment takes place in order to decide whether a given individual should be "hired" by an "employer," namely, the mission organization. Since these terms are rarely used in the context of candidate selection, few psychologists approach the task from an employee selection perspective. Instead, they approach it as an evaluation of the candidate's mental health. An employee selection perspective utilizes wisdom from organizational and personnel psychology as well as clinical approaches.

We will now consider some ethical principles and their potential for misuse. We hope to encourage psychological assessment practices that are legal and virtuous.

Problematic Areas

The APA Ethical Principles of Psychologists and Code of Conduct (APA, 1992) offers ten standards relevant to psychological assessment. Of these, five are most likely to be misused.

Psychological assessment techniques are used competently and appropriately (Standard 2.02).

Because of limited funds and lack of knowledge regarding testing, psychological tests are often administered and interpreted by individuals who have not been trained to do so competently. The availability of computer-generated printouts for commonly-used tests such as the MMPI-2 contributes to this misuse, giving the impression that test interpretation by a professional is unnecessary.

The professionals performing the assessment should have specific training in the tests used and be knowledgeable regarding personnel assessments. They should also have a strong familiarity with the specific roles a missionary performs, including stressors and pitfalls. Ideally, psychologists trained in organizational and personnel matters would collaborate with clinicians and mission administrators to establish these standards.

This standard also states, "Psychologists who... use psychological assessment techniques... do so in a manner and *for purposes* that are appropriate in light of the research on or evidence of the usefulness and proper application of the techniques" (n.p.). In other words, the purpose of the assessment must be clear in order to evaluate whether the techniques are appropriate.

The overarching purposes are relatively clear: screening, placement, and training/development. The picture becomes blurred when we attempt to operationalize these purposes. What specific characteristics should be screened for? What factors are important in placement issues? What training and development issues should be evaluated and identified?

Basic steps for determining specific goals have been established in Industrial and Organizational employee selection literature. It is required ethically in standards for educational and psychological testing (American Psychological Association, et al, 1999, Chapter 14) that: (a) A job analysis must be done in order to identify relevant job elements and the corresponding candidate characteristics; (b) appropriate instruments that address these criteria must be identified or constructed; (c) criterion-related validity of the instruments must be established; and (d) a strategy for selection decisions must be formulated.

A job analysis must be performed to identify the relevant personnel competencies and characteristics. What "jobs" do missionaries have? Two job domains must be evaluated: (a) the specific tasks that will be performed by the missionary, with the attendant job skills, personality characteristics, and spiritual characteristics; and (b) the task of adapting cross culturally. Once these characteristics are determined, the overarching goals of screening, placement, and training/development can be operationalized.

This "job analysis" varies from the traditional job analysis found in personnel selection literature, because mission employment has characteristics that differ significantly from general employment:

- It is a round-the-clock, 24/7 job, rather than a 9 to 5, clock-in/out job.
- Many aspects of the work environment (e.g., the streets of Bogota) cannot be controlled, because there are too many variables to predict.
- It is a representative job, in that the person functions as a representative of God in his or her context.
- It requires a cross cultural transition.

Given the unique work characteristics, missionary jobs tend to have very high stress levels. Characteristics needed to perform the job adequately include stress resilience and the absence of psychopathology which is magnified under prolonged stressful conditions. Knowledge of existing psychopathology may also be necessary in order to make appropriate placements.

For example, an individual with bipolar disorder may be able to function adequately as a missionary, but only in contexts where medications and other support treatment are easily available. An overly ambitious customs agent might confiscate all medications because they appear to be illegal drugs – leaving the missionary without treatment in a stressful transition.

A job analysis will yield desired characteristics that are common to all missionaries, and others that vary from placement to placement. Some literature is available for each of these two job domains (the specific task or role and general cross-cultural living). Specific job-related characteristics will vary depending on the organization and the assignment. Characteristics related to the missionary's spiritually-representative role and cross-cultural adjustment are more universal.

Cross-cultural adaptability is a concern of many secular organizations, and has been studied from a variety of perspectives. A summary of these and an application to a missionary population can be found in Hall, Duvall, Edwards, and Pike (1999).

A number of other articles have been written detailing the desired characteristics of missionaries. Some of these reflect the experience of the authors (e.g. Foyle, 1988). Others are the result of a broader consensus. For example, Ferguson, Kliewer, Lindquist, Williams, and Heinrich (1988) reported the results of a survey of 39 agencies. Wickstrom and Andrews (1993) and Powell and Andrews (1993) used a consensus methodology for establishing criteria for boarding school personnel.

To date, we are aware of only two studies reporting the results of a formal job analysis for missionaries (Cureton, 1988; Graham, 1988). Cureton administered three standardized job analysis instruments to mental health professionals and missionary personnel, and identified minimal job performance skills, personal and demographic traits, and interpersonal factors necessary for adequate job performance. Graham presented a profile of a church planter based on a job analysis, and identified twelve relevant factors.

Tests are administered, scored, interpreted, and otherwise used with appropriate awareness of reliability, validity, and standardization issues, and the uses appropriate for them. (Standard 2.04)

Assessment instruments must address relevant issues regarding the individual's ability to adjust cross-culturally and fitness for the assigned task. Unfortunately, at times psychologists appear to administer tests indiscriminately, without a clear sense of how the information gathered will address issues of job fitness. Tests must be pertinent to the goals of the assessment, reliable and valid, normed on an appropriate sample, and used in a legal manner.

Validity concerns. Criterion-related validity refers to a test's ability to predict an individual's behavior. How well are variables identified by our instruments able to predict cross-cultural adjustment, effectiveness, or longevity? This type of validity is established by comparing performance on the test with the desired goal, that is, the criterion. The dilemma is that psychological tests commonly used were developed primarily to assist clinical diagnosis and treatment planning, and do not specifically address cross-cultural adaptability or fitness for missionary service. We do not know how valid they are in addressing these issues.

Unfortunately, most assessment continues to be based on norm-referenced clinical instruments. Some criterion-related validity research is available, but these studies are not based on a preliminary job analysis.

Norming concerns. Given that the average missionary candidate is not seeking treatment psychologists should not rely too heavily on instruments that have been normed on clinical populations. For example, the MCMI-III was normed on individuals presenting for clinical services, and tends to overestimate pathology in non-clinical populations (Choca & Van Denburg, 1997).

Legal concerns. Questions have been raised regarding the legality of current missionary assessment practices, given anti-discrimination laws. Please note that these brief comments should not be construed as legal advice. The Equal Employment Opportunity Commission (EEOC) regulates selection procedures in order to help employers avoid discriminatory practices. In addition, the 1990 Americans with Disabilities Act prohibits employers from discriminating against qualified individuals with disabilities, and requires that employers make reasonable accommodations to the physical or mental impairments of a qualified applicant if it would not impose an undue hardship on normal business operations. These regulations are relevant to assessment because they directly address the use of psychological assessment to detect mental disabilities.

In 1994 and 1995, the EEOC ruled that medical examinations for applicants can be conducted only after an offer of employment has been made (EEOC Notice No. 915.002, 1995). Personality tests are considered to be medical examinations when administered and interpreted by a psychologist, and when their use might result in the detection of a mental disorder or impairment. Under these regulations, pre-employment assessments using instruments such as the MMPI-2 and 16PF appear to be illegal. However, under certain conditions assessment can be conducted after a conditional job offer. Also, in certain situations religious corporations are exempt.

Once a conditional job offer is made, the employer may judiciously ask disability-related questions and require medical examinations. If the individual is then screened out because of a disability, the employer must demonstrate that the reason for the rejection is job-related and consistent with business necessity (EEOC Notice 915.002, 1995). If the individual is screened out for safety reasons, the employer must demonstrate that the individual poses a significant risk of substantial harm to him/herself or others, and that the risk cannot be reduced below the direct threat level through reasonable accommodation (EEOC, 1999).

Reasonable accommodation must be provided unless the mission organization can show that the accommodation would impose an undue hardship (EEOC, 1999). "Undue hardship" refers to a significant difficulty or expense for the employer. "Difficulty" refers to accommodations that would be unduly extensive, substantial, disruptive, or that would fundamentally alter the nature or operation of the business.

This information is relevant to a missions context because the absence of certain types of psychological disorders (e.g., personality disorders) is necessary in order to do the job of a missionary. Other types of psychological disorders (e.g., bipolar disorder, recurrent major depression) may be safety risks because of limited availability of medications or psychiatric monitoring in remote locations overseas.

The Code of Federal Regulations 29CFR1607 (2000) also provides guidelines on employee selection procedures that are intended to assist in complying with anti-discrimination laws. Among other things, it requires that a thorough job analysis be conducted (Sec. 1607.9), and that the validity of tests be established for the purposes for which they are used (Sec. 1607.10).

Note that religious corporations are exempt from the Civil Rights Act of 1964. Membership or employment with a religious corporation may be discriminatory in a number of ways. For example, many religious organizations discriminate against individuals involved in extramarital sex, certain sexual orientations, certain religious belief systems, and against females for certain leadership positions.

Our recommendation is that mission organizations implement a two-step process in which the individual is offered conditional employment after a screening process that does not include a psychological assessment. In the second step, the individual would undergo a psychological assessment to determine whether impairments exist that would render him or her unable to perform the missionary job, or would present a safety risk to self or others. Further guidance on implementing this can be found in the EEOC Notice 915.002 (1995).

Interpretations and recommendations are not based on outmoded, obsolete instruments. (Standard 2.07)

It is often easier to stay with "tried-and-true" instruments than to make the effort to learn about and be trained in current assessment tools. However, psychological assessment is a rapidly-developing area, and practitioners who conduct assessments should be aware of advances in the field.

Assessment results are explained appropriately to the person being assessed.
(Standard 2.09)

If feedback will not be given to the candidate because of the preemployment nature of the assessment, this must be clearly explained to the missionary candidate in advance (APA, 1992). In all cases, the question of defining the "client" must be clarified before conducting the assessment. Whether the mental health professional is part of the mission organization or is a consultant, the professional's obligations to the organization and to the candidate must be clear. In most cases, understandable feedback will be beneficial to the candidate for training and personal development.

The integrity and security of tests is maintained. (Standard 2.10)

Because of constraints on time and money, as well as physical distance between the professional and the candidate, there is a temptation to use nonstandard practices that violate the integrity and security of tests. For example, photocopies of instruments may be used in order to save money. This is illegal as well as unethical. Or tests may be sent to candidates to be proctored by untrained individuals, violating the security of the instruments and making it impossible to ensure that standard test-taking conditions are in place. In addition to violating ethical and legal standards, this may undermine our ability to obtain accurate results.

Reasons for Assessment Misuse

There are a number of factors that promote the misuse of psychological assessments. Some of these relate to attitudes of the consulting professional; others to attitudes and views of mission administrators.

Administrators' Unrealistic View

Many mission administrators have an unrealistic view of what psychological testing can accomplish. They may assume that testing will allow the evaluator to overcome the subjectivity inherent in recommendations and interviews, and be able to scientifically predict missionary effectiveness. They may assume that psychological tests measure aspects of the person that cannot be uncovered through other means.

Although tests can be helpful in uncovering abilities, skills, personality characteristics, and even unconscious dynamics, these must be verified through other means. Mission administrators may also have an unrealistically high view of the consultant, assuming that he or she is sufficiently trained and will know what to do, when this may not be the case. In reality, consulting professionals often do candidate assessment as a side endeavor and have little time to read relevant literature or obtain training.

The opposite is just as prevalent: mission administrators may devalue psychological evaluation, doing it only because they are mandated to, or because other mission organizations are doing it. They may not recognize its value and reliability compared to other methods of assessment such as references, limited interaction impressions, self-reported motivations and non-structured interviews.

Psychologists' underlying assumptions

Many psychologists simply do not understand missionary competencies, and do not know exactly what needs to be evaluated. They may lack adequate training to conduct missionary assessments and fail to differentiate the role of evaluator from that of clinician. They are likely to adopt the procedures most familiar to them—those that have been a part of their graduate training and their ongoing clinical practice. In too many cases, this results in indiscriminate use of testing.

Logistical Complexities

Logistical complexities in attempting a comprehensive assessment with individuals from all around the continent may make unethical practices appealing. Comprehensive assessment is often abbreviated because of financial constraints or because the mission is attempting to be cost effective.

Conclusions

Psychological assessment can be an extremely valuable part of the overall candidate fit-for-placement process when it is used thoughtfully and competently. We hope this review of common pitfalls will encourage professionals to become better equipped in the wise, discretionary use of psychological instruments. Virtuous assessment entails clarity of purpose that is communicated clearly to all involved, the use of methodology that meets that purpose, accuracy, as little discrimination as is possible, and an attitude of caring for the well-being of the missionary candidate.

We have named a number of deficits in our unstandardized methodology for missionary candidate assessments. Our call is for more criterion studies on missionary candidates, looking at outcome criteria of adjustment, attrition/longevity, and effectiveness. We need more input from people with experience and expertise in legal parameters of consulting with religiously-based, non-profit organizations to assess potential missionaries for screening, placement, and training.

Finally, we desire that psychologists proficient in personnel and organizational psychology will contribute their knowledge. Our hope is that the end result will be symposiums and articles reporting the results of job analyses, promising instruments, and validity studies which will further enhance our God-given task to pick, train and sustain cross-cultural messengers of the forgiveness and peace found only through Jesus Christ.

References

American Educational and Research Association, American Psychological Association, & National Council on Measurement in Education. (1999). *Standards for educational and psychological testing.* Washington, DC: Authors

American Psychological Association. (1992). *Ethical principles of psychologists and code of conduct.* Washington, D. C.: Author.

Ascano, R. P. (2000). Ethical and legal considerations in psychological assessments with missions. Presentation at annual conference on Mental Health and Missions. Angola, IN: November 2000.

Choca, J. P., & Van Denburg, E. (1997). *Interpretive guide to the Millon Clinical Multiaxial Inventory* (2nd ed.). Washington D.C.: American Psychological Association.

Code of Fed. Reg. 29CFR1607 (2000). *Uniform guidelines on employee selection procedures (1978)* [On-line].
Available: frwebgate.access.gpo.gov/cgi-bin/get-cfr.cgi?TITLE:29&PART=1607

EEOC. (1999). *Enforcement guidance: Reasonable accommodation and undue hardship under the Americans with Disabilities Act* [On-line]. Available: www.eeoc.gov/docs/accommodation.html

EEOC Notice No. 915.002 (1995). *Enforcement guidance: Preemployment disability-related questions and medical examinations* [On-line]. Available: www.eeoc.gov/policy/guidance.html

Ferguson, L. N., Kliewer, D., Lindquist, S. E., Williams, D. E., & Heinrich. R. P. (1988). Candidate selection criteria: A survey. In *Helping missionaries grow: Readings in mental health and missions* (pp. 35-45). Pasadena, CA: William Carey Library.

Foyle, M. (1988). How to choose the right missionary. In *Helping missionaries grow: Readings in mental health and missions* (pp. 26-34). Pasadena, CA: William Carey Library.

Graham. T. (1988). How to select the best church planters. In *Helping missionaries grow: Readings in mental health and missions* (pp. 46-54). Pasadena, CA: William Carey Library.

Hall, M. E. L., Duvall, N. S., Edwards, K. J., & Pike, P. L. (1999). The relationship of object relations development to cultural adjustment in a missionary sample. *Journal of Psychology and Theology, 27*(2), 139-153.

Pope, K. S., & Vasquez, M. J. T. (1991). *Ethics in psychotherapy and counseling: A practical guide for psychologists.* San Francisco: Jossey-Bass.

Powell, J. R., & Andrews, L. A. (1993). Qualities desired in MK boarding school personnel: A preliminary study. *Journal of Psychology and Theology, 21*(1), 86-92.

Schultz, D. P., & Schultz, S. E. (1998). *Psychology and work today: An introduction to industrial and organizational psychology* (7th ed.). Upper Saddle River, NJ: Prentice-Hall.

Wickstrom, D. L., & Andrews, L. A. (1993). Personality characteristics of staff members at selected overseas missionary boarding schools. *Journal of Psychology and Theology, 21*(1), 74-85.

Appendix

Ethical Guidelines and Where to Find Them

American Disabilities Act: janweb.icdi.wvu.edu/kinder/

Equal Employment Opportunity Commission: www.eeoc.gov/publicat.html

American Psychological Association Ethical Principles of Psychologists and Code of Conduct: www.apa.org/ethics/code.html

Standards for Educational and Psychological Testing: Can be purchased at www.apa.org/science/standards.html

54

Professional Use of the Internet: Legal and Ethical Issues in a Member Care Environment

Christopher H. Rosik and
Roger K. Brown

The use of the Internet and e-mail has revolutionized communications in missions. This chapter looks at legal and ethical implications, including what constitutes a professional relationship over the Internet, ethical practice in member care via e-mail, and managing legal risks. A summary of interventions to limit legal liability and promote ethical practice in member care via Internet shows actions which mission agencies and mental health practitioners can take.

*I*ntroduction

The Internet has revolutionized communication technology and opened new horizons for the dissemination of mental health information and services. This is especially true for therapists and physicians involved in member care who communicate with missionaries in geographically diverse and distant areas. However, in many respects, these technological advances have outpaced the ability of our existing ethical and legal guidelines to adequately address them.

Critical issues include confidentiality, competence, consent, jurisdiction, record keeping, and the treatment of children. While there have been a few attempts to provide guidelines for e-mail correspondence between professionals and patients in established relationships, there is scant literature regarding standards of practice for professional Internet services where there has been no prior face-to-face relationship.

Complicating matters is the fact that the professional relationship with patients via electronic technology is not well defined. Courts and ethics boards are likely to make such determinations with reference to existing case law and ethics codes. Thus, member care therapists and physicians must act with prudence when utilizing electronic technology, having to operate with significant uncertainty as to whether their services might be deemed to constitute a professional relationship and thus be beholden to the prevailing standards of care.

The terms "telehealth" and "telemedicine" as used here are defined as the use of e-mail and the Internet to accomplish health and medical care over distance.

Case Examples

The following case examples illustrate some of the complex issues involved in providing member care via e-mail.

Case 1: Sexual Abuse of an MK

A field based missionary therapist provided an assessment of an 8-year-old male MK who had been sexual abused by a 14-year-old MK and the abusing MK's 16-year-old national friend. The abusers lived in a rural area of another third world country where communication was difficult other than by e-mail.

The therapist attempted to learn the reporting guidelines and laws regarding sexual abuse in the country where the abuse occurred. He learned that the typical response by the government was to either ignore the report or to lock abusers in prison without a trial and beat them severely. With the family's permission, the therapist e-mailed the referring missionary doctor located in the vicinity of the abuse in order to communicate recommendations for each of the abusive boys' families to seek professional counseling assistance.

The missionary doctor was a friend of each of the missionary families involved. He was reluctantly willing to speak with the abusing MK's family, but found them resistant to seeking assistance. The doctor was unable to make contact with the family of the national abuser, as they had moved from the area. The abused MK's family was reluctant to report the abuse to local authorities, but they did give the missionary therapist permission to contact the parents of the abusing MK.

The therapist e-mailed the family to explain to them the seriousness of the situation and insist that they have their son evaluated by a professional counselor. The family eventually responded back by saying that they would take their son to a counselor in another country, not their home country. No feedback was received as to whether this family ever indeed sought professional assistance. Further contact indicated that they headed an independent mission that did not have accountability protocols in place for such situations.

Case 2: Inadvertent Breach of Confidentiality

A missionary living in a remote setting in another country came to see a field missionary psychiatrist who diagnosed him as having a major depression. The missionary was unwilling to interrupt his field service to seek assistance other than treatment with an antidepressant medication. The missionary psychiatrist agreed to start the missionary on an antidepressant medication as long as he agreed to have regular medical checks with a local doctor, seek further evaluation and therapy within the next nine months, communicate with the psychiatrist by e-mail regarding medication response, and agree to a no-suicide contract.

The missionary followed through several times over the next four months with e-mail reports. In his reports he indicated that he was not noticing any improvement from the medication. The psychiatrist wrote back to the missionary and strongly urged him to return for further clinical evaluation or to return to their home country for a medical leave of absence.

Unknown to the psychiatrist, the missionary's field administrator had access to the missionary's e-mail account for purposes of passing on messages to the missionary by short-wave radio. Upon opening this particular e-mail, the mission administrator became alarmed and asked the psychiatrist for a report of what was going on with this missionary. As the psychiatrist did not have a release form signed for communicating with the mission administrator, he informed the administrator of this. In addition, he wrote another e-mail message to the missionary informing him of what had happened and apologized for the inadvertent release of information, as he had no idea that anyone other than the missionary had access to his e-mail account.

What Constitutes a Professional Relationship Over the Internet?

Currently, the question of whether electronic communication, especially via typed words alone, can or should constitute the practice of therapy or medicine remains unresolved. Key factors are the structure and nature of the telehealth and telemedicine services being provided and the subsequent expectations likely to be developed by consumers.

Therefore, mission organizations, licensed mental health professionals, and physicians must carefully examine the exact nature of what professional member care services are occurring over the Internet to determine their degree of risk or liability. Aspects of Internet communication which are likely to be seen as establishing a legally binding professional relationship include repeated communication with the same provider, professional advice being provided in a situation-specific manner rather than in the abstract, the presence of an expressed agreement, and the lack of a disclaimer that no professional relationship is offered.

Repeated Communication. Repeated electronic correspondence with the same professional is likely to occur at significantly higher levels in overseas settings, where a large number of missionaries may rely on a relatively small number of member care mental health professionals and physicians in their local geographic region. The missionary who escalates the number and detail of e-mail questions over time to the same professional may come to depend on that individual's expertise. At least in the United States, courts might decide that the client was misled into believing the professional could be relied upon to provide a relationship not unlike traditional psychotherapy.

Specific Responses. The concept of reliance is also more likely to be perceived when the professional member care specialist responds with specific answers to specific client situations. While trying to keep responses general and in the abstract may reduce liability, it is difficult to carry this out when situation-specific replies are requested.

Expressed Agreement. The existence of an explicit agreement between the member care professional and the missionary involving an offer to teleadvice, acceptance of that offer, and the payment of a fee legally establishes a professional relationship between the therapist and the client. However, the absence of such an expressed agreement does not insulate therapists or physicians from risk, as they may also imply a relationship through their actions.

Disclaimer. The inclusion of a disclaimer that no professional relationship is being offered is a helpful step in limiting expectations and defining boundaries. However, because many people do not really know what a therapist or physician specifically does, there is a need to indicate in any disclaimer how the services differ from psychotherapy or psychiatry and thus spell out in some detail the nature of the service offered. This provides another reason for member care professionals to carefully think through the type of services they are providing and how these could be construed by the missionaries they assist.

We still lack a clear and simple definition for determining when a professional client-therapist or patient-physician relationship is occurring over the Internet. Consequently, it is prudent for member care specialists to be aware of the many legal and ethical issues that exist even if they believe their electronic services do not surpass the threshold for creating a professional relationship. It is to these considerations that we now turn.

Promoting Ethical Practice in Member Care Telehealth and Telemedicine

Several measures can be taken to insure a more ethical atmosphere in which to conduct member care telehealth and telemedicine. Interventions aimed at protecting confidentiality, insuring consent, and creating competence with professional use of the Internet need to be considered and implemented.

Confidentiality. The literature addressing confidentiality concerns with electronic communication is emphatic on the need for some kind of security tool. Such electronic security tools include password-protected screen savers, personal access codes, electronic signatures, and encryption programs. These devices can significantly enhance the protection of sensitive patient information from unauthorized use and disclosure, though this typically makes the accessibility of electronic communication more difficult. Encryption technology is perhaps the most touted of the options to enhance security and protect confidentiality. Encryption software acts as a type of envelope and can provide a guarantee of the message's authenticity and integrity. Spielberg (1998) recommends that physicians use encryption whenever they communicate with or about a patient by e-mail, unless the patient has explicitly waived that option.

Encryption does have some limitations. It cannot assure legal or ethical use of electronic technology. The use of encryption is politically charged because of United States government proposals to retain the deciphering codes. Internationally, the use of encryption is banned or controlled by many countries, so member care professionals need to investigate the host nation's regulations before encrypting communications. Moreover, Spielberg warns that encrypted messages to patients using a workplace e-mail address may still be susceptible to an employer's view. It is therefore prudent to inform the patient that confidential and sensitive information should not be sent via office e-mail even with encryption.

When transmitting health information electronically, the American Academy of Pediatrics task force has recommended that clinicians verify that security protocols are in place to ensure against unauthorized changes or attempts to modify electronic records. The AAP also suggests the use of cover sheets with confidentiality/privacy disclaimers and requests for return receipts for transmitted data.

Spielberg (1998) additionally recommends that all patient-related e-mail should contain a notice at the top of the page informing the reader that the message is a confidential communication. He also suggests that, when professional teams are involved, each staff member should have their own personalized electronic address that makes the writer's identity clear to patients and ensures the authenticity of the message.

Forwarding of patient e-mail without the expressed authorization of the patient should not occur. Using the blind copy feature in software is also recommended. However, it appears that many professionally operated Web sites may not be employing precautions such as secure servers or encryption technology for messages transmitted directly from the site.

Consent. Obtaining informed consent from patients is foundational in the establishment of therapist-client and physician-patient relationships. Member care professionals engaged in telehealth and telemedicine need to carefully consider the nature of their services to determine what information should be disclosed. There is some consensus in the relevant literature that the initial consent be in written form and occur prior to using e-mail for direct correspondence.

Several aspects of telehealth and telemedicine practice have been targeted for inclusion in consent disclosures. These include:

- The lack of complete privacy and confidentiality guarantees (even with encryption)
- Whether and in what form patient e-mail messages and other electronically transmitted information will become part of their medical record
- How electronic records will be stored and who will have access to these records
- Differences between e-mail and traditional treatment
- Advantages and limitations of electronic services
- The experimental nature of professional services provided via Internet
- The duration of the telehealth or telemedicine relationship
- Normal response times
- Ways to confirm the practitioner's identity and qualifications
- Assurance that responses will be written by the treating therapist or physician
- Whether e-mail message will ever be forwarded
- Arrangements during the member care professional's vacation and/or furlough
- Any prohibited topics
- Details of the security measures in place.

Consent should also be obtained to indemnify the health care institution or mission organization for information loss due to technical failure. Finally, minors need to know that if the electronic interactions are stored, their parents probably will have a legal right to them.

Competence. At present, there is no separate standard for determining competence to perform telehealth or telemedicine. However, as the technology advances and becomes more embedded in professional practice, requirements for specific training, continuing education, and credentialing are likely to take place. For the meantime, member care professionals who routinely employ electronic technology in the provision of services should consider getting specialized training and continuing education in providing treatment over the Internet. The interested reader is encouraged to review articles in the suggested readings.

Competence at the organizational level implies an onus on mission organizations who sanction member care telehealth and telemedicine services to develop administrative controls and policies concerning the appropriate use of, access to, and dissemination of personal health information which is transmitted and/or stored electronically. In-house education to ensure ethical use of telehealth and telemedicine services can also be developed.

A mission working group could be convened to discuss and develop preliminary guidelines. Such education should include clear delineation of the missionary patient's right to keep medical and psychological information confidential and the security strategies that are being employed to ensure this. The extent to which member care telehealth and telemedicine records will be considered confidential within the mission organization's personnel department should be explicitly stated in the mission's policy handbook.

Additional Measures. Member care professionals utilizing Internet technology to provide services should also have a plan for how emergencies and/or technological failure will be handled. Professionals must be prepared to respond to e-mails regularly and in a timely fashion. The literature generally discourages trying to manage crisis situations by electronic communication. When a patient being treated over the Internet encounters a serious emergency, ethical practice mandates that provision be made for face-to-face treatment immediately, even if this means removing the missionary from the field. A less drastic option, where possible, is to provide the patient with the names and telephone numbers of qualified professionals in the patient's locale.

Limiting Legal Risk in Member Care Telehealth and Telemedicine

Recommendations for reducing legal exposure in telehealth and telemedicine practice are related to the general categories noted earlier: patient care, liability, jurisdiction, and privacy.

In treating minors over the Internet, the most conservative approach is to ask parents before providing any psychological or medical service to their children. This is a good idea even if the professional does not believe that a professional relationship will be established.

Reducing legal risk is also greatly enhanced by requiring an initial face-to-face evaluation. Therapists can insure the client is of age to consent and identify visual cues that might counter-indicate e-mail therapy. Therapists may wish to require patients to be evaluated by a physician prior to e-mail therapy in order to rule out any physical basis to the complaints. Internet and e-mail should be used only as an accompaniment or support for traditional face-to-face psychotherapy, so that knowledge of the presenting problem can enable sound clinical judgment.

Member care professionals and their mission organizations should check with their professional liability insurers to determine if electronic services would be covered in the event of a lawsuit or complaint. If they are not, an attempt to acquire such additional coverage is advisable.

Navigating the uncertainties surrounding jurisdiction issues remains a daunting task. However, some guidelines can be offered. Since there are no federal or international standards for child abuse reporting, the most prudent approach is to be knowledgeable regarding the reporting laws and child protective services procedures in the states and/or countries where the practitioner and patients reside. At a minimum, member care professionals should consider obtaining this information for those jurisdictions where the greatest number of their telehealth or telemedicine patients live.

Similarly, the most conservative approach to the issue of licensure is for therapists and physicians to hold a professional license in the state or jurisdiction in which the patient resides. While it is unlikely that many member care therapists or physicians providing services over the Internet adhere strictly to this guideline, the closer it is approximated, the less the potential legal exposure. Because the legal picture is evolving so rapidly, member care professionals and mission organizations would be wise to regularly update their knowledge.

Safeguarding electronic records from inadvertent loss is important legally and protects the integrity of the treatment. It is imperative that the system be backed up regularly, at maximum weekly intervals, and/or hard-copy files be created in order to avoid the potential loss of patient records. Storing e-mail electronically or printing it in hard copy and placing it in the patient's record insures accurate documentation of the communication. There is no advantage in deleting the e-mail communications, as even deleted messages are recoverable and legally discoverable.

In spite of this ambiguous and rapidly evolving environment, the existent literature does offer some common sense suggestions for limiting legal risk and promoting ethical care. Several of the practice recommendations described in this article are categorized by ease of execution and summarized for quick reference in Table 1. Member care professionals and mission organizations are encouraged to carefully consider what strategies can be implemented immediately into their practices and which need to be included in future planning so as to advance electronic care that reflects high legal and ethical standards. These measures, if employed, will enable us to be wise stewards of the tremendous advances in communications technology taking place in the 21st century.

Table 1
Interventions to Limit Legal Liability and Promote Ethical Practice in Member Care Telehealth and Telemedicine Via Internet

Lower Cost and/or Time Expenditure Interventions

- Contact your professional liability insurer to inquire about and, if needed, obtain coverage for Internet services.
- Obtain a written agreement from your carrier regarding their coverage of your specific program and/or services.
- Obtain informed consent in written form before engaging in electronic communication. This consent should include:

  - The lack of complete privacy and confidentiality.
  - The advantages and limitations of telehealth or telemedicine.
  - Indication if and how electronic correspondences will become part of the patient's medical record.
  - The experimental nature of telehealth or telemedicine treatment.
  - The normal response time to be expected by the patient.
  - An explanation of how vacations, furloughs, and emergencies will be handled.
  - A statement to indemnify the mission agency or health care institution for information loss due to technical failure.

- Use cover sheets with confidentiality and privacy disclaimers.
- Use encryption technology whenever communicating with patients.
- Configure an automatic reply to acknowledge the receipt of message and use blind copy features in your software.
- Use password protected screen savers for all desktop workstations in the office or home.
- Never forward patients' e-mail communications without their expressed permission.
- Back up electronic records regularly and no less than on a weekly basis.

Moderate Cost and/or Time Expenditure Interventions

- Obtain direct, face-to-face assessment with patients whenever possible before providing telehealth or telemedicine services.
- Know the abuse reporting and other health care related laws in the jurisdictions where most of your patients reside
- Educate yourself regarding telehealth and telemedicine practice.
- Regularly update your knowledge about the legal and ethical status of professional services provided via Internet through continuing education or specialized training.

High Cost and/or Time Expenditure Interventions

- Obtain professional licensure in the jurisdictions where your patients reside.

- Develop organizational administrative controls and policies concerning telehealth and telemedicine practice, including the confidentiality and privacy of professional member care communications with missionaries.
- Provide educational opportunities within the mission organization regarding legal and ethical issues in telehealth and telemedicine.

Suggested Readings

Barak, A. (1999). Psychological applications on the Internet: A discipline on the threshold of a new millennium. *Applied & Preventive Psychology, 8,* 231-245.

Gostin, L. (1997). Health care information and the protection of personal privacy: Ethical and legal considerations. *Annals of Internal Medicine, 127,* 683-690.

Koocher, G. P., & Morray, E. (2000). Regulation of Telepsychology: A survey of State Attorneys General. *Professional Psychology: Research and Practice, 31,* 503-508.

Kuppersmith, R. B. (1999, April). Is e-mail an effective medium for physician-patient interactions? *Archives of Otolaryngology—Head and Neck Surgery, 125,* 468-470.

Maheu, M. M., & Gordon, B. L. (2000). Counseling and therapy on the Internet. *Professional Psychology: Research and Practice, 31,* 484-489.

Reed, G. M., & McLaughlin, C. J., & Milholland, K. (2000). Ten interdisciplinary principles for professional practice in telehealth: Implications for psychology. *Professional Psychology: Research and Practice, 31,* 170-178.

Rosik, C.H., & Brown, R. K. (2001). Professional Use of the Internet: Legal and Ethical Issues in a Member Care Environment. *Journal of Psychology and Theology, 29,* 106-120.

Shapiro, D. E., & Schulman, C. E. (1996). Ethical and legal issues in e-mail therapy. *Ethics & Behavior, 6*(2), 107-124.

Spielberg, A. R. (1998). Sociohistorical, legal, and ethical implications of e-mail for the patient-physician relationship. *Journal of the American Medical Association, 280* (15), 1353-1359.

Note: This chapter is excerpted and condensed from a much longer article by the same title, which was published in 2001 in the *Journal of Psychology and Theology, 29,* pp 106-120. See the original article for more details. Used by permission.

Correspondence concerning this article should be addressed to: Christopher H. Rosik, Ph.D., Link Care Center, 1734 West Shaw Avenue, Fresno, California 93711. Electronic mail may be sent via Internet to: CRosik@worldnet.att.net

Part IX

Research

55

Research in Mental Health and Missions

William F. Hunter

eed for Research
The publication of this volume is ample evidence that the findings of the behavioral sciences have a significant impact on missions development and practice.

That impact can be more focused and productive as research data is available to guide mental health professionals in optimizing missionary experience and thereby furthering the work of God around the globe. However, research has not kept pace with the more robust clinical thrust of the mental health and missions movement.

The *Journal of Psychology and Theology* published special issues devoted to psychology and missions in 1983, 1987, 1993, and 1999. With the exception of the 1983 special issue, the editors have bemoaned the paucity of empirical research in psychology and missions.

The guest editors of the 1999 issue wrote:

> Most published work in this area continues to be the result of dissertations or theses, which generally means that they are not part of an ongoing empirical exploration of a certain area. In addition, although descriptive research is a necessary first step in exploring uncharted areas, it is important to implement research projects that utilize increasingly sophisticated research methodologies and that build on previous studies to explore specific research hypotheses. (Hall & Schram 1999, p. 86)

What is needed is empirical research that will help mission leaders and mental health practitioners make the right kinds of decisions for resolving dilemmas of strategy

The field of mental health and missions has developed an impressive body of practice-based wisdom, especially in recent decades. Research which could give a firmer foundation for practice has not kept pace. This chapter surveys the current state of the art and makes a plea for more long-term, rigorous empirical research which could help guide practice decisions in mental health and missions.

and practice. Researchers can help provide purpose and objectives in research to assist mission leaders and practitioners with resolution of dilemmas relating to missionary mental health issues. Research driven by what needs to be known and responding to the questions of mission leaders and mental health practitioners is the key to research making a difference.

Because there are few published studies of psychopathology in missionary personnel, Richardson (1992) concludes: "The paucity of solid empirical research thus affects our ability to make reliable conclusions about the incidence and nature of missionary psychopathology" (p. 91).

In recent years much of mental health in missions emphasis has come under the umbrella of *member care*. Much of the member care literature is theoretical and applied in nature. However, O'Donnell (1992) affirms the necessity of scientific research to "further identify member care issues, evaluate the effectiveness of member care programs, and study the nature of the missionary experience" (p. 293).

Adequate research requires "great chunks of time and long-term commitment from post-doctoral researchers with adequate funding for their work from evangelical sources" (Hunter, 1993) but the obstacles to these types of research efforts are great, including limited financial and time resources and the difficulty of doing research with missionary participants.

Research Issues

Missionaries constitute a special research population. We may think of missionaries as having marks of an ethnic minority group. Becker (1998) quotes sociologist Everett C. Hughes:

> [A group of people] is an ethnic group . . . because the people in and the people out of it know that it is one; because both the *ins* and *outs* talk, feel, and act as if it were a separate group.

Whether *in* or *out* of the missions enterprise, missionaries themselves as well as others think of them as a distinctive group.

What do we want to know about the mental health of missionaries? Why do we want to know these things? And, what will we do with what we discover about them? Can we really expect that research can be a viable resource harnessed in the service of Christ and mission?

The overarching response to such questions will to a large extent concern change that will help make the missions enterprise more effective, whether in member care practices and policies, organizational structure and responsiveness, understanding of the place and function of the missionary family, the education and nurture of MKs, reentry or an amelioration of problems that foster missionary attrition.

The whole continuum of mental health/mental illness needs to be addressed in mental health in missions research. Not only is there a large population to study but there are researchable issues affecting them that have received sparse or spotty attention. Becker (1996), referring to behavioral science research in general, calls for "expanding the reach of our thinking, of seeing what else we could be thinking and asking, and increasing the ability of our ideas to deal with the diversity of what goes on in the world."

Much of what concerns mental health in missions appears to be based on clinical theory or hunches, with insufficient science-based research to validate or undergird what is done. Expanded clinical research would provide a more reliable foundation for clinical practice.

Research should not be driven merely by what we need to know, but designed to inform us as to "where we actually are at any point in time" so that "we no longer plan our way into the future as much as we learn our way" (Myers, 1996, p. xvii). Research should be given a place of prominence in mission strategy as a valuable and indispensable dimension of accountable ministries.

Some of the same old questions continue to haunt the missions enterprise. We have not reached definitive, final conclusions on issues relating to candidate screening, missionary families, MK schooling, missionary attrition, cross-cultural adjustment, unique sources of stress for missionaries, and the like. For example, as I stated at my workshop at ICMK, Nairobi, "Anyone discussing the mental health of missionaries will surely bring up issues related to MKs and missionary families—they are that important in the total picture of missionary mental health" (Hunter, 1989, p. 2).

In the 21st century we will be confronted relentlessly with new issues that need framing as research questions. These include:

- The impact on missionaries reared in families with an alcoholic parent
- What is effective or not in on-field short-term counseling or mental health consultation with missionaries
- MKs and AMKs (adult or former missionary kids) who themselves become missionaries
- Factors involved when some AMKs reject their faith or become involved in cults or other religions
- "Boomer" and "generation-X" missionaries and how to provide member care that meets their mental health needs
- Preparing for dangerous and potentially traumatic situations and events

Well-designed clinical studies conducted by competent research teams will provide the needed scientific foundation for the counseling and consulting work of mental health professionals. We need to know what works with missionaries and what doesn't. For example, Rosik (1993) has introduced an intriguing discussion regarding the implications for member care of counselors who are mission-affiliated versus those who are not. Continued use of mental health professionals in various aspects of member care will surely raise other kinds of researchable questions that even now have yet to surface.

The Research Process

The term *research* conjures up a variety of perceptions in the missions community. Some may see it as a panacea for problems they face while others may look on it as merely a fanciful, hard-to-understand collection of numbers or graphs or statistics. Others may see it as a gratuitous waste of time and resources devoted to something that has little to do with what mission is at its spiritual core. Researchers may face opposition and even uncooperativeness if they do not go about their work wisely and purposefully.

The task which merits specific attention of missions-oriented mental health research concerns identifying mental health issues in missions issues with sound theory construction, formulation of testable hypotheses, and sophisticated research design. It is not within the scope of this chapter to tease out the full panoply of research possibilities. In at least some areas relating to mental health in missions or member care, this has been done well by others (e.g., Austin & Jones, 1987; Powell, 1999; Richardson, 1992; Taylor, 1997; Vander Pol, 1994).

Forgatch (1990) conceptualizes the research process as a vortex comprising three basic steps endlessly recycled and refined:

(a) generating hypotheses,
(b) developing measurement strategies, and
(c) testing the hypotheses.

The first cycles in the vortex are necessarily rough and exploratory. Hypotheses are broadly defined, measurement strategies are crude, and trials are usually only weak tests of the theory. Rounds within the vortex reflect refinement in each step. Surviving hypotheses are better specified, erroneous hypotheses are eliminated and alternative hypotheses are posited. Measurement strategies become more accurate and generalizable. Trials of the hypotheses become more crucial tests of the theory. (Forgatch 1990, p. 291).

Following completion and publication of an experimental study, others concerned with the problem function as helpful critics of its method and results. Publication of research studies is the accepted form of intra- and inter-disciplinary communication. Its importance cannot be overestimated.

Integrative peer-reviewed Christian psychology journals, e.g., *Journal of Psychology and Christianity* and *Journal of Psychology and Theology* are prepared to accept submissions of high quality that deal with mental health in missions issues. The review and editorial practices of peer-reviewed journals often lead to considerable refinement and overall improvement in the quality of article submissions.

Quantitative vs. Qualitative Research

Quantitative or empirical research requires measurement of variables and usually employs a sizeable sample, i.e., the larger the sample the greater the likelihood of generalizability of results. By contrast, qualitative research involves non-numerical study and analysis of observations from which the investigator attempts to tease out underlying dynamics (Søgaard, 1996). Much of quantitative research makes use of paper and pencil measures to garner responses. Questions of reliability and validity are consuming issues in empirical research. E.g., do instruments actually measure what they purport to measure? But it is impossible to construct measures that are not impersonal, and they will only measure responses given at a specific moment in time. This leads Becker (1996) to speculate that

> The people we study often do not give stable or consistent meanings to things, people and events. They change their minds frequently. Worse yet, they often are not sure what things *do* mean; they make vague and wooly interpretations of events and people. It follows … that we ought to

respect the confusion and inability to be decisive by not giving things a more stable meaning than the people involved do. But doing so makes the researchers work more difficult, since it is hard to describe, let alone measure, such a moving target.

Qualitative studies involve much smaller research populations and are based largely on personal interviews whether open-ended or structured. Part of the attractiveness of qualitative research is that it may provide deeper access to the dynamics underlying responses given by "moving targets."

There should not be a question of whether quantitative or qualitative methods are better. Indeed, some studies could benefit from creative use of both. It may be that rather than using either one or the other, creative researchers could find ways of combining these approaches.

Research Evaluation

The extant research in mental health and missions, no matter how "soft" it may be in respect to methodology and rigor, has "early stage" value. Early studies help to lay the foundation for later, more sophisticated studies. For that reason, we should neither minimize the importance of continued pre-experimental thinking and theorizing nor overlook the small though growing corpus of research that has been accumulating in recent years. Taken together, such results are suggestive and contributory even when falling short of desirable standards for more definitive studies.

We need to revisit the old questions, review previous studies, sharpen theory, develop hypotheses from real issues and, if necessary, design studies for greater sophistication. With little exception, no issue or area of mental health in missions has yet to be subjected to the kind of exhaustive, definitive and in-depth programmatic study that would lead to more substantive results and analyses.

The work of individual researchers has undoubted value and should continue to be validated through the scholarly publication process. However, a better approach has been modeled in the creation of the MK Consultation and Research Team/Committee on Research and Endowment (MK-CART/CORE). (See Chapter 56.)

A unique and extremely important facet of MK-CART/CORE structure is the inclusion of representatives of several missions who can raise questions and identify issues for the benefit of the CORE researchers. This not only helps engage mission representatives in initiating research but helps guarantee missions agencies' greater responsiveness to results of research studies.

In the MK-CART/CORE structure these representatives have the function of keeping research efforts grounded in the realities of agency and missionary personnel needs. Because they are confronted on a day by day basis with the issues they understand missionary families and children (MKs); can identify viable, researchable issues; and are able use the research results to bring about change in mission strategy and policies. They are the consumers and the movers and shakers who can take research results and give them life in more enlightened missions strategies and policies.

MK-CART/CORE is a model that not only has proved itself but should be emulated in the formation of new groups that could initiate research in other areas of missions-oriented mental health concern.

ReMAP (Reducing Missionary Attrition Project), a major study in missionary attrition (Taylor, 1997), utilized quantitative methodology to "identify causes and "cures." Researchers designed a questionnaire for the project which involved more than 500 mission agencies in 14 countries.

Unfortunately, Taylor's (1997) edited volume and the manner in which the study and its results are presented is confounding to the research community that looks to the presentation of data and results in a standard and efficient research format. It is difficult to find the scattered and disorganized information about this massive research project that would permit scholarly dialogue and critique. The motivation for the study is admirable and the publication of its results, in spite of its many inadequacies as a scholarly and definitive study, makes a major contribution to attrition literature. It fails, however, to provide a base for effective communication and validation. However helpful in raising researchable issues, the study is neither conclusive nor definitive.

It is unfortunate that qualitative research was not utilized as a precursor for setting up a better-designed and more professional quantitative study. There are lessons to be learned from ReMAP that will help guide future and more definitive attrition studies.

There is a rich research field to mine in missionary biographical materials. Beck (1992) has received little recognition for his major, well-researched retrospective study of the mental illness of William Carey's wife, Dorothy. This account demonstrates clearly that mental health issues in missions are far from new. Tucker and Andrews (1992) also offer briefer historical sketches of other missionaries with mental health issues that could become subjects for more extensive research based on Beck's model.

Conclusions

Research in mental health and missions should be considered, as does Beavers (1977), as an elegant expression or outgrowth of common sense rather than an exotic and basically impractical activity. Making headway in quality research in mental health in missions is dependent on the caliber of methods, measures, and strategies of data analysis that investigators employ. As our knowledge base in mental health and missions broadens and deepens researchers will discover that they will need to address questions of greater subtlety and complexity.

An objective or scientific approach to research is essential in mental health in missions because its methods are reasonably objective, subject to public view, and potentially replicable. Nielsen (n.d.) believes that

> Scientific research progresses best through experiments because they allow us to test our theories. Ideally, we begin with a theory about why things happen, and conduct an experiment to test the theory's usefulness. If the results support the theory, we gain confidence in it. If they fail to support the theory, we search for flaws in the experiment and in the theory that might account for the results. Experiments are important to science, and until experiments become more common . . . we will have a relatively superficial understanding.

It is important to continue encouraging greater progress in quality research through "greater chunks of time and long-term commitment from post-doctoral researchers with adequate funding for their work from evangelical sources" (Hunter, 1993). The model put in place by MK-CART/CORE should be adapted in structuring other groups of researchers/consumers that can take on other pieces of member care or mental health in missions research.

Christian graduate school faculties are a potential resource for competent researchers which could contribute mightily to the integration of psychology and theology. Members of these faculties are not exempt from the Great Commission. Mission agencies should be encouraged to contract with schools and faculties for programmatic research that would systematically address the problems and needs of mission administrators and missionary personnel.

It is time for Christian graduate schools to foster closer contact with potential researchers and missions administrators/missionaries through joint participation in conferences and seminars. The better both understand each other the more certain we can be that research efforts will be relevant and worthy of consideration for the implementing change in missions strategies and policies. Graduate faculty ignited with a passion for world missions have the skills and competencies to work with as yet unanswered but researchable questions that concern the mental health of missionary personnel. Christian behavioral science faculty in secular universities and graduate schools should also be encouraged to use their research skills on behalf of the missions enterprise.

Longtime editor of *Evangelical Missions Quarterly* James Reapsome (1998) suggests that "scientific discoveries generally are achieved by advancing in small steps from the current state of knowledge" and implies that researchers must keep current on the work of others as well as have sufficient experience to be able to interpret the data. Modern methods of communication should insure that researchers nurture consultative relationships and frequent contact with other researchers.

In studies related to mental health in missions, researchers need to balance superior research skills and competencies with a deep spiritual commitment and biblical/theological grounding in carrying out their work. Research has Great Commission implications and should always be viewed as such. The admonition of Reapsome (1998) to researchers in missiology should apply equally to researchers in mental health in missions: "Prayer and pure, objective research—carried out by [researchers] well versed in the current state of knowledge—will be powerful tools used mightily by God in the 21st century."

It is essential that researchers check and recheck their position and trajectory in comparison to their vision "lest our turbulent environment push us off course unawares and we invest our work in directions we do not wish to go" (Bryant, 1996, p. xvi). Again, returning to the wise counsel of Reapsome (1998),

> Our cause will only advance when we get on our knees and confess our need of the Holy Spirit. Even our most mature judgments resulting from fair, objective research must be guided by the Holy Spirit. Jesus said the Holy Spirit will guide us into all truth, and I believe that includes the results of our...research. (p. 7).

The ultimate goal of research in mental health in missions is to be able to obtain the data leading to potential solutions for problems and needs that will optimize missionary experience and thereby further the work of God on the mission fields of the world. We have a good start that should encourage us to move ahead in fitting together the pieces of the puzzle through the highest quality and most sophisticated research possible.

References

Austin, C. N., & Jones, B. V. (1987). Reentry among missionary children: An overview of reentry research from 1934-1986. *Journal of Psychology and Theology, 15,* 315-325.

Beavers, W. R. (1977). *Psychotherapy and growth: A family systems perspective.* New York: Brunner/Mazel.

Beck, J. R. (1992). *Dorothy Carey: The tragic and untold story of Mrs. William Carey.* Grand Rapids, MI: Baker Book House.

Becker, H. S. (1996). The epistemology of qualitative research. In R. Jessor, A. Colby, & R. A. Schweder (Eds.), *Essays in ethnography and human development: Context and meaning in social inquiry.* Chicago: University of Chicago Press. Retrieved July 27, 2001 from http://www.soc.ucsb.edu/faculty/hbecker/qa.html

Becker, H. S. (1998). *Tricks of the trade: How to think about your research while you're doing it.* Chicago: University of Chicago Press. Chapter 1 retrieved August 18, 2001 from http://www.press.uchicago.edu/Misc/Chicago/041247.html

Forgatch, M. S. (1990). The clinical science vortex: A developing theory of antisocial behavior. In D. J. Pepler & K. H. Rubin (Eds.) The development and treatment of childhood aggression (pp. 291-315). Hillsdale, NJ: Lawrence Erlbaum Associates.

Hall, M.E. L., & Schram, J. L. (1999). Psychology and missions: The role of the mental health professional in member care. *Journal of Psychology and Theology, 27,* 83-86.

Hunter, W. F. (1989). *MKs and missionary families: Some outstanding research issues.* Paper presented at the meeting of the International Conference on Missionary Kids (ICMK), Nairobi, Kenya.

Hunter, W. F. (1993). Missions and mental health: Introduction to a special issue. *Journal of Psychology and Theology, 21,* 5-8.

Myers, B. (1996). Foreword. In V. Søgaard, *Research in church and mission* (pp .xv-xviii). Pasadena, CA: William Carey Library.

Nielsen, M. (n.d.). Research in psychology and religion. In *Psychology in Religion pages* [On-line]. Retrieved August 18, 2001 from http://www.psywww.com/psyrelig/research.htm

O'Donnell, K. (1992). An agenda for member care in missions. In K. O'Donnell (Ed.), *Missionary care: Counting the cost for world evangelism* (pp. 286-298). Pasadena, CA: William Carey Library.

Powell, J. R. (1999). Families in missions: A research context. *Journal of Psychology and Theology, 27,* 98-196.

Reapsome, J. (1998). Research and the ginger ale syndrome. *Evangelical Missions Quarterly, 34,* 6-7.

Richardson, J. (1992). Psychopathology in missionary personnel. In K. O'Donnell (Ed.), *Missionary Care: Counting the cost for world evangelism* (pp. 89-109). Pasadena, CA: William Carey Library.

Rosik, C. H. (1993). Mission-affiliated versus non-mission counselors: A brief research report on missionary preferences with implications for missionary care. *Journal of Psychology and Christianity, 12,* 159-164

Søgaard, V. (1996). *Research in church and mission.* Pasadena, CA: William Carey Library.

Taylor, W. D. (Ed.). (1997). *Too valuable to lose: Exploring the causes and cures of missionary attrition.* Pasadena, CA: William Carey Library.

Tucker, R., & Andrews, L. (1992). Historical notes on missionary care. In K. O'Donnell (Ed.), *Missionary care: Counting the cost for world evangelism* (pp. 24-36). Pasadena, CA: William Carey Library.

Vander Pol, H.M. (1994). *Missionary selection, stress, and functioning: A review of the literature.* Doctoral Research Paper, Rosemead School of Psychology, Biola University. (ERIC Document Reproduction Service No. ED 384 839)

56

MK-CART/CORE:
A Multi-Mission Research Model

John R. Powell

*C*oncern for families in North American missions has increased noticeably over the past three decades. Although this concern has drawn variable attention throughout the history of missionary societies, several factors combined to bring greater focus on it in the early to mid 1970s.

These have included observable shifts in American cultural values such as greater permissiveness, more materialism and less family cohesion, greater emphasis on family concerns within the broader Christian community, increased international interest and mobility, and different felt needs and characteristics in newer generations of missionaries.

Although this chapter focuses on North American missionary families, there is a growing recognition that family issues are frequently implicated as reasons for field attrition in both old and new sending countries.

During this past quarter century, specific questions have been voiced regarding the education and development of missionaries' children (MKs) and how this may affect missionary service. Hunter (1983), in a perceptive article, raised 45 research questions which could guide work in this area with results leading potentially to a more comprehensive understanding of missionary families. Some have now been researched, and helpful answers found. Others await investigation.

A major point in his article was the need for theory-based research and sound conceptualization regarding the study of missionary families and MK development. In the context of research on missionary families there remain the ever-important issues of spiritual growth and development, the integration of biblical principles in

More research on topics related to mental health and missions is needed to help determine the best use of limited resources. One of the most extensive cooperative inter-mission efforts in the field of research on missionary life is MK-CART/CORE. It provides a model for designing and carrying out sound, practical research which has maximum relevance to the missions community.

family matters and dynamics, and satisfaction for family members in their lives, ministry, and spiritual disciplines.

This model of research collaboration among missions and researchers on MKs and families may serve as an example for research in other areas of concern to missions. See Figure 1 on page 488 for an overview of the structure.

Families and Missions

A fundamental assumption is that a missionary family with healthy dynamics, manifesting biblical principles in relationships within and outside the family, with good levels of satisfaction in ministry, spiritual growth, and family relationships is most likely to remain on the field. Also, a family with such characteristics is most likely to develop healthy, spiritually integrated, and satisfied children who become mature Christian adults.

Ward (1987) has pointed to the potential for such mission families not only to provide significant ministry as their children are growing up, but also to develop MKs who become "world Christians," persons with global perspective, cross-cultural skills, and spiritual integration who can make substantial contributions to the world Christian movement.

In the USA and Canada, stories and myths about MKs, positive and negative, appeared to increase in the 1970s and early 1980s, and efforts were directed toward better understanding the serious issues evoking such stories. There were no identifiable coordinated research efforts on the part of North American missions up to that time, however, and research tended to be largely independent in nature, the majority of which was thesis and dissertation work.

The International Conferences on Missionary Kids (ICMKs), held in Manila in 1984 and Quito in 1987, gave significant impetus to steps for better understanding and assisting MKs and their families. Participants at the 1989 ICMK in Nairobi adopted Resolution IX, committing themselves "to engage in appropriate, rigorous and systematic research into those additional areas which will enhance the database and provide for better understanding of the MK situation." (Bowers 1998, p. 432)

However, such a resolution points to the dearth of empirical, theoretically based research in this area as encourages research to be done. Andrews (1989), in searching for research on missionary families published in North America between 1934 and 1989, found 181 entries, the majority of which were doctoral dissertations or master's theses. Even in the most recent period reviewed, 1984-1989, 57% of the entries were doctoral dissertations. Though these have made useful contributions, and other researchers have contributed importantly, there had not yet developed a comprehensive picture of missionary families and their numerous variations, based on empirical research.

MK-CART/CORE

Stimulated in part by MK and missionary family issues raised at the 1984 ICMK and in part by emerging concerns regarding boarding school effects on MKs, a group of representatives from several missions were invited to meet in Nyack, NY, in 1986 to share their perspectives on MK issues. Eight missions were represented. Also present were qualified researchers who could listen to these issues and assist in framing researchable questions, put them into a research design, and conduct relevant research.

A distinction, perhaps uniqueness, of this meeting was that the issues to be researched were identified by people who were closest to them and who could use the results to effect change as might be indicated. The availability of researchers who would be directed by the concerns of missions rather than their own particular research programs or interests was an important aspect, as was the emergence of a coordinated effort among missions.

Thus the MK-Consultation and Research Team/Committee on Research and Endowment (MK-CART/CORE) came into being. CART is composed of missions representatives who raise questions and identify issues, and CORE is made up of six researchers who design and conduct the research. Figure 1 illustrates the essential process by which MK-CART/CORE works.

A variety of principles and procedures were developed, including how the database was to be handled, ethics and procedures for its use both by CORE and other researchers, cooperative arrangements with interested others, methods for dissemination and application of the findings, and procedures for data collection within the member mission organizations. Further, a statement of core values underlying these procedures was developed:

MK-CART/CORE is motivated by the following core values:

- God is glorified in the fulfillment of the Great Commission in worldwide missions.
- Christian churches, individuals, and mission organizations share this responsibility.
- Mission personnel, including singles and all family members, are our greatest resource in the fulfillment of this task and, therefore, their care and nurture should be the best we can provide.
- We affirm the primary role of parents in the spiritual, social, moral, educational, and physical development of their children but also recognize the crucial role of mission policy and administration in influencing the experience of families and the provision of a variety of educational opportunities for children.
- Parents can fulfill both parental and ministry responsibilities if called of God to cross-cultural ministry, and that ministry is enhanced by the improvement of the quality of family life.

These values can be realized through the following *objectives:*

1.   To seek an understanding of the experience of mission personnel and families from a broad developmental and interdisciplinary perspective and to understand ways to enhance ministry effectiveness and, thus, assist those who serve in missions. This would include a better understanding of and ability to predict the effects of growing up in other cultures and to understand and define any long-term and crucial effects by the isolation of contributing variables.

2.   To respond to the research needs identified by those primarily involved in

Figure 1. **MK-CART/CORE structure and function.** The flow chart represents the interactive process between mission leaders (Consultation and Research Team; CART) who identify research needs and provide direction and consultation to the projects, the researchers (Committee on Research and Endowments; CORE) who design, implement and interpret the research, and the mission organizations who may use the results to shape policy and determine practices for care and nurture of families.

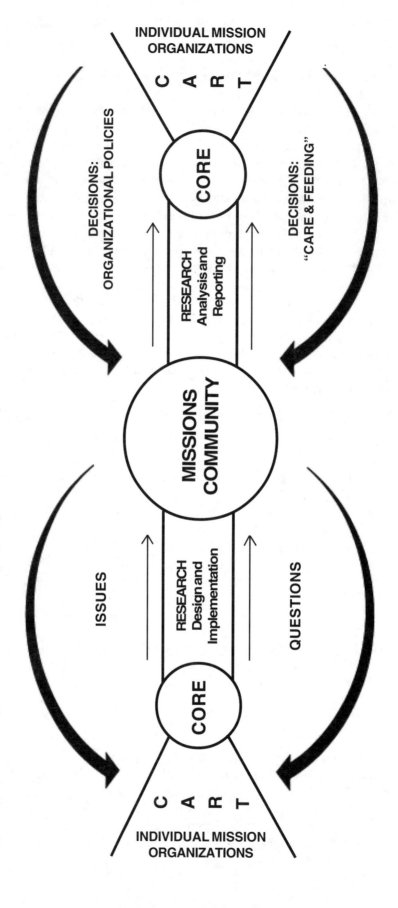

the care and education of missionary families through the design of a comprehensive research plan that includes identifying of key research areas, instrument design, implementation, coordination, and supervision of research.

3. To encourage networking among missions, other agencies and other researchers that will lead to cooperative efforts and the sharing of research through the creation of a data bank and maintenance of a resource center.

4. To provide families and mission organizations the best possible information for informed choices and decisions that sound, scholarly research can furnish and thus encourage the best possible member care.

5. To publish and circulate research results contributing to the body of literature that seeks to understand the missionary experience and, thus, to provide families and mission organizations the best possible information for informed choices that sound, scholarly research can furnish.

Some Distinctives

First, MK-CART/CORE is multi-mission in nature. By combining perspectives and coordinating efforts, a more comprehensive approach and broader, more meaningful results could be achieved. The initial eight missions included denominational, nondenominational, large, small, well-established, and newer mission agencies. There has been some slight turnover and addition in membership, with constituent missions now numbering 11. Dr. Leslie Andrews has remained chair of the group since its inception.

Second, the research is mission driven. Issues are discussed, questions raised, directions formulated, and research projects decided in discussions by all CART/CORE members. The mission organizations themselves participate in data gathering and contribute invaluable perspectives in providing direction and reviewing the preliminary designs.

Third, representatives of member missions are the first to receive results. These are presented by CORE members and discussed within the CART group to enrich perspective, understanding, and application. Further, individual consultation is provided to each representative by a CORE member for specific applications and/or where data specific to or confidential for that mission is involved. Results as appropriate are disseminated to the broader missions community and interested others through papers, articles, and presentations.

Fourth, CORE members are available to assist researchers in the area of MK and missionary families so as to encourage and enhance other research in this area and avoid duplication of efforts among constituent missions. This includes the controlled use of MK-CART/CORE's database under specified conditions. To date, CORE members have consulted significantly with a variety of other researchers or potential researchers and coordinated explorations and activities with several other projects.

Fifth, CORE researchers receive no personal remuneration for their services. Arrangements exist to cover expenses for research materials, data entry, travel to meetings, and other associated costs through support from missions, outside funding, and personal contributions.

The Boarding School Personnel Study

A prevailing issue at the time of MK-CART/CORE's formation related to boarding schools and their effect on MK development and later outcome. Virtually all mission representatives presenting 'white papers" about current MK issues reflected boarding school and educational concerns in the context of broader concerns for the healthy development and welfare of MKs.

The first project (Powell & Andrews, 1993), preliminary to the major boarding school study, was based on a sampling of those closest to boarding schools. A major finding was that, once technical competency was assumed, the greater emphasis was put on capacity to care, relate well, integrate biblical knowledge with other knowledge, and convey spiritual depth and truth as relational models and mentors.

The larger study involved measuring variables among staffs of 20 boarding schools worldwide. Schools were selected to reflect differences in size, sponsorship, and global location. Most had some relationship to one or more participating missions in MK-CART/CORE. (See Taylor & Pollock, 1995; Wickstrom, 1994; Wickstrom & Andrews, 1993, for selected results.) These findings added specific understanding to qualities for consideration in selection, assignment, and evaluation of boarding school staff. It was also clear that communication with and involvement by parents had important implications and that seeing boarding school personnel, themselves constituting a system, in interaction with other mission systems was an important concept.

The Adult Missionary Kid (AMK) Study

This is perhaps the largest, multi-mission study undertaken to date for assessing and understanding the processes and outcomes of growing up as an MK. The CART/CORE research project undertook a large cross-generational and multi-mission approach, surveying adult MKs (AMKS) between the ages of 20 and 80 years.

Beginning with a pool of some 12,000 AMK names and addresses, the study gained a representative sample of responses through a lengthy questionnaire involving standardized instruments and researcher generated items. A random sample of questionnaire respondents who volunteered to participate in telephone interviews (83% volunteered) provided further data. Results have been shared in considerable detail with constituent missions, and various results are available through other sources (see Andrews, 1994a, 1994b, 1995; Pauls & Pauls, 1993; Wickstrom, 1998).

Results indicated a high degree of educational achievement among AMKS, a significant extent of involvement in Christian ministry including return to the mission field, statistically significant correlations between the perception of having been included in family ministry and a sense of present well-being, and fathers being ranked as the most important person influencing them while growing up. Also found were indications of untoward events, family dysfunctionality, and abuse and trauma from various sources, from which some AMKs in the study were recovering. Some respondents indicated they had either rejected or were struggling with their faith, based wholly or in part on their MK and/or family experiences.

The Missionary Family Study

Not surprisingly, a strong and persistent theme emerging from these first two major studies was the implication of the family's importance to MK development and later outcome, in spite of significant periods of separation from parents, the influence of schooling, and other experiences.

Although a consistent concept in studies on personality and development has been the influence of early experiences and family-of-origin relationships, specifics of how, and perhaps how differently, this development may be influenced by family dynamics in mission situations is not well understood. Missions have begun seeing how newer missionaries and present candidates view both their past and their projected family experience, and how experiences of AMKs who look back on their growing up, implicate the family in both positive and negative ways.

CART representatives were enthusiastic and unanimous about undertaking a study which would look in some depth at missionary families. The objective was to study current missionary families, including adolescents and late elementary school children, and develop a profile including a number of variables which would provide a broad understanding of families in missions. This would involve not only descriptive characteristics such as age, time in mission service, location, and so forth, but also major activities, parent-child relationships interaction with the mission, host culture, and sending churches, practice of spiritual disciplines, influences on the family members from within and without, areas of satisfaction, marital relationship, dynamics, and various correlations. A better understanding of these areas *vis-à-vis* families could provide information for training, member care, interventions, and long-term development.

Utilizing a variety of standardized inventories designed to measure aspects of family life and dynamics, along with researcher-designed items and instruments, each participating mission gathered data from family members in its organization. Data collection and statistical summaries were completed early in 1998, and initial results were shared with constituent missions at the April 1998 meeting. "Spiritual, Family, and Ministry Satisfaction Among Missionaries" (Andrews, 1999) was the first public dissemination of results from this project.

Concluding Comments

This has been an attempt to provide one type of contextual information for research occurring in the area of MKs and missionary families in North American missions. Although the activities of MK-CART/CORE constitute only one approach to research in this important area, it is one which features direction by mission organizations, an evolving development of projects, and ongoing interaction between mission leadership and qualified researchers. It is a serious effort at coordination intended to reduce duplication of effort and allow for timely consolidation and application of research findings to mission concerns, practices, and policies.

The family in missionary service today is critical to the vitality and effectiveness in cross-cultural communication of the Gospel. Not only must families be spiritually, physically, and psychologically healthy to remain on the field, but they must also remain healthy as a context for effectiveness in both their particular ministries and in the provision of a holistically integrated family climate.

It is important to note that families, as systems or communities themselves, function in the context of other communities or systems and, as such, both influence and are influenced by these interacting systems. When a change is made in the part of any system it affects other parts of that system, a given which adds to the challenge of missionary family research.

The larger context for this research is two-fold: First is always the truth of Scripture and its practice in loving relationships (Eph. 4:15). In this larger context, one can hope that the result of well designed and conducted research ultimately adds to the experience of love, joy, and health in missionary families, leads to more effective ministry, helps make contributions to the broader missions systems and communities, and stimulates those observing to say, "See how they love one another!"

Secondly, MK-CART/CORE may serve as a helpful model for missionary organizations within Asia, Africa, and Latin America, suggesting a means by which mission organizations within these regions can coordinate data collection, analyses, collaboration, and consultation with one another. Related possibilities have also been explicated by Ward (1998).

Future research in the area of missionary families might concentrate on further understanding family dynamics, the influence of developmental and prefixed experiences on family development and satisfaction on the field, and the effects of various mission experiences on family relationships, health, and growth. These could include areas such as stressors, trauma, systemic dynamics, mission practices and policies, leadership, relationships with nationals, in-service training, and the practice of spiritual disciplines, among others. Empirical finding from such studies could not only serve to inform mission leadership, but also to guide effective professional interventions.

There is a need for research regarding intergenerational perspectives and systemic issues in mission organizations as they affect members (see Donovan & Myors, 1997, generally and especially pp. 60-61) and studies on the effects and out-comes of various practices and programs (e.g., family orientation/prefield training, language learning, mentioning, in-service training, shifts in assignments, etc.). Finally, there is a need for studying and understanding the dynamics, challenges, and effects of internationally mixed co-workers (including both families and single missionaries) and the co-laboring relationships between missionaries and nationals.

Studies on the missionary family such as those within the context noted here, as well as those suggested for the future, need to be extended into and conducted by mission agencies in the newer sending countries. Such studies and the application of their findings may assist in avoiding mistakes made by older sending countries, enhance the health of missionary families, and encourage more effective and satisfying missionary service.

Note: Appreciation is expressed to Dr. Leslie Andrews, Chair of MK-CART/CORE, and to Dr. Nancy Duvall, Rev. David Pollock, Rev. Glenn Taylor, and Dr. David Wickstrom, members of the research group, for their invaluable contributions.

References

Andrews, L. A. (1989). *Bibliography of research on the missionary family* (Research Brief). Nyack, NY: MK-CART/CORE.

Andrews, L. A. (1994a, September). *Life satisfaction of adult missionary kids* (Research Briefing #1). Wilmore, KY: MK-CART/CORE.

Andrews, L A, (1994b, September). *Educational experiences of adult missionary kids.* (Research Briefing #2). Gilmore, KY: MK-CART/CORE.

Andrews, L. A. (1995). Measurement of adult MKs well-being. *Evangelical Missions Quarterly, 31,* 442-449.

Andrews, L. A. (1999). Spiritual, family, and ministry satisfaction among missionaries. *Journal of Psychology and Theology, 27,* 107-118.

Bowers, J. M. (Ed.). (1998). *Raising resilient MKs: Resources for caregivers, parents, and teachers.* Colorado Springs, CO: Association for Christian Schools International.

Echerd, P., & Arathoon, A. (Eds.). (1989a). *Compendium of the International Conference on Missionary Kids, Quito, Ecuador, 1987: Vol. 1. Understanding and nurturing the missionary family.* Pasadena, CA: William Carey Library.

Echerd, P., & Arathoon, A. (Eds.). (1989b). *Compendium of the International Conference on Missionary Kids, Quito, Ecuador, 1987: Vol. II. Planning for MK nurture.* Pasadena, CA: William Carey Library.

Hunter, W. F. (1983). MKs and missionary families: Some outstanding research issues. *Journal of Psychology and Theology, 11,* 113-122.

Pauls, N., & Pauls, D. (1993, November). CART-CORE research on MKs. *Parents teaching overseas.* Dallas, TX: Wycliffe Bible Translators.

Powell, J. R., & Andrews, L. A. (1993). Qualities desired in MK boarding school personnel: A preliminary study. *Journal of Psychology and Theology, 21,* 86-92.

Taylor, G. C., & Pollock, D. C. (1995). Boarding school staff: How to get the best. *Evangelical Missions Quarterly, 31,* 29-36.

Tetzel, B. A., & Mortenson, P. (Eds.). (1986). *New directions in missions: Implications for MKs. Compendium of the International Conference on Missionary Kids, Manila, 1984.* Pasadena, CA: William Carey Library.

Ward, T. (1987, January). *MKs as global Christians.* Plenary address at the International Conference on Missionary Kids, Quito, Ecuador.

Wickstrom, D. L. (1994). The right stuff in boarding school staff. *Evangelical Missions Quarterly, 3 0,* 413-423.

Wickstrom, D. L., & Andrews, L. K. (1993). Personality characteristics of staff members at selected overseas missionary boarding schools. *Journal of Psychology and Theology, 21,* 74-85.

Note:

This chapter was adapted from an article titled "Families in Missions: A Research Context," published in the *Journal of Psychology and Theology,* 1999, Vol. 27, No. 2. 98-106. Used by permission.

Contributors

Alford, Linda Leitsch – Therapist, LakeSide Center, Lake Zurich, Illinois

Andrews, Leslie, Ph.D. – Vice President of Academic Development and Distributed Learning, Asbury Seminary, Wilmore, Kentucky

Blomberg, Janet R. – Director of Educational Services, Interaction, Wheaton, Illinois; editor of *Interact*; co-editor of *Fitted Pieces: A Guide for Parents Educating Children Overseas*

Bowers, Joyce M., M.S.W. – Editor of *Raising Resilient MKs*, member of Evangelical Lutheran Church in America, former missionary to Liberia.

Brown, Roger K., M.D. – psychiatrist, Tumaini Counseling Center, Nairobi, Kenya; missionary with AIM International

Carr, Karen F., Ph.D. – Psychologist; Clinical Director, Mobile Member Care Team, Abidjan, Ivory Coast

Carter, Joan, Ph.D. – Professor of Counseling, Canadian Theological Seminary, Regina, Saskatchewan, Canada

Crawford, Nancy, Psy.D. – Counselor, Tumaini Counseling Center, Nairobi, Kenya

Davis, Barney, Jr., M.D. – Psychiatrist; Executive Director, Godspeed Missionary Care, Easton, Maryland

Dodds, Lois A., Ph.D. and Lawrence E., M.D. – Co-founders of Heartstream Resources, Liverpool, Pennsylvania

Eckblad, Thomas, M.A. – (former) Director for Training, Mission Training International, Palmer Springs, Colorado

Friesen, Timothy P., Psy.D. – Project Stefanas, Christian Counseling Center, Grand Rapids, Michigan

Gamble, Kenneth, M.D. – Executive Director, Missionary Health Institute, North York, Ontario, Canada

Gardner, Laura Mae, D. Min. – International Vice President for Personnel, SIL International, Dallas, Texas

Hall, M. Elizabeth Lewis, Ph.D. – Associate Professor of Psychology, Rosemead School of Psychology, Biola University, La Mirada, California

Hunter, William F., Ph.D. – professor emeritus, Rosemead School of Psychology, Biola University, La Mirada, California; former editor, *Journal of Psychology and Theology*

Jensma, Jeanne, Ph.D. – Director of Counseling, ALONGSIDE, Inc., Richland, MI

Jerome, Darlene, M.I.A. – Director of Personnel and Training, Mobile Member Care Team, Abidjan, Ivory Coast; SIL/Wycliffe

Kellogg, Miriam E., M.A., NCC, LMHC – Counseling Ministries, Wycliffe USA, Orlando, Florida

Leverington, Rebecca, LMFT, LMSW-ACP – Counseling Development and Orientation Coordinator, Wycliffe Bible Translators, Dallas, Texas

Lindquist, Brent, Ph.D. – President, Link Care Center, Fresno, California

Lindquist, Lareau, D.Min. – Executive Director, Barnabas International, Rockford, Illinois

McKaughan, Paul, D.D. – Executive Director, Evangelical Fellowship of Mission Agencies (EFMA), Atlanta, Georgia

McLain, Ronald, M.A. – Director of Pastoral Care, Link Care, Fresno, California

Miller, Rev. Carl, M.A. – Director, Department of Clinical Ministries to Ministers and Missionaries, EMERGE Ministries, Akron, Ohio

Nelson, Paul E., M.A. – Executive Director, The Crowell Foundation, Colorado Springs, Colorado; formerly president of Mission Training International

Powell, John R., Ph.D. – Psychologist and mission consultant; Professor Emeritus, Michigan State University; co-founder of Mental Health and Missions Conference

Pruitt, Roni R., Ph.D. – Heartstream Resources; Columbia International University Graduate School, Columbia, South Carolina; program coordinator for Mental Health & Missions Conference

Richardson, Jarrett III, M.D. – Psychiatrist, Mayo Clinic, Rochester, Minnesota

Roembke, Lianne, Ph.D. – Educational Consultant, Campus Crusade for Christ International, Magdeburg, Germany

Rosik, Christopher H., Ph.D. – Clinical psychologist, Link Care Center, Fresno, California.

Schram, Judith L. – Summer Institute of Linguistics, Catalina, Arizona

Schubert, Esther, M.D. – Psychiatrist in private practice, New Castle, Indiana; serves missionaries and mission boards

Schulz, Dorris M., Ph.D. – Director, Cornhusker Center for Human Development and Associate Professor of Psychology and Family Studies, York College, York, Nebraska

Schumm, Dale H., D.Min – Mennonite Board of Missions, Elkhart, Indiana

Sieges, Timothy R. – JAARS Counseling Ministries, Waxhaw, N. Carolina; Wycliffe Bible Translators

Steere, O'Ann – Former Director of Member Care for World Relief Corporation. Consultant caregiver for mission organizations. Wheaton, Illinois.

Stringham, Edward M., Ph.D. – Psychologist, Lincoln Counseling and Enrichment Associates, Lincoln, Nebraska

Swanson, Bruce – Vice President, Organizational Change, CBInternational, Littleton, Colorado

Sweatman, Stephen M., Ph.D. – President, Mission Training International, Palmer Lake, Colorado; former professor, Columbia International University

Taylor, Rev. Glenn C., M.A., M.Th., M.Ed. – Missionary Health Institute, Mansfield, Ontario, Canada

White, Frances J., Ph.D. – Consultant to mission boards; professor, Wheaton Graduate School, Wheaton, Illinois

Wickstrom, David L., Ph.D. – Psychologist in private practice with Palmetto Counseling Associates, Columbia, South Carolina, and co-founder of the Mental Health and Missions Conference

Williams, Ken, Ph.D. – President, International Training Partners; International Training Consultant with Wycliffe Bible Translators and SIL International

Yeaman, Jan, Ph.D. – Associate Professor of Psychology, Spring Arbor College,

Index